Guanzi

管子

李亞農譯注

GUANZI

Political, Economic, and Philosophical

Essays from Early China A STUDY

AND TRANSLATION BY W. Allyn Rickett

Volume One

CHAPTERS I, 1 – XI, 34, AND XX, 64 – XXI, 65 – 66

Princeton University Press : Princeton, New Jersey

Published by Princeton University Press, 41 William Street,
Princeton, New Jersey 08540
In the United Kingdom: Princeton University Press,
Guildford, Surrey

Library of Congress Cataloging in Publication Data will be
found on the last printed page of this book

ISBN 0-691-06605-1

Publication of this book has been aided by a grant from the
Paul Mellon Fund of Princeton University Press

This book has been composed in Monophoto Times Roman
by Asco Trade Typesetting Limited, Hong Kong

Clothbound editions of Princeton University Press books are
printed on acid-free paper, and binding materials are chosen
for strength and durability. Paperbacks, although satisfactory
for personal collections, are not usually suitable
for library rebinding

Printed in the United States of America by Princeton
University Press, Princeton, New Jersey

CONTENTS

LIST OF CHARTS

PREFACE

Work on this first full translation and study of the *Guanzi* in a Western language was begun in 1948 while I was still a student of Professor Derk Bodde at the University of Pennsylvania. The present volume is the first of three, the first two of which will be devoted to a full translation with notes and bibliography, the third to separate studies by various scholars working in the field and by me.

The work has been a long time in coming. A rough draft was completed at Qinghua and Yanjing Universities during the years 1948–1951, when I had the opportunity to work with some of China's finest scholars. Among them was Professor Xu Weiyu, who compiled the first draft of the most comprehensive commentary on the *Guanzi*, the *Guanzi ji jiao*, later edited and published by Guo Moruo in 1956 after Xu's untimely death in 1951. In the summer of 1951, my work was brought to an abrupt halt when I was arrested by the Chinese authorities on charges of espionage. However, the Chinese prison officials took excellent care of my books and papers so that very little of the extensive material I had collected on the *Guanzi* was lost.

On my return home in 1955, I revised part of my translation of the *Guanzi*'s surviving seventy-six chapters and submitted eight of them as a Ph.D. dissertation to the University of Pennsylvania. One of these, dealing with the *You guan* (III, 8), appeared in *T'oung Pao*, 48 (1960): 195–251. In 1965 the University of Hong Kong Press published my *Kuan-tzu: A Repository of Early Chinese Thought*, which contained twelve chapters, including the original eight of my dissertation.

Since then the translation has progressed very slowly. Teaching and administrative commitments at the University of Pennsylvania as well as research interests in other fields kept me from any sustained work on the *Guanzi*. In 1969–70, I received a Guggenheim fellowship to continue the translation, but one year proved to be too short a time to do more than revise the previously published chapters and add a few new ones. Finally, approaching the age of sixty, I realized the time had come either to finish it or forget it.

Fortunately, in 1980 the National Endowment for the Humanities awarded me a translation grant to finish the project, and the University was also generous with leave time and a reduced work load. Hence, after many years the first volume of the complete translation has arrived.

In the preparation of this work I have received help and advice from many different people and organizations. In addition to the generous grants from the John Simon Guggenheim Memorial Foundation and the Translation Program of the National Endowment for the Humanities, an independent Federal agency, I was supported by Fulbright and Social Science Research Council grants while doing my original research in China, and I was able to spend the summer of 1970 working in Taiwan as a guest of the Academia Sinica.

The people who have helped me are too numerous to mention, but include such scholars as D. C. Lau, W.A.C.H. Dobson, and Timoteus Pokora, who reviewed, often very critically, my 1965 translation, and the two unknown readers for Princeton University Press. I owe an especially deep debt of gratitude to Professors Xu Weiyu, Feng Youlan, and Qian Zhongshu from the time I was at Qinghua University and just getting started. Qian and Professor Wu Xinghua of Yanjing University read much of the manuscript when it was at its most primitive stage. Ying Ruocheng, who was then a student at Qinghua, helped me with the initial work on the translation. I also wish to thank Professor Zhu Dexi of Beijing University, who has provided me material, some of it as yet unpublished, from the Yinqueshan tombs in Linyi Xian, Shandong. Special thanks are further due to Professor Ma Feibai, who has given me several of his unpublished manuscripts dealing with chapters that will appear in the second volume. I am deeply indebted to Professor Wallace Johnson of the University of Kansas, who published an invaluable concordance to the *Guanzi*, and to Professors Nathan Sivin and Robert Hartwell, my colleagues at the University of Pennsylvania, who provided encouragement and help with special problems. Nancy Cheng, Chinese bibliographer at the University of Pennsylvania, has also been of continuous assistance in all phases of this work.

My final and deepest thanks are reserved for Derk Bodde, teacher, colleague, and friend, who not only supervised and corrected the original dissertation, but may be said to have begun it all, and for Adele Austin Rickett, who has had to live with it, reading and criticizing countless drafts, not to mention supporting me while I was working on the original dissertation. It is to them that this work is dedicated.

Philadelphia, Pennsylvania
January 1984

Guanzi

INTRODUCTION

The *Guanzi* 管子 [Book of Master Guan], which bears the name of a famous seventh-century B.C. minister of the state of Qi 齊, Guan Zhong 管仲 (d. 645 B.C.), has been described by Gustav Haloun as an "amorphous and vast repository of ancient literature." [1] It is certainly one of the largest of the pre-Han 漢 or early Han politico-philosophical works, exceeding 135,000 characters in length and containing material written by a number of anonymous writers over a long period of time. Noted for its wealth of material concerning early Chinese economic and political theory, the *Guanzi* is especially famous for its concept of *qing zhong* 輕重, "light and heavy," which advocates the manipulation of the amount of coinage in circulation to control the supply of grain and commodities, and thus may constitute the world's earliest statement of quantitative theories of money. [2] However, the *Guanzi* also contains a great deal of other material, including military theory, sociological information, as well as a particularly rich store of early historical romance literature and Daoist, Naturalist, and Huang-Lao 黃老 writings. [3] The political writings are usually described as Legalist, but "Realist" might be a better description. [4] For the most part they tend to present a point of view much closer to that of the realistic Confucian, Xunzi 荀子 (c. 298–238 B.C.), than either the highly idealistic Confucianism of Mencius 孟子 (371–289 B.C.) or the Draconian Legalism advocated by Shang Yang 商鞅 (fl. 359–338 B.C.) and his followers and supposedly implemented in the state of Qin 秦, especially under the First Emperor 始皇帝.

How all this came together and what it all means would constitute a major study in itself. Therefore, only those considerations pertinent to

---

[1] "Legalist Fragments," p. 94.

[2] Most studies of the *Guanzi* since the 1930s, whether in Chinese, Japanese, or Western languages, have concentrated on the political and economic content of the text as does the first translation of a significant portion of the text into English. See Lewis Maverick, *Economic Dialogues in Ancient China: Selections from the Kuan-tzu.*

[3] The diversified nature of the *Guanzi*'s content created a problem of classification for early Chinese cataloguers. In the *Yiwen zhi* 藝文志 [Treatise on Literature] of the *Qian Han shu* [History of the Former Han Dynasty], 30/16a13, it is listed among Daoist works, but in the bibliography section of the *Sui shu* [History of the Sui Dynasty], 34/3b, and in subsequent catalogues it is classified as Legalist.

[4] See Kung-chuan Hsiao, *A History of Chinese Political Thought*, trans. by F. W. Mote, p. 321; and Yu Dunkang 余敦康, *Lun Guan Zhong xuepai*, pp. 39–40 (trans. pp. 3–4).

the translation of the *Guanzi*, as we now know it, will be dealt with in this Introduction and in the Introductory Comments to individual chapters. Other problems will be dealt with in the third volume of "Studies."

Arrangement of Text

The table of contents lists twenty-four *juan* or "books" containing eighty-six titled *pian* or "chapters," [5] of which ten are now missing. These ten include: VIII, 21; IX, 25; XI, 34; XIX, 60–63; XXI, 70; and XXIV, 82 and 86. Since they are generally located at the end of *juan*, most of them were probably lost when the ends of the silk or paper scrolls rotted away.

Of the remaining seventy-six chapters, III, 8, *You guan* 幼官, and III, 9, *You guan tu* 幼官圖 [*You guan* Chart], are identical except for a different arrangement of their various subsections. It is generally believed that the original text of one chapter, probably III, 9, was lost and later replaced by the present text. Another chapter, XVI, 50, *Feng Shan* 封山 [On the Feng and Shan Sacrifices], is identical with a passage in the chapter on the Feng and Shan sacrifices in the *Shi ji*, 28/4a–5b. According to a note appended to the title of this chapter in the *Guanzi*, [6] the original text was lost and later scholars replaced it with the passage from the *Shi ji* chapter that has to do with Guan Zhong and his prince, Duke Huan 桓 (685–643) of Qi. Four other chapters, XX, 64 through XXI, 67, consist of *Jie* 解 [Explanations] of other chapters. [7]

In addition to being grouped in twenty-four books, the chapters have also been arranged in the text under eight sections:

1. *Jing yan* 經言 [Canonical Statements] includes I, 1, to III, 9, supposedly the oldest portion of the book.

2. *Wai yan* 外言 [Outer Statements] includes III, 10, to VI, 17, a group of misellaneous essays representing different schools of thought.

---

[5] The *pian* 篇 were originally bundles of bamboo slips on which the text was written. The *juan* 卷 were scrolls or rolls of silk or paper that gradually supplanted the bamboo slips from Han times on. Since silk or paper *juan* were much less bulky than the bamboo, they usually contained the text of several *pian*.

[6] This note appears to be part of the standard commentary usually attributed to Yin Zhizhang 尹知章 (d. A.D. 718).

[7] Originally there were five "Explanations," covering chapters I, 1 (XIX, 63), I, 2 (XX, 64), the *Jiu bai* 九敗 section of I, 4 (XXI, 65), II, 7 (XXI, 66), and XV, 46 (XXI, 67), but the first, XIX, 63, which dealt with *Mu min* 牧民 (I, 1), is one of the ten missing chapters. Judging from the style and content of the four extant chapters, they would seem to represent the work of a single commentator, probably a Han Confucian writer with strong Legalist tendencies.

3. *Nei yan* 內言 [Inner Statements] includes VIII, 18, to X, 26, mostly devoted to stories about Guan Zhong and Duke Huan, but also containing some important sociological and philosophical materials.

4. *Duan yu* 短語 [Short Discourses] includes X, 27, to XV, 44, miscellaneous essays of varying length, including some that are important for their naturalistic or military content.

5. *Qu yan* 區言 [Minor Statements] includes XV, 46, to XVI, 49, a group of relatively short Legalist and Daoist essays.

6. *Za pian* 雜篇 [Miscellaneous Chapters] includes XVI, 50, to XIX, 62, essays covering a wide variety of subjects. Some of them appear to be fragments of very early texts.

7. *Guanzi jie* 管子解 [Explanations of the *Guanzi*] includes XIX, 63, to XXI, 67, line-by-line explanations of other chapters of the text.

8. *Qing zhong* 輕重 [Light and Heavy] includes XXI, 68, to XXIV, 86, essays concerned primarily with economics.[8]

Earliest References to the *Guanzi*

What appears to be the earliest reference to the *Guanzi* occurs in the *Hanfeizi*, XIX, 49/6a10 (Liao, *Han Fei Tzu*, II, p. 290), where it is stated: "[Every] household has those who preserve the laws of Shang [Yang] and Guan [Zhong]."[9] It is not entirely clear that actual writings are referred to here, but Jia Yi 賈誼 (201–169 B.C.) in his *Xin shu* [New History] quotes passages to be found in the present *Guanzi*, and identifies them with the words 管子曰, "Guanzi says."[10]

The first clear and specific reference to an actual *Guanzi* collection occurs in the *Huainanzi* (c. 122 B.C.), 21/7a, which also presents a picture of what the author believes is its origin:

In the time of Duke Huan of Qi, [the position of] the son of Heaven had become humble and weak, while the feudal lords used their energies in attacking [one another]. The Southern Yi and Northern Di[11] engaged the Central States in battle, and the continued existence of the Central States seemed [to hang by] a

---

[8] We do not know who was responsible for dividing the text into these sections. It may have been the Han scholar, Liu Xiang 劉向 (79–8 B.C.), who was responsible for the general editing of the text. Except for the *Jing yan* section, there appears to be no clear rationale for the sections. For an attempted explanation, see Machida Saburō's 町田三郎 article, *Kanshi no shisō*.

[9] Hanfeizi 韓非子 died in 233 B.C.

[10] For example, the *Xin shu*, IV, 4/9a5, quotes *Guanzi*, I, 1/1a9 (1 : 1.8), and the *Xin shu*, VI, 3/8b11, quotes *Guanzi*, I, 2/5b11 (1 : 5.12).

[11] 夷狄; two of the non-Sinified peoples of central and northern China.

thin thread. The territory of the state of Qi was backed against the sea on the east and confined on the north by the Yellow River. Its territory was narrow and fields few in number, so its people [had to be] very wise and clever. Duke Huan was troubled about the distress of the Central States and the rebelliousness of the Yi and Di. He wished to keep alive what was dying and preserve what was ceasing to exist, to bring esteem to [the position of] the son of Heaven, and broaden civil and military occupations. Therefore the books of Guanzi 管子 之書 grew out of this situation.

It is Sima Qian 司馬遷 (c. 145–c. 86 B.C.), in the epilogue to his biography of Guan Zhong (*Shi ji*, 62/3b12–4a4), however, who gives the first information we have about the specific contents of the collection as it existed before the first century B.C.:

I have read Mr. Guan's "On Shepherding the People," [12] "On Mountains that are High," [13] "On Military Taxes," [14] "Light and Heavy," [15] and "Nine Treasuries," [16] as well as the *Yanzi chunqiu*. Their words are presented with such care that having seen their writings, I wished to study their actions. Therefore I have attached their biographies. Their writings are very common in our times so I have not discussed them but only little known things [about the men themselves].

Thus we know that by the second century B.C. there was a collection of works attributed to Guan Zhong. The present arrangement of the text in

[12] *Mu min* 牧民; I, 1, of the present text.

[13] *Shan gao* 山高; these are the opening characters of I, 2, of the present text. It is the same chapter cited above by Jia Yi, and is now known as *Xing shi* 形勢 [On Conditions and Circumstances].

[14] *Sheng ma* 乘馬; I, 5, of the present text. The meaning of this title is not completely certain.

[15] *Qing zhong* 輕重; the *Qing zhong* section, as mentioned above, contains the last nineteen chapters of the present text. The last seven of these are specifically entitled *Qing zhong jia* 甲 through *geng* 庚 (i.e., A through G). It is questionable whether Sima Qian is referring to these chapters. There is considerable controversy about their date. Most scholars believe they were written during the Han. However, Xu Qingyu 徐慶譽, in his article, *Guanzi zhengzhi sixiang de tantao*, pp. 74–76, argues that they predate Hanfeizi, while Ma Feibai 馬非百 insists they were composed during Wang Mang's 王莽 interregnum (A.D. 8–23). See his *Guanzi Qing zhong pian xinquan*, pp. 3–50.

[16] *Jiu fu* 九府; this title does not appear in the present text. Moreover, according to the Liu Xiang preface to the *Guanzi*, which cites this passage from the *Shi ji*, "The text of the 'Nine Treasuries' is not found among the people." Whether the chapter was actually lost or simply known by another name in Liu's time, we cannot tell. It is probable, however, that it dealt with economics, as indicated by passage in the *Shi ji*, 129/2b: "Guanzi ... established the light and heavy [relationship between grain and money] and the nine treasuries." According to Zhang Shoujie 張守節 (fl. A.D. 737), in his *Zheng yi* commentary to this passage, the nine treasuries were bureaus concerned with finance. It is to be noted that of the five titles mentioned by Sima Qian, the first three are to be found in the *Jing yan* [Canonical Statements] section.

6

eighty-six *pian*, however, represents the work of Liu Xiang, who was in charge of cataloguing the Han imperial library under Emperor Cheng 成 (32–7 B.C.).

Liu Xiang's Editing

In a preface contained in most present editions of the *Guanzi*, Liu tells how he set about collating and editing the text:

> The Commissioner of Water Conservancy for the Eastern [Metropolitan Area] and Imperial Counsellor First Class [Liu] Xiang, says: "The books of Guanzi which Your Servant has collated consisted of 389 bundles (*pian*) in the palace, twenty-seven bundles belonging to the Imperial Counsellor Second Class Bu Gui 太中大夫卜圭, forty-one bundles belonging to Your Servant, Fu Can 富參, eleven bundles to the Colonel of the Bowman Guards Li 射聲校尉立,[17] and ninety-six bundles in the office of the grand historian 太史, making a total of 564 bundles of books inside and outside the palace. In collating them, he [Liu Xiang] has eliminated 484 duplicate bundles and made eighty-six bundles the standard text. He has written them on bamboo slips cured over fire so copies can be made.[18]

It would seem that Liu must have divided several of the larger bundles when making his collation, because the difference between 564 and 484 is only eighty instead of eighty-six. Furthermore, a number of the present chapters are clearly made up of two or more fragments that appear to have been lumped together because of some similarity in content. If each of these fragments originally made up one of the bundles, the discrepancy would be even larger. In any case, as a result of Liu's work, we find that the "Treatise on Literature" of the *Qian Han shu*, 30/16a13, lists a *Guanzi* in eighty-six *pian*.[19]

---

[17] Nothing is known of these men except that Fu Can apparently worked with Liu Xiang in cataloguing the library. See Piet van der Loon, "On the Transmission of the *Kuan-tzu*," pp. 360–362 and notes.

[18] Translation adapted from van der Loon, "Transmission," pp. 360–361. Van der Loon thinks (p. 360) that this preface was originally submitted to Emperor Cheng by Liu Xiang as a memorial accompanying his collation of the *Guanzi*. We do not know exactly when either the collation or the presentation took place, but the former probably occurred about 26 B.C. when Liu Xiang was actively engaged in such work. See van der Loon, p. 359, n. 5.

[19] This "Treatise" was based on the catalogue known as the *Qi lüe* 七略 [Seven Summaries], which was compiled by Liu Xin 劉歆 (d. A.D. 23). Liu Xin, in turn, based his work on the *Bie lu* 別錄 [Separate Lists], which he and his father, Liu Xiang, had prepared in cataloguing the imperial library.

The *Guanzi* and Guan Zhong

Chinese scholars have long recognized that the *Guanzi* could not have been written by Guan Zhong, in its entirety at least. Fu Xuan 傅玄 (217–278) has been quoted by Liu Shu 劉恕 (1032–1078) in his *Tong jian wai ji* [Unofficial Records of the Universal Mirror of History] as saying, "More than half the Book of Guanzi has been added by later mischief-makers who spoke of things which happened after the death of Guan Zhong." [20] His suspicions have been re-echoed by many others, including Kong Yingda 孔穎達 (574–648), Du You 杜佑 (735–812), Su Zhe 蘇轍 (1039–1112), Ye Shi 葉適 (1150–1223), Zhu Xi 朱熹 (1130–1200), and Huang Zhen 黃震 (fl. 1270). [21] Some of these men and many of the later commentators, who will be discussed below, have also noted the disparate nature of its ideological content and expressed the belief that therefore the text must represent the work of different men writing at different times.

The question then arises: How did the name of Guan Zhong come to be associated with such mishmash? Any attempt to offer an explanation is bound to be highly speculative, but an understanding of the historical position of Guan Zhong and how he appeared in the eyes of the different schools of thought that evolved in China from the time of Confucius on may help to clarify the matter.

According to the traditional account of his life in Sima Qian's *Shi ji*, 62, [22] Guan Zhong, who died a natural death at an advanced age in 645 B.C., was a native of Yingshang 潁上, a district controlled by the state of Chu 楚 and situated in what is now northwest Anhui. He seems to have come from a poor family and, for a time at least, engaged in trade before entering the service of Duke Xi 僖 (730–698) of Qi. Later he became tutor to Jiu 糾, one of the younger sons of Duke Xi. In 686 a civil war broke out and Xi's successor, Duke Xiang 襄, was killed. Jiu, with the help of Guan Zhong, attempted to seize the throne but finally lost out to

---

[20] Cited in the *SKQSZM*, 101/1a. Among the historical anachronisms are the mention of the two beauties, Xi Shi 西施 and Mao Qiang 毛嬙 (XI, 32/9b4; 2:39.1), both of whom belong to the fifth century B.C., and such terms as *qing xiang* 卿相 and *xiang shi* 相室 for the chief minister, a usage which did not become prevalent until the Warring States 戰國 Period (481–221 B.C.). Ideological anachronisms are also numerous and include clear references to the thought of Song Xing 宋鈃 (or Song Keng 宋牼), Mo Di 墨翟, and Yang Zhu 楊朱 (I, 4/16b6–9; 1:15.12–14), who also date from the period of the Warring States. Furthermore, the complicated essay style in which the various chapters are written could not have developed until after the time of Confucius 孔子 (551–479 B.C.). See Fung Yu-lan, *A History of Chinese Philosophy*, I, pp. 7–8.

[21] See Zhang Xincheng 張心澂, *Weishu tongkao*, II, pp. 763–765.

[22] For translations of this biography, see Evan Morgan, *A Guide to Wenli Styles and Chinese Ideals*, pp. 118–122, and Georges Margouliès, *Le kou-wen chinois*, pp. 77–83.

8

the future Duke Huan. Though Guan Zhong had fought against him, Duke Huan was impressed with his ability and had him brought back from abroad to become his chief minister. The story of this relationship is vividly told in chapters VII, 18, and VIII, 20.

Once in power, Guan Zhong persuaded his prince to institute a number of political, military, and economic reforms that soon raised Qi to a position of strength among the Chinese states. Particularly famous among the economic reforms attributed to him were the introduction of state monopolies over salt and iron, and the fiscal policy known as balancing the light and heavy (*qing zhong*).

Actually we know very little about the specific nature of these reforms.[23] The richest and most reliable source for the history of this period is the *Zuo zhuan*, but there is little in it about the internal political and economic system of Qi.[24] The *Guo yu*, 6, which forms the basis of VIII, 20, is devoted entirely to the exploits of Duke Huan and Guan Zhong, but it obviously incorporates much of later tradition and its credibility is difficult to assess. It goes into some detail concerning Guan Zhong's political and military reforms,[25] but says little about those concerned with economics, except to indicate that Guan Zhong fostered trade as well as agriculture and industry.[26] Fish and salt are mentioned but nothing is said about iron or salt monopolies, or the *qing zhong* fiscal policies.

As a result of Guan Zhong's reforms and clever use of diplomacy, Qi soon became the most powerful of all the feudal states, and in 680 Duke Huan was recognized as the first *ba* 霸, lord protector or chief over the feudal lords, with the responsibility of controlling the various so-called

[23] For a study of Guan Zhong, the man, see Sydney Rosen, "In Search of the Historical Kuan Chung." See also Henri Maspero, *China in Antiquity*, pp. 180–191.

[24] The *Zuo zhuan* forms the basis of the *Da kuang* chapter of the *Guanzi*, VII, 18. See the Introductory Comments to that chapter.

[25] There is no English translation of the *Guo yu*, 6, but the *Xiao kuang* chapter of the *Guanzi*, VIII, 20, adheres to its general content in spite of numerous minor differences and some additional material.

[26] According to tradition, at least, there must have been considerable economic development in Qi even before Guan Zhong's time. The *Shi ji*, 32/3a (Chavannes, *Mémoires historiques*, IV, pp. 39–40), states: "When Duke Tai 太 (trad. 1122–1078) arrived in his country [Qi], he improved the government, conformed to the [local] customs, simplified the rites, extended the work of merchants and artisans throughout the country, and facilitated the making of profit from fish and salt. Thus people came to Qi in large numbers and Qi became a great country." Although these activities of Duke Tai fall completely within the realm of traditional history, tradition is supported to some extent by considerable archaeological evidence showing Qi in later times as one of the first countries to make wide use of coins. See Wang Yu-ch'uan, *Early Chinese Coinage*, and two articles by Sun Shande 孫善德 and Zhu Huo 朱活 in the 1980, no. 2, issue of *Wenwu* 文物, pp. 63–72, on recent excavations of Qi knife money in Shandong Province.

barbarian peoples and enforcing respect for the Zhou 周 king. In this capacity the duke was able to maintain relative order among the lords of the central feudatories for a number of years. He conducted several highly successful campaigns against non-Sinified peoples, especially in the north and west, and for a short time was even able to bring the powerful southern state of Chu to terms.

For this reason Confucius was later moved to say:

> Through having Guan Zhong as his minister Duke Huan became protector over the feudal lords. He brought unity and order to the entire realm so that even today people enjoy his gift to them. Were it not for Guan Zhong we would now be wearing our hair loose and folding our clothes to the left [as the barbarians do].[27]

According to Chinese tradition, many famous ministers have served their rulers by exemplary conduct and good advice, but few of them have ever achieved such spectacular success or have been responsible for the introduction of such radically new policies as Guan Zhong. Thus, during the period of increasing change that accompanied the break-down of the old feudal society from the seventh century on, he became one of the chief models for a new type of professional bureaucrat and political adviser who came to the fore as the old hereditary officials proved inadequate for their tasks.[28] For these new professionals, he served as a shining example of what could be accomplished if only the ruler would listen to the advice of his ministers and advisers and thus he became a hero in the historical romance[29] and political philosophy literature that developed from the fifth century on.

As mentioned above, Guan Zhong is usually identified with the Legalist school, even though philosophical Legalism did not develop

[27] *Lun yu*, XIV, 18/2.

[28] For an interesting examination of the change that took place in the leadership during this period, see Richard Walker, *The Multi-State System of Ancient China*, pp. 59–72, and Melvin Thatcher, "A Structural Comparison of the Central Governments of Ch'u, Ch'i and Chin."

[29] The term "historical romance" was used by Henri Maspero to describe what he believed to have been a large corpus of fictionalized history that developed in China during the fifth and fourth centuries B.C. and served as the basis for such works as the *Zuo zhuan*. See his *China in Antiquity*, pp. 357–365. Maspero probably overstated his thesis for there is little evidence to support the existence of such a corpus at that time, but I believe the term is very appropriate to describe some of the later works centered around heroes such as Guan Zhong, and is particularly apt in describing the content of such chapters in the *Guanzi* as the *Da kuang* (VII, 18) and *Xiao kuang* (VIII, 20). For discussions of early Chinese historical writing, see Burton Watson, *Early Chinese Literature*, pp. 19–36; Ronald G. Egan, "Narratives in *Tso Chuan*," pp. 323–352; and J. I. Crump, Jr., *Chan-kuo Ts'e*, pp. 1–22.

until long after his time. The prime reason for this undoubtedly lies in the fact that, as a practical politician, he was concerned with the efficient administration of the state, and therefore instituted numerous regulations to see that this was accomplished.[30]

However, if Guan Zhong can be considered a Legalist at all, it is certainly not in the same sense as Shang Yang (d. 338 B.C.) and Hanfeizi (d. 233 B.C.).[31] In fact, judging from what is said of him in the *Zuo zhuan*, he could qualify, at least in most respects, as an ideal Confucian minister. At a conference held in 653 B.C., called to deal with the minor state of Zheng 鄭, Guan Zhong is reported to have advised Duke Huan: "Summon the wavering with courtesy (*li* 禮) and cherish the remote with virtuous conduct (*de* 德). So long as your virtuous conduct and courtesy never falter, there will be no one who will not cherish you."[32]

At this same conference the eldest son of the Zheng ruler approached Duke Huan with a plan to remove from power the ruling clans in his state and substitute his own group in their stead. Duke Huan was about to agree, but was warned against such action by Guan Zhong, who pointed out that the Duke had won the adherence of the feudal lords by "being polite (*li*) and trustworthy (*xin* 信), and it would be foolish to end with treachery."[33]

Such concern for *li*, *de*, and *xin* sounds very Confucian, or at least not at all Legalist. It is true that Confucius, in spite of his respect for Guan Zhong's administrative ability, had a rather low opinion of the minister's knowledge of the rules of propriety (*li*). He once said: "Guan Zhong was a man of small capacity.... If Guan knew the rules of propriety, who does not know them."[34] But when one of his disciples, Zilu 子路, charged that Guan Zhong had lacked essential goodness (*ren* 仁), because, rather than die along with his former prince, he had lived to serve Duke Huan, Confucius came to his defense: "It was due to Guan Zhong that Duke Huan was able to assemble the feudal lords on numerous occasions[35] without resorting to the use of his war chariots. Such was his goodness! Such was his goodness!"[36]

---

[30] Fung Yu-lan, *History*, I, p. 312, has also pointed out that during the Warring States Period, Qi was one of the states where Legalist thought flourished, and that this may quite possibly be attributed to the institutional reforms made by Guan Zhong.

[31] It is interesting that the *Shangjun shu*, which was put together by Shang Yang's followers, does not even mention Guan Zhong.

[32] *Zuo zhuan*, Xi, 7 (Legge, *Ch'un Ts'eu*, V, 7/4).

[33] Ibid.

[34] *Lun yu*, III, 22/2–3.

[35] 九合, lit., "nine times assembled." For a discussion of this phrase, see VII, 18/13a3–4 (1:93.3), and note.

[36] *Lun yu*, XIV, 17/2.

Authoritarian Mozi 墨子 (c. 479–c. 381 B.C.) was also sympathetic toward this aspect of Guan Zhong: "Duke Huan of Qi came under the influence of Guan Zhong and Bao Shu 鮑叔.... Therefore he became protector over the feudal lords and his achievements were handed down to posterity."[37]

The later, more idealistic Confucians, represented by Mencius (371–289 B.C.) and his followers found Guan Zhong very objectionable, however. Curiously enough their objections arose out of the very action that brought approval from Confucius, namely, his implementation of the *ba* or lord protector system. To Mencius the concept of the *ba* was one of the major causes of destructive violence and misery in the world, and only by returning to the rule of the sage kings could this evil be corrected:

> He who makes a pretense of goodness while using force is the lord protector.... He who practices goodness with virtuous conduct is the king.... When force is used to make men submit, they do not submit in their hearts. [They submit] because their own strength is inadequate. But when virtue is used to make men submit, they are happy in their hearts and sincerely submit of themselves.[38]

The Mencian attitude toward Guan Zhong may best be summed up by Zeng Xi's 曾西[39] statement: "How dare you compare me with Guan Zhong! Considering how completely Guan Zhong possessed [the confidence of] his prince, how long he ran the government of the state, and yet how little he accomplished, how can I be likened to this?"[40]

It is not difficult to find reasons for the difference in attitude between the Mencians and Confucius toward Guan Zhong. By Mencius's time the struggle for controlling power among the major states of Qi, Qin, and Chu had led to an interminable succession of bloody wars. This struggle for power in Mencius's mind was symbolized by the lord protector system. Where Confucius could look upon this system as having brought a measure of peace and security to Chinese society, for Mencius it had only intensified violence and destruction. In the time of Confucius there could still be the illusion that the lord protector acted in the name of the king, but after 370 B.C. even his title, *wang* 王, had been usurped by the feudal lords. Mencius was intensely conscious of the

---

[37] *Mozi*, I, 3/5a–b (Mei, *Mo Tse*, p. 10).

[38] *Mengzi*, IIA, 3/1–2.

[39] A descendant of Zengzi 曾子, a famous disciple of Confucius. He was probably somewhat older than Mencius, but seems to have shared his views.

[40] *Mengzi*, IIA, 1/3.

growth of violent authoritarianism and he rejected it in favor of an idealistic quest for the return of the sage king.

This Mencian idealism was ill-equipped, however, to withstand the march of history, and the next generation of Confucians, typified by Xunzi (c. 298–238 B.C.), rejected it for a more realistic approach. For Xunzi the ideal ruler still remained the sage king, but there was a difference between him and the ideal of Mencius. The sage king of the latter ruled chiefly by example; Xunzi's sage king, on the other hand, required absolute power.[41]

Toward Guan Zhong, Xunzi's attitude indicated a swing back to that held by Confucius. He criticized Guan Zhong's disregard for proper rites,[42] while at the same time he recognized his ability. After enumerating many vices of Duke Huan, he says: "Alas, Duke Huan of Qi had the greatest talent in the world; who could destroy him? In a glance he perceived that the ability of Guan Zhong was sufficient to be entrusted with the state. This was the greatest wisdom in the world."[43]

It was Xunzi's pupil, Hanfeizi (d. 233 B.C.), however, who brought his teacher's tendency toward authoritarianism to its logical Legalist conclusion, and Guan Zhong is cited extensively throughout the *Hanfeizi* text in support of Legalist theories.[44]

The Daoists, too, made use of Guan Zhong's name, but not because they were concerned with practical efficiency. It was simply their practice to make use of the names of all important figures in the past, no matter what their original ideology may have been. A Daoistic Confucius is one of the main heroes of the *Zhuangzi*, and in the same work we find a very Daoist-sounding apothegm attributed to Guan Zhong: "A small bag cannot hold a large object; a short rope cannot draw water from a deep well."[45]

[41] See Fung Yu-lan, *History*, I, p. 302; also *Xunzi*, XII, 18/6b (Dubs, *Hsüntze*, p. 198).

[42] *Xunzi*, V, 9/3b1–2 (Dubs, *Hsüntze*, p. 126).

[43] Ibid., III, 6/14a1–3 (Dubs, *Hsüntze*, p. 82).

[44] One such example appears in IX, 30/10a–b (Liao, *Han Fei Tzu*, I, p. 298). This tells us that Duke Huan, afraid that the people were exhausting the wealth of the country in lavish funerals, asked Guan Zhong how to stop them. "Guan Zhong replied, 'If the people do anything it is either for profit or fame.' Thereupon he issued orders that if the thickness of the inner and outer coffins went beyond the [legal] limit, the corpse was to be cut into pieces and the mourners held guilty of a crime. Now to cut the corpse into pieces would produce no fame for the mourners, and to be held guilty of a crime would produce no profit for them, so why should people [carry on expensive funerals]?" It is interesting to note that while Hanfeizi himself extensively cites the example of Guan Zhong, he recommends that others who do so be suppressed (*Hanfeizi*, V, 19/11a; Liao, *Han Fei Tzu*, I, p. 166).

[45] *Zhuangzi*, VI, 18/18b2–3 (Watson, *Chuang Tzu*, p. 194). Though the *Zhuangzi* specifically states that this was a saying of Guan Zhong, it does not appear in the present *Guanzi*.

In view of Guan Zhong's reputation as a model minister and his widespread acceptance by the Confucians, Mohists, Legalists, and Daoists, it is not surprising that he should become a hero in the propaganda literature of various schools of thought that developed during the Warring States Period on into the Han,[46] and that the authorship of certain of these texts should even be attributed to him. In the present *Guanzi* collection, the name of Guan Zhong appears in some thirty of the extant seventy-six chapters,[47] and we know from references in such works as the *Xin shu* of Jia Yi that some of the chapters were early attributed to his name.[48] It is the nature of this type of literature that once a few such works had been gathered together under the name of Guan Zhong, the collection was bound to grow with the addition from time to time of other pieces that had become popularly associated with his name, until the collection as a whole was stabilized by a person such as Liu Xiang.

The Origin of the Present Text

Although there has been seemingly endless speculation on the origin of the *Guanzi* and its individual chapters since at least the third century A.D., we still are very far from any positive answers. Given the diversified nature of its content, it would seem best to approach the questions of dating and authorship by studying its individual chapters rather than considering the work as a whole. A number of people, including me,[49] have tried to date individual chapters with varying degrees of success, but only Luo Genze 羅根澤, in his *Guanzi tanyuan* [On the Origin of the *Guanzi*], published in 1931, has attempted to deal realistically with the entire text on a chapter-by-chapter basis. He has examined each chapter for internal evidence, including the use of particles and technical terms, to date it, and he concludes that none of the *Guanzi* chapters predates

---

[46] The propaganda value of Guan Zhong's name is further borne out in Huan Kuan's 桓寬 *Yan tie lun*, which was compiled about 81 B.C. Here Guan Zhong is cited on several occasions by the Grand Secretary, Sang Hongyang 桑宏羊, in defense of his economic policies. But the quotations he gives are not to be found in the present *Guanzi* or any other extant work of the time. One is left with the strong possibility, therefore, that they may have been mere inventions of Sang or Huan.

[47] Chapters mentioning Guan Zhong include: IV, 12; VII, 18; VIII, 19–20; IX, 22; X, 26; XI, 32–33; VII, 35; XIV, 39–40; XVI, 50–51; XVIII, 56–57; XIX, 58; XXI, 68–69; XXII, 71–72, 74–76; XXIII, 77–80; XXIV, 81, 83–84.

[48] See the Introductory Comments to I, 1, and I, 2. It is perhaps worth noting, however, that none of the *Jing yan* chapters, which are generally considered to be the oldest in the *Guanzi*, mention the name of Guan Zhong.

[49] See my 1965 translation of twelve chapters.

the Warring States Period and that most of them come from either the end of that period or from the Han, that is, the fourth to first centuries B.C. Luo's conclusions are sometimes questionable,[50] but his method was basically sound as far as it went. My major criticism is that Luo's work is too limited in approach. As one of the young iconoclasts of his day, Luo was primarily interested in proving that the *Guanzi* could not be a work of the Spring and Autumn 春秋 Period (722–481 B.C.), a point which almost everyone is willing to concede now but which was still a subject of considerable debate in the early 1930s.[51] Therefore his approach was often negative in the sense that he spent much more effort telling us what the text is not rather than what it is.

The most widely accepted theory concerning the origin of the *Guanzi* holds that the so-called proto-*Guanzi*, that is, the core around which much of the present *Guanzi* finally took shape about 250 B.C., originated with the Jixia 稷下 Academy founded by King Xuan 宣 of Qi in his capital of Linzi 臨淄 in about 302 B.C.,[52] and additional materials were gradually added until its final shape was determined in about 26 B.C.[53]

[50] For example, Luo maintained that the *Dizi zhi* (XIX, 59) was probably a product of the Han, while Haloun (with greater justification) believed it to be one of the earliest chapters in the text. Luo has also dated the explanatory chapters as coming from the end of the Warring States or Qin periods. I believe they are much later, at least later than 122 B.C. See my Introductory Comments to I, 2. Xu Qingyu, in his article *Guanzi zhengzhi sixiang de tantao*, pp. 74–76, has attempted to refute the ten points given by Luo for dating the controversial *Qing zhong* economic chapters as Han and to prove that they predate Hanfeizi (d. 233 B.C.), but to me Xu's arguments are not very convincing. An even more elaborate, but equally unsuccessful, attempt to refute Luo's thesis is a privately published manuscript by Lou Liangle 婁良樂, *Guanzi pingyi*.

[51] A large section (pp. 11–54) of Ho Tin-Guang's *Kwantze* thesis, written in 1935, is taken up by a discussion of whether or not the *Guanzi* could actually have been written by Guan Zhong.

[52] That is, the eighteenth year of King Xuan. During this period the chronology of Qi is very confused. Edouard Chavannes has given the date as 325; Matthias Tchang, whose *Synchronismes chinois* I have used throughout this work to convert Chinese dates to a Western calendar unless otherwise stated, has given 315. In this case, I have followed the corrected chronology for the state of Qi given by Maspero in his "La Chronologie des rois de Ts'i au IVe siècle avant notre erè," p. 371, and Qian Mu 錢穆 in his *Xian Qin zhuzi xinien* [Chronological Studies of pre-Qin Philosophers], II, p. 599.

[53] Henri Maspero (*China in Antiquity*, p. 322) believed the original *Guanzi* was probably composed by Jixia scholars. Lewis Maverick, *Economic Dialogues*, pp. 2–3, also supports this thesis as presented by Huang Han 黃漢 in his study of the economic thought in the *Guanzi*, *Guanzi jingji sixiang*, which is translated in Maverick's work. It was also a commonly held view among Chinese scholars I met in China, such as Xu Weiyu 許維遹 and Sun Yutang 孫毓棠, who were among the main contributors to the *Guanzi jijiao* edited by Guo Moruo. for similar Japanese views, see Takeuchi Yoshio 武内義雄, *Shina shisō shi* [A History of Chinese Thought], p. 85, who has expressed the opinion that the *Guanzi* consists of remnants of Jixia texts; and Toda Toyosaburō 戸田豊三郎 in his article, *Gogyō setsu seiritsu no ichikōsatsu* [A Study of the Formation of the Theory of Five Phases], p. 38.

This theory also holds that the contents of the *Guanzi* had nothing to do with Guan Zhong himself, and that his name was simply borrowed because of his fame as a political leader. Some scholars, however, while accepting the composite nature of the *Guanzi* and the fact that none of its chapters were actually written by him, still believe that there is a connection and maintain that a careful examination of the political thought embodied in the entire book shows that a very great part of it is directly relevant to the historical background of the Spring and Autumn Period and the political philosophy of Guan Zhong. In his *History of Chinese Political Thought*,[54] Kung-chuan Hsiao enumerates four basic points to illustrate this: (1) the text discusses the role of the lord protector in favorable terms; (2) it expresses a high regard for the family and clan-law institutions; (3) it does not repudiate government by men (as did the later Legalists) but stresses rites and proprieties; (4) it elevates the ruler without abandoning the concept of following the people's wishes.

Another scholar, Yu Dunkang, would push this line of reasoning a bit further.[55] He maintains that there were three basic schools of political philosophy that developed in China during the Warring States Period: the Confucians originating in the state of Lu 魯, the Legalists in Jin 晉, and the School of Guan Zhong in Qi. The latter was devoted to maintaining clan-law and its morality based on the rules of propriety and to strengthening the system of feudal rule. It also took from Guan Zhong himself certain concepts such as: (1) integrating the internal administration and military command structure; (2) relying on both rules of propriety and law as instruments of government; (3) adopting a philosophical approach based on the way of Heaven and the nature of man; (4) following a policy of giving in order to receive. According to Yu Dunkang this school had been in existence long before the foundation of the Jixia Academy under King Xuan in 302 B.C. and continued its independent existence thereafter. He believes that the major political works in the *Guanzi* are all products of this school and that it was these works that made up the proto-*Guanzi* known to Jia Yi and Sima Qian. The remaining material that came from the Jixia Academy probably had nothing to do with the *Guanzi* until after the old Qi library was taken over by the Han and the present *Guanzi* was edited by Liu Xiang.

I have grave doubts about the methodology of both these scholars.

---

[54] Translated by F. W. Mote; I, pp. 320–321 and n. 7.

[55] Yu Dunkang, *Lun Guan Zhong xuepai* [On the School of Guan Zhong]. Yu's belief in a school of thought based on the ideas of Guan Zhong is shared by Zhao Shouzheng 趙守正 in his recently published *Guanzi zhuyi* [*Guanzi* with Notes and Translation into Modern Chinese], p. 1.

Aside from stating his position, Kung-chuan Hsiao does nothing to explain his basis for believing that the forty-two or so chapters from which he quotes are in any way connected with Guan Zhong or his thought except that they happen to adhere generally to the four criteria mentioned above. He also makes no effort to resolve the many contradictions that exist in the contents of these chapters. Yu, who quotes from twenty-seven chapters, is quite straightforward about his approach (p. 46): "If we cut out the works of the Jixia writers from the present *Guanzi*, the rest belongs to the works of the School of Guan Zhong." He does not explain how it is possible to include in this School of Guan Zhong both the writer of the *Xing shi* chapter (I, 2) and the writer of its explanatory chapter (XX, 64), who must have lived at least two hundred years later and who at times clearly interprets the *Xing shi* differently than was intended by its author; in one case he bases his misinterpretation on a corruption that must have entered the text long after the demise of Qi and any School of Guan Zhong.[56]

However, both of these scholars are correct in one respect. There is a basic point of view pervading most of the text that clearly sets it apart from the works of major Legalist and Confucian writers except perhaps for Xunzi, and this point of view encompasses most of the criteria listed by Hsiao and Yu.[57] The question then arises: How could the *Guanzi* be such a mishmash as described above and yet maintain such consistency in basic point of view? I think the answer lies in the fact that, aside from the Legalists and the more contemplative Daoists, all early Chinese political thinkers were basically committed to a reestablishment of the golden age of the past as early Zhou propaganda described it. This goal set great limits on their range of options, but there were differences in approach that came to a head when the Zhou finally lost all semblance of authority during the first quarter of the fourth century B.C.

These differences tended to be centered around different approaches toward political power and the best way to bring order to the realm— approaches which may be categorized as realistic or idealistic but which differed little in terms of ultimate goal. The idealists believed that the realists' stress on the need for law and order violated the traditional concept of social harmony. The lord protector system mentioned by

[56] See the Introductory Comments to I, 2, and XX, 64.

[57] The first of the criteria listed by Yu, i.e., the policy of integrating the internal administration and military command structure, is somewhat questionable, since it is explicitly mentioned only in the *Xiao kuang* (VIII, 20/9b5; 1 : 103.2), which in turn seems to have been based on the chapter dealing with Qi in the *Guo yu*, and thus may or may not have had anything to do with the original *Guanzi* collection. See the Introductory Comments to VIII, 20.

Xiao continued to be an important consideration to the realists of the Warring States Period, not just because of some national loyalty to Guan Zhong but because there was a desperate need for someone to bring the various warring states under unified control while at the same time supporting those traditional institutions and values that are associated with Zhou feudal society. The struggle between these two approaches also led to considerable philosophizing about the nature of man and the universe and bolstered respective positions against each other and against the main enemy, who were the Legalists.

I feel too much has been made of so-called schools of thought, but there is no doubt that the people of the Warring States Period and on into the Han were sensitive to the differences in these approaches and the philosophical arguments that went with them. It is not surprising, therefore, that texts which, no matter how different in detail, fell within a certain range on the general spectrum of political thought and which were not clearly identified with a specific person such as Xunzi, should be lumped together in a growing collection of materials attributed to the most famous realist of them all, Guan Zhong.

Certainly in the writing of political propaganda the name of Guan Zhong carried considerable weight in his home state of Qi.[58] Thus the Jixia Academy would have been a likely place for the development of a body of literature centered around his name. Association of the *Guanzi* with the Academy would not only account for the composite nature of the collection, but also for the high degree of eclecticism revealed in so many of its individual chapters. It is therefore possible that the original collection may have developed around some of the romance literature such as that contained in the *Da kuang* (VII, 18) or *Xiao kuang* (VIII, 20), with other pieces about him or supposedly written by him added to it.[59]

According to the *Shi ji*, 46/10b (Chavannes, *Mémoires historiques*, V, pp. 258–260):

King Xuan liked traveling scholars who talked of literary matters. He conferred ranks upon seventy-six men, such as Zou Yan 騶衍, Shunyu Kun

---

[58] Qi's nationalistic pride in Guan Zhong is brought out clearly in the *Mengzi*, IIA, 1/1–2. When Gongsun Chou 公孫丑 asked Mencius if he could repeat the accomplishments of Guan Zhong and Yanzi 晏子 (another famous statesman of Qi who lived about a century after Guan Zhong), if given direction of the government, Mencius replied, "You are indeed a man of Qi. You know about Guan Zhong and Yanzi but nothing more."

[59] Of course, some of the material later added to the collection may have been written long before. See Gustav Haloun, "Legalist Fragments," p. 96, for a diagram giving his concept of the evolution of the *Guanzi* text up to the time of Liu Xiang.

淳于髡, Tian Pian 田駢, Jie Yu 接輿, Shen Dao 慎到, and Huan Yuan 環淵, making them great officers of the upper grade. They did not take part in government but only carried on discussion. Hence the scholars at Jixia became very numerous, amounting to several hundred or thousand.

Shunyu Kun was a well-known sophist; Tian Pian, Jie Yu, and Huan Yuan were Daoists; Shen Dao was a Daoist who was also one of the early Legalists; and Zou Yan, perhaps the most famous of all the Jixia scholars during his day, was one of those chiefly responsible for the development of theories of the Five Phases (*wu xing* 五行). In addition to these men, Confucians such as Mencius and Xunzi, Mohists such as Song Xing, and Daoists such as Peng Meng 彭蒙, Yin Wen 尹文, and probably Zhuangzi 莊子, also visited there.[60]

The Jixia scholars must have produced hundreds of works during the three-quarters of a century or so that the Academy was in operation, although only a few of them are known to have survived the burning of the books in 213 B.C. and the subsequent destruction of the imperial library at the end of the Qin. Therefore we know very little about the thought of many of the men who are supposed to have been associated with the Academy or the ideological orientation of their works. In an atmosphere of such intense intellectual activity there must have been a great deal of give and take and blending of ideas. One of these blends appears to have been an amalgam of Daoist and Legalist concepts in what became known as the doctrine of Huang-Lao (Huang Di 黃帝 and Laozi 老子).

According to the *Shi ji*, 74/2–6: "Shen Dao was a man of Zhao 趙, Tian Pian and Jie Yu were from Qi, and Huan Yuan from Chu. They all studied the methods (*shu* 術) of Huang-Lao Daoism (*dao de* 道德)." According to 63/5a11, the doctrines of the well-known Legalist, Shen Buhai 申不害 (d. 337 B.C.), were rooted in Huang and Lao; he emphasized the relationship between form and name (*xing ming* 刑名). Furthermore, the same passage goes on to say of an even more famous Legalist, Hanfeizi, that he delighted in the study of the relationship between form and name, law, and methods, while basing [his doctrines] on Huang and Lao. Until recently most scholars have tended to treat these mentions of Huang-Lao doctrine as references to a highly mystical branch of Daoism that developed into a major religious movement during the Han. Recent discoveries make it clear, however, that the Huang-Lao doctrines referred to here constituted an important school

---

[60] See Jin Shoushen 金受申, *Jixiapai zhi yanjiu*.

of political thought which, besides having a base in Qi, also seems to have developed in the area belonging to Chu.[61]

In December 1973, Han tomb III, dated 168 B.C., was excavated at Mawangdui 馬王堆 in Changsha 長沙, Hunan. Discovered in this tomb, among many other relics, was a wide range of pre-Han and Han texts including those dealing with medicine, Yin-yang-Five Phases 陰陽五行 cosmology, astronomy and astrology, history, corporal punishment, as well as three maps and two versions of the *Laozi* written on silk scrolls.[62] These two *Laozi* manuscripts, now designated as "A" 甲 and "B" 乙, and their attached texts are extremely important in that they have enhanced our understanding of Huang-Lao thought and its connection with portions of the *Guanzi*.

Both the "A" and "B" versions of the *Lao-tzu* differ in arrangement and wording from the eighty-one-chapter Wang Bi 王弼 (A.D. 226–249) text that has been our standard in modern times. In terms of overall organization, the main difference is that neither of the Mawangdui versions has separate chapters, and both reverse the order of the *Dao* 道 and *De* 德 sections into which the text is divided, placing the more sociopolitical *De* section first. This is the arrangement to be found in the *Jie Lao* 解老 [Explaining the *Laozi*] chapter of the *Hanfeizi* (VI, 20), and would appear to represent a somewhat Legalist approach to the text.[63]

Postfixed to the *Laozi* "A" text are a series of four other unnamed texts, the first of which is clearly Confucian and was probably written by a follower of Mencius. It emphasizes the five characteristics (*wu xing* 五行): human goodness (*ren* 仁), righteousness (*yi* 義), propriety (*li* 禮), wisdom (*zhi* 智), and sageliness (*sheng* 聖). The fourth, a very short text of some ten lines, also discusses these same characteristics, while the third discusses the importance of having a strong military. The second of these texts, some fifty-two lines in length, purports to be a record of

[61] See Long Hui 龍晦, *Mawangdui chutu Laozi Yi ben qian guyi shu tanyuan*. Long adds that, in addition to a concern for name and form, Huang-Lao thought is characterized by an emphasis on timeliness instead of the timelessness of Daoism, a belief that law originated in the Way, and an acceptance of standard Confucian virtues.

[62] For a general survey of the Mawangdui materials, see Jeffry K. Riegel, "A Summary of some Recent *Wenwu* and *Kaogu* Articles on Mawangdui Tombs Two and Three," and "Mawangdui Tomb Three: Documents." See also Jan Yün-hua, "The Silk Manuscripts on Taoism," and Tu Wei-ming, "The 'Thought of Huang Lao': A Reflection on the Lao Tzu and Huang Ti Texts in the Silk Manuscripts of Ma-wang-tui." For a reconstruction of both versions of the *Laozi*, see *Wenwu* (1974), no. 11, pp. 8–20.

[63] See Robert G. Hendricks, "Examining the Ma-wang-tui Silk Texts of the *Lao-tzu*," and Paul J. Lin, *A Translation of Lao Tzu's Tao Te Ching and Wang Pi's Commentary*, pp. x–xi, as well as the articles of Jan and Tu cited in n. 62, above.

advice concerning different types of rulers given to Tang 湯, the founder of the Shang 商 dynasty, by his chief minister, Yi Yin 伊尹; it represents a mixture of Daoist and Legalist thought and is the most closely related to the *Guanzi*, especially chapters XV, 46, and XVII, 52.[64] It also asserts that the successful ruler must model himself on the pattern of Heaven and Earth 法天地之則, which is very reminiscent of a similar statement in XXI, 66/3a9: "In order to provide for the proper administration of the realm, laws are modeled after the positions of Heaven and Earth" 法者法天地之位. Chapter XXI, 66, is an explanation for chapter II, 7, and almost certainly dates from the Han.

Prefixed to the *Laozi* "B" text were four other texts: *Jing fa* 經法 [The Scriptures and Law], *Shi da jing* 十大經 [Ten Great Scriptures],[65] *Cheng* 稱 [Balancing], and *Dao yuan* 道原 [Dao, the Origin].[66] Tang Lan 唐蘭 identifies these four as being the lost *Huang Di si jing* 黃帝四經 [Four Scriptures of the Yellow Emperor]. The *Jing fa* stresses laws as the ultimate of government and says that they are produced by the Way (*dao*). The *Shi da jing* pays special attention to methods of warfare while *Cheng* is mostly concerned with the function of the Way and the relationship between it and forms and names. *Dao yuan* presents a classical exposition of the Way and its oneness.

The origin of these texts, like that of the *Guanzi*, is somewhat of a mystery. Tang Lan, writing in 1975, felt that the *Laozi* "B" texts were probably produced about 400 B.C. by a person from the small state of Zheng in present-day north-central Henan. Tang reasons that Shen Buhai, who is the earliest political philosopher known to have been influenced by Huang-Lao thought, had served in Zheng before it was wiped out by the state of Han 韓 in 376 B.C. and must have formulated his basic ideological approach before this time. Therefore, Huang-Lao thought and these texts must have been in existence by then. Tang's assumptions about the dating of Huang-Lao thought may be correct, but he really presents no evidence to show that these particular texts were in existence at that time, or for that matter that they had anything to do with the state of Zheng.

Both the *Laozi* "A" and "B" manuscripts themselves are much later than this. The former is judged to have been copied sometime during the

[64] See Ling Xiang 凌襄, *Shilun Mawangdui Hanmu boshu Yi Yin jiu zhu*, p. 26.
[65] There is some question about the reading of the second character in this title. Some would read *da* 大 as *liu* 六. Thus the title would be translated, "The Sixteen Scriptures." See Qiu Xigui 裘錫圭, *Mawangdui Laozi Jia Yi ben juanqianhou yishu yu Daofajia*, p. 68.
[66] For a discussion of these four texts see Tang Lan 唐蘭, *Mawangdui chutu Laozi Yi ben juanqian guyi shu de yanjiu*; Long Hui, *Mawangdui chutu Laozi Yi ben qian guyi shu tanyuan*; and Jan Yün-hua, "The Silk Manuscripts on Taoism."

Qin dynasty (221–207 B.C.), since it is written in the small seal characters that became standard during the Qin but were replaced in the Han by the more practical clerical script. It also continues to write *bang* 邦, which would have been a taboo character during the early Han because it appears in the name of the dynastic founder, Liu Bang 劉邦. The *Laozi* "B" manuscript is written in clerical script and avoids *bang*, writing *guo* 國 instead. However, it does not avoid the personal names of the two succeeding emperors, Liu Ying 劉盈 and Liu Heng 劉恒. Therefore, even though the clerical script was employed to a limited extent during the Qin, the *Laozi* "B" manuscript would seem to have been copied during the reign of the first emperor of the Han, 206–194 B.C.

A recent study further indicates that at least the Mawangdui copy of the *Laozi* "A" text was made in the area of the old state of Chu, since some of the characters deviate slightly from standard Qin forms in favor of Chu prototypes.[67] Long Hui, in his study, deals with the rhymes found in the texts prefixed to the *Laozi* "B" and concludes that the rhyme scheme is largely similar to that of the *Huainanzi* and thus that these texts were products of scholars from the state of Chu. Several chapters of the *Guanzi*, most notably V, 13; XIII, 36 and 38; XVI, 49; and XVII, 52, employ a similar rhyme scheme and it would seem, therefore, that they too were written by persons who at least originally came from Chu.[68] The connection between these texts attached to the *Lao-tzu* "B" and the *Guanzi* is further indicated by the fact that several chapters (III, 8; IV, 12; V, 15; VI, 17; XIII, 36, 37, and 38; XV, 42; XVI, 49; XVII, 55) contain passages either identical or similar to passages in them.

It is possible, of course, that the authors of some of the chapters in the *Guanzi* that appear to have some connection with Chu were also associated with the Jixia Academy. In fact, Qiu Xigui believes that chapters XIII, 36 and 38, were written by followers of Shen Dao and Tian Pian, both of whom were Jixia scholars.[69] If such were the case, these chapters could then have been part of the original protocollection. However, I think it is more likely that they originated in the old state of Chu and entered the *Guanzi* through a group of scholars centered around the court of Liu An 劉安 (180–122 B.C.), the second King of

[67] See Li Yumin 李裕民, *Mawangdui boshu chaoxie niandai kao.*

[68] On the basis of his study, Long further believes that these texts were probably written during the fourth century B.C.

[69] Qiu Xigui, *Mawangdui,* pp. 88ff.

Huainan 淮南, who is best known as the reputed author of the *Huainanzi*.[70]

Liu An, from his early youth on, seems to have been more interested in literary pursuits than political power and, by the time he had become king in 164 B.C., had accumulated an extensive library. After becoming king, he gathered around him a large group of scholars who concentrated on the study of a wide range of pre-Han philosophers as well as the cultural traditions of the old state of Chu. From all this activity emerged a number of works, including what seems to have been a trilogy: the *Nei shu* 內書 [Inner Book], which later became known as the *Huainanzi*; the *Zhong pian* 中篇 [Middle Part], dealing with alchemy; and the *Wai shu* 外書 [Outer Book]. The latter work has been lost, but according to the "Treatise on Literature" in the *Qian Han shu*, 30/21b13, it consisted of thirty-three *pian*. The commentator Yan Shigu 顏師古 (581–645) adds that while the *Nei shu* discussed the Dao, the *Wai shu* dealt with miscellaneous theories. Given the fact that Guan Zhong came from Yingshang, an area belonging to Chu, the *Guanzi* must have received considerable attention from Liu An's scholars.

According to the *Qian Han shu*, 36/5a10–11, after Liu An was accused of treason, and committed suicide in 122 B.C., Liu De 劉德, (d. 56 B.C.), the father of Liu Xiang, was sent to Huainan to take charge of Liu An's estate. Since Liu De could not have been born much before 120 B.C. and could not have been sent to Huainan much before 85 B.C., some commentators believe that this mission was actually carried out by Liu De's father, Liu Piqiang 劉辟彊 (164–85 B.C.). In any case, it appears certain that after Liu An's death, his library was incorporated into the imperial collection where it became known to Liu Xiang. No other text contains so many parallel passages to the *Guanzi* chapters contained in this volume as the *Huainanzi*. Thus it is very possible that some of the present chapters in the *Guanzi* may have entered the imperial library through the Huainan collection and may be partially, if not wholly, the work of the Huainan scholars.

In April 1972 another major discovery of ancient Chinese texts occurred during the excavation of two Han tombs at Yinqueshan 銀雀山 in Linyi 臨邑 Xian, Shandong. Over five thousand bamboo slips were recovered from these tombs, which date about 134 B.C. Most of the slips

---

[70] For a discussion of the history of the *Huainanzi*, see two unpublished dissertations: Charles Y. Le Blanc, "The Idea of Resonance (*Kan-ying*) in the *Huai-nan Tzu*" and Harold David Roth, "The Textual History of the *Huai-nan Tzu*."

were either badly fragmented or contained only three or four characters, but some 750 of them have been identified as coming from a number of pre-Han or early Han texts, mostly dealing with military affairs, and including such well-known works as the *Sunzi*, the *Mozi*, *Liu tao*, and the previously lost *Sun Bin bing fa*.[71] Also included among the finds were two documents directly related to the *Guanzi*. The first, entitled *Wang bing* 王兵 [On the Armed Forces of the King], is composed primarily of passages that more or less duplicate portions of three of the major military works in the *Guanzi*, *Qi fa* (II, 6), *Di tu* (X, 27), and *Can huan* (X, 28). The *Wang bing* material is in a somewhat abbreviated form and there are some differences in individual characters, but the connection is obvious.[72] The second, as yet unpublished, is entitled *Sanshi shi* 三十時 [The Thirty Periods] and consists of a calendar of activities that should be conducted during the thirty periods of twelve days each into which the year has been divided.[73] The text is fairly short and does not duplicate anything in the present *Guanzi*, but its twelve-day divisions are similar to those mentioned in the *You guan* (III, 8).

Thus it would appear that Haloun's use of the term "amorphous" to describe the *Guanzi* is more appropriate than even he realized, and that there must have been a large number of works vaguely attached to a recognized *Guanzi* core. Some of these were incorporated into Liu Xiang's work and thereby became permanently attached to it; others were incorporated but continued to have an independent existence;[74] and still others were rejected for one reason or another and, not being attached to any major work, quickly disappeared.

[71] *Wenwu* (1974), no. 2, pp. 15–35. Reconstruction and study of the *Sunzi* materials was published in 1976 by the Wenwu Chubanshe 文物出版社 under the title *Sunzi bingfa*. A similar reconstruction of the *Sun Bin bing fa* was published by the same organization in 1975. A third major discovery of early documents occurred in a Qin tomb dated about 217 B.C., which was excavated at Shuihudi 睡虎地 in Yunmeng 雲夢 Xian, Hubei, in December 1975; but aside from throwing much light on the practical application of Legalism and helping to clarify some terms that appear in the *Guanzi*, they do not appear to have any direct bearing on the *Guanzi* itself. See A.F.P. Hulsewé, "The Ch'in Documents Discovered in Hupei in 1975."

[72] See *Wenwu* (1976), no. 12, pp. 36–43, for a reconstruction of this text and a comparison with relevant material in the *Guanzi*.

[73] I am indebted to Professor Zhu Dexi 朱德熙 of Beijing University, who very graciously supplied me with a copy of his reconstruction of these materials.

[74] Some of the present *Guanzi* chapters appear to have had an independent existence even after Liu Xiang's editing. The *Bing fa* (VI, 17) and *Can huan* (X, 28) chapters seem to have been listed separately in the *Qi lüe* among the military works. See Tao Xianzeng 陶憲曾 (19th century), cited in Wang Xianqian's 王先謙 *Han shu buzhu*, 30/3189. They were later omitted by Ban Gu 班固 when he compiled the "Treatise on Literature" for the *Qian Han shu*. The "Treatise," 30/10b, however, still lists the *Dizi zhi* (XIX, 59) separately.

Transmission of the Text to Tang 唐 Times[75]

Can we assume, however, that the *Guanzi* that was collected and collated by Liu Xiang is basically the same as the text we have today? Henri Maspero believed not. He held that Liu Xiang's edition of the *Guanzi* was later lost and the present *Guanzi* is entirely a modern forgery, ancient parts being buried in a mass of chapters written probably during the fourth and fifth centuries A.D.[76] As proof, Maspero has made three main points: (1) *Guanzi*, V, 14/7b12–8a1, quotes the pseudo-*Tai shi* 泰誓 chapter of the *Shang shu* [Book of History], V, 1a/8, which is a forgery of the third century A.D.; (2) *Guanzi*, VII, 18, copies the *Zuo zhuan*, preserving even the Lu chronology;[77] (3) according to Zhang Shoujie's *Zheng yi* commentary to the *Shi ji*, 62/4a1: "The *Qi lüe* says, 'The *Guanzi* in eighteen *pian* belongs to the Legalist school.'" This indicates that the *Qi lüe* originally listed the *Guanzi* as having only eighteen sections. Therefore the present Liu Xiang preface must be a forgery and the reading in the *Qian Han shu's* "Treatise on Literature" of eight-six *pian* must be a later interpolation.

Maspero's first two points have been dealt with by Bernhard Karlgren in his *Authenticity of Ancient Chinese Texts* (pp. 173–176). He shows that the passage in *Guanzi*, V, 14, is not entirely the same as that in the pseudo-*Tai shi*, and that where it differs from the *Tai shi* it resembles another similar passage in the *Zuo zhuan*, Zhao, 24. After comparing the three passages, Karlgren concludes that the *Guanzi* passage was not based on the *Tai shi*, but that the forger of the *Tai shi* borrowed from both the *Guanzi* and the *Zuo zhuan* to create his text.

Concerning Maspero's second point, Karlgren remarks that, even though the *Guanzi* does cite the *Zuo zhuan*, this merely proves that it was written after the *Zuo zhuan* (which Karlgren, p. 65, maintains was

---

[75] For much of the material contained in this and the following section, I am deeply indebted to Piet van der Loon for his excellent study, "On the Transmission of the *Kuan-tzu*."

[76] *China in Antiquity*, pp. 479–480, nn. 6 and 7. See also his review in the *Journal Asiatique*, XII (1927), no. 9, pp. 147–151, of Gustav Haloun's *Seit wann kannten Chinesen die Tocharer oder Indo-germanen überhaupt?*. Here Maspero gave a diagram showing his concept of the history of the *Guanzi*; he believed that remnants of the original work are to be found in the *Zuo zhuan*, *Guo yu*, *Lüshi chunqiu*, *Hanfeizi*, *Han shi wai zhuan*, and *Shi ji*. I doubt if many scholars today would agree with Maspero's opinion, but at one time it was widely accepted. See, for example, Charles Gardner, *Chinese Traditional Historiography*, p. 26, and Esson Gale, *Discourses on Salt and Iron*, p. 7. Robert Shafer, "Linguistics in History," p. 299, also quotes Peter Boodberg to the effect that less than ten percent of the work may belong to the beginning of the fourth century B.C., the balance being post-Han.

[77] VII, 18/3b11 (1.85.1).

compiled between 468 and 300 B.C.) and has nothing to do with its being a post-Han forgery.

Maspero's third point is most effectively dealt with by van der Loon, who shows that the *Qi lüe* mentioned by Zhang Shoujie is a misreading for the *Qi lu* [Seven Lists], a catalogue prepared by Ruan Xiaoxu 阮孝緒 (479–536).[78] The reading of eighteen *pian* in Zhang's commentary is clearly a mistake for eighteen *juan*. Ruan's catalogue is now lost, but, as will be seen below, the standard edition of the *Guanzi* during Sui 隋 and Tang times was either in eighteen or nineteen *juan*, and we know that the text of the *Guanzi* that was excerpted for the *Zi chao* [Extracts from the Philosophers], an anthology compiled by Yu Zhongrong 庾仲容 (476–549), also consisted of eighteen *juan*.[79]

As further proof that the *Guanzi* was not a later forgery, we have positive evidence showing that, as a whole, the transmission of the text from Han to Tang times was uninterrupted. A number of references to the *Guanzi* appear in the literature of this period, and some quotations were taken from it as well. We have already mentioned the comment of Fu Xuan (217–278). The *Fengsu tongyi* [Popular Traditions and Customs] of Ying Shao 應劭 (fl. 178–196) makes reference to the work and originally contained a paraphrase of a passage from its *Dizi zhi* chapter (XIX, 59/7a4), which it specifically attributed to *Guanzi*.[80] Liu Xie 劉勰 (c. 465–522), in his work on literary criticism, the *Wen xin diao long* [The Literary Mind and the Carving of Dragons], frequently referred to the *Guanzi*, and in V, 18/13b (Shih, *Literary Mind*, p. 137), has cited a passage that appears in the present *Guanzi* text, XVIII, 56/4b–5a.

This evidence, of course, in no way proves that the *Guanzi* did not undergo considerable tampering during this period. Indeed, we have already seen that at least two chapters of the present text, III, 9 (or III, 8), and XVI, 50, were probably later substitutions for chapters that had been lost after the text was edited by Liu Xiang. Furthermore, any attempt to ascertain the degree of even such major altering as the addition or substitution of chapters is made difficult by the fact that, in spite of the notations appearing in other texts mentioned above, we do

---

[78] As van der Loon, "Transmission," p. 367, n. 3, points out, Zhang twice refers to this catalogue as the Ruan Xiaoxu *Qi lüe* (*Shi ji*, 63/4b–5a) and several times as the *Qi lu*.

[79] The *Zi chao* is now lost but a list of the works from which Yu compiled his anthology and the number of *juan* in each is given by Gao Sisun 高似孫 (fl. 1184) in an appendix to his *Zi lüe*.

[80] See the collection of lost passages contained in the Centre franco-chinois d'études sinologiques edition, p. 95. The *Fengsu tongyi*, IX, 2/67, especially quotes from the *Book of Guanzi* 管子書, but the quotation does not appear in our text today. It was probably taken from one of the chapters now lost.

not have, until much later, a description of the text as a whole, its number of chapters, or its general content.

Some information is found in the descriptive bibliographies beginning in the sixth century with Ruan Xiaoxu's *Qi lu*. But it is useless for studying the transmission of the text, because by the sixth century the *Guanzi* had long since been copied onto silk or paper scrolls[81] and is only recorded in terms of *juan*.[82] This means there is no way of making any comparison with information contained in the Han literature, which records the text in terms of *pian*. Thus, while the authenticity of the present text as a whole appears to be well attested, the same cannot be presumed for its individual parts.

Transmission from Tang to Song 宋

As mentioned above, by Tang times the standard division of the *Guanzi* text was in terms of *juan*. The *Sui shu* catalogue, 34/3b, submitted to the throne in A.D. 656, gives nineteen *juan*, as does that of the *Xin Tang shu* [New History of the Tang Dynasty], 55/8a–b, which was published in 1061–1063. That of the *Jiu Tang shu* [Old History of the Tang Dynasty], 47/5b, completed in 945, lists a *Guanzi* in eighteen *juan*,[83] and the *Nihonkoku genzaisho mokuroku* [Catalogue of Present Books in Japan] by Fujiwara no Sukeyo 藤原佐世 (d. 898) lists one in twenty.[84] As van der Loon points out, the difference between eighteen and nineteen *juan* may not indicate any real rearrangement of the text, but merely that the preface and table of contents of the nineteen *juan* text were on a separate scroll.[85] It is more difficult to explain why the text that reached Japan should be in twenty *juan*. Probably it was an unauthorized copy taken from some private collection and for this reason did not conform to the standard arrangement given in the Chinese catalogues.[86]

The oldest surviving copies of the *Guanzi* do not go back before the Southern Song (1127–1278), and are all divided into twenty-four in-

---

[81] Van der Loon, "Transmission," p. 367, believes that this probably took place before the end of the Han.

[82] As mentioned above, Zhang Shoujie has cited the *Qi lu* of Ruan Xiaoxu in terms of eighteen *pian*, but this is undoubtedly a mistake for eighteen *juan*.

[83] This catalogue was based on the now lost *Gujin shulu* [List of Ancient and Modern Books], which was compiled by Wu Qiong 毋嫈 soon after A.D. 721.

[84] See Onagaya Keikichi 小長谷惠吉, *Nihonkoku genzaisho mokuroku kaisetsukō*, supplement, p. 12.

[85] Ibid., p. 368.

[86] Ibid., pp. 369–370.

stead of eighteen or nineteen *juan*. To gain a picture of the text as it existed in Tang times, we must turn to another source.

In 631, Wei Zheng 魏徵 compiled his anthology, the *Qunshu zhiyao* [Important Passages from Assembled Books], which includes selections from twenty chapters of the *Guanzi*.[87] This work disappeared in China about the beginning of Song times but has been preserved in Japan. It is therefore particularly valuable not only because of its early date but also because of its independent history. From an examination of these selections in the *Qunshu zhiyao*, it appears that the arrangement and content of the *Guanzi* at the beginning of the Tang, at least, were the same as in the present text. The chapters missing from the text as we now have it also seem to have disappeared before Wei Zheng's time, because none of them are included in his collection.[88]

Since Wei Zheng's work must have been based on the official eighteen- or nineteen-*juan* edition mentioned in the imperial catalogues of the time, we can be relatively certain that the content and arrangement of these editions were also approximately the same as the work we have today. But how the eighteen- or nineteen-*juan* edition of that time became the twenty-four-*juan* edition of the Southern Song remains another mystery in the uncertain history of the *Guanzi*.

We know that the eighteen-*juan* edition still remained the official version of the text down until Song times, because it is mentioned in the *Chongwen zongmu* [Complete Catalogue of Honored Writings].[89] Even after the fall of the Northern Song in 1126, this edition is mentioned twice more before disappearing completely: once in a catalogue of a private collection compiled by Chao Gongwu 晁公武 about

---

[87] The *Qunshu zhiyao*, 32, includes excerpts from the following chapters: I, 1–4 (I, 4, is here entitled *Li jun* 立君 instead of *Li zheng* 立政); II, 6; III, 10; VI, 16; VIII, 19–20; IX, 22–23; X, 20 and 30; XI, 32; XV, 40; XVIII, 56; XX, 66–67; XXIV, 81. Other sources showing that the text we have now was in existence at this time are the Sui and early Tang encyclopedias such as the *Beitang shuchao*, *Yiwen leiju*, and *Chuxue ji*, which contain extensive quotations.

[88] Other evidence that these chapters were no longer extant during the early years of the Tang comes from Li Shan's 李善 (d. 689) commentary to the *Wen xuan* [Anthology], 28/1b. After repeating a quotation from the *Guanzi* given in the *Wen shi* [Literary Comments] of Jiang Suizhi 江邃之 (fl. 420) but missing today, Li adds: "When we now examine the text of the *Guanzi*, we find that more recently several chapters have been lost. I suspect Sui 邃 [i.e., Jiang Shuzhi] found his quotation in a lost chapter." This would indicate that at least the chapter cited by Jiang was still in existence about 420, but it is also possible that Jiang obtained it from a quotation in another text and not from the *Guanzi* itself.

[89] *Chongwen zongmu fubuyi* [*Chongwen zongmu* Reconstructed], 3/138. The original *Chongwen zongmu*, a descriptive catalogue of the Song imperial library, was compiled between 1034 and 1038 by Wang Yaochen 王堯臣 and others. The original version was lost and only preserved in abridged form to 1799, when large parts of the original were re-collected by Qian Dongyuan 錢東垣 in the reconstruction cited above.

1151,[90] and once in the *Tong zhi* [Comprehensive Collection of Treatises] of Zheng Qiao 鄭樵 completed about 1161.[91]

In discussing his eighteen-*juan* edition, Chao mentions that it has a commentary for fifty-eight of its *pian*.[92] The association of the eighteen-*juan* edition with a commentary represents a difficult problem. Neither the *Chongwen zongmu* nor any other previous text mentions such a commentary. This would seem to indicate that it was inserted in the eighteen-*juan* edition after the compilation of the *Chongwen zongmu* (1038). Van der Loon, however, suggests another alternative. Chao's copy may have been without a commentary, but having heard about such a work from some source such as the *Chongwen zongmu*, he may have noted it in his catalogue accordingly.[93]

The mention of fifty-eight (fifty-nine) *pian* indicates that this is the same commentary that is included in most modern editions of the *Guanzi* under the name of a well-known scholar-official of the early Tang period, Fang Xuanling 房玄齡 (578–648). Since it seems to have direct bearing on the development of the twenty-four-*juan* edition, a word or two should be said about it here. Unfortunately the history of the commentary is no clearer than that of the text. In his great encyclopedia on government, the *Tong dian*, Du You 杜佑 (735–812) gives extensive commentary. These quotations must have been taken from another work written by Du on the *Guanzi*, namely his *Guanshi zhilüe* [Summary of the Main Points of Mr. Guan], which consisted of ten chapters of excerpts from the work.[94] In his preface to this latter work, Du ascribes the commentary to Fang. This is the only reference we have in Tang times to a commentary on the *Guanzi* by Fang.

On the other hand, the *Chongwen zongmu*, III/139, cites the *Wushi xizhai shumu* [Catalogue of Mr. Wu's Western Study] of Wu Jing 吳兢 (d. 749) as listing an annotated edition of the *Guanzi* in thirty *juan* with a commentary by Yin Zhizhang 尹知章 (d. 718).[95] It adds, however, that

---

[90] *Zhaode xiansheng junzhai dushu zhi* [Treatise by Mr. Zhaode on Books Read in the Prefectural Study], IIIA/16b–17a. Zhaode 昭德 was the sobriquet of Chao Gongwu.

[91] 64/797a. The works listed by Chao Gongwu were supposed to have been examined by him personally. Zheng Qiao, however, is known to have relied heavily on other catalogues for his information and it is quite possible he never actually saw this eighteen-*juan* edition.

[92] 五十八篇有注解 fifty-eight should probably read fifty-nine since that is the number of *pian* covered by a full commentary in the present *Guanzi*.

[93] Van der Loon, "Transmission," p. 381, n. 1. Chao's reference is further confused by the fact that an enlarged edition of his catalogue, which was prepared by one of his students, Yao Yingji, no longer mentions an eighteen-*juan Guanzi*, but only one in twenty-four *juan*. See quotation in the *Wenxian tongkao*, 212/1737a–b.

[94] The *Guanshi zhilüe* was lost after the Song, but the preface is cited by Chao Gongwu in his *Junzhai dushu zhi*, IIIA/17a.

[95] Yin's biography in the *Jiu Tang shu*, 189B/9a, also mentions such a commentary.

29

at that time (1038) only nineteen of the original *juan* remained, and the commentary, beginning from XX, 64, onward, had been lost.

It is, of course, possible that two entirely different commentaries existed, one by Fang, quoted by Du You and preserved in the present editions of the *Guanzi*, the other now lost. But an examination of the surviving commentary makes this possibility doubtful. We find that the chapters in the first nineteen *juan* of the present text have a very full commentary, whereas the remaining chapters contain only brief scattered notes that are obviously not part of the same commentary. Indeed, in his study[96] van der Loon has shown without doubt that these notes were actually taken from Du You's work and later inserted into the text of the *Guanzi*.[97] All of them are to be found in the economic chapters of the *Tong dian*, and though the *Tong dian* occasionally contains more of this commentary than the *Guanzi* text itself, the reverse is never true. Moreover, as van der Loon points out, Du You himself says in regard to XXII, 76: "I have found nobody who made a commentary on it." This statement seems to apply not only to XXII, 76, but also to the rest of the economic chapters in the *Qing zhong* section (XXI, 68 through XXIV, 86).[98]

That the commentary attributed to Fang Xuanling and used by Du You, and the one attributed to Yin Zhizhang by the *Chongwen zongmu*, should both consist of nineteen *juan* cannot be mere coincidence. They must be the same work.

Wu Jing (the source of the *Chongwen zongmu's* information) and Yin Zhizhang were born about the same time, even though the latter died in 718 and the former in 749. Since they were both prominent scholars and must have known about each other, we can be fairly certain that Wu Jing was correct in attributing a thirty-*juan* commentary to Yin. However, it is also possible that Yin's commentary was later lost, perhaps in the destruction accompanying An Lushan's 安祿山 rebellion (756–757). In this case, the commentary that the *Chongwen zongmu* attributed to him could actually have been by Fang Xuanling. Another possibility, suggested by Zhou Guangye 周廣業 (1730–1798) in his *Yilin zhu* [Commentary to the Forest of Ideas], I / 17b, is that the commentary was begun under Fang and completed by Yin. Still a third suggestion is that Du You did not really know who wrote the com-

---

[96] "Transmission," pp. 374–375.

[97] These notes, however, do not include a special series of short glosses that appear at the end of *juan* I, III, VIII, IX, and X (see the *SBCK* edition), and are scattered throughout the text, beginning with the *Xing shi jie* (XX, 64). The glosses do not appear in the *Tong dian* and there is reason to believe that they are the work of someone else. See n. 99 below.

[98] *Tong dian*, 12/68a.

mentary but attributed it to Fang as one of the foremost political scholars of the time.

Most modern critics of the *Guanzi* have tended to accept Yin's authorship with certain reservations. Guo Moruo 郭沫若, for example, seems to be of the opinion that the original commentary was composed by Yin, and that some additions were made by others later on.[99] Haloun has stated categorically that Yin was the author.[100] Therefore, throughout the translation I have referred to this commentary as Yin's, though I think its authorship is still a very open question.

In any case, we know that in 1038 when the *Chongwen zongmu* was compiled, there existed an annotated edition consisting of sixty-three *pian*[101] in nineteen *juan*. We also know that this text was later completed by adding to it the remaining twenty-three *pian* in five *juan* (beginning with XX, 64) from some other text to make the present edition of twenty-four *juan*.

Printed Editions

The earliest available printed edition of the *Guanzi* is known by the name of the author of its preface, Yang Chen 楊忱.[102] It contains a short colophon by Zhang Nie 張嵲 (1096–1148) who, during the period from 1135 to 1138, occupied various positions in the Bishu Sheng 秘書省, an office responsible for rebuilding the imperial library after its destruction in 1126. Zhang's colophon, entitled *Du Guanzi* 讀管子 [On Reading the Guanzi], gives an interesting insight on the problem of finding a suitable text at this time:

I had been trying to find the *Book of Guanzi* for a long time when in the *jiwei* 己未 year of the Shaoxing 紹興 period [1139] I was able to borrow [a copy] from someone. Thereafter I read it for several months before beginning to see its meaning. However, there were numerous corruptions and deletions, twenty or

[99] See Guo Moruo's preface to the *Guanzi jijiao*, I, 1.
[100] "Legalist Fragments," p. 89. Haloun based his statement on the fact that part of the commentary as found in XVIII, 55, is expanded in the commentary to the parallel chapter, B12, of the *Guiguzi*. Since Yin was the only scholar known to have commented on both works, Haloun felt that the present *Guanzi* commentary must have been written by him. Van der Loon, however, points out that the expanded portion only constitutes a small part of the *Guanzi* commentary. Moreover, since Fang lived considerably before Yin, there is no reason to suppose that the latter could not have known of the parallel chapter in the *Guanzi* and made use of its commentary when making one for the *Guiguzi*.
[101] Undoubtedly these sixty-three *pian* were not complete, but their titles must have been given.
[102] This is the edition photographically reproduced in the *SBCK*, about which more will be said later.

thirty percent of which I was not able to explain. By making use of the context and comparing references to punishments and government in the classics and histories, I made some corrections of these errors. Those which were doubtful I set forth in a list; those which I could not explain I left, not daring to force a meaning. Then I further made a selection [those passages which were] profound in principle and earnest in purpose. I made a copy and kept it in my home in the hope of obtaining a better edition to complete my work.[103]

That Zhang, with his official position in the Bishu Sheng, should find it so difficult to get his hands on a copy of the *Guanzi* is rather surprising. Copies of the work should have been available during the Northern Song (960–1126) since it was included among those required for study by candidates for certain degrees;[104] and even though the imperial library had been destroyed, one would expect a number to be in private circulation. Yet it was probably not until the year 1138–1139, when Zhang left the capital to travel in Fujian and Sichuan,[105] that he finally came upon a copy of the book. This fits the time mentioned in the colophon, and since neither of these areas had been touched by the war, books were certainly more easy to obtain there.

Zhang's copy contained the commentary attributed to Fang Xuanling. He mentions it in the colophon, complaining about its poor quality and expressing the belief that it therefore could not have been written by Fang. Furthermore, the presence of the colophon at the end of the full twenty-four *juan* and the fact that Zhang does not mention that any large block of chapters is missing indicate that the text he obtained was complete.

We do not know who actually did the work of combining the surviving nineteen *juan* of the Yin Zhizhang (or Fang Xuanling) annotated edition with the last five *juan* from some other unannotated edition. Nor do we know who added the notes of Du You to the text and the anonymous glosses mentioned above.[106] It is a fact, however, that this

---

[103] Van der Loon, whose study also contains a partial translation of this colophon, adds the following note ("Transmission," p. 383, n. 2): "There must have existed a collection of passages which Zhang Nie had selected together with brief remarks of the edifying type called *ping* 評, because more than forty of these remarks are preserved in the edition of Zhu Yanghe 朱養和 and others (1625) [better known as the Huazhai 花齋 edition]. Cf. *Hubei tongzhi*, p. 2051. Perhaps such a collection formed part of the original version of his works." The enclosure in brackets is my addition.

[104] Edward Kracke, *Civil Service in Early Sung China*, p. 96. I suspect that these degree candidates relied primarily on quotations to be found in the encyclopedias and anthologies rather than the work itself.

[105] *Ziwei ji*, 31/15bff.

[106] The position of the glosses at the end of the *juan* in the first nineteen *juan* and their insertion in the text in the remaining five indicates that they must have been part of the text from which the last five *juan* were originally taken. See van der Loon, "Transmission," p. 380.

twenty-four-*juan* edition gradually replaced the old one in eighteen *juan* as the standard text. The *Tong zhi*, 68/797a, lists a twenty-four-*juan* edition with a Fang Xuanling commentary side by side with the unannotated one in eighteen *juan* and the incomplete edition in nineteen *juan* containing the commentary by Yin Zhizhang.[107] The enlarged edition of Chao Gongwu's *Junzhai dushu zhi* by Yao Yingji 姚應績 lists the *Guanzi* as having twenty-four *juan* instead of the eighteen given in the original edition of the catalogue.[108] Finally, the *Zhongxing guange shumu*, the official catalogue of the Southern Song which was submitted in 1178, lists only the twenty-four-*juan* edition,[109] as does Chen Zhensun's 陳振孫 (fl. 1234) *Zhizhai shulu jieti* [Zhizhai's, i.e., Chen Zhensun's Descriptive Catalogue], X/283. After the Song we hear no more about an eighteen-*juan* edition.

A copy of the Yang Chen edition with its Zhang Nie colophon is stored in the Beijing National Library, but there are two reprints of it in general circulation. One is a Guangxu 光緒 period reprint of about 1879, the other is contained in the *Sibu congkan* 四部叢刊], first series, published in 1920.[110] As mentioned above, this edition goes by the name of Yang Chen, but who he was and what exact connection he had with the text is unknown. Yang's preface is dated the twenty-third day of the ninth month of autumn, *jiashen* 甲申 year of the Great Song (dynasty); but since no reign name is given, it is impossible to tell which *jiashen* year is meant.

A certain Yang Chen (1024–1062) was associated with the Northern Song statesman, Wang Anshi 王安石.[111] It is possible that he was the one responsible for the editing of the edition of the *Guanzi* discovered by Zhang Nie. However, several points argue against this: (1) The *jiashen* year of this period came in 1044, which would have made Yang only twenty when he wrote the preface, something possible but not probable. (2) If Yang were in a position to be associated with Wang, it is strange that his edition of the *Guanzi* did not receive some official recognition at

---

[107] This reference to a twenty-four-*juan* edition may even predate our earliest known Song print of 1152, because much of the bibliography section of the *Tong zhi* is a summary of an earlier work by Zheng, the *Qunshu huiji* [Collected Records of Assembled Books], presented to the throne in 1149. Unfortunately this work is now lost, so we have no way of proving that this particular reference did not come from another source that may be as late as 1161, the date of the *Tong zhi*.

[108] Cited in the *Wenxian tongkao*, 212/1737a.

[109] Cited in the *Yu hai*, 53/17b.

[110] The *SBCK* and Guangxu prints may have some minor discrepancies. I have not been able to compare the two texts, but Guo Moruo's *Guanzi jijiao*, which was based on the Guangxu print, when commenting on II, 7/7b2 (1.28.2), writes 飭; the *SPCK* photo reproduction writes 飾, as does the *SBBY* print of the Zhao edition discussed below.

[111] See Jiang Liangfu 姜亮夫, *Lidai mingren nian li bei zhuan zongbiao*, p. 185.

the time and was not mentioned in one of the catalogues. (3) The preface concentrates on the *Guanzi*'s relationship to the problem of dealing with the barbarians. This was certainly a problem in Wang's time, but it would seem more logical that any friend of Wang who was working on the *Guanzi* would be more likely to concentrate on its economic and political aspects, since these were the really controversial issues of the day. Admittedly these points, even taken collectively, are not enough to rule out this Yang, but they would seem to make his choice unlikely.

Most writers, including Haloun and Guo Moruo, have taken the Yang Chen preface to be later than the Zhang colophon, and therefore have looked for a date after 1139. The first *jiashen* year after this time is 1164 (the date chosen by Haloun)[112] and the next is 1224. Guo Moruo, however, believes that this is really not a Song date at all, and that the omission of the usual reign name indicates that the preface was written by a Chinese who refused to admit the legality of the Mongol Yuan 元 dynasty and therefore dated his preface as Song. He supports this view by pointing out that the preface is primarily concerned with honoring the king and controlling the barbarians. The first *jiashen* date of Mongol times is 1284, five years after the fall of the Southern Song. Guo believes that the wood blocks were probably first cut under the Song, but that the actual printing of the book did not take place until after the Mongol victory, at which time the Yang Chen preface was drafted.

Actually the Yang edition was probably based on another Song print known as the Cai Qiandao's 蔡潛道 Mobao Tang 墨寶堂 [Mo-pao Bookshop] edition, a copy of which was still preserved in Dalian up to 1945 but since then seems to have disappeared.[113] I have not been able to find anyone who has made a collation of the two texts, but a very good description of the Mobao Tang edition is contained in Yang Shaohe's 楊紹和 *Yingshu yulu* [Initial Catalogue of the Yan Library], III/24bff. The copy he saw also contained the Zhang Nie colophon, and the end of the first *juan* had an imprint from a wooden seal: "Newly cut and printed by the Mobao Tang of the house of Cai Qiandao of Quyuan 瞿源." At the end of the final *juan* is another such imprint: "Published by the house of Cai Qiandao, first day of the first month of spring in the *renshen* 壬申 year of the Shaoxing period [February 8, 1152]." This was thirteen years after Zhang Nie had obtained his copy and only four years after his

---

[112] "Das Ti-tsï-tsï," p. 487, and "Legalist Fragments," p. 99. In the latter work he expresses some doubt about this.

[113] Personal communication from Professor van der Loon, who also added that he has collected considerable material concerning this and other printed editions of the *Guanzi* and plans to publish it.

death. It is likely that the Mobao Tang had obtained Zhang's manuscript copy of the *Guanzi* (he mentions in the colophon that such a copy was made) and used it as the basis for this printed edition. Then, toward the end of the Song or beginning of the Yuan, the blocks were re-cut and the Yang Chen preface was added.

The Yang edition eventually served as the basis for Zhao Yongxian's 趙用賢 (1535–1596) edition that appeared in his *Guan Han heke* [Combined Printing of the *Guanzi* and *Hanfeizi*], published in 1582. In his preface Zhao explains that the editions of the *Guanzi* that were current in his time were so corrupt that they were barely readable. It took him almost twenty years of searching before he was able to obtain a good old edition through a friend. The text was complete but it contained so many corruptions that even though he wrote some 30,000 characters in an attempt to correct them, twenty percent still remained in doubt. Though there are at least ten other known Ming 明 editions, this is by far the best and, since the Qing 清 period, it has been the most popular. It appears in many reprints including the *Sibu beiyao* 四部備要, which I have used with the *Sibu congkan* photographic reprint of the Yang edition as the basis for my translation.

Though the earliest available printed text is the Yang edition, another edition exists that may have a history going back to Liao 遼 times. This is the so-called Liu 劉 edition, deriving its name from Liu Ji 劉績, author of the *Guanzi buzhu* [Supplementary Commentary to the *Guanzi*], which is contained in this edition. Its history is discussed in some detail by Guo Moruo in his preface to the *Guanzi jijiao*. Unfortunately, a number of the texts mentioned by Guo have not been available to me, and so I can only summarize his conclusions.

According to Guo, a copy of Liu Ji's *Guanzi buzhu* is in the Beijing National Library, printed on yellow cotton paper. Because it lacks a preface, we do not know when the blocks were cut, but throughout the book are found stamped a number of small elliptical seal impressions, 宋本 [*Song ben*], indicating that someone considered it a Song edition.[114] The blocks were cut rather roughly and there are many abbreviated characters, some 514 by Guo's count. The book appears to have gone through at least one reprinting, for the style of the characters in the title differs from that of the text. Guo thinks that the Beijing Library copy is not the original print of the Liu edition, for if it were, it is

---

[114] Others, however, have taken it as either a Yuan or Ming edition. See the *Chijing zhai shumu* [Catalogue of Chijing's Study], 3/1a; the *Bi Song lou cangshu zhi* [Treatise on Books Stored in the Two Hundred Song Editions Tower], 42/11b, and the *Shanben shushi cangshu zhi* [Treatise on Books Stored in the Rare Book Room], 16/1a.

unlikely that it would lack a preface. The book contains a number of Liao, Jin 金, and Song *hui* 諱 [taboo characters], for which substitutes have been used.[115] This would indicate that the work must have originated in Liao times and undergone revision under the Jin and Song. Guo believes that when it was republished under the Jin or Song, the original preface bearing a Liao date was omitted because of hostility to that regime, and many of the Liao taboo characters were restored to their original forms. The yellow cotton paper edition later served as the basis for Zhu Dongguang's 朱東光 *Zhongdu sizi* edition published in 1579.[116] This is the best-known edition of Liu Ji's work.

Most modern catalogues, including the *Siku quanshu zongmu*, 101/1b, assign Liu Ji to the Ming dynasty. He is usually identified as a *jinshi* 進士 of the Hongzhi 弘治 period (1488–1505) from Jiangxia 江夏, Hubei, who, among other works, compiled a *Chunqiu Zuo zhuan leijie* [Classified Explanations on the *Chunqiu* and *Zuo zhuan*]. According to Guo, this work was published during the Jiajing 嘉靖 period (1522–1566) but contains a statement, signed by a Liu Ji of Luquan 蘆泉, that it was written under Hongzhi.

In Zhu Dongguang's (1579) edition of the *Guanzi buzhu*, the comentators are listed as Liu Ji of Luquan and Fang Xuanling of Linzi,[117] but Zhu's introduction (*tici* 題辭) says: "Mr. Fang of the Tang dynasty had a commentary and Liu Ji made a supplement, but from the Song on people have deleted it. There are few printed editions." Zhao Yongxian, in the introduction (*fan li* 凡例) to his edition discussed above, also says: "The *Guanzi* commentary came from Fang Xuanling. Some say it was by the *Guozi boshi* 國子博士, Yin Zhizhang of the Tang dynasty. Liu Ji of Luquan made intermittent supplements to it. However, none of the Song editions carries them." From this it is clear that Zhu and Zhao both considered Liu Ji to be pre-Song or Song.

Four reliable historical figures named Liu Ji are listed by Guo. One, who lived at the time of the Liu Song 劉宋 (420–477), can be ruled out immediately as being far too early. Another, who was president of the Guanli Bu 官吏部, lived during the Liao, in about 1012. The third, whose *zi* 字 or adult name was Mengxi 孟熙, lived from Yuan into Ming times. The fourth was the Hongzhi period *jinshi* from Jiangxia just mentioned. Guo says that the Liu Ji of the *Guanzi* commentary was most

---

[115] An extensive list of these by one of Guo's colleagues, Ren Linbu 任林圃, has been appended to the *Guanzi jijiao*, vol. II.

[116] This is made clear in that Zhu's print repeats almost all the variations appearing in the yellow paper copy.

[117] Fang came from Linzi 臨淄, the ancient capital of the Qi state, situated in present-day Shandong.

Chart 1. Transmission of the *Guanzi* from the Third
Century B.C. to the Song

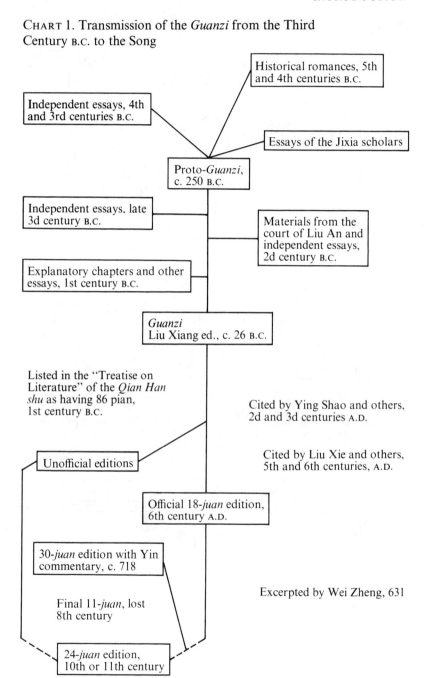

Historical romances, 5th
and 4th centuries B.C.

Independent essays, 4th
and 3rd centuries B.C.

Essays of the Jixia scholars

Proto-*Guanzi*,
c. 250 B.C.

Independent essays, late
3d century B.C.

Materials from the
court of Liu An and
independent essays,
2d century B.C.

Explanatory chapters and other
essays, 1st century B.C.

Guanzi
Liu Xiang ed., c. 26 B.C.

Listed in the "Treatise on
Literature" of the *Qian Han
shu* as having 86 pian,
1st century B.C.

Cited by Ying Shao and others,
2d and 3d centuries A.D.

Cited by Liu Xie and others,
5th and 6th centuries, A.D.

Unofficial editions

Official 18-*juan* edition,
6th century A.D.

30-*juan* edition with Yin
commentary, c. 718

Excerpted by Wei Zheng, 631

Final 11-*juan*, lost
8th century

24-*juan* edition,
10th or 11th century

CHART 2. Transmission of the *Guanzi* from the Song to Present

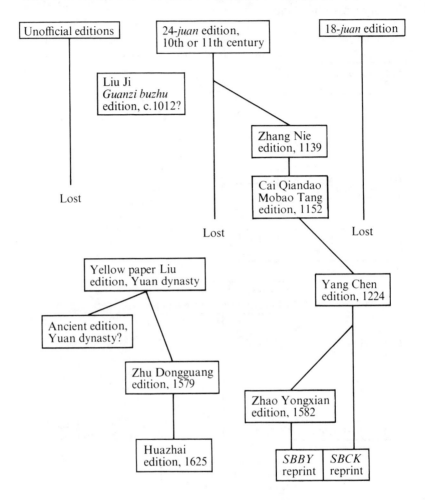

likely the Liao man.[118] But then, how are we to explain that both the Hongzhi period *jinshi* who wrote the *Chunqiu Zuo zhuan leijie*, and the Liao dynasty man who wrote the *Guanzi buzhu*, were given as Liu Ji of Luquan? Luquan does not appear among the lists of regular Chinese place names, but it could have been a place name under the Liao. Thus Guo maintains that when the *Chunqiu Zuo zhuan leijie* was published during the Jiajing period, the bookseller, not realizing that its author actually came from Jiangxia, mistakenly added "Luquan" before his name because he confused him with the Liu Ji who had written the better-known *Guanzi* commentary.[119]

Guo Moruo describes another old edition in his possession. It has ten columns on the folio, with twenty-one characters to the column. The beginning of the volume is missing, it is without title or table of contents, and it lacks a commentary. When Guo compared the textual variants of this print with those that Yasui Ko 安井衡 (1799–1876), in *Kanshi sanko* [The *Guanzi*, Edited and Annotated], cited as appearing in an "Ancient edition" (*gu ben* 古本), they were found to be the same. Mo Youzhi 莫友芝 (1811–1871), in his *Song Yuan jiuben shu jingyan lu* [Record of Personally Examined Old Song and Yuan Editions], also listed what seems to be the same edition: a ten-column edition without commentary that he says was probably published between the Yuan and Ming.[120] A Ming reprint of this edition is extant. It was published by the Anzheng Shutang 安正書堂 [Anzheng Bookshop] and bears the cyclical date *guisi* 癸巳. Unfortunately, this *guisi* date cannot be precisely fixed in terms of our Western calendar, since the Anzheng Shutang is known to have carried on publishing activities for over a century. This

---

[118] One difficulty in assigning a date of approximately 1012 to the *Guanzi buzhu* is that Liu Ji's comment on the *Guanzi* passage, XIX, 58/2b10 (3:22.4), cites the *Guang yun* [Expanded Rhyme Dictionary]: 螫 (*SBBY* ed. writes 勢) 音豪吾高七, 廣韻健也. Since the *Guang yun* was published during the Song in 1011 (Guo says 1007–1008), it was most certainly not available to the Liao dynasty Liu Ji. A check of the *Guang yun*, however, reveals no such definition for 螫. On the other hand, Guo points out that a Liao work of 997, the *Longkan shoujian* [Hand Mirror of Dragon Coffins] by a monk, Xingjun 行均, contains (III, 力部) the passage 螫音毫俊健也. Since this predates the *Guang yun*, Guo believes that both this work and the *Guanzi buzhu* must have derived their definition from the *Tang yun* [Tang Rhyme Dictionary], which was published in 751 and served as the basis for the *Guang yun*. The reference to the *Guang yun* in Liu Ji's commentary is thus either a later interpolation or "*Guang yun*" is a typographical error for "*Tang yun*."

[119] Guo's conclusions have been questioned by Luo Jizu in the *Shixue jikan* (1956), 2, pp. 31–33. According to Luo, the name Liu Ji in the *Liao shi* is possibly a corruption of Liu Jing 劉涇, and Luquan was not a place name but the sobriquet of the Ming scholar Liu Ji, who became a *jinshi* in 1490 and who was the author of several other works. The mutilated characters in the *Guanzi buzhu* may be explained as survivals of Song forms, as vulgar variants or as family taboos.

[120] Cited by Guo, *Guanzi jijiao*, I, 4.

means that any one of three *guisi* dates, 1473, 1533, or 1593, is possible.

When Guo compared the variant forms of characters in this "Ancient edition" (to borrow Yasui's terminology) with the Liu edition, he found that they agreed. Thus the Liu, Zhu Dongguang, and Ancient editions make up one system, the Yang and Zhao another.

I do not have access to a copy of the Liu edition. However, the Chinese commentators have carefully collated the Yang-Zhao editions with those belonging to the Liu system, as well as some other Ming editions that show occasional independent variants. Since these later works are either of unknown ancestry or belong to one of the above-mentioned systems, they will only be listed in the bibliography.

Commentaries

The *Guanzi* is not only one of the longest but also one of the most corrupt texts to have come down to us from Han and pre-Han times. We have already seen how Zhang Nie and Zhao Yongxian expended considerable effort in trying to correct the corruptions found in the copies that they were able to obtain. Even so, they still had to leave many questions unanswered. It is only through their editing and the work of numerous other commentators that the *Guanzi* becomes readable at all. So far we have mentioned the commentaries by Yin Zhizhang (d. 718) or Fang Xuanling (578–648), Du You (735–812), and Liu Ji (fl. 1012?). The comments of Du and Liu, though rather brief, are both quite helpful. Yin's commentary is extensive but has been generally criticized for its poor quality. Yin's major fault is that he usually attempts to read the text exactly as it stands, no matter how forced the resulting interpretation may be or how obvious the need is for textual emendation.[121]

The "Treatise on Literature" in the *Song shi* [History of the Song Dynasty], 205/11a, lists a *Guanzi yaolüe* [Summary of the *Guanzi*] by Ding Du 丁度 (990–1053), which may have contained a commentary. This, however, is now lost. On the other hand, some of Zhang Nie's work on the *Guanzi* is reflected in the present Yang edition. The Yao Yingji revision of Chao Gongwu's *Junzhai dushu zhi*[122] mentions that Chao also corrected characters and determined their pronunciation and meaning. Unfortunately, no trace of his labors has survived, and it is even doubtful whether what he did was ever actually published as a

---

[121] For example, VII, 18/2a4 (1.83.7), contains the character 凡, which, from the context, obviously should be read as 況. Yin, however, attempts to force a reading as 凡, even though it destroys the sense of the passage.

[122] Cited in the *Wenxian tongkao*, 212/1737b.

formal commentary. Another well-known Song literary figure, Huang Zhen 黃震 (fl. 1270), has left us some notes in his *Huangshi richao*, 55/7a–10a, but they are not particularly valuable.

During the Ming period the *Guanzi* again enjoyed minor popularity and numerous commentaries were written. For the most part the commentators were more concerned with moral interpretation than textual criticism and thus contributed little of value for our purposes. With the exception of Zhao Yongxian, only Mei Shixiang 梅士享 deserves special mention. In his *Quanxu Guanzi chengshu* [Complete Text of the *Guanzi* Annotated and Rearranged], published in 1625, Mei rearranged the various *pian* into fifteen *juan*, the *Jie* [Explanations] being placed after the chapters with which they dealt. The work is well worth consulting for its introduction and notes.

During Qing times the *Guanzi* received attention from many of the foremost scholars of the new school of philological criticism. Wang Niansun 王念孫 (1744–1832), Sun Xingyan 孫星衍 (1753–1818), Hong Yixuan 洪頤烜 (1765–1837), Wang Yinzhi 王引之 (1766–1834), Chen Huan 陳奐 (1786–1863), Ding Shihan 丁士涵 (nineteenth century), Zhang Wenhu 張文虎 (1808–1885), and Yu Yue 俞越 (1821–1906) all wrote special studies of the *Guanzi*. Then in 1873, Dai Wang 戴望 published his *Guanzi jiaozheng* [The *Guanzi*, Collated and Corrected], bringing together the works of these various commentators with added comments of his own. This became the standard collected commentary on the *Guanzi* and has been reprinted many times.

After Dai, a number of other prominent scholars, some of them important political figures of their day, continued to produce separate works on the *Guanzi*. They include Guo Songdao 郭嵩燾 (1818–1891), He Ruzhang 何如璋 (fl. 1886), Sun Yirang 孫詒讓 (1848–1908), Zhang Peilun 張佩綸 (1848–1903), Li Zheming 李哲明 (1857–?), Tao Hongqing 陶鴻慶 (1859–?), Liu Shipei 劉師培 (1884–1919), and Zhang Binglin 章炳麟 (1868–1936).[123]

Still more recent commentaries of importance have been made by such contemporary scholars as Yin Tongyang 尹桐陽, Yu Xingwu 于省吾, Ma Feibai 馬非百, and Shi Yishen 石一參. Shi attempts a total reorganization of the text to make it conform with what he

[123] It would be interesting to know how much of this relatively recent interest in the *Guanzi* has been due to a desire to find in Chinese traditional political and economic theory answers to problems that developed in the nineteenth century as a result of pressure from the West. As pointed out in the Introductory Comments to VIII, 20, Bai Chongxi 白崇禧 and Li Zongren 李宗仁 attempted to copy the militia system attributed to Guan Zhong in developing their base in Guangxi during the 1930s.

considers to have been its original arrangement. I have not found the results of his efforts in this respect very useful. With the assistance of Yu Xingwu, the Jilin Sheng Zhexue Shehuikexue Yanjiusuo 吉林省哲學社會科學研究所 (The Jilin Provincial Institute for Philosophy and Social Science) published a *Guanzi xuanzhu* [*Guanzi* Selections with Commentary] in 1975, covering some twenty chapters. Stripped of its "Gang of Four" verbiage, it can be very helpful. There are two partial translations into modern Chinese. One is *Guanzi jingji pianwen zhuyi* [Economic Sections of the *Guanzi* with Notes and Translation into Modern Chinese], prepared by a group from the Zhongguo Renmin Daxue (The Chinese Peoples' University) in Beijing and published in 1980. The other, by Zhao Shouzheng 趙守正, is projected as a two-volume work covering all the political and economic chapters. Volume I of this work, entitled *Guanzi zhuyi* [*Guanzi* with Notes and Translation into Modern Chinese], was published in 1982.

In addition to these works by Chinese, the Japanese have produced two first-rate commentaries, one by Igai Hikohiro 猪飼彦博, published in 1798, and another by Yasui Kō 安井衡 (Sokken 息軒), published in 1864. Translations of the *Guanzi* into Japanese have been made by Koyanagi Shigeta 小柳司氣太 (1922), Kimita Rentarō 公田連太郎 (1924), and Matsumoto Kazuo 町田三郎 (1973).

During the anti-Japanese war a number of Chinese scholars moved to Kunming 昆明 in southwest China. There they helped to found a temporary Lianhe Daxue 聯合大學 (Union University), where, under great physical hardship and with an almost complete lack of research materials, they turned out a remarkable number of constructive scholarly works, including the compilation of a comprehensive commentary for the *Guanzi* under the editorship of a Qinghua 清華 University professor, Xu Weiyu 許維遹. Xu based his work on that of Dai Wang and also incorporated later material written by Sun Yirang (1848–1908), Zhang Peilun (1848–1903), and others. He added new comments written by himself and other modern scholars, especially Wen Yiduo 聞一多, Sun Yutang 孫毓棠, Tang Lan 唐蘭, and Sun Shucheng 孫蜀丞.

When I went to China in 1948, I met Xu Weiyu at Qinghua University in Beijing. He was still working on the final draft of the manuscript, which by then ran to about 400,000 characters in nineteen volumes. When he heard I was working on a translation of the *Guanzi*, he immediately offered me free use of his work.

Unfortunately, Xu never lived to see his commentary published, for he died of cancer in the early spring of 1951. The work was eventually brought to the attention of Guo Moruo, head of the Academy of Sciences, who added material of his own as well as comments by some of his colleagues, including Zhang Dejun 張德鈞, Ren Linbu 任林圃, and Wang Tingfang 王廷芳. This work was finally published in Beijing in 1955 as the *Guanzi jijiao* [Collected Collations of the *Guanzi*]. To the student of the *Guanzi* it is absolutely indispensable for it supersedes all previous commentaries. All references to commentators in the following translation are taken from it unless otherwise indicated in the notes.

Technical Terms

This volume is meant to be primarily a work of translation rather than of interpretation; but a certain amount of interpretation is inevitable in any translation involving classical Chinese, and it becomes especially so when dealing with a work so disparate in nature and so textually corrupt as the *Guanzi*. One of the major problems is how to handle technical terms that often have, in addition to their general meanings, special ideological significance in certain contexts. Some of these terms will be discussed in the Introductory Comments to each chapter and in the notes, and where it has seemed appropriate a romanized transcription has been inserted in the translation.

Several terms that present particular problems, however, deserve special mention. These include *dao* 道 and *de* 德. The former basically means "road," "path, " "way"; by extension, "the proper or moral way of doing things," or "guiding principle." For the Daoists especially (though at times for the Confucians, too), the term takes on strong metaphysical implications, referring to the way of the universe or an all-embracing first principle. The Legalists interpret it more mechanistically, using it to describe the mechanical functioning of the universe or of a government when it operates in accordance with impersonal law.[124] In this expanded sense, I have translated *dao* as "the Way."

The term *de* is often translated as "virtue." As such it may refer to ordinary personal morality or it may have to be interpreted in the original Latin sense of *virtus*. Thus it is an inner quality of strength or power that makes a thing what it is. In this sense there can be both good and bad *de*, but the term is usually used in reference to what is morally good. For the Confucians it often takes on the meaning of a benevolent or moral force as opposed to that which is purely physical. For the Daoists in particular, it becomes a psychic force, power, or quality

---

[124] It should be noted, however, that in the *Hanfeizi*, which is also a composite work, *dao* sometimes appears in a sense very close to that accorded it by the Daoists.

inherent either in the natural universe as a whole ("Heaven and Earth") or in individual beings. In this sense, I have usually rendered it as "the Power."

Another term that appears frequently in the *Guanzi* with different connotations is *chang* 常 or *chang jing* 常經. In Confucian and Legalist parlance, *chang* or *chang jing* may be translated as "constant standards," but with differing meanings between the two schools. The Confucians mean by the term the constant or normative moral standards of Heaven that serve as the basis for the direction of society. The Legalists mean unvarying rules that are set up by the ruler as a basis for determining rewards and punishments. For the Daoists, the meaning of *chang* (*chang jing* does not appear in Daoist texts) is much broader. It refers to the invariables of the universe. According to the *Hanfeizi* chapter, *Jie Lao* 解老 [Explaining the *Laozi*], VI, 20/9a (Liao, *Han Fei Tzu*, I, P194):

> Things which exist and then perish, which are suddenly produced and suddenly die, which at first flourish but later decay, cannot be called invariable. Only what were produced along with the separation of Heaven and Earth and will not die or decay until Heaven and Earth themselves dissipate and scatter can be called invariables.[125]

Other terms that cause some difficulty are *shi* 士 and *junzi* 君子. Along with the titled nobility, the *shi* made up the aristocracy of ancient China. They were the lesser landholders and local elites who possessed surnames (*xing* 姓), lived in accordance with the rules of propriety (*li* 禮), were supported by the peasantry, and made war a chief occupation. They were men who possessed various specialized professional and technical skills, so that they served as the civil and military officers of their state. Thus the term *shi* in the *Guanzi* must be translated in different ways, depending upon the context, as "members of the aristocracy" or "gentry,"[126] or as "gentleman," "scholar," or "warrior knight." As a knight the *shi* ranked all the way from chariot-mounted officer and member of a hereditary elite guard to professional cutthroat, who wandered from state to state offering for sale his physical strength, skill with sword or bow, or cunning in intrigue or espionage. The *junzi* was a

---

[125] For a further discussion of *chang*, see III, 8/1b1 (1 : 29.10), and n. 52. *Jing* 經 appears also by itself, usually with the meaning of basic precept.

[126] I realize that using the word "gentry" to translate *shi* is bound to call forth some objections because of its wide range of connotations in Western literature and frequent use to denote the scholar-official class of later China. However, it is often the least cumbersome of various possibilities and here it is used in its strict dictionary definition: "The condition or rank of a gentleman; upper or ruling class; aristocracy."

man of superior moral qualities and presumably also one of the upper classes. The term is usually translated as "man of quality" or "superior man." In this text, when the reference is to the ruler I have followed the translation of "virtuous prince."

Two terms that often appear very close in meaning are *shi* 勢 and *quan* 權. *Shi* may be translated as "situation" or "circumstances," "force of circumstances," or "authority" derived from a specific position or situation. *Quan*, which originally referred to the weight on a steelyard, is usually translated as "political power." It may also be used to refer to whatever is expedient under varying circumstances.

Several terms are used to refer to the ordinary ruler: *jun* 君, *zhu* 主, and *shang* 上. Since all three terms may appear in the same chapter, I have attempted to distinguish them by translating *jun* as "prince," *zhu* as "ruler,"[127] and *shang* as "sovereign," or "the throne." *Shang*, however, basically means "to be above" so it may also mean "on high," "upper classes," or "superiors." Contrasted with *shang* is *xia* 下, which basically means "to be below," and so may mean in differing contexts "below," "lower classes," "inferiors," or when opposed to *shang* in the meaning of "sovereign," "subordinate officials," or "subjects" in general.

Also worth noting are: *yi* 義, "righteousness' or "correct social behavior"; *li* 禮, "rules of propriety" or "politeness"; *ren* 仁, "human goodness" or "benevolence"; *xin* 信, "trustworthiness" or "credibility"; *zheng* 正, "correct," "to be in proper balance," to rectify," or "to place in proper order."

Several different systems are presented pertaining to the organization of the state, each presenting an array of names for administrative units and official titles. These are not only difficult to translate, but confusing as well since the same term can be used to indicate different levels of units or different ranks of officials in different chapters. Therefore I have placed both the romanization and characters in parentheses after such names and titles.

Translation Procedures and Methods of Notation

Two texts have been used in making the translation: the *Sibu congkan* photographic reprint of the Yang Chen edition and the *Sibu beiyao* reprint of the Zhao Yongxian edition. The former is the oldest while the latter is the best of all widely available editions.

---

[127] *Zhu* is also frequently used to refer to a military commander.

Introductory Comments have been added to each chapter to provide the reader with some information about its specific history, general substance and organization, relation to other texts, and, where possible, some tentative conclusions about its date of composition.

As mentioned above, were it not for the tremendous work of a large number of commentators, it would be impossible to even read the *Guanzi*, let alone attempt this translation. However, I have tried to be as conservative as possible in following their often conflicting suggestions, preferring a sometimes forced reading of the original text to a poorly supported emendation. Where it seemed appropriate, I have given alternative readings in the notes. The names of the commentators have been given in brackets after their comments, and where I have cited. other texts, I have accompanied them with reference to their standard translations. These are for reference purposes only, since the translation given has often been changed or adapted. Information concerning the commentators is listed in the first section of the Bibliography.

Two systems of pagination accompany the translation. Roman type is used for the volume, page, and line numbers for the *Guoxue jiben congshu* 國學基本叢書 print of the Zhao edition, which Wallace Johnson used as the basis for his invaluable *Guanzi yinde* 管子引得 [*A Concordance ot the Kuan-tzu*]. Thus Johnson's *Concordance* can serve as a Chinese index to the translation. Pagination for the *Sibu beiyao* print of the Zhao edition appears in italics. Page and line breaks are sometimes approximate either because of the translation or to avoid more than one break in a single line.

The *Guanzi* contains many rhymed passages. A study of these rhymes by Jiang Yougao 江有誥 (d. 1851) and contained in his *Xian Qin yun du* [A Study of Pre-Qin Rhymes] lists some seventy-eight rhymed passages scattered throughout twenty-six different chapters. If these rhymed passages, which may be of considerable length, were rendered in a poetic format, the number of pages required for the translation would be increased to a point where publication would become very difficult. Therefore I have only made use of a poetic format when it appeared necessary to set off a part of the translation.

Detailed bibliographical data for books and articles, including the translation of Chinese and Japanese titles, will be found in the Bibliography. Works cited in the introductory comments and notes to the translation will be listed in the Index. The Index also provides the Chinese characters for names and technical terms. Page numbers for technical terms are given only in cases where the terms themselves are considered significant.

For all Chinese texts divided into both *juan* and *pian*, roman numerals are used to designate the former and arabic numerals the latter; for texts that are simply divided into either *juan* or *pian*, arabic numerals alone are used. Page and line numbers follow the hash mark.

All citations to archaic and ancient pronunciations have been taken from Chou Fa-kao's *Hanzi gujin yinhui* [*A Pronouncing Dictionary of Chinese Characters in Archaic and Ancient Chinese, Mandarin and Cantonese*] with the following modifications: ġ = ɣ; ė = ɛ; ê = ə; ī = ɪ.

GUANZI

Mu Min
牧民

ON SHEPHERDING THE PEOPLE

Introductory Comments

Mu min is the first of the nine chapters that constitute the *Jing yan* 經言 [Canonical Statements] section of the *Guanzi*. It is perhaps the most famous piece in the entire work. The line (1a9; 1:1.8), "When the granaries are full, the people will know propriety and moderation. When their food and clothing is adequate, they will know the [distinction between] honor and shame," has been cited by historians and social reformers throughout Chinese history from Sima Qian 司馬遷 to Sun Yat-sen 孫逸仙. Ideologically, the work reflects the practical thinking of the realist wing of Confucianism. While emphasizing the importance of rewards and punishments and the economic well-being of the state, it also stresses the preservation of traditional feudal values and government by men of virtue.

The importance of morality is expressed in the concept of the four *wei* 維, "cords" or "guy lines," supporting the state. These four cords, which I have called "cardinal virtues" in the translation, consist of *li* 禮, "propriety"; *yi* 義, "righteousness"; *lian* 廉, "integrity;" and *chi* 恥, "sense of shame." They are often mentioned by later writers as one of the special features of Guan Zhong's thought, and it is interesting that *lian*, which is not an important virtue in either the *Lun yu* or the *Mengzi*, is frequently mentioned along with *chi* by Xunzi,[1] who may have been influenced by this chapter.

Mu min is certainly one of the earlier chapters of the *Guanzi*. It is mentioned or quoted in a number of early works, including the *Shangjun shu* (V, 23/9a6–7; Duyvendak, *Lord Shang*, p. 316); *Hanfeizi* (XVI, 38/7a3ff.; Liao, *Han Fei Tzu*, II, pp. 187–188); *Wenzi* (A, 2/14a9–12); the *Xin shu* (III, 1/a10ff.) of Jia Yi 賈誼 (201–169 B.C.); and the *Shi ji* (62/2a5ff.) of Sima Qian (145–86? B.C.). Its emphasis on practical economic concerns in the pursuit of good government makes it perhaps as close to the original ideas of Guan Zhong as any chapter in the *Guanzi*.

[1] See, for example, *Xunzi*, I, 2/12a10 (Dubs, *Hsüntze*, p. 52) and II, 4/11b3 (Dubs, p. 61).

However, the language and style of writing are certainly post-Confucius. I would date it as coming from the early or middle part of the fourth century B.C.

The chapter is divided into short sections, with the title placed at the end of each. For convenience of translation, these titles have been shifted to the beginning of their respective sections. The first section is largely in rhyme. While the others contain rhymed passages, for the most part they are written in a relatively simple straightforward prose. *Mu min* originally seems to have had an explanatory chapter; at least a *Mu min jie* is listed as the name of the now lost chapter XIX, 63, in the table of contents.

Translation

1:2.1
1b9
1.7
1a7

CONCEPTS OF STATE (*Guo Song* 國頌)

All those who possess territory and shepherd people must pay heed to the four seasons and watch over the granaries. If the state has an abundance of wealth, people will come from afar; if the land has been

1.8

opened for cultivation, they will settle down. / When the granaries are full, they will know propriety and moderation; when their clothing and food is adequate, they will know [the distinction between] honor and shame.[2] If the sovereign complies with the rules [regarding proper dress and expenditure], the six relationships[3] will be secure; / if the

1.9

four cardinal virtues[4] prevail, the prince's orders will be carried out.

Therefore the essential component in reducing punishments is to prohibit luxury and artfulness. The [primary] measure for preserving the state is to promote the four cardinal virtues. The basic precepts for

[2] *Rong ru* 榮辱; "Honor and Shame," is the title of chapter II, 4, of the *Xunzi*. According to the *Xunzi*, II, 4/9a (Dubs, *Hsüntze*, p. 55): "The general distinction between honor and shame depends on the usual circumstances attendant on being peaceful or uneasy, beneficial or injurious to others. The man who first thinks of righteousness (*yi*) and secondly of gain is honorable; he who first thinks of gain and second of righteousness is shameful." The *Mengzi*, IIB, 4/1, states: "If there is goodness (*ren*), then there is honor. If not, there is shame."

[3] *Liu qin* 六親; the six relationships are generally given as either father and son, older and younger brother, husband and wife, or father and mother, older and younger brother, and wife and children.

[4] *Si wei* 四維; *wei* was a term used to designate the four guy lines or ropes used to support a target or lines attached to the four corners of a fish net to pull it in. Here, as defined below, the *si wei* refer to the cardinal virtues that support the state: propriety, righteousness, integrity, and a sense of shame. Thus the term is sometimes translated as "the four guiding principles."

52

achieving obedience among the people are: to honor the spirits, respect the mountain / and river gods, revere the ancestral temples, and venerate ancestors and great men of the past.[5]

If [the prince] does not heed the seasons of Heaven, wealth will not flourish. If he does not heed the fruits of Earth, the granaries will not / be full. If wastelands are left wild and uncleared, the people will run about unrestrained.[6] If the sovereign lacks proper restraint, the people will behave recklessly. If luxury and artfulness are not prohibited, the people will become licentious. If the source of these two evils is not kept in check,[7] punishments will proliferate. / If the spirits are not honored, crude common folk will take no notice of them.[8] If the mountain and river gods are not respected, orders intended to inspire awe will go unheeded. / If the ancestral temples are not revered, the people will emulate the sovereign [in their lack of respect]. If ancestors and great men of the past are not venerated, filial piety and respect for elders will be lacking. If the four cardinal virtues do not prevail, the state / will perish.

The Four Cardinal Virtues (*Si Wei* 四維)

The state has four cardinal virtues. If one is eliminated, [the state] will totter. If two, it will be in danger. If three, it will be overthrown. If all four are eliminated, it will be totally wiped out. What totters may be set straight. What is endangered may be made safe. What has been overthrown may be reestablished. But what has been totally wiped out / can never be restored.

What are these four cardinal virtues? The first is propriety, the second is righteousness, the third is integrity, and the fourth / is a sense of shame.[9] Propriety consists in not overstepping the bounds of proper

---

[5] In a similar passage, XI, 33/13a4 (2:42.3), 祖舊 is rephrased as: 先古之大臣, "great ministers of the past."

[6] Emending 管 to 荒 [Igai, Dai, and Guo Moruo].

[7] Reading 璋 as 障 [Mei, Igai, and Yu Yue]. Yin would read it as 章 "to clarify."

[8] Igai and Ding would emend 悟 (*ngag*) to 信 (*sjien*) in order to complete the rhyme with 神 (*zdjien*) in the preceding passage. Thus, "The crude common folk will not believe in them."

[9] Jia Yi (201–169 B.C.), in his *Xin shu*, III, 1/1a, cites this passage as 醜(愧) instead of *chi* 恥. The meaning is the same. The term *chi* appears frequently in these early chapters of the *Guanzi*. It also appears frequently in the *Mengzi*. For example, VIIA, 7, states: "A sense of shame is of great importance to a man. Those who form contrivances and versatile schemes distinguished for their artfulness do not allow their sense of shame to come into action. When one differs from other men in not having this sense of shame, what will he have in common with them?"

restraint. Righteousness consists in not pushing oneself forward [at the expense of others]. Integrity consists in not concealing one's faults. / Having a sense of shame consists in not following those who go awry.

Therefore if no one oversteps the bounds of proper restraint, the position of the sovereign will be safe. If no one pushes himself forward, the people will be free of artfulness and deceit. If no one follows / those who go awry, evil practices will not arise.

FOUR [DESIRES) TO BE FOLLOWED (*Si Shun* 四順)

Success in government lies in following the hearts of the people. Failure lies in opposing them. The people hate trouble and toil, so [the prince] should provide them with leisure and freedom from care. The people hate poverty and low position, so [the prince] should provide them with riches and honor. The people hate danger and disaster, / so [the prince] should insure their existence and provide them with security. The people hate death and annihilation, so [the prince] should enable them to live and propagate.

If [the prince] can provide them with leisure and freedom from care, the people will be willing to endure trouble and toil for him. If he can provide them with riches and honor, / they will be willing to endure poverty and low position for him. If he can ensure their existence and provide them with security, they will be willing to endure danger and disaster for him. If he enables them to live and propagate, they will be willing to endure death and annihilation for him.

Therefore punishment alone is not enough to terrify[10] the minds of [the people], nor is killing sufficient / to make their hearts submissive. Thus, if punishments are numerous yet the minds of the people are not terrified, / orders will not be carried out. If killing abounds, yet the hearts of the people are not submissive, the position the sovereign will be endangered. /

Therefore if [the prince] complies with their four desires, even those in distant places will of themselves rally around him. But if he imposes on them the four things they hate, then even those who are near at hand will turn against him.

Thus knowing that "to give is to receive" is the most precious thing in government.

---

[10] Emending 畏 to 恐 in accordance with the *Qunshu zhiyao* and the following passage of the *Guanzi* text.

The Eleven[11] Precepts (*Shiyi Jing* 十一經)

Place the state on a firm foundation.[12] Accumulate [grain] in inexhaustible granaries. Stock [supplies] in storehouses that may never be depleted. Hand down orders like the wellspring of a flowing stream. Place people in offices where they are not at cross-purposes. Make clear the road to certain / death. Open the gates to certain gain. Do not undertake to do what cannot be completed. Do not seek what cannot be obtained. Do not assume positions which cannot be maintained for long. Do not do what cannot be undone.[13]

To entrust [the government] to men of virtue is what is meant by placing the state on a firm foundation. / To pay heed to the five grains[14] is what is meant by accumulating [grain] in inexhaustible granaries. To cultivate the mulberry and hemp and raise the six domestic animals[15] is what is meant by stocking [supplies] in storehouses that can never be depleted. To issue orders that accord with the will of the people is what is meant by handing down orders like the wellspring of a flowing stream. / To employ each person according to his skill is what is meant by placing people in offices where they are not at cross-purposes. Having severe punishments is what is meant by making clear the road to certain death. Having trustworthy rewards is what is meant by opening the gates to certain gain. / To measure the strength of the people is what is meant by not initiating what cannot be completed. Not forcing the people to do what they hate is what is meant by not seeking what cannot be obtained. Not seizing momentary advantages[16] is what is meant by not assuming positions that cannot be maintained for long. / Not cheating the people is what is meant by not doing what cannot be undone.

Therefore if [the government] is entrusted to men of virtue, the state will be safe. / If heed is paid to the five grains, food will be sufficient. If mulberry and hemp are cultivated and the six domestic animals are raised, the people will be prosperous. If the orders accord with the will of

---

[11] Emending 土 to 十一 [Gu Guangqi].

[12] A similar statement appears in XVIII, 57/5a8 (3 : 16.2), but there it clearly refers to the geographical setting of the capital. Here, as explained in the text below, the reference is to the state's political foundations.

[13] This paragraph appears with minor variations in the *Wenzi*, A, 2/14a.

[14] The five grains are variously enumerated as wheat, two kinds of millet, pulse, and hemp or rice.

[15] The six domestic animals are usually given as the horse, ox, sheep, pig, dog, and fowl.

[16] Emending 世 to 時 [He and Zhang Peilun]. 偷取一時 is a common phrase, appearing in such works as the *Hanfeizi*, XV, 36/1a13 (Liao, *Han Fei Tzu*, II, p. 139), and the *Shi ji*, 69/9b4.

the people, they will be carried out as though inspiring awe.[17] If each person is employed according to his skill, he may be used to the full. If the punishments are severe, / the people will keep away from evil. If the rewards are trustworthy, the people will treat difficulties lightly. If the people's strength is measured, nothing will be undertaken which will not be completed. If the people are not forced into doing what they hate, deception will not arise. If there is no seizing of momentary advantages,[18] the people / will not harbor resentful hearts. If the people are not cheated, his subjects will rally around their sovereign.

FOUR CATEGORIES TO BE OBSERVED[19] AND FIVE RULES
(*Si Guan Wu Fa* 四觀五法)

A district cannot be managed as one would manage a household; a state cannot be managed as one would manage a district; the realm cannot be managed as one would manage a state. / Manage the household as a household, the district as a district, the state as a state, and the realm as the realm.

Do not say: "You are not of the same family [as I]," for then outsiders / will not listen to you. Do not say: "You are not of the same district [as I]," for then outsiders will not carry out your orders. Do not say: "You are not of the same state [as I]," for then outsiders will not follow you.

Be like / Earth. Be like Heaven. (*t'en*)
What partiality or favoritism have they? (*ts'jien*)
Be like the moon. Be like the sun. (*njiet*)
Such is the constancy of a [true] prince. (*tset*)[20]

The reins that direct the people consist of those things the sovereign / honors. The gate through which they are led consists of those things the sovereign puts first.[21] The road along which the people are guided consists of the likes and dislikes of the sovereign. Therefore when the prince / seeks something, his ministers obtain it for him. When the

---

[17] Deleting the character 令 following 威 as a superfluous interpolation [Igai and Guo Moruo].

[18] See n. 16 above.

[19] Emending *liu qin* 六親, "six relationships," to *si guan* 四觀 [Wen]. *Liu qin* makes no sense here in terms of the content of the section that follows. Wen points out that the seal forms of *liu* and *si* are very similar. *Qin* is also very close in form to *guan*. The *si guan* clearly refer to the household, district, state, and realm.

[20] According to the *Li ji*, XV, 29/12b–13a (Legge, *Li Ki*, 28, p. 281): "Confucius said, 'Heaven covers everything without partiality (私). Earth supports everything without partiality. The sun and moon shine on everything without partiality.'"

[21] This passage appears to be quoted in the *Shangjun shu*, V, 23/9a6–7 (Duyvendak, *Lord Shang*, p. 316).

prince relishes something, his ministers provide it for him to eat. When the prince likes something, his ministers serve it to him. When the prince dislikes something, his ministers keep it from his sight. [This is the first rule.]

Do not conceal / your dislikes. Do not be inconsistent in your regulations. [Otherwise] worthy people will not assist you. Words spoken in a room [should be addressed to] everyone in the room. Words spoken in a hall [should be addressed to] everyone in the hall. This is what it means to be a sage king.[22] [This is the second rule.]

City and suburban walls, moats and ditches will not suffice to secure one's defenses. / Arms and physical force will not suffice to meet the enemy. Vast territory and abundant wealth will not suffice to hold the masses. / Only those who adhere to the true Way are able to prepare for trouble before it arises so calamities will not occur. [This is the third rule.]

The trouble is not that the realm lacks ministers, but rather that there is no prince to employ them. Nor is it that it lacks / wealth, but rather that no one distributes it.[23] Therefore he who understands the times may be appointed head [of an office]. He who shows no partiality may be placed [in charge of] administration.[24] He who examines the times, finds out what is applicable to them, and so / is able to fill his offices [with men of ability], may be elevated as a prince. [This is the fourth rule].

He who procrastinates will be too late in his undertakings. He who is stingy with wealth will lose those close to him. He who trusts petty men will lose gentlemen of worth. [This is the fifth rule].

[22] The *Hanfeizi*, XVI, 38/7a3 (Liao, *Han Fei Tzu*, II, pp. 187–188), cites this passage from the *Guanzi* with minor variations in wording. It also cites a critic who goes on to say that what Guan Zhong meant was not restricted to talk connected with sport or play or following drinking and eating, but included serious discussion of important business.

[23] The meaning of the phrase 無人以分之 is not clear. I have followed Yin's interpretation. Yu Yue would interpret the phrase to mean "there is no one to employ with it."

[24] This passage appears to be related to another in the *Guanzi*, I, 3/8a5 (1 : 7.13–14): "Its population being large, the offices must have heads 長 . In shaping the destiny of the people, the court must have an administrative policy 政 ."

Xing Shi

形勢

Xing Shi Jie

形勢解

ON CONDITIONS AND CIRCUMSTANCES AND EXPLANATION OF *Xing Shi*

Introductory Comments

This chapter has the distinction of containing some of the most frequently quoted passages of the *Guanzi*. It is also one of the few chapters with a separate *Jie* 解 or "Explanation," in the form of a line-by-line commentary. Yet it has long been considered one of the least intelligible chapters in the entire work because the logical sequence of thought seldom extends over three or four sentences, thus making it impossible to read as an ordinary essay. However, with the possible exception of one passage (4b12; 1:4.14) 紂之失也, in particular, the sentences all appear to be complete and relatively free from corruption.

The short, disjointed passages that make up the text frequently have the distinct flavor of apothegms—short, pithy sayings containing a stated or implied moral—which are characteristic of some of the gnomic or wisdom literature to be found in other cultures, especially in India and the Near East. Indeed, just two examples from an Indian collection of gnomic verse, the *Cāṇakya-nīti-śāstra* [Cāṇakya's Science of Political Conduct],[1] will suffice to make this point: "When the king walks righteously, most righteous are the people; if he be evil, they also; if mediocre, the same with them; as the king, so the people." And again: "For this reason do kings gather to themselves men of high mind, that neither at the start, the crisis nor the finish may they play them false."

---

[1] This work, which exists in several different versions, has been traditionally attributed to Cāṇakya or Kautilya, the famous minister of Candragupta Maurya who reigned during the late fourth century B.C. See A. Berriedale Keith, *A History of Sanskrit Literature*, pp. 229–230, from which the following translations were taken.

Either of these statements would fit into the content of this chapter in regard both to form and general subject matter. Therefore, when read as a collection of wise sayings rather than an essay, the chapter begins to make sense and the choppiness of its content becomes understandable.[2]

At the same time its title, *Xing shi*, which in the past has also presented some difficulties in interpretation, begins to take on meaning.[3] The two characters *xing shi* in modern Chinese form a compound meaning "circumstances" or "conditions." Here, however, they should be rendered separately to refer to a specific condition or situation (*xing*) and its resulting circumstance (*shi*).[4] The opening line of the text may be taken as an example to show what is meant: "If a mountain rises high and never crumbles (the specific condition), sacrificial sheep will be presented to it (the resulting circumstance)." The same interplay of condition and resulting circumstance applies throughout a large portion of the text, thus making the title thoroughly relevant.

The apothegms that make up the text are mostly taken from Confucian or Daoist tradition. Some of them are direct quotations or paraphrases of the classics such as the *Shi jing*,[5] while others come from Confucian sources such as the *Lun yu* and *Mengzi*,[6] and still others from Daoist sources such as the *Laozi* and *Zhuangzi*.[7] For the majority we do not know the source, but some seem to stem from popular folk sayings, for example: "Whoever dislikes food will never grow fat," and "Disgraced and distrusted is the woman who acts as her own go-between." It is also probable that some were inventions of the author or, more accurately, compiler of the chapter. However, these seem to be

[2] Perhaps the reason this approach to an understanding of this chapter has not been generally adopted before is that gnomic literature of this type was rare in pre-Han China. It is true that both the *Lun yu* and the *Laozi* are largely made up of aphorisms or apothegms, but they both possess an internal unity lacking in this text, and their specific association with Confucius and Laozi has tended to set them apart in a special canonical category.

[3] At the time Liu Xiang and his son, Liu Xin, compiled their *Bie lu*, this chapter was also known under the name of the two opening characters of the text, *Shan gao* 山高 [If a mountain rises high]. See Pei Yin's (fl. 440) *Ji jie* commentary to the *Shi ji*, 62/3b13.

[4] Ch'i-yün Chen, in his *Hsün Yüeh and the Mind of Late Han China*, pp. 81–82, cites the *Han ji*, 2/12b, where the terms *xing* and *shi* appear together with *qing* 情. Ch'en's translation of the *Han ji* passage reads: "*Hsing* (*xing*) means the overall favorable or unfavorable conditions; *shih* (*shi*) means that which is appropriate at the moment and makes a time propitious for advancing or retreating; *ch'ing* (*qing*) means the mind and the intention [of men], which may or may not be appropriate [for the task]." Xun Yue (Hsün Yüeh) thus uses the terms *xing* and *shi* in a slightly different sense than they appear to have been used here in the *Guanzi*.

[5] See n. 27, below.
[6] See nn. 76, 78, and 79, below.
[7] See nn. 22 and 68, below.

relatively few in number as indicated by the fact that even though the compiler clearly had an eclectic interest in both Daoism and Confucianism, there is little mixing of the ideas and terminology of these separate schools within the individual apothegms themselves.

The very eclecticism of the *Xing shi* chapter with its blending of Confucian and Daoist ideas indicates that it cannot be dated before the third century B.C. The *Mengzi* and *Zhuangzi*, which it appears to quote, are both well established as works of this period. On the other hand, it could not have been written much after that time because it was well known to writers of the early Han. It is specifically quoted by Jia Yi 賈誼 (201–169 B.C.) who, in his *Xin shu*, VI, 3/8b11–12, cites passage 2/5b11 (1:5.12–13) prefacing his quotation with the words 管子曰, "Guanzi said."[8] Dong Zhongshu 董仲舒 (179?–104? B.C.), in his *Chunqiu fanlu*, appears to cite two passages from the text, but unfortunately he does not specifically mention the *Guanzi* by name.[9] Dongfang Suo 東方朔 (c. 161 – c. 87 B.C.) also appears to paraphrase another passage, but he, too, fails to give the source.[10] It is probable that the text dates from that first period of encyclopedic eclecticism highlighted by Lü Buwei's 呂不韋 *Lüshi chunqiu*, produced about 240 B.C.

Due to their terseness and metaphorical nature, many of the apothegms that make up the text border on the unintelligible without some additional explanation. Therefore, in spite of certain limitations, the *Xing shi jie* or "Explanation of the *Xing shi*," is often of considerable assistance in understanding the *Xing shi* text.

This is the longest of the four surviving explanatory chapters, all of which appear to have been written by the same person, probably a Confucian with strong Legalist tendencies. Though the *Xing shi* represents a mixture of Confucian and Daoist ideology, the writer of the *Xing shi jie* interprets most of the Daoist statements in the light of Legalistic Confucianism. He dwells at length on various Confucian virtues such as benevolence (*de* 德), kindness (*hui* 惠), compassion (*ci* 慈), loyalty (*zhong* 忠), and filial piety (*xiao* 孝), while at the same time making liberal use of such Legalist terminology as *shu shu* 術數, "political and statistical methods." Therefore his explanations for various Daoist passages are sometimes wide of the mark and he tends to turn vivid naturalistic concepts into stilted Confucian moralisms or mechanistic Legalist dicta.

[8] See n. 66, below.
[9] See nn. 45 and 86, below.
[10] See n. 75, below.

The tendency toward misinterpretation of Daoist passages was all the greater because the author does not seem to have been familiar with Daoist writings such as the *Zhuangzi*. Other misinterpretations arise from misreading characters or following corruptions. But for all its weaknesses, the *Xing shi jie* is valuable both for understanding the *Xing shi* and also for gaining some insight into Legalistic Confucian thinking during the Han. Where misinterpretations or mistakes are so serious that the explanation is rendered completely useless, however, I have placed it in the notes rather than in the translation proper. The *Xing shi jie* at the end of each explanation repeats the original text. I have omitted this repetition and merely commented on any differences in the notes.

The date of the *Xing shi jie* can hardly be before the first century B.C. The style of writing is considerably different from that of the *Xing shi* or other chapters of the *Guanzi* that are generally recognized to be of the third or second century B.C. The sentences are long but grammatically clear, and in contrast to the rest of the *Guanzi*, the text is remarkably free from corruptions. Moreover, it would appear fairly certain that it was written after the composition of the *Huainanzi* (c. 122 B.C.), because it interprets a passage (2/5a12; 1:5.7) of the original text in accordance with a corruption that must have entered the *Guanzi* after it had been used as the basis for a similar passage in the *Huainanzi*.

Translation

1:4.9
2/4b1

[*XS*] If a mountain rises high and never crumbles, sacrificial sheep will be presented to it.

3:28.9
64/1a5

[*XSJ*] A mountain is the highest of [all] things. Kindness is the highest conduct of the ruler. Compassion is the highest conduct of the father and mother. Loyalty is the highest conduct of the minister and subordinate official.[11] Filial piety is the highest conduct of the son and his wife. / Therefore, if the mountain is high and never crumbles, sacrificial

28.10

sheep will be presented to it. If the ruler is unfailingly kind, the people will care for him. If the father and mother are unfailingly compassionate, the son and his wife will be obedient. If the minister and

28.11

subordinate official are unfailingly loyal, ranks / and salaries will accrue to them. If the son and his wife are unfailingly filial, a good name will be attached to them. Therefore, so long as standards remain unfailingly high, desires will be fulfilled. Otherwise they will not.

[11] Inserting 下 below 臣 in accordance with the Ancient, Liu, and Zhu editions and the related sentence below.

61

1:4.9
2/4b1

[*XS*] If a pool is deep and never dries up, sacrificial[12] jade will be offered to it.

3:28.13
64/1a11

[*XSJ*] Pools are the source of life for a host of creatures. Since pools are capable of extremely great depth without ever drying up, sacrificial jade is presented to them. The ruler is one to whom men look for their livelihood. If he is capable of leniency and sincerity without oppres-

28.14

sion,[13] the people / will attach themselves to him. The father and mother are the ones from whom the son and his wife receive instruction. If they are capable of deep compassion and constructive teaching without neglecting principles, the son and his wife will be filial. The minister and subordinate official are the ones whom the ruler employs. If they are

29.1

capable of exhausting their strength in serving / the throne, they will fulfill their obligations to their ruler. The son and his wife are the ones on whom parents depend for security. If the son and his wife are capable of respect for age and are obedient toward their parents, they will fulfill their obligations to them.

Now, if a pool dries up and there is no water, sacrificial jade will not be

29.2

presented to it. If the ruler is oppressive / and lacking in generosity, the people will not attach themselves to him. If the father and mother are cruel and lacking in graciousness, the son and his wife will not treat them as parents. If the minister and subordinate official are indolent[14] and disloyal, they will be disgraced and impoverished. If the son and his wife do not provide security for their parents, calamities will befall

29.3

them. / Therefore so long as the pool does not dry up, what it desires will be presented to it. Should it dry up, nothing will be presented.

1:4.10
2/4b2
3:29.4
64/1b9

[*XS*] Heaven does not change its constant activities.

[*XSJ*] Covering all things, regulating cold and heat, setting in motion the sun and moon, maintaining the orderly sequence of the stars and planets—such are the constant activities of Heaven. It preserves order among them in accordance with principles, and when [one cycle of these activities] is completed, it begins all over again.[15]

Shepherding all the people, governing the realm, and supervising the

29.5

various officials—such are the constant activities of the ruler. / He preserves order among them in accordance with the law, and when [one cycle of these activities] is completed, it begins all over again.

Harmonizing the sons and grandsons, and holding relatives

---

[12] *Shen* 沈 is a special term for sacrifices to rivers during which jade or other objects, including animals, were cast into the water.

[13] The Yang edition for 奇 mistakenly writes 苟.

[14] Following the Yang edition, which for 隨 writes 墮.

[15] Following Yasui's interpretation of the phrase 終而復始 both here and below.

together—such are the constant activities of the father and mother. They preserve order among them in accordance with righteous conduct, and when [one cycle of these activities] is complete, it begins all over again.

Being respectful and loyal is the constant activity of the minister and subordinate official. / Thereby they serve their ruler, and when [one cycle of these activities] is completed, it begins all over again.

Loving their parents, providing a good living for them, thinking of them respectfully, and carrying out their instructions—such are the constant activities of the son and his wife. Thereby they serve their parents, and when [one cycle of their activities] is completed, it begins over again.

Therefore so long as Heaven does not neglect its constant activities, / cold and heat will have their proper season, and the sun and moon, stars and planets will have their proper order. So long as the ruler does not neglect his constant activities, the assembled ministers will practice righteousness, and the various officials will attend to their duties. So long as the father and mother do not neglect their constant activities, sons and grandsons / will be harmonious and obedient, and relatives will be at peace with each other. So long as the minister and subordinate official do not neglect their constant activities, there will be no mistakes in affairs and the offices will be well administered. So long as the son and his wife do not neglect their constant activities, old and young will keep to their proper place, and near and distant kin will be harmonious. Therefore / when these constant activities are properly carried out, there is order; when they are neglected, there is disorder. Heaven has never changed its means of maintaining order.

[*XS*] Earth does not alter its regular activities.

[*XSJ*] Giving[16] birth to and nourishing all things—such are the regular activities of Earth. Maintaining good order among the hundred surnames and making them secure—such are the regular activities of the ruler. Giving instruction and looking after the affairs of the family— such are the regular activities of the father and mother. Giving correct advice and being willing to die for their country—such are the regular activities of the minister and subordinate official. / Exhausting their strength in caring for the whole [family]—such is the regular activity of the son and his wife.

So long as Earth does not alter its regular activities, all things will have life. So long as the ruler does not alter his regular activities, the hundred

---

[16] Deleting the initial character 地 as a later interpolation [Guo Moruo].

29.12

surnames will be secure. So long as the father and mother do not alter their regular activities, family affairs will be well managed.[17] / So long as the minister and subordinate official do not alter their regular activities, the ruler will make no mistakes. So long as the son and his wife do not alter their regular activities, parents will receive complete care. Therefore, when these regular activities are properly carried out, there is security; otherwise there is danger. Earth has never altered its means of providing security.

1:4.10
2/4b3

[*XS*] Spring, autumn, winter, and summer do not vary their seasonal activities. From ancient times to the present, this has always been so.

3:29.13
64/2b3

[*XSJ*] In spring the vital force of Yang begins to rise so all things are born. In summer the vital force of Yang completes its ascendancy so all things reach maturity. In autumn the vital force of Yin begins to descend so all things are gathered in. In winter the vital force of Yin completes its

30.1

descent / so all things are stored away. Thus in spring and summer there is birth and maturity; in autumn and winter there is gathering in and storing away. These are the seasonal activities of the four seasons. Issuing rewards and punishments are the seasonal activities of the

30.2

ruler.[18] The four seasons never / fail to produce life and death. The ruler never fails to produce rewards and punishments. /

30.3

Heaven covers all things and regulates them. Earth supports all things and nourishes them. The four seasons give birth and maturity to all things, gather them in, and store them away. From ancient times to the present their way has never varied.

1:4.10
2/4b4
4.11

[*XS*] So long as the flood dragon has water, its divine nature / can be maintained.

3:30.5
64/2b10

[*XSJ*] The flood dragon is the divine spirit among water creatures. So long as it rides on the water, its divine nature is maintained. But when it is deprived of water, its divine nature fades away. The ruler of men holds a position of awe in the [human] world. So long as he retains [control over] the people, his awe-inspiring position is maintained. If he loses

30.6

[control over] the people, / his awesomeness fades away. The flood dragon depends on having water to maintain its divine nature. The ruler of men depends on gaining [control over] the people to achieve his awe-inspiring position.

---

[17] Following the Yang edition, which for 辨 writes 辦.

[18] According to the *Si shi* 四時 [Four Seasons] chapter of the *Guanzi* (XIV, 40/5a8–11; 2:78, 14–79, 1): "The Yin and Yang are the great principles of Heaven and Earth. The four seasons are the great course of the Yin and Yang. Punishment and the rewarding of virtue are the counterparts of the four seasons. If punishment and the rewarding of virtue correspond to the four seasons, good fortune will prevail. If not, disasters will occur." In general, summer was the time for rewards and winter for punishments.

1:4.11
2/4b5

[XS] So long as the tiger and leopard remain in[19] secluded places, their awesomeness is respected.

3:30.7
64/3a2

[XSJ] The tiger and the leopard are the most ferocious of beasts. So long as they dwell in deep forests and broad marshes, men will dread their awesomeness and respect them. The ruler of men is the most politically powerful person in the world. So long as he lives secluded,

30.8

men will dread his / power. Therefore, if the tiger and leopard leave their seclusion and approach men, men will catch them and disdain their

30.9

awesomeness. / If the ruler of men leaves his gates and presses himself upon the people, the people will treat him lightly and be contemptuous of his power.

1:4.11
2/4b6

[XS] Since the wind and rain are impartial, resentment and hatred are not directed toward them.

3:30.10
64/3a7

[XSJ] The wind blows upon things. When it blows it avoids neither the honored nor the lowly, the beautiful nor the ugly. Rain soaks things. When it comes down, it avoids neither the small nor the great, the strong

30.11

nor the weak. The wind and rain are fair and impersonal. / Their activity is impartial. Even though men may be blown about or soaked to the skin, there is no one who resents it.

:4.11
2/4b6

[XS] The honored possess the means to have their orders carried out. The lowly possess the means to forget their debasement.[20]

:30.12
4/3a11

[XSJ] The way for the ruler of men to have his orders carried out and his prohibitions put into effect is to be sure to issue orders on the basis of what the people like and issue prohibitions on the basis of what they hate. It is the nature of people always to desire life and hate

0.13

death, / always to desire benefit and hate harm. Therefore, so long as the throne issues orders that result in life and benefit to men, its orders will be carried out. So long as it issues prohibitions that result in executions and harm to men, its prohibitions will be put into effect. If the orders are carried out, it is sure to be because the people are content with the government. /

.1

The way for the ruler of men to have his subjects exert themselves to the utmost and give their allegiance to the throne is for him to be sure to

---

[19] Following the Yang edition, which for 得 writes 託.

[20] This and the above sentence also appear in the *Huainanzi*, 2/3b12 (Morgan, *Tao, the Great Luminant*, p. 36), in a slightly different context, "Now the Way has its principles and order. By grasping the Way in its unity, one may link together its thousands of branches and tens of thousands of leaves. Hence being in a honored position, one possesses the means to have orders carried out; in a lowly position, the means to forget debasement; when poor, the means to enjoy work; and when troubled, the means to endure in danger." The interpretation of these two sentences in the *Guanzi* should probably follow the *Huainanzi*. The *XSJ* has most certainly missed the point.

65

provide benefits to the realm and eliminate what is harmful. Therefore, when his benevolence is spread throughout the realm and his kindness is

31.2

extended generously to all things, fathers and sons / will find security and the myriad living things will find nourishment. Therefore all the people will happily exert themselves to the utmost and joyfully undertake employment on behalf of the throne. Within [their country] they will apply themselves diligently to essential production[21] and work quickly in order to fill the granaries. Abroad they will exhaust them-

31.3

selves and die [in resisting] the enemy in order / to secure the altars of Land and Grain. Even though they are belabored and debased, they will not dare complain. This is the way in which lowly men forget their debasement.

1:4.12
2/4b7

[*XS*] Long life and early death, poverty and opulence do not come about by accident.

3:31.4
64/3b10

[*XSJ*] If rising and retiring follow regular hours, if eating and drinking are done in moderation, and if cold and heat are met with suitable [clothing], the body will benefit and life will be lengthened. If these are not done, the body will become tired and life will be shortened. If a

31.5

man / is lazy and extravagant, he will become poor; if industrious and frugal, he will become rich. Now nothing comes about by itself; there must always be a reason for it.

1:4.12
2/4b8
3:31.5
64/4a1
31.6

[*XS*] When his commands are executed, the prince is honored.

[*XSJ*] Laws should be established so the people will be content with them. Orders should be issued / so the people will execute them. When laws and orders are made to accord with the hearts of the people just as tallies fit together, the honor paid to the ruler becomes evident.

1:4.12
2/4b8

[*XS*] When [the prince's] instructions are accepted, his fame spreads everywhere.

3:31.7
64/4a4

[*XSJ*] When the speech of the ruler of men conforms to principle and accords with the sentiments of the people, the people will accept his instructions. If they accept his instructions, his fame will be proclaimed [everywhere].

1:4.13
2/4b9

[*XS*] Even if the throne makes no demands, the people will make an effort on their own.[22]

---

[21] That is, agriculture.

[22] Cf. the *Laozi*, B, 52/13a8–9 (Waley, *The Way and Its Power*, p. 211): "So long as I do nothing, the people will of themselves be transformed. So long as I love quiescence, the people will of themselves go straight. So long as I act only by inactivity, the people will of themselves become prosperous. So long as I have no wants, the people will of themselves remain pure."

[XSJ] The enlightened ruler, in governing the realm, calms his people and does not trouble them, / gives them leisure and does not overwork them. Since he does not trouble them, the people will follow of their own accord. Since he does not overwork them, the people will make an effort on their own.

[XS] Though he may clasp the bell[23] in his arms and not say a word, everyone in the temple and hall will still follow him.[24]

[XSJ] If the ruler of men establishes procedures and measures, sets forth the duties and responsibilities, and clarifies laws and rules in order to control his people rather than placing primary emphasis on [his personal] statements, the people will follow what is correct.

[XS] Exquisitely lovely are the wild goose and swan; and so the people sing of them.[25]

[XSJ] The wild goose and swan in their exquisite loveliness represent beauty of form. Since their form is beautiful, the people sing of them. Benevolence and righteousness represent beauty of conduct. Since benevolence and righteousness are beautiful, the people take delight in them. What the people sing about and take delight in are beauty of form,[26] / benevolence and righteousness; and these are possessed by the enlightened ruler, the wild goose, and the swan.

[XS] Stately were the many officers [of Zhou 周],[27] and so the people of Yin 殷 were converted[28] by them.

[XSJ] King Wen[29] of Zhou was honest, upright, and made clearcut decisions in affairs. Therefore the ruler was enlightened. With the ruler / enlightened and the country in good order, all within the borders were enriched by his benefits. The people of Yin raised their heads and looked toward King Wen and wished to become his subjects.

[23] Emending *shu* 蜀 to *zhuo* 鐲 = *duo* 鐸 [Guo Moruo]. Zheng Xuan, in his commentary to the *Zhou li*, 3/5a3, says: "When the ancients were about to issue a new order, they were certain to ring a bell (*duo*) in order to arouse the masses and cause [the order] to be clearly heard." The *XSJ* says a *shu* refers to an implement used in sacrifices.

[24] Reading 修 as 循 [Wang Niansun].

[25] The *Shi ji*, 55/9b12–10a1, cites a song from the state of Chu praising the wild swan and goose 鴻鴈.

[26] Emending *xing* 行 to 貌. Reading *xing*, "conduct," here destroys the meaning of the passage [Igai and Wang Niansun].

[27] This is a direct quotation from the "Ode to King Wen 文王," *Shi jing*, no. 235 (Karlgren, *Book of Odes*, p. 186). The traditional chronology dates King Wen's reign 1184–1135 B.C.

[28] The *Yi Zhou shu*, IV, 35/1b8, says that King Wu 武王 (trad. 1134–1116) "was brilliant and violent. He attacked from all eight directions at once. High walls were as if [level] ground and the common people of Shang [Yin] were as if [already] converted."

[29] The *XSJ* here begins with a definition of 濟濟 and 多士.

1:4.14
2/4b12
3:32.1
64/4b7

[XS] [Consider] the fall of Zhou [Xin].[30]

[XSJ] Zhou, as a ruler, overworked the people, snatched away their wealth, and threatened them with death. Oppressive and cruel orders weighed upon the hundred surnames. Distressing and obnoxious service prevailed throughout the world. Therefore the great ministers would not

32.2

draw near him. The little people / hated him fiercely. The fact that the world revolted against him and wished to become subjects of King Wen was Zhou's own doing.

1:4.14
2/4b12
2/5a1

[XS] Advising[31] him were irresponsible vagabonds.[32] / Those lacking talent[33] were welcomed as guests.[34]

3:32.3
64/4b11

[XSJ] The advice of irresponsible vagabonds[35] may be described as lacking in rules of conduct and proper form, and erratic without settling anything. The enlightened ruler will not listen to it, nor will he permit reckless speech.

1:5.1
2/5a1

[XS] Gathered around him were the swallows and sparrows [among men].[36] Those who carried out the Way were disregarded.

3:32.5
64/5a5

[XSJ] When the Way is carried out, the prince and his ministers have a close relationship, fathers and sons feel secure, and all living things are nurtured. Therefore the duty of the enlightened ruler lies in carrying out the Way. He disregards petty things. Swallows and sparrows are such petty things.

[30] Zhou Xin 紂辛 (trad. 1154–1122) was the last ruler of the Shang or Yin Dynasty. This short phrase 紂之失也, for which I have rendered a rather forced translation, may be a corruption of some longer statement connected with a story appearing in the *Huainanzi*, 12/12b (Morgan, *Tao, the Great Luminant*, p. 126): After gaining release from Zhou Xin's prison by paying a huge bribe, King Wen returned home, and in order to allay suspicions, made a show of amusing himself with music and women, "thereby awaiting the fall of Zhou 人待紂之失也."

[31] The Yang edition mistakenly writes 間 for 問.

[32] *Fei peng* 飛蓬; *peng* is a type of bramble. "Flying *peng*" appears in the *Shi jing*, no. 52. Karlgren (*Book of Odes*, p. 43) translates it as "flying artemisia," Waley (*Book of Songs*, p. 50) as "tumbleweed." The metaphor is clear.

[33] *Zai* 在 is a mistake for *cai* 才. They are identical in their archaic and ancient pronunciations [Guo Moruo].

[34] According to the *Shang shu*, V, 2/6: "Only those who had fled after committing crimes in the four corners [of the world] were honored and exalted, trusted and employed, and made great officers and nobles."

[35] The *XSJ* for *fei* 飛 writes *fei* 蜚 throughout; 蜚 was commonly used for 飛 in early texts.

[36] The wild goose and swan 鴻鵠 and swallow and sparrow 燕雀 seem to have been common metaphors for great and petty men. The *Shi ji*, 481b3, quotes Chen She 陳涉 (d. 209 B.C.) as saying in reply to the ridicule of lesser men: "What can swallows and sparrows know of the aims of the wild goose and swan?"

68

[XS] Sacrificial animals and the *gui* and *bi*[37] are not [in themselves] enough when making offerings[38] to the spirits.

[XSJ] In movement and rest the enlightened ruler adheres to [correct] principles and righteous conduct. His orders conform with the hearts of the people. His punishments fit their crimes. His rewards fit their achievements. Therefore, even though he does not use sacrificial animals or the *gui* and *bi* in sacrificing to the spirits, the spirits / will help him, and Heaven and Earth will bestow favors upon him. He will meet with good fortune whenever he initiates an undertaking.

The movements of the muddle-headed ruler are devoid of righteous conduct and [correct] principles. His orders go against the hearts of the people. His punishments do not fit their crimes. His rewards do not fit their achievements. Therefore, / even though he may use sacrificial animals and the *gui* and *bi* in sacrificing to the spirits, the spirits will not help him, and Heaven and Earth will not bestow favors upon him. He will meet with misfortune whenever he initiates affairs.

[XS] If the achievements of the ruler are well established, why should he [use] precious gifts?[39]

[XSJ] A ruler's achievements are measured by wealth and strength. Therefore, when his country is rich and his soldiers strong, feudal lords will submit to his government, and neighboring enemies will fear its awesomeness. Even though [the ruler] does not use precious gifts to make the feudal lords serve him, they will not / dare go against him.

A ruler's faults are measured by poverty and weakness. Therefore, when his country is poor and his soldiers are weak, battles will not be won and its defenses will not be firm. Even though [such a ruler] presents neighboring enemies with famous objects[40] and precious jewels so they will serve him, he will be unable / to avoid the calamity of annihilation.

---

[37] The *gui* 圭 was a jade ceremonial tablet often conferred upon feudal princes as a symbol of rank and authority. The *bi* 璧 was a perforated jade disk believed to represent Heaven.

[38] For *xiang* 饗, the Yang edition and the *XSJ* both write *xiang* 享. Both terms mean "to make an offering," but the former specifies more particularly a sacrifice that is eaten by the participants, usually at a ceremonial feast.

[39] This and the above sentence of the text are reminiscent of the *Lun yu*, XVII, 11: "The Master said, 'Ritual! Ritual! Are jade and silk all that is meant by it?'"

[40] *Ming qi* 名器; according to the *Zhanguo ce*, 1/2a13–2b1, during the Western Zhou period there were many famous objects and precious jewels. The same work, 5/3a11–13 (Crump, *Chan-Kuo T'se*, p. 102), says that the states of Zhou, Song, Liang, and Chu each had precious objects. The art of making them had been lost, so they had become famous throughout the world.

1:5.2
2/5a4
3:32.13
64/5b4

[*XS*] Yi's[41] way did not lie merely in shooting [the arrow].

[*XSJ*] Yi was an excellent archer of ancient times. He kept his bow and arrow in careful adjustment and guarded them securely. When he grasped the bow, he carefully judged the elevation [for the arrow]. He had mastered the way of being sure to hit the mark. Therefore each time he released [the arrow] he was able to hit the mark.

32.14

The enlightened / ruler is like Yi. He harmonizes the laws. He judges which should be discarded and which maintained, and then guards them securely. He has mastered the way for being sure to govern well. Therefore, every time he undertakes something, he is able to do what is right. It is by mastering their [respective] ways that Yi could be sure of

33.1

hitting the mark / and the ruler can be sure of governing well. The mere act of shooting involves nothing more than the bow string releasing the arrow.

1:5.3
2/5a4
3:33.2
64/5b10

[*XS*] Zaofu's[42] technique did not lie in merely driving horses.

[*XSJ*] Zaofu was an excellent charioteer. He was good at looking after his horses, and was regular in watering and feeding them. He measured the horses' strength and judged their pace. Therefore he was able to take distant roads without tiring the horses.

33.3

The enlightened ruler is like Zaofu. / He is skilled in governing his people. He measures their strength and estimates their capabilities. Therefore he has achievements without distressing or injuring the people. Therefore it is by mastering their [respective] techniques that

33.4

Zaofu could take distant roads and the ruler / can have achievement and fame. The mere act of driving horses involves nothing more than holding the reins.

1:5.3
2/5a5
3:33.5
64/6a3

[*XS*] Xi Zhong's[43] skill did not lie in merely hewing and trimming.

[*XSJ*] When Xi Zhong made chariot parts, what was square, round, curved, or straight always matched the compass, T-square, bevel-compass, or marking line. Therefore, when the mechanism moved, each

---

[41] 羿; the legendary archer who was supposed to have lived during the time of Emperor Yao 堯 (trad. 2356–2257). When ten suns appeared in the sky at one time, he saved the world from burning up by shooting down nine of them. According to the *Guanzi*, XI, 32/10a11–12 (2:39.10–11): "Yi had an intuitive grasp of how to use the bow and arrow. Therefore, when shooting he could hit he mark."

[42] 造父; the charioteer of King Mu 穆 (trad. 1001–945) of the Zhou. According to the *Guanzi*, XI, 32/10a12–10b1 (2:39.11): "Zaofu had an intuitive grasp of how to use reins and whip. Therefore he could catch swift beasts and reach distant roads."

[43] 奚仲; the wheelwright of Emperor Yu 禹 (trad. 2205–2198). According to the *Guanzi*, XI, 32/10a11 (2:39.10): "The craftsman [Xi Zhong] had an intuitive grasp of how to use the axe handle. Therefore he could cut along the marking line."

part fitted into the other. When put to use, it was tight and secure, and the finished chariot was strong and solid.

33.6 The enlightened ruler is like Xi Zhong. His speech / and movements always accord with proper political and statistical methods. Therefore numerous principles are suitably applied, and a close relationship exists between the throne and those below. It is by mastering their [respective] skills that Xi Zhong could make his chariots and the ruler is able to govern well. The mere act of hewing and trimming involves nothing 33.7 more than the axe / and knife.[44]

1:5.4
2/5a6
[*XS*] For summoning [people] from afar, emissaries are of no use. For developing close relationships with those who are near, words are of no consequence.[45] Only those who act at night have [the capacity for] such things.[46]

3:33.8
64/6a8
[*XSJ*] When people are benefited, they come; when they are harmed, they leave. People follow after benefits just as water runs downhill.[47] It has no preference among the four directions. Therefore those who wish to make the people come must first initiate benefits for them. Then, even 33.9 though not summoned, / the people will arrive by themselves. [On the other hand] if what is harmful to them is instituted, the people will not come, even though they are summoned. /

33.10 If [the ruler] controls his people like a father and mother, the people will look on him as a parent[48] and love him. If he leads them with

---

[44] The above references to Yi, Zaofu, and Xi Zhong in the *XS* text are reminiscent of the story in the *Zhuangzi*, II, 3/1bff. (Watson, *Chuang Tzu*, pp. 50–51), concerning the cook who could cut up an ox with such skill that all his movements were in perfect harmony and his chopper was never dulled. When the prince praised his talent, he replied: "I have always devoted myself to the Way. It is more advanced than any talent." The *XSJ*, however, ignores the mystical Daoist implications of these apothegms and interprets them along practical Legalistic Confucian lines.

[45] Dong Zhongshu (179?–104? B.C.) in his *Chunqiu fanlu*, III, 5/8b1, paraphrases this and the above sentence: "Therefore it is said: 'For developing close relationships with [people] who are near, do not use words. For summoning those from afar, do not use emissaries.'" They are also cited with minor variations in characters in the *Huainanzi*, 6/3a11–12. See n. 46, below.

[46] Inserting 之 after 有 in accordance with the *XSJ* and Ancient, Liu, and Zhu editions. This and the preceding two lines of the text are repeated with slightly different wording in the *Huainanzi* (6/3a11–13) and the *Wenzi* (A, 2/9a4–5). The Gao You 高誘 commentary to the *Huainanzi* passage states that 夜行, "act at night," is a metaphor for "acting in secret," i.e., "not putting on a show of acting virtuously." The *XSJ* says it refers to heartfelt action.

[47] This appears to be a common simile. The *Mengzi*, IA, 6/6, says: "If there were one who did not find pleasure in killing men ... people would flock toward him as water flows downward with a rush which no one can stop."

[48] This passage is based on a play on the word 親, which can mean both "parent" or "to treat as a parent" as well as "to have a close relationship with someone."

6b

33.11

simplicity and generosity and receives them with truth[49] and actual [benefits], even though / he does not say, "I have a close relationship with my people," the people will still look on him as a parent. But if [the ruler] controls his people like a hated enemy, they will remain distant from / him. If he leads them without generosity and receives them with empty [promises], so that deception and hypocrisy both arise, then even though he may say, "I have a close relationship with my people," they will not look on him as a parent. /

33.12

The enlightened ruler's capacity for making those far away come to him and those near at hand have close relationships with him depends on his heart.[50] "Acting at night" refers to heartfelt action. If [the ruler] is able to exercise benevolence in a heartfelt manner, no one in the world will be able to contend with him.

1:5.4
2/5a7
3:33.14
64/6b7

[*XS*] How can a small rise[51] make a flat plain high?

[*XSJ*] The four major failings of men are for the ruler to be predatory, the father and mother to be cruel, the minister and subordinate official to be disloyal, and the son and his wife to be unfilial. Hence if any one of these [major] failings is present in a person, it is impossible / for him to become a worthy, even though he may have some minor good points. "A flat plain" refers to low marshland. Even though there may be a slight rise on it, it cannot be considered high.

34.1

1:5.5
2/5a10
3:34.2
64/6b11

[*XS*] How can a small depression make a lofty mountain low?[52]

[*XSJ*] The four highest forms of conduct for men are for the ruler to be kind, the father and mother to be compassionate, the minister and subordinate official to be loyal, and the son and his wife filial. If any one of these highest forms of conduct is present in a person, he cannot be considered unworthy, even though he may commit minor errors. / "A lofty mountain" refers to a mountain that is high. Even though it may have a small depression, it cannot be considered low.[53]

34.3

---

[49] Following the Ancient, Liu, and Zhu editions, which write 眞 for 有. This reading provides better balance with the above expression 純厚, "simplicity and generosity." The reading of the Yang and Zhao edition is 有實, "with what has reality."

[50] According to the *Lun yu*, XII, 16/2: "The Master said, 'Good government obtains when those near at hand are happy and those far away come.'"

[51] Emending 隖 to 陘 [Guo Moruo].

[52] These two statements are reminiscent of one of the paradoxes of the later fourth century dialectician, Hui Shi 惠施, which is cited in the *Zhuangzi*, X, 33/20b6 (Watson, *Chuang Tzu*, p. 374): "The heavens are as low as earth; mountains and marshes are on the same level."

[53] This rendering of the *XSJ* is analogous to the *Wenzi*, B, 21/31a7–9: "Laozi said, 'Crooked by the inch but straight by the foot; slightly bent but largely upright; such is the sage. When princes today judge a minister, they do not estimate his great achievements but

72

1:5.6
2/5a11

[*XS*] Men who slander and exaggerate should not be entrusted with great responsibilities.

3:34.4
64/7a3

[*XSJ*] To destroy the reputation of worthy men is called slander. To overstate [the ability of] the unworthy is called exaggeration. If men who slander and exaggerate obtain employment, the understanding of the ruler of men will be blinded, and destructive talk and overstatement will become prevalent. If [these people] are given responsibility for

34.5

great / affairs, nothing will be accomplished and calamities will result.

1:5.7
2/5a12

[*XS*] Those with large feet may take a long pace.[54] Those with clear sight[55] can attain the Way. Those whose machinations lead to hasty

5.8

[gains] / but later sorrow should, if they draw near [the ruler], be sent away and not summoned back.

3:34.10
64/7b1

[*XSJ*] Petty men distort the Way and seek what is convenient. They accommodate themselves to the ideas of the ruler so as to snatch pleasure surreptitiously. They pursue[56] profit so as to snatch gain surreptitiously. In this way they may get what they want quickly, but the arrival of calamities will also be sudden. Therefore the sage gets rid of

34.11

them / and does not employ them.

---

summarize his minute actions so as to seek out his petty goodness. This is the way to miss worthiness. Therefore, if a man is rich in virtue, do not raise questions about petty chastity.'" The *Huainanzi*, 13/14a ff. (Morgan, *Tao, the Great Luminant*, pp. 165 ff.) also expresses similar ideas.

[54] This sentence is clearly corrupt and should be emended to conform to a similar sentence in the *Huainanzi*, 13/15b4–6 (Morgan, *Tao, the Great Luminant*, pp. 167–168). Thus 譏 is a corruption of 蹠 and 臣 is a corruption of 巨. In both cases the forms are similar. The *Huainanzi* passage reads: "Those who are diligent in minor affairs will not achieve success. Those who slander will not get along with the masses. Those with large bodies have widely separated joints. Those with large feet take a long pace." The *XSJ* (64/7a6; 3:34.6) was written after the text had become corrupted and therefore attempts to explain its version of the text as follows: "In the planning of the enlightened ruler, those who make calculations about the world are called ministers who give good counsel 譏臣. If there are ministers who give good counsel, [all] within the seas receive their enrichment. If this enrichment is spread to the entire world, later generations will enjoy their accomplishments. Even after a long time the benefits will continue to increase. Therefore [the *Xing shi*] says, 'Ministers who give good counsel can effect long-lasting undertakings 遠舉.'"

[55] Taking 顧 as a noun and 憂, which here should be read as 優, as an adjective in order to balance the construction of the preceding sentence. The *XSJ*, having misinterpreted the preceding sentence, has also missed the point here and attempts to follow the original reading of 憂: "The sage determines what may be spoken and then speaks; he determines what may be done and then acts. To snatch at gain, which later leads to harm, or at pleasure, which later leads to sorrow, are things that the sage will not do. Therefore, when the sage chooses his words, he is certain to consider 顧 their implications. When he chooses his action, he is certain to consider any [resulting] sorrow 憂. Therefore [the *XS*] says, 'Those who consider the sorrow [that may result] can attain the Way.'"

[56] Emending 備 to 循 [Wang Niansun].

1:5.8
2/5b3
3:34.12
64/7b6

[XS] Those who initiate long-lasting [benefits] may be seen from afar.

[XSJ] If long-lasting [benefits] are initiated, the masses will receive their advantages, and the benevolence and righteousness of the initiators will be seen from afar.[57]

1:5.9
2/5b4
3:34.13
64/7b6

[XS] He who fashions great things is imitated by the masses.[58]

[XSJ] What Heaven fashions is great. Therefore it is able to cover all things equally. What Earth fashions is great. Therefore it is able to support all things equally. What the ruler of men fashions is great. Therefore he embraces many things and the masses succeed in imitating him.

1:5.9
2/5b5

[XS] If [the ruler] longs for[59] men to cherish him, he must set himself to following [the Way] untiringly.

3:35.1
64/7b9

[XSJ] High rank, wealth, honor, and fame are what attract and delight the people, so that every ruler of men desires the existence of these things. Now if he desires the people to cherish him and delight in him, he must untiringly follow the Way and its Power, and then the people will cherish and delight in him.

1:5.10
2/5b6

[XS] Undertakings that are deemed essential / [no matter what the circumstances] are not necessarily dependable.

3:35/3
64/7b12

[XSJ] When the sage wants something done, he first discusses its principles and rightness, and estimates its possibilities. If right, he pursues it; if not, he desists. If possible, he pursues it; if not, he desists.

35.4

Thus whatever he undertakes / is always like a personal treasure to him. But when the petty person wants something done, he does not discuss its principles or rightness, nor does he estimate its possibilities. Whether or not it is right or possible, he still pursues it. Therefore his

35.5

undertakings / are never dependable.

[XS] Speech that always promises is not necessarily trustworthy.

1:5.10
2/5b6

[XSJ] When the sage makes promises,[60] he first discusses their principles and rightness, and estimates their possibilities. If right, he makes the promise; if not, he refrains. If possible, he makes the promise; if not,

35.7

he refrains. Therefore his promises are always trustworthy. / But a petty person will still make a promise even though it is not right or possible.

---

[57] The *XSJ* here begins with a definition of the term 舉長, "to initiate long-lasting benefits," which has been omitted from the translation.

[58] Sun Xingyan and Zhang Peilun would read *cai* 裁, "to fashion," as *cai* 材, and Igai would emend *bi* 比, "imitate," to *bi* 庇. Thus the sentence would read: "He who has great talent will become a protector to the masses."

[59] Emending 美 to 羑 [Tan Jiefu].

[60] Emending 己 to 言 [Ding].

Whenever he speaks, he is certain to promise. Therefore his promises are not always to be trusted.

1:5.10
2/5b7[XS] Those who are diligent in minor matters will not accomplish great things.[61]

3:35.8
64/8a9[XSJ] When [a person] is diligent on behalf of one family, he will accomplish things for that one family. If he is diligent on behalf of one district, he will accomplish things for one district. If he is diligent on behalf of one country, he will accomplish things for that one country. If he is diligent on behalf of the entire realm, he will accomplish things for 35.9 the entire realm. / For this reason if the object of his diligence is of minor importance, so also will be his accomplishment. If the object of his diligence is of great importance, so also will be his accomplishment.

1:5.10
2/5b7
3:35.10
64/8b1[XS] Whoever dislikes[62] food will never grow fat.

[XSJ] The ocean does not reject water. Therefore it can achieve immense size. The mountain does not reject earth and rocks. Therefore it can achieve immense height. The enlightened ruler does not grow tired of men. Therefore he is able to acquire a large population.[63] The scholar 35.11 does not grow tired of study. Therefore he is able to become / a sage. Advice makes the ruler secure. Food makes the body fat. If the ruler dislikes advice, he will not be secure. If a man dislikes food, he will not become fat.

1:5.11
2/5b8
3:35.13
4/8b6[XS] Words that have an all-embracing [character] may surely be compared with Heaven and Earth.

[XSJ] Words that speak about the Way, benevolence, loyalty, trustworthiness, filial piety, and respect for seniority—these words are all-embracing. Heaven is fair and impartial. Therefore it covers all whether beautiful or ugly. Earth is fair and impartial. Therefore it supports all 5.14 whether small or large. / Words that are all-embracing are fair and impartial. Therefore they are applicable to everyone whether worthy or unworthy. Therefore words that are all-embracing are comparable to the impartiality of Heaven and Earth.

[61] This sentence is cited with slightly different wording in the *Huainanzi*, 13/15b4. See n. 54, above.

[62] For 訾 the *XSJ* and the Ancient, Liu, and Zhu editions all write 訾. The meaning here is the same. The definition of the latter term, which appears in the *XSJ* below, has been omitted.

[63] These ideas of the ocean not rejecting water, mountains not rejecting rocks, and the ruler not rejecting the people were common metaphors in pre-Han and Han texts. With slight variations in wording, they appear in a memorial presented by Li Si 李斯 to the King of Qin 秦 in 237 B.C. Other variations also appear in the *Zhuangzi, Hanfeizi*, and *Huainanzi*. See Bodde, *China's First Unifier*, p. 20.

1:5.12
2/5b10

[*XS*] To descend a cliff three *ren*[64] high is extremely difficult for men, but apes and monkeys will [do it simply for a] drink.

3:36.2
64/8b11

[*XSJ*] In granting office, the enlightened ruler gives men positions for which their capabilities are strong and not positions where they are weak. Therefore his undertakings are always successful and his merit established. The muddle-headed ruler does not understand that each

36.3

individual has his strong points and weak points, / so in assigning tasks he must make careful preparations.

Now men are strong in planning undertakings, in deciding upon things, and in distinguishing and clarifying proper ceremony and righteous conduct, whereas apes and monkeys are weak [in this respect]. But apes and monkeys are strong in climbing heights and going out onto

36.4

dangerous ground, / whereas men are weak [in this respect]. If [the ruler] assigns to men tasks that [require] the strong points of apes and monkeys, his orders will be disregarded and the assignments will not be completed.

1:5.12
2/5b10

[*XS*] Therefore it is said: "Aggressive arrogance and the desire to act alone leads to calamity in undertakings."[65]

3:36.6
64/9a5

[*XSJ*] When the enlightened ruler undertakes something, he entrusts it to the planning of a sage and uses the strength of the masses, without himself meddling in it. Therefore affairs are successful and prosperity arises. The muddle-headed ruler considers himself wise and does not rely

36.7

upon the planning of the sage. / He works strenuously for his own achievements and does not rely on the strength of the masses. He makes use of himself alone and does not listen to correct advice. Therefore his undertakings fail and calamities arise.

1:5.12
2/5b11

[*XS*] Even when a person is not traveling in the countryside, he does not abandon his horse.

3:36.9
64/9a9

[*XSJ*] To travel through the countryside, one rides a horse. Consequently, even when a person is not traveling through the countryside, he must still care for and feed his horse and not be remiss about it. To engage in battle, one uses people. Consequently, even when [a ruler] is

36.10

not engaged in battle, / he must never be lax in governing and caring for his people.[66]

[64] A *ren* 仞 is variously given as 8 Chinese feet or 5 Chinese feet, 6 inches. The latter is the most commonly accepted value. According to Swann (*Food and Money*, p. 362), a Zhou foot was equal to 0.909 English inches. Thus a 3-*ren* cliff at 8 Zhou feet per *ren* would be a little over 21 English feet in height.

[65] This passage appears to be out of order and should probably come after the statement (2/7b6–7; 1:7.6–7), which speaks of the prince who maintains his state in isolation.

[66] Jia Yi (201–169 B.C.), in his *Xin shu*, VI, 3/8b, relates the story of Duke Yi 懿 (668–660 B.C.) of Weii 衛, who loved cranes and held actors in high esteem, but neglected his people

1 : 5.13
2/5b12

[XS] Those who can give without taking [in return] are like Heaven and Earth.

3 : 36.11
54/9a12

[XSJ] Heaven produces the four seasons and Earth produces all resources, thereby nourishing all things but not taking anything [in return]. The enlightened ruler is like Heaven and Earth. He instructs the people in accordance with the seasons. He exhorts them to plough and

36.12

weave in order to enrich their livelihood, / and does not push his own achievements nor regard his gains as belonging to himself.

1 : 5.14
*/6a2
3 : 36.13
54/9b4

[XS] Those who weary of tasks will prove wanting.

[XSJ] If [a person] is lazy or tardy, he will be disloyal in serving the ruler, unfilial in serving his father and mother, and unsuccessful in all he undertakes.

: 5.14
*/6a2

[XS] Those who do not scatter [their attention]⁶⁷ may be compared with⁶⁸ the spirits. Those comparable⁶⁹ to the spirits will be [received] within [the palace], while those who have proved wanting will be left at

---

and slighted his ministers. Subsequently, when attacked by the Di barbarians, his ministers and people deserted him; he was killed and his country lost. Jia Yi then concludes: "Guanzi said, 'Even when a person is not traveling in the countryside, he does not abandon his horse.' This was [a case of Duke Yi] abandoning his horse." Thus Jia Yi and the author of the XSJ are in agreement on the meaning of this sentence. The Yin commentary, however, presents a different interpretation. It says, "A horse has a natural capacity for knowing the way. Do not abandon the horse and the horse itself will find it." This interpretation appears to be based on a story in the Hanfeizi, VII, 22/8b8–9 (Liao, Han Fei Tzu, I, p. 235): "[Once] when Guan Zhong and Xi Peng accompanied Duke Huan to attack Guzhu, spring [suddenly] left and winter returned. They became confused and lost the way. Guan Zhong said, 'We can utilize the wisdom of old horses.' He thereupon released an old horse and by following after it, they subsequently found the way."

⁶⁷ Emending 廣 to 曠 [Yasui, He, and Zhang Peilun].

⁶⁸ Reading yi 疑 as ni 擬 [Liu Shipei and Xu]. Cf. the story of the hunchback in the Zhuangzi, VII, 19/2b8–3a6 (Watson, Chuang Tzu, pp. 199–200), who could catch cicadas with his hands. When Confucius questioned him about his ability, he replied that he trained himself until Heaven and Earth and all creation might be around him, yet he would only be conscious of the wings of his cicadas. Confucius turned to his disciples and said: "He is single-minded and concentrates (ning 凝) his spirit." The same passage appears in the Liezi, 2/12b8–9 (Graham, Lieh-tzu, pp. 44–45), but its commentator, Zhang Zhan 張湛 (4th century) says: "If a person is single-minded, he will be like the spirits." The three characters, yi ni, and ning, being similar in form, are easily mistaken for each other, but only the reading of ni is applicable in the case of the Guanzi. The author of the XSJ (64/9b6; 3 : 36.14) also read yi as ni, but he interpreted 無廣 (無曠) as meaning "not being empty [of principles]." Thus, "To be successful in making squares and circles, use the compass and T-square. To obtain results in measuring length, use the foot and inch ruler. To be secure in maintaining good order among the people, use laws and statistical methods. Therefore those whose affairs are not empty of principles will achieve success comparable to the spirits." In my opinion, the interpretation of the XSJ here fails to achieve a proper balance of meaning with the preceding sentence in the XS text. Therefore I have not included it in the translation proper.

⁶⁹ Inserting yi 疑 (ni 擬) before 神 in order to complete the meaning of the sentence [Igai].

6.1

the gate.[70] / Those who are within will attain [their goal];[71] those left at the gate will be kept waiting.[72]

6.2

If a person is lazy at dawn's warning call, he will later meet with disaster at dusk.[73] / If [a person] is forgetful about his affairs in the morning, he will fail to achieve anything by evening.

3:37.2
64/9b9

[*XSJ*] If a person does not exhaust his strength when serving the ruler, he will be punished. If he does not exhaust it when serving his father and mother, he will not be close to them. If he is not attentive when receiving instruction or pursuing studies, he will not be successful. Therefore, if a person does not exert his strength and attend to advancing [himself] in the morning, / no achievement will be seen by evening.

37.3

1:6.2
2/6a6

[*XS*] If evil influences steal[74] into [the ruler's heart], his dignified appearance[75] will be marred.

3:37.4
64/9b12

[*XSJ*] If within [a person's heart] there is a feeling for trustworthiness and honesty, his fame will be great. If he has cultivated a diligent and respectful conduct, honor will be associated [with his name]. But if within [his heart] there is no feeling for truth, his reputation will be notorious. If he has cultivated an indolent and easygoing conduct, shame will result.

1:6.2
2/6a7
3:37.6
64/10a3

[*XS*] If the prince is not a prince, his ministers will not be ministers.

[*XSJ*] If the prince does not clearly manifest righteous conduct between ruler and minister so as to rectify his ministers, they will not understand the principles for acting as ministers in serving their ruler.

---

[70] This and the following two sentences have no explanation. He Ruzhang says that they were originally part of the commentary rather than the text. Guo Moruo, however, states that the style is not the same as the commentary and points out that other passages that follow also have no explanation.

[71] Emending 假 to 𝄇 [Dai].

[72] Wen would interpret this sentence differently. He reads 假 as 暇 and 待 as 殆. Thus, "Those who are within will find leisure; those left at the gate will be exhausted."

[73] The meaning of this sentence is not clear. I have followed the interpretation of Wen, who believes 曙戒 was probably the name for the warning drum in the morning. He also reads 勿 as 忽 and 稈 as 遲(暮). Tao would read 稈 as 徲. Thus, "thereafter he will meet with diaster."

[74] Following the Yang edition, which for 入, "to enter," writes 爇.

[75] According to Zhang Peilun, *Zheng se* 正色 should be written *yu se* 玉色. Li Shan 李善 (d. 689) in his commentary to the *Wen xuan* (Hu 胡 edition) twice (16/7b and 34/1b) cites this passage from the *Guanzi*, writing *yu* for *zheng*. Thus the sentence would read: "If evil influences steal into [the ruler's heart], his appearance, jadelike [in its purity], will be marred." A similar passage also appears in Dongfang Suo's (c. 161 – c. 87 B.C.) *Jian yuan si* 諫怨思 [Admonishment Against Resentful Thoughts], which reads 邪氣入而感內兮, 施玉色而外淫, "If evil influences enter and affect [the heart of the ruler] within, he will neglect his jadelike appearance, and the evil influences will show through." See the *Quan shanggu Sandai Qin Sanguo Liuchao wen*, 全漢文, 25/3b.

1:6.2
2/6a7

[*XS*] If the father does not act as a father, his sons will not act as sons.[76]

3:37.7
54/10a5

[*XSJ*] If the father does not clearly manifest righteous conduct between father and son in order to instruct and discipline his sons, they will not understand the way to act as sons in serving their father.

4:6.2
2/6a7
5.3

[*XS*] If the throne is remiss in maintaining its position, those below will overstep their bounds. / If harmony is lacking between the throne and those below, orders will not be carried out.

3:37.9
54/10a8

[*XSJ*] If the prince and minister have a close relationship and harmony exists between the throne and those below, the people will all live in concord. Therefore if the ruler issues orders, the people will carry them out. If the ruler[77] institutes prohibitions, the people will not violate them. But if the prince and minister do not have a close relationship and harmony is lacking between the throne and those below, the people will

7.10

not all live in concord. Therefore / what is ordered will not be carried out, and what is prohibited will not be stopped.

6.3
6a8

[*XS*] If clothing and caps are not worn correctly, guests will not be respectful.[78]

37.11
/10a11

[*XSJ*] If [the ruler's] speech is trustworthy, his movements sedate, and his clothing and cap are worn correctly, ministers and subordinate officials will be respectful. But if his speech is careless, his movements offensive, and his clothing and cap untidy, ministers and subordinate officials will treat him lightly.

6.3
6a9

[*XS*] If advancing and retiring do not accord with good form, governmental orders will not be carried out.

37.12
/10b1

[*XSJ*] Good form sets the pattern of conduct for all things. Laws and procedures set the standards of good form for people as a whole. Rules for propriety and righteous conduct set the standards of good form between the honored and lowly. Therefore, if [the ruler's] movements adhere to good form, his orders will be carried out. / Otherwise they will

13

not.

---

[76] This statement is reminiscent of the *Lun yu*, XII, 11: "Duke Jing 景 (547–490 B.C.) of Qi asked Confucius about government. Confucius replied: "Let the prince be a prince, the minister a minister, the father a father, and the son a son."

[77] Emending 上, "the throne," to 主 in order to preserve a balance in meaning with the preceding line [Ding].

[78] Cf. the *Lun yu*, XX, 2: "A gentleman sees to it that his clothes and hat are worn correctly and imparts such dignity to his glances that no sooner do [other people] look upon him than they are overcome with awe. Is this not inspiring awe without being ferocious?"

<table>
<tr><td>1:6.3
2/6a9
3:37.14
64/10b4</td><td>[XS] Kindly yet awe-inspiring, the way of the prince will be complete.
[XSJ] If the ruler of men is warm-hearted and generous, the people will love him. If he is orderly and sedate, the people will fear him. Therefore, since the people love him, they will give him their allegiance. Since they fear him, they will work for him. Now it is of vital necessity for the ruler to have the people give him their allegiance and work for him.</td></tr>
</table>

1:6.4
2/6a10
[XS] If [the prince] does not give pleasure [to the people], they will not grieve for him. If he does not give them life, they will not die for him.[79]

3:38.2
64/10b7
[XSJ] If the ruler of men is able to make his people secure, they[80] will serve their ruler as their father and mother. Therefore if the ruler grieves, they will grieve with him. If he encounters difficulties, they will die for him. But if the ruler looks on his people as dirt, they will not work for

38.3
him. / If he grieves, they will not grieve for him. If he encounters difficulties, they will not die for him.

1:6.4
2/6a11
[XS] If what goes out is not adequate, what returns will not be the best.

3:38.4
64/10b11
[XSJ] The generosity with which the throne treats the people is what makes them keep fighting to the death. Therefore, so long as it treats them generously, the people will respond in the same way. But if it is

38.5
mean to them, / the people will respond with meanness. Therefore, the prince cannot expect his ministers to respond generously to meanness, nor can the father expect it of his sons.

1:6.5
2/6a12
3:38.6
64/11a3
[XS] What the Way says is one, but its applications vary.
[XSJ] The Way supports the multitude of things, brings life and nourishment to them, and brings each to its appointed end. That is why through it some govern districts, some govern countries, and some govern the entire realm.

1:6.5
2/6b1
6.6
[XS] The man who heeds the Way and so is good at managing a family is a man of a single family. / The man who heeds the Way and so is good at managing a district is a man of a single district.

3:38.7
64/11a5
[XSJ] Whoever heeds the Way in order to govern a district, brings into close relationship its fathers and sons, makes its elder and younger brothers obedient, rectifies its habits and customs, causes its people to

38.8
rejoice in their superiors and be secure on their land, / and himself becomes the pillar of the district—such a person is a man of that district.

[79] Cf. the *Mengzi*, IB, 4/3: "When [a ruler] rejoices in the joy of his people, they also rejoice in his joy. When he grieves at the sorrow of his people, they also grieve at this sorrow."

[80] Inserting 民 before 事 in accordance with the reading of the *Qunshu zhiyao* [Ding].

1:6.6
2/6b2
6.7

[*XS*] The man who heeds the Way and so is good at managing a country is a man of a single country. / The man who heeds the Way and so is good at managing the realm is a man of the entire realm. The man who heeds the Way and so is good at fixing the place of things is like

5.8

Heaven / and Earth.[81]

When the Way has left [the ruler], no one will come[82] to him. When the Way has come [to the ruler], no one will leave him.

3:38.9
54/11a9

[*XSJ*] People follow those who possess the Way, just as to the hungry food comes first, to the cold, clothing, and to the hot, shade. Therefore when [the ruler] possesses the Way, the people turn to him, but when he does not, they leave him.

:6.8
2/6b7
:38.11
4/11a12

[*XS*] The Way brings about the transformation of the self.

[*XSJ*] The Way is the means by which the self is transformed so a person will adhere to correct principles. Therefore, so long as the Way exists in a person, in speaking he will be naturally submissive, in doing things he will be naturally correct, in serving his prince he will be naturally loyal, in serving his father he will be naturally filial, and in dealing with others he will be naturally in accord with principles.

:6.9
/6b7

[*XS*] Maintaining fullness has to do with Heaven.[83] Alleviating danger has to do with men.

:38.13
4/11b3

[*XSJ*] The way of Heaven is full without overflowing. It flourishes without decay. The enlightened ruler patterns himself on the way of Heaven. Therefore, though honored he is not arrogant, though rich he is not extravagant. He acts in accordance with principles and is never

3.14

indolent. / Therefore he is able to preserve his honor and wealth for a long time and long possesses the realm without losing it. /

0.1

The enlightened ruler relieves the calamities of the world and alleviates the dangers of the world. Now he who would relieve calamities and alleviate dangers must wait until all the people are employed before he will be able to accomplish it.

---

[81] Emending 天下, "realm," to 天地 [Huang Zhen, Wang Niansun, and Yin Tongyang]. Reading "realm" does not make sense here. Furthermore, the expression 天地之配也 also appears in line 2/6a1 (1:5.13) above.

[82] The Yang edition mistakenly reverses the order of the two expressions 其人莫來 and 其人莫往.

[83] This and the following sentence appear to be part of a set of old apothegms that are expounded further in a passage in the *Guo yu*, 21/1a3–7: "When the King of Yue, Goujian [496–465 B.C.], had been on the throne three years, he wished to attack Wu. Fan Li warned him, 'Now in the affairs of state, there are the maintaining of fullness 持盈, the stabilizing of what is inclined to collapse 定傾, and the regularizing of affairs 節事.' The king asked, 'What do you mean by these?' The reply was, 'Maintenance of fullness has to do with Heaven; stabilization of what is included to collapse has to do with man; regularization of affairs has to do with Earth.'"

[XS] If [the ruler] disregards the limits [set by] Heaven, though [his country] be full to overflowing, it will certainly dry up.

[XSJ] Territory extensive, nation wealthy, population large, and armed forces strong—these are [the attributes of] a state that is flourishing and blessed with abundance. But even though it is already flourishing and blessed with abundance, if the benevolence and generosity to secure it are lacking, and there are no limits or calculations to keep it in good order, the state will not be [the ruler's] state, nor the people[84] be / his people.

[XS] If harmony is lacking between the throne and those below, though [the ruler] may feel secure, he will certainly encounter danger.

[XSJ] When ministers do not have a close relationship with their ruler, and the population does not trust his functionaries, the throne will become estranged from those below, and harmony will be lacking. Therefore, even though [the ruler may think] himself secure, he will certainly encounter danger.

[XS] He who wishes to become king of the realm yet disregards the way of Heaven can never attain such a position.

[XSJ] If the ruler adheres to the way of Heaven in controlling his people, they will be of one mind in serving the throne. Therefore [the ruler] will become honored and wealthy and long be king of the realm. But if he loses the way of Heaven, the people will become estranged and revolt against him, and neither obey nor follow him. / Therefore the ruler will be in danger and cannot long remain king of the realm.

[XS] If he aheres to the way of Heaven, his undertakings will appear to be spontaneous. / If he disregards the way of Heaven, though he be set upon [the throne], he will not be secure. When he adheres to the way [of Heaven], no one will understand how he accomplishes things. When he achieves success, no one will understand how he bestows[85] his benefits. Mysterious and formless—such is the way of Heaven.

[XSJ] When the ruler of men devotes himself to studying political and statistical methods and devotes himself to carrying out correct principles, progressive changes will be a daily occurrence. He will achieve great success, yet the simple people will not understand why. The muddle-headed ruler is lewd and indolent, wicked and depraved, and his

---

[84] Emending 無 to 非 in accordance with the Ancient, Liu, and Zhu editions [Igai, Yasui, and Dai].

[85] Following the Yang edition, writing 澤 for 釋.

9.9   daily activities are lacking in the way [of Heaven]. / He will perish without himself understanding why.

:6.11
/7a1
,12
    [*XS*] Those who would question the present should investigate the past. / Those who do not understand what is to come should look at what has gone before.[86]

:39.10
4/12a10
    [*XSJ*] In ancient times the Three Kings and Five Lords (*bo*)[87] were all rulers of men who brought advantages to the world. Therefore they themselves were honored and famous and their sons and grandsons enjoyed their benefits. Jie and Zhou, You and Li[88] were all rulers of

9.11
    men who brought harm to the realm. / Therefore they themselves encountered distress and injury and their sons and grandsons met with calamity.

6.12
7a1
    [*XS*] Handling[89] of the myriad affairs may lead in different directions, but they all reach a common goal. From ancient times to the present it has always been so.

39.11
/12b2
12
    [*XSJ*] Shen Nong[90] instructed in ploughing and raised grain in order to benefit the people. Yu / personally cleared the waterways, cut through[91] the high places and where it was too low [led the water] along

---

[86] Dong Zhongshu, in his *Chunqiu fanlu*, III, 5/10a1–2, paraphrases this apothegm: "A man of ancient times has said, 'Those who do not understand what is to come should look at all that has gone before.'" He then continues: "Now the reason for studying the *Chunqiu* is to understand what has gone before and clarify what is to come." By "a man of ancient times," Dong was probably referring to Guan Zhong.

[87] The term "Three Kings" is generally taken to refer to the three dynastic founders: Yu of the Xia 夏, Tang 湯 of the Shang 商, and Wen of the Zhou. *Bo* 伯 was a senior feudal rank. The five *bo* were the five *ba* 霸, lord protectors or chiefs of the feudal lords. The *Xunzi*, VII, 11/2b13–3a1, lists them as Huan 桓 (685–643) of Qi 齊, Wen 文 (635–628) of Jin 晉, Zhuang 莊 (613–591) of Chu 楚, Helü 闔閭 (514–496) of Wu 吳, and Goujian 句踐 (496–465) of Yue 越. In later texts the names of the last two are usually replaced by Xiang 襄 (650–637) of Song 宋 and Mu 穆 (659–621) of Qin 秦.

[88] Jie Gui 桀癸 (trad. 1818–1763) and Zhou Xin were the last rulers of the Xia and Shang, whose evil actions were said to have brought about the end of their dynasties. You 幽 (781–771) and Li 厲 (878–828) were the Western Zhou kings whose poor administration led to the decline of central Zhou power and the eventual removal of the capital to Loyang, the site of the weaker Eastern Zhou.

[89] Emending *sheng* 生 to *ren* 任 in accordance with the *XSJ* and Ancient, Liu, and Zhu editions. Guo Moruo would read *sheng* as *xing* 性. Thus: "The nature of the myriad affairs may lead in different directions, but they all reach a common goal." The *XSJ* mistakenly writes 起 for 趣.

[90] Shen Nong 神農, or the Divine Husbandman, is one of the early legendary emperors. He is said to have invented the plough and taught the people the art of husbandary.

[91] The character 斬 is obviously corrupt. Igai would write 墼, "to dig out," Yu Yue would write 墼, "to chisel out." According to the *Shi ji*, 29/1b1–2 (Chavannes, *Mémoires historigues*, II, pp. 520–521): "[Yu] directed the course of the Yellow River from Jishi past Longmen, south to Huayin." The *Zheng yi* commentary (pub. A.D. 737) of Zhang Shoujie adds that fifty *li* north of Hancheng he cut 鑿 a channel eighty paces wide.

higher terrain,[92] in order to benefit the people. Tang and Wu attacked those who did not adhere to the Way and killed those who were violent and disorderly, in order to benefit the people. Therefore the movements of enlightened kings may have been different, but their advantages to the people were the same.

[XS] A green ridgepole may cause a house to collapse, yet it will not arouse anger and resentment. A weak child may merely throw down a single tile, / but his gentle mother will seize the bamboo switch.

[XSJ] When a ridgepole is green it will bend and not fulfill its function, with the result that the house may collapse; yet no one will be resentful because this is its nature. A weak child is loved by his gentle mother. / Yet when he acts contrary to [what is considered] his nature[93] and throws down a tile, the affectionate mother will beat him. Therefore an action that accords with what is natural, even though it may cause the house to collapse, will not bring about resentment. But an action that is not in accord with what is natural, such as throwing down a tile, will certainly [result in] a beating.

[XS] When the way of Heaven is fulfilled, even those who are far off will of themselves seek close relationships [with the ruler]. But when the [selfish] affairs of men arise, even [close] relatives will harbor resentments.

[XSJ] If the way of Heaven is carried out and the principle of the common good put forth, those who are far removed will of themselves give their allegiance [to the ruler]. But if the way of Heaven is disregarded and selfish actions are carried out, even sons and mothers will resent each other.

[XS] The myriad creatures, in their relationship to men, are equally impartial toward those near at hand / and those far away.[94]

---

[92] Emending 橋 to 墙(墻), "high terrain" [Igai]. The same passage in the *Shi ji* goes on to say: "Yu thereupon became concerned that the source of the river was high and its water was rapid and violent. [This made it] difficult to conduct across the flat plain and brought about frequent disasters. He then detached two canals [from the main stream] in order to lead off the river. To the north he carried them along high terrain 高地 across the Jiang River to Dalu [the name of a large marsh said to have been located in Hebei]."

[93] Deleting the two characters, *dong zhe* 動者, which destroy the sense of the sentence here. They were probably inserted into the text by a copyist in assimilation of a similar phrase in line 12b8 (3 : 40.1) [Wang Niansun, Wang Shaolan, and Xu]. The Yang edition in place of these two characters writes 衍, "superfluous." This obviously represents a marginal note of commentary on *dong zhe* which was later incorporated into the text in their place by mistake.

[94] This sentence has no explanation, but the Yin commentary says: "Animals possess sensory perception 識, but lack reason 知. Plants possess life 生, but lack sensory perception. Therefore [both categories of living things] in their relationship to men are equally impartial toward those near at hand and those far away."

The clever will have a superabundance of things while the stupid will never have enough.

[XSJ] In ancient times the territory of King Wu did not exceed 100 *li*, and the number of his warriors did not exceed 10,000 men. But he was able to win battles, seize [territory], and set himself up as son of Heaven so that the world called him the sage king. This was because he understood / political methods of action. Jie and Zhou were honored as sons of Heaven. Their wealth included all within the four seas. Their territory was extremely large. Their warriors were extremely numerous. Yet they themselves were killed and their countries lost, and they became objects of contempt in the world. This was because they did not understand / political methods of action. Therefore, those who are capable of action can make the small large and the lowly honored, whereas those who are incapable of action, even though they may be the son of Heaven, will still have [their positions] wrested from them by others.

[XS] Heaven will assist those whose efforts accord with it and oppose[95] those whose efforts are contrary to it.

[XSJ] The enlightened ruler does not act contrary to Heaven above and does not waste [the fruits of] Earth below. Therefore Heaven bestows its seasons and Earth bestows its wealth. But the muddle-headed ruler acts contrary to the way of Heaven above and disrupts the principles of Earth below. Therefore Heaven does not bestow its seasons and Earth does not produce / wealth.

[XS] Whatever Heaven assists, even though small [at first], is certain to become large. Whatever Heaven opposes, even though successful [at first], is certain to fail.[96]

[XSJ] In ancient times, King Wu was assisted by Heaven. Therefore, even though his territory was small and his people few, he still became son of Heaven. Jie and Zhou were opposed by Heaven. Therefore, even though their territory was large and people numerous, they still met with trouble, / humiliation, and death.

[XS] Those who accord with Heaven will retain their achievements. Those who act contrary to Heaven / will embrace misfortune and cannot be saved.[97]

[95] The Yang edition for 違 mistakenly writes 圍 [Wang Niansun and Song].
[96] The XSJ, in its repetition of the XS text, writes: "Whatever Heaven opposes, even though large [at first], is certain to be pared down." Guo Moruo points out that this reading of the text is preferable since "large" (大, *dar*) forms a rhyme with "fail" (敗 *brwar*).
[97] This passage lacks an explanation.

Even though relationships[98] among a flock of crows may seem good, they are never really close.

3:40.14
64/13b4

[XSJ] When relationships among men involve frequent cases of deceitfulness, heartlessness, and general rapaciousness, they are said to be those of a flock of crows. Relationships among a flock of crows, even though happy at first, will eventually turn into dissonant cawing.

1:7.3
2/7a12

7b1

[XS] Agreements that do not take into account all possible difficulties, even though seemingly firm, will certainly be broken. When the Way is followed / such difficulties are treated with deference.[99]

3:41.1
64/13b7

[XSJ] When the sage makes an agreement with other men, on high he considers his service to the prince, and within the family he considers his service to his relatives. In each case he will certainly grasp whatever principles may be known before making the agreement. If the agreement does not accord with basic principles, it is certain to be repudiated by both sides later on.

1:7.4
2/7b1
3:41.3
64/13b11

[XS] Do not consort with those who lack ability.

[XSJ] The enlightened ruler consorts with sages in making his plans. Therefore his plans achieve their purpose. He consorts with them in initiating affairs. Therefore his affairs succeed. But the muddle-headed ruler consorts with unworthy people in making his plans. Therefore his estimates miscarry. He consorts with them in initiating affairs.

41.4

Therefore his affairs end in failure. / Now to have estimates miscarry and affairs end in failure are the evil consequences of consorting with those who lack ability.

1:7.4
2/7b1
3:41.5
64/14a2

[XS] Do not force people to do what they are incapable of doing.

[XSJ] The enlightened ruler measures what a man's strength is capable of accomplishing before assigning him a mission. Therefore, since the orders are in accordance with what the man is capable of doing, they will be carried out. Since he assigns to the man a mission he is capable of performing, the affair will succeed. Whereas the muddle-headed ruler,

41.6

without / measuring a man's strength, orders him to do what he is incapable of doing. Therefore [the ruler's] orders are disregarded. He commissions men to do what they are unable to do. Therefore his affairs end in failure. Now if orders are issued but are disregarded and affairs

41.7

are initiated but end in failure, / it is the evil consequence of forcing upon people what they are incapable of doing.

---

[98] Reading 狡 as 交 in accordance with the XSJ [Jiang Han].
[99] This passage is not clear. I have generally followed Yasui's interpretation.

1:7.4
2/7b1
3:41.8
54/14a7

[XS] Do not inform those who cannot understand.

[XSJ] A perverse and confused man, on being informed about the right conduct between prince and minister, the principles of father and son, and the distinctions between the honored and lowly, will not believe in them. Though the words of a sage, they will be turned to harm. Therefore the sage does not inform [such a person].

:7.4

[XS] Consorting with those who lack ability, forcing those who are incapable, and informing those who do not understand are called belaboring [oneself] to no avail.

:41.10
4/14a10

[XSJ] Initiate affairs with the unworthy, and those affairs will fail. Commission men to do what they cannot, and they will disregard your orders. Advise a perverse and confused man, and you will harm yourself.

:7.4
4/7b3
5

[XS] Those who parade concern for their friends[100] will hardly achieve close relationships with them./Those who parade sympathy[101] in their social contacts[102] will hardly create any strong bonds. Those who parade virtue will hardly be requited./[People] from the four directions will turn toward those who act from a [pure] heart.[103]

6

:41.12
4/14b1

[XSJ] The person who constantly uses words to express his concern for others, his pity toward others, and his virtue toward others, will not achieve close relationships when making friends, will not create strong bonds in his social contacts,/and will not be requited for his virtuous conduct toward others.

4.13

7.6
7b6

[XS] The state whose [ruler] acts on his own[104] will be overworked and encounter numerous disasters.

42.1
4/14b6

[XSJ] The enlightened ruler does not utilize his own wisdom but

[100] Emending 交 to 友 in accordance with XSJ and the Ancient, Liu, and Zhu editions.

[101] The XSJ for ai 哀 writes ai 愛. Their meanings are very close.

[102] Emending 役 to 交 in accordance with the XSJ [Wang Niansun].

[103] The final statement of the text is further explained by a passage in the Huainanzi, 1/7b11–8a1 (Morgan, Tao, The Great Luminant, p. 12): "Now it was only because he acted with a [pure] heart 心行 that [Emperor Shun 舜] was able to control the three Miao tribes, bring to court the Yu people, transform the country of Naked Men, obtain revenues from Sushen, and without issuing orders or promulgating commands [the SBBY ed. mistakenly writes 生 for 命], change habits and alter customs. How could laws and punishments achieve so much?" See also the Guanzi, chapters XVI, 49, and XIII, 36 and 37, for similar ideas.

[104] Emending 王 to 壬 = 任 in accordance with the XSJ [Wang Niansun and Guo Moruo]. Dai and Wen would leave the text as it stands: "The country of the king who stands alone . . . ."

rather employs the wisdom of the sage.[105] He does not utilize his own strength but rather employs the strength of the masses. Therefore, he who uses the wisdom of the sage in his deliberations will understand everything. He who uses / the strength of the masses in initiating affairs will accomplish everything. So long as he is able to dispense with his own [wisdom and strength] and rely on that of the world,[106] he will enjoy personal ease and good fortune. But the muddle-headed ruler utilizes only his own wisdom and does not employ that of the sage. / He utilizes only his own strength and does not employ that of the masses. Therefore he overworks himself and encounters numerous disasters.

42.2

42.3

1:7.6
2/7b6

[*XS*] The prince who maintains his state in isolation will be despised and not inspire awe.

3:42.4
64/14b12

[*XSJ*] The enlightened ruler carries out his laws and procedures at home and his principles and righteousness abroad. Therefore neighboring states give him their allegiance and allies trust him. When he encounters misfortunes, the neighboring states grieve for him. When he encounters difficulties, they come to his aid.

42.5

But the muddle-headed ruler / who neglects the hundred surnames at home and abroad does not put any faith in neighboring states. Therefore, when he encounters misfortunes, no one will grieve for him. When he encounters difficulties, no one will come to his aid. Both [abroad and at home] all will be lost. He will stand alone without partisans. Therefore his state / will become weak and its ruler humiliated.

42.6

1:7.7
2/7b7

[*XS*] Disgraced and distrusted is the woman who acts as her own go-between.

3:42.7
64/15a5

[*XSJ*] When the enlightened ruler governs the realm, he must utilize the sage before it can be well governed. When a woman seeks a husband, she must utilize a go-between before the marriage can be completed. Therefore if [a ruler] tries to govern the realm without / utilizing a sage, it becomes disorderly and the people will not give him their allegiance. If [a woman] seeks a husband without using a go-between, she[107] will be disgraced and men will distrust her.

42.8

---

[105] Igai, Dai, and Guo Moruo throughout this passage would emend 聖, "sage," to 衆, "masses," in accordance with the reading of the Huazhai edition and the statement below linking wisdom and strength to the world. The *Shang shu*, II, 3/3, contains the famous passage: "Heaven hears and sees as our people hear and see." The *LSCQ*, IV, 5/9b9–10 (Wilhelm, *Frühling und Herbst*, p. 53), also says: "With the wisdom of the masses one need not stand in awe of a Yao or Shun."

[106] Deleting 起 in accordance with the Ancient, Liu, and Zhu editions. The character is meaningless and has obviously been mistakenly copied from the preceding line.

[107] Inserting 身 below 則 in accordance with the Ancient, Liu, and Zhu editions [Dai and Guo Moruo].

[XS] When [the ruler] has never been seen, yet [the people] still give him their allegiance, they may [be said to] have gone to him.[108]

[XSJ] The reason people feel allegiance in their hearts to the enlightened ruler even though they have never seen him is that he possesses the way to accomplishing this. Therefore his position is secure and the people will go to him.[109]

[XS] When after a long time [the ruler] is still not forgotten, it may [be said] that the people have come to him.

[XSJ] Yao and Shun were enlightened rulers of ancient times. The fact that the world has never become weary of esteeming them and has never become bored with singing their praises, so that they have not been forgotten over a long period of time, is because they possessed the way to accomplish this. Therefore their position / was secure and the people came to them.

[XS] If the sun and the moon do not shine, it is not because Heaven itself has changed.

[XSJ] The sun and moon illumine and survey all things. But when there are many clouds in the heavens that cover everything, the sun and moon cannot shine through. The ruler of men is like the sun and moon. If the various ministers commit many wicked deeds and institute selfish [schemes], thereby concealing the ruler, the ruler / is then unable to illumine and survey his subjects, nor are their sentiments able to reach the ruler. Therefore wickedness and depravity daily increase and the ruler of men becomes ever more obscured.

[XS] If a mountain, being high, becomes invisible, it is not because Earth itself has changed.

[XSJ] A mountain is the highest of things. If Earth's defiles [leading to a mountain] become overgrown and difficult [of access], the mountain can no longer be seen. The ruler of men is like the mountain. When parties[110] and cliques are formed on the left and right so that they block off their ruler, he can no longer be seen.

---

[108] The meaning of this and the following sentence of the XS text is not very clear because of the rather forced usage of the two characters 往, "to go," and 來, "to come," in order to achieve stylistic balance.

[109] This explanation may be further clarified by a passage from the *Mengzi*, IA, 2/18: "Now if Your Majesty will institute a government that spreads benevolence, this will cause all those holding office throughout the realm to wish to stand in Your Majesty's court, all those who plough to wish to plough Your Majesty's field, all merchants and traders to wish to store [their goods] in Your Majesty's markets, all traveling strangers to wish to go forth on Your Majesty's roads, and all those who feel aggrieved by their princes to wish to go and complain to Your Majesty." "To go" is written 赴, but its meaning here is the same as that of 往 in the text above.

[110] Emending 多 to 朋 [Wang Yinzhi].

1:7.9
2/7b10
3:43.4
64/15b10

[*XS*] The prince does not utter words that are not fit to be reiterated.

[*XSJ*] When the ruler of men utters words that neither go against the hearts of his people nor pervert principles and righteousness, and thus what he says is sufficient to bring peace to the realm, men only fear that he will not repeat his words. But words that break up the close relation-

43.5

ship between father/and son, alienate the way of the prince and minister, and harm the masses of the realm are not fit to be reiterated. Therefore the enlightened ruler does not utter them.

1:7.9
2/7b11
3:43.6
64/16a2

[*XS*] The prince does not act in a way that is not fit to be repeated.

[*XSJ*] When the ruler of men personally acts correctly, commissions men with proper ceremony, and meets them according to correct principles,[111] so that the actions emanating from himself become the pattern for the realm, then men only fear that he will not repeat them. But if

43.7

he were to act improperly himself, / to employ men with cruelty, and to meet them with deception, so that the actions emanating from himself were to become the laughingstock of the realm, such actions are not fit to be repeated. Therefore the enlightened ruler does not act in this way.

1:7.10
2/7b12

[*XS*] Any words not fit to be reiterated or actions not fit to be repeated are the most important prohibitions for those who possess states.

3:43.9
64/16a7

[*XSJ*] Words not fit to be reiterated are not trustworthy. Actions not fit to be repeated are predatory. Therefore, when words are not trustworthy, the people will not adhere to [the ruler]. When actions are

43.10

predatory, the realm / will be resentful. Unwillingness to adhere on the part of the people and resentment on the part of the realm are the origins of destruction. Therefore the enlightened ruler prohibits them.

---

[111] Following the Yang edition and the *Qunshu zhiyao,* which transpose the two characters 理 and 禮. Yasui and Guo Moruo would emend them to read 禮 and 信, "trustworthiness," in accordance with the reading of the sentence 16a4 (3:43.7) below.

Quan Xiu

權修

ON THE CULTIVATION OF POLITICAL POWER

Introductory Comments

This chapter follows *Mu min* (I, 1) as one of the basic political chapters of the *Guanzi*, and appears to represent much the same school of thought, even though it places more emphasis on law and rewards and punishments than its predecessor.[1] It makes extensive use of the term *mu min*, "to shepherd the people," and otherwise stresses the same Confucian values, such as propriety (*li*), righteousness (*yi*), integrity (*lian*), and a sense of shame (*chi*). The two chapters are also similar in terms of language and general style, and as in the case of *Mu min*, it is quoted by the *Hanfeizi* (XVI, 38/6b; Liao, *Han Fei Tzu*, II, pp. 186–187). In fact, the two chapters are so close that it is possible they were written by the same author. However, this chapter is much more pedantic in tone than *Mu min*. In any case, there is no real evidence to support either view. I would date this chapter as coming from the early or middle part of the fourth century B.C.

Translation

In a country of ten thousand chariots,[2] the armed forces must have a commander-in-chief (*zhu* 主). Its area being extensive, the countryside must have functionaries (*li* 吏). Its population being large, the offices must have / heads (*zhang* 長).[3] In shaping the destiny of the people, the court must have an administrative policy (*zheng* 正).

If its area is extensive, yet the state remains poor, it is because the countryside has not been brought under cultivation. If its population is large, yet its armed forces are weak, it is because there is nothing to motivate[4] the people. /

---

[1] Chapter III, 14, of the *Shangjun shu* is entitled *Xiu quan* 修權. The characters are reversed, but the meaning is essentially the same. Duyvendak (*Lord Shang*, p. 260) translates the title as "The Cultivation of the Right Standard."

[2] This is a common designation for a large state in pre-Qin China.

[3] Zhao Shouzheng would read 長 as *chang* = 常, "constant standards." I have followed the reading that appears necessary for the term in a similar context in I, 1/4a5 (1:4.4).

[4] Reading 取 as 趣 here and in the following paragraph [He Ruzhang and Guo Moruo].

91

8.1 Now, if nonessential production is not prohibited, the countryside will not be brought under cultivation. If rewards and punishments are not reliable, there will be nothing to motivate the people. When the countryside is uncultivated and there is nothing to motivate the people, the enemy cannot be challenged without nor the defenses secured within. /

8.2 Therefore it is said: "If [a state] bears the name of having ten thousand chariots, but [in reality] lacks the use of even a thousand, it is impossible to expect its power to be taken seriously."

8.3 If the land has been brought under cultivation, yet the state / remains poor, it is because boats and chariots are ornate and towers and pavilions are built on a vast scale. If the rewards and punishments are reliable, yet the armed forces are weak, it is because [the ruler] has been careless in employing the masses and overworking his people. /

8b If boats and chariots are ornate[5] and towers and pavilions are built on a vast scale, levies and exactions will be heavy. If [the ruler] is careless in

8.4 employing the masses / and overworks his people, their strength will be exhausted. If exactions and levies are too heavy, his subjects will resent their sovereign. When the strength of his people has been exhausted, his orders will not be carried out. When his subjects resent their sovereign and his orders are not carried out, it is impossible to expect his enemies to refrain from scheming against him. /

9.9
10a2 [If[6] the self is not well disciplined, how can discipline be applied to other individuals? If individuals are not well disciplined, how can discipline be applied to the household? If the households are not well

9.10 disciplined, how can discipline be applied to / the district (*xiang* 鄉)? If the districts are not well disciplined, how can discipline be applied to the state? If the states are not well disciplined, how can discipline be applied to the entire realm? The realm is based on the state,[7] the state on the

---

[5] The Yang edition mistakenly omits the character 飾.

[6] The following paragraph 有身不治···身者治之本也 is located in the text, 10a2–7 (9.9–11), where it is obviously out of place. I have moved it to this point as the most likely place for it in the chapter, but I suspect it may represent a misplaced passage from some other text.

[7] Beginning with this sentence to the end of the paragraph, the meaning of the text is not clear. Usually 天下者國之本也 would be rendered as "the realm is the basis of the state." (The same grammatical construction continues throughout the paragraph.) Such an interpretation, however, would mean making the larger unit the basis for the smaller one, something quite contrary to normal Chinese reasoning. For example, the *Mengzi*, IVA, 5, writes: 天下之本在國, 國之本在家, 家之本在身, "The foundations of the realm lie with the state, those of the state lie with the family, and those of the family lie with the self." Another famous passage of similar nature appears in the *Da xue* [Great Learning] chapter of the *Li ji*, XIX, 42/9a (Legge, *Li Ki*, 28, pp. 411–412): "The ancients who wished clearly to exemplify illustrious virtue throughout the empire first disciplined

9.11 district, the district on the household, the household / on the individual, individuals on the self, and the self on good discipline.] /

8.5
8b3 Whoever would control the entire realm must be careful how he uses his state. Whoever would control a state must be careful how he uses his people. Whoever would control his people must be careful how he uses
3.6 their strength. / If there is no way to feed them, they cannot be prevented from running away. If there is no way to shepherd them, they may remain at home, but cannot be employed. When people come from
8.7 afar / and do not leave, it is because there is a way to feed them. When they are numerous yet can be united, it is because there is the way to shepherd them.

On seeing conduct of which you approve, express your pleasure. On
3.8 seeing conduct / of which you disapprove, manifest[8] your displeasure. If rewards and punishments are reliable in regard to what you have seen, will people dare do [any wrong] even though it is something you do not
3.9 see? If on seeing conduct of which you approve, / you do not express your pleasure, or if on seeing conduct of which you disapprove, you do not manifest your displeasure, and if rewards and punishments are not
a reliable in regard to what you have seen, / it is impossible to expect people to change for the better in regard to what you do not see.

.10 Being generous / with love and benefits is sufficient to win the allegiance of the people. Manifesting wisdom and propriety is sufficient to instruct them. [However], the sovereign must himself adhere to [the law] in order to serve as an example for them and see that there is proper measure in exactions and expenditures in order to guard against [excesses]. /

.11 Place governors (*shi* 師) in the local districts to exhort and guide [the people]. Thereafter, keep them informed with laws and orders, encourage them with rewards, and overawe them with punishments. Then,
.12 since the hundred surnames will all be happy in doing good, / violent and disorderly conduct will have no cause to arise.

The land has seasonal limitations in the production of wealth; the people have a point of exhaustion when using their strength. However,

---

their own states. Wishing to discipline their states, they first regulated their families. Wishing to regulate their families, they first cultivated their own persons." The preceding passage in this chapter of the *Guanzi*, beginning 8b3, (8.5), also states: "Whoever would control the entire realm must be careful how he uses his state...." Thus I have followed Guo Moruo in reading 之 as 是.

[8] Emending 刑 to 形 both here and below [Igai, Yasui, Ding, and Yu Yue]. The *Hanfeizi*, XVI, 38b6 (Liao, *Han Fei Tzu*, II, pp. 186–187), which cites this passage with slightly different wording, also writes 形.

the desires of a prince may be insatiable. When what has seasonal limitations or a point of exhaustion is taken to support a prince who is insatiable, / sovereign and subject will come to hate each other if proper measure [in regard to exactions and expenditures] is not instituted [as a safeguard] between them. It is for this reason that ministers have killed their princes and sons have killed / their fathers.[9]

Therefore, if there is proper measure in taking from the people and limits are placed on their employment, even a small state is certain to be safe. But if proper measure is not exercised in taking from the people, and no limits are placed on their employment, even a large state is certain to be in danger.

Land left uncultivated, / is not my land.
People left unshepherded, are not my people.[10]

Those who would shepherd the people must pay careful attention to see that stipends accord with achievements. Those whose achievements are great should be given much. / Those whose achievements are few should be given less. Those who have no achievement should be given nothing. Should it happen that those who have achievements receive nothing, the people will turn away from the sovereign. Should those whose achievements are great receive less, the people will not exert themselves. Should those whose achievements are few / receive more, the people will resort to deceitfulness. Should those who have no achievements receive stipends for nothing, the people will merely trust to luck [in attempting to make a living].

Now if [the people] turn away from the sovereign, do not exert themselves, resort to deceitfulness, or merely trust to luck, they will neither complete [their sovereign's] undertakings nor be of any use in opposing the enemy. Therefore it is said: / "Investigate ability when bestowing offices; graduate the salaries when making awards. Such is the crucial factor when employing the people."

The countryside should rival the market place in population. Private households should rival public storehouses in goods. Grain should rival

----

[9] This would appear to be an allusion to what the *Mengzi*, IIIB, 9/7–8, says about the *Chunqiu*: "The world fell into decay and principles faded away. Perverse speech and oppressive action became prevalent. There were cases of ministers who murdered their princes and sons who murdered their fathers. Confucius was afraid and made the *Chunqiu*." The *Hanfeizi*, XIII, 34/3a (Liao, *Han Fei Tzu*, II, p. 92), contains a similar passage: "Zixia said, 'In the records of the *Chunqiu* there are over ten cases of ministers who have murdered their princes and sons who have murdered their fathers.'" See also the *Guanzi*, VI, 16/6b1, (1 : 75.1–2).

[10] This unrhymed couplet would appear to be a quotation from some other text, but the source is unknown.

9.5 gold[11] in value. / Local districts should rival the court in good government. Thus the countryside will not be overgrown with weeds because agriculture has been put first. The public storehouses will not be piled high with goods because they have been stored by the people.

9.6 Marketplaces will not be filled with / stalls because private households have enough for their needs at home. The masses will not gather at court because the local districts share in having good government. Now, when the countryside is not overgrown with weeds, the public storehouses are not piled high with goods, the marketplaces are not filled with stalls, and the masses do not gather at court [to submit their complaints], such is the acme of good government.

9.7 Human nature / is all the same. That is why it is possible to control the people.[12] By examining their likes and dislikes, their strengths and weaknesses may be known. By observing their associates, their worthiness or unworthiness may be learned. If these two are not

9.8 neglected, / those of ability among the people may be placed in office.

The preservation of territory depends on walls; the preservation of walls depends on arms. The preservation of arms depends on men, and the preservation of men depends on grain. Therefore, unless a territory is brought under cultivation, its walls will not be secure. /

9.11 10a7 Accordingly,[13] if the sovereign does not appreciate what is essential, nonessential production will not be prohibited. If it is not prohibited, the

9.12 people will neglect their seasonal work / and treat lightly the benefits of Earth. If they treat lightly the benefits of Earth, it is impossible to expect the fields to be cultivated and the granaries to be full.

If merchants and traders are received at court, goods and wealth will flow upward [in the form of bribes]. If women have a voice in the affairs

9.13 of men, / rewards and punishments will not be reliable. If men and women are not segregated, the people will have neither a sense of integrity nor a sense of shame. If goods and wealth flow upward,

9.14 rewards and punishments are unreliable, / and the people have neither a sense of integrity nor a sense of shame, it is impossible to expect either

10b the hundred surnames / to remain steadfast in times of trouble or the troops to be willing to sacrifice their lives.

If the dignity of the court is not preserved, and the positions of the honored and lowly are not clearly defined; if the old and young are not distinguished, and proper measure [in regard to exactions and expendi-

[11] Transposing 粟, "grain," and 金, "gold" [Tao and Li].
[12] Deleting 情 as a mistaken repetition of the same character in the preceding line [Chen, Yasui, and Tao].
[13] The preceding paragraph in the text has been transferred to 8b5 (8.5). See n. 5, above.

10.1 tures] is not observed; / if there are no gradations of clothing [according to rank], and sovereign and subject both exceed the proper limits,[14] it is impossible to expect the hundred surnames to honor the government and orders of their ruler.

If the sovereign indulges in cunning plots and false accusations while his ministers and subordinate officials compete with one another to get
10.2 their hands on the exactions and levies [of the state], / thus causing people to snatch at every opportunity [for personal gain],[15] the hundred surnames will then become resentful, and it will be impossible to expect the sovereign to have the allegiance of his subjects.

If [the sovereign], while possessing territory, pays no heed to essential production and, while serving as the prince over his state, is unable to
10.3 unite its people, / it will be impossible to expect the ancestral temples and the altars of Land and Grain to escape danger.

If the sovereign relies on divination by tortoise shell and milfoil plant, and indulges in the use of magicians and witch doctors, the spirits [themselves] will hasten calamities.[16]

10.4 Now, failure to establish merit or achieve fame stems from / three evils: having [ministers who] act on their own,[17] possessing [a state that] is poverty-stricken and treated with contempt, and having [a government that] cannot complete its daily tasks.

10.5 When planning for one year, / there is nothing better than planting grain. When planning for ten years, there is nothing better than planting trees. When planning for a lifetime, there is nothing better than planting men. Grain is something that is planted once and produces only a single harvest. Trees are things that are planted once but may produce ten
10.6 harvests. / Men are things that are planted once but may produce a
11a   hundred harvests.

Having once planted (*tjewng*) them,
Spiritlike I make use (*riewng*) of them. /
10.7 To undertake affairs as would the spirits (*zdjien*),
Such is the gate (*mwên*) to kingliness.

Those who would shepherd the people cause men to refrain from evil acts and women to refrain from illicit affairs. When men do not commit
10.8 evil acts, / it is because they have been [properly] instructed. When women do not engage in illicit affairs, it is because they have been

[14] The Yang edition for 淩 writes 凌. The meaning is the same. The *Qunshu zhiyao* for 上下淩節 writes: 下賤侵節, "the lowly and humble will transgress proper limits."
[15] Xu would emend 偷壹 to the much more common expression, 偷幸. Thus, "causing the people to trust to luck."
[16] The Yang edition mistakenly writies 崇 for 祟.
[17] Emending 王 to 壬(任) [Zhang Wenhu and Guo Moruo].

[properly] admonished. When instruction and admonition mold customary behavior, punishments decline.

Those who would shepherd the people desire them to be correct. Since they desire their people to be correct, they must prohibit even the slightest manifestations of evil. / Slight manifestations of evil are the source from which great evil springs. If these slight manifestations of evil are not prohibited, it is impossible to expect that great evil will not bring harm to the country.

Those who would shepherd the people desire them to observe propriety. / Since they desire their people to observe propriety, it must be meticulously observed even in minor matters. If propriety in minor matters is not meticulously observed throughout the country, it is impossible to expect the hundred surnames to observe it in major ones.

Those who would shepherd the people / desire them to practice righteousness. Since they desire them to practice righteousness, it must be practiced even in minor matters. If righteousness in minor matters is not practiced throughout the country, it is impossible to expect the hundred surnames to practice it in major ones. /

Those who would shepherd the people desire them to have integrity. Since they desire them to have integrity, it must be cultivated even in minor matters. / If integrity in minor matters is not cultivated throughout the country, it is impossible to expect the hundred surnames to have it in major ones. /

Those who would shepherd the people desire them to have a sense of shame. Since they desire them to have a sense of shame, it must be displayed even in minor matters. If a sense of shame in minor matters is not displayed throughout the country, it is impossible to expect the hundred surnames / to display it in major ones.

Since those who shepherd the people desire them even in minor matters to be meticulous[18] in observing propriety, practicing righteousness, cultivating[19] integrity, and displaying[20] a sense of shame, they must[21] prohibit even the slightest beginnings of evil. Such is the way to discipline the people. When the people, / even in minor matters, are meticulous in observing propriety, practicing righteousness, cultivating integrity, and displaying a sense of shame, and even the slightest beginnings of evil are prohibited, such is the basis of good order.

---

[18] Emending 修 to 謹 here and in the following sentence [Yasui and Xu].

[19] Emending 飾 to 修 here and in the following sentence.

[20] Emending 謹 to 飾 here and in the following sentence.

[21] Inserting 則必 before 禁. As Guo Moruo points out, "prohibiting even the minutest beginnings of evil" is the function of the ruler, not an act of the people.

97

Those who shepherd the people desire them to be controllable. Since they desire them to be controllable, they must pay serious attention[22] to the laws. / Laws [are created] to establish [the authority of] the court. [However], if they are to establish [the authority of] the court, noble ranks and ceremonial dress must be honored. If noble ranks and ceremonial dress are awarded to those lacking in righteousness, the people will treat noble ranks and ceremonial dress with contempt. If the people / treat them with contempt, the ruler will not be respected. If he is not respected, his orders will not be carried out.

Laws [are created] to make use of the people's strength. [However], if they are to utilize the people's strength, salaries and rewards must be / treated with importance. If salaries and rewards are given to those lacking in achievement, the people will treat salaries and rewards lightly. If the people treat them lightly, the sovereign will have no means to encourage his people. If he has no / means to encourage his people, his orders will not be carried out.

Laws [are created] / to make use of the people's ability. [However], if they are to utilize the people's ability, serious attention must be paid to the granting of offices. If serious attention is not paid to the granting of offices, the people will be cut off from government. If the people are cut off from government, the sovereign will not understand the true state of affairs. / If he does not understand the true state of affairs, his subjects will resent him. If they resent him, his orders will not be carried out.

Laws [are created] to make use of [the power of] life and death over the people. [However], if they are to utilize [the power of] life and death over the people, serious attention must be paid to punishments. / If serious attention is not paid to punishments, there will be evasion [of guilt] and involvement [of the innocent]. If there is evasion [of guilt] and involvement [of the innocent], the innocent will be killed and the guilty pardoned. If the innocent are killed and the guilty are pardoned, the country will not be free of rebellious ministers. /

Now, having noble ranks and ceremonial dress treated with contempt, salaries and rewards treated lightly, the people cut off from their government, and rebellious ministers initiate trouble—these are called the ways to ruin a state.

---

[22] Both the *Beitang shuchao*, 43/3a (p. 167), and the *Taiping yulan*, 638/3a–b (p. 2831), for 審 write 重, "treat with importance."

Li Zheng
立政
Li Zheng Jiu Bai Jie
立政九敗解

ON OVERSEEING GOVERNMENT AND

EXPLANATION TO THE SECTION ON NINE

WAYS TO FAILURE

Introductory Comments

Li zheng is also the title of chapter V, 19, of the *Shang shu*. Legge, in his translation of that work, renders *Li zheng* as "The Establishment of Government." Here I have followed Wen Yiduo in reading *li* 立 as *li* 莅, "to oversee," since the character appears in line 15b3 (14.11) with that meaning. To complicate matters further, in the *Qunshu zhiyao*, this chapter is entitled *Li jun* 立君, "On Establishing the Prince." Yasui believes that is the correct title.

The chapter is divided into a general introduction and nine titled sections dealing with various aspects of government. The *Jiu bai* or "Nine Ways to Failure" section is also provided with a line-by-line commentary in a separate *jie* or explanatory chapter, XXI, 65, which I have included here. The titles of each section have been translated at the beginning of their respective sections rather than at the end where they appear in the Chinese text. *Li zheng* provides one the most detailed descriptions to be found in the *Guanzi* of how a government was supposed to operate, including its organizational structure. The general terminology used is similar to that found in the *Zhou li*, but with some substantial differences, especially in its description of local government organization. Its content is also consistent with the statecraft of Confucian feudal tradition. For example, the term used for law is *xian* 憲, here translated as statute, rather than *fa* 法, which is more Legalist in tone.

Most of the text appears to have a linguistic and logical consistency, which would indicate it was probably written by a single person, though the writer undoubtedly made use of earlier material. However, both the section on clothing regulations, *Fu zhi*, which is duplicated with minor variations in the *Chunqiu fanlu* of Dong Zhongshu 董仲舒 (179?–104? B.C.), and *Jiu bai*, stand out as distinct from the rest. The former, for instance, mentions the son of Heaven, while the rest of the text deals with the government of a late feudal state headed by a prince (*jun* 君). The latter is not only distinguished by having a separate explanatory section, but in terms of content, it does not seem to fit in with the other sections.

I would date the text as probably coming from the end of the Warring States Period, about the middle of the third century B.C. This is partly because of its general style, which is similar to that of the *Xunzi* and other texts of the period. It also contains in the "Survey of Officials" or *Sheng guan* section several passages that are almost identical to parts of chapter V, 9, of the *Xunzi*. Furthermore, at least the *Jiu bai* section could not have been written much before Xunzi's time (c. 298–238 B.C.), since it refers to the thought of such people as Mo Di 墨翟, Yang Zhu 楊朱, and Song Xing 宋鈃 and Yin Wen 尹文, who lived in the late fourth and early third centuries B.C. I also do not believe it could date much later than the middle of the third century B.C. because it lacks that strong authoritarian Legalist flavor that became dominant in Chinese political thought after Xunzi and Hanfeizi.

Translation

1:11.11
12a11

Three things determine whether a state is to have order or disorder. To use executions and punishments [alone] is not enough. Four things determine whether a state is to know safety or danger. To defend it with

11.12

city and suburban walls and guarded passes [alone] is not enough. / Five things determine whether a state is to be prosperous or poor. To rely [solely] on lightening taxes and rents or making the levies and exactions more lenient is not enough. Maintaining the state in good order involves three fundamentals, keeping it safe involves four security measures, /

11.13

and assuring its prosperity involves five undertakings. These five undertakings are the five constant guides to action.

12.7
13a6
11.13
12b3

THREE FUNDAMENTALS (*San Ben* 三本)

The prince should be concerned about three things: The first is that a man's virtue is not equal to his position. The second is that his achieve-

100

11.14 ment is not equal to his salary. The third is that his ability is not / equal to his office. These three fundamental [areas of concern] are a source of order or disorder.

Therefore, if there are those in the country who have not demonstrated their virtue and righteousness to the court, they should not be given positions of honor. If there are those in the country who have not

12.1 shown to the country any achievement and service, / they should not be given large salaries. If there are those who, in overseeing affairs, are not trusted by the people, they should not be employed in high offices.

Accordingly, if a man has great virtue yet his position is lowly, this is called an oversight. However, if he has little virtue yet his position is

12.2 honored, this is called / a grievous error. It is better to overlook a virtuous man (*junzi*) than to commit a grievous error with one who is immoral. The resentment caused by overlooking a virtuous man will be slight, but the disasters created by committing a grievous error with an immoral person will be serious indeed.

Now, if positions of honor in the country are held by those who have

12.3 not demonstrated their virtue and righteousness / to the court, good ministers will not be advanced. If large salaries are obtained by those

12.4 who have not shown to the country any achievement and service, hardworking ministers will not be encouraged. If high offices are occupied by

12.3a those who, in overseeing affairs, are not trusted by the people, / talented ministers will not be employed.

If concern is paid to the three fundamentals, those in low station will not dare to seek [more than they deserve]. However, if concern is not paid to the three fundamentals, wicked ministers will move upward and those who speciously curry favor will command awe.

Under such circumstances, an understanding [of what is going on

12.5 below] / will be kept from the sovereign and good government will be denied to his subjects; the correct way will be cast aside, and evil conduct will daily increase.

If concern is paid to the three fundamentals, those who speciously curry favor will not command awe in the country, and the highways will

12.6 not be filled with roving beasts;[1] those who are isolated / and distant [from friends and relatives] will not be subjected to secret criminal actions, and the widowed and orphaned will not be subjected to clandestine penal proceedings. Therefore it is said that if punishments are

---

[1] There is some question about the character 禽, "beasts." Yu Yue would read it as 囚, "prisoners." Thus, "the highways will not be filled with marching prisoners." Liu Shipei believes it is a corruption of the character 竊, "robbers." Thus, "the highways will not be filled with roving robbers."

reduced and the number of criminal actions is diminished, the masses
will not gather at court [to submit their complaints].

THE FOUR SECURITY MEASURES (*Si Gu* 四周)

The prince should exercise caution in regard to four things: The first is
that those who have great charismatic power (*de*) but are deficient in
terms of basic goodness (*ren*) should not be given control of the state.
The second is that those who on seeing worthiness are unable to yield to

12.9

it should not be given positions of honor. / The third is that those who
avoid punishing their relatives and men of high rank should not be
commissioned to lead the armed forces. The fourth is that those who
neither appreciate essential undertakings nor pay heed to the benefits of
Earth, and [at the same time] treat lightly the imposition of levies and
exactions [upon the people] should not be assigned [to administer] cities

12.10

(*du*) and towns (*yi*).[2] These four security measures[3] / are basic to [the
question of] safety or danger.

Therefore it is said that the state will be endangered if the prime
minister (*qing xiang* 卿相) does not obtain [the support of] the masses, if
there is disagreement among the great ministers, if the commander-in-
chief (*zhu* 主) of the armed forces is not sufficiently awe-inspiring, or if
the people are not devoted to their production. /

12.11
13b

Accordingly, if [the prime minister] has great charismatic power and
is perfect in terms of basic goodness, he will control the state and obtain
[the support of] the masses. If on seeing worthiness the great ministers
are able to yield to it, they will be in harmonious accord. If [the
commander-in-chief] does not avoid punishing his relatives and men of
high rank, his ability to inspire awe will extend to neighboring enemies.

12.12

If there is appreciation for / essential undertakings, heed is paid to the
benefits of Earth, and there is concern about levies and exactions, the
people will devote themselves to their production.

13.5
14a3
12.14
13b5

THE FIVE UNDERTAKINGS (*Wu Shi* 五事)

The prince should pay heed to five things. The first is that the state will
be impoverished if mountains and lowlands are not saved from fire and

---

[2] The terms *yi* 邑 and *du* 都 are sometimes difficult to translate. According to the *Zuo
zhuan*, Zhuang, 28 (Legge, *Ch'un Ts'eu*, 28/5), both were urban centers, but a *yi* differed
from a *du* in that the former did not have an ancestral temple containing the tablets of
former rulers. As Legge points out, this is much the same as the difference between cities
and towns in England, cities being distinguished by having a cathedral and a bishop.
However, in other chapters of the *Guanzi* (I, 5, for example) *yi* can have the meaning of a
feudal manor, a residential area, or a small agricultural unit consisting of four well fields.
A *du* can refer to a region, usually a border region, of a feudal territory or state, or a
regional capital.
[3] Emending 務 to 固 [Zhang Peilun].

plants and trees do not flourish.[4] The second is that the state will be impoverished if canals and ditches are not kept within banks and dammed-up water is not kept safely in reservoirs. / The third is that the state will be impoverished if mulberry and hemp are not planted in the countryside and the five grains are not suited to their soil. The fourth is that the state will be impoverished if the six domestic animals are not raised in [peasant] households and there is not a full supply of melons, vegetables, and various fruits. / The fifth is that the state will be impoverished if in the work of artisans there is a striving for [overly ornate] carving and if in the work of women there is a proliferation of [overly elaborate] design.

Therefore it is said that the state will flourish if mountains and lowlands are saved from fire and plants and trees flourish, / if canals and ditches are kept within banks and dammed-up water is kept safely in reservoirs, if mulberry and hemp are planted in the countryside and the five grains are suited to their soil, if the six domestic animals are raised in [peasant] households, and there is a full supply of melons, vegetables, and various fruits, / and if artisans avoid [overly ornate] carving and women avoid [overly elaborate] design.

ORGANIZATIONAL AND PROCEDURAL STATUTES (*Shou Xian* 首憲)[5]

The country proper (*guo* 國)[6] shall be divided into five rural districts (*xiang* 鄉) with each administered by a governor (*shi* 師). A rural district shall be divided into five subdistricts (*zhou* 州) with each administered by a prefect (*zhang* 長). A subdistrict shall be divided into ten villages (*li* 里) with each administered by a commandant (*wei* 尉). A village shall be divided into ten circuits (*you* 游)[7] / with each administered by a clan elder (*zong* 宗). Ten households shall form a group of ten (*shi* 什), and five households shall form a group of five (*wu* 伍). Both of these shall have leaders (*zhang* 長).[8]

---

[4] The Yang edition for 不植成 writes 不得成. In the following passage 植 is written 殖. The meaning remains essentially the same.

[5] *Shou* 首 here means "to come before" and refers to those organizational and procedural statutes that must be set in place before other statutes can be implemented.

[6] In addition to being the general term for the state, *guo* 國 specifically meant the capital and its environs, as opposed to the outlying areas (*bi* 鄙) or dependencies (*shu* 屬). Chapter VIII, 20/6b1 ff. (1:100.5), of the *Guanzi* and the *Guo yu*, 6/4a9 ff., give the details of a somewhat different administrative system than that presented in the following paragraph.

[7] The most common meaning of *you* is to wander or travel about. Therefore I have translated it as circuit. However, another early meaning is to wave a flag, and thus Zhang Peilun would read *you* to mean something like a banner unit.

[8] I have translated *zhang* here as "leader" and above as "prefect" to distinguish the obvious difference in rank implied in the text. The organizational structure given here is

Set up strong points and close off [the approaches to villages] with barricades.[9] Let there be but a single road [leading into each village], and let [people] leave or enter only one at a time.[10] Let the village gates be watched and careful attention paid to keys and locks. The keys shall be kept by / the village commandant, and a gatekeeper shall be appointed to open and close the gates at the proper time. Let the gatekeeper observe those who come and go in order to report on them to the village commandant.

All cases of leaving or entering at improper times, wearing improper clothing, or members of households[11] or their retainers / not conforming to the accepted norms shall be reported by the gatekeeper immediately, no matter what the time. If [such irregularities] involve the sons, younger brothers, male or female slaves, retainers or guests[12] of the head of a household,[13] the village commandant shall warn the clan elder of the circuit. / The clan elder shall [in turn] warn [the leader] of the group of ten or five who shall [accordingly] warn the head of the household.

If the warning is respected, there need be no report [to higher authority]. / The first or second [offenses] shall be treated leniently, but there shall be no pardoning of a third.

All [special] cases of filial piety / and respect for elders, loyalty and faithfulness, worthiness and goodness, or refinement and talent on the part of the sons, younger brothers, male or female slaves, and retainers or guests of the head of a household shall be reported accordingly by the leaders of the groups of ten or five to the clan elder of the circuit. The clan elder shall report them to the village commandant who [in

---

somewhat similar to that presented in the *Zhou li*, 10/7a2–4 (Biot, *Tcheou-li*, I, p. 211): "[The *da situ* 大司徒] orders each five households (*jia* 家) to form a group (*bi* 比) and requires them to protect each other [from enemies]; each five groups to form a compound (*lü* 閭) and requires them to provide for each other [in time of need]; each four compounds to form a clan settlement (*zu* 族) and requires them to help each other in burying their dead; each five clan settlements to form a league (*dang* 黨) and requires them to aid each other [in times of famine]; each five leagues to form a subdistrict (*zhou* 州) and requires them to assist each other [on ceremonial occasions]; each five subdistricts to form a district (*xiang* 鄉) and requires them to cooperate with each other in providing for honored guests."

[9] Reading 賓 as 匵 or 偃 [Xu].

[10] Emending 博 to 搏 [Igai, Wang Niansun, and Hung].

[11] Reading 圈 as 眷 [Tao].

[12] These guests 賓客 formed a special social stratum made up of scholars, political advisors, soldiers of fortune, etc., who traveled around to various courts and feudal households offering their services to whoever would employ them.

[13] Reading 長家 as 家長 here and in the following passage (14b5; 13.12) [Yasui].

13.12 turn] / shall report them to the subdistrict prefect. He shall summarize them for the district governor who will record them for the chief justice (*shishi* 士師).

In all cases where the participants in a crime are members of a household, [collective responsibility] shall extend to the head of the household. If [the participants include] the heads of households, [collective responsibility] shall extend to the leaders of the groups of ten and 13.13 five. / If [the participants include] these leaders, [collective responsibility] shall extend to the clan elder of the circuit. If [the participants include] clan elders, [collective responsibility] shall extend to the village commandant. If [the participants include] village commandants, [collective responsibility] shall extend to the subdistrict prefect. If [the participants include] subdistrict prefects, [collective responsibility] shall 13.14 extend to the district governor. / If [the participants include] district governors, [collective responsibility] extends to the chief justice.

Reports shall be made once every three months, summaries once every six, and [permanent] records once every twelve. Whenever the worthy are promoted, they shall not be allowed to exceed their proper rank. When the able are employed, they shall not be allowed to hold 14.1 more than one office at a time. / When punishments are imposed, they shall not be applied to the guilty person alone. When rewards are granted, they shall not be bestowed merely on the person [credited with] the achievement.

At the beginning of the first month of spring, the prince himself shall listen to the court [hearings] and discuss the award of ranks and the reassignment of offices. This will last for five days. At the end of the last 14.2 month of winter, / the prince himself shall listen to court [hearings] and discuss the infliction of punishments and executions. This will also last five days.[14]

On the first day of the first month all officials shall come to court. The 5a prince will then issue his orders and proclaim his statutes to / the country. The governors of the five districts and the great officers (*dafu* 4.3 大夫) of the five dependencies (*shu* 屬)[15] / shall all receive the statutes from the grand scribe (*taishi* 太史).

On the day of the great court, the governors of the five districts and

---

[14] This passage reflects the strong influence of Yin-Yang thought on the ceremony of the court. Since winter was considered to represent the Yin or negative principle, punishments were discussed at that time. A similar statement appears in the *Zhou li*, 35/5a1 (Biot, *Tcheau-li*, II, p. 325). For the manner in which this same principle operated in Han times, see Hulsewé, *Remnants of Han Law*, I, pp. 103–109.

[15] The five dependencies refer to those territories lying outside the country proper. See n. 4, above.

105

the great officers of the five dependencies shall all acquaint themselves
with the statutes before the prince. The grand scribe shall then proclaim
the statutes and deposit a record of them in the grand archives (*taifu*
太府). / [Copies of] the record of the statutes shall be distributed in the
presence of the prince. The five district governors shall then leave the
court and proceed to their district headquarters, where they shall assemble[16] their subordinates in the districts down to the clan elders of the
circuits so all may receive [copies of] the statutes. /

When the statutes have thus been proclaimed, [the governor] shall
return to report [to the prince] concerning [the execution of] his orders.
Only then dare they return home [to rest]. Until the statutes have been
proclaimed and the report concerning the orders is sent, they dare not
return home because so doing shall be deemed delaying the orders, for
which crime[17] the punishment is death with no pardon.

The great officers of the five dependencies / shall all use traveling
carriages to come to court. When they leave the court, they dare not
return home, but shall commence their travels. On the day that they
arrive at their capitals (*du*) they shall proceed to the ancestral temple,
where they shall assemble their subordinate functionaries so all may
receive [copies of] the statutes. When the statutes have been proclaimed,
messengers shall be dispatched / to report [to the prince] concerning [the
execution of] the orders. This shall take place on the day the statutes are
proclaimed, whether the hour be early or late. Only after the messengers
have been sent out, dare [the great officers] return home [to rest]. Until
the statutes have been proclaimed and the messengers dispatched, they
dare not return home because so doing / shall be deemed delaying the
orders, for which crime the punishment is death with no pardon.

When the statutes have thus been proclaimed, failure to implement
them shall be deemed a refusal to follow orders, for which crime the
punishment is death with no pardon. On examining [the execution of]
the statutes, if there is anything which is not in agreement with the
record in the grand archives, going too far[18] / shall be deemed assump-
tion of independent authority, whereas not going far enough shall be
deemed inadequate implementation. For both of these crimes the punishment is death with no pardon.

Only after these organizational and procedural statutes have been
proclaimed shall [other] statutes be promulgated.[19]

---

[16] Deleting 于 [Wang Yinzhi, Yu Yue, and Wen].
[17] The Yang edition mistakenly writes 死罪 for 罪死.
[18] The Yang edition mistakenly writes 曰侈 for 侈曰.
[19] Ding would emend 布 to 行, "be implemented."

Procedures for Undertakings (*Shou Shi* 首事)[20]

Whenever an undertaking is to be initiated, orders shall first be issued stating [the nature of] it. The extent of the rewards and punishments [involved] must also be made clear beforehand. Those who oversee[21] these undertakings shall carefully adhere to the orders in carrying out rewards / and punishments. When summing up the results of the undertaking and reporting on [the execution] of the orders, they shall submit an account of which rewards and punishments have been applied. If there is anything that is not in agreement with what the orders have stated, even though it may be of merit, it shall be deemed assuming independent authority, for which crime the punishment is death with no pardon.

Only after these procedures for undertakings have been proclaimed shall [specific] undertakings be initiated.

Survey of Officials (*Sheng Guan* 省官)[22]

To regulate statutes concerning [the use of] fire, care for[23] the natural[24] products of the mountains and marshes, forest preserves, and luxuriant grasslands, and to close or open them in proper season, thereby ensuring the people sufficient[25] [materials] for dwellings and stores of[26] firewood—such are the duties of the warden of parks and ponds (*yushi* 虞師). /

To direct the course of flooding rivers, open canals and ditches, build dams and dikes, keep the reservoirs from overflowing so that seasonal floods will not harm the five grains even though they be excessive, and there will be a harvest even though the year be poor and dry—such are the duties of the minister of works (*sikong* 司空).[27]

To inspect / high and low land, examine fertile and stony soils, observe the suitability of land [for certain crops], determine the periods for levying public service labor,[28] set the priorities [in the work schedule] of

---

[20] Here again *shou* 首 actually means "to come before" but refers to those matters of procedure that must be implemented before other undertakings can be initiated.

[21] Reading 立 as 位 [Yu Xingwu and Xu].

[22] A similar, but more extensive, list of officers appears in the *Xunzi*, V, 9/8b10–10b8 (Dubs, *Hsüntze*, pp. 139–144).

[23] Emending 敬 to 救 = 養 [Liu Shipei and Xu].

[24] Emending 夫 to 天 [Ding and Xu].

[25] Inserting 足 after 民 [Dai and Wen].

[26] Deleting 所 [Yu Yue and Dai].

[27] A similar description of the duties of the minister of works also appears in the *LSCQ*, 3/2a6–9 (Wilhelm, *Frühling und Herbst*, p. 28).

[28] Reading 詔 as 召 = 招 [Zhang Peilun and Wen].

107

15.3 the peasants[29] so everything[30] is done at the proper time, and see that the five grains, mulberry, and hemp will do well in their places—such are the duties of the minister of agriculture (*shentian* 申田).[31]

15.3 To make inspection tours of / his district and villages, examine dwellings, observe the planting of trees, survey the six domestic animals so everything is done at the proper time,[32] and encourage the hundred surnames so they will work with energy, refrain from theft, be happy in their homes, and be impressed with the gravity of leaving their district and village—such are the duties of the district governors. /

15.4 To supervise the various artisans, examine their seasonal activities, separate the fine from the coarse, promote the well-made and useful, oversee and standardize [the work of] the five districts so everything is done at the proper time, and see that no one dares produce goods that are [overly] carved and decorated—such are the duties of the superintendent of artisans (*gongshi* 工師). /

15.11
16b5
15.6
16a8

THE REGULATION OF CLOTHING (*Fu Zhi* 服制)[33]

Let clothing be regulated according to gradations in rank. Let wealth be spent according to gradations in salaries. Let there be restraints on the consumption of food and drink and regulations governing the wearing of clothing. Let there be gradations in dwellings, limitations on the number of animals and retainers, and restrictions on boats, chariots, and military equipment.[34]

15.7 In life,[35] / let there be distinctions in regard to carriages and official caps, clothing and positions, stipends[36] and salaries, and fields and dwellings. In death, let there be gradations in coffins, shrouds, and tombs. Let no one, even if worthy[37] and honored,[38] dare wear clothing

---

[29] For 前後農夫 the similar passage in the *Xunzi* (V, 9/9b1) writes 省農功, which Dubs (*Hsüntze*, p. 140) translates as, "to examine into the merits of the farmers." A similar interpretation is possible for the *Guanzi* passage here.

[30] The *Xunzi* version of the above passage consistently writes 順 for 均. Dubs (ibid., p. 140) translates the phrase as "obediently do each at the proper time."

[31] For *youtian* 由田, the *Xunzi*, V, 9/9b2, writes *zhitian* 治田, which Dubs (ibid., p. 140) translates as "bailiff," and explains as "an officer who had oversight of the fields." I have followed Liu Shipei and Xu, who state that *youtian* 由田 should be written *shentian* 申田, another term for *sitian* 司田 or minister of agriculture.

[32] Emending 鈞 to 均 here and below to conform to the passage above.

[33] The following section is duplicated in a similarly named chapter of the *Chunqiu fanlu*, VII, 26/12b13 ff.

[34] The *Chunqiu fanlu* for 陳器 writes 甲器, "weapons."

[35] Deleting 修 in accordance with the *Chunqiu fanlu* [Wang Niansun and Sun Xingyan].

[36] For 穀, the *Chunqiu fanlu* writes 貴, "honors."

[37] For 賢身, the *Chunqiu fanlu* writes 賢才, "worthiness and talent."

[38] For 貴體, the *Chunqiu fanlu* writes 美體, "handsome."

that does not befit his rank. Let no one, even if / coming from a rich family and possessing extensive property, dare spend wealth that exceeds his salary.

Let the clothing of the son of Heaven be decorated with insignia,[39] and the royal concubines / never dare wear leisure dress when making sacrifices in the temple. Let generals and great officers [wear their ceremonial robes only] at court and officials and functionaries / [wear them only] in the performance of their duties. Let the gentry be limited to decorations on their belts and on the hems of their robes.[40]

Let ordinary people never dare wear mixed colors, nor the various artisans, merchants, and traders be permitted to wear long-haired sable.[41] Let [criminals] who have undergone castration and people who have undergone mutilation as a punishment never dare / wear silk,[42] own[43] handcarts,[44] or ride in chariots.[45]

The Nine Ways to Failure (*Jiu Bai* 九敗) and Explanation (*Jiu Bai Jie* 九敗解)

[*JB*] If talk of abolishing the use of arms[46] prevails, the strategic passes will not be defended.

[*JBJ*] Even if the prince of men merely listens to [talk of] abolishing the use of arms, the multitude of ministers and guest retainers will not dare talk about them. Thus internally, he will know nothing about the strengths and weaknesses of the feudal lords. Such being the case, / when the city and suburban walls are in ruins, there will be no one to rebuild and repair them. When armor is inferior in quality and weapons defec-

---

[39] Emending 文有章 to 有文章 in accordance with the *Chunqiu fanlu* [Hong].

[40] The following passage 而夫人 … 帶緣 appears to be corrupt both in the *Guanzi* and *Chunqiu fanlu* versions. Xu would emend it to read 而夫人不敢以燕服以饗, 將軍大夫不敢以廟, 官吏不敢以朝, 命士止於帶緣. "…, and the royal concubines never dare wear leisure dress when making sacrifices. Let generals and great officers never dare wear them in temples and officials and functionaries never dare wear them at court. Let the gentlemen of the court be limited to decorations on their belts and on the hems of their robes."

[41] For 長鬃貂, the *Chunqiu fanlu* writes 狐狢, "fox and raccoon."

[42] Emending 縄, "ceremonial cap," to 絲 in accordance with the *Chunqiu fanlu* [Hong and Wang Niansun].

[43] Deleting 不敢 in accordance with the *Chunqiu fanlu* [Xu and Guo Moruo].

[44] For 畜連 the *Chunqiu fanlu* writes 玄纁, "[wear] black and red [clothes in place of the usual ones made of yellow hemp]."

[45] For 乘車, the *Chunqiu fanlu* writes 乘馬, "ride horses."

[46] *Qin bing* 寢兵; this refers to the doctrines of Song Xing and Yin Wen, who were contemporaries of Mencius and Zhuangzi during the late fourth and early third centuries B.C. According to the *Zhuangzi*, X, 33/16b8 (Watson, *Chuang Tzu*, p. 368): "They sought to put an end to strife among the people, to outlaw aggression, to abolish the use of arms, and to rescue the world from warfare."

tive,[47] there will be no one to improve or repair them. Such being the case, preparations for defense will be impaired. Distant territories will hatch schemes, knights situated on the borders will become lackadaisical,[48] and the hundred surnames / will have no mind to besiege the enemy.

[JB] When talk of universal love[49] prevails, the troops will not fight.

[JBJ] Even if the prince of men merely listens to talk of universal love, he will look upon the people of the entire realm as his people and the various states as his state. Such being the case, he will have no mind for annexation or capture, and no efforts will be made to vanquish [enemy] armies or defeat / [enemy] generals. Such being the case, knights who are skilled in archery and charioteering and who possess courage and strength will not receive high salaries, and ministers who can vanquish [enemy] armies and kill their generals will not be granted high ranks. Such being the case, knights who are skilled in archery and charioteering and who possess courage and strength will go abroad. / How will we be able to avoid attacks from others?

It is not our desire to be unable to prevent attacks from others and give them our territory if they seek it. If we do not give it to them, but fight, we will certainly be defeated. They will be using trained knights / while we will be using the masses prodded [into action]. They will be using good generals while we will be using those with no ability. Our attempts to vanquish their armies and kill their generals will certainly be defeated.

[JB] If talk of living to the full[50] prevails, integrity and a sense of shame will not be established.

[JBJ] Even if the prince of men merely likes [the idea of] living to the full, the multitude of ministers will all live their lives to the full, and in doing so, further take [special] care of themselves. What does "taking [special] care" mean? It means [the multitude of ministers will indulge in] gluttonous tastes, music, and sexual pleasures, and then consider this to be caring for their lives. Thus they will follow / their desires and behave with reckless abandon. Men and women will not be kept separate, but

[47] Reading 彫 as 凋 [Yin Tongyang].
[48] Emending 修 to 偷 [Guo Moruo].
[49] *Jian ai* 兼愛; this refers to the doctrine of Mo Di (c. 479 – c. 381 B.C.). Chapters IV, 14–16, of the *Mozi* (Mei, *Motse*, pp. 78–97) are entitled *Jian ai* 上, 中, and 下.
[50] *Quan sheng* 全生; this refers to the teachings of Yang Zhu (fourth century B.C.). According to the *Huainanzi*, 13/7b10, Yang Zhu believed in "living to the full (here 生 is written 性), preserving what is genuine, and not allowing outside things to entangle one's person."

44.3

1:15.12
4/16b7
3:44.4
65/1b1

44.5

44.6

44.7

1:15.13
4/16b8

3:44.8
65/1b9

44.9

revert to being animals. Consequently the rules of propriety, righteous conduct, integrity, and a sense of shame will not be established, and the prince of men will have nothing with which to protect himself.

[JB] If talk expressing private criticism and self-importance prevails, orders from the sovereign will not / be carried out.

[JBJ] Even if the prince of men merely listens to talk expressing private criticism and self-importance, people will retreat into solitude, conceal themselves, take to living in caves, flee to the mountains, renounce the world, disdain ranks and salaries, and look down on holding office. Thus the orders will not be carried out, and what is prohibited will not / be stopped.

[JB] If talk [motivated by] partisanship and factionalism prevails, no distinctions will be made between the worthy and the unworthy.[51]

[JBJ] Even if the prince merely listens to talk [motivated by] partisanship and factionalism, the multitude of ministers will form cliques and conceal the good while praising the bad. Thus the country's true state of affairs will be falsified and obscured from the sovereign. Such being the case, large[52] factions will come to the fore while smaller / ones are pushed back. Now, if large[53] factions come to the fore, and no distinctions are made between the worthy and the unworthy, turmoil resulting from their infighting / will arise, and the prince will be placed in the midst of danger.

[JB] If talk of gold and jade, goods and wealth prevails, official ranks and attire will flow downward.

[JBJ] Even if the prince of men merely listens to talk of gold and jade, goods and wealth, he will certainly desire to obtain what he likes. Thus he will certainly have things to exchange for them. What can he exchange for them? [He can exchange] great offices and honored positions; if not these, then honored / ranks and high salaries. Such being the case, the unworthy will come to occupy the highest positions. Consequently the worthy will make no effort,[54] and the wise will make no plans, the trustworthy will make no commitments, and the brave will not be willing to face death. Such / being the case, [the prince] may urge the country [to action], but it will still be destroyed.

---

[51] The "Explanation" for this line is out of sequence. See 2a10 (3:45.3).
[52] Emending 朋 to 多 [Igai and Wang Niansun].
[53] Emending 朋 to 多 [Yu Yue].
[54] Emending 下 to 力 to accord with the Ancient edition [Yasui and Xu].

[*JB*] If talk of seeking pleasure and enjoyment prevails, depraved people will occupy / the highest positions.

[*JBJ*] Even if the prince of men merely listens to talk of seeking pleasure and enjoyment, he will fail. Seeking pleasure always entails palaces and mansions, pavilions and pools, pearls and jade, and music. These are all ways to waste wealth, exhaust energy, and bring ruin to the state. Moreover, / those who serve the prince in this way are all depraved persons, and in listening to them, the prince of men will only meet with failure. Such being the case, his treasury and storehouses will be emptied and his reserves dissipated. Moreover, if depraved people occupy the highest positions, they will obstruct those who are worthy so they will not / advance. Such being the case, if it so happens that the country should meet with disaster, entertainers and dwarfs will arise to discuss the affairs of state. In this way the state will be driven to destruction.

[*JB*] If talk that involves the seeking of private audiences and recommendations[55] for promotion / prevails, the guidelines [for appointment to office] will be distorted.

[*JBJ*] Even if the prince of men merely listens to talk that involves the seeking of private audiences and recommendations for promotion,[56] the multitude of ministers will all make such requests, and if permitted by the sovereign, factions and alliances will be formed in the districts. Such being the case, goods and wealth will be circulated throughout the state [in the form of bribes], and laws and regulations / will be undermined by officials. The multitude of officials will devote themselves to trickery rather than seeking to be meritorious.[57] Thus, even without rank, they will still be honored; even without salaries, they will still / be rich.

[*JB*] If talk that flatters and covers up mistakes prevails, clever sycophants / will be employed.

[*JBJ*] Even if the prince of men merely listens to talk that flatters and covers up mistakes, he will fail. How do we know this to be so? Now ministers who flatter constantly cause their rulers to fail to repent their mistakes and correct their failures. / Therefore the ruler is misled with-

---

[55] Reading 任 as 保 [Yin Zhizhang and Xu].

[56] Emending 譽 to 舉 to accord with the *Jiu bai* text and the Ancient, Liu, and Zhu editions [Yasui and Dai].

[57] Inserting 不 before 求 in accordance with a similar passage in chapter XV, 46/11a1 (2:94.5–6).

out knowing it. Such being the case, ministers who issue warnings[58] will be killed, while those who flatter will be revered.

SEVEN POINTS TO OBSERVE (*Qi Guan* 七觀)[59]

To set a date and have it observed, to send out messengers and have them go, to have the hundred surnames renounce their own [interests] and take the sovereign as their heart—such is the expectation of teaching.

To begin with what cannot be seen and end with what cannot be equaled, to have one man act and ten thousand follow / —such is the expectation of instruction.

To have orders carried out before they are issued, to have messengers go forth before being sent, to have people exert themselves to the utmost without any pressure being applied from on high / —such is the expectation of customary procedures.

To have the hundred surnames transformed below in accordance with the likes and dislikes that form in the heart [of the prince], to have the people feel fearful even before punishments have been executed, to have them feel encouraged even before rewards have been applied / —such is the expectation of unswerving good faith.

To act without suffering harm, to achieve without suffering criticism,[60] to obtain with no one able to struggle against it—such is the expectation of [adhering to] the way of Heaven. /

To act and achieve, to seek and obtain, to carry out whatever is wished on high whether it be great or small—such is the expectation of undertakings.

To issue orders and have them carried out, to establish prohibitions and have them obeyed, to have the customs [of the people] accord with the aims of statutes / just as the various parts of the body conform to [the direction of] the mind—such is the expectation of government.

[58] Emending 謀 to 諫 in accordance with a similar passage in chapter V, 13/6b1 (1:62.11–12).

[59] Ding would emend 觀 to 期, "Expectations," in order to accord with the wording used in the text that follows.

[60] A similar passage in the *Heguanzi*, I, 4/8a3–4, for 議, "criticism," writes 敗, "failure."

Sheng Ma
乘馬

ON MILITARY TAXES

Introductory Comments

The term 乘馬 appears in the title of three other chapters in the *Guanzi*, XXI, 68, 69, and 70, of which XXI, 70, is now lost. Pronounced *cheng ma* it merely means "to ride" or "drive a horse," and it is with this meaning that it appears in line 19b1 (1 : 18.11) of this chapter. Both *cheng* and *ma* are also terms used in reference to accounting, and for this reason He Ruzhang, Ma Feibai, and the Zhongguo Renmin Daxue group would interpret the title to mean something like "On Government Finances." Although this interpretation would seem to fit the content of the chapter very well, I have adopted another approach. Pronounced *sheng ma* the term refers to a chariot and team of four horses, and I believe that in the titles of this and chapters XXI, 68, 69, and 70, it refers to a system of military taxation or levies known as the *sheng ma zhi fa* 乘馬之法, which is best explained in *Qian Han shu*, 23/2b2–9:[1]

[Ancient rulers] instituted a system of military taxes (*jun fu* 軍賦) based on the well field (*jingtian* 井田) system. An area one *li*[2] square constituted a well-field (*jing* 井), ten well fields a division (*tong* 通), and ten divisions a small estate (*cheng* 成) ten *li* square. Ten small estates constituted a large estate (*zhong* 終) and ten large estates a fiefdom (*tong* 同) a hundred *li* square. Ten such fiefdoms constituted a feudal state (*feng* 封) and ten feudal states made up the royal domain (*qi* 畿) a thousand *li* square.[3]

There were general taxes (*shui* 稅) and military taxes.[4] General taxes were to provide sufficiency in food and military taxes sufficiency in arms. Therefore, [for military tax purposes] four well fields formed a colony (*yi* 邑) and four colonies a section (*qiu* 丘) covering sixteen well fields and having [a military tax of] one war horse and three head of cattle. Four sections formed a sector (*sheng* 甸)

---

[1] See Hulsewé, *Remnants of Han Law*, I, pp. 322–323.

[2] A Zhou *li* 里 equaled 1364.1 English feet or approximately .26 English miles. See Swann, *Food and Money*, p. 362.

[3] The terminology employed here seems to be based in part on the *Zhou li*, 42/1b2–3 (Biot, *Tcheou-li*, II, p. 566).

[4] Emending 租 to 賦 in accordance with the Yan Shigu 顏師古 (581–645) commentary.

covering sixty-four well units and having [a military tax of] four war horses, one chariot, twelve head of cattle, three gentlemen in armor, and seventy-two foot soldiers completely provided with shields and halberds.[5] This was called the *sheng ma zhi fa.*[6]

Although the terminology employed in the above quotation differs considerably from that used in the relevant section of this chapter (20a1–10; 19.4–8), the system described is basically the same.

The chapter is made up of nine titled sections of varying length that deal with various aspects of the state and especially its fiscal support for the military. Several of the shorter sections, particularly the last three, appear to have little to do with the central core of the chapter and probably represent later additions or insertions. The final section, "On the Management of Land," for example, uses the character *shi* 室 for household rather than *jia* 家, the term used in the rest of the text.

The bulk of the chapter contained in the three sections, "On Yin and Yang," "On Paying Attention to Markets and Production," and "On Gentlemen, Peasants, Artisans, and Merchants," hang together quite well. However, the text presents many problems, especially in the large number of obscure technical terms to which I have assigned arbitrary, and often rather unsatisfactory, translations. The terms used for various political divisions and fiscal units frequently differ from those appearing elsewhere in the *Guanzi*, in such chapters as I, 4, and VIII, 20, for example. In addition there are a number of textual corruptions that make certain passages doubtful.

Various Chinese scholars, including Luo Genze and the members of the Jilin Institute, have indicated their belief that this chapter is a product of the Warring States Period. On the basis of its general style and content I would agree. However, because of the problems mentioned above, it is difficult to come to any conclusion concerning its relevance to either the political theory or realities of that period. Despite all this, the text remains extremely interesting because of its presentation

---

[5] The organizational structure presented here appears to come from the *Zhouli*, 11/2b9–3a1 (Biot, *Tcheou-li*, I, pp. 226–227): "[The *xiao situ* 小、司 徒] measures the land and divides cultivated and uncultivated areas into well fields and pasturage. Nine individual tracts (*fu* 夫) form a well field and four well fields a colony (*yi* 邑). Four colonies form a section (*qiu* 丘) and four sections a sector (*sheng* 甸). Four sectors form a district (*xian* 縣) and four districts a region (*du* 都). [These divisions are instituted] in order to take charge of work on the land, and regulate tribute, military taxes, and all matters involving general taxes and levies."

[6] Although the above material appears to be based, at least in part, on the *Zhou li*, the *Zhou li* itself makes no mention of a *sheng ma zhi fa*, and I have been unable to discover the origin of the term.

of concrete ideas and discussion of such concepts as land and tax equalization.

Translation

ON SITUATING THE CAPITAL (*Li Guo* 立國)

Always situate the capital and urban centers (*du* 都) either at the foot of a great mountain or above [the bank of] a broad river. To insure sufficient water, avoid placing them so high as to approach the drought [level]. To conserve on [the need for] canals and embankments, avoid placing them so low as to approach the flood [level]. Take advantage of the resources of Heaven and adapt yourself to the strategic features of Earth. / Hence city and suburban walls need not [rigidly] accord with the compass and square, nor roads with the level and marking line.[7]

16.14

17.3
17b11
17.2
17b9
ON THE GRAND DESIGN (*Da Shu* 大數)

To avoid action is [the way of] the emperor. To act, but without any deliberate purpose, is [the way of] the king. To act, but not for honors [either for oneself or others], is [the way of] the lord protector. To avoid action designed to honor oneself is the way of the prince. To seek honors, but not exceed proper measure, is the way of the minister.

17.13
18b5
17.4
17b12
ON YIN AND YANG (*Yin Yang* 陰陽)

Land is the basis of government. The court sets the pattern for righteous conduct. The marketplace determines the value of goods. Gold is the measure of expenditures. / The territory of a feudal lord, constituting a state with a thousand chariots, is the unit for [assessing] armaments. The rationale underlying these five [propositions] being comprehensible, there is a proper way to implement them.

17.5
18a

Land is the basis of government. Hence land can [serve as a basis for] proper order in government. / If land is not [distributed] equally and harmoniously, the government cannot be properly ordered. If it is not in proper order, its affairs will not be well managed. /

17.6

Spring and autumn, winter and summer represent shifts in the Yin and Yang. The shortening and lengthening of the seasons represent the functioning of their beneficence. The alternations of day and night / represent their transformations. Thus the Yin and Yang main-

17.7

17.8

---

[7] In theory, Chinese cities were laid out according to a strict geometrical pattern in the form of a square with major streets running straight along the lines of the four cardinal directions.

116

tain proper order. But even if they lacked this proper order, what was excessive could not be lessened, nor what was deficient be increased. / No one can add to or detract from Heaven.[8]

Thus it is only land that can [serve as a basis for] proper order in government. / Therefore it must be [distributed] in an orderly fashion. If the land [is to be distributed] in an orderly fashion, the facts concerning it must be correct. No matter whether [its shape] be long or short, [its area] small or large, / [the figures] must be accurate. Regardless of shape or size, there must be accuracy in every respect.

If the land[9] is not [distributed] in an orderly fashion, government offices will not be well managed. / If offices are not well managed, production will be poorly organized. If production is poorly organized, goods will not be plentiful. Now, how can we know if goods will be plentiful? The answer is that production is well organized. How can we know that production is / well organized? The answer is that goods are plentiful. When goods are plentiful and production is well organized, little need be sought from the rest of the world.[10] There is a proper way [to distribute land].

RANKS AND POSITIONS (*Jue Wei* 爵位)

The court sets the patterns for righteous conduct. Thus ranks and positions are bestowed in orderly fashion, so the people will not be resentful. When the people are not resentful, disorders do not arise. Only then can a pattern be established for righteous conduct. Without[11] proper order [in the bestowal of ranks and positions], it would be impossible to establish a pattern [for righteous conduct]. /

Now, it is not possible for all people of a state to have honored positions. If they did, production would fail, and the state / would suffer. However, if [for fear] that production will fail and the state will suffer, one were to eliminate honored positions entirely, the people would not be able to establish a pattern [for correct social behavior] on their own. For this reason we differentiate between honored and lowly ranks so we may know the order of precedence and the proper relationship between the honored and humble. There is a proper way [to bestow ranks and positions]. /

---

[8] Deleting 地 [Zhang Wenhu and Tao].

[9] Emending 正 to 地 [Igai, Wang Niansun, and Zhao Shouzheng]. Zhang Peilun and Guo Moruo would read 正 as 政. Thus, "If the government lacks proper order...."

[10] Tao would delete 下. Thus, "... little need be sought from Heaven."

[11] The sentence, 理不正則不可以治而不可不理也, is obviously corrupt. I have followed Guo Moruo in emending it to read: 不正則不可以理也.

117

18.8
19a7

On Paying Attention to Markets and Production
(*Wu Shi Shi* 務市事)

18.5
19a1

The marketplace determines the value of goods. Hence, if goods are kept cheap, there will be no [exorbitant] profits. If there are no [exorbitant] profits, production will be well organized, and if it is well

18.6

organized, expenditures will be properly controlled. / Now production materializes through planning, succeeds through diligent attention, but fails through negligence. Without planning it will never materialize, without diligent attention it will never succeed. However, unless there is

18.7

negligence, it will not fail. Therefore / it is said that the marketplace may know order or disorder, abundance or scarcity. However, it is incapable of bringing about abundance or scarcity [on its own]. There is a proper way to manage [markets and production].

21.3
22a5

On the Gentlemen, Peasants, Artisans, and Merchants
(*Shi Nong Gong Shang* 士農工商)

18.9
19a8

Gold is the measure of expenditures. If [the prince] is discerning in the management of gold, he understands [the difference between] extravagance and penuriousness. If he understands this, his expenditures will be properly controlled.

Now, penuriousness harms production; extravagance wastes goods.

18.10

Penuriousness / leads to a fall in the value of gold, and when gold is cheap, production declines, it is for this reason that [penuriousness] is harmful to production. Extravagance leads to a rise in the value of gold, and when gold is high, the value of goods is depressed. It is for this reason that [extravagance] causes goods to be wasted.

If it is only after goods are exhausted that one realizes there is a shortage, this is not knowing how to exercise proper measure. If it is only

18.11

after production has ceased / that one realizes there is a surplus of goods, this is not knowing when to be economical. [When the prince] does not know how to exercise proper measure nor when to be economical, he

19b

cannot be said / to possess the proper way.

When [the people of] the world harness horses and yoke oxen, a limit

18.12

is placed on the weight of their loads. / Since there is [an established distance for] a single-stage journey, the [total] distance of the road may be measured.[12] Similarly, by knowing that the territories of the feudal lords constitute states of a thousand chariots, one may know the

---

[12] According to the *Zhou li*, 13/7b5–7 (Biot, *Tcheou-li*, I, p. 228): "Along all the highways of the state proper and outlying areas, every ten *li* there is a shelter 廬 in which one can find food and drink. Every thirty *li* there is a stopover 宿 with a lodge 路室 and provisions. Every fifty *li* there is a market with a hostel 候館 and supplies."

strength of their armament[13] / and the extent of their [tax] burden. If it is too heavy so that later it has to be reduced, this is to fail to understand their burden. If it is too light so that later it has to be increased, this is to fail to understand [the strength of] their armament. When [the prince] fails to understand either [a feudal state's tax] burden or [the strength of] its armament, he cannot be said / to possess the proper way.

Unproductive land and treeless mountains should be assigned a ratio of one in a hundred [for tax purposes]. The same should be the case for dry marshes and land barren of grass and trees as well as places so overgrown with hedges and brambles / that people cannot enter. Marshlands that can be entered with sickles and cords[14] should be assigned a ratio of one in ten[15] [for tax purposes]. The same should be the case for foothills[16] which have trees that can be made into lumber or axles, / and high mountains[17] which have trees that can be made into coffins and carts when these areas may be entered with axes and hatchets. Free-flowing streams in which fishing nets can be placed should be assigned a ratio of one in five [for tax purposes]. The same should be the case for forests / which have trees that can be used for coffins or carts and which can be entered with axes and hatchets as well as marshes which can be entered with fishing nets. / This is called equalizing [the tax on] land in accordance with actual yields.

An area of six *li* square / is called a village (*bao* 暴).[18] Five villages are called a section (*bu* 部), and five sections are called a subdistrict (*ju* 聚). Each subdistrict should have a marketplace. If it does not, the people will suffer shortages.[19] Five subdistricts are called such and such a district (*xiang* 鄉). Four districts / are called an area (*fang* 方). This is the organization for administrations under direct rule (*guan* 官).

When [the organization of] administrations under direct rule has been completed, set up the areas administered through rural towns (*yi* 邑). Five households (*jia* 家) form a group of five (*wu* 伍), and ten households a group (*lian* 連). Five groups form a village (*bao*), and five villages a headquarters unit (*zhang* 長) known as such and such a district

[13] Emending 地 to 器 [Wang Niansun].

[14] Following the Yang edition, which for 纏 writes 繹.

[15] Emending 九, "nine," to 十 both here and below [Ding].

[16] The meaning of 蔓 山 is not clear. I have followed Yu Xingwu. Yasui says that it refers to mountain spurs close to towns and villages.

[17] The meaning of 汎 山 is also not clear. Again I have followed Yu Xingwu. Yasui says it refers to high mountains distant from towns and villages.

[18] Zhang Peilun both here and below would emend *bao* to 箄 *bi*, "a fence," and by extension "a fenced-off village."

[19] The Yang edition mistakenly writes 之 for 乏.

119

(*xiang* 鄉).[20] Four districts are called / a region (*du* 都). This is the organization of areas administered through rural towns.

When [the organization of] of these areas has been completed, organize production. Four strips (*ju* 聚) constitute a plot (*li* 離), and five plots a lot (*zhi* 制). Five lots constitute a field (*tian* 田), and two fields an individual tract (*fu* 夫). Three such tracts constitute [the land] of a household. This is the organization for production.[21] /

When [the organization for] production has been completed, organize [the system of taxation for] armaments. An area of six *li* square constitutes the territory for one chariot. Each chariot has four horses, and for each horse there should be seven armored soldiers (*jia* 甲) and five guards (*bi* 蔽). Thus, for each four horses[22] there should be twenty-eight / armored soldiers and twenty guards. Thirty untrained conscripts (*bai tu* 白徒) should also assist with the [baggage] wagons.[23] This is the organization for armament [taxes].

An area of six *li* square is the territory for one chariot; an area of one square *li* contains nine individual tracts.[24]

One *yi*[25] of gold / is the fee[26] for one night's lodging for a hundred chariots. If gold is unavailable, silk may be used. Thirty-three *zhi*[27] of

[20] Liu Shipei would insert 五長而鄉 after 五暴而長. Thus, "Five communities form a village and five villages a headquarters. Five headquarters form a district known as such and such district." The *xiang*, "district," given here is probably the same basic unit as the *xian* mentioned in the *Zhou li*. See n. 4.

[21] The Zheng Xuan 鄭玄 commentary to the *Zhou li*, 11/3b5–7, quotes a passage attributed to the *Sima Fa*, but it does not appear in present editions of the work: "Six Chinese feet (*chi* 尺; 9.094 English inches) equaled one double pace (*bu* 步; 54.564 English inches). One hundred double paces (i.e., 1 × 100) equaled one Chinese acre (*mou* 畝; 0.04746 English acres), and one hundred Chinese acres equaled one individual tract (*fu* 夫; 4.746 English acres). Three such tracts equaled a household holding (*wu* 屋, for which this text writes *jia* 家; 14.238 English acres), and three household holdings equaled one well field (*jing* 井; 42.714 English acres). The English equivalents for these Zhou measurements are taken from Swann, *Food and Money*, p. 363.

[22] Emending 乘 to 馬 [Igai and Ding].

[23] 車兩; this may refer to the chariots rather than separate baggage wagons.

[24] Zheng Xuan's commentary to the *Zhou li*, 11/3a6, also states that a well field was one square *li* in size. According to the *Qian Han shu*, 23/2b10–3a1 (Hulsewé, *Remnants of Han Law*, I, p. 323): "A fiefdom (*tong* 同) was 100 *li* [square], all in all [covering an area of] 10,000 well fields (*jing*). Deducting the area of 3,600 well fields for mountains, rivers, marshlands, walls, moats, communities and dwellings, gardens, large and small roads, it can be determined that there will be produced a tax on 6,400 well fields [amounting to] 400 war horses and 100 chariots." Thus 36 well fields were required to support a chariot and four horses along with their attendant personnel.

[25] 鎰; variously stated to equal 20 or 24 Chinese ounces (*liang* 兩). According to Swann, *Food and Money*, p. 364, a Qin *yi* equaled 20 Chinese ounces or 9.8 ounces troy or 10.75 ounces avoir or 305 grams.

[26] Reading 盡 as 賮 [Igai and Ding].

[27] 制; a *zhi* equaled 18 Chinese feet.

high grade thin silk[28] is the equivalent of one *yi* [of gold]. If silk is unavailable, plain cloth may be used. One hundred bolts (*liang*)[29] of
9.10   loose woven[30] cloth made from hemp[31] is / the equivalent of one *yi* [of gold]. Since one *yi* of gold will feed a hundred chariots overnight,[32] each six double-paces of land surrounding a market area [should be assessed a tax of] one peck (*dou*)[33] of grain. This is called the mean annual harvest [tax]. When there should be a marketplace, if there is none, the
9.11   people will[34] / suffer shortages.[35]

Six *li* square is called an altar area (*she* 社).[36] When it contains a town (*yi* 邑), it is called a center (*yang* 央).[37]

Establish[38] custom and market levies. For each hundred *yi* in gold, [the tax] should be one *qie*[39] [of gold]. For goods [with the value of] a
9.12   basket (*long* 籠) of grain / it should be ten *qie* [of grain]. The elder[40] [of each group] of thirty traders in the market should [see to it that] one *yi* of gold [is paid] during the first and twelfth month [of the year]. This is called establishing proper order in the apportionment [of levies].

Spring is said to be the time for publishing [the tax] rates, summer[41]
9.13   for estimating the conditions for each month, and fall / for making comprehensive calculations and figuring the gains and losses of the people.

---

[28] 季絹 ; following Jin Tinggui. The Yin commentary says that it is a poor quality silk, below third grade.

[29] 兩 ; 40 Chinese feet in length.

[30] Reading 暴 as 薄 [Wen].

[31] Emending 經 to 絵 [Zhang Peilun].

[32] The relationship between this phrase 一鎰之金食百乘之一宿 and the rest of the sentence is not clear. Zhang Peilun feels it was originally part of the commentary mistakenly inserted into the text. I feel it is more likely that something has been omitted between the end of the phrase and the beginning of the latter part of the sentence.

[33] Reading 斜 as 斗 [Ding and He Ruzhang]. A *dou* equaled 1.81 U.S. dry quarts.

[34] Deleting 不 [Igai, Yasui, and Tao].

[35] There is some question as to how this line 命之曰中歲,有市無市,則民(不)之矣, should be punctuated. I have followed Yasui and others. Xu and Guo Moruo would end it with 中. Thus, "This is called the mean [tax]. If at the time of harvest there should be a market but there is none, the people will suffer shortages."

[36] The meaning of *she* here is not entirely clear. I have interpreted it to mean a rural area possessing a small altar to Land. According to the *Zuo zhuan*, Chao 25 (Legge, *Ch'un Ts'eu*, X, 25/6): "The Lord of Qi said, 'From the borders of Ju westward, I will hand over 1,000 *she* and await Your Lordship's commands.'" The *Shuowen jiezi* says that a *she* consisted of 25 households.

[37] This short paragraph seems out of place here and probably represents a misplaced slip from some other text.

[38] Emending 亦 to 立 [Guo Moruo].

[39] 筐 ; a small box-shaped measure, the capacity of which is unknown.

[40] Emending 茍 to 者 = 耆 [Zhang Peilun].

[41] Deleting 立 [Sun Yirang].

Every three years repair the earthen banks [between fields]. Every five years repair the boundaries [between household lands]. Every ten years redefine [the boundaries]. This is to set standards for maintaining proper order [in the distribution of land].

If the water [table] is observed to be [below] the one-*ren*[42] mark there will be no serious flood. If it is observed to be [above] the five-foot (*chi* 尺) mark, / there will be no serious drought. However, if it is observed to be [below] the one-*ren* mark,[43] lighten taxes by one-tenth [because of possible drought]. [If it drops to the two-*ren* mark, lighten them by two-tenths, to the three-*ren* mark, by three-tenths, to the four-*ren* mark, by four-tenths, / and to the five-*ren* mark, lighten them by half. This is comparable to mountain [land].

If the water [table] is observed to be [above] the five-foot mark, lighten taxes by one-tenth [because of possible flooding]. [If it rises to] the four-foot mark, lighten them by two-tenths,[44] / to the three-foot mark, by three-tenths, to the two-foot mark, by four-tenths. When it is observed at the one-foot mark, this is comparable to marsh [land]. /

Beyond the gates of the capital (*guo* 國), everywhere / within the four borders, able-bodied adult males [should be responsible for] two plowings during their three days of public service; boys [under] five feet should be responsible for one. In the first month, order the peasants to begin work on the public fields.[45] Their plowing should start when the snow melts. [Their spring work] begins with plowing / and ends with weeding.

Gentlemen who may be broadly[46] informed, widely learned, and discerning in judgment, but who are unwilling to act as ministers to their prince, should take part in public work, but not share in allotments [from the public fields]. Traders who understand prices / and who daily go to the market, but do not engage in official trade, should take part in public work, but not share in allotments [from the public fields].

[42] Emending 十, "ten," to 一 to accord with the content of the following passage [Yu Yue]. A *ren* 仞 is variously given as 8 Chinese feet or 5 Chinese feet, 6 inches. The former is the most commonly accepted value.

[43] This passage 十一仞見水…五則去半 is obviously corrupt. I have followed the emendations of Igai and Wen, writing: 一仞見水輕征, 十分去一, 二則去二, 三則去三, 四則去四, 五則去半.

[44] The figures given in this passage are again obviously corrupt. I have followed Yasui and Yu Yue in emending 三, "three," to 二; 二 "two," to 三; 一, "one," to 四; and 三, "three," to 一.

[45] *Gong tian* 公田; according to the *Mengzi*, IIIA, 3/19: "A well field (*jing*) covers an area one *li* square consisting of 100 *mu*. Of these the central plot is a public field, while the other eight, consisting of 100 *mu* each, are the private fields of eight households who together care for the public field. Only when work on the public field is completed, dare they tend to their private work."

[46] Emending 閒 to 聞 = 燗 [Sun Yirang].

Artisans who are well versed in [producing articles of suitable] form and function, and who go daily to the market but do not engage in official work, / should take part in public work, but not share in allotments [from the public fields]. Those who cannot be used in performing public service[47] should be seen as in default on what they owe and required to pay grain [amounting to that derived] from an individual tract (*fu*).

Now then, the people should not be instructed to do either what can only be understood by the intelligent / but not by the stupid or what can only be done by the skilled but not by the unskilled. / Unless it is something that the people may carry out as the result of a single order, it cannot be considered very good. Unless it is something that everyone[48] can do, it cannot be considered to have great merit.

Now then, unless a trader is honest, he should not be permitted to make a living as a trader. / Neither should this be permitted in the case of artisans and peasants. Unless a gentleman is trustworthy, he should not be permitted to hold a position at court.

Now then, even if an office is vacant, no one[49] should dare to make a request for it. Even though the prince may possess costly chariots / and armor, no one else should dare to have them. When the prince initiates an undertaking, his ministers should never dare to lie about their lack of ability. Let the prince know his ministers, and let the ministers likewise know the prince knows them. In this way no minister will dare fail to exert his utmost effort, and all of them will maintain / their integrity when coming forward.

There is a saying: "Equalize the land, apportion the work, and let the people know the proper time [for doing things]. Then will they be aware of how quickly morning turns to evening, how short are the days and months, and how [suddenly] they may be beset by cold and hunger." Hence / they will retire late and rise early, and neither father nor son, elder brother nor younger brother will forget their public work but perform it / tirelessly. Even the hardest work, the people will not fear. It follows that evil lies in not equalizing [the land].

The benefits of Earth are inexhaustible; the strength of the people is unlimited. / However, unless instructed as to the proper time [for doing things], the people will not know about it, and unless you guide them in their work, the people will not do it. Whereas if you share the proceeds with them, the people will understand gain and loss,[50] and if you are

[47] Reading 工 as 功 [Ding].
[48] Following Xu's interpretation of 夫人.
[49] The Yang edition mistakenly writes 其 for 莫.
[50] Emending 正 to 亡 [Xu]. Guo Moruo would read 得 as 德 and 正 as 政. Thus, "the people will know a virtuous government."

21.2 judicious in giving them their proper share, the people will work with all their might. / Indeed, even without being pushed, fathers and sons, elder and younger brothers will not forget their public work.

21.7
22b1
21.4
22a7

THE SAGE (*Shengren* 聖人)

What makes a sage is his skill in giving the people their proper share. A sage who is unable to give them their share is merely [an ordinary member] of the hundred surnames. [Furthermore], if he does not even have enough [to support] himself, how can he be called a sage? / Thus
21.5 when he has an undertaking, he uses [the resources of the people], but when he has none, he returns these to them.

It is only the sage who is skilled in entrusting the people with
21.6 duties. / People's nature is such that when it is allowed to develop, it becomes kindly,[51] but when it is repressed, it becomes perverse.[52] When the sovereign sets an example, his subjects will follow.

21.10
22b5
21.8
22b2

ON NEGLECTING OPPORTUNITIES (*Shi Shi* 失時)

Opportunity is crucial in handling affairs. It cannot be stored up or set aside. Therefore it is said: "If you do not act today, tomorrow you will
21.9 lose[53] your wealth. Yesterday has already gone / and will not come again."

21.13
22b10

ON THE PRINCIPLES UNDERLYING [THE DISTRIBUTION OF] LAND (*Di Li* 地里)

21.11
22b6

It requires an area eighty *li* square of superior quality land [to support] one capital city (*guo*) of ten thousand households and four urban centers (*du*) of a thousand households each. For medium-grade land, it requires an area one hundred *li* square, and for inferior land, it requires an area
21.12 one hundred twenty *li* square. / An area eighty *li* square of superior quality land and an area of one hundred twenty *li* square of inferior land are both equivalent to an area one hundred *li* square of medium-grade land.

---

[51] Emending 愚, "stupid," to 惠 [Guo Moruo].
[52] Emending 頹 to 纇 [Guo Moruo].
[53] Following the Yang edition in reading 亡 for 忘.

Qi Fa

七法

THE SEVEN STANDARDS

Introductory Comments

Qi fa, which is divided into four titled sections, is the first of several chapters in the *Guanzi* dealing with the art of war, a subject of very broad interest in early China. A number of works ascribed to the pre-Han period dealt extensively with military tactics and strategy, the most famous being the three known as the *Sunzi* containing the injunctions of Sun Wu 孫吳 (d. 496 B.C.?), the *Wuzi* attributed to Wu Qi 吳起 (d. 381 B.C.) or one of his disciples, and the *Sun Bin bing fa*. The latter work, attributed to Sun Bin 孫臏 who served King Wei 威 (357–320 B.C.) of Qi, was lost until some fragments of it were discovered in a Han tomb at Yinqueshan 銀雀山 in Linyi 臨邑 Xian, Shandong, in 1972. Indeed, many of the major works of the Warring States Period, including in particular the *Shangjun shu*, the *Mozi*, and *Xunzi*, discuss military affairs at some length.

Most relevant to this chapter in general is the *Shangjun shu*, the Legalist classic that is devoted to a political philosophy aimed at assuring victory in war. Chapter III, 10 of that work, entitled *Zhan fa* 戰法, which Duyvendak (*Lord Shang*, p. 244) also translates as "Methods of Warfare," expresses (5b8) its thesis very well: "The methods of warfare must always be based on the supremacy of the government." Chapter III, 11/6b9ff. (Duyvendak, pp. 247–248) goes on to explain:

When employing armed forces there are generally three stages to victory: before armed forces are committed to action, laws should be fixed; laws being fixed, they should become the custom; when they become customary,[1] supplies should be provided. These three things should be done within the country before the armed forces can be sent abroad. For performing these three things, there are two conditions; the first is to support the law, so that it can be applied; the second is to obtain the right men in appointments so the law is established. ... Therefore it is said that when the armed forces are born of orderly government, there is a marvelous result; when customs are born of law, ten thousand changes of circumstances are brought about; when strength is born of a state of mind, it

---

[1] Inserting 俗成 before 而用 [Duyvendak].

is outwardly manifested in a condition of preparedness. If these three points are all taken into consideration the result will be that the strong will be firmly established.... Therefore it is said that the way to orderly government and strength is to discuss fundamentals.

While this chapter of the *Guanzi* is very similar in general approach to the *Shangjun shu*, its verbiage is not as harsh, and its content is much more sophisticated and imaginative. Of particular interest is the opening section variously subtitled as *Qi fa* 七法, "Seven Standards," or *Si shang* 四傷, "Four Harms," which discusses seven standards or considerations—laws of nature, physical qualities, standards for measurement, forms of transformation, permissive or inhibitory actions, patterns of mental behavior, and categories of mensuration—as aids in the process of government.[2] The first of these is of particular interest in view of the controversy over whether or not the early Chinese indeed had any real concept of the laws of nature.[3] The explanation given in this text for the term *ze* 則, which I have translated as "laws of nature," would seem to indicate they did.

The last two sections of this chapter, *Wei bing zhi shu* and *Chen xuan*, deal specifically with military matters and are extensively cited by three other chapters in the *Guanzi* dealing with military matters: III, 8, paraphrases lines 5a12–5b4 (26.2–4) and 5b11–12 (26.9–10); VI, 17/11b7–12 (1:79.12–80.1), repeats with some minor variations in wording lines 6a9–6b2 (26.14–27.3); while X, 28/9a2–5 (2:22.6–7), does the same with lines 5b9–6a1 (26.8–10).

Furthermore, from the finds at Linyi Xian's Yinqueshan, Chinese researchers have been able to piece together from a mass of scattered and fragmented slips some twenty-three that constitute an essay on military affairs entitled *Wang bing* 王兵 [On the Armed Forces of the King]. The reconstructed text of this essay was published in the 1976, no. 12, issue of *Wen wu*, pp. 36–43. What makes this work so fascinating is its close relationship to three of the military chapters in the *Guanzi*. Almost the entire *Xuan chen* section (5b9–7a8; 26.8–27.12) as well as a portion (5a6–5b7; 25.13–26.6) of *Wei bing zhi shu* are covered in abbreviated form by paragraphs 2 through 6 and part of 7 of the

[2] The term *qi fa* also appears in the *Jing fa* 經法, one of the documents contained in the *Laozi* "B" silk manuscript (1.6.52) discovered in Han Tomb no. III at Mawangdui in Changsha, Hunan, in 1973. See Tang Lan's reconstruction, *Kaogu xuebao* (1975), no. 1, p. 30. Another Chinese scholar, Long Hui, writing in the same journal, pp. 23–32, attempts to establish a connection between this text and the *Guanzi*. I doubt there is a connection since the meaning of *qi fa* in the *Jing fa* differs from that given here.

[3] See Joseph Needham, *Science and Civilisation in China*, II, pp. 118–183, and Derk Bodde, "Chinese 'Laws of Nature': A Reconsideration," in *Essays*, pp. 299–315.

reconstructed *Wang bing* text. The sequence of passages differs from that of this chapter and there are differences in the use of individual characters, but the close relationship of the two texts is obvious. The first paragraph of the *Wang bing* also shows a similar relationship to the second part of chapter X, 28, and part of paragraph 7 and all of 8 are covered by chapter X, 27, though the differences in content and language are greater in this latter case. Two remaining important military chapters of the *Guanzi*, III, 8, and VI, 17, also contain passages that parallel the *Wang bing* essay, but this is probably due to their citation of this chapter rather than the existence of an independent relationship.

It is extremely interesting that the *Wang bing* essay should tie together three of the most important military essays in the *Guanzi*, but what relationship it may have had with the developing *Guanzi* collection remains unclear. I suspect that the *Wang bing* text, which probably existed in several copies besides this one buried in the Yinqueshan tomb about 134 B.C., may have been among those *Guanzi* materials collected by Liu Xiang, but was later rejected by him because it was completely duplicated by material to be found in other chapters.

Unfortunately, as interesting as this find is, it does not help very much with the problem of dating except to reinforce our conviction that the present *Guanzi* is not a late forgery, as maintained by Maspero. It is also impossible at this point to say which came first, the *Wang bing* essay or its related chapters in the *Guanzi*. However, it is my belief that this is the basic military chapter in the *Guanzi*, and was probably part of the proto-*Guanzi* core that took shape about 250 B.C. However, its language, style, and content are relatively complex and thus I doubt it could date any earlier than the end of the fourth or beginning of the third century B.C. Luo Genze (*Guanzi*, p. 31) would date the text as coming from the end of the Warring States Period.

Translation

:22.5
a6

When correct theories cannot be implemented, nor incorrect ones rejected; when the meritorious cannot be rewarded, nor the guilty punished—under such conditions it has never been possible to govern

2.6

the people well. / If correct [theories] are certain to be implemented, and incorrect ones rejected; if the meritorious are certain to be rewarded, and the guilty punished—under such conditions, will there then be

2.7

orderly government? If not, / what is the reason? The answer is that unless [favorable military] conditions and weapons are fully present, orderly government will still not be assured. Whereas if these are fully present and the four [above-mentioned] factors are complete, there will be orderly government.

22.8   Never has [a prince] who was unable to govern / his people well been able to strengthen his armed forces. However, even if he were able to

1b   govern them well, it still / would not do for him to lack understanding of the art of warfare. /

22.9   Never has [a prince] who was unable to strengthen his armed forces been able to achieve certain victory over enemy countries. However, even if he were able to strengthen his armed forces, he still would not be victorious should he lack understanding of the principles involved. /

22.10   Never has [a prince] whose armed forces were unable to achieve certain victory over enemy countries been able to bring order to the realm. However, even if his armed forces were certain of achieving

22.11   victory over enemy countries, / it still would not do for him to lack understanding of the different areas of concern involved in bringing order to the realm.

Therefore it is said that for assuring good government of the people there are weapons, for warfare there is an art, for achieving victory over enemy countries there are principles, and for bringing order to the realm there are different areas of concern.

23.12
2b11
22.12   THE SEVEN STANDARDS (*Qi Fa* 七法)[4]
1b7
Laws of nature (*ze* 則), physical qualities (*xiang* 象), standards for measurement (*fa* 法), forms of transformation (*hua* 化), permissive or inhibitory actions (*jue se* 決塞), patterns of mental behavior (*xin shu* 心術), and categories of mensuration (*ji shu* 計數)—[these constitute the seven standards].

What are rooted in the vital forces of Heaven and Earth, the harmonious balance between cold and heat, the properties of water and earth, the life of human beings, birds, animals, plants, and trees, and, which in

22.13   spite of the great variety[5] of things, / are inherent in all of them and never changing—these are called laws of nature.

Bearing, designation, position in time, similarity, classification, comparability, and shape are called physical qualities. /

22.14   The foot rule, marking line, compass and square, / beam and weight,

2a   peck and bushel, and grain leveler are called standards for measurement. /

23.1   Gradualness, compliance, friction, persistence, submissiveness, and repetitiveness are called forms of transformation. /

---

[4] The Yang edition for *Qi Fa* writes *Si Shang* 四傷, "The Four Harms."
[5] Deleting 不 [Xu].

23.2   Giving or taking away, endangering or making secure, benefiting or harming, encumbering or facilitating, opening or closing, and killing or permitting to live are called permissive or inhibitory actions. /

23.3   Being factual, sincere, liberal, generous, temperate, or altruistic are called patterns of mental behavior.

23.4   Consistency, weight, size, degree of solidity, distance, / and amount are called categories of mensuration.

Hoping to institute rules of behavior and formulate institutions[6] while remaining ignorant of the laws of nature is like trying to determine [the directions of] the sunrise and sunset / on a revolving potter's wheel[7]

23.5
23.6   or seeking to hold the tip steady while shaking[8] a rod. / Hoping to grade materials and investigate their usage while remaining ignorant of physical qualities would be like cutting off what is [naturally] long to make it short or stretching something that is [naturally] short to make it long.[9] Hoping to govern the people well and unite the masses while remaining ignorant of standards for measurement is like attempting to

23.7   write with the left hand / while holding it in check with the right.
2b

Hoping to change customs and alter teachings while remaining ignorant of forms of transformation is like bending wood for wheels in the

23.8   morning and expecting to ride in the [finished] chariot by night. / Hoping to exhort the masses and move the people while remaining ignorant of permissive or inhibitory actions is like trying to make water flow against the current. Hoping to have men carry out your orders while remaining ignorant of patterns of mental behavior is like turning one's back on a

23.9   target and being confident of hitting the mark.[10] / Hoping to initiate great undertakings while remaining ignorant of categories of mensuration is like expecting to navigate a river gorge without boat or oars.

Therefore it is said that it will not do [to attempt] to institute rules of behavior and formulate institutions while remaining ignorant of laws of

23.10   nature. / Nor will it do [to attempt] to grade materials or investigate their usage while remaining ignorant of physical qualities, [to attempt] to

---

[6] Emending 出號令, "to issue orders," to 錯儀畫制 in accordance with the summary passage, 2b6 (23.9) [Ding].

[7] This simile also appears in the *Mozi*, IX, 25/1b4–5 (Mei, *Motse*, pp. 182–83): "To expound doctrine without regard to the standard would be like determining [the direction of] sunrise and sunset on a revolving potter's wheel."

[8] Emending 檐 to 搢 = 搖 [Wang Yinzhi].

[9] This is reminiscent of a passage in the *Zhuangzi*, IV, 8/2b12ff. (Watson, *Chuang Tzu*, p. 100): "Even though the duck's legs are short, to stretch them would trouble him; even though the crane's legs are long, to cut them down would make him sad. What is long by nature needs no cutting down; what is short by nature needs no stretching."

[10] Reading 倍 as 背 and emending 拘 to 射 [Wang Yinzhi].

govern the people well[11] and unite the masses while remaining ignorant of standards for measurement, [to attempt] to change customs and alter teachings while remaining ignorant of forms of tranformation, [to attempt] to exhort the masses and move the people while remaining ignorant of permissive and inhibitory actions, / [to attempt] to proclaim orders and be confident they will be carried out while remaining ignorant of patterns of mental behavior, or [to attempt] to initiate undertakings and be confident of their completion while remaining ignorant of categories of mensuration.

THE FOUR HARMS AND ASSORTED HIDDEN EVILS[12]
(*Si Shang Bai Ni* 四傷百匿)

Assorted hidden evils are harmful to the majesty of the sovereign. Wicked functionaries are harmful to laws governing officials. Wicked / people are harmful to customary teachings. Robbers and brigands are harmful to the country's masses.

If the majesty[13] [of the sovereign] is harmed, / real authority will lie with his subordinate officials. If laws are harmed, goods will flow upward [in the form of bribes]. If the teachings are harmed, those who follow orders will fall into discord. If harm is done to the masses, the hundred surnames will not be secure in their places.

When real authority lies with subordinate officials, orders [from the sovereign] will not / be carried out. When goods flow upward, officials and their retainers become corrupt. When those who would carry out the orders fall into discord, the undertakings [of the sovereign] will not be successful. When the hundred surnames are not secure in their places, riffraff will settle down, / while people of substance scatter.

If riffraff settle down while people of substance scatter, the land will remain uncultivated. If it remains uncultivated, the six domestic animals will not / be raised. If they are not raised, the state will be impoverished, and its needs will not be sufficiently supplied. If the state is impoverished and its needs are not sufficiently supplied, its armed forces will be weak and its knights dispirited. Weak and dispirited, they will neither be victorious in attack nor firm in defense. / If they are neither victorious in attack nor firm in defense, then indeed the state will not be safe.

Therefore it is said that if [the sovereign] does not pay careful attention to his fundamental orders, hidden evils will prevail. If he does not

[11] Emending 和 to 治 in accordance with the preceding passage, 2a12 (23.6) [Dai and Tao].

[12] The Yang edition merely writes 百匿, "Assorted Hidden Evils."

[13] The Yang edition mistakenly writes 眾 for 威.

pay careful attention to his bestowal of offices and ranks, wicked functionaries will prevail. If he does not pay careful attention to tallies and records, / wicked people will prevail. If he does not pay careful attention to his penal laws, robbers and brigands will prevail. If these four constant guidelines for the state are undermined, and the prince is negligent,[14] there will danger. / If the prince is negligent, gentlemen who speak the truth will not come forward, and if they do not come forward, the true situation affecting the state will not be fully grasped on high.

Precious things[15] are what the ordinary ruler values [most]. / Relatives are what he holds [most] dear. People are what he [most] loves. Ranks and salaries are what he considers [most] important. But the enlightened[16] prince is different. What he values [most] are not precious things, what he holds [most] dear are not relatives, what he loves [most] / are not people, and what he considers [most] important are not ranks and salaries.

He[17] does not neglect his orders because precious things are considered [more] important. therefore it is said that orders are more to be valued than precious things. He does not endanger / the altars of Land and Grain because relatives are held [more] dear.[18] Therefore it is said that the altars of Land and Grain are to be considered dearer than relatives.[19] He does not twist the law because he loves his people [more]. Therefore it is said that laws are more to be loved than the people. / He does not share his majestic power because he considers ranks and salaries [more] important, and therefore it is said that the majesty [of the prince] is to be considered more important than ranks and salaries.

If [the prince] does not fully comprehend these four [principles], he will end up with nothing. / Therefore it is said that governing the people is like controlling a flood, nurturing them is like feeding the six domestic animals, and employing them is like making use of grass and trees. /

If the prince[20] himself studies the way [of orderly government] and acts on its principles, his numerous ministers will submit to his instruction, his various functionaries will be strict when deciding cases, and no one will dare pursue their self-interest in regard to them. / If he studies the achievements [of his officials], assesses their degree of service, and never neglects his laws, specious attendants, advisors, members of the

---

[14] Emending 見 to 則 [Wang Niansun].
[15] The Yang edition mistakenly writes 實 for 寶 [Igai, Dai, and Wang Niansun].
[16] Emending 亡 to 明 [Igai, Yasui, He Ruzhang, and Zhang Peilun].
[17] Deleting 故 [Zhang Peilun].
[18] Emending 愛親 to 親戚 [Ding and Xu].
[19] Emending 戚於親 to 親於戚 [Chen].
[20] Emending 身 to 君 [Ding].

great clans, high nobles, and great ministers will not be able to exaggerate their merit, and the distant, / lowly, and people who have not been
brought to the attention of the court will not have their service forgotten. Therefore those who are guilty will not resent the sovereign, nor will
those who receive[21] rewards harbor greedy hearts. Then knights drawn
up for battle will all / treat death lightly and remain calm in the face of
difficulties in seeking to accomplish the undertakings of [the prince].
These are the ultimate principles underlying [success in] warfare.

THE ART OF CONDUCTING WARFARE (*Wei Bing zhi Shu* 爲兵之數)

The art of conducting warfare consists in amassing material resources, examining [the skill of] artisans, / manufacturing weapons,
and selecting knights, issuing administrative instructions, training,
acquiring / a broad knowledge of the realm and an understanding of
strategy—all to an unrivaled degree. / Therefore, even before the armed
forces have crossed the borders, [the prince must be] unrivaled in these
eight respects. / For this reason, it is impossible for him to hope to bring
order to the realm if his material resources do not excel those of the rest
of the realm. It is [also] impossible even if he excels in material resources,
but fails to excel in [the skill of] his artisans, / or if he excels in [the skill]
of artisans, fails in weaponry. [Likewise] it is impossible even if he excels
in weaponry, but fails in [the quality of] his knights, / or if he excels in
[the quality of] his knights, fails in his instructions. It remains impossible even if he excels in his instructions, but fails to do so in
training, / or if he excels in training, but fails in terms of having a broad
knowledge of the realm, or excelling in terms of his broad knowledge,
fails in his understanding of strategy. /

Therefore understanding strategy is a powerful force / when using
one's armed forces. Most important is timing; of lesser importance are
tactics.

It is because of his correctness that the way of the king is not rejected
and no one throughout the realm dares encroach upon him. / Weighing
[everything] and storing it up [in his mind] is the guiding principle[22] of
the son of Heaven.[23] /

It is for this reason that when the weapons have been completed and
troops selected, the knights will know victory. / Having acquired a
broad knowledge of the realm and a mastery of strategy, [the prince] will
have freedom of action and be unrivaled [in battle]. Since he is free to

---

[21] Emending 愛 to 受 [Igai and Chen].

[22] Emending 禮 to 理 [Wen and Guo Moruo].

[23] As Dai points out, this paragraph does not fit the context of the passage in general and
is clearly an interpolation.

26.1 benefit those countries he likes or harm those he dislikes, his orders are carried out and his prohibitions observed. / It is because of this that the sage kings valued [freedom of action].

26.2 By vanquishing one [enemy, the prince] will cause a hundred to submit, and then the entire realm will fear him. By supporting a few [states], he will encourage[24] many, and then the entire realm will embrace him. / By punishing the guilty and rewarding the meritorious, he will then cause the entire realm to follow him.

26.3
5b Therefore he amasses the finest materials of the realm, and examines the sharp weapons of the artisans. During the spring and autumn / there are competitive trials in order to make a selection. The fine and sharp are given top rating. Finished weapons are not used until they have been examined and not stored until they have been tested.

26.4 Since he has collected the [most] heroic men of the entire realm and acquired [the services of] its / most valiant, when he sends them forth, it is like birds in flight. When he commits them to action, it is like thunder and lightning, and when he deploys them, it is like wind and rain. No one can stand before him; no one can harm him from the rear. He goes and comes freely without anyone daring to resist him.

6.5 To achieve success and establish / his undertakings, [the prince] must be in accord with correct principles[25] and righteous in conduct. Therefore, if he is not in accord with correct principles, he will not win over the entire realm. If his conduct is not righteous, he will not win over other men. Therefore, the prince who is worthy and wise is certain to occupy a victorious position and thus will set the realm in order without anyone daring to oppose[26] him.

ON SELECTING AND DEPLOYING [TROOPS] (*Xuan Chen* 選陳)

7.13
29
5.8
59 Now military units should be sent forth in a timely fashion with no lack of regard for the seasons of Heaven, and no lack of attention to[27] the benefits of Earth.[28] The numbers required must be derived from

9 detailed plans.[29] / Therefore the proper way of preparing for an attack is always to be certain that these detailed plans have been completed at home before troops are dispatched beyond the borders.

.10 If this has not been done / before troops are dispatched beyond the

---

[24] Reading 觀 as 勸 [Xu].

[25] Emending 禮 to 理 here and in the following sentence [Ding].

[26] Reading 御 as 禦 [Igai and Dai].

[27] Reading 壙 as 曠 [Igai, He Ruzhang, and Jiang].

[28] That is, the prince must pay attention to the needs of agriculture. It was for this reason that the appropriate season for conducting military campaigns was after the autumn harvest.

[29] Deleting 數 in accordance with a similar passage, X, 28/9a4–5 (2:22.7) [Ding].

133

26.11 borders, their battles will be self-defeating[30] and their attacks self-destructive. It is for this reason that if any one of these three occurs—an army is committed but unable to fight, a town is besieged but cannot / be taken by assault, territory is occupied but cannot be secured—it can lead to destruction.

26.12 Therefore, if there is no understanding of the enemy's administrative system, [armed force] cannot be applied. If there is no understanding of the enemy's / situation, no treaties[31] can be made. If there is no understanding of the enemy's generals, armies cannot be led against them. If there is no understanding of the enemy's knights, formations[32] cannot be led against them.

26.13 The reason for this is that / the many should be used to attack the few, the well organized to attack the disorganized, the well equipped to attack the poorly equipped, the able to attack the incompetent, well-instructed troops and trained knights to attack impressed hordes and untrained conscripts. As a result, in ten battles there will be ten victories;
26.14 in a hundred / battles, a hundred victories.

Therefore, if preparations for the venture have not been made and the armed forces lack a commander, the enemy[33] will not be known in time. If the countryside is left uncultivated and the land lacks civil functionaries, there will be no accumulated stores. If the officials lack
27.1 constant standards and those below come to resent the sovereign, / the weapons will not be well made. If the court does not have a [strong] government, rewards and punishments will not be clear. If they are not clear, the people will merely trust to luck for their livelihood.

27.2
6b
Now if the enemy is known in time,[34] one may move freely. / If stores are accumulated, there will be no shortages for a long time. If weapons are well made, they will not be worn out in the attack. If rewards and punishments are clear, men will not trust to luck [for their livelihood]. If they do not trust to luck, brave knights will be encouraged.[35] /

27.3 Therefore, in military affairs it is the duty of the military commander
27.4 to examine maps, consult with the court astronomer,[36] / estimate the

[30] Emending 勝 to 敗 [Ding and Zhang Peilun].

[31] The meaning of 約 here is not clear. I have followed Yasui. The members of the Jilin Institute would read it as "declarations of war."

[32] Following the Yang edition, which writes 陳 for 陣.

[33] Inserting 敵 after 知 in accordance with the following passage, 6a12 (27.1), and a similar passage in VI, 17/11b7 (1:79.12) [Igai, Ding, and Xu].

[34] Emending 如 to 則 in accordance with the passage in VI, 17, mentioned above [Ding].

[35] Emending 之 to 矣 [Wen].

[36] This phrase 謀十官, 日量蓄積, appears to be corrupt. I have followed He Ruzhang in emending it to 謀于日官, 量蓄積.

accumulated stores, organize the brave knights, acquire a broad knowledge of the realm, and determine strategy.

Since[37] he moves like the wind and rain, he will be able to consider no
road or village as being too far. Since he sallies forth like a bird in flight,
he will be able / to consider no mountain or river as being impassable.
Since he strikes like thunder and lightning, he will be able to move freely
and be unrivaled in battle. Since his effectiveness is like a flood or
drought [in its destructiveness], he will be able / to attack capital cities
and uproot[38] towns. Since his defenses are like metal walls, he will be
able to secure the ancestral temples and care for his men and women.
Since his rule is united as one body, he will be able to issue orders and
make his laws clear. /

He can move like the wind and rain because of his speed. He can
sally forth like a bird because of the lightness [of his equipment]. He can
strike like thunder and lightning because his knights and troops[39]
are well organized. His effectiveness is like a flood or drought in its
[destructiveness], / because [he causes the enemy's] uncultivated and
cultivated fields to be without harvests. / His defenses are like metal
walls because he uses his wealth to provide eyes and ears [to spy on the
enemy]. / His rule is united as one body because he banishes unorthodox
doctrines and prohibits extravagant customs.

Since he does not consider any road or village too far, he is able to
overawe the people of remote lands. Since he does not consider any
mountain or river impassable, / he is able to subjugate states that rely on
these for defense. Since he moves freely and is unrivaled in battle, his
orders are carried out and his prohibitions observed. Since[40] he can
attack capital cities and uproot towns and does not rely on powerful
allies, what he directs is certain to be obeyed. /

Only after [the prince] has secured his ancestral temples, cared for his
men and women, and no one in the entire realm can harm him, will he be
able to possess his state. Only after he has instituted rules and laws and
issued orders with no one failing to respond, will he be able to govern his
people well and unite the masses.

[37] Deleting the initial 故 [Zhang Wenhu].
[38] Emending 救, "save," to 拔 here and below, 7a5 (27.10) [Wen].
[39] Emending 不, "not," to 卒 [He and Xu].
[40] Deleting the initial 故 [Igai].

Ban Fa

版法

Ban Fa Jie

版法解

Introductory Comments

Ban fa is a short chapter that presents some basic guidelines for successful rule beginning with the need for the ruler to conform to the will of Heaven. It is distinguished by being one of the few chapters to have a separate *jie* or explanatory chapter providing a line-by-line exposition of the text.

The title, *Ban fa*, is difficult to translate. *Ban* probably refers to a tablet made of wood or bronze on which a document had been inscribed. *Fa* usually refers to laws, but in this chapter it primarily means a "model" or "guideline," or as a verb, "to model." The Yin commentary explains the title by saying that important political policies were inscribed on tablets in order to establish them as constant models.

The *Ban fa* text itself appears to be quite old, perhaps late fourth or early third century B.C. The language is terse, and there is extensive use of rhyme. The considerable emphasis in the text on the ruler extending his love to everyone and the specific use of the term *jian ai* 兼愛, often translated as "universal love," would seem to imply Mohist influence. However, the text is too short and too general in nature to support any conclusion in this regard.

The *Ban fa jie* or "Explanation of the *Ban fa*" is certainly Han or later. It interprets the *Ban fa* in terms of the naturalism and Legalistic Confucianism prevalent during the Han. See the Introduction and the Introductory Comments to I, 2, and XX, 64, for a discussion of these explanatory chapters. The *Jie* here consists of three distinct parts. The main part (XXI, 66 / 3a8–7b12; 3 : 48.11–49.3) provides a line-by-line explanation of the text of the *Ban fa*; the last two parts, which I have referred to as "Addendum I" (8a1–6; 50.8–10) and "Addendum II" (8a7–8b3; 50.11–51.1), are of a summary nature. "Addendum I," which appears to cite the *Shiji* (1/17b10–18a3), has little to do with the *Ban fa*

136

text itself. Igai and Ding Shihan feel that it as well as "Addendum II" represent misplaced slips from one of the lost chapters. However, the style of both addenda is close to that of the rest of the *Ban fa jie*, and "Addendum II" does comment on the content of the *Ban fa* text (8a12–8b1; 28.14), using the technique of an imaginary conversation between Duke Huan and Guanzi.

It should be noted that the explanatory passages usually conclude by repeating the text of the *Ban fa* following the words, "Therefore [the *Ban fa*] says." Unless these summary statements are an inherent part of the explanation or required for clarification, I have deleted them from the translation in order to avoid unnecessary repetition.

Translation

1:28.2
7/7a12

[BF] Whenever [the prince] is about to initiate affairs of state, he should make them conform to the will[1] of Heaven.

3:46.2
56/3a9

[BFJ] In order to provide for the proper administration of the realm, laws[2] are modeled after the positions of Heaven and Earth and imitate the movements of the four seasons. The movements of the four seasons [have their times for creating life and causing death][3] and bringing cold and heat. Since the sage takes them as his model, he assumes civil and military functions.

46.3

The positions of Heaven and Earth / include front, back, left, and right. The sage takes them as his model in order to establish standards and rules. [As the prince sits on the throne facing south], spring brings life on his left, fall brings death on his right, summer brings growing before him, and winter brings storing to his rear.[4] Matters related to creating life and growing / are civil matters. Matters related to gathering and storing are military functions. For this reason, civil matters are treated on the left and military matters on the right.

6.4

b

The sage [follows this pattern] as his model / when executing his laws and orders and when administering affairs and the principles [of government]. He who executes laws and administers affairs / must be correct in

6.5

---

[1] Reading 植 as 志 [Xu].

[2] Deleting 版 as an interpolation taken from the title [Wang Niansun]. The *Beitang shu chao*, 43/1a6–7, and the *Taiping yulan*, 638/3b5, cite this passage omitting this character.

[3] Inserting 有生有殺 before 有寒有暑 to accord with what follows [Tao].

[4] These direction front and back, left and right, assume the ruler is sitting on the throne facing south. Thus spring, equated with his left and east, brings life. Fall, equated with right and west, brings the killing of animals in the hunt as well as the execution of prisoners and captives. Summer, equated with the south and lying before him, brings growth. Winter, equated with the north and lying behind him, brings the storing of food.

his grasp of them. Otherwise, he will not be just in his administration. If he is unjust, neither will his administration fully adhere to the principles [of government] nor will his management of affairs fully fit the true situation. If his administration does not fully adhere to the principles [of government], the distant and humble will have no / way to voice their complaints. If his management of affairs does not fully fit the true situation, what is beneficial will not be promoted. If what is beneficial is not promoted, his country will become impoverished. If the distant and humble have no way to voice their complaints, his subordinate officials will cause trouble.[5] Therefore [the *Ban fa*] says: "Whenever [the prince] is / about to initiate affairs of state, he should make them conform to the will of Heaven."

The will of Heaven is its mind. When [the prince] conforms to Heaven's will, he neither bestows personal favoritism on those who are close to him nor treats with disdain those who are far removed. Since he does neither of these things, he never neglects what is beneficial nor conducts his administration in secret. / Since he does neither of these things, affairs of state are always presented properly and nothing is neglected.

[*BF*] The wind and rain turn their backs on no one.[6] The distant and near, high and low, all are sustained by them.[7]

[*BFJ*] If one wishes to observe the mind of Heaven, it manifests itself in the wind and rain.

[*BF*] The three standards[8] being set, the prince may then possess his state.

[*BFJ*] All things revere Heaven and esteem the wind and rain. The reason for revering Heaven is that everything receives its life from it. The reason for esteeming the wind and rain is that everything waits upon them to be moved / and watered. If without Heaven, all things still received life, or without the wind and rain, they still were moved and watered, there would be no reason to revere Heaven / or esteem the wind and rain.

Now, the reason the prince of men is revered and secure is that his

---

[5] The Yang edition mistakenly writes 饒 for 饒 = 擾 [Jin].

[6] Guo Moruo would emend 違 (*gjwêr*) to 慝 (*t'nêk*) to complete the rhyme with 事 (*dziêg*) and 植 (*diêg* or *djiêk*)above and 飭 (*t'iêk*) below. Thus, "The wind and rain are false to no one."

[7] Yu Xingwu would read 嗣 as 嗣 = 治. Thus, "all are controlled by them."

[8] There is some debate as to the meaning of "the three standards," 三經. The *BFJ* takes them as: the will of Heaven, wind and rain, and high and low. Guo Moruo takes them as: the will of Heaven, benefits of the Earth, and harmony among men.

majestic position has been established and his orders are carried out. The reason he is able to establish his majestic position and have his orders carried out is that control of the benefits associated with his majestic position lies / with none other than the prince alone. If such control does not lie with the prince alone, but is shared with others, the prince will be treated more lightly day by day, and day by day the benefits associated with his majestic position will decline. Such is the way to usurpation and violence.

[*BF*] When pleased, do not respond with rewards. When angered do not respond with killing.[9] / If [the prince] responds to being pleased or angered with rewards or killing, resentments will arise and orders will be disregarded. If he capriciously issues orders and[10] they are not carried out, the hearts of the people will turn to outsiders. When outsiders develop a following, disasters will begin to sprout.[11] / [However], if only a few things[12] anger the masses, [outsiders] will not be able to hatch their schemes.

[*BFJ*] If [the prince] takes advantage of summer to make things grow, is judicious in administering punishments and rewards, makes certain that his standards and rules are clear, displays righteousness in creating laws, decides matters in accordance with principles, is calm in spirit and peaceful in mind, he will rid himself of being angered or pleased. If, [however], he responds to being angered or pleased by repudiating his laws and discarding his orders, / disaster and turmoil will ensure, and his high position will be endangered.

[*BF*] When promoting what he considers good, [the prince] should be certain to examine the end results. / When rejecting what he dislikes, he should be certain to count the cost.

[*BFJ*] When winter arrives, storehouses are closed, and all business comes to a halt. Past business is finished, and future business has yet to begin. It being winter with no business, [the prince] carefully considers the end results and beginnings of things, and judiciously examines affairs and the principles [of government]. There are undertakings that at first appear easy, but later proved difficult, / as well as those that are not examined sufficiently in the beginning so in the end they were not completed. This is why their long-term benefits do not materialize and is

[9]A similar statement appears in the *Deng Xizi*, 1/2b1–2, but 殺 is written 罰, "punishing."
[10]Following the Ancient, Zhu, and Liu editions, which write 而 above 不 [Guo Moruo].
[11]Reading 牙 as 芽 [Igai, Yasui, and Wen].
[12]Emending 置 to 寡 in accordance with the *BFJ* [Liu Ji].

the reason for their difficulty. When undertakings at first appear easy, men attach little importance to carrying them out. If they attach little importance to carrying them out, / there will certainly be difficulties. When undertakings that are difficult to complete are not examined sufficiently in the beginning, men attach little importance to expediting them. If men attach little importance to expediting them, there will certainly be failures from insufficient effort. Now, having numerous undertakings that are difficult to complete, / and frequent failures from insufficient effort is the way to decline and ruin.

For this reason the enlightened prince judiciously examines the affairs and principles [of government] and carefully considers the end results and the beginnings of things. When undertaking something, he must be certain to know that it will be completed, when completed, what its use will be, / and when used whether it will be beneficial or not. When undertaking something, if he does not know [these things], he is said to be foolish in the promotion of affairs. Those who are foolish in promoting affairs will not have them completed and their / efforts will not stand.

[*BF*] [The prince] should commend and encourage those he respects to give them prominence. He should provide wealth / and salaries to those who have merit to urge them on, and award ranks and honors to those who have achieved fame to bring them good fortune.

[*BFJ*] The prince of men always desires his people to exhibit propriety and righteousness. Now, if the people lack propriety and righteousness, there will be turmoil above and below, and conflict between the honored and the humble.

[*BF*] Spreading love universally (*jian ai*) and neglecting no one, this[13] is called being of a princely mind. [The prince] should first be certain to provide instruction,[14] and then the myriads of people / will respond as if bending before the wind. If morning and evening he benefits them, the masses / will perform their tasks well.

[*BFJ*] The prince of men always desires the masses to feel attached to their ruler and respond to his wishes. He desires them to perform their tasks well when pursuing his affairs. However, if the masses do not love him, they will not feel attached to him. If they do not feel attached to him, [his instructions] will not be clearly apprehended.[15] If he does not instruct them, / they will not respond to his wishes. For this reason, the

---

[13] The Yang edition mistakenly omits 是.
[14] Inverting the two characters 順教 [Liu Shipei].
[15] This sentence appears out of context and probably should be deleted [Liu Ji, Chen Huan, and Yu Yue].

enlightened prince spreads his love everywhere so [the people] will feel attached to him. In order to lead them, he makes his instructions clear, and in order to benefit them, he is relaxed in exercising his authority, facilitates their [obtaining] what they need, and is solicitous about expending their strength so as not to deprive them of time [to make a living]. This being so, / the masses feel attached to their sovereign, respond to his wishes, and perform their tasks well when pursuing his affairs.

[*BF*] [The prince] should select men on the basis of his own character[16] and dispose of affairs on the basis / of their substance.

[*BFJ*] The basis of good government is twofold: one is called men, the other is called affairs. In regard to men, [the prince] desires to be certain of employing them. In regard to affairs, he desires to be certain of good results. Among men there are those who resist and those who comply. For affairs there are proper calculations. Men cannot be employed if their minds resist. The results will not be good if [the prince] fails to make proper calculations in regard to affairs. / If the results are not good, it will be harmful. If men are not properly employed, it causes resentments.

[*BF*] [The prince] should be judicious when expending resources and the strength[17] [of the people], careful when distributing rewards, and meticulous when making calculations. Therefore, when expending resources, he must not / be miserly; when expending the strength [of his people], he must not be overly demanding. If he is miserly when expending resources, it leads to waste.[18] If he is overly demanding, when expending the strength [of the people], it leads to their being overworked.

[*BFJ*] Those who dispose of affairs on the basis of their substance utilize proper calculations. Those who select men on the basis of / their own character take action after assessing [men] according to the principle of reciprocity. Those who assess [men] according the principle of reciprocity assess others on the basis of their own character. What they do not feel comfortable about themselves, they do not inflict on others.

---

[16]This statement is similar to the *Zhong yong*, 20/4: 故爲政在人，取人以身，脩身以道，脩道以仁, "Therefore the administration of government lies in [selecting the right] men, such men being selected on the basis of [the ruler's] own character. He cultivates his character in accordance with the moral way, and cultivates the moral way on the basis of innate human goodness."

[17]Inserting 力 to accord with the content of the text below [Ding].

[18]Liu Shipei would read 費 as 拂, "opposition," to better accord with the *BFJ*.

1:28.10
7/8a5
28.11

[BF] If the people lack sufficiency, [the prince's] orders will be scorned. If the people suffer hardships, / his orders will not be carried out. If he distributes rewards in an inappropriate manner, misfortunes will begin to abound. If misfortunes abound without [the prince] becoming aware of them, the people will seek their own devices.

3:48.3
66/5b1

[BFJ] How do we know this is so? If [the prince] is too demanding in expending the strength [of the people], undertakings will not produce / good results. Should his undertakings lack good results, they will have to be done over many times. Therefore, this is said to be overworking [the people].[19] If, in expending resources, he is too miserly, he will not command the hearts of the people. Should he not command the hearts of the people, resentments will arise. Since he is expending resources while creating resentments, it is therefore said to be wasteful. If resentments arise with no relief, / and the masses are overworked with no respite, they will certainly have hearts [bent on] destruction and ruin.

48.4

48.5

1:28.11
7/8a7

[BF] If [the prince] rectifies the laws and straightens out the regulations, there will be no [need to] pardon the execution of criminals. / When the people definitely believe the [threat of] executions, they will tremble in fear. Since [the prince's] military might will be clear, his orders will need no repeating before they are carried out.

28.12

3:48.7
66/5b8

[BFJ] Whenever a state lacks laws, the masses do not know what to do. If it lacks regulations, affairs will not accord with the rules of social behavior.[20] If there are laws but they are not correct, and if there are regulations but they are not set straight, the administration will be perverse. Should the administration be perverse, the state will be in turmoil.

1:28.12
7/8a8
28.13

[BF] [The prince] should treat harshly those who are remiss and lazy so as to shame them. / He should punish those who commit crimes and make[21] mistakes so as to discipline them, and execute those who violate the prohibitions so as to terrify[22] [would-be violators].

3:48.9
66/5b12

[BFJ] Among the people, there is no one who does not hate punishment and fear committing a crime. For this reason, the prince sternly instructs them to keep them informed / and clarifies his punishments to admonish[23] them.

6a

---

[19] Deleting 矣 [Tao].
[20] Emending 機 to 儀 [Sun Xingyan and Hong].
[21] Emending 宥 to 有 to accord with the BFJ [Igai, Wang Niansun, Song, and Yasui].
[22] Reading 振 as 震 [Wen].
[23] Emending 致 to 敬 = 儆 [Guo Moruo].

[*BF*] If [the prince] is firm and unshakable, those whose behavior is strange[24] or depraved will be fearful. / When strange behavior is eliminated and depravity reformed, the orders will hardly have gone out before the people move.

[*BFJ*] There are three instruments for maintaining the state in good order and six attacks that will reduce the state to turmoil.[25] Since [26] the enlightened prince is able to overcome the six attacks and establish the three instruments, his state is well ordered. Since the incompetent prince is unable to overcome the six attacks and establish the three instruments, / his state is in disorder.

What are the three instruments? The answer is: commands and orders, battle-axes and halberds, salaries and rewards. What are the six attacks? The answer is:[27] having favorites, the awarding of honors, the acceptance of bribes, beautiful women, clever sycophants, and indulgence in pleasure. /

What about using the three instruments? The answer is: Were it not for commands and orders, there would be no means to employ one's subordinate officials. Were it not for battle-axes and halberds, there would be no means to instill fear among the masses. Were it not for salaries and rewards, there would be no means to encourage the people. What are the failures brought on by the six attacks? The answer is: / There will be those who even though disobedient, can still survive, who even though violating the prohibitions, can still escape [punishment], and who even though lacking merit, can still become rich.

Now, if a state contains those who are disobedient and yet able to survive, the commands and orders will not be / sufficient to employ subordinate officials. If it contains those who violate the prohibitions yet are able to escape [punishment], battle-axes and halberds will not be sufficient to instill fear in the masses. If it contains those who have no merit yet are able to become rich, salaries and rewards will not be sufficient to encourage / the people.

If commands and orders are not sufficient / to employ his subordinate officials, battle-axes and halberds are not sufficient to instill fear in the

[24] Reading 倚 as 奇 [Igai and Wang Niansun].

[25] A more developed version of this section dealing with the three instruments (*san qi* 三器) and six attacks (*liu gong* 六攻) appears in the *Zhong ling* chapter (V, 15/13b8–14a10; 1:69.5–12) of the *Guanzi*. Guo Moruo concludes (*Guanzi*, I, p. 230) that both the *Zhong ling* and the *BFJ* were written by the same person, but he gives no evidence to show that this version was not simply adapted by its author from the *Zhong ling* text. The *Zhong ling* was most likely available to him along with other sections of the *Guanzi*.

[26] Emending 則 to 故 in accordance with the *Qunshu zhiyao* and the following line [Wang Niansun].

[27] Inserting 曰 in accordance with the *Qunshu zhiyao* [Wang Niansun].

masses, and salaries and rewards are not sufficient to encourage the people, the prince of men will have no means to defend himself. In such a case, what can the enlightened prince do? The enlightened / prince does not, because of the six attacks, alter his commands and orders, create doubts about [the certainty of his] using battle-axes and halberds, or tamper with salaries and rewards.

[*BF*] [The prince] should model himself on Heaven by extending his benevolence to all in common. He should imitate the Earth[28] by being / impartial.

[*BFJ*] The prince of men [like Heaven] always covers and supports the myriads of people so they will completely belong to him. He shines down on the myriads of clans so they will serve him. For this reason, Heaven and Earth, the sun and moon, and the four seasons are taken as the master and the substance when administering the realm. / Nothing lies beyond Heaven's cover; its benevolence extends everywhere. Nothing is rejected by the Earth's support; it is steadfast and unshakable. Therefore there is nothing that does not enjoy birth and growth. The sage takes them as his model in covering and supporting the myriads of people. / Therefore there is no one who does not have a constant livelihood.[29] Since they have a constant livelihood, there is no one who cannot be employed.

[*BF*] [The prince] should make himself form a trinity with the sun and moon and a quintuplet[30] with the four seasons.

[*BFJ*] There is no self-interest in the brilliance of the sun and moon. Therefore no one fails to obtain its light. / The sage takes them as a model in shining down on the myriads of people. Therefore, since he is able to look into [everything], there is no ignoring of good conduct nor concealing of licentiousness. Since there is no ignoring of good conduct nor concealing of licentiousness, [people] believe punishments and rewards to be certain. Since there is faith in the certainty of reward or punishment, good conduct is encouraged / and licentiousness brought to a halt. Therefore [the *Ban fa*] says: "[The prince] should make himself form a trinity with the sun and moon."

Since [people] believe that the movements of the four seasons are certain and that they will be manifested clearly, the sage takes them as a model to employ the myriads of people. Consequently they do not

[28] The Zhao edition mistakenly writes 法 for 地.

[29] Reading 職姓 as 常生 [Guo Moruo].

[30] Emending 佐 to 伍 to accord with the *BFJ* and the Ancient, Liu, and Zhu editions [Igai, Wang Niansun, and Yasui].

neglect their seasonal work. Therefore [the *Ban fa*] says: "[The prince] should form a quintuplet with the four seasons."

[*BF*] The four[31] happinesses lie in bestowing love; possessing the masses lies in getting rid of self-interest.

[*BFJ*] Whenever [the prince] loves the masses, they feel attached to him. For this reason, the enlightened prince creates benefits to bring this about. He makes clear his love so they will feel attached to him. If he only bestows benefits on them, but does not love them, the masses will gather around, but not feel attached to him. If he only / loves them, but does not benefit them, the masses will feel attachment but not congregate around him. When love and benefits[32] are applied, there will be happiness between the prince and his ministers, friends, elder and younger brothers, and fathers and sons. [The attachment] created by the bestowal of love cannot be maintained [even by] having four firm [boundaries]. Therefore / [the *Ban fa*] says: "The four[33] happinesses lie in bestowing love."

Whenever / the prince possesses the masses, it is because of the beneficent power of his love. However, if love has been undermined[34] and benefits have been concentrated [on a few], it becomes impossible to possess [the masses] fully. Therefore [the *Ban fa*] says: "Possessing the masses lies in getting rid of self-interest."

[*BF*] [The prince] should summon the distant to cultivate the near.

[*BFJ*] Even though the beneficent power of love is applied and there is no self-interest, if there is no cultivation [of right conduct] within the country, [the prince] will not be able to face distant princes. For this reason, he conforms to the right conduct between prince and minister, and fosters right conduct between fathers and sons, elder and younger brothers, and husbands and wives. / He fosters the separation of men and women, differentiates the ranks of those from near and far, and sees to it that the benevolence of the prince, the loyalty of ministers, the compassion of fathers, the filial piety of sons, / the love of elder brothers, the respect of younger brothers, and the rules of propriety and right

[31] The line 悦在施有，聚在廢私, is clearly corrupt. I have followed Zang Yong's reconstruction based on Song notes and the *BFJ* emending it to read: 四悦在愛施，有聚在廢私. Guo Moruo would emend it to read: 聚悦在施齐(齊)，齐聚在廢私. Thus, "Happiness for the masses lies in the [prince] being equitable in what he bestows on them. Being equitable toward the masses lies in getting rid of self-interest." Guo believes 四 is a mistake for 聚, and 有 for 齐. he would emend the *BFJ* accordingly.

[32] Emending 施 to 利 [Ding].

[33] The Zhao edition mistakenly omits 四.

[34] Igai would emend 移 to 私. Thus, "If love involves self-interest, and benefits are concentrated [on a few] . . . ."

145

conduct are manifested. This being so, those who are near feel attached
to him, while those far away / come to him.

[*BF*] Closing the door on disaster lies in eliminating resentments.

[*BFJ*] "Closing the door on disaster lies in eliminating resentments"
does not mean having resentments and then eliminating them. Where
[closing the door] is practiced, there never are resentments. Disaster and
turmoil always stem from / resentment and blame. Resentment and
blame stem from unprincipled [action]. For this reason, the enlightened
prince must adhere to constant standards when dealing with the masses,
accord with the moral way when employing them, be appropriate when
issuing rewards, be to the point when making pronouncements, and
adhere to principles when imposing punishments. If he does this, the
masses will not have grieved and resentful hearts nor vexed and hateful
thoughts. / This being so, disaster and turmoil will not arise, and the
position of the ruler will not be endangered.

[*BF*] Preparation[35] for the future lies in employing the worthy.

[*BFJ*] It is always because of worthy assistants that the prince of men
is revered and made safe. If his assistants are worthy, the prince will be
revered, the state will be safe, and the people will be well ordered.
Lacking such assistants, the prince will be treated with contempt, the
state will be endangered, and the people will be in turmoil.

[*BF*] Ensuring the safety of persons on high[36] lies in spreading benefits throughout [the realm].

[*BFJ*] There is no one who does not desire benefit and hate injury. For
this reason, those who spread benefits throughout the realm are supported by it. Those who monopolize benefits for themselves are plotted
against. Those whom the realm plots against are certain to be
overthrown / even though their positions are well established. Those
whom the realm supports will not be endangered even though their
positions are high.

[Addendum I]

Shun 舜 is always taken as the example of being able to benefit others
with what does not benefit oneself. Shun tilled Mount Li,[37] fashioned

---

[35] Reading 修 as 備 to accord with the *BFJ*.

[36] The Zhao edition for 安高 mistakenly writes 高安.

[37] 歷山; located northeast of Jinan 濟南 in northeastern Shandong Province. This
description of the activities of the legendary Emperor Shun accords with the *Shi ji*,
17b10–18a3 (Chavannes, *Mémoires historiques*, I, p. 72). According to the *Shang shu*, II,
2/3, 21: "When [Shun] was living by Mount Li, he went into the fields and daily cried with
tears to compassionate Heaven and to his parents, talking to himself and bearing all guilt
and evil."

50.2

1:29.2
7/8b3
3:50.2
66/7b2

50.3

50.4

1:29.2
7/8b3
3:50.5
66/7b8

1:29.2
7/8b3

3:50.6
66/7b10

50.7

3:50.8
66/8a1

banks of clay for the Yellow River, and fished the Lei Marsh,[38] not for his own benefit, but to instruct the hundred surnames. They [in turn] benefited him. / This is what is referred to as being able to benefit others with what does not benefit oneself.

King Wu is always taken as the example of being able to give to others what oneself does not possess. When King Wu attacked Zhou,[39] the troops who went along obtained titles / to fiefs, and on the day he entered Yin, he distributed the grain in the Juqiao 鉅橋 Granary and disbursed the money in the Deer Pavilion 鹿臺.[40] The people of Yin were greatly pleased. This is what is referred to as giving to others what oneself does not possess.

[Addendum II]

Duke Huan spoke to Guanzi: "Now you have instructed me to model myself on Heaven and extend my benevolence to all in common[41] and have told me that if I extend this power to all in common for a long time so that it covers everyone, all [living] things will be content with their fate. [You also instructed me to] imitate Earth by being impartial,[42] and said that if I am steadfast in being impartial / so as to support everyone, all living things will enjoy birth and growth. [You instructed me to] form a trinity with the sun and moon,[43] and said that if my lack of self-interest radiates from within and shines on everyone, neither goodness nor evil will be concealed. According to this then, what makes a man of quality / is having no likes or dislikes. Is this all there is to it?"

Guanzi replied: "No, it is not. Now, learning is the means to reform and nurture oneself. Therefore a man of quality hates praise for the wickedness of others. He hates disloyalty, / which engenders resentment and envy. He hates having no public criticism but only constant[44] acclaim. He hates unwillingness to accept lower ranks, but only those that are high. He hates unwillingness to associate with those from abroad so those within [the inner circle] can do as they please. These five things are what a man of quality fears. They are the reasons for the demise of petty men, / and how much more so with the prince of men."

---

[38] 雷澤; located near Pucheng 濮城 on the border of Shandong and Henan.

[39] 紂; the last king of the Shang dynasty whose capital was known as Yin 殷.

[40] The *Shang shu*, V, 3/9, records these events inverting the last two phrases and for 決, "distributed," writes 發, "issued," and for 錢, "money," writes 財, "wealth." The *Shi ji*, 4/9b13–10a1, accords with the *Shang shu*, but 32/3a3 and 55/5b8–9 both write 錢.

[41] See II, 7/8a12 (1:28.14).

[42] Ibid.

[43] See II, 7/8b1 (1:29.1).

[44] The Yang edition mistakenly writes 當 for 常 [Yasui and Guo Moruo].

You Guan
幼官

Introductory Comments

The *You guan* is basically a Five Phases calendar supplemented by an essay on political and military strategy that has been cut up and rearranged under the seasonal divisions of the calendar. The five divisions have been correlated with the four directions and the center, so that when the different sections of the text are laid out geographically on paper they form a pattern reminiscent of a Yin-Yang and Five Phases numerology chart. The following chapter, III, 9, *You guan tu* 幼官圖, is identical in content except for a rearrangement of the various sections of the text.[1]

MEANING OF TITLE

The title itself presents a difficult problem. *You guan*, which literally means "The Office in Charge of Youth," has nothing to do with the content of the text that follows and therefore appears suspect. Igai Hikohiro reads *you* 幼 as *yao* 窈, rendering the title as "The Office in Charge of Esoteric Affairs." Shi Yi-shen reads *you* as *wu* 五 because the two characters appear somewhat similar in form in the seal script. Thus the title would be translated as "Five Offices" and, according to Shi, would refer to the duties associated with the four seasons and the center.[2]

However, most commentators, including He Ruzhang, Wen Yiduo, and Guo Moruo, interpret it differently. They would emend *you* to *xuan*

---

[1] It is the consensus of the Chinese commentators that the original *You guan tu* was lost and later replaced by a different arrangement of the *You guan*.

[2] Shi Yishen, *Guanzi jinquan*, p. 263. The *Zuo zhuan* under the year 513 B.C. (Zhao, 29; Legge, *Ch'un Ts'eu*, X, 29/4) speaks of the officers of the Five Phases who were known as the "Five Officers" (*wu guan* 五官). It goes on to say that these officers "received their several clan and family names and were enfeoffed as dukes of the first rank. They were sacrificed to as exalted deities, and at the altars of Land and Grain and in the five sacrifices they were honored and served. The Master of Wood was Goumang, the Master of Fire was Zhurong, the Master of Metal was Rushou, the Master of Water was Xuanming, and the Master of Earth was Houtu." This material is undoubtedly much later in origin than the 513 B.C. date assigned to it, since Five Phase theories did not really develop until the end of the fourth and beginning of the third centuries B.C. The *Zuo zhuan* itself is generally considered to have been composed in about 300 B.C. These officers also appear as the guardian spirits associated with the seasons in the *LSCQ* and the *Yue ling* 月令 [Monthly Ordinances] chapter of the *Li ji*, which will be discussed in detail below.

玄 and *guan* to *gong* 宫,[3] so the title would read *Xuan gong*, "Dark Palace," a term that appears frequently in Chou literature. According to the *Mozi*, V, 19/8a8 (Mei, *Motse*, p. 111): "Gao Yang then gave orders [to Yu] in the Dark Palace."[4] The *Zhuangzi*, III, 6/6a11 (Watson, *Chuang Tzu*, p. 82), says: "Zhuan Xu adhered to [the Way] and dwelled in the Dark Palace." The *Lüshi chunqiu*, X, 1/1b (Wilhelm, *Frühling und Herbst*, p. 117), refers to a Xuan Tang 玄堂 or "Dark Hall," which the commentator Gao You 高誘 (fl. A.D. 205) describes as the northern hall of the Ming Tang 明堂 or "Bright Hall," the palace where the emperor was supposed to have offered sacrifices and held audiences for the feudal princes.[5]

Traditionally the Ming Tang consisted of a nine-part square with five main halls located on the east, south, west, north, and center, and side halls on the four corners. The ruler was supposed to shift from one hall to another in a clockwise direction according to the seasons, beginning with the eastern hall in the spring. Thus the Ming Tang is connected with such seasonal calendars as are presented in this chapter.

It is also possible that this chapter had an alternative title, *Shi ling* 時令 [Seasonal Ordinances]. The *Zhou li zhusu*, 14/10a, compiled by Jia Gongyan 賈公彦 (fl. A.D. 650–655), refers to a *Shi ling* chapter of the *Guanzi* and cites a short passage from it. The *Guanzi* as we have it today contains no chapter by that name, but the passage cited seems to be a paraphrase of a section in the *You guan*, and contains one phrase (2b10; 30.13) that is identical, 合男女.

Since another famous calendar, the *Yue ling*, is also known as the *Ming Tang yue ling* 明堂月令 [Monthly Ordinances of the Bright Hall],[6] by analogy, the full title of this chapter actually might have been *Xuan Gong shi ling* 玄宫時令 [Seasonal Ordinances of the Dark Palace].

BACKGROUND OF CALENDAR IN *You guan*

In predominantly agrarian societies, the relationship between man and the forces of nature is bound to play an important part in the thinking of its people. This was particularly true of China, where we find

---

[3] In Zhou bronze inscriptions, the two characters *you* and *xuan* are often written in a similar manner [Wen and Guo]. *Guan* and *gong* are also often mistakenly written for each other in this text.

[4] The *SBBY* edition for *xuan* writes *yuan* 元, a substitute character for *xuan* that was under taboo during the Qing dynasty because it appeared in the name of Kangxi.

[5] Gao's comment appears in the *LSCQ*, I, 1/1b5–8. For a detailed study of the Ming Tang, see Maspero, "Le Ming T'ang et la crise religieuse chinoise avant les Han"; and Soothill, *The Hall of Light*.

[6] Cf. Cai Yong 蔡邕 (133–192), *Ming Tang yue ling lun* 論.

at an early date agricultural calendars that listed the fluctuating natural phenomena of the seasons and the activities in which men should then be engaged. As time went on, these calendars became closely associated with the theory of Five Phases (earth, wood, metal, fire, and water), which had assumed a major role in the cosmological outlook of the Chinese.[7] The Chinese attempt to correlate the Five Phases with the four seasons of the year presented definite problems. The *Yue ling* 月令, which in its present form dates from about 240 B.C., sought to solve these problems by creating a special center season for earth. It was placed at the end of summer, but had no time allotted to it in terms of actual days.[8]

Later on, in the *Shi ze xun* 時則訓 [Teachings on the Rules for the Seasons], which makes up chapter 5 of the *Huainanzi*, compiled about 122 B.C., we find that the third month of summer has been assigned to a center season. It was unnatural, however, to solve the problem in this way, since it not only violated the traditional calendrical scheme but also disrupted the mathematical harmony of four seasons of three months each.[9]

Another approach was to construct a chart with earth forming a square in the center and the four seasons arranged around it. The east was equated with spring, the south with summer, the west with autumn, and the north with winter. This accorded with the popular concept 天圓地方, "Heaven round, Earth square," and made it possible for the relationship between the center and earth, with the other seasons and phases to be shown clearly without upsetting the normal calendrical order. According to this theory, the phase earth, as the central phase, was not correlated with any specific portion of the year, but was believed to operate throughout all four seasons of the year equally.

[7] It is not known just when the concept of the Five Phases originated, but the earliest literary reference appears to be in the *Hong fan* 洪範 or "Grand Norm" chapter of the *Shang shu*, V, 4/5. (Unfortunately there is considerable doubt concerning the dating of the *Hong fan*. Most modern scholars consider it to be at least post-Confucius if not much later.) The earliest archaeological evidence appears to be an inscription on a jade sword handle that is thought to have come from the state of Qi not long after 400 B.C. (See Chen Mengjia, *Wuxing zhi qiyuan*, p. 35.) It was under Zou Yan 騶衍, a Jixia 稷下 Academy philosopher who became famous some time after Mencius (371–289 B.C.), that Five Phases ideas developed into the complex cosmological theory that later, along with the concept of Yin-Yang, provided the perspective for Chinese naturalistic thought.

[8] Since the four regular seasons continued to have their usual full three lunar months, Legge believed that the arrangement for the center season probably represented a later insertion into an earlier calendar. See Legge, *The Li Ki*, XXVII, p. 281.

[9] Actually, because of the disparity between the lunar and solar cycles, a thirteenth month had to be added every so often to bring the two calendars back into reasonable accord, but this is not taken into account in seasonal calendars such as the *Yue ling*.

CHART 3. *Guanzi*, III, 8, Xuan Gong Chart

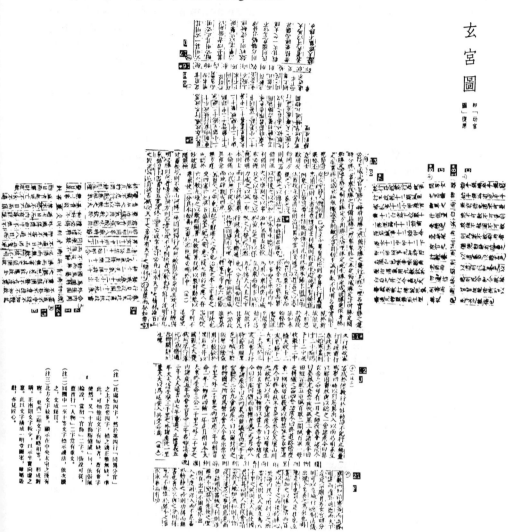

It is apparent that the *Guanzi* text was intended to form the content of such a calendar chart. Each section is accompanied by a brief notation assigning it to a specific geographical section. On the basis of these notations, Wang Tingfang 王廷芳 and Guo Moruo[10] have produced a reconstruction of the original chart, a photographic reproduction of which (chart 3) accompanies this text.

It would have been impossible to construct such a complicated chart on the usual narrow bamboo slips; only a relatively large area such as that provided by a silk scroll, tablet of wood or stone, or perhaps a bronze vessel would have sufficed.[11] Later, however, for convenience, the text must have been copied on bamboo slips in regular literary form. This may have been accompanied by a small outline of the chart showing the various geographical sections, or perhaps, because of its size, the chart was not reproduced at all.[12]

The presentation of the text in standard literary form automatically established a specific order in which these sections had to be read, something the original chart did not necessarily do. It is therefore not surprising that there should be some disagreement on the proper sequence of sections and that this should, in turn, give rise to different arrangements of the text. Thus, even though the overall content remains the same, there is not only a different arrangement of the various sections as they appear in the two chapters, III, 8, and III, 9, but also as they appear in the Yang and Zhao versions of III, 9.[13] (See chart 4.)

A brief glance at this list of sections immediately gives rise to the question: If the chart maker's intention was merely to show the relation-

[10] *Guanzi jijiao*, I, facing p. 140.

[11] The original form of the chart may well have resembled the famous Chu silk manuscript from Changsha. This manuscript, discovered in 1936–37, was written in archaic characters with a brush pen and black ink on a piece of silk 30 cm wide by 39 cm high. The main text of over six hundred characters is divided into two paragraphs placed upside down in relation to each other. On the edges of the manuscript are other short inscriptions and drawings of various leafy branches and mythical creatures in red, blue, and brown (see Noel Barnard, "Preliminary Study," for a description of this Chu silk manuscript).

[12] There is actually little evidence to prove the existence of a chart accompanying the text, except that the opening characters of the present text 若因 are unintelligible as they stand. Guo has suggested that they are a corruption of 右圖, "to the right is the chart." He is probably correct, especially since this arrangement would conform to the standard procedure in dealing with complicated charts in later times. The title of III, 9, *You guan tu*, it should be noted, means "Chart of the *You guan.*"

[13] In the text each of the major geographical sections has been divided into two parts. The notations in III, 9, distinguish these as the basic 本圖 and supplementary 副圖 parts of the chart. I have used the terms "inner" and "outer" as descriptive of their actual position. The capital letters accompanying the word "Essay" indicate Wang and Guo's opinion as to the order in which the original essay was read.

CHART 4. Arrangement of Sections in *You guan*, III, 8, and
Yang and Zhao Versions of *You guan tu*, III, 9

	III, 8	III, 9 (Yang)	III, 9 (Zhao)
1	Inner Center: Center Calendar and Essay A	Inner West: Autumn Calendar and Essay G	Inner Center: Center Calendar and Essay A
2	Inner East: Spring Calendar and Essay I	Outer West: Autumn Calendar continued and Essay C	Outer Center: No Calendar Essay B
3	Inner South: Summer Calendar and Essay H	Inner South: Summer Calendar and Essay H	Inner East: Spring Calendar and Essay I
4	Inner West: Autumn Calendar and Essay G	Inner Center: Center Calendar and Essay A	Outer East: Spring Calendar continued and Essay E
5	Inner North: Winter Calendar and Essay J	Inner North: Winter Calendar and Essay J	Inner South: Summer Calendar and Essay H
6	Outer Center: No Calendar Essay B	Outer South: Summer Calendar continued and Essay D	Outer South: Summer Calendar continued and Essay D
7	Outer East: Spring Calendar continued and Essay E	Outer Center: No Calendar Essay B	Inner West: Autumn Calendar and Essay B
8	Outer South: Summer Calendar continued and Essay D	Outer North: Winter Calendar continued and Essay F	Outer West: Autumn Calendar continued and Essay C
9	Outer West: Autumn Calendar continued and Essay C	Inner East: Spring Calendar and Essay I	Outer North: Winter Calendar and Essay J
10	Outer North: Winter Calendar continued and Essay F	Outer East: Spring Calendar continued and Essay E	Outer North: Winter Calendar continued and Essay F

ship between the four seasons and the Five Phases, why did he divide each of the geographical sections into two parts, making a total of ten? Simply having the five sections represent the four directions and the center would have solved this problem. The answer to this question becomes clear as soon as this reconstruction of the III, 8, chart is compared with one of the traditional representations of the so-called River Chart or *He tu* 河圖, which was supposed to have emerged from the Yellow River on the back of a "dragon horse" during the reign of the legendary emperor Fu Xi 伏羲.

Before discussing the relationship between these two charts, however, something should be said about the history of the River Chart itself. The earliest references to it occur in the *Shang shu*, V, 22/19, *Lun yu*, IX, 8, and the *Mozi*, V, 19/9a11 (Mei, *Motse*, p. 113), but of particular importance is the reference that occurs in the "Appended Treatise A" 繫辭 of the *Yi jing*, VII, 11/10a1–2 (Wilhelm, *I Ching*, I, p. 344): "The Yellow River brought forth a chart and the Luo River brought forth a writing. The sages took these as models." [14] Undoubtedly this chart and writing never actually existed except in popular legend, but supposed reconstructions of them began to appear as far back as the Warring States Period.

The *Zhuangzi*, V, 14/19b (Watson, *Chuang Tzu*, p. 154), states: "With the event of the nine [part] Luo [Writing] 九洛之事 good government prevailed and virtue was complete." The *Shi ji*, 6/16b11 (Chavannes, *Mémoires historiques*, II, p. 167), refers to a "Book of the Lu Chart" 錄圖書, which was presented to the First Emperor of the Qin in 215 B.C. by one of his magicians, a man from the state of Yan 燕 named Lu 盧. Some scholars believe the latter may have been the River Chart.[15] An intense interest in the Luo Writing and River Chart developed during the Han period, as shown in the apocrypha (*wei shu* 偽書) and prognostication texts (*chan shu* 讖書). About one-quarter of all these works are said to have been devoted to them; we know the titles of some thirty-seven apocrypha dealing with the River Chart alone.[16]

Unfortunately, most of these apocrypha and prognostication texts have long been lost, and though there are some general literary descriptions of the chart dating back to the fifth century A.D., the oldest surviving reconstruction only goes back to Zhu Xi 朱熹 (1130–1200) and his edition of the *Yi jing*. In a group of diagrams at the beginning of

---

[14] The "writing" refers to the so-called Luo Writing or *Luo shu* 洛書, another mysterious diagram or chart that was supposed to have emerged out of the Luo River on the back of a tortoise during the reign of the legendary emperor Yu.

[15] Needham, *Science and Civilisation in China*, III, pp. 56–57, n. a.

[16] See Gu Jiegang and Yang Xiangkui, *San huang kao*, p. 221.

this work, Zhu Xi presents one that he labels as the River Chart. Under it he quotes a passage from the "Appended Treatise A" (*Yi jing*, VII, 10/8b; Wilhelm, *I Ching*, I, p. 331), which assigns numerical correlates to Heaven and Earth beginning with Heaven as one and alternating up to ten. These, he adds, are the numbers of the River Chart.

The origin of Zhu Xi's chart, however, is much in question. It seems to have been supplied, along with a Luo Writing diagram, by one of Zhu's former students, Cai Yuanding 蔡元定, who is quoted by Zhu (*Yixue qimeng*, A/2b) as saying: "The symbolism of the [River] Chart and Luo [Writing] came down from Kong Anguo 孔安國 (c. 156–c. 74 B.C.) and Liu Xin 劉歆 (d. A.D. 23) of the Han dynasty, and Guan Lang 關朗 (fl. 477–500) of the Wei. . . . All spoke about them in the way [depicted here] until Liu Mu 劉牧 (1023–1063) for the first time reversed their two names. Various other writers followed him. For this reason we now restore [their original names] and follow their old [forms]."

Can we accept Cai's statement that the symbolism of the River Chart given in Zhu Xi's work goes back to the Han? We do know that the chart was in existence considerably before Cai's time. It was contained in a work, now lost except for its preface, known as the *Yi long tu* [Dragon Chart of the *Yi jing*], which was attributed to the well-known Daoist, Chen Tuan 陳摶 (c. 906–989).[17] We also know that Liu Xin associated the River Chart with the symbolism of the *Yi jing*,[18] and the *Yi zhuan* attributed to Guan Lang contained an accurate description of the Zhu Xi chart as having "seven in front, six at the back, eight to the left, and nine to the right."[19]

Furthermore, as can be seen from chart 5, when Zhu Xi's version of the River Chart is compared with the general framework of the chart reconstructed by Wang Tingfang and Guo Moruo from the text of this chapter, a remarkable parallel becomes evident. The groups of dots in the center and on the four sides in the River Chart correspond to the arrangement of the inner and outer divisions of the Wang-Guo reconstruction.[20] Moreover, the inner center and outer side dots of the River Chart exactly correspond both in numerical value and in position to the numbers of the Five Phases as these are found correlated with

[17] See the *Qinding gujin tushu jicheng, Jingji dian* 經籍典, 51/25a.

[18] *Qian Han shu*, 27A/1a.

[19] The *Yi zhuan*, which now appears to be lost, was quoted by Zhu Xi in his *Yi xue qimeng*, A2b. The question is, however, whether or not the *Yi zhuan* was really by Guan Lang. Later scholars have usually attributed it to Ruan Yi 阮逸, who lived during the first part of the eleventh century. See Zhang Xincheng, *Weishu tongkao*, I, pp. 88ff.

[20] The River Chart forms a mathematical diagram, the sets of dots being so arranged that, disregarding the three sets of five in the center, the remaining sets, which are odd (1,3,7,9) and even (2,4,6,8), both add up to twenty.

CHART 5. Zhu Xi River Chart and *You guan* Chart

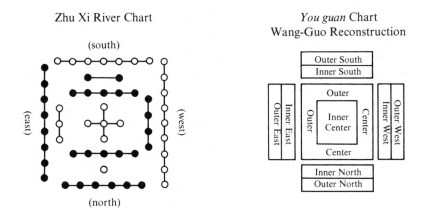

each direction and season in this chapter, that is, five for the center, and, along the outer sides, eight for east and spring, seven for south and summer, nine for west and autumn, and six for north and winter. Clearly this is not merely a calendar chart but a calendar chart patterned on a River Chart. As such, it not only explains the reason for the ten sections but also proves conclusively that Zhu Xi's River Chart did actually go back to Former Han times.

This still does not explain its origin, however. For that we must first turn to the origin of the Luo Writing. As seen from the *Zhuangzi* reference cited above, the Luo Writing was early associated with the number nine, and from its descriptions and later representations in other works dating from the Han dynasty on, it is clear that it was based on a magic square of three in which the numbers one to nine were arranged so they would add up to fifteen in any direction.

The relationship between the Luo Writing and this magic square has been discussed by Schuyler Cammann in his article, "The Magic Square of Three in Old Chinese Philosophy and Religion." Cammann maintains that this magic square came to play an increasingly important role in Chinese philosophy and religion after 400 B.C., largely because of its adaptability to the inherent Chinese doctrine of centrality.[21] From the

[21] The central number five dominates the square. Multiplied by three (the base number of the magic square of three) it results in fifteen, the constant sum of the rows, columns, or diagonals; multiplied by nine it results in forty-five, the sum total of all the squares, and so on.

156

Chart 6. Magic Square of Three and Luo Writing

Magic Square of Three   Luo Writing

(south)

4	9	2
3	5	7
8	1	6

(east)   (west)

(north)

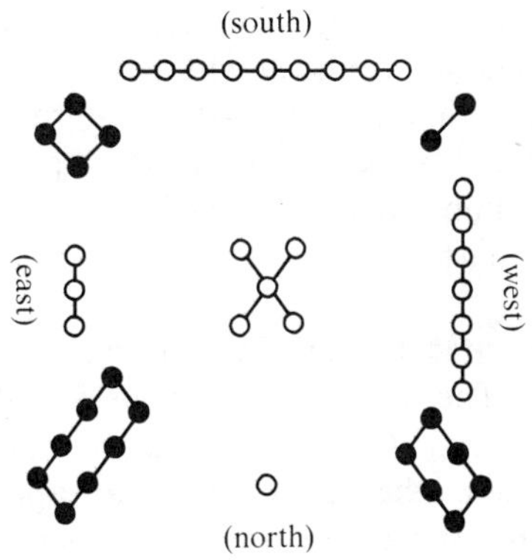

time of Zou Yan at least, it became intimately connected with Five Phases theories and was used to depict the rotation of the seasons.[22] Zou arranged the sequence of the phases on the principle that each was conquered by its successor, beginning with earth, then wood, metal, fire, and water, and then back to earth to begin the cycle anew.[23] This cycle was then assimilated to the cycle of the four seasons and made to accord with the positions of the magic square. Spring was assigned the phase wood and the northeast corner of the square, with its numbers three and eight (5 + 3); summer, metal and the southeast, with its numbers four and nine (5 + 4); autumn, fire and the southwest, with its numbers two and seven (5 + 2); winter, water and the northwest, with its numbers one and six (5 + 1). This left the central five (present in all the other numbers) to represent the prime phase earth. (See chart 6.)

However, such an arrangement emphasized the corners and was bound to come into conflict with the strong tendency in Chinese thought to place major consideration on the cardinal points. Therefore, Cammann maintains, another school of thought adopted a rival diagram in the form of a cross, with five as the center and the arms consisting

[22] The reader has probably noted the similarity between the Ming Tang and the magic square.
[23] That is to say, earth was overcome by growing plants and trees (wood) and wood by metal axes and knives; metal was melted by fire, fire extinguished by water, and water clogged or dammed up by earth.

of the paired numbers eight and three, four and nine, two and seven, and six and one, with the larger numbers occupying the extremities. The same numerical correlates for the phases were kept, but the sequence was changed so that fire, with its numbers two and seven, became identified with summer, while metal, with its numbers four and nine, became identified with antumn. Then, to complete the Yin-Yang balance and conform to the pattern of alternating numbers for Heaven and Earth as set down in the "Appended Treatise A" of the *Yi jing*, the number ten was added to the center.[24] This then became the River Chart.

OTHER EARLY CALENDARS

The *You guan* calendar is only one of a number of such works surviving from Han and pre-Han times. It is possible to date some of these other calendars at least approximately and by comparison arrive at some idea of the development of the art of making them. Generally speaking, as time went on the calendars tended to become less concretely natural and more abstractly cosmological, less agricultural and more political in content.

Included among them were:

1. *Xia xiao zheng* 夏小正 [Little Calendar of the Xia], comprising the second part of chapter II in the *Da Dai li ji*. While difficult to date, it is considered the earliest of all the surviving calendars, going back at least to the early Warring States Period.[25] In it the year is divided into twelve months, commencing with the third month after the winter solstice, which is reckoned as the beginning of spring. A number of terse maxims,

[24] As Cammann points out, this was easily done without disturbing the shape of the cross because in Han times five was commonly written as an X, and ten was written in the shape of a Greek cross. Thus they could be written on top of each other, to form a star-shaped device pointing outward in the eight directions. The most commonly accepted Chinese explanation for these numerical correlates is one proffered by Zheng Xuan 鄭玄 (127–200) and Kong Yingda 孔穎達 (574–648) and discussed by Fung Yu-lan, in his *A History of Chinese Philosophy*, II, p. 14, note. It is based on the order of the phases as they are listed in the *Hong fan* and correlated with the numbers one to ten assigned to Heaven and Earth in the "Appended Treatise A." Another somewhat similar Chinese explanation, attributed to Cai Yong, is to be found in the chapter on music of the *Nan Qi shu*, 11/4a. For a discussion of the weakness of both these explanations, see my article, "an Early Chinese Calendar Chart," pp. 206–209.

[25] According to Herbert Chatley in his article on "The Date of the Hsia Calendar *Hsia hsiao cheng*," p. 529, the astronomical data of the calendar are consistent with conditions about 350 B'C. Needham, *Science and Civilisation*, III, p. 194, adds: "The brevity of the details given would permit a dating as far back as the −7th century, though that would be unlikely. A fair estimate would perhaps be the −5th." Translations of this calendar are to be found in Soothill, *Hall of Light*, pp. 237–243, and Wilhelm, *Li Gi, Das Buch der Sitte des älteren und jüngeren Dai*, pp. 223–243.

mostly concerned with natural phenomena and agricultural activities, are listed under each month. There is no mention of the Five Phases.

2. *Shi xun jie* 時訓解 [Explanations of the Teachings on the Seasons], which is chapter VI, 52, of the *Yi Zhou shu*, a work purporting to be a collection of documents from Zhou times. The text was taken from a tomb in A.D. 281, together with other texts that are known to have been tampered with thereafter. Therefore its authenticity has been questioned by Chinese and Western scholars alike. Henri Maspero, however, believed the *Shi xun jie* to be a genuine Zhou text, probably dating from the middle of the fourth century B.C.[26]

The calendar divides the year into twenty-four fifteen-day periods, which are, in turn, subdivided into three periods of five days each. The first day of each of the longer periods has a name that with minor variations in order, is precisely the same as those listed for the twenty-four periods given in the astronomical chapter of the *Huainanzi* (see below). These names are still in popular use today.[27] Under each five-day period is listed a phenomenon of nature suitable to that time, such as the stirring of insects or arrival of wild geese. At the end of each fifteen-day period there is then listed the evil that will befall man if the phenomenon does not occur at the proper time.

3. *Shi ji* 時紀 [Seasonal Record], which is the title of a series of subsections of the first twelve chapters of the *Lüshi chunqiu*. It is better known, however, as the *Yue ling*, the title under which it was later incorporated into the *Li ji*. It also appears as the *Yue ling jie* 解 [Explanations on the Monthly Ordinances] in VI, 53, of the *Yi Zhou shu*. Since the *Lüshi chunqiu* was compiled about 240 B.C., we know that this calendar was at least in existence by this time. However, the original date of its composition remains in doubt. The complexity of its contents would seem to indicate that it could not have been put together in its present form much before the middle of the third century B.C., but parts of it may be much earlier.[28]

This *Yue ling* calendar divides the year into four seasons of three months each. The content is more political than the previous two texts,

[26] See *China in Antiquity*, pp. 358–359.

[27] This fact might lend support to a conclusion that the text was not genuine, since these names appear only sporadically in calendars that are definitely known to predate the *Huainanzi* (c. 122 B.C.). However, the predominantly naturalistic and agricultural content of the work as well as its brevity of style suggest a date comparable to the *Xia xiao zheng*. Furthermore, the smaller divisions of five days (not found in the *Huainanzi* version) may indicate early Zhou dynasty peasant origin. See n. 30, below.

[28] Needham, *Science and Civilisation*, III, p. 195, cites a Japanese scholar, C. Noda, to the effect that the star data contained in the "Ordinances" would seem to come from about 620 B.C., with a range of a couple of centuries on either side.

being primarily concerned with the action of the ruler in each season. It is also the first of the calendars to deal with the Five Phases and their correlates, and it resolves the problem of the fifth phase, earth, by creating for it a special section following the last month of summer, without, however, assigning it any actual time in terms of specific days. For a list comparing the Five Phases correlates found in the *Yue ling* with those given in the present chapter of the *Guanzi*, see chart 7.[29]

4. *Shi ze xun* 時則訓 [Teachings on the Rules for the Seasons], which constitutes chapter 5 of the *Huainanzi*, compiled shortly before 122 B.C. Though similar in form to the *Yue ling*, it includes several more correlates, such as the directions, weapons, and animals. On the other hand, it lacks the emperors and guardian spirits. For the fifth phase, earth, it creates a separate center season out of the last month of summer, thus taking care of the Five Phases while retaining the pattern of four basic seasons and twelve months. The *Tian wen xun* 天文訓 [Teachings on Astronomy], which makes up chapter 3 of the same work, divides the year into twenty-four periods of fifteen days each, but this system does not appear in the *Shi ze xun*. It should be noted that the terms used to designate these periods are frequently to be found in the text of the *Xia xiao zheng* and *Yue ling* to describe the characteristics of the seasons.

In addition to III, 8, and III, 9, the *Guanzi* itself contains three other calendars of importance:

1. XIV, 40, *Si shi* 四時 [Four Seasons], which resembles the *Yue ling* in content but divides the year into four seasons under the four directions, east, south, west, and north. The center is simply included as a subsection in the middle of the passage relating to the south and summer. The phases are listed under their appropriate directions, but the system of correlates is completely different from that of the *Yue ling*, and does not even mention the colors.

2. XIV, 41/11aff., *Wu xing* 五行 [Five Phases], which begins its reckoning with the winter solstice and divides the year into five periods of seventy-two days' duration. Each period is under the influence of one of the Five Phases in their normal seasonal rotation: wood, fire, earth, metal and water; each phase determines the type of political activity and agricultural work then to be done. Upon completing the first cycle for a year, the text describes a second, using the same calendar system but prescribing slightly different activities and work for each period. It is

---

[29] I have listed only those correlates in the *Yue ling* assigned to each of the four seasons as a whole and to the center. Those assigned to the individual months, such as a position of the sun, an evening and morning star, or one of the twelve pitch pipes (*lü* 呂), are not included because the *Guanzi* calendar contains no monthly divisions.

CHART 7. Comparative Chart of Five Phases Correlates
for the *Yue ling* and *Guanzi*, III, 8

Phases						
	Yue	wood	fire	earth	metal	water
	Guan	wood	fire	earth	metal	water
Seasons	*Yue*	spring	summer	center	autumn	winter
	Guan	spring	summer	center	autumn	winter
Days	*Yue*	*jiayi*	*bingding*	*wuji*	*gengxin*	*rengui*
	Guan	none	none	none	none	none
Emperors	*Yue*	Tai Hao	Yan Di	Huang Di	Shao Hao	Zhuan Xu
	Guan	Qing Hou	Chi Hou	Huang Hou	Bai Hou	Hei Hou
Guardian Spirits	*Yue*	Goumang	Zhurong	Houtu	Rushou	Xuanming
	Guan	none	none	none	none	none
Creatures	*Yue*	scaly	feathered	hairless	furry	shell
	Guan	feathered	furry	hairless	shell	scaly
Notes	*Yue*	*jiao*	*zhi*	*gong*	*shang*	*yu*
	Guan	*jiao*	*yu*	*gong*	*shang*	*zhi*
Numbers	*Yue*	eight	seven	five	nine	six
	Guan	eight	seven	five	nine	six
Tastes	*Yue*	sour	acrid	sweet	bitter	salty
	Guan	sour	bitter	sweet	acrid	salty
Smells	*Yue*	fleshy	burning	fragrant	rank	rotten
	Guan	none	none	none	none	none
Sacrifices	*Yue*	door	stove	mid. court	gate	path
	Guan	none	none	none	none	none
Organs	*Yue*	spleen	lungs	heart	liver	kidney
	Guan	none	none	none	none	none
Colors	*Yue*	green	red	yellow	white	black
	Guan	green	red	yellow	white	black

probable that this second cycle is simply another version of the same calendar and that it was included by Liu Xiang in the *Wu xing* chapter along with the first cycle when he edited the *Guanzi*.

3. XXIV, 85, *Qing zhong ji* 輕重己 [Light and Heavy, F], which contains a list of orders concerning court ceremony and agricultural activities. It divides the year into four seasons, which, in turn, are each divided into two periods of forty-six days. The Five Phases are not mentioned nor are any of their standard correlates, except the colors.

CHART 8. Names of the Twelve-Day Periods

Spring	Summer	Autumn	Winter
Vital Force of Earth Comes Forth 地氣發	Lesser *Ying* 小郢	Seasonal Wind Arrives 期風至	First Cold 始寒
Lesser *Mao* 小卯	*Jue* Vital Force Descends 絕氣下	Lesser *Mao* 小卯 [Lesser *You*] 小酉	Lesser *Yu* 小榆
Vital Force of Heaven Descends 天氣下	Middle *Ying* 中郢	*White Dew Falls 白露下	Middle Cold 中寒 [Middle *Yu*] 中榆
Vital Force of Well-Being Arrives 義氣至	Middle *Jue* 中絕 Greater *Ying* 大郢	Markings Restored 復理	Middle *Yu* 中榆 [Greater Yu] 大榆
Clear Brightness 清明	Greater Heat Arrives 大暑至 [Lesser Heat Arrives] 小暑至	First Temporal Division 始節	Cold Arrives 寒至 [Lesser Cold Arrives] 小寒至
First *Mao* 始卯	Middle Heat 中暑	First *Mao* 始卯 First *You* 始酉	(First) *Greater Cold 大寒 [Middle Cold] 中寒
Middle *Mao* 中卯	*Lesser Heat 小暑 [*Greater Heat] 大暑	Middle *Mao* 中卯 Middle *You* 中酉	(Second) *Greater Cold 大寒 [*Greater Cold] 大寒
Final *Mao* 下卯		Final *Mao* 下卯 [Final *You*] 下酉	

Note: Brackets indicate emended reading. Asterisks indicate those names that also appear in the astronomical *Tian wen xun* chapter of the *Huainanzi* and the *Shi xun jie*.

But even here the system is different. Only four colors are given. Red, the normal color for summer and fire, is missing, and replaced by yellow, the normal color for the center and earth.

CONTENT OF CALENDAR IN *You guan*

A brief comparison of the calendar in the *You guan* and *You guan tu* with the calendars listed above shows that it most closely resembles the *Yue ling* with respect to its Five Phase correlates, but the list includes only number, color, taste, musical note, and creature (here called animals). Moreover, the order of the last three correlates differs. Divine rulers or emperors are given, but they are known only by color names rather than by the proper names presented in the *Yue ling*. There are no guardian spirits. Weapons, a category lacking in the *Yue ling*, are listed for the four seasons as part of the calendar included in the outer sections. None is given for the center, since its outer section contains no calendar. Three of these weapons are similar to those in the *Shi ze xun*. Like the *Yue ling*, *Shi ze xun*, and *Si shi*, each season contains a passage describing what will happen if policies only suitable to other seasons are carried out during the one in progress.

The greatest difference between this calendar and those discussed above is that, in addition to the four seasons, it also divides the year into thirty twelve-day periods, assigning eight each to spring and autumn and seven each to summer and winter. Each period has a name relating to some aspect of natural phenomena and is followed by a short command concerning the appropriate human activity of the time. Some of the period names are similar to those in the astronomical chapter of the *Huainanzi* and the *Shi xun jie*, but most of them are entirely different and many of them appear to be corrupt. The passage containing these periods stands out so sharply from the rest of what appears to be a common *Yue ling*-type calendar that one is tempted to believe it must represent a completely different system, perhaps going back to a much earlier type such as that found in the *Xia xiao zheng* or *Shi xun jie*. Its similarity with the latter is particularly noteworthy, except that the *Shi xun jie* is based on the number five, while this one is based on twelve or at least on a multiple of three.[30]

---

[30] Actually, several different systems of number classification seem to have existed in ancient China. According to Hsü Chung-shu in his article on the "Well-field System of Shang and Chou" (John de Francis and E-tu Zen Sun, *Chinese Social History*, pp. 1–17), the Shang based its calculations on the number four. By Zhou times this system seems to have declined, and two other systems appeared to be very common, one based on the number five, the other on multiples of three. Marcel Granet, in his *Danses et légendes de la Chine ancienne*, pp. 6–7, suggests this may have been due to two different civilizations in

As mentioned in the Introduction, the documents unearthed at Yinqueshan 銀雀山 Linyi 臨邑 Xian, Shandong, in 1972 from two Han tombs dated 134 B.C. contain an as yet unpublished fragment entitled *Sanshih shi* 三十時 [The Thirty Periods]. This document consists of a calendar listing activities to be performed during thirty periods of twelve days each into which the year has been divided. Clearly, the *You guan* and the *Sanshi shi* share a common calendrical system, but the connection between the two texts is unclear.

The names of the twelve-day periods as they appear in the *You guan* are extremely confusing. No doubt this is because, as technical terms unfamiliar to later copyists, they were very easily corrupted. So the reader may clearly see the names of the thirty periods, they are presented in chart 8 with both their original and emended forms.

ESSAY PORTION OF *You guan*

The second part of the text, which I have described as an essay on political military strategy, presents a baffling problem. It is reasonably clear what the author (or perhaps I should say editor or compiler) of this chapter has done. On making up his original calendar chart, he found that the calendar alone did not provide him with enough material to fill up the square; so he took the present essay, which formerly had no connection with the calendar, cut it up, and freely inserted it into the appropriate sections as filler. It is possible, of course, that he could have composed the essay himself, but if he did, it must originally have been for another purpose. There is no connection at all between the content of the essay, which is primarily concerned with how to be a successful military ruler, and the seasonal changes of the year. Moreover, if he had written the essay for the chart, he could at least have made each section a complete unit. But as it is, the outer center section starts with a dangling sentence that is clearly left over after filling up the inner center.

The most frustrating aspect of the essay is that there is no way of telling how it should be read. Some of the sections appear to follow one another quite logically, but others seem to defy any sense of order, and one passage (4b12–5b12; 32.11–33.9) concerning the meetings of the

---

contact, but unfortunately he does not make his point very clear. Later on he states that five seems to have been used as the method of calculation of the peasants and predominated in legends affecting the patricians (the local aristocracy?), while six predominated in matters concerning the (urban?) nobility (pp. 10–11). He further says that the classification system based on multiples of three was associated with the rise of urban military power. The administrative organization of the *Zhou li* was based on six and the Zhou military structure on six and three (pp. 617–618).

feudal lords appears to have been lifted out of some other context and inserted here as additional filler simple because it speaks of the Dark Emperor 玄帝 and Dark Palace 玄宮(官). Wang Tingfang and Guo Moruo, in their reconstruction of the chart, have attempted to establish a sequence for reading the text, but I am afraid the results are hardly satisfying.

Some conclusions can be drawn, however, about the essay portion of the text. First of all, it shows an extremely high degree of eclecticism. The entire essay presents a wide array of Daoist, Confucian, and Legalist ideas and technical terms interwoven with an ease that could only be achieved by someone who felt no close identity with any of these schools. The opening paragraph of section A of the essay, for example, uses varying terminology to describe the attributes of the various classes of rulers of the past. Thus, with regard to the sovereign (*huang* 皇), it uses such Daoist terms as "dwelling in emptiness" and "preserving quiescence," whereas in the discussion about the king (*wang* 王), the Confucian virtues of goodness (*ren* 仁), righteousness (*yi* 義), loyalty (*zhong* 忠), and trustworthiness (*xin* 信) appear. The lord protector (*ba* 霸) is supposed to perform the Confucian task of making clear the rules of propriety (*li* 禮), but he also carries out the more Legalistic-sounding work of examining stratagems (*mou* 謀). A little further on, the text takes on a strong Legalist tone by speaking of paying attention to essential activities (*ben* 本), making laws (*fa* 法) clear, and setting up constant standards (*chang* 常). I suspect that this essay is a product of the Huang-Lao thinking that seems to have developed rapidly during the fourth and third centuries B.C.

We also know that the writer was most likely the same person who wrote *Guanzi*, VI, 17, *Bing fa* 兵法 ["Methods of Warfare"], which, as explained in its Introductory Comments, is even more identifiable as a product of the Huang-Lao school. Not only do the two texts have a number of passages in common, but they each contain passages that can only be understood in the light of passages in the other. Line 7a7 (34.11) of the present chapter, for instance, contains a brief reference to the nine symbols (*jiu zhang* 九章), explained in detail in VI, 17/12a11–b3 (1:80.6–7). Chapter VI, 17/13b3–4 (1:81.7), contains a long list of categories, many of which can only be explained by references to this chapter. The writer also paraphrases several passages to be found in chapter II, 6, and cites a number of categories to be found in other chapters of the *Guanzi*. For example, the three fundamentals (*san ben* 三本) in passage 2a11 are clearly taken from I, 4/12b3–13a5 (1:11.13–12.6). All of this indicates that the author of this chapter had knowledge of the proto-*Guanzi* collection, which probably began to take shape in the early part of the third century B.C.

DATING OF CALENDAR PORTION

Over the years Japanese scholars have displayed a special interest in the *You guan*, with three of them attempting to reach some conclusions concerning its date of composition. Aihara Shunji, in an article on Five Phases thought in the *Guanzi, Kanshi sho to gogyō setsu*, concludes that the *You guan* is pre-Han and postdates the *Shi ze xun* of the *Huainanzi*. On the other hand, Machida Saburō in his *Kanshi Yōkan kō*, maintains that the *You guan* calendar is more primitive than the *Shi ji* (*Yue ling*) of the *Lüshi chunqiu* and thus the chapter is of earlier origin. Toda Toyosaburō, in his study *Gogyō setsu seiritsu no ichikōsatsu*, attempts to show that the *You guan* is a work of the fourth century B.C. Space does not permit a proper treatment of the arguments of these three scholars, but Toda's study requires some special consideration because it involves an earlier dating of the calendar portion of the *You guan* than I believe is possible.

Briefly, Toda maintains that the numerical and other correlates given here have nothing to do with the Five Phases. He points out that there is no mention of them in the text and argues that before the time of Zou Yan, the Five Phases were only one of a number of fivefold categories. Toda believes that the number correlates were derived from the numerology of the *Yi jing*, with the numbers of Heaven and Earth assigned to the various sections of the chart: north, one; south, two; east, three; west, four; center, five; and beginning around again until the center was reached with ten.[31] The numbers six, seven, eight, and nine were used in the text because they included both the initial number and the number of completion. Five was kept rather than ten because it represented both itself and ten, the latter being merely a multiple of the former.

Toda cites a statement in the *Zhou li*, 19/1a8 (Biot, *Tcheou-li*, I, p. 441): "The assistant director of sacred ceremonies presides over ... the erection of altars to the Five Emperors in the suburbs," and concludes that these "Five Emperors" are the same as the five seasonal rulers—Yellow Ruler (Huang Hou 黄后), Green Ruler (Qing Hou 青后), etc.—mentioned in this chapter of the *Guanzi*. To support his argument he cites the chapter on the Feng and Shan sacrifices in the *Shi*

---

[31] Toda cites the *Tai xuan* of Yang Xiong 揚雄 (53 B.C.–A.D. 18) as another work in which the numbers of Heaven and Earth were assigned to the five directions twice around. For a translation of the passage that he probably had in mind here, see Fung, *History*, II, p. 146.

ji, 28/2b–13b (Chavannes, *Mémoires historiques*, III, pp. 419–449), to show that sacrifices had been instituted for some deities with color names as far back as the eighth century.[32]

It seems to me, however, that Toda's conclusions cannot be accepted. First of all, since it is almost certain that the calendar and essay portions stemmed from different origins, they must be treated separately. Second, although it is true that the Five Phases are not specifically mentioned, the various correlates (both numerical and otherwise) in the text are closely associated with the Five Phases, and there would be no reason for introducing a fifth, center season except to make the calendar conform to Five Phase concepts by giving each phase its turn to exert an influence in that year. Third, the date of the *Zhou li* itself being very uncertain, it cannot be used in dating other works, even though it is useful in other ways in studying pre-Han China. Finally, though the *Shi ji* describes sacrifices to emperors with color names as far back as the eighth century, "five emperors" as a category does not appear in any datable text before the *Lüshi chunqiu*, and the earliest datable list of emperors with color names actually does not appear until Han times.[33]

In my opinion the calendar portion of the text cannot be dated much before the middle of the third century B.C.[34] Though it does not actually

---

[32] According to the *Shi ji*, 28/2b12–13 (Chavannes, *Mémoires historiques*, III, pp. 419–420): "When Duke Xiang 襄 [777–766] of Qin became lord, he lived on the western frontier. Since he considered himself head of [the cult of] the divinity of Shao Hao 少皞, he built a western terrace and performed sacrifices to the White Emperor (Bai Di 白帝)." Here these color deities are called *di* 帝, "emperor," instead of *hou* 后, "ruler," but the meaning is the same. Thus "White Emperor" would appear to be simply another appellation for Shao Hao, who appears in the *Yue ling* as the seasonal emperor for autumn. (See chart 7, which gives the correlates for the *Yue ling*.) Subsequently, similar sacrifices were instituted for the Green Emperor or Qing Di 青帝 under Duke Xuan 宣 of Qin in 672 B.C. (*Shi ji*, 28/4a8; Chavannes, *Mémoires historiques*, III, p. 423). The *Shi ji*, 28/6a11 (Chavannes, III, p. 429) also informs us that sacrifices were instituted for Yan Di 炎帝 (who is usually associated with the color red, but is not actually called "Red Emperor" or Chi Di 赤帝 here) and for the Yellow Emperor, or Huang Di 黄帝, by Duke Ling 靈 of Qin in 422 B.C. However, the same source (*Shi ji*, 28/13a13–b1; Chavannes, III, p. 449) states that sacrifices to the Black Emperor, or Hei Di 黑帝, were not instituted until Han times in 205 B.C.

[33] The earliest list of emperors with color names appears in the astronomical *Tian guan* 天官 ["Heavenly Offices"] chapter of the *Shi ji*, 27/34a–b (Chavannes, *Mémoires historiques*, III, pp. 411–414), which refers to them as the "Five Celestial Emperors" (五天帝). Lu Deming 陸德明 (early 7th century), in his *Shiwen* 釋文 commentary to the *Zhou li*, lists the "Five Emperors" mentioned in that text as the Green, Red, Yellow, White, and Black Emperors, representing the east, south, center, west, and north, respectively. (See the *Zhou li zhusu*, 2/11a.) However, Lu offers no support for his statement and, indeed, it seems to be a mere speculation based on this material about the Five Celestial Emperors contained in the *Shi ji*.

[34] This does not refer to that portion of the calendar dealing with the twelve-day periods, which, as said, would appear to be much earlier.

mention the Five Phases, it appears to be based on Five Phases concepts and correlates, and these do not seem to have been associated with agricultural calendars until after Zou Yan developed his ideas during the early part of the third century B.C. Furthermore, of all the extant early calendars, the one it resembles most closely in style and content (especially in regard to the introduction of a center season) is the more sophisticated *Yue ling*, which in its present form also dates from about the middle of the third century B.C.

I also think we can feel fairly safe in saying that this *You guan* calendar predates the latter half of the second century B.C., since it does not assign the center to a special season in the third month of summer, as became the custom about the time of the *Huainanzi* (c. 122 B.C.).

DATING OF ESSAY PORTION

I feel that the essay portion of the text also could not date much before the middle of the third century B.C. for the following reasons: (1) It uses the term *qingxiang* 卿相 (2a7; 30.6) to refer to the prime minister of state, a usage that did not develop until late in the Warring States Period.[35] (2) It cites a passage (8a2–3; 35.7) that is very similar to, and may have been taken from, the *Lüshi chunqiu*, XIX, 5/11a12 (Wilhelm, *Frühling und Herbst*, p. 333), compiled about 240 B.C.[36] (3) The opening paragraph of Essay A (1a6; 29.7) contains a political progression from sovereigns through emperors, kings, and finally to lord protectors. Presumably the author also had in mind here the numerical progression of the Three Sovereigns, Five Emperors, Three Kings, and Five Lord Protectors.[37] The categories of the Three Kings and Five Lord Protectors are first mentioned in the *Mengzi*, VIB, 7/1, but the Three Sovereigns and Five Emperors only appear later. The *Zhou li*, 26/11b7 (Biot, *Tcheou-li*, II, p. 119), refers to them, but the dating of this text is very uncertain. The earliest datable reference is the *Lüshi chunqiu*, which

[35] See Luo Genze, *Guanzi tanyuan*, pp. 26–29.

[36] See n. 195, below.

[37] The Three Sovereigns have been variously listed by later commentators, but the most frequent groupings are Huang Di, Fu Xi 伏羲, and Shen Nong 神農, or Sui Ren 遂人, Fu Xi, and Shen Nong. The earliest list of Five Emperors is one cited above in the chart of correlates for the *Yue ling*: Tai Hao 太皞, Yan Di, Huang Di, Shao Hao, and Zhuan Xu 顓頊. However, in later texts the lists of names vary greatly. One of the most common is Huang Di, Zhuan Xu, Di Ku 帝嚳, Tang Yao 唐堯, and Yu Shun 虞舜. The Three Kings are usually identified as the three dynastic founders, Yu 禹 of the Xia 夏, Tang 湯 of the Shang 商, and Wen 文 of the Zhou 周. The Five Lord Protectors are listed in the *Xunzi*, VII, 11/2b–3a, as Huan 桓 (685–643) of Qi 齊, Wen 文 (635–628) of Jin 晉, Zhuang 莊 (613–591) of Chu 楚, Helü 闔閭 (514–496) of Wu 吳, and Goujian 句踐 (496–465) of Yue 越. In later texts the names of the last two are often replaced by Xiang 襄 (650–637) of Song 宋 and Mu 穆 (659–643) of Qin 秦

mentions them several times (see, for example, I, 4/9a5–6; Wilhelm, p. 9). They were subsequently placed chronologically ahead of the Three Kings and Five Lord Protectors.[38] Hence, the fact that all four terms are here listed in descending sequence (even though without specifying the alternating numbers, three and five) supports the above statement concerning the earliest possible date for this portion of the text.

If further proof were needed, the fact, as mentioned above, that the author of the essay must have had access to a proto-*Guanzi* collection would be enough. Since the majority of the essays in the *Guanzi* from which he appears to have borrowed, including I, 4, and II, 6, do not predate the late fourth century B.C., he could hardly have composed his work before that time.

There is almost no evidence to indicate the later limit for the date of the essay except that it must have been composed some time before Liu Xiang included it in the present *Guanzi* work. But works on military affairs, the subject of the chapter and its companion piece, VI, 17, seem to have reached their peak of popularity at the end of the Warring States Period and beginning of the Han. The major military classics, such as the *Sunzi, Wuzi, Sun Bin bing fa*, and *Shangjun shu*, III, 10, are all from the later years of the Warring States.

DATING OF CHART

The reorganization of the calendar and essay into chart form is most likely Han. It was during the middle and later years of the Han dynasty that the construction of river charts became particularly popular, and though this chart represents a rather crude piece of work, it could not date much before that time. In other words, the chart itself could not have been made much more than a century or so before it was incorporated into the present *Guanzi* by Liu Xiang about 26 B.C.

Translation

29.7
.6

To the right is the chart.[39]

[INNER CENTER]

[Calendar] Since it is the season when five is in harmony, the prince

.8

wears the color yellow, / tastes sweet flavors, and listens to the *gong*

[38] See Gu and Yang, *San huang kao*, pp. 20–112 and p. 277.

[39] The opening line of this chapter, 若 因 … 則 皇, is clearly corrupt and, as it stands, appears to be unrelated to the text that follows. To render it intelligible, I have followed Guo Moruo, who believes that the two characters 若 因 were originally written 右 圖, "to the right is the chart." Their forms are somewhat similar. These first two characters would

29.9

29.10

1b

29.7
1a6

note.[40] He governs with the vital force which brings harmony[41] and / utilizes the number five.[42] He drinks from the well of the Yellow Ruler[43] and uses the fire of hairless animals when cooking.[44] His temper[45] is mild and yielding.[46] / His activities are devoted to caring for[47] and nurturing [his people].

As the equable vital force [of the phase earth] circulates and permeates,[48] / all creatures [appropriate to this season] leave the state of quiescence and their forms acquire markings. /

[Essay A] Those who dwelt in emptiness,[49] preserved quiescence, and [were in perfect accord with] all men and things[50] became

---

then constitute a separate explanatory heading indicating that, to the right, was the chart and this following text is its explanation. This interpretation accords with the accepted practice of putting headings preceded by the character 右 at the end of their respective sections rather than at the beginning. I have further followed Ding in transferring the remaining portion of the line 夜虛…則皇, which concerns the sovereign, to line 1b1 (29.10) above the phrase in order to fill out the passage there. Thus the text of this chapter should open with the words 五和時節.

[40] The color yellow, sweet taste, and *gong* 宮 note (the first of the five tones of the classical Chinese pentatonic scale) are all associated with the phase earth.

[41] That is, the phase earth that dominates the activity of the center.

[42] The Yang edition lacks this phrase 用五數.

[43] Wen would identify the Yellow Ruler 黃后 as the Yellow Emperor, one of the Five Celestial Emperors mentioned in n. 33. According to the *Zhou li zhusu*, 2/11a9, the Yellow Emperor is the ruler of the center and has the alternative name, Hanshu Niu 含樞紐. He is also popularly associated with the Earth Star (i.e., the planet Saturn), and his nature is said to be that of the *qilin* 麒麟, a mythical beast often compared with the Western unicorn.

[44] The meaning here is not clear. *Luo* 倮 literally means "naked" and the naked animal is often identified as man. The same adjective *luo* appears in the section on the center in the *Yue ling* (*Li ji*, V, 6/15b9), but instead of 獸, "animals," the text writes 蟲, "insect" or "creature." In his commentary, Zheng Xuan says that these naked or hairless creatures refer to short-haired animals such as the tiger and leopard. The Gao You commentary to the *LSCQ*, VI, 1/3a1, version would identify them with the category headed by the *qilin*. Yasui says that fire was obtained by boring the bone of these animals.

[45] 藏: literally, "what is stored within."

[46] The Yang edition for 濡 writes 儒, which implies the same meaning. Wang Niansun says they are both a mistake for 偄, "weak."

[47] Following Yu Yue, who here and in several passages below reads 敺 as 嫗 = 姁.

[48] This sentence is repeated in each of the first five sections of the chapter. The Yin commentary and Yasui explain 氣 in each of these occurrences as representing the vital force of the appropriate phase. I have also followed Wen, who would emend 修 to 循, two characters that are often confused in this text.

[49] As mentioned in n. 39, above, the sentence (1a6; 29.7) 夜虛…則皇 has been transferred to this point. The character 虛 here does not make good sense and is probably a corruption of *chu* 處. The parallel passage of the *You guan tu*, III, 9/9a12 (1:36.11), writes *chu*. The two characters are easily confused since *chu* is often written 処.

[50] The *You guan tu* version, III, 9/9a12 (1:36.11), for 人物人物 simply writes 人物. Guo Moruo believes, however, that the text as it stands here is correct since the two extra characters are needed to make this sentence balance with those that follow. The meaning is the same as when written 人人物物.

29.10
1b1
29.11

29.12

29.13

29.14

sovereigns. / Those who adhered to the constant standards,[51] perfected their commands,[52] / honored the worthy, and bestowed [ranks and salaries] on the virtuous became emperors. Those who embodied goodness, practiced righteousness, gained the adherence of the loyal, and employed the trustworthy / became kings. Those who examined stratagems, made clear the rules of propriety, selected knights, and sharpened their weapons became lord protectors.

Those who were able to give security to the living, find a resting place for the dead, take care of the worthy, and form the groups of five [gained] a large population. Those who were trustworthy in issuing rewards, were discriminating in exacting punishments, gave ranks to the talented and salaries / to the able became strong. Those who kept a record of all [expenditures] and tallied[53] the results, paid attention to essential [activities], and regulated those that were nonessential became prosperous. Those who made the laws clear, examined the estimates [of their officials], set up constant standards,[54] and prepared men of ability achieved a well-ordered government. / Those who allotted the offices in

[51] A character appears to be missing before *chang* 常, since each of the other rulers listed in this paragraph is described by two four-character phrases. Zhang Peilun would supply the character 率, which appears in combination with *chang* in the *Zuo zhuan*, Ai, 6 (Legge, *Ch'un Ts'eu*, XII, 6/6). Here *chang* refers to the constant moral standards of Heaven, which is the meaning of the term when used by Confucians. Since the two concluding descriptive phrases of this passage that deal with the emperors, i.e., "honored the worthy and bestowed [ranks and salaries] on the virtuous," are also Confucian in tone, I have accepted Zhang's interpretation.

To the Daoists, however, *chang* had a broader meaning, referring to the invariables of the universe, and it is possible this may be the implication here. The *Laozi*, A, 16/8b–9a (Waley, *The Way and Its Power*, p. 162) contains a passage that bears some similarity in the use of terms to this and the following phrase of our text: "All things howsoever they flourish return to the root. Returning to the root is called quiescence. This is called submitting to fate. Submitting to fate is called [adhering to] the invariables (*chang*). Understanding (*zhi* 知) the invariables is called enlightenment." Therefore it is also possible that the missing character may be *zhi*. Thus the phrase would read: "Those who understand the invariables . . . ."

[52] The meaning of this phrase *zhi ming* 至命 is also unclear. Ming may refer to ordinary commands or the commands of Heaven, i.e., "destiny" or "fate." In view of the predominantly mundane context of the other phrases in this passage describing the emperors, I have interpreted *ming* to mean ordinary commands. If one were to follow the Daoist interpretation of *chang* given in the note above, however, *ming* should certainly be read as "fate." The *Shuo gua* 說卦 [Discussion of the Trigrams] chapter of the *Yijing*, IX, 1/1a8–9 (Wilhelm, *I Ching*, I, p. 281), contains the passage: "[The sages] by thinking through the principles [of the world] to the end, and by exploring their nature to the deepest core, arrived at [an understanding of] fate 至於命." Following this interpretation, *zhi ming* should be read as "arrived at [an understanding of] fate."

[53] Reading 付 as 符 [Igai, Zhang Peilun, and Xu].

[54] Here *chang* 常, "constant standards," must be taken in the Legalist sense of unvarying rules that are set up as the basis for determining rewards and punishments.

accordance with similarities or differences [in affairs] became secure.[55]

Extend [your influence to the people] by means of the moral way. Care for them with kindness. Draw them to you with humaneness. Nurture them with / righteousness. Requite them with benevolence. Bind them with trustworthiness. Receive them with propriety. Harmonize them with music. Set a time limit for them in affairs. Test them with words.[56] Send them forth with strength. Overawe them with warnings.[57]

When the first [of the nine bases of government][58] is set in operation, both sovereign and subject will be able to live out their lives.[59] / When the second is set in operation, the people will all comply. When the third is set in operation, land will be opened up and government[60] perfected. / When the fourth is set in operation, farmers will enjoy leisure time yet cereals will be abundant.[61] When the fifth is set in operation, [corvée] services may be lightened yet funds will be plentiful.[62] / When the sixth is set in operation, fluctuations in affairs may be measured and understood. When the seventh is set in operation, [people from both] outside and inside [the country] may be employed. When the eighth is set in operation, [the prince's] supremacy will hold sway and his prestige be established. When the ninth is set in operation, the emperor's[63] undertakings will achieve fruition. /

30.1

30.2

30.3
2a

30.4

[55] Judging from the construction of the other sentences in this paragraph, four characters must be missing from the beginning of this one, but there is no way to reconstruct them.

[56] As it stands, this line 攻之以官, "attack them with officials," is unintelligible. Therefore I have followed the text of the parallel passage in the *You guan tu*, III, 9/9b8–9 (1 : 37.1), which writes 攻之以言. However, 攻 should be emended to 玫 in accordance with the writing of III, 9, in an old edition mentioned by Liu Ji and Yasui.

[57] Emending *cheng* 誠, "sincerity," to 誠 [Yasui and Guo Moruo]. The two characters are close in form and the reading of *cheng* here would be repetitious, since 信, "trustworthiness," in line 1b9 (30.1) expresses the same idea.

[58] The Yin commentary interprets this and the following eight sentences as referring to the traditional nine meetings of the feudal lords, which were supposed to have been called by Duke Huan of Qi between the years 681 and 651 B.C. The passage, 4b12–5b3 (32 : 11–33.4), also lists in detail the orders issued at nine meetings of the feudal lords, but without any apparent logical relation between the sequence of the orders and the results given here. In my opinion, the reference is probably to the nine bases [of government] mentioned in the following paragraph. See n. 65, below, for a discussion of these.

[59] The meaning of the two characters 得終 is not clear. The Yin commentary says they mean that both the high and low will fulfill the prince's orders.

[60] Emending 歟 to 政 [Igai, Hong, and He]. Zhang Peilun and Xu would emend it to 穀. Thus, "the grain crop will be successful."

[61] Emending 十 to 丰 = 豐 [Guo Moruo].

[62] The character 九 here is unintelligible. It is probably a corruption of 充 [Guo Moruo].

[63] 帝 here probably refers to the present emperors rather than to those of antiquity. It is a concept that was stressed by Li Si 李斯 (280?–208 B.C.). See Bodde, *China's First Unifier*, p. 130.

30.5   It is for the ruler of men to maintain the broad application[64] of the
nine bases [of government].[65] It is for the prime minister (*qing xiang*) to
30.6 maintain the employment of the eight / divisions [of officeholders].[66] It is
for the general to maintain complete awesomeness in the seven victories.[67] It is for the worthy to maintain a meticulous examination of the
six records.[68] It is for the common people to maintain unremitting
effort[69] toward the five tasks to be completed.[70] /

30.7   [When you move, no one will fail to follow; when you are quiescent,
no one will fail to be the same.][71]

---

[64] Emending 搏 to 博 [Igai, Wang Niansun, and Zhang Peilun].

[65] He Ruzhang and Zhang Peilun suggest that the nine bases of government (*jiu ben*
九本) are the "Nine Things to be Preserved" (*Jiu shou* 九守), the title of *Guanzi*, XVIII,
55. The nine are: the ruler's benevolence 德, clear sight 明, ability to listen 聽, rewards 賞,
questions 問, responses 因, communication 周, counsel 參, supervision of terminology
督名. Gustav Haloun translates this chapter in his "Legalist Fragments."

[66] These eight divisions 八分 most likely refer to the 八職 of the *Zhou li*, 3/5b6ff., which
Biot (*Tcheou-li*, I, p. 59) translates as the "huit degrés de la subordination administrative."
Zhang Peilun says they may refer to the eight guiding principles 八經 of *Guanzi*,
III, 10/17a8–9 (1:44.4): "For the sovereign and his subordinate officials there is
righteous conduct. For the honored and lowly there are separate roles. For the old and
young there are gradations in status. For the poor and rich there is proper
measure."

[67] The phrase 十官飾 has been badly corrupted. Other editions for 十, "ten," write 七,
"seven," which fits the numerical sequence of this passage. Moreover, the phrase here in
four characters destroys the balance with the two-character pattern above and below. I
have followed He Ruzhang and Zhang Peilun, who delete the characters 官飾 as an
interpolation. The seven victories listed in *Guanzi*, IV, 12/12b6–7 (1:56.12) are: the many
over the few, the speedy over the slow, the brave over the cowardly, the wise over the
stupid, the good over the bad, those who practice righteousness over those who do not,
those who follow the way of Heaven over those who do not.

[68] The six records (*liu ji* 六紀) are further mentioned in lines 2a10–11 (30.7): "There
are six records of flourishing and decay." The reference may be to legendary records of
the six ages from the reign of Sui Ren Shi to Fu Xi. Zhang Peilun gives an entirely
different interpretation to *liu ji*, which he reads as the "six regulators." He Ruzhang
identifies them with the six handles [of power] (*liu bing* 六秉) listed in *Guanzi*, VIII
20/6a10–12 (1.100.3–4): to kill, to nurture, to honor, to degrade, to impoverish, and to
enrich.

[69] Reading 解 as 懈 [Guo Moruo].

[70] Emending 紀 to 終 [Guo Moruo]. The two characters are similar in form, and the
following passage (2a10; 30.7) writes 富貧之終五. The writing of 紀 here represents an
assimilation of the same character in the line above. The "five tasks to be completed"
probably refer to the "five undertakings" 五事 that will determine prosperity or poverty.
First mentioned in *Guanzi*, I, 4/12b1 (1:11.12), they are discussed in considerable detail in
a special section, I, 4/13b5–14a8 (1:12.14–13.4). In short, they refer to the need for
conservation, water control, agriculture, animal husbandry and gardening, and simplicity
in handicrafts.

[71] This sentence is repeated in the following section under the eastern part of the chart
(3a5; 31.3). It appears out of context here, and since it is not to be found in that portion of
III, 9, concerned with the center, but only in that concerned with the east, Igai and Guo
Moruo believe it is an interpolation here and should be deleted.

There are three fundamentals that will determine order or disorder,[72] four relationships between the lowly and honored,[73] five tasks to be completed that will determine prosperity or poverty, six records of flourishing and decay, seven crucial concerns that will determine safety or danger,[74] / eight obligations that will determine strength or weakness,[75] nine propositions that will determine existence or extinction.[76]

Become well versed in these so they may be made known to the many categories of executive offices and all offices that estimate / resources.[77] Execute [officials] if they amass [private] wealth.[78] Exhort them to be

[72] The three fundamentals (*san ben* 三本) are also discussed in detail in I, 4/12b3–13a5 (1:11.13–12.6); they are that a man's virtue should be equal to his position, his achievement equal to his salary, and his ability equal to his office.

[73] Zhang Peilun believes that this phrase 卑尊之交 should be transposed with the phrase 安危之機 in the following line. Thus, "There are four crucial concerns that determine safety or danger." Another passage, 7b5–6 (35.3), mentions the crucial concerns as being four in number. Zhang cites the passage, I, 4/12a12 (1:11.11) 國之所以安危者四, "Four things determine whether a state is to know safety or danger," to show that the four crucial concerns are the four securities 四固. These are enumerated in a special section, I, 4/13a7–13b3 (1:12.8–12): "(1) Those who have great charismatic power but are imperfect in terms of basic goodness should not be given control of the state. (2) Those who on seeing worthiness are unable to yield to it, should not be given positions of honor. (3) Those who avoid punishing relatives and men of high rank should not be commissioned to lead armed forces. (4) Those who neither appreciate essential undertakings nor pay heed to the benefits of Earth and at the same time treat lightly the imposition of levies and exactions [upon the people] should not be assigned to administer cities and towns." I know of no reference elsewhere to the four relationships 四交 between the lowly and honored.

[74] As mentioned in n. 73, Zhang Peilun believes this sentence should read 卑尊之交七. He would also read 交 as 效. Thus, "There are seven categories that affect both the lowly and honored." Zhang explains these as the seven standards 七法, which are enumerated in detail in *Guanzi*, II, 6/1b7–2b10 (1:22.11–23.11). They include: laws of nature 則, physical qualities 象, standards for measurement 法, forms of transformation 化, permissive or inhibitory actions 決塞, patterns of mental behavior 心術, and categories of mensuration 計數.

[75] Zhang Peilun says these refer to the "Eight Observations" 八觀, the title of *Guanzi*, V, 13.

[76] Zhang Peilun says these refer to the "Nine Ways to Failure" 九敗, the title of a subsection in I, 4/16b6–17a1 (1:15.12–16.2). The first three of these "ways to failure" refer to the teachings of Song Xing 宋鈃 (Song Keng 宋牼), Mo Di 墨翟 (Mozi 墨子), and Yang Zhu 楊朱. The fourth may refer to those of Wei Mou 魏牟, a hedonist follower of Yang Zhu.

[77] This sentence 練之···則署 appears badly corrupted but none of the commentators is able to present a clear reconstruction. I have tried to read the text as it stands, but the translation is forced.

[78] This and the following sentences are also unclear. Guo Moruo would emend 殺 to 敦 and read 僇 as 繆 = 穆. Thus, "Honor [officials] if they amass [public] wealth."

diligent in improving[79] [the morals of] the masses. Have two categories [of officials record] all essential [matters]. / When distributing gratuities, be certain to examine the situation in minute detail. When exercising authority, be certain to understand the [golden] mean.[80]

The preceding is situated in the central part of the chart.

[INNER EAST]

[Calendar] In spring, if government [suitable only to] winter is carried out, things will shrivel with cold.[81] If government [suitable only to] autumn is carried out, there will be thunder.[82] If government [suitable only to] summer is carried out, [growth] will be stifled [by an excess of Yang].[83] /

During the twelve [days] when the vital force of Earth is coming forth, issue warnings about spring affairs. During the twelve [days] of the lesser *mao*,[84] go out / to plough. During the twelve [days] when the vital force

[79] Following the Yang edition, which for *xuan* 選 writes *qian* 遷 [Guo Moruo]. Ding would also follow the Yang edition, but would interpret *qian* to mean "move about." Thus, "Exhort [officials] to be diligent in circulating among the masses." Dai and Xu would keep to the Zhao edition reading of *xuan*. Thus, "Exhort [officials] to be diligent in taking count of the masses."

[80] This paragraph should be concluded by the opening sentence of the second portion of the central part of the chart (6a1; 33.10) 必得(德)文威武, "Be certain to have virtuous civil [officials] and awe-inspiring military [officials]."

[81] The *Si shi* chapter of the *Guanzi*, XIV, 40/5b9 (2:78.6), for *su* 肅, "to shrivel," writes 雕, which Dai reads as 凋, "to wither." The *Yue ling* (*Li ji*, V, 6/9a6; Legge, *Li Ki*, XXVII, p. 267) writes *su*: "If in the third month of spring, orders [suitable only to] winter are carried out, a period of cold will break out and the plants and trees will all shrivel (*su*)."

[82] For 雷, "thunder," XIV, 40/5b9 (2:78.7), writes 霜, "frost."

[83] For 閣, XIV, 40/5b9 (2:78.7), writes 欲, which Guo Moruo reads as 欯, "to become exhausted."

[84] *Mao* 卯 is the fourth of the so-called twelve earthly branches (*di zhi* 地支). In the *Shi ze xun* of the *Huainanzi*, one of them is assigned to each month beginning with the second month of winter, the time of the solstice. Here (5/2b) *mao* is associated with the second month of spring. The *Shuowen jiezi* of Xu Shen 許慎 (d. A.D. 120?), XIV, B/14a3, gives an interesting though hardly scientific rationale for this: "*Mao* 夘 (the ancient script form of 卯) means mao 冒, 'to burst forth.' During the second month all things burst forth from the earth and come up. The form of the character gives the appearance of an open gate. Therefore the second month is the gate of Heaven." Thus, at least from the time of the *Huainanzi*, the character *mao* is definitely associated with spring. This however, would not explain why it should also appear in connection with autumn in passage 3b11–4a1 (31.12–13).

Therefore Chen and Guo Moruo offer another suggestion. They believe *mao* was originally written *luan* 卵. The form is very close and, as Chen points out, in this calendar none of the other seasons uses one of the earthly branches to designate its periods. (There is some question on this point. See n. 110, below.) Guo supports Chen by saying that spring and autumn are the two mating periods, and it is for this reason that the term *luan*, which refers to the male and female sex organs as well as eggs, is used for both these seasons.

of Heaven descends, bestow favors. During the twelve [days] when the vital force of well-being[85] arrives, repair the gates. During the twelve [days] of clear brightness,[86] issue prohibitions. During the twelve [days] of the first *mao*, unite the men and women.[87] During the twelve [days each] of the middle and final *mao*, / carry out the same activities.

Since it is the season when [the number] eight is elevated, the prince wears the color green, tastes sour flavors, and listens to the *jiao* note.[88] He governs with the vital force that brings desiccation[89] / and utilizes the number eight. He drinks from the well of the Green Ruler[90] and uses the fire of feathered animals when cooking. / His temper is unrestrained. His activities are devoted to caring for and nurturing [the people].

As the equable vital force [of the phase wood] circulates and permeates, all creatures [appropriate to this season] leave the state of quiescence and their forms acquire markings.

[Essay I] Unite [the people] at home[91] and bring those abroad within your orbit. Then strong countries will become like members of your family[92] while weak ones / will become dependencies. When you move, no one will fail to follow; when you are quiescent, no one will fail to be the same.

Initiate [undertakings] and issue [orders] in accordance with the rules of propriety. Then timeliness and propriety will certainly be achieved. / Be harmonious and agreeable and refrain from perniciousness.[93]

---

[85] Reading 義 as 和 [Guo Moruo].

[86] *Qing ming* 清明 is the name of one of the present twenty-four solar periods. It extends from approximately April 5 to 19.

[87] According to the *Zhou li*, 14/6b6 (Biot, *Tcheou-li*, I, p. 307): "In the middle month of spring [the officer in charge of marriages] orders the assembling 會 of men and women. At this time there is no restriction on people being married without preliminary formalities." It is also stated that he orders men of thirty and women of twenty to marry. Granet, in his *Festivals and Songs of Ancient China*, p. 126, cites this passage in the *Guanzi* as evidence for a spring mating festival, which in the autumn resulted in marriage if the girl became pregnant.

[88] The color green, sour taste, and *jiao* 角 note are all associated with the phase wood and spring.

[89] 燥; the Yin commentary explains that the frequent spring winds cause dryness.

[90] Wen would identify the Green Ruler 青后 as the Green Emperor, one of the Five Celestial Emperors mentioned above. See n. 33. According to the *Zhou li zhusu*, 22/11a, the Green Emperor is the ruler of the east and has the alternative name, Ling Weiyang 靈威仰. He is also popularly associated with the Wood Star (i.e., the planet Jupiter) and his nature is said to be that of a green dragon.

[91] Following Dai, who says 空 is a corruption of the preceding character 内 (repeated by mistake) and should be deleted.

[92] Emending 圉 to 眷 [Igai]. The two characters are also confused elsewhere in the *Guanzi*.

[93] Reading 基 as 甚 [Yin Tongyang].

30.14

31.1
3a

31.2

31.2
3a3

31.3

31.4

Then the honored and lowly will not engage in litigations.[94] [If these are done] the fluctuations in seasonal affairs will occur on the proper day.

The preceding is situated on the outer side of the eastern part of the chart.

[INNER SOUTH]

[Calendar] In the summer, if government [suitable only to] spring is carried out, there will be winds. If government [suitable only to] winter is carried out, [plants] will droop. [If this is repeated, there will be rain and hail.][95] If government [suitable only to] autumn is carried out, there will be floods.[96]

During the twelve [days] of the lesser *ying*,[97] perfect your virtue.[98] / During the twelve [days] when the *jue*[99] vital force descends,[100] grant ranks and rewards. During the twelve [days] of the middle *ying*, bestow favors. During the twelve [days] of the middle *jue*,[101] gather [crops]. During the twelve [days] when the lesser heat[102] arrives, make full use of

[94] Reading 司 as 辭 [Guo Moruo].

[95] This sentence seems to violate the structural pattern of the passages concerning the other seasons. Xu suggests that it was originally a marginal note later incorporated into the text.

[96] The parallel passage of XIV, 40/6b5 (2:79.3), reads: "In summer, if government [suitable only to] spring is carried out, there will be winds 風. If government [suitable only to] autumn is carried out, there will be floods 水. If government [suitable only to] winter is carried out, [plants] will droop 落."

[97] *Ying* 郢 was the name of the capital of the state of Chu and appears elsewhere only as a proper name. He Ruzhang and Liu Shipei say it should be written *ying* 盈 "to fill" or "be overflowing." The *Er ya*, 5/4b7, contains the passage 夏為長嬴 (= 盈): "The summer is for growth and fulfillment." Thus *ying* here probably refers to the growth and fulfillment that take place during the summer.

[98] He Ruzhang would interpret 至德 as "summon [men of] virtue."

[99] *Jue* 絕 means "to cut off." Yasui explains that when the Yin reaches its low ebb in the cycle during the summer, it is cut off by the Yang.

[100] The second character 下 is redundant and probably represents an error on the part of the copyist. It should be deleted [Ding].

[101] The term *zhong jue* 中絕 here is not clear. *Jue* probably refers to the *jue* vital force mentioned above, but the use of *zhong* would seem to imply that another period, which also uses the term *jue*, should follow. The only other alternative is that this is the middle period of the summer season. However, this does not fit the pattern of names of the other periods. I am of the opinion that the two characters *zhong jue* are corrupt and should be emended to read *da ying* 大郢 (= 盈), "greater *ying*." Thus the series of *ying* periods (limited as the text now stands to a "first" and "middle" *ying*) would be complete.

[102] Emending *da shu* 大暑, "greater heat," to *xiao shu* 小暑, "lesser heat"; they must have been reversed by mistake in the text. The greater heat, one of the twenty-four solar periods, begins about one month after the summer solstice, extending from about July 23 to August 6, which is the actual period of the greatest summer heat; to put it before the lesser heat is

those who are skillful. During the twelve [days each] of the middle heat and greater heat[103] [the complete dominance of the Yang] comes to an end. / During these three heats carry out the same activities.

Since it is the season when [the number] / seven is elevated, the prince wears the color red, tastes bitter flavors, and listens to the *yu* note.[104] / He governs with the Yang vital force[105] and utilizes the number seven. He drinks from the well of the Red Ruler[106] and uses the fire of furry animals for cooking. / His temper is simple[107] and sincere. His activities are straightforward and generous.

As the equable vital force [of the phase fire] circulates and permeates, all creatures [appropriate to this season] leave the state of quiescence and their forms acquire markings.

[Essay H] Arrange the bureaus and offices. Clarify their names and responsibilities. Examine and criticize the various ministers and office-holders. Then those in inferior positions will not take advantage of their superiors and the lowly will not take advantage of the honored. When the laws have been established, estimates obtained, and no cliques permitted among the people, those in superior positions will be honored, / their inferiors will be humble, and neither those far removed nor those near at hand will be perverse.

The preceding is situated on the outer side of the southern part of the chart.

[INNER WEST]

[Calendar] In autumn, if government [suitable only to] summer is carried out, [plants will sprout] leaves. If government [suitable only to]

---

unnatural. The Yang edition, for the final of the three periods of heat, writes *da shu* instead of *xiao shu*; thus in this edition, even though the name of the first period had been altered to *da shu*, the name of the last period was still given correctly.

[103] Emending *xiao shu* 小暑, "lesser heat," to *da shu* 大暑, "greater heat." See n. 102, above.

[104] The color red and bitter taste are associated with the phase fire and summer, but the *yu* 羽 note is usually correlated with winter and the *zhi* 徵 note with summer. See the *Yue ling* (*Li ji*, V, 6/22b4 and 9b5; Legge, *Li Ki*, XXVII, pp. 296 and 268).

[105] This clause 治陽氣 does not appear in the Yang edition.

[106] Wen would identify the Red Ruler 赤后 as the Red Emperor, one of the Five Celestial Emperors mentioned in n. 33. According to the *Zhou li zhusu*, 2/11a9, the Red Emperor is the ruler of the south and has the alternative name, Chibiao Nu 赤熛怒. He is also popularly associated with the Fire Star (i.e., the planet Mars), and his nature is said to be that of a scarlet bird.

[107] Emending *bao* 薄, "mean" or "stingy," to *pu* 樸 [Ting]. *Pu* is often used together with *chun* 純, "simple," whereas *bao* does not make much sense here.

spring[108] is carried out, [plants] will flower [but not bear fruit].[109] If government [suitable only to] winter is carried out, / [plants] will wither away.[110]

During the twelve [days] when the seasonal wind arrives, issue warnings about autumn affairs. During the twelve [days] of the lesser *mao*,[111] distribute the various ranks widely.[112] During the twelve [days] when the white dew[113] falls, gather [crops]. During the twelve [days] when markings are restored,[114] bestow favors. During the twelve [days] of the first temporal divisions,[115] / [fix] taxes and duties.[116] During the twelve [days] of the first *mao*, unite the men and women.[117] During the twelve [days each] of the middle / and final *mao*, carry out the same activities.

Since it is the season when [the number] nine is brought into harmony, the prince wears the color white, / tastes acrid flavors, and listens to the

---

[108] The Ming (1582) cutting of the Zhao edition mistakenly writes 秋 for 春.

[109] The *Shi ze xun* of the *Huainanzi*, 5/18b1, contains an inverted version of these two sentences: "In autumn, if orders [suitable only to] summer are carried out, [plants] will flower [but not bear fruit]. If orders [suitable only to] spring are carried out, [plants will sprout] luxuriant foliage 榮."

[110] The parallel passage in XIV, 40/7a10–11 (2:79.11–12), reads: "In autumn, if government [suitable only to] spring is carried out, [plants will sprout] luxuriant foliage [but not bear fruit]. If government [suitable only to] summer is carried out, there will be floods 水. If government [suitable only to] winter is carried out [plants] will wither away 耗 = 秏."

[111] The use of the character *mao* 卯 in this paragraph in connection with autumn is extremely doubtful. *Mao* 卯 (written 戼 in the ancient script) is very close in form to *you* 酉 (written 丣 in the ancient script), the tenth of the earthly branches. According to the *Shuowen jiezi*, XIV, B/16a4: "*Mao* is the gate of spring; all things have already come up. *You* is the gate of autumn; everything has already gone back into [the earth]. The line on top (一) gives the appearance of closing the gate." Therefore *mao* is probably a mistake for *you*. Guo Moruo, however, believes that *mao* here should also be written *luan* 卵 as in the previous passage, 2b8–10 (30.13–14). See n. 84, above.

[112] Emending 薄 to 博 [Guo Moruo].

[113] *Bai lu* 白露, one of the twenty-four solar periods, from about September 8 to 22.

[115] The meaning of the term 復理 is not clear. I have followed the suggestion of Professor Derk Bodde that this is a meteorological term for when animals and birds grow new fur and feathers before the forthcoming cold.

[115] The meaning of this term *shi jie* 始節 is not completely clear. *Jie* is a dividing point in time. It probably refers here to the autumn equinox. Assuming that the first twelve-day period began about the same time as *Li chun* 立春, "Beginning of Spring," the first of our present twenty-four solar periods, which commences about February 5, it would require approximately 229 days to reach the autumn equinox; in fact the 19 twelve-day periods preceding this one total 228 days. The solstices and equinoxes are commonly referred to as *jie*, or temporal divisions; the character *shi*, "first," used here would tend to indicate that, in this calendar, the autumn equinox was considered as the beginning.

[116] *Guanzi*, III, 9/12b7 (1:39.14), before 賦 has the character 弟, which Liu Shipei reads as 第. Thus, "[fix] the graduated taxes and duties."

[117] The *Zhou li* makes no special mention of an autumn marriage festival. Granet, *Festivals and Songs*, pp. 126–127 and 200, believed that at this autumn union young men came to fetch their brides. See n. 87, above.

shang note.[118] He governs through the vital force of moisture and utilizes the number nine. He drinks from the well of the White Ruler[119]

32.1   and uses the fire of shell creatures[120] / when cooking. His temper is respectful and reverential. His activities are devoted to grasping sharp-pointed [weapons].[121]

32.2   As the equable vital force [of the phase metal] circulates / and permeates, all creatures [appropriate to this season] leave the state of quiescence and their forms acquire markings.

32.2   [Essay G] Separate[122] the rearing of male and female [children].
4a6   Organize the groups of ten and five in the districts and villages.

32.3   Measure / the amount of the public stores. Determine the calculations of the bureaus and offices. Nurture the old and weak and do not neglect them.[123] Remain trustworthy through both profit and loss,[124] without regard for self-interest.

The preceding is situated on the outer side of the western part of the chart.

[INNER NORTH]

32.4   [Calendar] In winter, if government [suitable only to] autumn is
4a10   carried out, there will be fog.[125] If government [suitable only to] summer is carried out, there will be thunder. If government [suitable only to] spring is carried out, there will be steamy mists and exudations.[126]

[118] The color white, acrid taste, and *shang* 商 note are all associated with the phase metal and autumn.

[119] Wen would identify the White Ruler 白后 as the White Emperor, one of the Five Celestial Emperors mentioned above in n. 33. According to the *Zhou li zhusu*, 222/11a9, the White Emperor is the ruler of the west and has the alternative name, Baizhao Ju 白招拒. He is also popularly associated with the Metal Star (i.e., the planet Venus), and his nature is said to be that of a white tiger.

[120] Igai and Wang Yinzhi suggest that 蟲, "creatures," was originally written 獸, "animals," in accordance with the examples in the other seasons, all of which speak of animals.

[121] Guo Moruo would emend 搏銳 to 博悅, in order to accord with the pattern of the parallel sentence under the other seasons. Thus, "His activities are devoted to being liberal and pleasing." However, weapons go with the phase metal, which is inherent in the meaning of 銳, "pointed."

[122] Ding would read 間 as 簡 = 閒, "to supervise."

[123] Emending 通 to 遺 [Wu Zhizhong].

[124] Emending 周 to 害 in accordance with the parallel passage III, 9/12b12 (1:40.3) [Zhao and Wang Niansun].

[125] XIV, 40/8a1 (2:80.6), writes 旱, "drought."

[126] According to the commentators, one of the two characters, *zheng* 烝 or *xie* 泄, is a later interpolation, since it destroys the balance of the related passages above and below. Xu and Dai would omit *zheng*, "steamy mists," basing their decision on XIV, 40/8a1

During the twelve [days] of the first cold, complete the punishments. During the twelve [days] of the lesser *yu*,[127] bestow favors, / During the twelve [days] of the middle cold,[128] gather [firewood].[129] During the twelve [days] of the middle *yu*,[130] [conduct] the great collection.[131] During the twelve [days] when the cold[132] arrives, be quiescent.[133] During the [first] twelve [days] of the greater / cold,[134] utilize the Yin. During the [last] twelve [days] of the greater cold, [the complete dominance of the Yin] comes to an end. During these three colds, carry out the same activities.[135]

(2:80.6), which only writes *xie*, "exudations." Igai would omit *xie*, basing his decision on a parallel passage in the *Chunqiu fanlu*, XIV, 64/3b13, which writes *zheng*.

[127] *Yu* 榆 usually means an "elm tree," but here the meaning would hardly seem to apply. Yasui is the only commentator to attempt an explanation: "*Yu* ought to be *yu* 揄 and *yu* 揄 = *chui* 垂. During the second month of winter the sun is in the extreme south. It is suspended (*chui*) 15,000 *li* beyond the equator. Therefore this is taken as the name of a period." Yasui is clearly referring to the solstice, but if our calculations concerning the autumn equinox are correct (see n. 115, above), this is too early, there having been a lapse of only five periods, or sixty days. The logical reference in the calendar at this point would be to the closing up of the earth which takes place at this time, but this idea is not to be found in the present writing of the text.

[128] 中寒, "middle cold," should probably be read 中榆, "middle *yu*." The next period is called "middle *yu*" but there is no third one to complete the series. There also seems to be an inordinate number of periods with the same name ("cold") in this section as compared with those of the other seasons.

[129] The meaning of 收聚 here is not clear. It would seem to be too late in the season for the harvesting of crops, as was the case in line 3b11 (31.12). Therefore I have followed *Guanzi*, XVIII, 57/8a4 (3:18.8–9), which states that firewood should be collected after the agricultural work is finished.

[130] 中榆, "middle *yu*," should probably be 大榆, "greater *yu*," to complete the series. See n. 128, above.

[131] Again, this would seem too late in the season to refer to the harvesting of crops. Therefore I have interpreted 大收 to mean the collection of revenues due the state after the harvest.

[132] 寒, "cold," here should probably be written 小寒, "lesser cold." These last three periods of winter should correspond to the last three periods of heat in summer. Under the twenty-four solar period system the year ends with the lesser and greater cold, just as summer ends with the lesser and greater heat.

[133] This is clearly the time of the winter solstice when people are supposed to remain indoors. *Guanzi*, XIV, 40/7b8–9 (2:80.3), states that the ruler should prohibit the movement of people so the earth will have no exudations. According to the *Yue ling* (*Li ji*, V, 6/26a8–26b1; Legge, *Li Ki*, XXVII, pp. 304–305): "In this month the shortest day arrives. The Yin and Yang struggle [for supremacy] and all living things begin to stir. Superior men give themselves to self-adjustment and fasting. They keep retired within their houses and seek to be at peace with themselves.... They seek [complete] quiescence in order to await the settlement of [the struggle between] the Yin and Yang."

[134] 大寒, "greater cold," here should probably be written 中寒, "middle cold." See n. 132, above.

[135] That is, they carry on inside activities.

32.6   Since it is the season when [the number] six is functioning, / the prince wears the color black, tastes salty flavors, and listens to the *zhi* note.[136]

32.7   He governs with the Yin vital force and / utilizes the number six. He drinks from the well of the Black Ruler[137] and uses the fire of scaly

32.8   animals when cooking. His temper is compassionate and kind. / His activities are simple[138] and sincere.

As the equable vital force [of the phase water] circulates and permeates, all creatures [appropriate to this season] leave the state of quiescence and their forms acquire markings.

32.8   [Essay J] The weapons should be completed in grand style.[139] The
4b7
32.9   instructions should be carried out in minute detail.[140] / Movement and rest should not be recorded; marches and stopovers should not be measured. Take care[141] to dwell[142] in different places during the four

32.10   seasons. / Take different [roads] when going out and returning so both will be safe.[143] Make clear [the need for] nurturing life in order to dispel any resistance. Examine receipts and bequests in order to summarize them.[144] /

32.11   At the first meeting of the feudal lords[145] the order was proclaimed:

[136] The color black and salty taste are both associated with the phase water and winter. However, the *zhi* 徵 note is usually correlated with summer and the *yu* 羽 note with winter. See the *Yue ling* (*Li ji*, V, 6/9b5 and 22b4; Legge, *Li Ki*, XXVII, pp. 268 and 296).

[137] Wen would identify the Black Ruler 黑后 as the Black Emperor, one of the Five Celestial Emperors mentioned above in n. 33. According to the *Zhou li zhusu*, 2/11a9, the Black Emperor is the ruler of the north and has the alternative name, Xieguang Ji 叶光纪. He is also popularly associated with the Water Star (i.e., planet Mercury) and his nature is said to be that of a dark warrior 玄武.

[138] Emending 薄 to 横. See n. 107, above. Here the text refers to the prince's activities rather than his temper, as in line 3b4 (31.9).

[139] Emending 僇 to 繆 = 穆 [Ding and Guo Moruo].

[140] Emending 鈔 to 眇 [Song and Dai].

[141] The phrase 戒審四時 contains four characters, while the pattern for the following sentence is three each. Therefore I have followed Ding and Xu in deleting 審 as an interpolation taken from the passage 審取予 (4b11; 32.10).

[142] This passage is unclear. I have followed Li in reading 息 as 處. He explains that the ruler dwells in separate parts of the Ming Tang during each of the four seasons.

[143] Again, this passage 異出入以兩易 is unclear. I have followed Li because this section appears to be primarily concerned with the ruler's security and his political and military relations with his neighbors. There is also a somewhat similar passage in *Guanzi*, VI, 17/14a7 (1:82.1), 出入異塗，則傷其敵: "If different roads are used for going out and returning, it will be harmful to the enemy."

[144] Dai and Guo Moruo would read the final 之 as 乏, "in order to summarize your deficits."

[145] This and the following eight meetings of the feudal lords certainly appear to be a reference to the six military and three civil conferences that Duke Huan of Qi was supposed to have called between 681 and 651 B.C. In my opinion, the content of this passage is not in harmony with the remainder of the essay, which is primarily a list of do's and don'ts to ensure success for the ruler. Compared with the rest of the text, it also contains surprisingly few textual corruptions. Thus I feel it represents a portion of some

Unless the command comes from the Dark Emperor,[146] do not embark on a single day of military activity. /

At the second meeting of the feudal lords the order was proclaimed: Nurture the orphaned and old. Feed the chronically ill and take in widowers[147] and widows.

At the third meeting of the feudal lords the order was proclaimed: The land tax shall be five percent, / the market tax two percent, and the customs tax one percent. Avoid shortages of implements for ploughing and weaving.

At the fourth meeting of the feudal lords the order was proclaimed: Build roads. Make your measurements uniform. Standardize your weights. / Do not tax[148] the marshlands but open and close them according to the season.

At the fifth meeting of the feudal lords the order was proclaimed: When arranging the regular sacrificial offerings of spring, autumn, winter, and summer, and the ancient sacrifices to / Heaven, soil, mountains, and rivers, be sure to accord with the proper time.

At the sixth meeting of the feudal lords the order was proclaimed: Supply the Dark Palace[149] with the products of your soil and request the four aides[150] / to use them in ceremonies to the Lord on High (*Shang Di* 上帝).

At the seventh meeting of the feudal lords the order was proclaimed: Those who lack propriety in the four aspects [of behavior][151] should be banished. /

---

other essay inserted here by the chart maker because he needed a filler to match the longer outer northern section. It is also possible that this particular passage was used because it appears to refer to the Dark Palace—the only reference, it should be added, to be found in the entire chapter.

[146] That is, the emperor is in residence in the northern Dark Palace or Dark Hall (Xuan Tang) during the winter.

[147] Emending 孤 to 矜 [Zhang Peilun and Xu].

[148] This sentence as it stands lacks a verb and should be emended to accord with III, 9/13b10 (1:40.2), by inserting the two characters 毋征 at the beginning.

[149] Emending 官 to 宫 [Zhang Peilun].

[150] According to the *Li ji*, VI, 8/18a4 (Legge, *Li Ki*, XXVII, p. 350), in the time of Emperor Yu and during the Xia, Shang, and Zhou dynasties, there were the four aides (*si fu* 四輔) and three supreme ministers (*san gong* 三公). Kong Yingda in the *Li ji zhusu*, 20/16b3, says that the four aides were a counsellor (*yi* 疑), assistant (*cheng* 丞), aide (*fu* 輔), and attendant (*bi* 弼), who occupied positions to the front, behind, left, and right, respectively.

[151] Following Yu Yue, Xu, and Guo Moruo, who would delete 宫 because it destroys the balance of this sentence with the one that follows and appears unintelligible here. Guo further explains the four aspects [of behavior] 四體 as seeing, hearing, speaking, and movement.

33.3   At the eighth meeting of the feudal lords the order was proclaimed:
Those who are not devious[152] in instituting the four [kinds of] righteousness[153] should be elevated to the Dark Palace[154] to wait upon the
three supreme ministers.[155] /

33.4   At the ninth meeting of the feudal lords the order was proclaimed:
5b
Use as presents [to the court] products of your fiefs and possessions of
your states. /

33.5   The great commands of the nine meetings having thereupon been
issued, it regularly happened that:

         The feudal lords who lived over a thousand *li* [from court] but within
33.6   two thousand *li* / came to court every three years to study the commands. Every two years their three ministers of state (*qing* 卿) were
dispatched to the four aides. Every year a senior great officer[156] on the
first day of the first month came [to court] to review and receive
33.7   commands from the three / supreme ministers.

         Those feudal lords who lived over two thousand *li* [from the court] but
within three thousand *li* came to meet every five years to study the
commands. Every three years a specially appointed minister[157] made
33.8   requests about affairs. Every two years a great / officer reported the
fortunes or misfortunes [of his state].

         Those[158] feudal lords living further away than three thousand *li* /
33.9   arrived [at court] once in a generation. Every ten years the primary
heir entered [the court] to be given correct guidance in propriety and

[152] Emending 議 to 儀 [Yu Yue and Guo Moruo]. The two characters were similar in
their archaic pronunciation (*ngia* and *nga*).

[153] According to the Yin commentary, the four kinds of righteousness 四義 are: to
refrain from barricading valleys, hoarding grain, changing the legitimate heir, and taking
a concubine as the legal wife. The *Huainanzi*, 15/14b2–3, lists them for a general as:
"When pacifying the country do not count [the number of] your troops; as a commander
do not take [special] care of your own person; when you see difficulties do not be afraid to
die; when deciding doubtful cases do not put to death the guilty." Guo Moruo says that 義
probably ought to be 儀, "rules of conduct or ceremony." The *Yi Zhou shu*, III,
29/10b2–5, presents a list of these as: filial piety, respect for elders, compassion and
kindness, magnanimity.

[154] Emending 官 to 宮. See n. 149.

[155] According to the *Shang shu*, V, 20/5, the three supreme ministers (*san gong* 三公)
under the Zhou were the grand tutor (*taishi* 太師), grand secretary (*taifu* 太傅), and grand
guardian (*taibao* 太保).

[156] *Ling dafu* 令大夫 is an unusual term. It appears also in the *Guanzi*, XXIII, 81/18a10
(3:99.6), where it clearly refers to an official with a rank higher than that of an ordinary
great officer (*dafu* 大夫).

[157] Reading 名 as 命 [Zhang Peilun and Zhang Binglin].

[158] The two sentences 十年...受變 are clearly out of place; they should follow the
phrase 世一至 (5b10–11; 33.9). The translation has been rendered accordingly.

righteousness. Every five years a great officer requested to receive any changes [in the commands].

[The feudal lords] would install a great officer [in the capital as an official] to inquire into the safety of the court.[159] They would present tribute[160] and receive commands.

The preceding is situated on the outer side of the northern part of the chart.

[OUTER CENTER]

[Essay B] [There should be virtuous[161] civil (officials) and awe-inspiring military (officials).][162]

Training of officials is a necessity for victory.[163] Timing is the ultimate factor in victory. / Flexibility is the secret of victory. The practice of righteousness is the principle of victory. Making names accord with reality is a vital concern for victory. Timely division [of spoils] is the business of victory. / Investigation [of places] to be attacked is the [prerequisite] activity for victory. Being complete in preparations is the origin of victory. / Inscrutability is the basis for victory.

To be victorious: Be sure you are alone in your awesomeness. Be sure to calculate your resources. Be sure to ascertain [the enemy's situation]. / Be sure in the selection of your knights. Be sure to regulate salaries. Be sure of the direction of your expenditures. Be sure of guiding principles. / Be sure [to differentiate] between life and death, success and failure, conformity and nonconformity, reality and emptiness, growth and decay.

Be conscientious about essentials when developing tactics so the enemy will not be able to measure / them. Be completely conscientious when utilizing your advantages[164] so the enemy will not be able to contend against you. Clarify the meaning of terms and commend real performance[165] so your knights will be willing to sacrifice their

---

[159] Guo Moruo says 安, "safety," is a corruption of 官 and that a 廷官 is a hostage. Thus, "[The feudal lords] would install a great officer in the capital as a hostage."

[160] Reading 共 as 貢 [Guo Moruo].

[161] Emending 得 to 德 [Dai, He Ruzhang, and Zhang Peilun].

[162] This sentence clearly concludes the final paragraph of the central part of the chart (2b4; 30.10). See n. 80.

[163] The Yang edition lacks the successive 之 characters throughout the following paragraph.

[164] Guo Moruo would emend 利, "advantages," to 制. Thus, "Be completely conscientious when making use of your regulations."

[165] The relationship between 名, "names" or "terminology," and 實, "reality," in general was a popular concern among various schools of thought during the late Warring

34.3 lives. / Conduct attacks[166] in an unanticipated manner so knights will welcome being in your employ. Exchange[167] materials in accordance with the areas [where they are produced] so weapons will be fully
34.4 prepared. Rely upon the able and take advantage of preparations / so what you seek will certainly be obtained. When assigning duties, clarify what is essential so the knights will not be remiss. Do not have a fixed pattern to your preparations so[168] you will be flexible in meeting [the enemy]. /

34.5 Listen for the minutest [sound][169] and you will be able to hear what has not yet come within bounds. Look for the newest and you will be
34.6 able to see what has not yet taken form. / Think about the abstruse and you will be able to understand what has not yet begun. Attack with surprise and you will be able to achieve [your objective] without being detected. Move when [your power] is in the ascendancy[170] and you will
34.7 be able to gain their treasure. / Establish yourself by means of stratagems and you will be able to realize [your objective] with no one able to attack you.[171]

See that the weapons are complete and instructions observed. Then
34.8 no road or village will be too far removed. / See that orders are examined
7a and instructions widely applied. Then no mountain or river will be too dangerous. Be single-minded[172] and steadfast. Then you will be able to
34.9 move freely and / be unrivaled [in battle]. Be careful of your orders and examine the symbols [on your signal flags]. Then in case of attack you need not wait upon powerful allies. Make clear the necessity for
34.10 victory. / Then the mild-mannered will become bold. Avoid [tricky] techniques in [the employment of] weapons. Then even the stupid will

---

States Period. Here the reference is to giving substantial rewards to those persons whose conduct fully lived up to such terms as loyalty or bravery.

[166] The phrase 奇舉發不意 contains five characters and is thereby out of balance with the passages above and below, which contain only four. I have followed Wang Niansun in deleting *qi* 奇 as a later interpolation. The *Sanko* edition of Yasui lacks *qi*. Guo Moruo, however, would omit 發. Thus, "When making unorthodox attacks, act in an unanticipated manner."

[167] Yu Yue would read 交 as 校: "When examining materials, take into consideration the areas [where they are produced]."

[168] Inserting 則 in accordance with the format of the other sentences in this paragraph.

[169] Emending 鈔 to 眇 [He Ruzhang].

[170] The character 昌 here appears doubtful. I have followed the interpretation given by Yasui. Dai would emend it to 冒. Thus, "Move under cover and you will be able to gain their treasure."

[171] Emending 古 to 攻 [Dai and Zhang Peilun].

[172] Emending 博 to 搏 [Igai and Wang Niansun].

[use] them wisely. Attack where [the enemy] is defenseless. Then even the
clumsy / will be skillful. Such is the art [of war].

Be diligently[173] careful concerning the ten orders.[174] Distinguish
clearly the nine symbols.[175] Systematically[176] practice the ten
weapons.[177] Be well drilled in / the five instructions.[178] Painstakingly
cultivate the three means of command.[179]

Be certain to set up a permanent commander.[180] Be certain that
detailed plans are prepared beforehand.[181] Seek for the finest materials
in the world. Examine the sharp / weapons of the various artisans. When
the weapons have been completed, distinguish the bad from the
good through competitive trials.[182] Collect the martial heroes of
the world. Gain possession of the recognized talent in the world.
Move [183] like the wind and rain. Deploy [your forces] like thunder
and lightning.[184]

The preceding is situated in the center of the chart.

[173] Emending 動 to 勤 [Guo Moruo].

[174] I have not been able to identify specifically these ten orders 十號.

[175] The nine symbols 九章 are listed in detail in *Guanzi*, VI, 17/12a11–b3 (1:80.6–8).

[176] Reading 飾 as 飭.

[177] For "ten weapons" 十器, VI, 17/13b4 (1:81.7), writes "nine weapons" 九器, but
this passage appears to be corrupt. I have not been able to identify specifically either a
category of ten or nine weapons except that the *Zhou li*, 32/2b7 (Biot, *Tcheou-li*, II, p. 237)
speaks of the five arms 五兵 and five shields 五盾.

[178] Emending 官 to 教 [Hong]. The latter is mistakenly assimilated with the former in
the following sentence. The five instructions are discussed in detail in VI, 17/12a3–6
(1:80.4–6).

[179] The three means of command 三官 are drums, metal instruments (cymbals and
gongs), and banners, as listed in VI, 17/12a3–6 (1:80.2–4).

[180] Ding would emend this passage 必設常主 to 主必設常 to accord with the structural pattern of the following sentence. Thus, "The commander must set up constant
standards."

[181] According to *Guanzi*, II, 6/5b11–12 (1:26.9–10): "Therefore the proper way of
preparing for an attack is always to be certain that detailed plans have been completed at
home before troops are dispatched beyond the borders."

[182] Again according to II, 6/5a12 (1:26.2–3): "Therefore [the ruler] amasses the finest
materials of the realm and examines the sharp weapons of the artisans. During the spring
and autumn there are competitive trials in order to make a selection. The fine and sharp
are given top rating. Finished weapons are not used until they have been examined and not
stored until they have been tested."

[183] Deleting 說, since it destroys the structural balance with the following sentence and
appears to have no meaning here [Igai, Zhang Wenhu, and Xu].

[184] According to *Guanzi*, II, 6/5b2–4 (1:26.3–4): "Since he has collected the [most]
heroic men of the entire realm and acquired [the service of] its most valiant, when he sends
them forth, it is like birds in flight. When he commits them to action, it is like thunder and
lightning, and when he deploys them, it is like wind and rain. No one can stand before him;
no one can harm him from the rear. He goes and comes freely without anyone daring to
resist him."

[OUTER EAST]

[Calendar] [In spring] green is esteemed as the color for banners. The lance is esteemed as the weapon. For punishment / the feet are encased in a wooden block or shackled to a cross bar.[185]

[Essay E] Their weapons may be ready but [the enemy] will be defenseless because your passage [through their territory] will not be known [until too late]. Their instructions may be practiced but [their effectiveness] will not be manifested because your onslaught will be unanticipated. / Since your passage [through their territory] will not be known, no one will be able to stop you. Since your onslaught is unanticipated, no one will be able to meet it. Since no one will be able to meet it, you will be completely victorious without any harm to yourself.[186] Since no one will be able to stop you,[187] you will certainly be victorious / and unrivaled [in battle].

If the four crucial concerns[188] are not clearly understood, before nine days have passed roving soldiers will throw fear into your army. If the barricades are not examined, before eight days have passed robbers from the outside will find openings in them. / If care is not taken concerning the warnings[189] and preparations for defense, before seven days have passed there will be slanderous plotting within your own borders. If prohibitions against craftiness are not instituted, before six days have passed thieves and robbers will arise.[190] / If the death-defying knights[191] are not provided with stipends, before four days[192]

[185] The actual meaning of these punishments is uncertain. The commentators for the most part agree that some type of shackles is involved, but beyond that they are of little help. I have made the following emendations based on the suggestions of the various commentators: 交 to 校; 寒 to 寋; 害 to 轄. Xu points out that the block and crossbar, both made of wood, correspond to the phase of the season. The *Yue ling* (*Li ji*, V, 6/5a2; Legge, *Li Ki*, XXVII, p. 259), under the second month of spring, says: "Command the officer in charge to inspect the prisons, remove shackles and handcuffs 桎梏, and not use the bamboo beating stick to excess." The wood radical 木, in the characters for shackles and handcuffs, would indicate they were probably made of wood. In contrast to the *Guanzi*, the *Yue ling* has punishments involving wood relaxed in the spring.

[186] See similar passage in VI, 17/12b8–10 (1 : 80.11–12).

[187] The Yang edition and the Ming (1582) cutting of the Zhao edition for *yu* 圉 mistakenly write 害, "to harm." III, 9/11b5 (1 : 38.13), writes *yu*.

[188] For the four crucial concerns 四機, see nn. 73 and 74, above.

[189] Emending 由 to 申 [Yu Yue and Xu].

[190] The concluding portions of these two sentences may have been inverted. The sentences should probably read: "If care is not taken concerning warnings and preparations for defense, before seven days have passed thieves and robbers will arise. If prohibitions against craftiness are not instituted, before six days have passed there will be slanderous plotting within your own borders."

[191] Emending 亡 to 士 [Wang Yinzhi].

[192] Zhang Peilun would emend 四, "four," to 五, "five," in order to preserve the numerical sequence.

have passed the material for your army will belong to the enemy.

The preceding is situated on the outer side of the eastern part of the chart.

[OUTER SOUTH]

[Calendar] [In summer] red is esteemed as the color for banners. The halberd is esteemed as the weapon. / For punishment there is burning[193] at the frontier.

[Essay D] Be certain to clarify the unity [of your purpose]. Be certain to clarify who your generals are. Be certain to clarify your policies. / Be certain to clarify who your knights are. When these four things have been done, you may attack disorder with good order and defeat with success.

If there are numerous battles, the knights will become weary.[194] If there are numerous victories, the prince will become arrogant. If an arrogant prince forces into action a wearied people, the country will be endangered.[195] It is best to have no battles at all; / next best is to have only one of them.

Those who achieve great victories are those who collect the masses and in victory never lack righteousness. This can be considered a great victory.[196] / A very great victory means being victorious in every respect.

The preceding is situated on the outer side of the southern part of the chart.

[OUTER WEST]

[Calendar] [In autumn] white is esteemed as the color for banners. The

---

[193] Emending 交 to 焌 [Zhang Peilun and Xu]. The use of fire as punishment corresponds to the phase of the season. Why the punishment should be executed at the frontier is not clear unless, in addition to destroying the corpse by fire, the ashes were then scattered, thus depriving the dead soul of all contact with home and descendants.

[194] In a similar passage in VI, 17/13b7 (1:81.8), 疲, "weary", is written 罷. The meaning is the same.

[195] This statement, which is repeated in VI, 17/13b6-8 (1:81.8-9), is also contained with slight verbal changes in the *LSCQ*, XIX, 5/11a12-13 (Wilhelm, *Frühling und Herbst*, p. 333), where it is attributed to the early fourth-century statesman, Li Ke 李克. See also the *Huainanzi*, 12/5b7-10 (Morgan, *Tao, the Great Luminant*, p. 111).

[196] The phrasing of this passage is somewhat redundant, suggesting that the text may be corrupt. Dai and Ding would delete the three characters 大勝者, "Those who achieve great victories," as an interpolation. Thus, "Those who collect the masses and are never lacking in righteousness can then be considered as having achieved a great victory."

35.10

sword is esteemed as the weapon.[197] For punishment there is mutilation[198] / and dismemberment.

35.10
8a7

[Essay C] Begin[199] in the limitless. End in the inexhaustible. Beginning in the limitless refers to the Way; ending in the inexhaustible refers to the Power. The Way cannot be measured; the Power cannot be calculated. / Since [the Way] cannot be measured, neither the numerous nor strong can plot [against the one who clearly perceives it]. Since [the Power] cannot be calculated, neither the false[200] nor deceitful will dare approach [the one who comprehends it].[201] When these two have been applied throughout, there will be achievement in both movement and rest.

35.11

35.12

Rear [your people] in accordance with the Way. Nurture them with the Power.[202] / If reared in accordance with the Way, the people may be harmonized. If nurtured with the Power, the people may be united. Since they are harmonious and united,[203] they can live on intimate

8b

terms.[204] Since they live on intimate terms, / they can cooperate. Since they live in complete cooperation and on such intimate terms, no one can harm them.[205] /

---

[197] In the *Shi ze xun* chapter of the *Huainanzi*, 5/8a2, the sword is assigned to the center season, and the weapon for autumn (5/9a11) is the spear 戈.

[198] The Yang edition for *shao* 紹 writes *zhao* 詔. Xu says that in early texts they were used interchangeably and here should be read as *zhao* 刽 = *wan* 元. Both these punishments involve the use of metal implements and thereby accord with the phase of the autumn season. The *Yue ling* (*Li ji*, V, 6/19a1; Legge, *Li Ki*, XXVII, p. 288) says: "Then command the officer in charge to review with strict accuracy the various punishments. Beheading and other capital punishments must precisely accord [with the law] with no excess or deficiency." Punishments involving metal appear to be relaxed in the *Yue ling*, in contrast to the *Guanzi*.

[199] The following paragraph is repeated with slight differences in wording in VI, 17/12b4ff. (1:80.9–11). However, there these two opening commands are part of a longer sentence: "The three means of command, the five instructions, and the nine symbols begin in the limitless and end in the inexhaustible." It is difficult to know which is the original version. See also the Introductory Comments for VI, 17, for discussion of a somewhat similar statement that appears in *Shi da jing* 十大經 (2.12.133), one of the Huang-Lao texts attached to the *Laozi* "B" silk manuscript discovered at Mawangdui.

[200] Emending 爲 to 僞 in accordance with the parallel passage in VI, 17/12b7 (1:80.10) [Igai, Sun Xingyan, Yu Yue, and Zhang Peilun].

[201] The parallel passage in VI, 17/12b7 (1:80.11), for 鄉 writes 響; here it has the same meaning [Liu Ji].

[202] Here 德 must be interpreted in its Daoist sense of an innate force or power capable of affecting others rather than the Confucian meaning of benevolence or virtue. The remainder of this paragraph is repeated with slightly different wording in VI, 17/13b (1:81.6).

[203] The Yang edition mistakenly omits the two characters 和合.

[204] Emending *xi* 習 to *ji* 輯 throughout this passage [Liu Ji, Ding, and Xu]. The corresponding passage in VI, 17/13b2 (1:81.6), writes *ji*.

[205] The Yang edition mistakenly omits 之 after 莫.

5.13 The preceding is situated on the outer side of the western part of the chart.

5.13 [OUTER NORTH]
b1   [Calendar] [In winter] black is esteemed as the color for banners. The shield is esteemed as the weapon.[206] For punishment there is drowning in flowing water.[207]

5.14 [Essay F] Delve[208] into the art [of warfare][209] and you will know how b3   to control [the masses].[210] Examine the weapons and you will become familiar with victory. Make your stratagems clear and victories will occur.[211] Extend your benevolence everywhere and the entire realm will be made secure. Secure the ancestral temples. Provide for the men and 5.1   women. / Control[212] the four classes.[213] Then you may establish your majestic power, practice benevolence, regulate laws and rules of conduct, and issue orders.

      The best way to employ arms is not by demanding [the enemy's] 5.2   territory but by applying punishments to their prince alone. / Institute righteousness and apply it in your victories. Maximize your prestige and make it real by [exercising] benevolence. Observe these [two] and afterward you will conquer the minds [of the enemy] and encompass all within the seas. /

      Institute what is advantageous to people and get rid of what is .4   harmful to them. Then the people will follow you. / Establish yourself as .5   lord of six thousand *li*. Then men of high position will follow you. / See to it that the princes of states have good government. Then they will

---

[206] The shield, being defensive, exemplifies the Yin. The *Shi ze xun* chapter of the *Huainanzi*, 5/13a3, instead of the shield, assigns a type of spear with a guard 鏔 as the weapon for winter.

[207] Drowning in flowing water also means that the corpse is separated from home and descendants. As with the other punishments, the type given here accords with the phase of the season, in this case, water.

[208] The following paragraph is repeated with some differences in wording in VI, 17/11b (1 : 79.10–121).

[209] The reference seems to be to the art of war 為兵之數. According to II, 6/1a12–1b1 (1 : 22.7–8): "Never has [a prince] who was unable to govern his people well been able to strengthen his armed forces. However, even if he were able to govern them well, it still would not do for him to lack understanding of the art of warfare." VI, 17/11b3 (1 : 79.10), speaks of 治眾有數, "There is an art to governing the masses," but this does not fit the context here.

[210] Reading 治 in accordance with VI, 17/11b3 (1 : 79.10).

[211] Wang Niansun would emend 適勝 to 勝敵, "and the enemy will be vanquished." His emendation is based on the parallel passage in VI, 17/11b3 (1 : 79.11) 明理而勝敵: "Make the principles clear and the enemy will be vanquished."

[212] Reading 官 as 管 [Guo Moruo].

[213] The four classes 四分 are: gentry 士, peasants 農, artisans 工, and merchants 商.

9a   follow you. / Make your requests and commands compatible with Heaven and Earth and come to know the harmony of the vital forces. Then all living things will follow you. Estimate the relative urgency in
36.6   affairs. Then even though you may be involved in danger / there will be no difficulty. Make clear [to your troops] the advantages of their weapons. Then even though they may be involved in difficulties they will not have a change [of heart]. Investigate the principles of what lies ahead
36.7   and behind. Then the armed forces / may be sent out without encountering trouble. Become familiar with the passages out of and into [a country]. Then even though you may penetrate deep [into enemy territory] there will be no danger. Examine where movement and rest are necessary. Then success may be achieved without harm. Make known the difference between receiving and giving. Then territory may be
36.8   obtained / without fear.[214] Take care [when appointing] officials who issue orders. Then you may initiate undertakings with success.

The preceding is situated on the outer side of the northern part of the chart.

---

[214] Reading 執 as 慹 [Yasui and Yu Yue].

192

Wu Fu
五輔

THE FIVE AIDS

Introductory Comments

Wu fu is the first chapter of the *Wai yan* [Outer Statements] section of the *Guanzi*, which includes a group of miscellaneous essays representing various schools of thought. For the most part they appear to be later in composition than those of the *Jing yan* [Canonical Statements] preceding them. The bulk of this chapter consists of a fairly well-constructed essay reflecting a late Confucian point of view somewhere between the idealism of Mencius and the authoritarian philosophy of Xunzi. Law is important, but most important is the benevolence of the ruler, which enables him to win the hearts of his people. The *wu fu* or five aids listed 16a7–8 (43.5–6) consist of manifestations (*xing* 興) of benevolence (*de* 德), forms (*ti* 體) of righteous conduct (*yi* 義), standards (*jing* 經) of propriety (*li* 禮), duties (*wu* 務) dictated by law (*fa* 法), and considerations (*du* 度) underlying political power (*quan* 權), all of which can serve as guides to the Confucian ruler. The remainder of the chapter, from 18b11 (45.10) on, probably represents fragments from other texts that were tacked on to the *Wu fu* essay by Liu Xiang or some other editor because of similarity in general subject matter.

Although I believe this chapter is certainly later than most of the chapters in the *Jing yan* section, it is difficult to date. The author (17b4–5; 44.9) cites the *Zuo zhuan*, indicating, as Luo Genze points out, that it must have been written no earlier than the late Warring States Period since the *Zuo zhuan* is generally considered to have been produced about 300 B.C. I believe the chapter probably was written sometime during the middle or late third century B.C., before the unification of China and suppression of Confucian classics under the Qin. The text's general language, style, and content, including its reference to feudal rulers desiring to become king over the entire realm, would tend to support such a conclusion.

Translation

1:42.6
15a5

Never has there been heard of an ancient sage ruler[1] who enjoyed illustrious fame and widespread praise, and whose rich achievements and great works were celebrated by the entire realm and not forgotten by later generations that this was not due to his having won the hearts of

42.7

men. / Never has there been heard of a cruel ruler who lost his country, endangered his altars of the land and grain, caused the collapse of his ancestral temples, and whose [memory] was completely obliterated throughout the entire realm that this was not due to his having lost the hearts of men. /

42.8

Nowadays, princes who possess territory all desire to be secure when at rest, awesome in action, victorious in battle, and firm in defense. The great ones desire to become king over the entire realm, lesser ones

42.9

protectors over the feudal lords. / Yet they still do not pay heed to winning the hearts of men. For this reason the lesser ones have their armed forces crushed and their lands pared away, while the greater ones lose both their lives and countries.

42.10
15b

Therefore it is said: / "[The prince] must pay heed to [the hearts of] men. This is the ultimate principle of the realm."

How[2] do we know this to be so? The answer is that among the ways of winning the hearts of men, nothing is as good as benefiting them. Among the ways of benefiting them, nothing is as good as teaching

42.11

them.[3] / Therefore [the sovereign who] is skilled in conducting his government has well-developed fields and his capital city and towns are well populated. His court is calm and his offices well run. Public laws are carried out while individual crookedness is prevented. The granaries are

42.12

full and the jails empty. Worthy men come forward while wicked / people retreat. His high officials[4] esteem honesty[5] and correctness and look down on cajolery and flattery. His citizens honor martial bravery and despise profit seeking. His common people like agricultural work and

42.13

abhor [gluttonous] drinking and eating. / Whereupon his fiscal resources are sufficient and drink, food, and firewood are plentiful.

[1] Following the *Qunshu zhiyao*, which both here and in the sentence below writes 主 for 王, "king."

[2] Following Xu, who in accordance with a similar pattern 18b8–9 (45.9) would emend 曰然則 to 何以知其然也？曰....

[3] Deleting 以政, in accordance with the *Qunshu zhiyao*.

[4] The term *junzi* 君子 here does not have the usual Confucian meaning of a man of quality or virtue.

[5] For 中, "honesty," the *Qunshu zhiyao* both here and in the contrasting passage below writes 忠, "loyalty."

For this reason, such a sovereign is certain to be liberal [in his administration] and undemanding [of taxes and services]. Subordinate officials are certain to be obedient / and lacking in resentments. Since above and below there is harmony and accord, propriety and righteousness, [the sovereign] is secure when at rest, awesome in action, victorious in battle, and firm in defense. For this reason, with one battle he is able to establish order among the feudal lords.

[However, the sovereign who] is incompetent in conducting his government has barren fields / and his capital city and towns are empty [of people]. His court is uneasy and his offices in disarray. Public laws are ignored while individual crookedness prevails. The granaries are empty and the jails full. Worthy men withdraw while wicked people advance. / His high officials esteem cajolery and flattery and look down on honesty and correctness. His citizens honor profit seeking and despise martial bravery. His common people love [gluttonous] drinking and eating and abhor agricultural work. Whereupon his fiscal resources / are exhausted and drink, food, and firewood are insufficient.

Such a sovereign is extremely severe[6] and demanding while subordinate officials are exceedingly destructive and disobedient. / Since above and below there is struggle and discord, [the sovereign] is never secure when at rest, nor awesome in action, victorious in battle, / or firm in defense. For this reason the lesser ones have their armed forces crushed and their lands pared away while the larger ones lose both their lives and states.

It is clear from this point of view that care must be exercised in the conduct of government.

Benevolence has six manifestations, righteous conduct seven forms, / propriety eight standards, the law five duties, and political power three considerations.

What are these so-called six manifestations [of benevolence]? The answer is: open up fields, regulate[7] shops[8] and dwellings, cultivate horticulture, exhort the citizenry, encourage farming, and repair / walls and buildings. This is called enriching the lives [of the people].

Develop hidden resources, circulate hoarded reserves, build roads, make customs and markets convenient, / and take care to provide travel lodgings. This is called circulating wealth among them. /

Channel flood waters, improve dams and ditches, clear whirlpools

---

[6] Emending 荀 to 苛 [Igai, Liu Ji, and Wang Niansun].
[7] Emending 利 to 制 [Wang Niansun and Xu].
[8] Reading 壇 as 廛 [Wang Niansun].

43.9 and sandbars, / remove mud and other obstacles, open places blocked by weeds, and make fords and bridges passable.[9] This is called presenting them with benefits.

43.10 Ease exactions, / lighten levies, relax punishments, pardon crimes, and forgive minor errors. This is called liberalizing the government.

Care for the adult and old, be compassionate toward the young and orphaned, have sympathy for the widower and widowed, inquire after 43.11 the sick, and console the unfortunate and bereaved. / This is called assisting [people] in their time of crisis.

Clothe the freezing, feed the starving, assist the poverty stricken, aid[10] the exhausted, and comfort the distressed. This is called aiding [people] 43.12 in dire straits. / All six of these are manifestations of benevolence.

When these six appear, every desire of the people is certain to be fulfilled. Now, once people are certain to obtain what they desire, they 43.13 will listen to their superiors. Once they listen / to them, government can be skillfully conducted. Therefore it is said: "Benevolence must be manifested."

It is also said: "Once the people have come to know the meaning of benevolence, if they still do not know the meaning of righteous conduct, then clarify your actions in order to lead them in the path of righteous- 43.14 ness." Righteous conduct has / seven forms. What are these seven forms? The answer is: being filial and respectful toward elders, compassionate in caring for relatives, respectful and trustworthy when serving the prince and their superiors, honest and correct when carrying 44.1 out the rites, / proper and humble when exacting punishment, frugal *17a* and economical in preparation for famine, generous and steadfast in 44.2 preparation for calamitous / disorders, cooperative and friendly when preparing for bandits[11] and barbarians. All seven of these are forms of righteous conduct.

Now, once the people are certain to know the meaning of righteous conduct, they will become honest and correct, and having become honest and correct, they will be harmonious. Since they are har- 44.3 monious, / [the prince] can be secure when at rest. Once he is secure when at rest, he can be awesome in action. Since he is awesome in action, he can be victorious in battle and firm in defense. Therefore it is said: "Righteous conduct must be practiced."

---

[9] Reading 慎 as 順 [Hong].

[10] Following the Yang, Liu, Zhu, *Sanko*, and Ming Print of the Zhao edition, which write 賑 for 振 throughout the chapter.

[11] The Yang edition mistakenly writes 冠 for 寇. Although the text states clearly that there are seven forms of righteous conduct, there would appear to be eight listed here.

44.4 It is also said: "Once the people have come to know the meaning of righteous conduct, if they still do not know the meaning of / propriety, then propagate the eight standards in order to lead them to it." What are the eight standards? The answer is: For the sovereign and his sub-ordinate officials there is righteous conduct. For the honored and lowly there are separate roles. For the old and young there are gradations in status. For the poor and the rich there is proper measure. All eight of

44.5 these / are standards for propriety.

Now, should the sovereign and his subordinate officials lack righteous conduct, there will be discord. Should the honored and the lowly not play their separate roles, there will be struggle [between them]. Should the old and young not maintain their gradations in status, there will be rejection. Should the poor and rich lack proper measure, excesses[12] will prevail.

Never has there been heard of a country in which there was discord between the sovereign and his subordinate officials, struggle between the

44.6 honored / and the lowly, mutual rejection on the part of the old and young, and excesses on the part of both poor and rich that it was not in chaos. For this reason the sage kings propagated[13] [these standards of]

7b propriety in order to lead their / people.

4.7 If these eight [classes of people] are all righteous in their conduct, / the prince will be honest, correct, and unselfish, ministers trustworthy and nonpartisan, fathers compassionate in their instruction, the sons filial in

4.8 their reverence, elder brothers / kindly in their admonishment, younger brothers submissive in their respect, husbands generous in their firm-ness, and wives encouraging in their purity.

Now, when this is so, subordinate officials do not turn their backs on

4.9 the sovereign, / ministers do not murder their princes, the lowly do not encroach upon the honored, the young do not abuse their elders, distant friends do not cause the alienation of close ones, new ones do not cause the alienation of old ones, the petty do not coerce the great, and licentiousness does not destroy righteous conduct.[14] All eight of these are standards for propriety.

---

[12] The meaning of 矢 is not clear. I have followed Yu Yue, who would write 軼. Wang Niansun would write 佚, "laxity."

[13] Emending 飭 to 飾, in accordance with the above passage 17a7 (44.4) [Xu and Sun Shucheng].

[14] A similar passage appears in the *Zuo zhuan*, Yin, 3 (Legge, *Ch'un Ts'eu*, I, 3/7): "Now there are what are called the six insubordinations: when the lowly obstruct the honored, the young abuse their elders, distant friends cause the alienation of close ones, new ones cause the alienation of old ones, the petty coerce the great, and licentiousness destroys righteous conduct."

44.10   Now, / once people are certain to know the meaning of propriety they will become respectful, and being respectful, they will become deferential. Since they are deferential, the young and old, the honored and lowly do not encroach upon each other. Since the old and young, honored and

44.11   lowly do not encroach on each other, disorders do not / arise and calamities are not produced. Therefore it is said: "Careful attention must be paid to propriety."

It is also said: "Once people have come to know the meaning of propriety, if they still do not know their duties,[15] then propagate the law in order to make them responsible and industrious." For making them

44.12   responsible and industrious there are the five duties. / What are the five duties? The answer is: The prince selects ministers to take charge of offices. Great officials take charge of offices and discuss affairs. The heads of offices take charge of affairs and attend to their responsibilities.

44.13
18a   The knights discipline themselves and perfect their talents. / The common people engage in agriculture and horticulture.

When the prince selects ministers to take charge of offices, there is no confusion in [the handling of] his affairs. When great ministers take charge of offices and discuss affairs, whatever they undertake will be timely. When the heads of offices take charge of affairs and attend to their responsibilities, whatever they do will be in accord [with their

44.14   instructions]. / When the knights discipline themselves and perfect their talents, the worthy and good emerge. When the common people engage in agriculture and horticulture, [the state's] fiscal resources are sufficient. Therefore it is said: "All five of these are duties [dictated by] law."[16]

Now, once people are certain to know their duties, their hearts will be

45.1   united, / and being united, they will have a singleness of purpose. Since their hearts are united and they have a singleness of purpose, their achievements are notable. Therefore it is said: "Dutiful attention must be paid to the law."[17]

It is also said: "Once the people have come to know the law,[18] if they

45.2   still do not know the meaning of political power, / then examine the three considerations in order to move them." What are the three considerations? The answer is: Above there is the auspiciousness of Heaven, below the suitability of Earth, and in the middle the submissiveness of man. These are the so-called three considerations.

---

[15] Ding and Zhang Peilun would emend 務, "their duties," to 法, "the law," in accordance with the pattern followed above.

[16] Emending 力, "work," to 法 [Zhang Peilun].

[17] Emending 力, "work," to 法 [Ding].

[18] Emending 務, "duties," to 法, in accordance with the pattern followed above [Ding].

45.3 Therefore it is said: "If the seasons of Heaven / are not auspicious, there will be floods and drought. If the way of Earth is not suitable [to man's activity], there will be starvation and famine. If the way of man is not submissive, there will be disasters and chaos. The arrival of these three—the auspiciousness of Heaven, the suitability of Earth, and submissiveness of man—is brought about by government."

45.4 It is also said: "Pay attention to the seasons [of Heaven] to initiate undertakings. / Use undertakings to move the people, the people to move the state, and the state to move the realm. Once the realm has been

45.5
*8b moved, merit and fame can be / be achieved."

Now, once the people are certain to know the meaning of political power, what you initiate will be accomplished, and when it is accomplished, the people will be content. Since the people are content, your merit and fame will be established. Therefore it is said: "Political

45.6 power / must [be based on] these considerations."

Once these five essential elements [of government] have been propagated, [the prince] may chase away wicked people, punish deception, reject slander, and neither listen to insidious rumors nor engage in tricky practices. Death or banishment will be the punishment for anyone among the people who engages in licentious conduct, has a depraved /

45.7 nature, or produces insidious rumors and engages in tricky practices in order to flatter[19] the prince and superiors on high or delude the hundred surnames below, or who incites the country and influences the masses in order to harm the people's performance of their duties.

45.8 Therefore it is said: / "Never has there been heard of a prince who internally neglected the hundred surnames and externally neglected the feudal lords, whose armed forces were crushed and lands pared away, whose name was despised, whose country was lost, whose altars of the land and grain were destroyed, and who himself was endangered that all

45.9 this was not produced by flattery and licentiousness. / How do we know this is so? The answer is that licentious sounds beguile the ear; licentious sights beguile the eye. What is pleasing to the ear and eye beguiles the heart, and [under these circumstances] what is pleasing to the heart is harmful to the people. Never has there been heard of people being

.10 harmed without [the prince] himself / being endangered."

It is also said: "Fill empty[20] spaces [with people], develop arable fields, build walls and houses, and then the state will be enriched. Be temperate in the consumption of drink and food, practice restraint in regard to clothing and then [the state's] fiscal resources will be sufficient.

[19] The Yang edition for 諂 throughout the rest of the chapter consistently writes 諂, "to create suspicion."

[20] Reading 壙 as 曠 [Xu].

199

45.11

19a

Elevate the worthy and good, pay heed to / merit and hard work, propagate benevolence and compassion, and then the worthy will come
forward. Chase away / the wicked, punish deception, get rid of slander,
and then the wicked will be restrained. Prepare[21] for famine, provide
help in disasters, aid the exhausted, and then the state will be on a firm
foundation."

45.12

The enlightened ruler[22] / pays heed to strengthening essential production and getting rid of what is useless. Thereafter the people can be
enriched. He selects[23] worthy men and utilizes their abilities. Thereafter
the people can be well governed. He lightens taxes and exactions and is

45.13

not / cruel[24] to his people, treating them with loyalty and affection so the
people can be drawn close to him.

Three things should concern the lord protector to the king: that
production is devoted to essentials and that goodness and righteousness
are both treated as his prime considerations. Now, when the artisans are

45.14

skilled, yet / the people still do not have enough to meet their needs, it is
because [the ruler's] pleasure is derived from idle amusements. When the
peasants have worked hard yet the realm still suffers from hunger, it is
because his pleasure is derived from exotic things being spread before

46.1

him [on a table] ten-foot square. / When the women are skilled and yet
the realm suffers from cold, it is because his pleasure is derived from the
ornate.

46.2

For this reason, wide belts should be split in two, / large sleeves
trimmed down, and ornate [clothing] dipped in [plain] dye. The highly
carved should be planed down, and highly engraved smoothed over.

At the customs posts, [traders] should be inspected but not charged

46.3

duties. / In the marketplace, [merchants] should be charged a ground
rent[25] but not taxed.[26]

19b

The good / artisans of old did not belabor their knowledge and skill in
order to produce what was [simply] amusing. For this reason, useless
things are not produced[27] by those who uphold the law.

[21] Emending 修 to 俗 = 備 [Yu Yue and Xu].
[22] Emending 王, "king," to 主.
[23] Reading 論 as 掄 [Xu].
[24] Emending 苟 to 奇 [Igai and Wang Niansun].
[25] The Yang edition for 廛 writes a variant form of the character 廛.
[26] This paragraph, which is repeated several places elsewhere in the *Guanzi*—see VIII,
18/16b1–2 (1 : 109.2); IX, 22/2a3 (2 : 2.3); and X, 26/4a2–3 (2 : 17.11)—does not seem to fit
the context here and is probably a later interpolation.
[27] Emending 矢 to 生 [Guo Moruo].

Zhou He

宙合

THE ALL-EMBRACING UNITY

Introductory Comments

This is a rather perplexing chapter combining Daoist, Yin-Yang, and, to some extent, Five Phases as well as Confucian political concepts. It is divided into two distinct parts. The first (1a6–1b6; 46.9–47.1) consists of a series of thirteen short statements that appear to have been excerpted from one or more earlier texts. The second part consists of thirteen short essays explaining each of the original statements in much the same manner as the *jie* or explanatory chapters that deal with the *Xing shi* (I, 2) and other texts. However, in this case, the explanations are provided within the same chapter instead of being presented separately. It may be that because of the brevity of the original statements, Liu Xiang, or perhaps the author of the explanations, felt it was better to keep them together. I have numbered both the original statements and the explanations to facilitate cross-checking.

Although the political implications of the various statements as presented in the explanations provide the chapter with an overall logic, it is often difficult to see the connection between one statement and the next. Even within a single statement, its separate sentences sometimes appear to have no relationship to each other and could very well have been taken from entirely different sources. Ambiguity is further enhanced by a terseness of the language that often leaves the subject of a given sentence in doubt. Where necessary, I have provided a subject based on a reading of the explanations.

The strong Yin-Yang flavor of many of the original statements as well as their references to Five Phases correlates would seem to indicate that in general they do not date much before the early part of the third century B.C. when these ideas began to gain widespread popularity. The relative terseness of language would also support a pre-Han origin. Moreover, one would assume that the author of the explanations must have felt they were old enough to make his special comments worthwhile. However, there is no way of being certain that they are indeed pre-Han or even that they were not composed by the author of the explanations himself.

I suspect that the explanations, which constitute the heart of the chapter and which appear to be by the same author, are the work of some writer at the court of Liu An. The mixture of Daoist (particularly *Laozi*), Yin-Yang, Five Phases, and Confucian rhetoric, is characteristic of their approach, and several passages in the explanations are reminiscent of the *Huainanzi*.

Translation

[STATEMENT I]

1:46.9
1a6
The left regulates the five tones; the right controls the five tastes.

[STATEMENT II]

Treasuring the marking line and complying with the level and bevel-compass, preparing many perfectly round axles and distributing them without reserve in a complete range of sizes, such is [the great worthy's] coordination of timeliness and virtue.

[STATEMENT III]

46.10
In the spring vegetables are grown; in the fall they are harvested. / In the summer they dwell in the Yin and in the winter the Yang.[1] The virtue of a great worthy will long endure.[2]

[STATEMENT IV]

Being farsighted, he is wise. Being wise, he is farsighted. Were he overly aggressive, he would fall as a withered leaf, but being both farsighted and wise, how great his accomplishments.

[STATEMENT V]

Should he be maligned, he is not given to anger; should he be
46.11
wronged, he says nothing; / should he have desires, he does not indulge in scheming.

[STATEMENT VI]

Grand in his calculations and measured in respect to customary practices, it is as if he were in repose while awake yet able to see the light

---

[1] That is, in the summer they are planted in the earth (Yin), and in the winter they are exposed to the sun (Yang) to dry.

[2] The Yin commentary would include this sentence in the following Statement. However, the Explanation makes it clear that it belongs here.

while in the dark. It is as though he were sojourning in [the time of] Yao.[3]

[STATEMENT VII]

46.12
Do not seek advice from sycophants. Do not succor those who engage in flattery. Do not nurture those prone to violence. Do not / give supervisory positions to those who indulge in slander. If one is not correct [in this], great will be [the resulting] devastation.

[STATEMENT VIII]

[The prince who causes resentments] cannot make use of his deserted lands,[4] but the flight of birds is like the level and marking line.

[STATEMENT IX]

1b
[The great worthy's] mental capacity[5] / being complete and its extensions well balanced, he conducts his government with ease and benefits the people.

[STATEMENT X]

46.13
Do not arouse the violent anger [of the prince who causes resentments]. / Do not be a party to his desires. Remain detached from his grief. Exalted though he may consider his position, nothing can save him from danger and collapse.

[STATEMENT XI]

46.14
[The great worthy] is able to be shallow or deep, to sink or float, to be bent or straight, to speak or be silent. / Heaven has more than a single season, Earth more than a single source of benefit, and man more than a single activity.[6]

---

[3] This short passage 若敖之在堯 is difficult to interpret. The Explanation is unusually silent except to repeat the original Statement, and none of the commentators is very helpful. Probably these six characters represent an incomplete and misplaced slip that was inserted here because of its syntactical similarity to the preceding passage.

[4] The reduplication of the character 區 is probably a copyist's mistake. The Explanation (5b2; 50.6) also contains a note, probably representing an erroneous insertion into the text of a later commentary, which states: " 區 means 虛, 'deserted.' Since he has no good men, therefore [the Statement] says it is deserted."

[5] The meaning of 謥 is unclear. I have followed Guo Moruo, who says that it is probably a mistake for 滑 = 胸.

[6] According to Yin Zhizhang's commentary, this phrase 天不一時，地不一利，人不一事 belongs to Statement XII. I have followed Liu Ji, who considers it part of Statement XI.

[STATEMENT XII]

Whoever is correct in his observations and walks with resolve will leave deep footprints.

[STATEMENT XIII]

Now, Heaven and Earth alternate hard times with the easy. It is like a drum having sticks / that [alternately] beat *ti dang* (*diek tang*).[7] Heaven and Earth are the receptacles for all things. The All-Embracing Unity serves as a receptacle for Heaven and Earth.

[EXPLANATION I]

"The left regulates the five tones; the right controls the five tastes." This refers to the distinction between the prince and his ministers. / The prince issues his orders and then retires. Therefore his position is on the left. The ministers exert themselves in hard work. Therefore their position is on the right. / Now, the five tones consist of different sounds, but they can be harmonized. This means that since the orders issued by the prince are not undisciplined, / they are always submissively received. Because of this submission, they are carried out, and political order comes into being. The five tastes are different, but they may be blended together. This means that the ministers in exerting themselves never lack discipline, / so there is nothing they cannot achieve. Having achievement, they become [even more] energetic in performing their duties, and the [state's] wealth increases.

Therefore the prince, in issuing his orders, sets the correct standard for the state and does not [merely] satisfy[8] his own desires. / In applying his love by a single standard, he does not consider himself alone as being right.[9] Since the correct standard[10] prevails and there is no self-interest, [people come from everywhere within] the [four] seas to serve as retainers. The ministers / in exerting themselves are alike in their loyalty and so do not compete for their own benefit. No one neglects his duties and so no one takes credit for them. Since they maintain their distinctions and respect for each other and there is no jealousy between them, they live in harmony and encourage each other in the manner of husbands and wives.

47.1

47.2

47.3

47.4

47.5
2a

47.6

47.7

---

[7] The passage 摘擋則擊 appears to be corrupt. Most of the commentators agree that the first two characters, *ti dang*, represent the sound of a drum. Guo Moruo would invert the sentence to read 擊則摘擋. The meaning would remain essentially the same.

[8] Reading 齊 as 濟 [Yasui and Yu Yue].

[9] Reading 與 as 為 [Xu].

[10] Emending 王 to 正 [Wang Niansun and Yasui].

47.8   If the prince neglects the [five] tones, custom and law will certainly / diverge. Diverging, they will fall into disorder and decay. If the ministers part from the [five] tastes, the common people will not be nourished. Not being nourished, they will scatter and flee en masse. When the prince and his ministers are individually able to perform their separate functions,

47.9   the country / will be at peace. Therefore, this is called "[virtue that is] unvirtue."[11]

[EXPLANATION II]

    "Treasuring the marking line and complying with the level and bevel-compass, preparing many perfectly rounded axles and distributing them without reserve in a complete range of sizes, such is [the great worthy's] coordination of timeliness and virtue." Now, the marking line assists in

47.10   making the crooked straight. The level reduces rough places / to make them smooth. The bevel-compass is inserted into the uneven to produce a concentric [curve]. This refers to the sagely prince's selecting worthy

47.11
2b   assistants through [appropriate] institutions. / It is broad in scope and misses nothing. Thereby, [the prince] can call on every sort of ability and none will be lacking.

    The state was the same state and the people were the same people, but

47.12   Jie and Zhou[12] / lost them by causing disorder, while Tang and Wu[13] brought them prosperity by creating good order. The latter manifested the Way through their teachings and clarified their laws through their expectations. It was due to[14] the merits of Tang and Wu that the people became so prosperous and good. /

47.13
47.14   In preparing many perfectly round axles, they provided a complete range of sizes. / Now, with many axles in a complete range of sizes, if the place [they needed to fit] was large there was no slack;[15] if the [hole] they were to enter was small, it would not be too tight. It was

48.1
48.2   like / determining the pattern of a shoe from a footprint. Where would they fail to fit? Since there was always a perfect fit, / there was never a lack of selection.[16] Therefore those who issue edicts and instruct [the people] should take [this metaphor of axles and shoes] as a lesson.

---

[11] 不德; Yasui and Yu Xingwu explain this phrase by citing the *Laozi*, B, 38/1a4, 上德不德，是以有德, "Superior virtue is unvirtue (i.e., natural). Therefore it possesses [real] virtue." Ding would emend 不 to 丕, thus, "great virtue."

[12] 桀 and 紂; the last kings of the Xia and Shang dynasties.

[13] 湯 and 武; the founders of the Shang and Zhou dynasties.

[14] Following the Yang edition, which for 此 writes 化 [Wang Niansun and Zhang Dejun].

[15] Emending 究 to 窕 [Igai and Wang Niansun].

[16] Reading 傻 as 僕 = 選 [Guo Moruo].

48.3
3a

Heaven's provision of nourishment / and care[17] is without measure. Earth's transforming and giving birth is without limit.[18] As for saying

48.4

there is the true with no / false or the false with no true, since they both exist, they are certain to emerge interacting together. If a [prince] believes that he is [always] right and so is incapable of planning

48.5

ahead, / there are certain to be [events] he could never contemplate that

48.6

will suddenly occur[19] without warning. / Therefore the sage is comprehensive in his listening and extensive in his observation. He cultivates the Way in anticipation of events.[20] When events occur, they stand in contrast to each other with both the crooked and the straight being

48.7

present.[21] / Therefore [the Statement metaphorically] says that [the great worthy] distributes [axles] without reserve in a complete range of sizes." /

48.8

The art of successful achievement requires having standards of measurement,[22] being replete in virtue, and discriminating in regard to

48.9

time. / The coincidence of virtue and timeliness is the culmination of an

3b

affair. It is as though / they were matching halves of a tally. Therefore [the Statement] says, "Such is [the great worthy's] coordination of timeliness and virtue."

[EXPLANATION III]

48.10

"In the spring vegetables are grown; in the fall they are harvested. / In the summer they dwell in the Yin; in the winter they dwell in the Yang." This refers to the fact that the sage must be timely in being active or quiescent, outgoing or secluded, yielding or assertive, quick[23] or slow,[24] acquisitive or forgoing. When it is the [proper] time, he is active; when it

48.11

is not, he is quiescent. For this reason / [there were times] when gentlemen of old had [excellent] intentions that they were unable to realize. Consequently, they bundled together[25] [the slips] containing their words

[17] Emending 陽 to 義 [Ding and Xu].
[18] Emending 法 to 洋 [Wang Yinzhi and Xu].
[19] Emending 然將卒 to 將然卒 [Xu].
[20] The *Huainanzi*, 16/12a3–5, contains a similar passage: 事或不可先規,·物或不可豫慮. 卒然不戒而至. 故聖人畜道以待時: "There are matters for which we cannot plan ahead, and events that we cannot have contemplated. They may suddenly occur without warning. Therefore the sage cultivates the Way in anticipation of this day."
[21] A brief note, which was probably part of a separate commentary mistakenly inserted into the text, follows: "*Jian* 減 means *jin* 盡, 'to the full' ('without reserve'). *Liu* 溜 means 發, 'to distribute.' [The sentence] means that when the dissemination [of axles] everywhere has been completed, no one will be without full access to them."
[22] Reading 巨獲 as 矩矱 [Wang Niansun and Yasui].
[23] Reading 浧 as 逞 [Jin].
[24] Reading 儒 as 濡 [Jin].
[25] Reading 愁 as 摯 [Wang Niansun].

about good government and, keeping them concealed,[26] stored them away.

48.12   Since worthy men / living in an age of disorder know the Way cannot be carried out, they hold back in order to avoid[27] punishment and remain quiet in order to escape [notice].[28] It is like being able to avoid

48.13 the misery resulting[29] from heat or cold by going / somewhere cool in the summer or somewhere warm in the winter. It is not that fearing

48.14 death, they become disloyal. / However, speaking out will subject them to punishment with no advantage either in terms of merit [for themselves] or benefit [for others]. If they were to push forward, they would

49.1 undermine the dignity due the prince. / If they were [summarily] to withdraw they would jeopardize the lives of those serving as ministers. The disadvantages would be great indeed. /

49.2
4a   Therefore [worthy men] withdraw, but do not abandon what is proper. They cultivate themselves and never cease to read [the words of

49.3 the sages] while awaiting the clear brightness [of a new day]. / Thus Weizi did not share in the difficulties of King Zhou, but was enfeoffed in Song as Lord Yin.[30] [The sacrifices to his] ancestors were not disrupted, nor was the line of descent broken. Therefore [the "Statement"] says, "the virtue of a great worthy will long endure." /

[EXPLANATION IV]

9.4   "Being farsighted, he is wise. Being wise he is farsighted. Were he overly aggressive, he would fall as a withered leaf, but being both farsighted and wise, how great his accomplishments." This means that if [the prince] monopolizes fame, is too possessive of his wealth, and is overly aggressive in his own interests, he will become dissolute[31] and

9.5 oppress others.[32] Men / are constantly being ruined by this.

    For this reason, documents and records written by the sages have been handed down to warn those who came after, saying: "Being overly aggressive and concerned with wealth means to fall as a withered leaf.

---

[26] Emending 含 to 佘 (陰) [Wang Niansun].

[27] Reading 辟 as 避 [Yasui].

[28] Deleting 也 as a later interpolation [Wang Niansun].

[29] The Yang edition for 及 writes 反, "to avoid the misery of unseasonable heat or cold . . . ."

[30] Weizi 微子, the viscount of Wei whose personal name was Qi 啓, was the elder brother and chief minister of the infamous last king of the Shang, Zhou 紂. Disgusted with the conduct of the court, he withdrew. When King Wu of the Zhou dynasty eliminated the Shang, Weizi Qi, because of his recognized virtue, was enfeoffed in the state of Song 宋 as Lord Yin 殷主 in order to continue the sacrifices to the Shang royal ancestors.

[31] Reading 琅 as 浪 and 湯 as 蕩 [Ding].

[32] Reading 淩 as 陵 [Yasui].

49.6 Never has there been a person too concerned with wealth who did not fall." Consequently, those who possess the Way / do not [insist that] the steelyard be exactly level, the grain measure be completely full, the calculations[33] be strictly adhered to, or metrical standards be carried out to the limit. Noble ranks are honored so that gentlemen are re-

49.7 spected. Salaries are plentiful so[34] that / duties are assiduously performed. Though [the prince's] achievements be great, he does not make a display of them. Though his cultivation be brilliant, he never boasts of it.

Now, contradictions between name and reality have existed for a long

4b time. / For this reason they are dissociated, and [men] make no connec-

49.8 tion between them. The wise[35] [prince], / knowing he cannot meet the demands of both, holds fast to one of them. Therefore he is secure in mind without worry.

[EXPLANATION V]

49.9 "Should he be maligned [the wise prince] is not given to anger." / This means he suppresses any trace[36] of his anger and desists from undermining the law. "Should he be wronged, he says nothing." When he

49.10 does speak, / he must be very cautious. If his words are not discreet, they will be turned against him and bring harm to himself.

"Should he have desires, he does not indulge in scheming."[37] This

49.11 means schemes cannot leak out. When schemes leak out, / the evil consequences are extremely grave. Now, if he gives vent to his anger and consequently undermines the law, he will certainly be afflicted by the evil consequence of having bandits arise, his words treated lightly, and his schemes leaked [to the world].

49.12 Therefore [the Statement] says: "Should he be maligned, / he is not given to anger; should he be wronged, he says nothing; should he have desires, he does not indulge in scheming."

[EXPLANATION VI]

"Grand in his calculations and measured in respect to customary practices, it is as if he were in repose while awake yet able to see while in

49.13 the dark." / This means he is sincere and benign in his self-restraint,

---

[33] *Yue* 樂, "music," does not seem to fit this context. Therefore I have followed Yu Xingwu and Xu in emending 樂 to 數 in accordance with the passage, 7b11–12 (52.7–8), 世用器 ··· 品有所成.

[34] The Yang edition for 則 writes 即.

[35] Reading 惠 as 慧 [Sun Xingyan, Yasui, Yao, and Yin Tongyang].

[36] Emending 速 to 迹 = 跡 [Guo Moruo].

[37] This sentence begins with the two characters 故曰, which are clearly interpolations from the following sentence and should be deleted [Wang Niansun, Igai, and Yasui].

tranquil and serene in his deliberations. He relies on the worthy and talented and employs / the compassionate and good.[38] His coming to understand clearly the principles of what may or may not be done and of what is beneficial or harmful is like[39] dispelling the ignorance of a child.

Therefore [the Statement] says: "It is as if he were in repose while awake yet able to see the light while in the dark. / It is as though he were sojourning in the time of Yao."

[EXPLANATION VII]

"Do not seek advice from sycophants." This means that one should not employ them, for if one does, their self-interest will prevail every-where. "Do not succor those who engage in flattery." This means that one should not listen to them, for if one does, they will deceive their superiors. "Do not nurture those prone to violence." This means that one should not / grant commissions to those who are cruel, for if one does, they will harm the people. "Do not give supervisory positions to those who indulge in slander." This means that one should not listen to slander, for if one does, one will lose the allegiance of gentlemen.

Now, the employment of these four—those who promote their pri-vate interests, deceive their superiors, harm the people, and cause one to lose the allegiance of gentlemen—is the reason why the righteousness of the prince is jeopardized / and his correctness lost. Now, once the prince on high loses his righteousness and correctness, he will perversely strive for fame and glory. Once the minister loses his loyalty, he will de-pravedly chase after ranks and salaries. They will both corrupt the customs[40] of the people and bring ruin to their generation in the process of stealing / leisure and embracing pleasure.

Even though [the prince's territory] may be vast, his majestic power can be destroyed.[41] Therefore [the Statement] says: "If one is not correct [in this], great will be [the resulting] devastation."

[EXPLANATION VIII]

It is for this reason that men of old blocked their roads and closed their village streets. They kept to themselves, and everything was well managed. Consequently, they compiled records and documents for us, / which have been handed down to warn later generations, saying: "[The prince] caused deep resentments. Thus his majestic power was

---

[38] The passage 依賢可用也仁良 appears corrupt. I have followed Zhang Peilun in emending 可 to 才 and deleting 也 as a misplaced character that should follow 審慮 in the preceding line.

[39] Emending 循 to 猶 [Wang Niansun].

[40] The Yang edition for 俗 mistakenly writes 數, "calculations."

[41] The Yang edition for 損 mistakenly writes 須.

exhausted and he could not make use of his deserted lands."[42]

50.7   Invariably he hesitated / and would not move, impeded [others] and would not take action [himself]. He inevitably missed opportunities, and having missed them, was ruined beyond relief. If [the prince] lacks concern for correctness of purpose, even though he makes no mistakes, he cannot be considered worthy. If he has a [proper] purpose, but lacks

50.8   ability, he cannot be considered skillful. / The worthiness and [administrative] skill[43] existing in a sage [prince] depends on his changing along with change. Deep as a spring, [his virtue] is never exhausted; in a fine and diffused stream, it flows forth. For this reason the outward flow of

50.9   his virtue brings enrichment that extends to all things / Therefore it is said: "The sage forms a triad with Heaven and Earth."

"The flight of birds is like the level and marking line." This refers to the righteousness of the great man. Now, in their flight, birds must fly

50.10   around mountains and settle in valleys. / If they do not fly around mountains, they will encounter difficulty. If they do not settle in valleys they will die.[44] The location of mountains and valleys may not be in a straight line so that in flying around mountains and assembling in valleys, they take one turn after another, yet [the Statement] calls [their

50.11   flight] a marking line. This is because a bird rising in the north, / with the intention of flying south, arrives in the south; arising in the south with the intention of flying north, arrives in the north. If the one major purpose [of an effort] is attained, it should not be considered ruined because of a minor defect. /

50.12   Therefore the sage praises [this metaphor of birds in flight] and
6a   [further] elucidates, saying: "A road, a thousand *li* long, cannot be

50.13   straightened with a marking line. / An administrative region (*du* 都) of 10,000 households cannot be made flat with a level." This means that the actions of a great man need not follow the constant standards of the former emperors.[45] When righteous conduct has been established, it is

50.14   called worthiness. / Therefore when the sovereign examines his subordinate officials, he must not ignore this technique [of government].

[EXPLANATION IX]

"[The great worthy's] mental capacity[46] being complete," refers to his mind. His mind desires loyalty. "Its extensions well balanced," refers to

---

[42] See n. 4, above.

[43] Emending 失 to 夫, in accordance with the preceding sentence [Yue Yue].

[44] Yasui explains that they will die of thirst.

[45] Wang Niansun would delete 帝, "emperors," as a reduplication of the following character 常. Thus, "the constant standards of the past."

[46] See n. 5, above.

the ears / and eyes. The ears and eyes seek uprightness. People who are honest and correct are the basis of good government. The ears control hearing. Hearing is certain to be accompanied by listening. If listening is discerning, it is called "sharp." The eyes control sight. Sight is certain to be accompanied by / seeing. If seeing is perceptive, it is called "clear." The mind is in charge of thought. Thought is certain to be accompanied by speech. If speech is to the point, it is called wise. If [the prince] is sharp, clear, and wise, he will have a broad grasp of things.[47] Having a grasp of things and not being confused / makes the conduct of government easy. If the conduct of government is easy, the people will benefit. If they benefit, they will be encouraged. Being encouraged, they will be happy.[48]

If hearing[49] / is not discerning, it will not be sharp. If it is neither discerning nor sharp, [the prince] will make mistakes. / If sight is not perceptive, it will not be clear. If it is neither perceptive nor clear, [the prince] will commit errors. If thought fails to grasp the point, it will not be wise. If it neither grasps the point nor is wise, [the prince] will be confused. [A prince who] makes mistakes, commits errors, and is confused / is stupid. Stupidity leads to being perverse and petty. Perversity and pettiness lead to rashness in government. If there is rashness in government, the people will be harmed. If they are harmed, they will become resentful. Being resentful, they will become violent.

Therefore [the Statement] says: "[The great worthy's] mental capacity being complete, and its extensions well balanced,[50] he conducts his government with ease and benefits his people."

[EXPLANATION X]

"Do not / arouse the violent anger [of the prince who causes resentments]." This refers to being honest and correct in maintaining a cautious attitude. "Do not be a party to his desires." This refers to the sovereign corrupting the constant standards and coveting gold, jade, horses, and women so he has little regard for [the production of] grain and goods. If he imposes heavy exactions / upon the hundred surnames, the masses of the people will become enraged.

"Remain aloof from his grief." This refers to [the prince] on high

[47] Emending 博 to 搏 [Xu].

[48] Emending 告 to 古 in order to provide proper balance with the following passage 怨則凶 [Liu Ji and Xu].

[49] Deleting the two characters 不順 in accordance with the following balanced phrases concerning seeing and thinking [Liu Ji, Ding, and Guo Moruo]. The Ancient and Zhu editions lack these two characters. The Yang and Liu editions write 不慎.

[50] Deleting 言, which does not appear in the Statement [Igai and Wang Niansun].

211

losing his country. If he constantly pursues his own pleasure and awards positions to actors and clowns[51] so that outside [the court] he may indulge in fast horses and hunting while inside he lets himself go with
51.8   beautiful women / and licentious music, those below will become lazy and careless. If the various functionaries lose their sense of uprightness, trouble and disorder will result in his losing his country.

"Exalted though he may consider his position, nothing can save him
51.9   from danger and collapse." This refers to his self-esteem being high / and his self-satisfaction great so that he likes to boast to others of his beauty. Being a master of abundance and occupying a worthy position, he considers himself a hero, but his abundance is bound to be lost, and as a hero he is bound to fail.

51.10   Now, the ruler, / being master of abundance and occupying a worthy position, controls the citizens [of his country], but when the state is beset
7a   by trouble and disorder, / the hearts of all the people will harbor resentment [against him]. This means the certain loss [of the country] as though [the prince] were thrown from a ten-thousand-*ren*[52] peak into a deep abyss. Certain will be his death, with no [hope of] salvation. /

51.11   Therefore [the Statement] says: "Do not be party to his desires and remain aloof from his grief. Exalted though his position may be, nothing can save him from danger and collapse."

[EXPLANATION XI]

"Able to be shallow or deep, to sink or float, to be bent or straight,
51.12   spoken / or unspoken." This refers to [the manner in which] he expresses his meaning and demands for achievement. "Heaven does not have a
51.13   single season, Earth a single benefit, / nor man a single activity." For this reason there are bound to be many [aspects to the prince's] endeavors, and the men [who serve him] must have a variety of titles and
51.14   positions.[53] / All[54] those who understand this do not [try] to manage everything, but [try] to comprehend the Way. /

[51] Emending 美 to 笑 [Zhang Peilun and Xu].

[52] A *ren* 仞 was a measure eight Chinese feet in length.

[53] Ding and Xu believe the text here is corrupt and this sentence should accord with a similar passage in the *Huainanzi*, 20/6a8–10: 天不一時, 地不一利, 人不一事, 是以緒業不得多端, 趨行不得不殊方: "Heaven does not have a single season, Earth a single benefit, nor man a single activity. For this reason there are bound to be many aspects to his endeavors and different facets to his pursuits." Thus they would emend this sentence to read: 是以人之緒業不得不多, 端名位不得不殊方, including the character 方 with which the Yin commentary begins the following sentence. Thus, "For this reason there are bound to be many aspects to man's endeavors and different facets to his titles and positions."

[54] 方; according to Ding and Xu this character should be part of the preceding line. See n. 53, above.

52.1   Those [who comprehend] the Way reach the highest, roam the inexhaustible, and share the life cycles of all creatures. Consequently, those who are capable of only one argument, who are familiar with only one

2.2   jurisdiction, and who master only one activity are capable of / making tortuous statements, but are incapable of dealing with matters in a comprehensive fashion. /

b   The sage, because of this, knows that [one] word cannot be used to

2.3   cover every situation. Therefore / he tempers [his speech] with wide knowledge and carefully considers his meaning. He knows that [one] example cannot be used to cover every situation. Therefore he explains each[55] of them and compares their merits. /

2.4   The year has its spring and autumn, winter and summer. A month has its first, last, and middle ten-day periods. The day has its morning and

2.5   evening, and the night its dusk and dawn. Each star culmination[56] / in its cyclical order[57] has its dominion. Therefore [the Statement] says: "Heaven does not have a single season."

2.6   Mountain peaks and precipices, / deep springs and wide rivers, springs from which the water drips slowly but which are never exhausted, marshy lakes into which water runs slowly and are never

.7   filled, / high and low land, the fertile and barren, all have that for which they are suitable. Therefore [the Statement] says: "Earth does not have a single source of benefit."

The countryside has its customs and the state its laws. The tastes of food and drink differ, and for clothing there are different colors. Daily

8   necessities, / implements, the compass and square, marking line and level, weights and measures, each kind of thing has that for which it is just right. Therefore [the Statement] says: "Man does not have a single activity." /

[EXPLANATION XII]

)   The behavior proper to each of these activities involves endless detail. / "Whoever is correct in his observations" means that when [the prince] examines the beautiful and ugly, and distinguishes between[58] the good and the harmful, he must be careful to grasp the distinctions so they are not confused. Then in his exercise of government there are no

0   regrets. "To walk with resolve" means that / in occupying his position,

[55] Emending 名 to 各 [Wang Niansun and Yasui].

[56] 半星; the meaning of this term is not clear. I am indebted to Professor Nathan Sivin for this translation.

[57] That is, the twelve earthly branches.

[58] Deleting 審 as an interpolation of the same character from the following phrase [Wang Niansun].

52.11

he walks the right road in conducting his affairs so the people will stick to their assigned functions and not be disorderly. Thereby he will protect his ancestral domain and [rule] well to the end of his life. "To leave deep footprints" means that if [the prince] makes his ink-lines clear, his writings intelligible,[59] and is consistent in his virtue, later / generations will practice[60] his principles and not go astray. Therefore his fame will never cease.

[EXPLANATION XIII]

52.12

"Now, Heaven and Earth alternate hard times with the easy. It is like a drum having sticks that [alternately] beat *ti dang* (*diek tang*)."[61] / This means that if [the drum] is to produce a rhythm, [the sticks] must be synchronized. Perfect synchronization is the result of their being in

52.13

complete accord with the way of Heaven and Earth. / The shadow of something crooked will not be straight, nor will the echo of a discordant sound be sweet.[62] For this reason the sage who wishes to see clearly the

52.14

nature of things / must consider the category from which they have come. Therefore the virtuous prince is careful to heed what he puts first.

53.1
8b

"Heaven and Earth are the receptacles for all things. / The All-Embracing Unity serves as the receptacle for Heaven and Earth." Since

53.2

Heaven and Earth / contain all things, [the Statement] says that they are the receptacles for all things. The scope of the All-Embracing Unity penetrates above the heights of Heaven and reaches[63] below the depths

53.3

of Earth. Externally it extends beyond the four / seas. It binds together Heaven and Earth to make them a single bundle and then separates them so that there is nothing in between. We cannot name it, but we

53.4

describe[64] it / as being so great there is nothing beyond and so small there is nothing within. Therefore [the Statement] says: "[The All-Embracing Unity] serves as the receptacle for Heaven and Earth."

---

[59] This phrase 明墨章書 is reminiscent of the *Chu ci*, IV, 6/19b1–2, 章畫志墨兮, which David Hawkes (*Ch'u Tz'u*, p. 70) translates as "I make my marking clear; I set my mind on the ink-line." Wang Niansun would emend 書, "writings," to 畫, "markings."

[60] Emending 修 to 備 [Wang Niansun].

[61] See n. 7, above.

[62] The *Huainanzi*, 15/12b12–13, contains a similar passage: 夫景不爲曲直，響不爲清音濁, "Now the shadow of something crooked will not be straight nor will the echo of a pure tone be muddy." According to the *Chunqiu fanlu*, XIII, 57/3a3, 美事召美類, 惡事召惡類: "Good attracts the good, evil attracts the evil."

[63] Emending 泉 to 象 [Wang Yinzhi].

[64] The character 山, "mountain," is clearly a mistake here. I have followed Guo Moruo, who would emend it and the following character 是 to read 字之. Thus the line accords with the *Laozi*, A, 25/14a3–4 (Waley, *The Way and Its Power*, p. 174): 吾不知其名, 字之曰道, "We do not know its name, but we call it the Way."

214

Its true meaning is not known to the world. If we were to compile [all that has been said about it, the results] / would not exceed a single wooden tablet.[65] However, such a compilation is unmanageable. When [knowledge of it] has been extensively internalized, it provides a richness, and when it emanates / in a timely manner [from the sage], there is appropriate action. Thus it is the way of the sage to value its richness and its production of appropriate action.

What is meant by appropriate action? Basically appropriate action means maintaining order without recklessness, acting naturally in the face of matters for which there is no precedent, and responding to change rather than ignoring it. There is no change / to which [the sage] does not respond, and no response that is not appropriate. From beginning to end he is not distracted from this.[66] Therefore, in speaking about it, he gives it the name "All-Embracing Unity."

[65] This passage is not at all clear. I have generally followed Guo Moruo's interpretation reading 薄 as 簿, "a wooden tablet."

[66] The passage 變無不至, 無有應當, 本錯不敢忿 is clearly corrupt, but none of the commentators offers a satisfactory solution. I have followed Guo Moruo in emending it to read: 變無有不應, 應無有不當, 本鏢(剽)不敢分心.

Shu Yan
樞言

CARDINAL SAYINGS

Introductory Comments

This essay consists of short statements attributed to Guanzi, a number of which echo ideas expressed elsewhere in the text. For example, line 9a9 (53.12) refers to *qi* 氣, "vital force," which is discussed at length in the *Nei ye*, XVI, 49. However, none of the statements appears to be a direct duplication of material found in our present recension of the *Guanzi*.

The style of writing is rather well developed in its use of imagery. The sentence structure is complex and varied, and rhyme is fairly common. Given its rather well developed style and the fact that at least one rhymed passage (10a5–6; 54.8–9) is consistently ancient rather than archaic in pattern, I suspect this chapter comes from the early Han period. Its easy mixture of Confucian, Daoist, Yin-Yang, and Legalist concepts is also quite consistent with the work produced at the court of Liu An during the early years of the second century B.C. One line, 13a1 (57.2), which discusses the three categories of terms, is similar to a passage (1.6.55) in the *Jing fa*, one of the Huang-Lao texts from Mawang-dui. The closing paragraph is of special interest, being a very personal statement rather than the usual pompous moral pronouncement to be found in the *Guanzi*.

Translation

1:53.11
9a7
53.12

Guanzi said: "In Heaven the Way is [manifested by] the sun. In man it is [manifested by] the mind. / Therefore it is said that when the vital force is present, things live; when not, they die. What lives does so by virtue of its vital force.[1] When there is [proper] terminology, good order prevails;

53.13

when there is not, / disorder ensues. What is ordered is so by virtue of [proper] terminology."

---

[1] The Yang edition omits this line 生者以其氣. It may well represent the insertion into the text of a later marginal note.

216

His [other] cardinal sayings were:

"Love them, benefit them, make them prosper, and make them secure. These four emanate from the way [of good government]. / The [former] emperors and kings used it and so the realm became well governed."

"The [former] emperors and kings took care when establishing priorities. Since they gave precedence to people and land, they were successful. / If they had given precedence to honor and pride, they would have failed. For this reason, the former kings took care when establishing priorities." [2]

"A ruler of men must consider carefully the bestowing of honors. / He must [also] consider carefully his people and his wealth. Careful consideration in regard to bestowing honors lies in promoting the worthy. In regard to people, it lies in establishing offices; in regard to wealth, it lies in paying heed to the land. Since the status and importance of the ruler of men / depends on these three, they must be given careful consideration."

"A state has its precious assets, its guiding instrument, and its media of exchange.[3] Its urban and suburban walls, its defensible passes and defiles, and what has been accumulated and stored away are its precious assets. / The wisdom of the sages is its guiding instrument. Pearls and jade are its media of exchange.[4] The former kings / valued the precious assets and guiding instrument, but looked down on the media of exchange.[5] Therefore they were able to rule the realm."

"There are two things, [precious assets and guiding instrument], that will give life to the realm and prevent its death. There are four things that will bring about its demise[6] and prevent its [secure] establishment. / Indulgence in pleasure or anger, hatred or desire, will bring ruin to the realm, and so worthy men keep [these feelings] to a minimum."[7]

---

[2] Deleting 貴在 as an interpolation from the following line [Wang Niansun and Xu].

[3] Following Guo Moruo's explanation of 用. He cites the often-repeated statement in the economic chapters of the *Guanzi* that pearls and jade were the most valued currency, gold was second, and knife and spade money were third. See XXII, 73/8a12–8b1 (3:70.3), and XXIII, 78/8b2–3 (3:90.2–3), as examples.

[4] Following Liu Ji and Guo Moruo, who would delete 末, "nonessential," both here and in line 9b10 (54.5) below as interpolations taken from the Yin commentary. The Yang edition also omits the second 末.

[5] Guo Moruo would interpret this passage very differently. He would emend 輕, "look down on," to 經. Thus, "The former kings valued the precious assets and guiding instrument and standardized the medium of exchange." This fits the importance attached to money in the economic chapters cited above, but it is not necessarily relevant here.

[6] Emending 立 to 亡 [Guo Moruo].

[7] Reading 實 as 寡 [Guo Moruo].

54.7 "Contrived goodness is not goodness. There is no way [true] goodness can be contrived. / Thus the former kings valued [true] goodness."

"The treasure of the kingly ruler is spent on his people, while that of the lord protector is spent on his generals and troops. The treasure of the weak ruler is spent on those in high positions, while that of the ruler who 54.8 is about to perish is spent on / women and precious stones. Therefore the former kings were careful with their treasure."

"Be diligent! Be diligent!

For all things there is a pattern (*sier*; *ṣizi*).

Be active! Be active!

For all things there is a time (*djiêg*; *dźi*).

Be strong! Be strong!

For all things there is meaning (*tjier*; *ts'izi*)." [8] /

54.9 "[In the matter of] of control, there are three classes of states: those that control others, those that are controlled by others, and those that cannot control others or be controlled by them. How do we know this is so?

54.10 "Abundant in this virtue, / respected for his sense of justice, yet lacking any desire to gain fame; his population large and his army strong, yet unwilling to use his state to stir up trouble and create 54.11 suffering; the whole realm at war, / yet desirous of keeping his own country in the background—[a state possessing a ruler] such as this, is one that controls others.

"Neither abundant in virtue nor respected for his sense of justice, yet 54.12 desiring to gain fame; his population small and his army weak, / yet willing to use his state to stir up trouble and create suffering; dependent upon allies and trusting to their favor for fame and fortune—[a state possessing a ruler] such as this, is one that is controlled by others. /

54.13 "Advancing as others advance, retreating as others retreat, striving as
10b others strive, relaxing as others relax; whether advancing or retreating, striving or relaxing, always in accord with others—[a state possessing a 54.14 ruler] such as this, is one that cannot / control others or be controlled by them."

"One may love others deeply, yet be unable to benefit them, hate others intently, yet be unable to harm tham. Therefore the former kings 55.1 valued what was appropriate / and profound. What is profound does not issue from the mouth or appear on the face. At one moment like a dragon, at another like a serpent, it may transform itself five times in a

---

[8] The Yang edition mistakenly writes 脂 for 指(旨). The Ancient, Liu, and Zhu editions agree with the Zhao edition in writing 指. According to the reconstructions of both Karlgren and Chou Fa-kao, the rhyme pattern in this brief poem appears to be irregular in the archaic, but is consistent in the ancient.

single day. This is the meaning of what is profound. / Therefore the former kings did not exaggerate one [by calling it] two. Nor did they initiate affairs on their own or take sole credit for achievements."

"The former kings did not restrain [people by treaties] or bind them [through oaths]. They released those restrained [by treaties] / and dissolved the bonds of those bound [by oaths]. Therefore, when [people] attached themselves to [the former kings], it was not because of restraints or bonds. The former kings [also] did not engage in the exchange of gifts or carve up territory [to grant fiefs] / in order to maintain control over the realm. [However], the realm's [institutions] were inviolable / and so the whip could be used to enforce them.[9] [Thus] whether it be the seasons [of Heaven] or the benefits [of Earth], generation after generation[10] took advantage of them."

"Extra eyes would not have given them clearer sight nor extra ears sharper hearing. Thus [the former kings] were able to sustain / the majestic bearing of the son of Heaven. The same was true of their officials."

"Those who are timely obtain [the rewards of] Heaven; those who are just obtain [the loyalty of] men. Being both timely and just, [the former kings] were able to obtain [the rewards of] Heaven and [the loyalty of] men."

"Since the former kings did not rely on / bravery and fierceness to maintain their frontiers, their frontiers were peaceful. Since they were peaceful, neighboring countries were friendly. Being friendly, they did what was appropriate."

"Men in ancient times were hostile to each other, and their hearts were cruel. Therefore laws were made for them. / The laws emanated from rules of propriety, and these [in turn] from [the requirements for] good order. Good order and customary rules of behavior constitute the moral way. All beginnings await the security that comes when good order and the rules of propriety prevail."

"Now all things are born of the two, Yin and Yang, so that a third comes into being.[11] Because of this third aspect, the former kings were careful [to observe] / both what went in and what came out."

"If one looks only at the lowly when considering lowliness, lowliness cannot be understood. If one looks only at the honored when considering honor, honor cannot be understood. Jie and Shun[12] were examples of this. That is why the former kings attached extreme importance to it."

---

[9] This sentence is not at all clear and seems to contradict what was said above.

[10] Emending 出 to 世 [Guo Moruo].

[11] Reading 視 as 活 [Yin Tongyang and Sun Shucheng].

[12] Jie 桀, the last king of the Xia dynasty, fell from honor to banishment and death, while Shun 舜 rose from a lowly position to become one of the legendary Five Emperors.

55.10
"What is it that when possessed leads to certain life, / and when lost leads to certain death? It can only be the vital force.[13] Yao, Shun, Yu, Tang, Wen, Wu, and Xiaoji[14] depended on [understanding] this for

11b
their success. The realm must depend on such [understanding] / for its very existence. Therefore the former kings [also] attached importance to this."

55.11
"To go one day without eating / is like having a poor harvest. Three days without eating is like having a crop failure. Five days without eating is like a famine. Seven days without eating and the nation's knights[15] will be no more. Ten days without eating and mankind will be gone, everyone dead."

55.12
"The former kings valued / honesty and trustworthiness. The honest and trustworthy hold the realm together. High officials who are worthy do not presume on their family connections.[16] Gentlemen do not rely on external pressure."

"Petty gains do not bring success (*kewng*)."

55.13
"Petty / expedients are not effective (*riewng*). Therefore preserving the state and securing the altars of Land and Grain depend on thorough planning."

"When engaged in mental effort, the [thoughts of] the sage are:

"Swirling, around (*dwan*) encompassing everything (*grwan*), /

55.14
Elusive (*dwan*),[17] so none may know them (*mwan*),

Complex (*p'jwan*), like an entangled skein of silk (*sjiêġ*),

Methodical (*ts'jiwan*),[18] as though adhering to a scheme of order (*diêġ*)."[19]

"Therefore [the former kings] would say: 'Those who wish to be considered wise, I consider wise. / Those who wish to be benefited, I

56.1

[13] The meaning of the phrase 唯無得之 is not clear. I have followed Guo Moruo in emending 無 to 炁 = 氣.

[14] Yao 堯 and Shun were two of the legendary Five Emperors, Yu 禹 is the legendary founder of the Xia, Tang 湯 of the Shang, and Wen 文 and Wu 武 were the founders of the Zhou. Xiaoji 孝己, or Xiaoyi 孝巳 (the Yang edition writes the former; the Zhao edition the latter), was the son of the Shang emperor Wuding 武丁. Xiaoji is frequently mentioned in early texts under both names as an example of filial piety. Since Xiaoji hardly seems to fit the sequence here, Guo Moruo would emend 孝己 or 孝巳 to 老子, Laozi. Guo supports this rather dubious solution to the problem by arguing that the chapter was written during the Warring States Period by someone who revered Laozi and Huang Di 黃帝, the Yellow Emperor.

[15] Emending *tu* 土 to *shi* 士 [Yin Tongyang, Xu, and Guo Moruo].

[16] Following the Yang edition, which for 至 writes 室.

[17] Reading 豚 as 遯 [Ding].

[18] Emending 遺遺 (*ġriwêr*) to 遒遒 (*ts'jiwan*) to complete the rhyme with 氾氾 (*dwan*), 豚豚 (*dwan*), and 紛紛 (*p'jwan*) [Guo Moruo].

[19] Inserting 所 after 有 in accordance with the Ancient, Liu, and Zhu editions [Yasui and Xu].

benefit. Those who wish to be considered brave, I consider brave. Those who wish to be honored, I honor. When others wish to be honored and I honor them, they say I have propriety. When they wish to be considered brave and I do so, they say I am respectful. / When they wish to be benefited and I benefit them, they say I am good. When they wish to be considered wise and I do so, they say I am brilliant.'"

"Be cautious! Be cautious! Be subtle and unpredictable.[20] / Consider your actions, but let no man know your mind. Be prepared for the unexpected. Whoever trusts others is good. Whoever cannot be deceived is wise. To be both wise and good—such is called being a complete man."

"The lowly indeed serve / the honored. The unworthy indeed serve the worthy. [However], what makes the honored truly honored is that they use their honored [position] to serve the lowly. What makes the worthy truly worthy is that they use their worthiness to serve / the less worthy."

"Ugliness is the basis[21] for [appreciating] beauty. Humility is the basis for [measuring] high status. Lowliness is the basis for [gauging] honor. Therefore the former kings honored [these bases]."

"Heaven serves with its seasons, Earth with its natural resources, man with his virtue, / the spirits with their omens, and animals with their strength."

"What is called virtue is said to be that which is put first. In exercising[22] virtue, there is nothing better than being first. In confronting enemies,[23] there is nothing better than being last."

"Of the former kings, those who used one Yin and two Yang / became lord protectors. Those who used the pure Yang became true kings. Those who used one Yang and two Yin declined, and those who used nothing but pure Yin perished."[24]

"If you calculate, you will not consider less as more. If you weigh, you will not consider light as heavy. If you measure, you will not consider short as long. If you do not seriously consider / these three, you will not be able to initiate major undertakings."

"Can you be cautious? Can you give orders? Can you keep secrets?

[20] Reading 異 as 翼 [Guo Moruo].
[21] Reading 充 as 統 = 本 here and below [Xu].
[22] Emending 故 to 致 [Guo Moruo].
[23] Reading 適 as 敵 [Yasui, Dai, and Tao].
[24] This paragraph refers to the composition of the trigrams of the *Yijing*, the broken line representing Yin and the unbroken, Yang. Thus one Yin and two Yang refers to the trigram ☲ while the pure Yang 畫以陽 is represented as ☰ and the pure Yin 畫以陰 as ☷.

221

Can you be like[25] panicled or unpanicled millet—no planting in the spring, no harvest in the fall?"[26]

"For the mass mind, / love is the beginning of hatred and virtue is a cause for resentment. Only [the mind of] the worthy is different."[27]

"The former kings conducted their affairs to assure harmony in their relations. They practiced virtue to create harmony among men. If in these two respects there is no harmony, / there will neither be success nor close support."

The demise of states and the defeat of individuals stem from their strengths. Therefore, those who are skilled in swimming die in dammed up ponds.[28] Those who are skilled in / shooting die in fields."

"Life depends on having food to eat. Good government depends on managing affairs. From ancient times down to the present there has never been good government without skill in managing affairs."

"The many will be victorious over the few, the speedy over the slow, / the brave over the cowardly, the wise over the stupid, the good over the bad, those who practice righteousness over those who do not, and those who follow the way of Heaven over those who do not. When all seven of these victories are appreciated and brought together,[29] a great many people will be able to live out their full lives."

"Rulers / who are given to idleness and indulge in their desires, who forget[30] their own safety and neglect their country are in danger. Those who make a display of punishments and degrade the members of the gentry are in danger. Those who delegate their majestic powers to feudal lords and even after a long time / fail to recognize the crisis facing them are in danger. Those who are old but know no respect for their heirs apparent are in danger. Those who store up grain, keeping it for a long time until it rots, and are unwilling to share it with others are in danger."

"Generally speaking, there are three [categories of] terms involved in [governing] men: those dealing with good order in government, a sense of [honor and] shame, / and management of affairs. There are two terms

---

[25] Reading 而 as 如 [Sun Shucheng].

[26] According to the *LSCQ*, XIX, 4/9a2–3 (Wilhelm, *Frühling und Herbst*, p. 329.): "Now no one wonders that when unpanicled millet is planted, one obtains unpanicled millet, or that when panicled millet is planted, one obtains panicled millet. Employing people also involves planting. For [a ruler] not to examine his planting, but to expect people to be employed, is an illusion of major proportions."

[27] This passage 眾人之用心…唯賢者不然 appears to be a condensed version of 13a9–12 (57.5–7) below.

[28] The Yang edition mistakenly writes 也 for 池.

[29] The meaning of the two characters 貴眾 here is doubtful. I have followed Guo Moruo in emending 眾 to 聚.

[30] Reading 亡 as 忘 [Yasui and Yao].

involved in the management of affairs: rectification and investigation. With these five, one can[31] institute good order throughout the realm. When these terms are correctly adhered to, there is good order; when they are distorted, disorder prevails. If there is not terminology at all, death ensues. Therefore / the former kings valued terminology."

"The former kings gained control over distant peoples of the realm by using the rules of propriety. For those close at hand, they relied on personal contact. Personal contact and the rules of propriety were the means by which they gained control over the realm. 'Far' and 'near' were the means by which they differentiated [the forms of] intercourse."

"Those who daily bring benefits / and cause few problems are indeed loyal. Those who incur losses and many problems are indeed greedy. Having much loyalty and little greed is wisdom. It is the great moral way for ministers."

"When ministers do not work / for their country, their great crime is that their own families become rich while the state is impoverished or that they enjoy ranks and honors while their ruler occupies an inferior position. / Is anyone who[32] is not working for his country and yet enjoys honor and wealth to be considered worthy?"

"For the mass mind, love is the beginning of hatred, and virtue is / a cause for resentment. If, when serving[33] relatives, wives and children are given everything, respect for the father will decline. If, when serving the prince, the prince is pleased with the work [of his ministers] so their families are enriched, the activity of [his ministers] will decline. / Only those who are [truly] worthy are not like this. Therefore the former kings were never satisfied." /

"The ruler should be resolute in his consistency; the minister should be resolute in his obedience."

"The former kings emphasized honor and shame. Honor and shame lie in what men do. The realm has no room for partisan love or partisan hate. / Those who do good bring prosperity; those who do not cause misery. Misery and prosperity lie in what men do. Therefore the former kings paid serious attention to what men did."

"The former kings made it clear that rewards should not be extravagant and punishments should not be cruel. When rewards and punishments are clear, / there comes the perfection of virtue. Therefore the former kings valued clarification."

"The way of Heaven being great, the [former] emperors and kings

[31] Reading 而 as 能 [Guo Moruo].
[32] Reading 唯 as 誰 [Guo Moruo].
[33] Following the Yang edition, which omits the character 生.

made use of love and hate. With love and hate they could bring the realm close together. With love and hate they gave weight to closing the door [against outsiders] and assured the firmness [of their defenses]." [34]

57.10   "When the *fu* and *gu* measures[35] are too full of grain, / people level them. When people are too satisfied, Heaven levels them. Therefore the former kings were never satisfied."

"The writings of the former kings inspire the mind with admiration, but the masses do not understand them. Therefore, if there is something they should do, they do it. [However], if there is something they should not do, / they still do it."

57.11   "Since I fear [involvement in] affairs, I dare[36] not act. Since I fear [the consequences of] words, I dare not speak. Therefore, after sixty years, I have grown decrepit and hesitant in speech."

---

[34] The meaning of this sentence 愛惡天不可祕, 愛惡重必固 is not clear.

[35] The *fu* 釜 was a large grain measure said to contain six *dou* and four *sheng* 升, about twelve U.S. dry quarts. A *fu* contained four *gu* 鼓.

[36] Following the *Bo Kong liu tie*, 30/3a7–8 (p. 437), and the *Taiping yulan*, 740/7b3–4, which, in quoting this passage both here and below, for 欲 write 敢 [Sun Xingyan, Dai, and Guo Moruo].

Ba Guan

EIGHT OBSERVATIONS

Introductory Comments

Following a brief introduction describing various security precautions and the need for maintaining order at the local level, the bulk of this chapter is devoted to eight short sections listing various matters to be observed if one is to ascertain the general health of a state. Hence the title *Ba guan*.

The detail provided concerning political and social problems is interesting, but unfortunately the chapter appears to be rather late, probably dating from the early Han or at least no earlier than the end of the Warring States Period. Its sentence structure is generally more involved than that of earlier periods. Luo Genze (*Guanzi*, pp. 45–48) dates the chapter as coming from the period following the reigns of the Han emperors Wen 文 and Jing 景 (179–141 B.C), citing two passages from a speech on the value of grain by Chao Cuo 鼂錯 (d. 154 B.C) recorded in the section on food and money in the *Qian Han shu*, 24A/8b9 (Swann, *Food and Money*, p. 159) and 9a9 (Swann, pp. 161–162), which are similar in content to ideas expressed in this chapter. Luo also maintains that the chapter's references to such practices as taxing the six domestic animals and selling ranks, as well as such expressions as 民有鬻子, "the people will sell their children" (3b11; 60.7–8), and 道有損瘠, "the roads will be filled with the corpses of displaced persons" (3b9; 60.7), were current during the Han, but not pre-Han literature. While in general I have no argument with Luo's conclusions regarding a Han date for this chapter, I believe his attempt to tie it to Chao Cuo and the reigns of Wen and Jing is questionable. The passage he cites from Chao Cuo's speech is somewhat similar to, but in no way parallels, the content of this chapter except for one short statement (24A/8b9), 民貧則姦邪生, "When the people are impoverished, wickedness and depravity arise," which is almost the same as this chapter's statement (2b12; 59.9) that 民貧則姦智生, "When the people are impoverished, wicked ideas arise." It should also be pointed out that, as discussed in the Introductory Comments to chapters IX, 23, and X, 28, Chao Cuo seems to have been familiar with at least some of the material that now makes up the *Guanzi*. Therefore, if any borrowing took place, it is more likely that he took his ideas from this chapter rather than the other way around.

Translation

The main city wall must be well constructed, the suburban walls impenetrable, village boundaries secure from all sides, gates kept closed,
and residential walls and doorlocks / kept in good repair. The reason is that if the main walls are not well constructed, rebels and brigands will plot to make trouble. If suburban walls[1] can be penetrated, evil fugitives and trespassers will abound. If village boundaries can be crossed, thieves
and robbers / will not be stopped. If gates are not kept closed and there are passages in and out, men and women will not be kept separated. If residential walls are not solid and locks are not secure, even though people may have rich possessions, they will not be able to protect
them.

Now, if conditions do not permit / wrongdoing, wicked and depraved men will become honest. If prohibitions and penalties are awesome and
severe, troublemakers will behave. If the statutes and orders are clear, / [even] the Man 蠻 and Yi 夷 barbarians will not dare violate them. If rewards are dependable, those having merit will be encouraged. If there are many [who accept the ruler's] teachings and put them into
practice, the people[2] will be transformed without realizing it. /

For this reason, when an enlightened prince occupies the throne, he is sparing in his punishments and exacts few penalties. Unless the punishments are necessary, he does not punish; unless the penalties are necessary, he does not exact them.[3] The enlightened prince shuts the door [on depravity and crime], / blocks the way [to them], and does not allow
their manifestations to appear so there will be no place for people to come in contact with them. As a result, / his people follow a proper path and their actions are good. If this becomes natural to them, punishment and penalties will be few,[4] yet the people will become orderly. /

[1] Emending 郭周 to 周郭, in accordance with the above passage, 1a7 (58.2) [Xu].

[2] Deleting 君 as an interpolation taken from the following passage, 明君 [Yu Yue].

[3] The two appearances of 罰 in this passage should accord with the preceding passage and be written 罪 [Yasui and Xu].

[4] Emending 故罪罰寡 to 故刑省罪罰 to conform with the above passage 1b5 (58.7) [Xu].

[I]

58.10   Survey the fields, examine the plowing and weeding, and calculate the amount of agricultural activity to ascertain whether a state is hungry or wellfed. If the plowing is not deep and the weeding is not carefully done, if the land is not used to its best advantage and fallow fields are
58.11   overgrown / with weeds, if the land that is plowed is not necessarily good and that which is abandoned not necessarily bad, if in calculating the
2a   number of fields in relationship to the population, / a large number of fields are allowed to lie fallow while only a few are planted, then even
58.12   though there be neither flood nor drought, / these will be the fields of a state in which hunger prevails.

          Such being the case, if the population is small, it will not be sufficient to protect the land. If the population is large, the state will be impoverished and the people hungry. Under these conditions, if [the state]
58.13   meets with flood or drought, the masses will scatter and not / collect their harvests. [The prince] who lacks sufficient people to provide protection will not have secure city walls. A starving populace cannot be employed in war. If the masses have scattered and do not collect their harvests, the state will become a wasteland. A prince[5] who possesses
8.14   territory and rules a state yet / does not pay attention to plowing and weeding is dependent on others for his existence.

          Therefore it is said: "Survey the fields, examine the plowing and weeding, and calculate the amount of agricultural activity to ascertain whether a state is hungry or well fed." /

[II]

.1   Survey the mountains and marshlands, observe [the production of] mulberry and hemp, and calculate the production of the six domestic animals to ascertain whether a state is poor or wealthy. Now, if the mountains and marshlands cover a wide area, it is easy to have an
.2   abundance of grass and trees. If the soil is rich, / it is easy to plant mulberry and hemp. If fodder and grass are abundant, it is easy to propagate the six domestic animals.

          [However], the door to these products will be closed if mountains and marshlands cover a wide area but there are no restrictions on [the
3   harvest of] grass and trees, if the soil is rich / but there is no plan for [the production of] mulberry and hemp, and if fodder and grass are abundant but there are heavy taxes on the six domestic animals. / If[6] these

          [5] Deleting 故曰 "Therefore it is said" as an interpolation taken from the following passage.
          [6] Ibid.

227

59.4 products are not produced on time, even though there may be plenty of gold and jade, the country may be said / to be poor.

Therefore it is said: "Survey the mountains and marshlands, observe [the production of] mulberry and hemp, and calculate the production of the six domestic animals, to ascertain whether a state is poor or wealthy." /

[III]

59.5 On entering the capital (*guo* 國) and towns (*yi* 邑), examine the residences and observe the chariots, horses, and clothing to ascertain whether a state is wasteful or frugal. Now, if a state's borders[7] are extensive but its fields are small, there will not be enough to provide for 59.6 the people. / If the area contained within the city walls is large but the population is small, there will not be enough people to protect them. If courtyards[8] are large but buildings are few, there will not be enough 59.7 places for people to live. If buildings are numerous / but retainers are few, there will not be enough people to keep them occupied. If granaries and storehouses are few, but pavilions are numerous, there will not be sufficient reserves to meet expenses.

59.8 Therefore it is said: "If the ruler on high / has no stockpiles of provisions but his residences are splendid, if the households of the common people [also] have no stockpiles but their clothing is highly ornate, if those who ride in chariots make an elaborate display and those walking about are dressed in variegated colors, if basic commodities are scarce 59.9 but nonessential items are plentiful—these / are the practices of a wasteful state."

When the state is wasteful, it exhausts its resources. When its resources are exhausted, its people are impoverished. When the people are 3a impoverished, wicked ideas / arise. When wicked ideas arise, there are 59.10 evil and cunning acts. Thus the origin of wickedness and evil / lies in scarcity and insufficiency. The origin of scarcity and insufficiency lies in wastefulness. The origin of wastefulness lies in not setting proper limits.

Therefore it is said: "It is vital for the state to be judicious in setting limits, frugal in dress, economical in the use of resources, and to prohibit 59.11 extravagance." / Those who do not understand such calculations cannot make proper use of their states.

Therefore it is said: "On entering the capital and towns, examine residences and observe the chariots, horses, and clothing to ascertain whether a state is wasteful or frugal." /

[7] Emending 城 to 域 [Wang Niansun and Xu].
[8] The meaning of 宮營 is not clear. Yasui would read it as "grave areas." Another possible reading would be palace guardhouse. See IX, 23/6b7 (1:26.6).

[IV]

59.13 Take note of extensive hunger, calculate the amount of military and labor service, observe [the number of] pleasure pavilions, and measure the state's expenditures to ascertain whether a state rests on a solid basis or not. In general, it takes an area of land fifty *li* square to feed ten
59.14 thousand households. / If the number is less than ten thousand, the people may spread [freely] into the mountains and marshlands. If it is
60.1 more, they may [be required to] leave them.[9] / If the fields are fully developed yet the people have no stockpiles of provisions, it is because the area of the state is too small and food-producing land is spread too thin. If the fields are only half cultivated yet the people have surplus food
60.2 and grain is plentiful, it is because the area of the state is large and / food-producing land is ample. If the area is large yet the fields are not developed, it is because the prince likes possessions and his ministers like
3b profit. / If the developed land covers a wide area yet the people do not
60.3 have enough, / it is because levies exacted by the sovereign are heavy and the reserves [of the people] are drained away.[10]

Therefore it is said: "If grain travels three hundred *li*, the state will not
50.4 have reserves for even one year. / If it travels four hundred *li*, the state will not have provisions for even half[11] a year. If it travels five hundred *li*, the masses will appear starved. If one-third of the crop is then lost, it is
50.5 called a minor famine. / If minor famines extend over a three-year period, it becomes a major famine. If there is a major famine, the masses
50.6 will become refugees and die of starvation.[12] / If one-tenth [of the people] become soldiers and three-tenths do not engage in productive work, one-third of the crop will be lost. If one-third of the crop is
50.7 lost / and no reserves have been previously set aside, the roads will be filled with the corpses of displaced persons.[13] If one-tenth [of the people] become soldiers and are not released within three years, and if there was
0.8 no excess food [to begin with], the people / will sell their children."

Even though[14] the mountains and forests be near at hand and the
.9 grass and trees lush, proper limits must be set on residences / and the

---

[9] As noted by several commentators, the point of these two sentences is not clear. Perhaps it would be better to follow Yu Yue and Guo Moruo in transposing 下 and 上, which are easily confused in their early written forms. Thus the two sentences would read: "If the number is above ten thousand, [the people] may [freely] spread to the mountains and marshlands. If it is less they may [be required to] leave them."

[10] Following the Yin commentary's interpretation of 流. Tao would read it as "sent abroad."

[11] Emending 二 to 半 [Guo Moruo].

[12] Deleting the second 大 and reading 荀 as 莩 [Hong and Wang Niansun].

[13] Emending 損 to 捐 [Hong, Wang Niansun, and Wang Shaolan].

[14] Deleting 故曰 "Therefore it is said" as an interpolation, since this passage is clearly a statement summarized by line 4a4 (60.10) [Tao].

proper times set for the closing and opening [of mountains and forests]. Why is this? The answer is that large trees cannot be felled, lifted, or transported by an individual acting alone, nor can they be used for the thin walls [of small houses].[15] /

60.10   Therefore it is said: "Even though the mountains and forests be extensive[16] and the grass and trees lush, proper times must be set for the closing and opening [of the mountains and forests]."

Even though the state be overflowing [with riches] and possess an abundance of gold and jade, there must be proper limits set on resi-
60.11   dences. / Even though rivers and lakes be extensive, pools and marshes widespread, and fish and turtles plentiful, there must be regulations set on the use of nets and lines. Boats and nets cannot be the only resource
60.12   for there to be success. It is wrong to be partial toward / grass and trees or favor fish and turtles, and it is inadmissible to subvert people from the production of grain.

Therefore it is said: "When the former kings prohibited work in the mountains and marshlands, it was to expand [the efforts of] the people in the production of grain."

60.13   Unless the people have grain, they will have nothing to eat. / Unless there is land, [grain] will not be produced. Unless there are people, [the land] will not be worked. Unless people have the energy to work, there will be no way to acquire the resources [required by the state]. What the
60.14   world produces / emanates from the expenditure of energy. Such energy emanates from hard physical labor. For this reason, if the ruler on high is unrestrained in the use of resources, it means the people will have no rest in their expenditure of energy.

Therefore it is said: "If pleasure pavilions are [so numerous that they
61.1   stand] / in sight of each other, those above and below will harbor resent-
4b   ments against each other."

If the people have no surplus stores, prohibitions will certainly not be obeyed. If the masses become refugees and die of starvation, battles will certainly not be won. If the roads are filled with the corpses of displaced
61.2   persons, / defenses will certainly not be secure. Now if orders are not reliably carried out, prohibitions obeyed, battles won, and defenses
61.3   secure, danger / and destruction will follow.

Therefore it is said: "Take note of extensive hunger, calculate the amount of military and labor service, observe [the number of] pleasure

---

[15] The point of this sentence is not entirely clear. Perhaps it is referring to the fact that the handling of such large trees would require organized labor and thus take men away from grain production.

[16] The original statement (3b12) writes 近, "near at hand," instead of 廣.

pavilions, and measure the state's expenditures to ascertain whether a state rests on a solid basis or not." /

[V]

On entering the subdistricts (*zhou*) and villages (*li*),[17] observe the customs and pay attention to how people are transformed by their superiors to ascertain whether or not good order prevails within the state. If the subdistricts and villages are not separated from each other / and their gates are not properly constructed, if there are no established times [for people] to go in and out and there are no prohibitions against [going in or out] too early or too late, there will be no way to overcome thieves and robbers and persons who attack and pillage. If they drink from mountain streams and dig / wells along village lanes, if their gardens join each other and trees grow too abundantly, if residential walls are in disrepair and gates and doors are left unlocked so those inside and out can easily communicate, there will be no way to regulate the separation of sexes. /

If in the rural districts (*xiang*),[18] no one is in charge of the circuits (*you*), the villages lack schools,[19] there are no set times for meetings, people do not come together for funerals and the winter sacrifice, / and prohibitions and punishments are not severe, there will be no way to create harmony between the young and old. Now, if marriage ceremonies are not conducted with restraint, people will not cultivate modesty. If the discussion of worthiness is not promoted in the village, the conduct of the local gentry will not / be proper.[20] If goods and wealth

[17] According to Zheng Xuan's 鄭玄 commentary to the *Lun yu*, XV, 5/2a10, a *zhou* 州 consisted of twenty-five hundred households; a *li* 里 consisted of twenty-five. According to the *Guanzi*, XVIII, 57/5b2–4 (3:16.5–6), a *zhou* consisted of ten thousand households, a *li* of one hundred.

[18] According to the *Guanzi*, I, 4/14a4–6 (1:13.6–7): "The country proper shall be divided into five rural districts (*xiang* 鄉), with each administered by a governor (*shi* 師). A rural district shall be divided into five subdistricts (*zhou* 州), with each administered by a prefect (*zhang* 長). A subdistrict shall be divided into ten villages (*li* 里), with each administered by a security officer (*wei* 尉). A village shall be divided into ten circuits (*you* 游), with each administered by a clan elder (*zong* 宗). Ten households shall form a group of ten (*shi* 什) and five households a group of five (*wu* 伍). Both should have heads (*zhang* 長)."

[19] The term *shi she* 士舍 is not clear. The Yin commentary follows the *Guanzi*, I, 4, passage cited above, saying that *shi* 士 equals *wei* 尉, thus interpreting *shi she* as the living quarters for the village's security officer. I have followed Yasui and Song. Guo Moruo would agree.

[20] The character *ji* 及 is questionable. Xu would emend it to 反, in accordance with a similar passage XI, 31/8b4 (2:37.14). Thus the passage would read: "If the discussion of worthiness is not promoted in the village, the local gentry will not restore proper conduct." Yu Yue and Guo Moruo would emend *ji* to 服. Thus, "not be obedient in its conduct."

freely circulate throughout the country, laws and orders will be undermined by officials. If requests for audience are honored on high, factions will be formed below. If officials in the [rural] districts do not adhere to the system of laws, the hundred surnames and multitudinous retainers will not be obedient. These things / are what naturally give rise to the loss of states and the death of princes.

Therefore it is said: "On entering the subdistricts and villages, observe the customs and pay attention to how people have been transformed by their superiors to ascertain whether or not good order prevails within the state." /

[VI]

On entering the court, observe the officials of the left and right and the ministers who are essential to the court,[21] and inquire about who is honored or disdained above and below to ascertain whether a state is strong or weak. If meritorious service is mostly performed by those on high but salaries / and rewards are bestowed on those below, then ministers who have worked hard will not be concerned about putting forth their best effort. If government is conducted by those on high but noble ranks are bestowed on those below, / martial heroes and talented ministers will not be concerned about making full use of their abilities.

If specious attendants and officials of the left and right, regardless of merit and ability, have ranks and salaries, the hundred surnames will be resentful, blame the sovereign, have contempt for ranks, and look down on salaries. / If men who possess gold and jade, goods and wealth, and engage in trade acquire[22] ranks and salaries[23] regardless of whether their actions have any constructive purpose or not, orders of the sovereign will be treated lightly and the system of laws will be undermined. /

If people with great power, regardless of whether or not they have ability, still obtain honored positions, people will turn against serving in the military ranks of their own country and seek [the favor] of external forces. If those who have worked hard are [no longer] concerned with putting forth their best effort, the troops will not fight. If martial heroes / and men of talent are not concerned about making full use of their abilities, in internal administration there will be no distinction [between good and bad].

If the hundred surnames are resentful, blame the sovereign, have contempt for ranks, and look down on salaries, the sovereign will have

---

[21] The passage 本求朝之臣 is unintelligible. I have followed Wang Niansun and Xu, who would delete 求 as a reduplication of 本.

[22] The Yang edition writes 在 "occupy" for 有.

[23] The final 也 of this passage in the Zhao edition should be deleted.

232

no means to exhort the masses. If orders of the sovereign are treated lightly and the system of laws is undermined, / the prince will have no means to control his ministers and his ministers will have no means to serve the prince. If people turn against serving in the military ranks of their own country and seek [the favor of] external forces, the true situation affecting the state will be known to its rivals. /

Therefore it is said: "On entering the court, observe the officials of the left and right and the ministers who are essential to the court,[24] and inquire about who is honored or disdained above and below to ascertain whether a state is strong or weak." /

[VII]

Calculate the degree of strictness or leniency in setting up laws, issuing orders, supervising the masses, and employing the people to ascertain whether or not these things are effective among the people.[25] If laws are instituted in a thoughtless manner and are harmful to those removed [from court], / if from the moment orders are issued there are those who pay no attention to them, if the lowly are given ranks and those with no merit become rich, the masses will certainly treat orders lightly / and the position of the sovereign will be endangered.

Therefore it is said: "If good land is not [bestowed on] those who have served in battle, within three years [the state][26] will be weakened. If rewards and punishments are not dependable, / within five years it will be torn apart. If the sovereign engages in the sale of offices and ranks, within seven[27] years it will be lost. If [those on high] turn their backs on the [five] human relationships[28] and behave like animals, within ten years it will be wiped out [forever]."

To lack victories in battle is to be weak. For territory to be pared away on all sides and incorporated by the feudal lords is to be torn apart.[29] To leave / one's own state and shift the capital elsewhere is to be lost. For

---

[24] See n. 21, above.

[25] The opening sentence of this section does not fit the pattern of other sections and appears to be corrupt. I have followed Yasui and Dai, who would insert 而 after 惠 to accord with the summary passage, 6a10 (62.9). Zhang Peilun and Xu would insert five characters 而興滅之國 before 可知也. Guo Moruo agrees, but would insert 廢 instead of 滅. Thus the sentence would read: "In regard to setting up laws issuing orders, supervising the masses, and employing the people, calculate the degree of strictness and leniency and whether or not things are effective among the people, to ascertain whether a state will flourish or become extinct." For "become extinct," Guo would read, "decline."

[26] Deleting 兵, "armed forces," in accordance with the following passages [Yu Yue and Xu].

[27] Emending 十, "ten," to 七 [Guo Moruo].

[28] The five human relationships are: prince and minister, father and son, husband and wife, older and younger brother, and friends.

[29] The Yang edition mistakenly writes 被 for 破.

those who possess [one's state] to be of another surname is to be wiped out [forever].

62.10   Therefore it is said: "Calculate the degree of strictness or leniency in regard to setting up laws, issuing orders, supervising the masses, / and employing the people to ascertain whether or not these things are effective among the people." [30] /

[VIII]

62.11   Calculate [the relative strength of] enemies and allies, measure the intentions of the sovereign, examine the essential [production] of the country, and observe whether the production of the people results in

6b   surpluses or deficiencies / to ascertain whether a state will [continue to] exist or be lost. If enemy states are strong while allies are weak, if

62.12   ministers who offer criticism are killed / while those who curry favor are revered, if personal wishes are carried out to the detriment of public laws, allies will have no faith in maintaining close relationships and

62.13   enemies will not fear the strength [of such a state]. If martial heroes / are not safe in their positions and men who have worked hard are not content with their salaries, if there is a liking for trade but no concern about basic commodities, the people will trust to luck in making a living and forsake the accumulation of reserves. If martial heroes are not safe

62.14   in their / positions, good ministers will not come forward. If people who have worked hard are not content with their salaries, the troops will be of no use. If people trust to luck to make a living and forsake the accumulation of reserves, granaries and storehouses will be empty.

63.1   If it is like this and the prince does not make / changes, thieves and robbers, cruel brigands and invaders will arise. If internally the court has

63.2   no good ministers, the troops are of no use, and granaries / and storehouses are empty, and if externally there is anxiety caused by the presence of strong enemies, the state will have destroyed itself without doing anything.

Therefore it is said: "Calculate [the relative strength of] enemies and allies, measure the intentions of the sovereign, examine the essential

63.3   [production] of the country, and observe / whether the production of the people results in surpluses or deficits to ascertain whether a state will [continue to] exist or be lost."

Now, if one takes these eight [criteria] to observe the state of a

7a   ruler, / the ruler will have no way of hiding the true state of affairs.

---

[30] See n. 25, above.

Fa Jin
法禁

ON LAWS AND PROHIBITIONS

Introductory Comments

This relatively short chapter deals with the importance of having a legal system (*fa zhi* 法制) and presents a list of prohibitions that were supposed to have been implemented by ancient sage kings. It represents a mixture of Confucian and Legalist ideology, perhaps best described as authoritarian Confucianism. There is considerable stress on law, but not in the draconian manner of a Shang Yang or even Hanfeizi. At the same time much is made of such traditional Confucian virtues as goodness (*ren*) and propriety (*li*). Its approach is very similar to that of the *Xunzi* and probably dates from about the middle of the third century B.C. Its Confucian heritage is confirmed also by its citation of the *Tai shi* 泰誓 or "Great Declaration" chapter of the *Shang shu*, the existing text of which is generally considered to be spurious. As mentioned in the Introduction, this citation was one of the reasons given by Maspero for considering the entire *Guanzi* a post-Han forgery.

Translation

63.6
.4   If the legal system is not open to discussion, people will not unite to promote their self-interest. If there is no pardoning of punishments and
.7   executions, people will not take chances to do what they like. / If the awarding of ranks and salaries is not delegated to others, subordinate officials will not rebel against their sovereign. When these three have been assimilated by officialdom, they will become the law. When they have been put into effect throughout the country, they will become a
.8   matter of accepted practice. / Beyond this no effort will be required for good order to prevail.

The moment the prince establishes these rules of conduct, the various
.9   offices will enforce his laws. / When the sovereign has made his system clear, his subordinate officials will all accord with its measures.

If the prince is not consistent in establishing these rules of conduct, there are certain to be many of his subordinate officials who will turn their backs on the law and replace it with their own private reasoning.

63.10 Given this situation, men will apply / their own private reasoning, disregard the sovereign's legal[1] system, and advocate what they have heard from others. Now, if below [men] are at odds[2] with the [various]

7b offices / over the law while on high they share the majesty of the prince, this will certainly give rise to danger for the state. /

63.11 In ancient times, the sage kings, in governing their people, were not like this. Those who disregarded the sovereign's legal system were

63.12 certain to be put to shame. / By maintaining correct standards, they caused those who would spread about their wealth[3] so as to gain people's allegiance to rectify their own conduct.[4] The sage kings prohibited [the actions of] those who distorted the doctrines of the state, altered its constant standards, and bestowed rewards to suit /

63.13 themselves.[5]

When the sage kings passed away, those who succeeded them were weak, and since those who became princes were unable to comprehend

63.14 the doctrine of establishing princely rule / as the basis for managing the state, it inevitably became common for great ministers to consort with those below to capture the hearts of men. Since princes could

64.1 not / judiciously establish their laws as the system for managing those below, it inevitably became general practice for the hundred surnames to institute their own reasoning and follow their own interests.

64.2 In ancient times, the sage kings, in governing men, did not / value broad learning among their people. They wanted men to be unanimous in obeying orders. "The Great Declaration" says: "Zhou had countless

64.3 ministers; they also were of countless minds."[6] / King Wu had three
8a thousand ministers, but they were of one mind. Therefore Zhou with his countless minds lost, while King Wu with one mind survived.

Now, if the prince who possesses a state is unable to unite the minds of

64.4 people, concentrate the power of the state [in his hands alone], / spread

---

[1] Inserting 法 before 制, in accordance with the following passage, 7b2 (63.11) [Xu].

[2] Reading 列 as 裂 [Yu Yue and Dai].

[3] Inverting 財厚 to 厚財 [Wang Niansun].

[4] The translation of this sentence is doubtful since the original text is clearly corrupt. I have generally followed the interpretation of Tang Jinggao.

[5] This passage appears to be a misplaced slip that originally followed 故國之危也 (8a10; 64.7).

[6] The existing text of the *Tai shi*, or "Great Declaration," chapter of the *Shang shu* (VA, 1/8), which is now generally considered to be a late forgery, reads 受有臣億萬, 惟億萬心, "Shou 受 had countless ministers, but they were of countless minds." Shou is the same as Zhou 紂, the last king of the Shang who was overthrown by King Wu 武 of the Zhou.

the righteous conduct of gentlemen everywhere, and extend his government on high to become the law among those below, then even though his territory be vast and his population large, he still cannot be counted safe. If the prince neglects the doctrine [of princely rule], great ministers will band together with those who are powerful / in order to advance themselves within the country while lesser ministers, in the pursuit of gain, will be certain to join them.

Thus [these people] will promote the country's gentry to make them members of their own factions[7] and implement public doctrine to serve their private interests. / When coming forward they will recommend each other to the prince; when retreating they will praise each other to the people. Each will do what is advantageous for himself and forget the altars of land and grain in expanding his own base of operations. They will assemble huge numbers of retainers.[8] On high they will blind the prince [to what is going on] / while they squeeze the people below. All this is a doctrine that weakens the prince and disrupts the country. Therefore the state is endangered.

The sage kings prohibited [the actions of] those who:

[1] Distorted the doctrines of the state, altered its constant standards, and bestowed rewards to suit themselves.[9]

[2] Usurped the power of the state to further squeeze the people.

[3] Did not personally / assume the obligations due their sovereign.

[4] Came forward to accept salaries from the prince, but on retreating reserved them for their immediate household, failed to perform their governmental functions while expending their efforts on those attached to themselves, and turned the royal / offices and service to the prince to their private advantage, getting rid of those who were not their men so people would act in their interest.[10]

[5] Did not consider that the cultivation of morality / should begin with themselves or that managing affairs should be under the [appropriate] office, advanced those with no ability, and promoted those with no achievement.

[6] When associating with others, felt they were doing them a favor, / when advancing someone, considered it their own accomplishment, and when employing someone, took a share of his salary. /

[7] Associated with the wealthy while plundering the poor, felt no

---

[7] Emending 亡 to 己 [Wang Niansun].

[8] Emending 威 to 成 [Hong and Xu].

[9] See n. 5, above.

[10] As several commentators have pointed out, the latter part of this passage is very likely corrupt, but they provide no real help in solving the problem.

64.13 concern about taking from the people while taking care to present gifts to the prince, / exploited the sovereign to subsidize their underlings, and manipulated the law to make demands on the people.

64.14 [8] Possessed equipage not suitable to people [in their position], owned family wealth richer than others of the same rank, / and had small salaries but great wealth.

65.1
9a [9] Violated the customs of the time in conducting their activities, slandered their superiors in order to achieve fame, / and consistently opposed the sovereign's legal system to create a mass following.

65.2 [10] Gave the appearance of poverty, but while refusing[11] / to work were friendly with the poor and lowly, had no regular employment themselves or any regular source of livelihood[12] for their families, but circulated among those on high and those below, saying it was all for the sake of the people. /

65.3 [11] Recruited[13] knights for their own[14] use and produced armor[15]
65.4 for their own[16] / purposes so as to provide for knights who would certainly be willing to die for them personally,[17] and thereafter adopted
65.5 a belligerent attitude[18] / in intensive bargaining with the sovereign.

65.6 [12] Paid studious attention to minor details to show off before the people, incessantly commented on major / matters to impress the sovereign, established wide contacts to skip ahead of the [official] crowd, and took advantage of rank to dominate the court.

65.7
9b [13] [Pretended] to humble themselves to live among the masses, / secretly engaged in evil, surreptitiously entered [the court] to welcome those from afar while shunning both the sovereign and the people. /

65.8 [14] Offended against established custom, distorted the rules of propriety, overstated the difficulty of their activities, and exaggerated what they had done.

65.9 [15] Hoarded public stores and lived in idleness, / distributed them in order to entice the masses, busied themselves following the lead of

[11] Reading 發 as 廢 [Sun Xingyan].

[12] Reading 姓 as 生 [Ding].

[13] The Yang edition for 壺 writes 壹, "to bring together." I have followed the Zhao edition, which concurs with the Ancient, Liu, and Zhu editions and Yin Zhizhang's notation in the Yang edition. I have also followed Guo Moruo's explanation of 壺 as 鋪.

[14] Emending 亡 to 己 [Wang Niansun].

[15] Emending 田 to 甲 [He Ruzhang].

[16] See n. 14, above.

[17] The phrase 則生之養必死之士 does not make sense, but none of the commentators provides a well-argued reconstruction. I have generally followed Xu's suggested emendation, 則私養必死之士.

[18] Emending 失 to 矢 [Guo Moruo].

others, curried the favor of others on account of their wealth, assisted others to buy their praise, / or kept themselves very reserved to force others to seek them out.

[16] Persisted in perverse conduct, were argumentative in hypocritical speeches,[19] prolific in telling lies, and glossed over their connivance with evil.[20] /

[17] Considered forming cliques as [mere] friendship, concealing evil as goodness, calculating machinations as wisdom, levying heavy exactions as / loyalty, and giving way to anger as bravery.

[18] Monopolized[21] the essential production of the state, personally strove to deceive[22] the sovereign, and were deeply committed to the feudal lords. /

During the age when the sage kings personally exercised their rule, / virtuous conduct was certain to be prevalent, and moral standards were clear. Therefore none of the gentry dared offend against established custom / or distort the rules of propriety in order to make himself known throughout the country. None dared to spread favors, be lenient in executing [punishments] or establish special relationships with those above or below in order to gain the personal allegiance of the people. None[23] dared exceed his proper rank, skip ahead in office, fish for profit, / or scrounge for merit by catering to his prince.

The sage kings, in governing the people, made it so that coming forward would bring no profit, retreating would bring no / avoidance of harm. They were certain to cause people to return to being content with their positions, to being happy among the crowd [of officials], to devoting themselves to their duties, to taking pride in having a good reputation, and that was all.

Therefore those who skipped ahead in office and separated themselves from the crowd [of officials] / were certain to be brought to harm. Those who lacked ability and neglected their duties were certain to be brought to shame.

For this reason, when the sage kings instructed their people, they used goodness to manage them and a sense of shame to motivate them. They

[19] The *Xunzi*, VIII, 28/1b6–8, cites these two faults among a list of five, which, according to Confucius, the ancients hated. They are also cited by the *Li ji*, IV, 5/14b4 (Legge, *Li Ki*, XXVII, p. 237), as being among the crimes punishable by death. In both cases 詭 is written 偽.

[20] The *Xunzi*, VIII, 28/1b7, cited above for these two faults, writes: 記醜而博, 順非而澤, "prolific in recording nasty details and glossing over connivance with wrongdoing."

[21] Yasui would read 固 as 錮, "obstructed."

[22] Reading 往 as 廷 [Tao, Zhang Peilun, and Guo Moruo].

[23] Deleting 故 [Wang Niansun and Yasui].

66.4 cultivated their abilities / to attain that which they could do, and that is all.

Therefore it is said: "Being decisive, they insured stability; being calm, they maintained good order; providing security, they gained respect; in taking administrative action, they were consistent. Such was the way of the sage kings."

Zhong Ling
重令

On the Importance of Orders

Introductory Comments

This is a curious chapter, generally Legalist in tone as indicated by its title, but containing passages very reminiscent of the *Laozi*. It appears to be a work of the Huang-Lao school, which is primarily distinguished from other schools by its amalgamation of Legalist and Daoist concepts. One line, 13a12–b1 (69.1), is similar to a passage (1.5.41) in the *Jing fa*, one of the Huang-Lao texts discovered at Mawangdui.

Zhong ling is written in a very choppy and excessively repetitious style. Although it hangs together as a complete essay, this choppiness and occasional abrupt change in subject matter have led some commentators, including Wang Niansun and Guo Moruo, to suspect that there are ellipses in the text. It is also possible that the final section (13b8–14b2; 69.5–14) may have been a separate fragment that Liu Xiang or some other editor incorporated into this text because it speaks of the *san qi* 三器, "three instruments," of government, and thus helps to explain the opening sentence of this chapter: "Of all the important instruments (*qi*) for ruling a state...."

The final section is also very similar to the "Explanation" to the *Ban fa*, XXI, 66/6a3–6b3 (3:48.11–49.3), prompting Guo Moruo to believe that this chapter and the "Explanation" were written by the same person. I think it is more likely that the "Explanation" represents a paraphrase of this section, either as part of this chapter or as an independent fragment. The "Explanation" is not only simpler in content but is written in that much more straightforward style characteristic of Han. Luo Genze (*Guanzi*, p. 57) would date this chapter as coming from the end of the Qin or beginning of the Han. On the basis of its general style and content, I believe it may be of a slightly earlier date, perhaps as early as the middle of the third century B.C. If my earlier dating is correct, this *Zhong ling* chapter could constitute one of the earliest surviving texts of a Huang-Lao school.

Translation

Of all the important instruments for ruling a state, none is more important than orders. If orders are treated as important, the prince will be honored. If he is honored, the state will be safe. If the orders are treated lightly, the prince will be scorned. If he is scorned, the state will be endangered.

Therefore, ensuring the safety of the state depends on the prince being honored, / and such honor depends on having his orders carried out.
Having his orders carried out depends on his being strict in regard to punishments. If his punishments are strictly applied and his orders are carried out, the various functionaries will all be fearful of punishment. If punishments are not strictly applied and the orders are not carried out, the various functionaries will all be delighted.

Now, when the enlightened prince examines / the essentials involved in governing his people, nothing is more essential than [the proper execution of] his orders. Therefore it is said: "Death should be inflicted on those who scale down orders, exceed them, fail to see them carried
out, hold them back, or fail to obey them." / If these five mean death and no [hope of] pardon, [the proper execution of] orders will become the sole consideration [of the various functionaries]. Therefore it is said; "When [the orders] are treated as important, subordinate officials become fearful."

[However], if the sovereign is not enlightened, when orders are issued,
even though they emanate from on high, / his subordinate officials will discuss whether they are right or wrong. Now, if they may repudiate the orders of the sovereign to enhance their own authority and give themselves a free hand in pursuit of their / private interests, how can the various functionaries fail to be delighted?

Moreover, if orders are issued, but even though they emanate from on
high, / subordinate officials discuss whether they are right or wrong, it means the authority [of the prince] has moved downward, to be preempted by the people. / It is impossible to expect the sovereign not to be endangered if his authority has moved downward and been preempted by the people.

When orders are issued, if holding them back is not a crime, it teaches
the people disrespect. / When orders are issued, if there is no blame for failing to enact them or there is blame for carrying them out, both of
these teach the people disobedience. / When the orders are issued, if there is discussion in the offices as to whether they are right or wrong, it means the authority [of the prince] is being shared with his subordinates.

When orders are issued,[1] if exceeding or detracting is not a crime, it teaches people / the way to depravity.

If such is the case, men who are sycophants will take advantage of the situation to satisfy their self-interest and conspire with others; men who are connivers will take advantage of it to cater to / factions and obtain allies; men who covet profit will take advantage of it to accumulate goods and amass wealth; men who are cowardly and weak will take advantage of it to cater to the honored and rich[2] and serve specious attendants [of the prince]; men who are arrogant and boastful will take advantage of it to purchase praise and acquire / fame. Therefore, the moment the orders are issued, the [above] five crossroads on the way to depravity will be demonstrated to the people, / and it will become impossible to expect the sovereign not to be endangered or his subordinate officials / not to be rebellious.

When legumes and grains are insufficient and there are no prohibitions against nonessential production, the faces of the people are certain to show signs of starvation. Under such conditions, it is called sedition for artisans to vie arrogantly with one another in carving and engraving. / When hemp cloth and silk are insufficient and no sumptuary limits have been placed on clothing, the people are certain to suffer freezing and cold. Under such conditions, it is called sedition for women to vie arrogantly with one another [in producing] elegant clothing, / embroidery, and sashes.[3] When the troops of a state that possesses ten thousand chariots and stores of arms are not able to meet the enemy on the field of battle, the altars of Land and Grain are certain to face the calamity of being endangered or lost. Under such conditions, it is called sedition for knights to vie arrogantly with one another in not assuming their military duties. / When the bestowal of ranks entails no mention of ability and the granting of salaries entails no mention of accomplishments, knights are certain[4] to be neither willing to carry out commands nor die [for their country]. / Under such conditions, it is called sedition for the multitude of ministers to vie arrogantly with one another in communicating with outside forces, requesting [special] audiences, seizing political power, engaging in deceitful[5] activities, serving

---

[1] Inserting the three characters 令出而 before 益 to make this sentence conform to the general pattern [Zhang Peilun and Xu].

[2] Inverting the two characters 事當 to make the phrase conform to the general pattern for this sentence [Guo Moruo].

[3] Reading 綦 as 纂 [Wang Niansun].

[4] Inserting 必, which was mistakenly moved from here to below 群臣, "multitude of ministers."

[5] Emending 道 to 遁 [Tao].

specious [court] attendants, and using honored positions and wealth for [personal] glory. /

67.10 The court should have ministers, the state customary practices, and the people production, all adhering to constant standards. What is meant by the court having ministers who adhere to constant standards?

67.11
12a Such ministers examine their own ability / when accepting office and do not deceive their sovereign, pay careful heed to laws and orders and do not serve the interests of factions, use their utmost ability and full strength with no regard for [personal] gain, do not retreat from death

67.12 when encountering difficulties or facing disaster, / do not accept salaries that exceed their accomplishments, do not exaggerate their abilities when assuming office, and do not accept false credit for having done nothing. /

67.13 What is meant by the state having customary practices that adhere to constant standards? Such customary practices involve no conflict between the likes and dislikes [of the people] and those of the sovereign, no opposition to his orders in what they honor or denigrate, no activities that the sovereign opposes, no talk of factional interests on the part of

67.14 subordinate officials, / no extravagant living, no attire exceeding that appropriate to rank. They also involve careful attention being paid to conduct in the districts and villages so it does not become seditious in regard to matters essential to the court. /

68.1 What is meant by the people having production that adheres to constant standards? Such production involves raising animals, planting trees, sowing grain at the appropriate time, devoting energy to agriculture, opening grasslands, and preventing nonessential production.

68.2 Therefore it is said: / "If the court does not value ministers who adhere to constant standards, specious attendants will gain entrance, those with no accomplishments will falsely obtain [salaries], the depraved and wicked will be able to do as they please, and the incompetent will move upward. If the state does not support customary practices that adhere to constant standards, ministers and subordinates will not be obedient and

68.3
12b the orders of the sovereign will be difficult to carry out. / If the people do not pay attention to production that adheres to constant standards, granaries will be empty and necessities in short supply."

If specious attendants gain entrance [to the court], those with no accomplishments falsely obtain [salaries], the depraved and wicked are

68.4 able to do as they please, / and the incompetent move upward, great ministers will fall into discord. If ministers and subordinate officials are not obedient, and orders of the sovereign are difficult to carry out, there will be no success when responding to difficulties. If the granaries are

244

empty and necessities are in short supply, the state will have no means to / secure its defenses. If one of these three [conditions] appears, enemy countries will be in control.

Now, a state must not be ineffectual in establishing its importance [in the world], its armed forces must not be ineffectual in seeking victories, its people must not be ineffectually employed, and orders must not be ineffectually carried out. / The importance of the state inevitably depends on victories by its armed forces. Victories by its armed forces inevitably depends on the employment of its people. Employment of its people inevitably depends on / orders being carried out. The carrying out of its orders inevitably depends on establishing their precedence over those close [to the prince].

Now, it is impossible to be certain that orders will be carried out if two or three [of the following conditions exist]:[6] prohibitions do not take precedence over those close [to the prince] and those who are honored; punishments / are not applied to specious attendants; laws and punishments do not secure the execution of those who commit serious [crimes] but merely inflict harm on those who are distant [from the court]; commendations and rewards are not bestowed on the humble and lowly. /

It is impossible to be certain that people will be employed if: ability is not associated with office; salaries and rewards do not match accomplishment; / commands and orders are opposed in the hearts of the people; activity and rest do not accord with seasonal changes; those who have accomplishments are not certain of reward and those who have committed crimes are not certain of execution; the orders are not certain of / being carried out; prohibitions are not certain to be obeyed; those in high positions have no means to employ their subordinates.

It is impossible to be certain that the armed forces will be victorious if: generals are not strict in their authority; the people's hearts are not united; knights arrayed for battle are not willing to die in carrying out / their commands; the troops are not scornful of the enemy.

It is impossible to be certain that the country will be treated as important if: internally, defenses cannot be made complete; externally, attacks cannot be subdued; the field of battle cannot be controlled; when faced with enemy attack, / neighbors on all four sides cannot be overawed.

It is impossible to expect [a prince] to become lord protector over the

---

[6] Several commentators note that the two characters 二 三 "two or three," do not fit the pattern employed in the following sequence of paragraphs and probably represent a textual corruption.

feudal lords if: his benevolence is not extended to the weak and small; the strong and large do not believe in the awesomeness of his authority; his punitive expeditions are incapable of subjugating the entire realm. /

68.13   It is impossible to expect him to become king over the entire realm if: another shares his awesome authority; [control over] the armed forces is contested; his benevolence is incapable of embracing distant countries; his orders are incapable of uniting the feudal lords. /

68.14   Extensive territory, a wealthy state, a large population, and powerful armed forces, these are the basis for becoming a lord protector or a king. However, they will also bring [the prince] close to danger and destruction. The way of Heaven has its course;[7] the minds of men are subject to

69.1   change. / It is the course of Heaven's way to reach the extreme and then

13b   revert, to reach the full and then decline.[8] / The change in men's minds is to become arrogant when achieving too much. When there is arrogance, there is negligence. /

69.2   Now, those who are arrogant will be arrogant toward the feudal lords. If [the prince] is arrogant toward the feudal lords, he will lose [their allegiance] without. If there is negligence, the people will become rebel-

69.3   lious within. To lose feudal lords without, / and have the people become rebellious within—such is the way of Heaven.[9] This is the time for danger and ruin.

Now, such being the case, even though his territory be extensive, [the prince] should neither annex [the territory of others] nor plunder [their wealth]. Even though his population be large, he should be neither

69.4   negligent / nor overbearing toward his subjects. Even though the state be wealthy, he should avoid being extravagant and given to following his desires. Even though his armed forces be powerful, he should not insult the feudal lords. When activating the masses and employing his armed forces, it must be to provide government for the entire realm.[10] This is

69.5   the basis for bringing order to the realm, / and the guiding principle for lord protectors and kings.

[7] Reading 數 as 理. See Wang Bi's commentary to the *Laozi*, A, 5/3b–4a, and the *Guanzi*, IX, 23/10b10 (2:10.1).

[8] This line is reminiscent of the *Laozi*, B, 40/4a (Waley, *The Way and Its Power*, p. 192): "Reversion is the movement of the Way." the *Jing fa* (1.5.41) also contains a similar passage, the opening phrase of which is missing a crucial character. However, the remainder reads: 極而反, 盛而衰, 天地之道也, 人之李(理)也, "Reaching the extreme and then reverting, reaching the full and then declining—such is the way of Heaven and Earth, and the guiding principle of man."

[9] According to the *Laozi*, B, 77/22b (Waley, *The Way and Its Power*, p. 237): "Heaven takes away from those who have too much and gives to those who have not enough."

[10] Emending 理 to 治 to accord with the concluding statement of this chapter, 14b4 (70.1) [Yasui].

There were always three instruments (*san qi*) with which the former kings governed the state and six [evils] that attacked and harmed it.[11] The enlightened kings were able to overcome these attacks. Therefore, they did not add to these three [instruments], yet possessed their own states and brought order to / the entire realm. Muddle-headed kings were unable to overcome these attacks. Therefore, even though they did not detract from the three [instruments], should they have possessed the entire realm as their own, they would still have perished. /

What are the three instruments? The answer is: commands and orders, battle-axes and halberds, / salaries and rewards. What were the six attacks? The answer is: having favorites, awarding honors, / bribes, beautiful women, clever sycophants, and indulgence in pleasure.

What about using the three instruments? The answer is: were it not for commands and orders there would be no means to employ one's subordinate officials. Were it not for battle-axes and halberds, there would be no means to instill awe among the masses. Were it not for salaries and rewards, there would be no means to encourage / the people.

What are the failures brought on by the six attacks? The answer is: there will be those who even though disobedient can still survive, even though violating the prohibitions can still escape [punishment], and even though / lacking accomplishment can still become rich.

Whenever a state contains those who are disobedient yet able to survive, commands and orders will not be sufficient to employ subordinate [officials]. When it contains those who violate the prohibitions yet are able / to escape [punishment], battle-axes and halberds will not be sufficient to awe the masses. When it contains those who lack accomplishments yet become rich, salaries and rewards will not be sufficient to encourage the people.

When commands and orders are not sufficient to employ one's subordinate officials, battle-axes and halberds / are insufficient to awe the masses, and salaries and rewards are insufficient to encourage the people, they will be of no use to [the prince] himself. If they are of no use to him, / there will be no victories in battle. If there are no victories in battle, the defenses will not be secure. If the defenses are not secure, enemy countries will control [his state].

This being so, what would the former kings do? The answer is: they would not, because of the six [attacks], alter their commands and orders, create doubts / about [the certainty of their] using battle-axes and hal-

---

[11] This section, 13b8–14b2 (69.5–14), is very similar to the "Explanation" to *Ban fa*, XXI, 66/6a3–6b3 (3:48.11–49.3), which I suspect was adapted from this chapter by the Han author of the "Explanation."

14b

70.1

berds, or tamper with salaries and rewards. Such being the case, the near and far were of one mind. Being of one mind, the many and the few cooperated in their efforts. Cooperating in their efforts, they were certain to be victorious in battle / and the defenses were certain to be secure. This was not to annex and plunder, but to provide government for the entire realm. This is the way to bring order to the realm.

Fa Fa

法法

ON CONFORMING TO THE LAW

Introductory Comments

One striking feature of the *Fa fa* is that it consists of three separate fragments similar in content and even identical (or nearly so) in certain passages. Liu Xiang 劉向, or perhaps some earlier editor, probably lumped them together to form the present single chapter, introducing the second and third fragments with the phrase *yi yue* 一曰, "Another version says."

Whether all three versions are the work of one man, or of three men closely associated with one another in their viewpoint and use of language, it is impossible to say at this point. The versions are similar in philosophical approach as well as in their detailed treatment of specific ideas, and there are no obvious inconsistencies in grammatical usage. However, the style of the first version, the longest of the three, is more contrived than that of the other two, making extensive use of the classical Chinese chain argument with its monotonous repetition of "if ... then ...." clauses.[1] The text of this version is also much less corrupt than the other two.

Luo Genze (*Guanzi*, p. 48ff.) and others have labeled this chapter as Legalist primarily because of its title and emphasis on law. The opening passage (1a6–2a4; 70.6–71.3), for example, appears strictly Legalist; however, other passages are clearly more in line with the teachings of such authoritarian Confucians as Xunzi. The passage 2b2 (71.8) points up the importance of observing *li*, "propriety," and *yi*, "righteousness," and on page 3b (72.9ff.) there is a discussion of the *junzi* or man of quality, who is paid in accordance with his adherence to the moral way while ordinary men are paid in accordance with their physical effort. This is certainly a Confucian concept reflecting their distinction between those who labor with their minds and those who labor with their physical strength.

[1] For a fuller discussion of the chain argument device, see Bodde, *China's First Unifier*, pp. 228–232.

After another long Legalist-sounding chain argument advocating strict laws and punishments, we come to a passage on page 4b (73.7) that states that legal statutes, regulations, and procedures must be patterned on the moral way. However, immediately following this there is a frank Legalist statement that the sovereign loves his people because he employs them. On page 6a (74.10–11) there appears perhaps the most strikingly Confucian statement of all: "Thus, how can a country get along without the moral way or men get along without seeking after it."

The second version presents the same mixture of Legalist and Confucian-sounding phrases; the third version is perhaps the most Confucian of all. One passage on pages 8b–9a (77.3–5) states: "No gentlemen of high standing will be found among those who repudiate the past when discussing the present, and no gentlemen of [great] wisdom will be found among those who are ignorant of the past and are easygoing in their achievements. Even though one may be completely virtuous in his own conduct, if he repudiates the past he will be a mediocre person." This passage not only accords with Confucian views, but is precisely the opposite of the Legalist position, which holds that since times change, the past cannot be taken as a model. Finally, on page 9b (78.1–2) we find the statement that nothing impoverishes the people or destroys goods on such a scale as do armed forces; yet from ancient times to the present no one has been able to dispense with them. This pronouncement stands in marked contrast to the Legalist glorification of war, but is almost identical with Xunzi's position on the subject. Actually, except for the fact that laws are stressed here more than in any of Xunzi's writings, the basic philosophical approach of this chapter is more in line with his thought than with Legalism.

It would appear that the first part of the chapter, at least, could not have been written before the time of Mencius (d. 289 B.C.) because it contains (6a12; 75.1) a statement about the *Chunqiu* that directly parallels the Mengzi, IIIB, 9/7–8. Furthermore, the authoritarian school of Confucianism with which this text appears to be intimately associated did not develop until the middle and later part of the third century B.C. Xunzi himself died about 238 B.C., and the style is in general accord with that of this period. It is also doubtful that it was written after the fall of the Qin because by that time the kind of simplistic arguments stressing law presented here were no longer necessary or fashionable.

Translation

1:70.6
1a6

If [the ruler] does not conform to the law, government affairs will lack a constant standard.

250

If he conforms to what is unlawful, his orders will not be carried out.

If orders are issued yet are not carried out, it is because the orders do not conform to the law.

70.7 If they conform to the law yet / are not carried out, it is because those who issue the orders are not discerning in their judgment.

If they are discerning yet [the orders]are not carried out, it is because the rewards are paltry and punishments light.

70.8 If the rewards are generous and the punishments severe / yet [the orders] are not carried out, it is because they are not reliable.

If [the rewards and punishments] are reliable yet [the orders] are not carried out, it is because [the ruler] does not set an example [by obeying them] himself. /

70.9 Therefore, it is said: "When prohibitions take precedence over [the ruler] himself, his orders will be carried out among the people."

To hear of worthiness and not elevate it is dangerous. /

'b To hear of excellence and not seek after it is dangerous.

0.10 To see ability and not / employ it is dangerous.

To become intimate with men and not remain firm [of purpose] is dangerous.

To agree on a plan and then diverge from it is dangerous.

To make threats against others and not be able [to implement them] is dangerous.

To dismiss a person and then reinstate him is dangerous.

0.11 To fail to act when there is an opportunity to do so / is dangerous.

To have secret plans and not treat them discreetly is dangerous.

If the ruler of men is not discreet in all things, gentlemen who would
).12 speak truthfully and act in a straightforward manner / will be endangered.[2]

If the gentlemen who would speak truthfully and act in a straightforward manner are endangered, the ruler of men will find himself isolated and without an inner circle of supporters.

If the ruler of men is isolated and without an inner circle of supporters, his ministers will form factions and assemble their partisans. /

.13 If the ruler of men becomes isolated and without an inner circle of supporters and his ministers form factions and assemble their partisans, this is not the crime of his ministers but rather is the fault of the ruler himself.

---

[2] This statement is reminiscent of the *Xi ci* 繫辭 [Appended Treatise, A] of the *Yi jing*, VII, 7/6b1–3 (Wilhelm, *I Ching*, I, p. 330): "The Master said, 'Where disorder develops, words are the first step. If the prince is not discreet, he loses his ministers. If the minister is not discreet, he loses his life. If the secret matters are not treated discreetly, their successful completion will be harmed.'"

70.14   If the people do not commit serious crimes, / it is because they have committed no major faults.

If the people have committed no major faults, it is because the sovereign has granted no pardons.

If the sovereign pardons minor faults, the people will go on to commit many serious crimes. This is because [the latter] grow out of an accumulation [of the former]. /

71.1   Therefore it is said: "If pardons are granted, the people will not be respectful,[3] and if mercy is bestowed, their faults will daily increase."

If mercy and pardons are extended to the people, then even though the
71.2   prisons are full and executions numerous, depravity / will not be
2a   overcome.

Therefore it is said: "There is nothing better than preventing depravity at its inception."

If faults are pardoned and excellence neglected, the people will not be encouraged. Faults should not be pardoned; excellence should not be
71.3   neglected.[4] The way to encourage / the people lies in the application of this [principle].

Therefore it is said: "The enlightened prince is a keen judge of affairs."

The prince desires three things from his people, but if these desires are not kept within bounds, his position on high will be endangered. What
71.4   are the three? / The first pertains to what he seeks, the second to what he prohibits, and the third to what he orders. He certainly desires to gain what he seeks. He certainly desires to have stopped what he prohibits. He certainly desires to have carried out what he orders.

If he seeks too much, little will be gained. If he prohibits too
71.5   much, / little will be stopped. If he orders too much, little will be carried out. If what he seeks is not gained, his prestige will daily decrease. If
71.6   what he prohibits is not stopped, the punishments will be ridiculed. / If what he orders is not carried out, his subjects will have humiliated the sovereign.

Thus it is that no one has ever been able to seek too much and gain it
71.7   all, prohibit too much / and have all that is prohibited stopped, or issue too many orders and have them all carried out.

Therefore it is said: "If the sovereign is too demanding, his subjects will not be obedient."

If subjects, being disobedient, are forced [to conform] by means of punishments, the masses will scheme against anyone who becomes the
71.8   sovereign. When someone becomes the sovereign / and the masses
2b

---

[3] Dai and Yasui would read 苟 as 儆. Thus, "will not take warning."
[4] The Yang edition mistakenly writes 積 for 遺.

scheme against him, he cannot possibly avoid danger, even though he may want to.

If orders are changed once they have been issued, if rules of propriety and righteousness are abandoned once they have been put into practice, if procedures and measurements are altered once they have been instituted, if penal laws are modified once they are in place, / then even though the rewards are generous, the people will not be encouraged, and even though there are many executions, the people will not be fearful.

Therefore it is said: "If the sovereign lacks a firm purpose,[5] his subjects will harbor doubts in their hearts, and if the state lacks constant standards, the strength of the people / will certainly be exhausted. This is inevitable."

When an enlightened prince occupies the position on high, there will be no one among the people who will dare initiate private debates or consider himself better than others. Within the country there will be no monstrous / boasts,[6] heterodox customs, or peculiar rites. Among gentlemen there will be no private debates. Those who display arrogance, alter the orders, lay down their own rules of conduct, draw up their own regulations or engage in private debates will all be punished.[7] / Thus the strong will be bent, the sharp blunted, and the firm broken.[8]

He will guide them with the marking line [of the law] and set them straight with punishments. Thus the hearts of all the people will be subservient / and they will follow their sovereign. When he pushes them, they will go; when he pulls them, they will come. If, however, there are among his subjects any who initiate private debates or consider themselves better than others or any who are quarrelsome and draw themselves apart, the orders will not be carried out. /

---

[5] Reading 植 as 志.

[6] Reading 嚴 as 譀 [Xu].

[7] This opposition to private debates was not only characteristically Legalist, but also an essential part of Xunzi's authoritarianism. According to the *Xunzi*, XVI, 22/5b7 ff. (Dubs, *Hsüntze*, p. 289): "All heretical doctrines and perverse teachings that depart from the correct way and are fabricated without authority can be classed among the three deceptions.... Therefore the enlightened prince supervised [the people] with executive authority, led them with the [correct] way, ordered them through decrees, explained [things] to them through proclamations, and restrained them through punishments. Therefore the people's conversion to the [correct] way was as if by magic."

[8] A similar passage appears in the *Shangjun shu*, IV, 17/8a6–9 (Duyvendak, *Lord Shang*, p. 282): "What I mean by the unification of education is that all those partisans of wide scholarship, sophistry, cleverness, good faith, integrity, rites and music, and moral culture, whether their reputations are unsullied or foul, should for these reasons not become rich or honored, should not discuss punishments, and should not compose their private views independently and memorialize the sovereign. The strong should be broken and the sharp blunted."

Therefore it is said: "When private debates are initiated, the way of the ruler will be debased."

How much more will this be true[9] if there are any who are arrogant, alter the orders, lay down their own rules of conduct, draw up their own regulations, change the customs, wear strange clothes, voice heretical theories, or set themselves apart.[10] / Those who on high do not carry out the prince's orders, who are uncooperative in the districts and villages below, who act on their own to change things, and who alter the established customs of the country—these are called people who cannot be shepherded. / People who cannot be shepherded stand outside the marking line [of the law] and should be punished.[11]

See to it that worthy men are given salaries according to their ability and fighting knights according to their achievements. If worthy men / are given salaries according to their ability, the sovereign will be honored and the people obedient. If fighting knights are given salaries according to their achievements, troops will disregard misfortune and scorn the enemy. If these two things—the sovereign being honored and the people obedient, the troops disregarding misfortune and scorning the enemy—/ are achieved within the country, the realm may be well governed and the ruler made secure. /

In general[12] the granting of pardons is of little benefit and great harm, and in the long run nothing is more disastrous. The nongranting of pardons / is of little harm and great benefit, and in the long run nothing / can be more beneficial. Thus granting pardons is the same as releasing the reins of a runaway horse, / while not granting them is the same as [probing] a festering boil[13] with a stone lancet.[14]

If a person has neither high rank nor large salary, he will not share in preparing for difficulties or withstanding danger. When he is treated in such a way, / nothing may be expected from him. For this reason, former kings instituted official carriages and caps that were just adequate enough[15] to distinguish the honored from the lowly, but they did not strive for beauty. / They established ranks and salaries just adequate enough to insure service, but they did not strive for ostentatiousness.

---

[9] Deleting 主, "ruler," at the beginning of this sentence as an assimilation of the same character in the preceding sentence [Yu Yue and Zhang Peilun].

[10] Emending 猶 to 獨 [Dai and Zhang Peilun].

[11] According to the *Hanfeizi*, XI, 32/2a6 (Liao, *Han Fei Tzu*, II, p. 30): "If their words went beyond the limits of the law and their actions were far from meritorious, they were people outside the marking line [of the law]."

[12] Here begins a new paragraph in the Chinese text.

[13] Reading 睢 as 疽 [Liu Ji, Sun Xingyan, and Xu].

[14] The character 礦 here is unintelligible. I have followed Wang Niansun and Liu Shipei in emending it to 砭.

[15] Following the Yang edition, which writes 足 for 所.

72.10   They caused men of quality to be paid in accordance with [their ad-herence to] the moral way and ordinary men / in accordance with their physical effort.[16] When men of quality are paid in accordance with [their adherence to] the moral way, the sovereign is honored and the people submissive. When ordinary men are paid in accordance with their physical effort, wealth becomes abundant and nourishment ad-equate. When these four [conditions] have been fulfilled—the sovereign honored, the people submissive, wealth abundant, and nourishment adequate—then by awaiting the proper opportunity,[17] it is easy to become king.

72.11   In civil affairs / one may be lenient[18] three times, but in military affairs not a single pardon should be granted. One who is merciful grants many pardons. At first this is easy but later it becomes difficult, and in the long

72.12 run nothing is more / disastrous. The person who adheres to the law grants no pardons.[19] At first this is difficult, but later it becomes easy and in the long run nothing is more beneficial. Therefore, he who shows mercy is the enemy of the people, while he who adheres to the law is the

*a father and mother of the people. /

   It is best to institute regulations and procedures [which will prevent

*2.13 any errors]. Next best / is to be able to catch mistakes should they occur. Then, even though there may be errors, they will not be very serious.

   The enlightened prince builds his ancestral temple just adequate enough to provide for the guests[20] at sacrificial feasts, but does not strive for [lavish] beauty. He erects palaces and pavilions just adequate

---

[16] According to the *Mengzi*, IIIA/4: "Some labor with their minds, some with their strength. Those who labor with their minds govern others; those who labor with their strength are governed by others."

[17] Deleting 足上尊 as an interpolation from the preceding line [Wang Niansun].

[18] Reading 侑 as 宥 [Hong]. The concept of three leniencies 三宥 appears frequently in Confucian writings, but the exact meaning is not clear. In the *Guanzi* passage the context requires that it be rendered as above. However, according to the *Zhou li*, 36/1b7–2a1 (Biot, *Tcheou-li*, II, p. 355): "The master of executions (*sici* 司刺) presides over the regulation of the three executions, three leniencies, and three pardons.... The three leniencies are: (1) In case of ignorance; (2) in case of [involuntary] error; (3) in case of forgetfulness." The *Li ji*, VI, 8/20b (Legge, *Li Ki*, XXVII, p. 356), speaks of the three leniencies in connection with a royal relative guilty of a capital offense. After the judge had pronounced sentence, an officer would announce it to the ruler who would then request leniency three times. The officer would refuse twice, saying that such was the sentence. The third time, without making further reply, he would turn the criminal over to the proper official for execution.

[19] Following Ding who, after 法者, would insert the four characters 無赦者也 in order to make this sentence balance with the above.

[20] Ding would interpret 賓 as 賓尸, the impersonator of the deceased grandfather during the ancestral sacrifices. Thus the sentence would read: "The intelligent prince builds ancestral temples adequate to provide for the impersonation of the deceased at the sacrificial feasts."

72.14 enough to avoid dryness and dampness, cold / and heat, but does not strive for grandiosity. He sees that their carvings and engravings are just adequate enough to differentiate between the honored and lowly, but does not strive for ostentatiousness. Thus, the peasants do not neglect their seasonal occupations, the various artisans do not neglect their

73.1 work, the merchants do not lose their profits, the people / have no idle days, and wealth is not hoarded.[21]

Therefore it is said: "Frugality is the way."[22] /

73.2 It[23] is reckless of the sovereign to reward people who have acted on orders before they have been issued. If the sovereign rewards thus recklessly, meritorious ministers will become resentful. If meritorious

73.3 ministers / become resentful, stupid people will administer affairs in a reckless manner. If stupid people administer affairs in a reckless manner, it will form the basis for great confusion.

[On the other hand] it is reckless of the sovereign to mete out punishments before orders have been issued. If the sovereign metes out punish-

73.4 ments recklessly, / the people will have little regard for life. If the people have little regard for life, men of violence will flourish, factions will arise, and rebellions occur.

If the orders have already been issued but no rewards follow, the

73.5
4b
people / will become discouraged, no longer follow the regulations, or be willing to sacrifice their lives [for the sovereign]. If such is the case, they will neither be victorious in attack nor firm in defense. If they are neither

73.6 victorious in attack nor firm in defense, the country will indeed not / be safe.

If orders have already been issued but punishments are not meted out [to those who disregard them], the people are taught to be disobedient. If the people are disobedient, the strong establish themselves [in power]. If the strong establish themselves, the position of the ruler will be endangered.

Therefore it is said: "Legal statutes, regulations, and procedures

73.7 must / be patterned on the moral way, the orders must be publicized and made clear, and the rewards and punishments must be made reliable and absolute."[24] These are the standards for bringing order to people.

The prince of a great country is always honored, while the prince of a small country is held in low esteem. Why is the prince of a great country

[21] Reading 砥 as 底 [Yu Yue and Yasui]. This paragraph is very reminiscent of the stress on economy preached by the Mohists. See the *Mozi*, I, 5/10a–b, and VI, 20–21 (Mei, *Mo Tze*, pp. 20–21 and 117 ff.).

[22] This phrase 儉其道乎 seems to be an old popular saying. It appears in the *Hanfeizi*, III, 10/7a5 (Liao, *Han Fei Tzu*, I, p. 87), and the *Shuo yuan*, 20/5b10.

[23] Here begins a new paragraph in the Chinese text.

[24] Emending 密 to 必 [Wang Niansun].

73.8 honored? / The answer is that there are many in his employ. Why is the prince of a small country held in low esteem? The answer is that there are few in his employ. Thus, if one is honored because of employing many

73.9 and held in low esteem because of employing few, / how can a ruler fail to want the masses of the people employed on his behalf?

What are the means for employing the masses of the people on one's behalf? The answer is that when laws are established and orders carried

73.10 out, many of the people will be employed. / But if laws are not established and orders are not carried out, few of the people will be employed.

Therefore, if many laws are established and many orders carried out whereas only a few are disregarded, the people will not engage in

73.11 slanderous talk. If the people / do not engage in slanderous talk, they will be obedient.

5a If laws / that have been established and orders that have been carried out are equal in number to those that have been disregarded, the country will lack constant standards. If the country lacks constant standards, the people will act recklessly.

3.12 If few laws are established and few orders carried out / whereas many are disregarded, the people will not be obedient. If they are not obedient, men of violence will arise and depravity will become prevalent.

3.13 If one assesses the reason why a sovereign loves his people, / it is because he employs them. But if, because of loving them, he feels no reluctance toward undermining laws or neglecting orders, he will in this case fail in what is truly meant by loving the people. If he fails[25] to love the people when employing them, it will soon become evident that the

3.14 people are not being employed. / Now he who is skilled[26] in employing the people may kill them, endanger them, belabor them, make them

4.1 suffer,[27] starve them, or exhaust them. His employment / of the people may bring them to these extremes, yet no one among them will conspire to harm him.[28] /

4.2 When an enlightened king is on the throne, laws patterned on the moral way are carried out throughout the country, and the people all set aside what they like so as to do what they dislike. Therefore, he who is

---

[25] Emending 夫 to 失 and reading 愛民以 instead of 以民愛 [Tao].

[26] Emending 至 to 善, in accordance with the text of the second sentence (5a11; 74.2) in the following paragraph [Zhang Peilun and Xu].

[27] The two characters 苦之 have been deleted in the Yang edition.

[28] The phrase 害己者 appears to be corrupt. Tao would emend it to read 害者矣. Thus, "and yet no one among them would conspire to do harm." Xu, basing himself on a later passage in this same chapter (5b7; 74.6), says the two characters 害己 are a corruption of 始. Thus, "yet no one among them should be allowed to share in the consideration [of an undertaking] at its inception." I have attempted to keep to the original text.

257

74.3   skilled in employing the people does not take low rank into consideration / when bestowing official carriages and caps nor is he influenced by high position when applying the axe and halberd. /

74.4   In such a way, worthy men are encouraged while men of violence / are
5b   kept in check. If worthy men are encouraged and men of violence kept in check, [the sovereign's] merit and fame will be established for posterity. People will tread on naked blades, suffer arrows and stones,²⁹ and enter water and fire in order to obey the orders of their sovereign. When the orders of the sovereign are completely carried out and his prohibitions are completely effective, he may draw the people into service and they

74.5   will not dare shirk / their work. He may push them into battle and they dare not refuse to die.

When men dare not shirk their work, only then will there be achievement. When men dare not refuse to die, only then will [the sovereign] be unrivaled [in battle]. Advancing, he will be unrivaled; withdrawing, he

74.6   will be successful. / Hence the men in his three armies³⁰ will be able to preserve their heads and necks while their fathers and mothers, wives and children remain completely safe at home.

Now the people should never be allowed to share in the consideration [of an undertaking] at its inception, but they may be allowed to join in the rejoicing over its successful completion.³¹ For this reason, those

74.7   who are humane, / understanding, and possess the moral way will not share with others³² any consideration [of an affair] at its inception.

It is not because of its small size and misfortunes that a country suffers paring away [of its territory] or meets with destruction. Rather it is sure to be because virtuous conduct has been neglected by the ruler and his

74.8   great ministers; because official duties, / legal regulations, and political instruction have been neglected within the country; and because the schemes of the feudal lords have been neglected abroad.³³ It is be-

---

²⁹ The Yang edition for 石 mistakenly writes 后.

³⁰ During the Zhou dynasty, the Zhou king traditionally had six armies. The larger states among the feudal lords had three. The *Guanzi*, VIII, 206b2–3 (1 : 100.5–6), presents a description of the formation of these armies under Duke Huan of Qi. See also Maspero, *China in Antiquity*, pp. 53–55 and 180–181.

³¹ This seems to have been a common Legalist concept. See the *Shangjun shu*, I, 1/1b5–6 (Duyvendak, *Lord Shang*, p. 169) and *LSCQ*, XVI, 5/10a9–10 (Wilheim, *Frühling und Herbst*, p. 248).

³² Emending 大 to 人 [Wang Niansun].

³³ The meaning of this passage is doubtful. Xu would interpret 以 as 有, and read 與 in the sense of "allies." Thus, "When a country lacks even weak allies, suffers misfortune and paring away [of its territory], or meets with destruction, it is sure to be because virtuous conduct has been neglected by the ruler and his great ministers, because the official duties, legal regulations, and political instruction have been neglected within the country, and because the schemes of the feudal lords have been neglected abroad."

cause of this that territory is pared away and the country is imperiled.[34] /

74.9

It is not because of its large size and good fortune that a country achieves success and fame. Rather it is sure to be because virtuous conduct has been practiced by the ruler and his great ministers; / because official duties, legal regulations, and political instruction have been maintained within the country; and because the schemes of the feudal lords / have been dealt with abroad.[35] It is only then that success may be established and fame achieved.

6a

74.10

Thus, how can a country get along without the moral way or men get along without seeking after it?[36] / If [the ruler] finds the moral way and guides his people with it and if he finds worthy men and employs them, he may achieve his great expectations of promoting benefit and expelling harm. But in achieving such expectations nothing is more vital than his own conduct.

4.11

Moreover, if the prince stands alone and comes to extreme harm, it is sure to be / because he has neglected his previous orders.[37]

4.12

If the ruler of men neglects his orders, he will be kept in ignorance [of what is going on].

If he is kept in ignorance, / he will be stripped of his power.

4.13

If he is stripped of his power, he will be assassinated.

What makes a prince of men a prince is always his position of authority. Therefore, if he loses this position of authority, his ministers will control him. When the position of authority rests with his subordinate officials, the prince is controlled by his ministers, whereas when it rests with / the sovereign, the ministers are controlled by the prince. Therefore, when the prince and his ministers exchange positions, authority rests with his subordinates. Should it rest with the ministers for a year, then even though the ministers may prove to be disloyal, the prince will not be able to retrieve it. / Should it rest with a son for a year, then

.14

.1

---

[34] Ding and Xu would emend 危 to 亡 to accord with the Yin commentary and the above passage. The sentence would then read: "It is because of this that territory is pared away and the country meets with destruction."

[35] If Xu's interpretation of 以 as 有 and 與 as "allies" were to be followed here also, this passage would read: "When a country possesses great allies, enjoys good fortune, and achieves success and fame, it is sure to be because meritorious conduct has been practiced by the ruler and his great ministers, because official duties, legal regulations, and political instruction have been maintained within the country, and because the schemes of the feudal lords have been dealt with abroad."

[36] Zhang Peilun would emend 求 to 賢 in order to make this phrase accord with the meaning of the passage below. Thus, "or men get along without worthiness."

[37] This passage is very doubtful. There is wide disagreement among the various commentators about suggested emendations and punctuation. Therefore, instead of following any of them, I have tried to interpret the original text as it stands.

even though the son may prove to be unfilial, the father will not be able to bring him to submission. Thus, in the records of the *Chunqiu* there are cases of ministers who murdered their princes / and sons who murdered their fathers.[38]

Therefore it is said: "Those who stand at the head of the hall[39] may be further away than 100 *li*; those at the foot of the hall, 1,000 *li*; those at the gate, 10,000 *li*."

Now, by taking a single day's tour on foot one may come to know conditions within 100 *li*, / but if those who stand at the head of the hall have business and yet after ten days the prince still has not heard them, it may be said they are further away than 100 *li*.

By taking a ten-day tour on foot one may come to know conditions within 1,000 *li*, but if those who stand at the foot of the hall / have business and yet after one month the prince still has not heard them, it may be said they are further away than 1,000 *li*.

By taking a hundred-day tour on foot one may come to know conditions within 10,000 *li*, but if those who stand at the gate have business and yet after one year the prince still has not heard them, / it may be said they are further away than 10,000 *li*.

Therefore, when information[40] has been sent in but there is no outgoing reply, it is said to have been suppressed. When [information] has been sent out but there is no incoming confirmation, it is said to have been cut off. / When [information] has been sent in but does not reach [as far as the court], it is said to have been intercepted. When [information] has been sent out but is stopped on the way, it is said to have been blocked. / When a prince [is plagued by information] being suppressed, cut off, intercepted, and blocked, it is not because he has shut his gates and guarded his door, but because his administration is not functioning properly. /

Therefore it is said: "Orders are more precious than jewels. The altars of Land and Grain take precedence over family relations. The laws are more important than the people. Prestige and power are more to be valued than ranks and salaries."

---

[38] This is clearly an allusion to what Mencius said about the *Chunqiu*; according to the *Mengzi*, IIIB, 9/7–8: "The world fell into decay, and principles faded away. Perverse speech and oppressive action became prevalent. There were cases of ministers who murdered their princes and sons who murdered their fathers. Confucius was afraid and made the *Chunqiu*." The *Hanfeizi*, XIII, 34/3a10 (Liao, *Han Fei Tzu*, II, p. 92), contains a similar passage: "Zixia said, 'In the records of the *Chunqiu* there are over ten cases of ministers who murdered their princes and sons who murdered their fathers.'"

[39] That is, the chief ministers. The following refers to ordinary ministers and officials.

[40] Reading 請 as 情 [Ding, Tao, and Xu].

Thus, do not disregard orders because of precious jewels. Do not consider your altars of Land and Grain secondary because of family relations. / Do not twist laws and statutes because of love for the people. Do not share your prestige and power because of ranks and salaries.

Therefore it is said: "Your position of authority is not something to be granted to others."

To govern means to establish a correct order.[41] The establishment of a correct order / serves to correct and fix the terminology[42] of all things. For this reason the sage refines his virtue and takes a central stand in order to bring about this correct order. He makes this correct order clear [to the people] so the state will be well governed.

Therefore the establishment of a correct order / is the means to check what goes too far and push forward what falls too short. Neither what goes too far nor what falls too short is correct. Since neither is correct they are alike in harming the country.[43] /

Bravery without righteousness is harmful to the armed forces. Humaneness without correctness is harmful to the law.[44] Therefore military defeat may spring from lack of righteousness. / Transgression of the law may spring from lack of correct order.

So it is that speech may be argumentative and irresponsible, and conduct troublesome and evil. Therefore, / in speech one must be responsible and not given to needless argument. In action one must think of what is good and not be given to needless troublemaking.

The compass and T-square are [instruments for achieving] correctness in making squares and circles. Even though one may have a clever eye and a skillful hand, these are no match for correctness of the simple compass and T-square. / Therefore a clever person is able to produce a compass and T-square but is unable to make correct squares and circles without them.[45]

75.9

75.10

75.11

75.12

75.13

75.14
7b

76.1

[41] This statement appears in the *Lun yu*, XII, 17: "To govern 政 means to establish a correct order 正. If you lead [the people] with correctness 正, who will dare not be correct 正?" Here we have a play on the homophones *zheng* 政, and *zheng* 正.

[42] Reading 命 as 名.

[43] Though the setting is Legalistic, this is clearly from the Confucian "Doctrine of the Mean." See the *Lun yu*, XI, 15: "Zigong asked which was better, Shi or Shang. The Master said, 'Shi goes too far, and Shang does not go far enough.' Zigong said, 'If that is so, then Shi is the superior.' The Master said, 'To go too far is as bad as not to go far enough.'" See also the *Zhungyong*, passim.

[44] Emending 不法傷正 to 不正傷法 in order to accord with the sense of the following line [Sun Shucheng]. The original wording would read: "Humaneness without law is harmful to correctness."

[45] According to the *Mengzi*, IVA, 1/1: "The clearsightedness of Li Lou and cleverness of Gongshuzi were incapable of forming squares and circles without the compass and T-square."

[In the same way] even the sage, though able to produce laws, is unable to put the state in order without them. Therefore, even though a person / may be of brilliant wisdom and exemplary conduct, for him to attempt to put [the state] in order while turning his back on the laws would be like trying to make correct squares and circles without a compass and T-square.

Another version says:[46]

The virtuous conduct and majestic presence of the prince is never due to any unique capacity for being more worthy / than other men. Since he is called the prince of men, people follow and honor him without daring to discuss the extent of his virtue. / The reason for this is that in deciding their death or life, he is quicker than the Masters of Destiny.[47] /

It is he who enriches men, impoverishes them, or makes them care for each other. It is he who honors men, degrades them, or makes them serve each other. The ruler of men controls / these six conditions in sustaining his ministers. The ministers likewise look toward these six conditions in serving their prince. The six conditions form a bridge[48] in the relationship between the prince and his ministers. /

Should [control over] the six rest with the minister for a year, then even though the minister may prove to be disloyal, the prince will not be able to retrieve it. Should [control over the six] rest with the son for a year, then even though the son may prove to be unfilial, the father will not be able to retrieve it. Thus, in the records of the *Chunqiu* / there are cases of ministers who murdered their princes and sons who murdered their fathers. This is because [ministers and sons] have gained control over these six conditions without the prince or father realizing it.[49]

If [control over] these six conditions rests with the minister, the ruler will be kept in ignorance. If the ruler is kept in ignorance, / he will neglect his orders.

Therefore it is said: "If [a memorial requesting] an order has been sent in but there is no outgoing reply, it is said to have been concealed. If an order has been issued but there is no incoming confirmation, it is said to have been blocked. If an order has been issued but is not carried out, it is said to have been disobeyed. If [a report on] an order / has been sent in

---

[46] *Yi yue* 一曰. This phrase would seem to have been inserted by Liu Xiang to indicate that the following passage to 8a12 (76.11) represents another version of the material covered in the preceding pages.

[47] *Siming* 司命; these were the two gods in charge of the destiny of men, the Greater and Lesser Masters of Destiny. The *Chu ci*, 2/14a–18a (Hawkes, *Ch'u Tz'u*, pp. 39–41), contains two songs to them. They are also identified with the fourth star of Ursa Major.

[48] Reading 謀 as 媒 [Yu Yue].

[49] Reading 智 as 知 [Wang Niansun].

262

but it does not reach [as far as the court], it is said to have been dealt with in lax manner. When a prince [is plagued by] disobedience, laxity, concealment, and blockage, it is not because he has shut his gates and guarded his doors,[50] but because his orders are not being carried out properly. / This happens because worthy men do not come to him and loyal ministers are not employed. Therefore the ruler must pay careful attention to his orders. Orders are the greatest treasure of the ruler."

Another verion says: /

When worthy men are not presented, it is said they have been concealed. When loyal ministers are not employed, it is said they have been impeded. / When [the ruler] issues orders that are not carried out, it is said they have been obstructed. When prohibitions are not effective, it is said they have been opposed. When a prince [is plagued by] concealment, impediment, obstruction, and opposition, it is not because he / has shut his gates and guarded his doors,[51] but because worthy men have not been presented and his orders are not carried out.

When the people follow the sovereign, they never follow merely what his mouth says but what he really likes. / If the sovereign likes bravery, the people will not be afraid of death. If the sovereign likes goodness, the people will not be concerned with wealth. Therefore, what the sovereign likes the people are bound to like even more.[52] For this reason the enlightened prince, knowing the people must take the sovereign as their heart, / establishes laws for his own good order and establishes rules of behavior to ensure his own correctness. Thus, if the sovereign does not act, the people will not follow, and if the people are not willing to submit to the law and die for the regulations, the country will certainly fall into disorder. For this reason, when executing his laws and making regulations, the prince who possesses the moral way / sets an example for the people by acting first.

In all discussions about [the relative merits of] men, there are certain essential points:

No great gentlemen will be found among men given to boasting. Those given to boasting / [consider themselves] perfect, but their perfection is hollow. Perfection or hollowness is a matter of facts, and the facts are what decide the matter. Those given to boasting belong to the category of petty men.

---

[50] Deleting the two characters 事 and 敢 as interpolations [Wang Niansun].

[51] Deleting 敢 as an interpolation [Wang Niansun].

[52] The *Mengzi*, IIIA, 3/4, contains a similar passage: "What the sovereign likes, his subjects are bound to like even more. The relation between the sovereign and his subjects is like that between the wind and grass. The grass must bend when the wind blows upon it."

No gentlemen of high standing will be found among those who
repudiate the past when discussing the present,[53] / and no gentlemen of
[great] wisdom will be found among those who are ignorant of the past
and are easygoing in their achievements. / Even though one may be
completely virtuous in his own conduct, if he repudiates the past he will
be a mediocre person.[54] /

Those who lack natural talent in affairs and who, in spite of good
opportunities, are careless in their duties, are gentlemen of low
mentality.

No gentlemen of worth are to be found among men who fish for
fame. / No kingly rulers are to be found among princes who fish for
profit. In conducting himself, the worthy man forgets about fame. In
carrying out the moral way, the kingly ruler / forgets about achieving
success. Nothing can hinder the conduct of the worthy man or the moral
way of the kingly ruler.

The enlightened prince rules the country for the public good and
unites the people so as to gain the obedience of the realm. / The loyal
minister advances in a straightforward manner so as to have his ability
judged. The enlightened prince does not grant salaries and ranks to
those he [merely] likes personally. The loyal minister does not make false
claims of ability in order to seek / ranks and salaries. The prince should
not rule the country in his own interest and the minister should not make
false claims about his ability. Even though adherence to this way may
not produce great government, it does provide a [constant] standard for
establishing correct order among the people. /

Now, from ancient times down to the present, success and fame have
never been attained when a prince who ruled the country for his own
interest was served by a minister who falsified his ability. Men who
falsify their ability are easily known. / Ministers[55] should be measured
by [the example of] those of the former kings. / When Shun possessed
the world, Yu was his minister of works (*sikong* 司空), Xie was minister
of education (*situ* 司徒), Gaoyao was chief justice (*li* 李), and Houji

---

[53] Emending 人 to 今 [Zhang Peilun].

[54] This idea is completely Confucian. The Legalists stressed the need to do away with
past precedent in dealing with the present. According to the *Shangjun shu*, II, 2/11a
(Duyvendak, *Lord Shang*, p. 227): "The guiding principles 道 of the people are base and
they are not consistent in their value. As conditions in the world change, different
principles are practiced." And again II, 7/11b (Duyvendak, p. 228) says: "The sage does
not imitate antiquity . . . ." See also Fung, *A History of Chinese Philosophy*, I, pp. 316–317,
for his discussion of the Legalist concept of history.

[55] The Yin commentary would read 臣 as "I, Your Servant," meaning the author, i.e.,
Guan Zhong. Thus, "I, Your Servant, measure [ministers] by those of the former kings."

was minister of agriculture (*tian* 田).[56] These four gentlemen were the worthiest men in the world; / still, in serving their prince each was esteemed for refining his one particular virtue.

Nowadays men who falsify their ability to carry out affairs and fulfill their offices all try to combine the abilities of these four worthies. From this point of view, it is easy to see that they will achieve neither success nor fame. / But provided their ranks are honored and their salaries large, there is nothing they will not put up with. Provided their positions are profitable and their offices important, there is no one they will not follow. / He who serves the prince in such a way is known as the minister who falsifies ability and grasps for profits.

If in the world there is no prince who rules his country for the public good, there will be no gentlemen who will advance in a straightforward manner. If there are no rulers[57] who judge the abilities [of their ministers], there will be no successful ministers. /

When the three dynasties passed from one to another in ancient times, the killing took place in the same world [we have today].[58] Nothing impoverishes the people / or destroys goods on such a scale as do armed forces. Nothing endangers the country or causes the ruler concern as quickly as do armed forces. These four evil consequences are clear, yet from ancient times to the present, no one has been able to dispense with [armed forces].

Not to dispense with armed forces when they ought to be dispensed with shows confusion.[59] / But to wish to dispense with armed forces when they ought not to be dispensed with[60] likewise shows confusion. / These two situations are alike in their harm to the country. Huang Di, Tang, and Yu[61] were the most glorious emperors. They possessed the entire realm and its control lay in the hands of a single

---

[56] Shun 舜 (trad. 2255–2206) was the last of the five ancient sage emperors. Yu 禹 became his successor and is credited with founding the Xia dynasty. Xie 契, Gaoyao 皋陶, and Houji 后稷 were three of Shun's most famous ministers.

[57] Yu Yue would emend 主 to 士 in order to make this sentence accord with the above passage (9a8; 77.8). Thus it would read: "If there are no gentlemen who discuss their ability, there will be no ministers who achieve success."

[58] This passage 安待二天下而殺之 is very doubtful; the text is probably corrupt. I have generally followed the interpretation of Yasui and Guo Moruo, but have turned it from a question into a positive statement.

[59] Deleting the two characters 古今 as an interpolation taken from the preceding passage [Wang Niansun].

[60] Deleting the three characters 此二者 as an interpolation taken from the passage that follows. Also inserting 當 after 不 in order to make this sentence balance with that above [Wang Niansun].

[61] Huang Di 黃帝 Tang 唐 (i.e., Yao 堯), and Yu 虞 (i.e., Shun) are the most famous of the legendary sage emperors.

78.5   man. / Yet [even] during this time armed forces were not dispensed with. Nowadays, since the virtue [of our rulers] does not come up to that of these three emperors and the world is not obedient, would it not be difficult to try to dispense with armed forces? /

78.6   Therefore, the enlightened prince knows where to assume responsibility and what will have evil consequences. Seeing to it that the state is kept in good order and the people pay attention to their harvest—this is where he assumes responsibility. [Unsuitable] movement or rest—this is

78.7   what / will have evil consequences. For this reason, the enlightened prince is careful when assuming responsibility in order to prepare for what may have evil consequences.

Princes who are violent and reckless cannot avoid external difficulties.

78.8   Princes who are irresolute and weak cannot avoid internal / disorders.

Princes who are violent and reckless are irresponsible in their application of punishments. When the irresponsible application of punishments becomes prevalent, those whose way of conduct is correct are no longer safe. When those whose way of conduct is correct are no longer

78.9
10b   safe, ministers with talent and ability will flee. / Being knowledgeable men, they will know the real facts about us. If they scheme against us for the enemy, external difficulties will arrive. /

78.10   Therefore it is said: "The prince who is violent and reckless cannot avoid external difficulties."

The prince who is irresolute and weak finds it difficult to apply punishments. When this difficulty in applying punishments is carried to excess, those whose conduct is wicked will not be removed. If they are not removed over a period of time, the various ministers will form

78.11   cliques. If they form cliques, / they will conceal the good and elevate the evil. If the good is concealed and the evil elevated, internal disorders will arise.

Therefore it is said: "Princes who are irresolute and weak cannot avoid internal disorders."

The enlightened prince does not endanger his altars of Land and

78.12   Grain because of family relations. / The altars of Land and Grain are more dear than are his family relations. He does not alter his orders because of his own desires. Orders are more to be honored than the prince. He does not share his prestige with others because of precious jewels. His prestige is more to be valued than precious jewels. He does

78.13   not neglect the laws because of love for the people. / The laws are more to be loved than the people.

Bing Fa

兵法

Methods of Warfare

Introductory Comments

Bing fa (often translated as "The Art of War"), the title of chapter VI, 17, is also an alternative or primary title for three other famous pre-Han works on military affairs: the *Sunzi*, which contains the injunctions of Sun Wu 孫吳 (d. 496 B.C.?); the *Wuzi*, attributed to Wu Qi 吳起 (d. 381 B.C.) or one of his disciples; and the *Sun Bin bing fa*, attributed to Sun Bin 孫臏, who served King Wei 威 (357–320 B.C.) of Qi. In addition to these three works, the *Shangjun shu* contains a chapter entitled *Zhan fa* 戰法, III, 10, which Duyvendak (*Lord Shang*, p. 244) also translates as "The Method of Warfare."

Although these works all deal with the same general subject as this chapter, there are certain notable differences, especially in philosophical approach. The *Sunzi*, *Wuzi*, and *Sun Bin bing fa* are clearly the work of practical military men concerned primarily with matters of tactics and strategy, and it is difficult to associate them with any particular philosophical school.[1] The *Shangjun shu*, on the other hand, is a Legalist classic, and chapter III, 10, opens with a clearly Legalist statement: "The methods of warfare must always be based on the supremacy of the government." It continues with another statement, declaring that the people must be made to have no thought of self-interest in mind, but only the interest of the ruler. Only after this politico-philosophical groundwork has been laid does the discussion of tactics and strategy begin.

Guanzi, VI, 17, on the other hand, opens with a very Daoist-sounding paragraph, which speaks of understanding Oneness or the Unity of Nature (*yi* 一), discerning the Way (*dao* 道), and comprehending the Power (*de* 德). Throughout the text great stress is laid on understanding

---

[1] In the "Treatise on Literature" of the *Qian Han shu*, 30/12b–13a, these military writers are treated as a separate school. However, the classification of literature called *zi* 子, "philosophers," under which the school is listed, covers a much broader range of subjects than we would normally class as philosophy.

the Way and Power in order to become militarily proficient,[2] and there are a number of passages, particularly in the final paragraph, that are reminiscent of the *Laozi*. Finally, the text places considerable emphasis on numerical categories, a type of symbolism that appeared in Daoist writings from the latter part of the third century B.C. onward.

It would be a mistake, however, to classify this text as purely Daoist since it is primarily concerned with the ways to establish military superiority over one's neighbors, and instead of denouncing governments and institutions, it stresses their efficiency as a precondition for victory. It is this amalgamation of Legalist and Daoist ideas that forms the basis for what is known as the Huang-Lao School. One of the Huang-Lao texts, the *Shi da jing* 十大經 (2.12.133), attached to the Mawangdui *Laozi*, "B" silk manuscript, contains a phrase, 道有原而無端, "Though the Way had an origin, it is without limit," which describes the Way in a fashion similar to that employed in this text (12b5–6; 80.9–10), 始乎無端者道也, "Beginning in the limitless refers to the Way."

As mentioned in the Introductory Comments to chapters II, 6, and III, 8, there is a close relationship between those chapters and this work. This has led Guo Moruo to the conclusion that all three chapters were written by the same person.[3] For reasons stated in the Introductory Comments to III, 8, I agree with Guo that the essay portions of III, 8, and VI, 17, probably had a common origin.[4] Although both paraphrase certain passages from II, 6, an examination of the particle usage in all three chapters shows that chapter II, 6, was probably written by someone else. Both III, 8, and VI, 17, have a consistent pattern of using *ruo* 若 to mean "like," while in II, 6, *ruo* only appears with the meaning of "if," and *ru* 如 is used to mean "like." Furthermore, in II, 6, *yu* 于 frequently appears in place of *yu* 於, which does not appear at all in the other two chapters. Perhaps He Ruzhang's suggestion that VI, 17, was composed as an explanatory chapter for the final section of II, 6, *Xuan chen* 選陳 [On Selecting and Deploying Troops], is nearer the truth.[5] However, it is my opinion that II, 6, which is a relatively older text dating from the late fourth or early third century B.C. and part of the original proto-*Guanzi* collection, was simply used by the author of the essay portion of III, 8, and this chapter.

---

[2] In contrast to this chapter of the *Guanzi*, the other military texts mentioned above make relatively little use of these terms. The *Sunzi*, for example, mentions *dao* (1/2b–4b; Giles, *Sun Tzu*, p. 2) but contains no reference to *de*. It does, however, mention Yin and Yang (which this chapter does not), but places no stress on them.

[3] Guo Moruo, *Guanzi*, I, p. 256.

[4] This, however, would only apply to the essay portion of III, 8; the calendar portion was probably by an entirely different source.

[5] Guo Moruo, *Guanzi*, I, p. 82.

Since this chapter was probably written by the same author as the essay portion of III, 8, the same conclusion on its dating (i.e., it could not date before the middle part of the third century B.C) holds true here. Such a conclusion finds considerable support from the content of the opening paragraph of the chapter, mentioned above: "Those who understood the Unity of Nature became sovereigns (*huang* 皇). Those who discerned the Way became emperors (*di* 帝). Those who comprehended the Power became kings (*wang* 王). Those who schemed to gain military victories became lord protectors (*ba* 霸)." Aside from the progression from sovereign to lord protector,[6] we have here another progression of a metaphysical type from the Unity to Way to Power and then (breaking the metaphysical sequence) to schemes for military victories. Such metaphysical progressions are very common in Daoist literature. However, in the earlier Daoist texts the Way is generally considered superior to the Unity, in that it is the all-embracing first principle through which all things are brought into being rather than merely a given stage of development. In later texts, on the other hand, there is a gradual shift in attitude, so that the Way is equated with the Unity and then is even made subordinate to it.

For example, according to the *Laozi*, B, 42/5a9–10 (Waley, *The Way and Its Power*, p. 195): "The Way produced the Unity of Nature, the Unity produced duality, duality produced trinity, and trinity produced all things. All things support the Yin and embrace the Yang. It is on the blending of the vital forces [of the Yin and Yang] that their harmony depends." [7] In this progression it is clear that the Unity owes its origin to the Way. In the *Zhuangzi*, V, 12/5a4–7 (Watson, *Chuang Tzu*, p. 131), there is another progression, which, without actually mentioning the Way, implies the same idea: "In the Great Beginning there was Nonbeing. It had neither being nor name, but was that from which came the Unity of Nature. When the Unity came into existence there was Unity but as yet no form. When things obtained that by which they came into existence, it was called their Power." [8]

Thus the normal progression as presented in the *Laozi* and *Zhuangzi* would appear: the Way to the Unity to the Power. However, in the *Lüshi chunqiu*, an eclectic text of about 240 B.C., there is a shift in viewpoint, so that the Unity and the Way are equated.[9] In the *Huainanzi* (c. 122 B.C.)

---

[6] For further discussion of this progression, see the Introductory Comments to III, 8, "Essay Portion of *You guan*."

[7] Fung Yu-lan, *A History of Chinese Philosophy*, I, pp. 178–179, explains the Unity as Being, the duality as Heaven and Earth, and the trinity as the Yin and Yang and harmony resulting from the interactions of these two.

[8] According to Fung, ibid., p. 225, "The Non-being here spoken of is Tao (Dao)."

[9] *LSCQ*, III, 5/10a1–2 (Wilhelm, *Frühling und Herbst*, p. 39).

we find a passage (3/11b4–5) that takes the relationship a step further: "The Way began with the Unity of Nature.[10] There was the Unity but it did not produce anything. Therefore it divided and became the Yin and Yang. The Yin and Yang harmonized so that all things were produced." Here is expressed the idea that the Way is not simply the origin of all things (including the Unity), but is itself immanent in the total sequence of creative activity, beginning with the Unity but proceeding from there to all things. The same concept is implied in the phrase quoted from the *Shi da jing* above.

The progression we have in this chapter of the *Guanzi* then represents a step in the ideological development of Daoism, which appears to have begun in the closing years of the Warring States Period and to have become common during the early Han.

We do not know just when this essay was incorporated into the *Guanzi*, but its close connection with the protocollection from its very beginning is indicated by its references to material found in I, 4, as well as its paraphrases of II, 6. It also seems to have existed independently of the *Guanzi* until the end of the Former Han at least, since it was listed as a separate work under the military school in the *Qi lüe* of Liu Xin 劉歆.[11] By the time Ban Gu 班固 (A.D. 32–92) did his "Treatise of Literature" for the *Qian Han shu*, however, it is no longer mentioned as a separate work.

Translation

1.79.2
10b11

Those who understood the Unity of Nature became sovereigns. Those who discerned the Way became emperors. Those who comprehended the Power became kings. Those who schemed to gain military victories became lord protectors.[12] /

79.3
11a

Truly, though arms are not the same as the all-complete Way or supreme Power, they still at least served to provide aid to the kings and success to the lord protectors.[13] /

79.4

But such is not the case with those who employ arms today. They do not know how to weigh [the proper use of] arms. Thus, on the very day they take up arms, impoverishment descends within their own

[10] The *SBBY* edition writes 道日規始於一. According to Wang Niansun (see the *Huainan honglie jijie*, 3/21a3) the two characters 日 (Wang's edition for 日 writes 曰) 規 are an interpolation taken from a preceding line and should be deleted.

[11] See Introduction, nn. 19 and 74.

[12] For a listing of the Three Sovereigns, Five Emperors, Three Kings, and Five Lord Protectors, see III, 8, n. 37.

[13] The author has not done a very neat job of relating this last sentence to the progression he has established above. Here he speaks of arms not only in conjunction with lord protectors, but also with kings whom he earlier connects with the Power.

borders. / They are not certain of victory in battle, and even when victorious, many [of their men] die. Even though they acquire territory, their country is reduced to ruin. These four are misfortunes resulting from the employment of arms. / If these four misfortunes [befall] a country, there will be no escape from danger.

The *Book of Da Du*[14] says: ["Now,[15] military ventures are dangerous things. Being untimely in one's victories or unrighteous in one's acquisitions will not lead to good fortune. Suffering defeat through the neglect of (proper) stratagems is dangerous for the country. But by being careful in one's stratagems, one may protect the country."]

To avoid having impoverishment descend within one's own borders on the very day arms are taken up; / to be certain of victory in battle; to be victorious without any deaths; to acquire territory without one's own state being reduced to ruin—how should one act to achieve these four?

The avoidance of impoverishment within the borders on the very day arms are taken up is achieved through obtaining detailed plans.[16] / Certainty of victory in battle is achieved by being judicious in respect to one's methods[17] and procedures. Victory without many deaths is achieved by giving instruction in weapons and having them ready and sharp so the enemy will not dare enter into conflict. The acquisition of territory without your own state being reduced to ruin is achieved by relying upon the people. /

[14] *Da Du zhi shu* 大度之書; Zhang Peilun and Xu believe that this is the same as a work known as the *Liu tao* 六弢(韜), or the *Six Bow Cases*, which Xu further maintains should properly be read as *Da Tao* 大弢, the name of a Zhou dynasty historian 周史 mentioned in the *Zhuangzi*, VIII, 25/29a9 (Watson, *Chuang Tzu*, p. 289) and the *Qian Han shu*, 20/51a9. However, their arguments are not very convincing, and the passage that follows is not found in the present *Liu tao* text. In my opinion, the title should probably be rendered in translation as *The Book of Important Procedures*. The *Bohu tong* (*Bohu tongde lun*, 10/15b6, cites a *Da Du*, but *Lu Wenchao* 盧文弨 (1717–1796), in his edition of the work (*Bohu tong*, IV, B/299), says that the two characters are a corruption of *Wang zhi* 王制, the name of a chapter in the *Li ji* that is quoted in the preceding line, and he therefore deletes them. Tjan Tjo Som, in his translation, *Po Hu T'ung*, II, p. 647, follows Lu.

[15] Guo Moruo points out that the passage following 曰 could hardly be a quotation from another text because it continues the argument of the preceding passage with exactly the same phrasing. Therefore, either the phrase 大度之書曰 is an interpolation, or a portion of the text quoting this work has been omitted. Guo believes that a passage in IX, 24/14b5–7 (2:13.7–8), 夫兵···保國, which appears to be out of context there, actually belongs here. I have inserted it accordingly. This passage does not appear in the present *Liu tao*.

[16] According to the *Sunzi*, 1/25a6 (Giles, *Sun Tzu*, p. 7): "Many calculations mean victory; few mean defeat. How much more is this true if none have been made at all." The *Sunzi* writes 算 instead of 數.

[17] According to the *Sunzi*, 1/9b (Giles, ibid., p. 3): "Methods (*fa* 法) refer to organization into units, regulations, [gradation of] officers, [construction of] roads, [selection of] commanders, and [administration of] supplies."

79.9
11b

If the people[18] may be relied upon, it is because orders and regulations[19] have been / issued. If [the troops] have been instructed in their weapons and they are ready and sharp, it is because there are regulations. If methods and procedures are judicious, it is because they have

79.10 been [properly] observed. If detailed plans / have been obtained, it is because [the facts] are clear.

There is an art to governing the masses, and principles for being victorious over the enemy. Delve[20] into this art and you will come to know these principles. Examine the weapons and you will become

79.11 familiar with victory. / Make the principles clear [to your troops] and the enemy will be vanquished. Secure the ancestral temples. Provide[21] for the men and women. Control[22] the four classes.[23] Then you may make

79.12 your majestic position and benevolent power secure,[24] / regulate laws and rules of conduct, and issue orders. After this you may unite the masses and exercise control over the people.

If[25] the armed forces lack a commander, they will not know the enemy in time. If the countryside lacks civil functionaries, there will be

79.13 no accumulated stores. / If the officials lack constant standards, those below will come to resent those on high. If the weapons are not skillfully made,[26] the court will not be secure.[27] If rewards and punishments are

79.14 not / clear, people will pay little heed to production.[28]

Therefore it is said:[29] "If the enemy is known in time,[30] one may move freely. If stores are accumulated, there will be no shortages for a long time. If the weapons are skillfully made, they will not be worn out in the

[18] The Ming (1582) cutting of the Zhao edition mistakenly writes 利 for 民.

[19] Guo Songdao and Zhang Peilun would delete 號制 as an interpolation since it destroys the structural balance of this sentence in its relationship with those that follow. Xu would also emend 發 to 法 in order to preserve the balance in meaning. Following these two emendations, the sentence would then read: "If the people may be relied upon it is because there are laws."

[20] The following passage down to "issue orders" is closely paralleled by III, 8/8b3–6 (1:35.14–36.1).

[21] III, 8/8b5, for 遂 writes 育. The meaning is the same [Xu].

[22] Reading 官 as 管 [Guo Moruo].

[23] 四分; that is, the gentry, peasants, artisans, and merchants.

[24] III, 8/8b5 (1:36.1), for 定威德 writes 立威行德. By analogy 行 should be inserted before 德. Thus the clause would read: "Then you may make your majestic position secure and practice benevolence."

[25] The following two paragraphs appear to be a condensation of II, 6/6a9–b2 (1:26.14–27.3).

[26] For 巧, II, 6/6a10 (1:27.1), writes 功 (read as 工). The meaning is about the same.

[27] For 定, II, 6/6a11 (1:27.1), writes 政, "government."

[28] For 輕其產, II, 6/6a11 (1:27.1), writes 幸產, "trust to luck for their livelihood."

[29] *Gu yue* 故曰. The character *yue*, which is missing from the parallel passage II, 6/6a12, would appear to indicate the author's recognition of his borrowing from II, 6.

[30] The Yang edition for 則 writes 而. The meaning is the same.

80.1 attack. / If the rewards and punishments are clear, brave knights will be encouraged."

If the three means of command (*san guan* 三官) are not in error, the
12a five / instructions (*wu jiao* 五教) not confused, and the nine symbols (*jiu zhang* 九章) clear, then danger may follow on danger but there will be no harm; exhaustion may follow on exhaustion but there will be no
80.2 difficulty. Thus / the distant can be reached through [mastery] of the art [of war] and the strong can be made subservient[31] through regulation.

The three means of command are: (1) drums, by which [the troops] are
80.3 made to assume their posts, start [the attack], and advance; / (2) metal instruments,[32] by which the troops are made to halt, retreat, and desist [from battle]; (3) banners, by which [the troops] are made to take up their
80.4 arms, maneuver[33] them, and put them away. These / are said to be the three means of command. They are the three [means of] issuing orders so that the methods of warfare will be [carried out] in good order.[34]

30.5 The five instructions are: (1) to the eyes, the forms and colors of the banners; (2) to the / ears,[35] the numbers[36] of the orders; (3) to the feet,
30.6 the procedure of advance and retreat; (4) to the hands, the advantages of long and short [weapons]; / (5) to the heart, the reliability of rewards and punishments. These five instructions should each be made standard
30.7 practice so the knights may be relied upon for their bravery.

The nine symbols are: / (1) the sun for marching by day; (2) the moon
2b for marching by night; (3) the dragon for marching through water;
30.8 (4) / the tiger for marching through forests; (5) the crow[37] for marching over sloping terrain; (6) the snake for marching through swamps; / (7) the magpie for marching over hills; (8) the wolf for marching over mountains; (9) the bow case[38] for loading provisions and driving

---

[31] Reading 縱 as 從 [Yu Yue].

[32] That is, gongs and cymbals.

[33] Emending 利 to 制 [Tao].

[34] According to the *Sunzi*, 7/16a3–b3 (Giles, *Sun Tzu*, pp. 63–64); "*The Book of Military Management* says, 'The spoken word may not be heard by everyone [on the field of battle]. Therefore drums and gongs are used. [Ordinary] signs may not be seen by everyone. Therefore flags and banners are used. Now metal instruments and drums, flags, and banners are the means to unite the ears and eyes of the people.'"

[35] The character 身 here is obviously a mistake for 耳 [Hong and Xu].

[36] That is, the number of beats on the gongs and drums.

[37] *Niao* 鳥, "bird," here appears to be a corruption of *wu* 烏, "crow," since the specific names of other birds are listed among the other symbols to follow [Guo Moruo].

[38] The Yang edition for *gao* 韇 writes an alternate form 韔. Tang Lan suggests that *gao* is a corruption of 鴇, which he describes as a bird with markings like a wild duck. He argues that since all the other symbols except the sun and moon are birds or animals, this one should be the same.

80.9   away. / When the nine symbols are clearly fixed there will be no mistakes in either movement or rest.

The three means of command, the five instructions, and the nine symbols begin[39] in the limitless and end in the inexhaustible. Beginning
80.10 in / the limitless refers to the Way; ending in the inexhaustible refers to the Power. The Way cannot be measured; the Power cannot be calculated. Therefore, since [the Way] cannot be measured, neither the numerous nor strong can plot [against the one who clearly perceives it].
80.11 Since [the Power] cannot be calculated, the false and deceitful / will not dare approach [the one who comprehends it]. When these two have been applied throughout, there will be achievement in both movement and rest. Passage through [enemy territory] will not be known, and your onslaught not anticipated. Since it is not known, no one will be able to
80.12 stop it. Since it is not anticipated, / no one will be able to meet it.[40] Therefore there is complete victory without harm.

Follow what is expedient when issuing instructions. Weigh what is advantageous when taking action. In this way neither instructions nor
80.13 actions will follow a set pattern. When these two [principles] / have been fully developed, there will be success in movement.

When the weapons have been perfected and the instructions implemented, you may overtake fugitives and pursue the fleeing like a whirlwind, beat and stab like thunder and lightning. [The enemy] will be
80.14 unable to defend his isolated territory[41] / or maintain[42] his strongholds.
13a   You will hold the central position and remain invincible. Your orders will be carried out with no delay.

81.1   When the weapons have been perfected / and the instructions implemented, [your troops] may either be dispersed in no [set] direction or assembled without [the enemy] being able to calculate [their number]. When instruction has [been given] concerning the weapons and they are prepared and sharp, advances and retreats will be like thunder and lightning and nothing can hinder or exhaust[43] you.

When the spirit [of the troops] is united and their will resolute, you
81.2   may pass through neighboring [territory] without hindrance. / When the

---

[39] The following passage down to the words, "both movements and rest," directly parallels III, 8/8a7–10 (1.35.10–11).
[40] The *Sunzi*, 1/22b11 (Giles, *Sun Tzu*, p. 7), says: "Attack when [the enemy] is not prepared. Sally forth when he does not anticipate it."
[41] According to the *Sunzi*, 11/26a9 (Giles, ibid., p. 134): "Leaving one's country and crossing over [enemy] borders to employ troops [places] one in isolated territory."
[42] Emending 拔 to 枝 [Yu Xingwu].
[43] Ding would read 匱, "exhaust," as 潰, "scatter," while Zhang Peilun would read it as 讀 to form a compound with 疑, "stop."

knights have been disciplined and the weapons sharpened, you may be involved in difficulties without being exhausted. In advancing you may not be stopped; in retreating you may not be exhausted. Thus the enemy[44] may be turned to your own use. / When crossing mountain defiles, [the troops] will not wait for hooks and ladders. When crossing river valleys, they will not need boats and oars. When passing through isolated territory or attacking strongholds, they may go forth and return freely and no one / will be able to stop them.

How[45] precious, that they may return freely and[46] no one is able to stop them! How[47] precious, that they may go forth[48] freely and[49] no one is able to collect [troops to oppose them]! / They are the epitome of the Nameless,[50] being everywhere yet not anticipated. Therefore it is impossible to hinder their spirit. /

If[51] reared in accordance with the Way, the people may be harmonized. If nurtured with the Power, the people may be united. Since they are harmonious and united, they can be brought into agreement. Since they can be brought into agreement, they can live on intimate terms. Since they [live in] complete agreement and on such intimate terms, no one is able to harm them. /

Secure the One,[52] carry out the two important [principles],[53] control the three [instruments of] authority,[54] implement the four crucial concerns,[55] issue the five instructions,[56] establish the six practices,[57] dis-

---

[44] Guo Moruo would interpret the character 敵 here and below to mean "feeling of hostility," and have the sentence read: "Thus feelings of hostility [toward the enemy] may be put to use."

[45] Emending 不 to 才 = 哉 [Guo Moruo]. The text from here to the end of this paragraph, line 13a12 (81.5), is very corrupt. I have followed the emendations suggested by Guo simply because they provide some sense of contextual logic, and not because they can be considered accurate with any degree of certainty.

[46] Following the Yang edition, which for 故 writes 而.

[47] See n. 45, above.

[48] Emending 見 to 出 [Guo Moruo].

[49] Emending 故 to 而 [Guo Moruo].

[50] That is, the Way.

[51] The following passage down to the words, "harm them," is similar to III, 8/8a11–8b1 (1:35.12).

[52] That is, the Nameless or the Way.

[53] That is, instructions and action.

[54] That is, the three means of command.

[55] Following Zhang Peilun, who would transpose the characters 教 and 機 to make this passage read 施四機, 發五教, in order to accord with the above text, 12a6–11 (80.4–6), and that of III, 8/7b5–6 (1:35.3). Zhang equates the four crucial concerns with the four securities 四固 discussed in I, 4/13a7–13b3 (1:12.8–12). The four securites are: (1) Those who have charismatic power but are deficient in goodness should not be given control of the state; (2) those who on seeing worthiness are unable to yield to it should not be given positions of honor; (3) those who avoid punishing their relatives and men of high rank should not be

81.8

cuss the seven calculations,[58] observe the eight obligations,[59] examine the nine symbols,[60] take care[61] [in issuing] the ten orders. / Thus one can be completely victorious.

[Concerning the matter of] great victories,[62] since there is nothing over which you are not victorious, great victories can therefore be achieved. Since there is nothing that you do not preserve, victories can therefore be preserved.

81.9

If[63] there are numerous battles, the knights will become weary.[64] If there are numerous / victories, the prince will become arrogant. Now, if

---

commissioned to lead the armed forces; (4) those who neither appreciate essential undertakings nor pay heed to the benefits of Earth, and [at the same time] treat lightly the imposition of levies and exactions [upon the people] should not be given cities and towns [to administer].

[56] Emending 機 to 教. See n. 55, above.

[57] The meaning of this phrase *liu xing* 六行, which I have translated as "six practices," is unclear. The two characters also appear in III, 8/4b1 (1:32.5), under a section on winter: 六行時節, "Since it is the season when the [number] six is functioning...." Here the characters *liu xing* are used in an entirely different grammatical context from that of this passage, but Zhang Peilun, basing his opinion on the fact that most of the other numerical categories mentioned in this paragraph are to be found in III, 8, says that there is a connection. Unfortunately he does not explain himself further. In my opinion, originally there was some connection between the category six here and that in III, 8/2a8 (1:30.6), which speaks of the six records (*liu ji* 六紀), but one or the other text, or possibly both, became corrupted, and it is impossible now to tell which, if either, is correct.

[58] Almost the same applies here as above. III, 8/3b2–3 (1:31.8), in a section on summer, reads: 治陽氣用七數, "[the prince] governs with the Yang vital force and utilizes the number seven." Zhang Peilun says that *qi shu* 七數 both here and in this passage of III, 8, are the same, but the difference in context makes this unlikely. In my opinion, *qi shu* here may be a mistake for *qi fa* 七法, "seven standards," the chief subject matter and title of *Guanzi*, II, 6, already cited at length in this chapter. The seven standards are listed in II, 6/1b7 (1:22.11–12), as: laws of nature, physical qualities, standards for measurement, forms of transformation, permissive or inhibitory actions, patterns of mental behavior, and categories of mensuration.

[59] According to III, 8/2a11 (1:30.8): "There are eight obligations that will determine strength or weakness."

[60] Following Zhang Peilun who would invert the two characters 器 and 章 to make the text read 審有章器 (= 者)十號, in order to accord with a similar statement of III, 8/7a6 (1:34.11).

[61] Following Zhang Peilun in emending 章 to 器 and in turn to 者 (= 慎), in accordance with III, 8/7a7 (1:34.11). III, 8, however, gives no details concerning the ten orders.

[62] The following passage is obviously corrupt. I have followed Zhang Peilun in reconstructing it on the basis of a slightly similar passage, III, 8/8a4–5 (1:35.8–9). Thus the text would read, 大勝無不勝也, 故能大勝無不守也, 故能守勝.

[63] Except for a slight variation in wording, this paragraph directly parallels III, 8/8a2–3 (1:35.7–8). A similar statement is also contained in the *LSCQ*, XIX, 5/11a12–13 (Wilhelm, *Frühling und Herbst*, p. 333), where it is attributed to the early fourth century B.C. statesman, Li Ke. See also the *Huainanzi*, 12/5b7 (Morgan, *Tao, the Great Luminant*, p. 111).

[64] III, 8/8a2, for 罷 here writes 疲. The meaning is the same.

an arrogant prince forces into action a wearied people, how can the country avoid falling into danger? Therefore it is best to have no battles at all; next best is to have only one of them.[65]

To destroy the large and vanquish the strong is [the way] to achieve having only one [battle]. / To throw them into disorder without resorting to opportunism, to gain ascendancy over them without resorting to deception, and to vanquish them without resorting to treachery[66] is [the way] to realize having only one [battle]. / For those [countries] that are near, use the reality [of armed forces]. For those that are distant, implement the [ten] orders.

Incalculable strength, immeasurable force, unlimited spirit, and un-fathomable Power are the source of having only one [battle]. / To as-semble[67] like the seasonal rain and disperse[68] like the whirlwind is to bring to an end the one [battle].

Controlling[69] the enemy[70] [requires] the refinement[71] of weapons. / Turning the enemy[72] to one's own use [requires] thoroughness of in-struction. Those who are not able to refine their weapons will not be able to control[73] the enemy. Those who are not able to be thorough in their instructions will not be able to turn the enemy to their own use. / Those who are unable to turn the enemy to their own use will become im-poverished. Those who are unable to refine their weapons will encounter trouble.

[65]According to the *Sunzi*, 3/9a–11a (Giles, *Sun Tzu*, pp. 19–20): "Therefore those who are skillful in employing arms subdue the armed forces of the enemy without fighting. They capture enemy cities without making an attack. They destroy enemy countries without [remaining in the field] for a long time. Since they may contend throughout the world with the certainty [of their forces] being intact, they will gain complete advantage without losing a man. This is the method of attack in accordance with stratagems." This furthermore appears as the practical military application of the Daoist assertions con-tained in the *Laozi*, A, 22/12b6–7 (Waley, *The Way and Its Power*, p. 171): "[The sage] does not contend with anyone; therefore no one in the world can contend with him." And in A, 30/17b1–2 (Waley, p. 180): "The good [general] achieves his objective and stops. He does not dare to force [his advantage]."

[66]This statement appears in sharp contrast to the *Sunzi*, 1/15a3 (Giles, *Sun Tzu*, p. 6): "All warfare is based on deception."

[67]Emending 眾 to 聚. The two characters were confused because of similarity form [Xu].

[68]Emending *gua* 寡 to *fen* 分. *Gua* appears to be a mistaken emendation of *fen* introduced by a copyist in order to make the meaning balance with the already-corrupted reading of 眾 as 聚, discussed in n. 67, above.

[69]Emending 利 to 制 [Xu].

[70]Emending 適 to 敵 throughout this passage [Chen, Yu Xingwu, and Xu].

[71]Emending *zhi* 至 to *zhi* 致 throughout this passage in accordance with the Ancient, Liu, and Zhu editions, and reading *zhi* 致 as *zhi* 緻 [Chen].

[72]The Yang edition for 適 mistakenly writes 敵.

[73]Emending 利 to 制.

82.1   If the armed forces are employed with speed,[74] / victory will be certain. If different roads are used for going out and returning, it will be harmful to the enemy. When encountering danger as a result of penetrating deep [into enemy territory], the knights will prepare themselves. /

82.2   When preparing themselves, they will be united in heart and effort. Those who are skillful at manipulating armed forces are ones who cause the enemy to act as if they were grasping at empty air and striking at shadows. /

82.3   It has neither fixed place nor form, yet there is nothing it does not achieve. It has neither form nor action, yet there is nothing it does not

82.4
14b   transform. / Such is the Way.[75] It appears lost and yet it is there. It appears to be behind and yet it is to the fore.[76] The [mere] prestige [of being a prince] is inadequate to command it.[77]

[74]Emending 遠 to 速 [Zhang Wenhu].

[75] According to the *Laozi*, A, 37/21a1–2 (Waley, *The Way and Its Power*, p. 188): "The Way never acts, yet nothing is left undone. If lords and kings could but keep to it, all things would be transformed of themselves." The *LSCQ*, XVII, 2/4b3–4 (Wilhelm, *Frühling und Herbst*, p. 266) further says: "Heaven has no form, yet all things are accomplished. The perfect essence has no shape, yet all things are transformed."

[76]Cf. the *Laozi*, A, 7/4b2–3 (Waley, *The Way and Its Power*, p. 150): "For this reason the sage puts himself in the background, but he is always to the fore."

[77]Here I have followed Guo Moruo's suggestion and interpreted the text as it stands. Ding, however, would emend 威 to 我 and read 命 as 名 in order to make this sentence accord with another passage in the *Laozi*, A, 25/14a (Waley, ibid., p. 174): "I do not know its [real] name, but as a byname we call it the Way. If I were forced to name it, I would call it Great." Thus Ding would read the sentence here as: "I am inadequate to give it a [real] name."

Da Kuang
大匡

Introductory Comments

The *Da kuang* is the first chapter of the *Nei yan* 内言 [Inner Statements] section, which is mostly devoted to the exploits of Guan Zhong 管仲 and Duke Huan 桓 and the institution of the *ba* 霸 or lord protector. It is also the first of a series of three chapters (*Da kuang*, VII, 18; *Zhong kuang* 中匡, VIII, 19; and *Xiao kuang* 小匡, VIII, 20). The first and third of these are among the longest in the *Guanzi* and provide the most extensive coverage of the lives of Guan Zhong and Duke Huan to be found in the work. However, the significance of the three titles is not clear. *Da*, *zhong*, and *xiao* normally mean "large," "middle," and "small," and *kuang* basically means "square basket," and by extension "square," "to correct," "to regulate" or "to set in order," and finally "to aid," but none of the possible interpretations seems to apply here.

The *Yi Zhou shu*, IV, 37/5a, mentions *da kuang*, *zhong kuang*, and *xiao kuang* as names of three sets of regulations that were applied respectively to (1) feudal lords, (2) ministers and officials, and (3) people in general during Zhou times. If the *Guanzi* titles were based on these three sets of regulations, we would expect that each chapter would deal with three categories in turn. As a matter of fact, the *Da kuang* and *Xiao kuang* are similar in content, the main difference being that the *Xiao kuang* discusses in more detail the internal administration of the state of Qi. The *Zhong kuang* is a very short chapter made up of several unrelated conversations between Guan Zhong and Duke Huan about external as well as internal affairs, and could not be categorized as dealing primarily with ministers and officials. There would seem to be little reason, therefore, to apply the meaning of the *Yi Zhou shu* to the three titles.

The term *kuang* occurs frequently in the *Guanzi* in the same sense as it appears in a reference to Guan Zhong in the *Lun yu*, XIV, 18/2: 一匡天下, "Guan Zhong ... brought unity and order to the entire realm."[1] However, *Guanzi*, X, 26/4a9 (2.17.14), also contains the passage 果三匡天子而九合諸侯, which, if it is not corrupt, can only be translated as: "Consequently he three times aided the son of Heaven

---

[1]See, for example, *Guanzi*, VIII, 20/14b3–4 (1.107.6–7), and XIX, 58/1a6 (3.20.12).

and nine times assembled the feudal lords." [2] Reading *kuang* with either of these meanings still would not account for the use of *da*, *zhong*, and *xiao*, especially since the *Xiao kuang* is the longest of the three chapters.

Guo Moruo suggests an entirely different approach. In bronze inscriptions *kuang* was used for *fu* 簋, which also means "square basket." *Fu*, in turn, was confused with *bu* 簿, "a register," or the bamboo slips upon which registers were written. According to Guo, there were four sizes of these slips, varying in length from 2.4 Chinese feet to six Chinese inches. The short six-inch slips were used for tallies rather than records. Thus Guo believes that *da*, *zhong*, and *xiao* here refer to the length of the slips on which the material contained in the chapters was originally written.

It is also possible that *da* 大 and *xiao* 小 are corruptions of *shang* 上 and *hsia* 下, in which case the three titles might be interpreted as the "Rectification" [of Duke Huan], parts I, II, and III. In my opinion, these explanations are all too tenuous to provide a satisfactory solution to the problem, and I have therefore left the title untranslated.

The *Da kuang* itself is made up of two distinct parts representing the work of different authors. The first part (1a6–5b6; 82.10–86.9), which falls into three sections, is purely a historical romance depicting the rise to power of Duke Huan (685–643 B.C.) in Qi and his acceptance of Guan Zhong as his chief minister.

The first section (1a6–2b3; 82.10–83.13) consists of an imaginary conversation between Guan Zhong and two friends, Bao Shu 鮑叔 (or Bao Shuya 鮑叔牙) and Shao Hu 召忽, concerning the problem of succession in Qi. This depiction serves to set the stage for the action to follow much the same as the prologue or opening scene of a Shakespearian play.

The next section (2b3–4a2; 83.13–85.3) turns to an elaboration of the events described in the *Zuo zhuan* concerning the revolt in 686 B.C. against Duke Xiang of Qi, which eventually brought Duke Huan to power. Here the story is obviously borrowed directly from the *Zuo zhuan* or at least from a common source, since the phraseology is often directly parallel. Line 3b11 (85.1) even cites the chronology of the *Zuo zhuan* in the reference to the ninth year of Duke Zhuang 莊 of Lu. Maspero[3] and others have felt this is definite proof that the text was

---

[2] Guo Moruo believes the text is not corrupt and points out three conferences summoned by Duke Huan and Guan Zhong that were either attended by a representative of the Zhou king or dealt with matters concerning the House of Zhou. These were: Shouzhi 首止 (655), Kuiqiu 葵丘 (651), and Xian 鹹 (647).

[3] See the Introduction, "Transmission of Text to Tang Times."

taken from the *Zuo zhuan*. Guo Moruo (*Guanzi*, I, p. 270), however, believes that this was originally the note of some commentator that was later copied into the text by mistake. Aside from the addition of some explanatory background material in the *Da kuang*, the chief difference between it and the *Zuo zhuan* at this point is that the former contains a long speech by one Shu Man (3a2–12; 84.5–9). This may have been the invention of the author of the *Da kuang*, but it may also have come from a source common to both works but not used by the *Zuo zhuan*.

The third section (4a2–5b6; 85.3–86.3) consists primarily of two more imaginary conversations. The first is between Bao Shu and Duke Huan in which the duke is convinced by Bao Shu that he should employ Guan Zhong even though the latter had supported a rival in the struggle for the throne. The second conversation is between the ruler of Lu and one of his ministers about whether they should allow Guan Zhong, who had fled to their country, to return to Qi and perhaps strengthen Qi against themselves.

The entire first part is then summed up by a moral judgment on Guan Zhong introduced by the words 君子聞之曰, "A man of quality, hearing of this, has said." This is a standard formula used in the *Zuo zhuan* to introduce the historian's opinion about a matter. However, the judgment that follows does not appear in the *Zuo zhuan*. There are several possible explanations for this: (1) it may be a lost passage from the *Zuo zhuan*; (2) it may have been in a source common to both the *Zuo zhuan* and *Da kuang* but omitted by the compiler of the former; (3) it may have been written by the author of the *Da kuang* in an attempt to assimilate the style of the *Zuo zhuan* or its original source.

From the style and content it is clear that the author belonged to the tradition of historical writers who glorified the feudal institutions of the past and therefore naturally appeared Confucian in outlook, even though they might not have been doctrinaire members of any Confucian school. The author's primary concern obviously lay in telling a good story. The moral judgments passed on Pengsheng 彭生 and Guan Zhong are feudalistic rather than specifically Confucian. That is to say, they stem from the basic consideration of preserving the altars of Land and Grain and keeping the ancestral temples intact, rather than from any lofty concepts of systematized morality.

The second part of the chapter (5b6–15b1; 86.9–95.4) is clearly a fragment from some longer text. Both a proper beginning and end are missing. Introduced by a comment, perhaps appended by Liu Xiang 劉向 when he edited the text, "Someone else says," it falls into two sections. The first (5b6–6b5; 86.9–87.7) deals with Bao Shu's efforts to persuade Duke Huan to assume power in Qi and then to employ Guan Zhong. The second (6b5–15b1; 87.7–95.4) deals with Guan Zhong's efforts to make the duke into an ideal Confucian ruler who is able to unite the world through moral force rather than violence.

Of particular interest is that this part of the *Da kuang* represents a blending of two literary genres: historical romance, as typified by the first part of the chapter, and philosophical treatise, as typified by the other *Guanzi* chapters contained in this volume as well as by such well-known works as the *Xunzi* and Hanfeizi. As mentioned in the Introduction, the writers of philosophical treatises constantly borrowed from fictionalized history to support their points of view, but since they were mainly concerned with the discussion of a specific subject rather than the narration of a story, they tended to adhere to the treatise form.

The second part of the *Da kuang* is neither a simple story nor a philosophical treatise. Actually, it appears as an extension of the historical romance into what might be called a philosophical romance. That is, it retains what is primarily a story form, but through a highly romanticized account of the relations between Duke Huan and Guan Zhong, it attempts to describe the building of a feudalistic utopia in accordance with a specific philosophical point of view. The author weaves into this account many historical events also recorded in the *Zuo zhuan*, but it is obvious that he has made no reference to that work at all during his writing. Not only are the separate events treated with un-restricted romantic license as far as their general chronological sequence is concerned, but the details also differ from those of the *Zuo zhuan* to such a degree and in such a way that it could not be explained simply by literary convenience.

In spite of its blatant disregard for conventional history, this latter part of the text is an interesting piece of writing. In describing the transformation of Duke Huan from a timid young prince into an arrogant, impetuous tyrant and then into a mature and capable ruler, the author shows a real sense of character development. The same skill in characterization is extended to the picture of Guan Zhong as the grand statesman and Bao Shu as his respectful second. Though the purpose of the author is to drive home a lesson in political philosophy, he never indulges in the long-winded, repetitious moralizing that is characteristic of so many of the early political propagandists.

There can be no doubt that the author was a Confucian, however. The importance attached to filial piety, the emphasis on the efficacy of moral force rather than armed might, the concern that the government obtain men who practiced righteousness, as well as the stress on the need for the ruler to heed the advice of his ministers, all reflect a typically Confucian point of view.

In regard to particle usage, both parts conform closely to the general rules laid down by Karlgren for his third century B.C. literary language.[4] Two points, however, deserve special mention. The first concerns the use of the particles *ruo* 若 and *ru* 如. In most chapters of the *Guanzi*, both appear in the sense of "if" and "like." In the two parts of this chapter, *ruo* appears with both meanings, but *ru* appears only with the meaning of "like." This differs from the practice of the *Zuo zhuan* and Lu dialect texts such as the *Lun yu* and *Mengzi*,[5] but adheres closely to the practice of both the *Guo yu*[6] and texts written in third century B.C. literary language such as the *Shangjun shu*.[7]

The second point concerns the use of the particle *yu* 于, which in the literary language of third century B.C. is almost entirely replaced by *yu* 於, except for sporadic occurrences.[8] In this chapter, *yu* 于 appears a total of eight times: six times in the sense of "at" or "to" followed by a place name, and once in the sense of "to" or "toward" followed by the name of a person (8b11; 89.7). However, of the six cases where it appears in the sense of "at," four are to be found in a passage (3b3–3b10; 84.11–14) that directly parallels the *Zuo zhuan*. This is also true for the one example of its use in the sense of "in." This leaves only three cases (one in the first part, 1b11; 83.5, and two in the second part, 8b11; 89.7, and 12b7; 92.12) where the author used *yu* 于 instead of *yu* 於. Since 於 appears some eighty-two times throughout the text, it can still be said that the occurrence of 于 does not interfere with the general third-century B.C. pattern.

The sentence structure in both parts, except for those passages paralleling the *Zuo zhuan*, generally accords, in terms of complexity, with that of other texts coming from the third century B.C. The style of the first part tends to be more formalistic than that of the second, and to be slightly more economical in use of words. This may be indicative of earlier dating but it may also be due to the individual style of the writer.

In conclusion, the first part of the text was probably composed by an early third-century B.C. writer of historical romances showing Confucian tendencies but not Confucian orthodoxy. He was a person who had access to the *Zuo zhuan* or at least to one of the sources from

---

[4] Karlgren, *On the Authenticity and Nature of the Tso Chuan*, pp. 62–63.
[5] Ibid., pp. 35–39.
[6] Ibid., p. 58.
[7] Duyvendak, *Book of Lord Shang*, p. 152.
[8] Karlgren, *On the Authenticity and Nature of the Tso Chuan*, p. 62.

which the *Zuo zhuan* was taken, perhaps even the state records of Qi. Such a description could easily fit a member of the Jixia Academy.[9]

The second part, however, could hardly have been written by anyone connected with the Jixia Academy or, for that matter, in any way with the state of Qi, because of the ignorance displayed concerning the traditional history of that country. I believe it constitutes part of a longer work dating from later in the third century B.C. by a person from one of the central states. We have no way of knowing when the two parts were put together, but it may not have been until Liu Xiang edited the present *Guanzi* text in about 26 B.C.

In this chapter the terms *gong* 公, "duke"; *jun* 君, "prince"; and *hou* 侯, "lord," are used in such a way as to be very confusing to the reader. Therefore, I have generally used the title of duke when the text is referring specifically to Duke Huan or to one of the other feudal rulers with that title.

Translation

Duke Xi[10] [730–698 B.C.] of Qi had [three sons]: Gongzi[11] Zhuer,[12] Gongzi Jiu,[13] and Gongzi Xiaobo.[14] He commissioned Bao Shu[15] to tutor Xiaobo, but Bao Shu refused the appointment on the pretext of illness and would not come out [of retirement].

Guan Zhong went with Shao Hu[16] to see him and asked, / "Why won't you come out [and accept]?"

Bao Shu replied, "Our forefathers had a saying, 'No one knows the son better than his father and no one knows the minister better than his prince.' Now, the prince knows of my unworthiness and so has com-

missioned me to tutor Xiaobo. / I realize that I have been rejected."[17]

"If you are firm in your refusal and will not come out [of retirement], I'll vouch for your [integrity] even unto death," said Shao Hu. "[The duke] will certainly excuse you." /

---

[9]The Jixia Academy 稷下, which was founded in Qi about 302 B.C., continued in operation for the next three-quarters of a century or so.

[10]僖; reigned 730–698 B.C.

[11]公子: lit., "son of a duke," a title given to the legitimate sons of a feudal lord.

[12]諸兒: the later Duke Xiang 襄, who reigned in Qi 697–686 B.C.

[13]糺; also written 糾.

[14]小白; the later Duke Huan 桓 who reigned in Qi 685–643 B.C.

[15]鮑叔; also known as Bao Shuya 鮑叔牙 was a long-time friend of Guan Zhong. According to Guan Zhong's biography in the *Shi ji*, 62, the two men had engaged in trade before becoming involved in government.

[16]召忽; another long-time associate of Guan Zhong.

[17]That is, since he had been ordered to teach a son who was not the immediate heir.

13 Bao Shu replied, "If you will do this, how can he fail to excuse me?" /

14 "That won't do," said Guan Zhong. "Those who would uphold the altars of Land and Grain and the ancestral temples / may not resign from affairs or waste[18] their time. We cannot know yet who will eventually possess the country. How about coming out [of retirement]?"

1 Shao Hu agreed, "It won't[19] do. / We three men in Qi are like the feet of a *ding* tripod. If one of them is removed, it certainly cannot stand.[20]

2 In my opinion, Xiaobo will certainly not become / the successor."

"Not so," replied Guan Zhong. "The people of this country detest Jiu's mother and extend this [detestation] to Jiu himself, whereas they pity Xiaobo for being motherless. Zhuer is the eldest but also the

3 meanest. So we still can't tell what will happen. / Now there is no way to put Qi on a firm footing except through these two Gongzi [Jiu and

4 Xiaobo]. / Xiaobo is not a man of petty intelligence and though he may be a little wild,[21] he has great plans. I[22] am the only one who can put

5 Xiaobo's [talents] to use.[23] / If by some mischance Heaven should send down calamities and rain misfortune upon Qi, then even though Jiu were to gain the throne, conditions would not be relieved. So unless you [Bao Shu] secure the altars of Land and Grain, who will there be to do it?" /

6 Shao Hu [demurred] saying, "After our prince has fulfilled his years and dies,[24] if anyone violates his orders and, rejecting [the one] I have set upon the throne, deprives my Jiu [of what belongs to him], I will not

7 remain alive, even though I might gain the entire realm, / not to mention[25] [merely] sharing in the government of our country, Qi. I will accept the orders of the prince and not change them. I will serve whomever he sets up and not fail[26] him. This is my righteous duty." /

8–9 "As a minister," replied Guan Zhong, / "I will follow the orders of the prince and maintain the altars of Land and Grain in order to uphold our ancestral temples. But am I to be expected to die for one Jiu? As for

---

[18]Reading 廣 as 曠 [Yu Yue].

[19]The Yang edition mistakenly omits 不 before 可.

[20]Meaning that the three men should not divide their efforts by becoming associated with conflicting factions.

[21]Emending 惕 to 愓 here and wherever it appears throughout the chapter [Wang Niansun and Yasui].

[22]Yiwu 夷吾, i.e., the personal name 名 of Guan Zhong, which he uses in referring to himself. Zhong 仲 was the appellation of the second brother in a family and was Guan's adult name 字. He was also known as Zhongfu 仲父 (or 甫) and Jingzhong 敬仲.

[23]Reading 客 as 用 [Tao and Yasui].

[24]Emending 卜 to 下 [Yu Yue, Ding, Yasui, and Yao].

[25]Emending 兄 to 況 [Wang Niansun].

[26]Reading 濟 as 廢 [Yu Yue and Sun Shucheng].

83.10 dying, I will do so if the altars of Land and Grain are destroyed, or if the ancestral temples are demolished, or if the sacrifices / are cut off. But unless it is [a question of] these three, I will keep on living. If I live, Qi will prosper; if I die, it will not."

Bao Shu asked, "Then what do we do about it?" /

83.11 "Everything will be all right if you come out [of retirement] and comply with the order [to tutor Xiaobo]," replied Guanzi.

Bao Shu agreed and, leaving [his retirement], complied with the order. Subsequently he became tutor to Xiaobo.

Bao Shu said to Guan Zhong, / "What course should we follow?" /

83.12 "If a minister," replied Guan Zhong, "does not employ all his
2b strength in serving his prince, he will not be taken into [the prince's] confidence. If he is not taken into [the prince's] confidence, his advice will not be heeded. If his advice is not heeded, the altars of Land and
83.13 Grain cannot be made secure. / Whoever serves a prince must not be of two minds."

Bao Shu agreed.

Duke Xi's younger brother by the same mother, Yi Zhongnian 夷仲年, had [a son], Gongsun[27] Wuzhi 無知, who, having found favor with Duke Xi, [had been granted] clothing and rank the same as that
83.14 of / a royal heir. When Duke Xi died [698 B.C.], Zhuer, as the eldest son, became the prince. This was Duke Xiang [697–686 B.C.]. After Duke Xiang ascended the throne, he demoted Wuzhi. Wuzhi was filled with rage.

84.1 The duke had ordered Lian Cheng 連稱 and Guan Zhifu 管至父 to guard Kuiqiu.[28] He had told them, "You are going forth during the melon season. When the melons are in season again you may return."

They remained on guard for a year, but no word[29] came from the duke. When they requested relief it was refused. Therefore the two men followed Gongsun Wuzhi in starting a rebellion.[30]

---

[27] 公孫: lit., "grandson of a duke," was an honorific title given to the grandson of a feudal lord or gentleman of royal blood.

[28] 葵丘: situated about thirty *li* west of present-day Linzi 臨淄 Xian in north-central Shandong.

[29] Reading 問 as 訊 [Xu].

[30] This story of the beginning of the revolt against Duke Xiang appears to have been taken directly from the *Zuo zhuan*, Zhuang, 8 (Legge, *Ch'un Ts'eu*, III, 8/5), with only minor alterations in wording. See also *Shi ji*, 32/5a (Chavannes, *Mémoires historiques*, IV, p. 44). In similar fashion the following passage concerning the death of Duke Huan in Qi seems to have been taken from the *Zuo zhuan*, Huan, 18 (Legge, II, 18/2). See also *Shi ji*, 32/4b (Chavannes, IV, p. 43).

84.2 The wife of Duke Huan of Lu,[31] / Wen Jiang,[32] was a native of Qi.
When the duke was preparing to go to Qi [in 694 B.C.] accompanied by[33]
84.3 his wife, Shen Yu[34] warned him, "This won't do. / A woman has her
[husband's] house. A man has his [wife's] chamber. There should be no
defilement on either side. This we call having propriety."

But the duke would not listen and subsequently with Wen Jiang met
the duke of Qi at the Le,[35] where Wen Jiang had improper relations
with him. On hearing about it, Duke Huan scolded her. She then told the
84.4 duke of Qi, / who became enraged. After a feast given for Duke Huan,
3a [Duke Xiang] had [a strong knight], Gongzi Pengsheng 彭生, crush
Duke Huan in his arms while helping him into his chariot. Thus Duke
Huan died in his chariot.[36]

Shu Man[37] said, "A worthy man in order to save [his ruler's repu-
tation] from suspicion will sacrifice his life out of loyalty, regarding his
84.5 own body[38] as a mere hostel [for the spirit]. / But the wise man in-
vestigates the reason for things and makes long-term plans so his body
84.6 can avoid [death]. / Now, Pengsheng was an aide to Duke Xiang, but
instead of giving honest advice, he indulged in flattery in seeking to find
amusement for the duke, thereby causing him to abandon propriety in
84.7 his family relations. Now,[39] / in addition, his physical strength has
brought calamity to our duke by creating resentment between two

---

[31] Duke Huan 桓 of Lu 魯 reigned 711–694 B.C. Lu was an important state situated in
present-day Shandong to the south of Qi.
[32] 文姜; Jiang was her family name. After her death she was styled Wen, "Elegant."
During the Spring and Autumn Period (722–481 B.C.) women were generally known only
by their surnames while living. After death they received a posthumous style supposedly
based on their outstanding characteristic.
[33] Reading 皆 as 偕 [Li].
[34] 申俞; a great officer of Duke Huan of Lu. The *Zuo zhuan*, Huan, 18 (Legge, *Ch'un
Ts'eu*, II, 18/1), for Yu writes Xu 繻.
[35] 濼; a river marking the traditional boundary between Qi and Lu.
[36] *Shi ji*, 32/4b (Chavannes, *Mémoires historiques*, IV, p. 43), presents the circumstances
of Duke Huan's death in a little more detail: "Duke Xiang of Qi entertained the duke of Lu
at a drinking bout and made him drunk. He then sent a strong knight, Pengsheng, to pick
up in his arms the duke of Lu and put him in a chariot. Whereupon he crushed Duke Huan
of Lu in his embrace and killed him. When they took the duke down from his chariot, he
was dead."
[37] 豎曼: perhaps this should be translated as "the Servant Man." Neither this man nor
the speech that follows appears in the *Zuo zhuan* or *Shi ji* versions of the story.
[38] The phrase containing the two characters 百姓 appears to be corrupt. The Yin
commentary attempts to interpret it without making any emendations. Thus it would
read: "so the hundred surnames will then have someone in whom to place their confidence." Since this interpretation lacks logical balance with the following passage, I have
followed Tao in emending 百姓 to 身如.
[39] Emending 命 to 今 [Xu].

states. Since the reason for the calamity devolves on Pengsheng, can he
avoid [death]? / The duke, having been led into this calamity through his
own rage, does not fear hostile relations or general censure and feels no
shame at having destroyed [the purity of] the family.[40] / How can [the
blame for] this stop short of Pengsheng? If Lu wants someone punished,
we should certainly say it was Pengsheng who did it." /

In the second month[41] a man of Lu told the duke of Qi: / "Our
prince, fearing your might, did not dare remain quietly at home but
came to renew old friendships. The rites have been completed but he has
not returned. We do not blame[42] [the crime on] anyone, but we request
that you expiate it with [the life of] Pengsheng." /

The men of Qi then killed Pengsheng in order to mollify Lu.

In the fifth month,[43] Duke Xiang went hunting at Beiqiu,[44] where he
saw a boar. An attendant exclaimed, "It's Gongzi Pengsheng!" /

The duke angrily replied, "How dare Gongzi[45] Pengsheng show
himself here!"

When he shot at it, the boar stood up like a man and screamed. Falling
down from his chariot in terror, the duke injured his foot and lost his
shoe. When he returned home he demanded the shoe from his attendant
Bi 費, and when it could not be found, whipped him until the blood
flowed. Bi, running out, / met some rebels at the gate. They seized and
bound him, but after he had stripped off his clothes and showed them his
back, the rebels trusted him and sent him back into [the palace] ahead of

---

[40] The meaning of this passage is unclear. I have followed the interpretation of Dai,
Ding, and Liu Shipei, emending 閒容 to 閒咎 and reading 昏生 as 泯姓. Yu Xingwu
agrees with Dai on the latter reading, but would read the former as 惛庸. According to his
interpretation the passage would read: "He is shameless in not fearing hostile relatives and
being stupid and boorish [in his conduct]."

[41] From this point on the story again parallels the text of the *Zuo zhuan*, Huan, 18
(Legge, *Ch'un Ts'eu*, II, 18/2). However, as He Ruzhang points out, the writing of "second
month" would seem to be a mistake. According to the *Chunqiu*, Huan, 18 (Legge, *Ch'un
Ts'eu*, II, 18/2), Duke Huan was killed in the fourth month of the summer of 694 B.C. The
Zuo zhuan commentary records the arrival of the messenger from Lu under the same year.

[42] Following Wang Niansun, who would emend 死 to 咎 to accord with the text of the
Zuo zhuan.

[43] Here the story returns to the events surrounding the revolt against Duke Xiang and
the text again parallels the *Zuo zhuan*, Zhuang, 8 (Legge, *Ch'un Ts'eu*, III, 8/5). However,
for "fifth month" the *Zuo zhuan* writes "twelfth month." Legge, in his translation,
mistakenly writes "eleventh month."

[44] 貝丘; situated south of present-day Boxing 博興 Xian in northern Shandong. The
Shi ji, 32/5a9, for *bei* 貝 writes *pei* 沛.

[45] The title *gongzi* does not appear in the *Zuo zhuan* version and it would seem to be an
interpolation here since the duke would hardly have used this honorific title when speaking
in anger.

288

84.14 them. [Once there], he hid the duke and came out fighting to die at the gate. Shizhi Fenru 石之紛如 died / at the foot of the stairs. Meng Yang 孟陽 posed as the duke asleep in his bed, but when the rebels killed him, they said, "This is not the duke. It's not at all like him."

Then they saw the duke's foot under the door [behind which he was hiding]. They subsequently killed him and placed Gongsun Wuzhi upon the throne.[46]

85.1 Bao Shuya, / serving the Gongzi Xiaobo, had fled with him to Ju.[47] Guan Yiwu and Shao Hu, serving Gongzi Jiu, had fled with him to Lu.[48] In the ninth year,[49] Gongsun Wuzhi oppressed [the people] in Yonglin[50] and they killed him. /

85.2 Duke Huan,[51] [returning] from Ju, was the first to enter [Qi], but the men of Lu attacked Qi [in an attempt] to install Gongzi Jiu. There was a
4a battle at / Ganshi.[52] Guan Zhong shot at Duke Huan and hit him on the belt buckle. However, the troops of Lu were routed completely, and Duke Huan ascended the throne.[53] He thereupon threatened Lu and
85.3 forced / them to kill Gongzi Jiu.

[46] Here ends the parallel with the *Zuo zhuan* passage.

[47] 莒; a small principality of the Eastern Yi, situated near present-day Ju 莒 Xian in south-central Shandong.

[48] According to the *Zuo zhuan*, Zhuang, 8 (Legge, *Ch'un Ts'eu*, III, 8/5): "In the beginning after Duke Xiang was established on the throne, he indulged in irregularities. Bao Shuya said, 'The duke is making the people despise him. Disorders will soon break out.' Thus, serving Gongzi Xiaobo, he fled [with him] to Ju. Yiwu and Shao Hu, serving Gongzi Jiu, fled here [to Lu]."

[49] The "ninth year" here obviously refers to the reign of Duke Zhuang 莊 of Lu (i.e., 685 B.C.).

[50] 雍廩; there is some question about this name. The *Zuo zhuan*, Zhuang, 9 (Legge, *Ch'un Ts'eu*, III, 9/1), treats the name as that of a person. The *Shi ji*, 32/5b9 (Chavannes, *Mémoires historiques*, IV, p. 46), treats it as the name of a place, but for *lin* 廩 writes *lin* 林. The *Zuo zhuan*, Zhao, 11 (Legge, X, 11/9), says that Wuzhi was killed by Quqiu 渠丘 of Qi. Yin Tongyang believes that Wuzhi was killed by an official named Quqiu at Yonglin, which he locates west of Linzi 臨淄 at present-day Ququili 渠丘里 in Shandong.

[51] 桓; that is, Xiaobo.

[52] 乾時; situated on the Shi 時 River, which flows to the north of present-day Boxing 博興 Xian, Shandong. It probably received its name (lit., "Dry Shi") from the fact that the river dried up here during part of the year.

[53] According to the account in the *Shi ji*, 32/6a (Chavannes, *Mémoires historiques*, IV, p. 47): "When the duke of Lu heard of the death of Wuzhi, he sent troops to escort Gongzi Jiu [to Qi] and dispatched Guan Zhong in charge of another column to block the road from Ju. [In the fighting that followed], an arrow hit Xiaobo on his belt buckle. Xiaobo then feigned death and Guan Zhong sent a messenger at full speed to carry the [false] news to Lu. The men of Lu who were escorting Jiu slackened their pace. When they arrived at [the capital of] Qi six days later, Xiaobo had already entered it and [the great officer] Gao Xi 高傒 had placed him on the throne." It was after this that the troops of Lu were defeated at Ganshi.

Duke Huan asked Bao Shu, "How can I make the altars of Land and Grain secure?"

"Obtain Guan Zhong and Shao Hu and then the altars of Land and Grain will be secure," Bao Shu replied. /

85.4 "Yiwu and Shao Hu have rebelled against me," said the duke.

Bao Shu then told the duke about their former plan.

"But can we get them?" asked the duke.

85.5 "If we summon them quickly, / we can," Bao Shu responded, "otherwise we cannot. Now, in Lu, Shi Bo[54] knows that Yiwu is a man of great wisdom. His plan will certainly be to have Lu turn its government over 85.6 to him. If Yiwu accepts / it, they[55] will be able to weaken Qi. If he does not accept, they will know that he expects to return to Qi and will certainly kill him."

85.7 "Then / will Yiwu accept the government of Lu or not?" asked the duke.

"He will not accept," replied Bao Shu. "When Yiwu did not die for Jiu it was because he wished to make Qi's altars of Land and Grain 85.8 secure. Now, if he were to accept the government of Lu, / this would weaken Qi. Yiwu is single-minded in serving his prince. Even though he knows he may die, he certainly will not accept [the government.]" /

85.9 "Will he be like this with me?" asked the duke.
4b
Bao Shu replied, "It is not for you but for our late prince. He cannot be on as good terms with you as he was with Jiu. If he would not die for Jiu, how much less [would he do so] for you. But if you wish to make Qi's 85.10 altars of Land and Grain secure, / then be quick about welcoming him."

"I fear we will be too late," said the duke. "What can we do about it?"

85.11 Bao Shu replied, "Now Shi Bo is a man / who is clever but extremely fearful. If Your Grace acts first, he[56] will be afraid of arousing your anger and certainly won't kill him." /

85.12 "Agreed," said the duke.

Shi Bo went before the duke of Lu and said, "Guan Zhong is wise,[57] but in this affair he has not been successful. Now since he is in Lu, you 85.13 should offer him the government of Lu. / If he accepts, Qi may be weakened. If he does not accept, kill him. Kill him and thereby placate Qi. [To show that] we share the same dislike for him is still better than doing nothing at all." /

[54] 施伯: a great officer of Lu.
[55] Following Wang Niansun who would delete 知 after 彼 as an interpolation taken from the following line. A similar passage in the *Xiao kuang*, VIII, 20/4a8 (1.98.5–6), says: 則魯能弱齊矣, "then Lu will be able to weaken Qi."
[56] Emending 反 to 皮 = 彼 [Yu Yue and Guo Moruo].
[57] Emending 悫 to 慧 [Tao].

85.14 "Agreed," said the duke.[58]

Before Lu could offer the government to Guan Zhong, however, an emissary arrived [with an ultimatum] from the duke of Qi, saying:
86.1
5a "Yiwu and Shao Hu are rebels against me. They are at present in Lu. / I want them alive. If I do not get them, it means that you are collaborating with rebels against me."

When the prince of Lu questioned Shi Bo [about it], Shi Bo said, "Give them to him. I have heard the prince of Qi is wild and extremely arrogant, so even though he obtains these worthies, is it certain that he
86.2 will be able / to make use of them? If it happens that the prince of Qi is able to make use of them, then Guanzi's career will be successful. Since
86.3 Guan Zhong is one of the world's great sages, if he now / returns to Qi, all the world will esteem him. How can Lu stand alone? Now supposing we were to kill him. Since he is Bao Shu's friend, Bao Shu will cause
86.4 trouble over it. You certainly would not be able to withstand it. / It would be better to give him up."

The prince of Lu subsequently had Guan Zhong and Shao Hu bound. Guan Zhong said to Shao Hu, "Are you afraid?"

86.5 Shao Hu replied, "Why should I be afraid? I have not / died before this because I have been waiting[59] for things to be settled. Now that they have been settled, [the new duke] will make you chief minister[60] of the left in Qi. He would certainly make me chief minister of the right,[61] but
6.6 for him to employ me after having killed my prince / would be a double shame for me. You become a live minister, but I shall be a dead one. I shall die knowing that I might have had [charge of] the government of a

---

[58] The *Shi ji*, 33/9b3–6 (Chavannes, *Mémoires historiques*, IV, p. 110), gives a slightly different account of Shi Bo's advice to Duke Zhuang: "A man of Lu, Shi Bo, said, 'When the duke of Qi wishes to obtain Guan Zhong, it is not to kill him. He will use him. If he uses him, it will mean trouble for Lu. It would be better to kill him and present [Qi] with his corpse.' But Duke Zhuang paid no heed."

[59] The Yang edition for 俟 mistakenly writes 耳.

[60] *Xiang* 相; the basic meaning of this term is to "observe" or "assist." From this it came to be a term for a high-level minister. The *Zuo zhuan*, Xiang, 25 (Legge, *Ch'un Ts'eu*, IX, 25/2), states: 崔杼立而相之, 慶封爲左相, "Cui Zhu established [Duke Jing upon the throne in 548 B.C.] and became his chief minister. Qing Feng became chief minister of the left." According to Melvin P. Thatcher, *Structural Comparison*, p. 147, this was a new ministerial position developed during the sixth century B.C. as a means of circumventing hereditary high officials. Later the term appears with specific reference to the chief minister either when used alone or in compounds, such as *qing xiang* 卿相, *xiang guo* 相國, or *zai xiang* 宰相. Luo Genze (*Guanzi*, pp. 26–29) maintains that this later meaning did not develop until the Warring States Period. Indeed, the compounds *qing xiang, xiang guo*, and *zai xiang* do not seem to appear before this time, but *xiang* by itself seems to have been used as a general term for a chief minister before then.

[61] The left was usually concerned with civil affairs, the right with the military. See Dubs, *History of the Former Han Dynasty*, I, p. 123, n. 1.

10,000-chariot [kingdom]; in this way, Gongzi Jiu may be said to have
had a minister who died for him. / But you will live [to raise to power] a
protector over the feudal lords; in this way, Gongzi Jiu may be said to
have had a minister who lived for him. The one who dies will have
[virtuous] conduct. The one who lives will have fame. Fame is not to be
established in both ways. / [Virtuous] conduct is not to be come by
lightly. You must exert yourself so that the one who dies and the one
who lives will each achieve what is [proper] for him."

And so as they were crossing the border into Qi, he cut his own throat
and died, while Guan Zhong went on to enter [the country].[62]

The man of quality, hearing of this, / said,[63] "Shao Hu's dying was
preferable to his living. Guan Zhong's living was preferable to his
dying."

Someone else said:[64]

In the following year[65] / Duke Xiang drove out Xiaobo. In the third
year after Xiaobo had fled to Ju, Duke Xiang met his death and Gongzi
Jiu mounted the throne. The people of the country called for Xiaobo.

Bao Shu said, "Why don't you go?" /

"It wouldn't do," replied Xiaobo. "Now Guan Zhong is knowledgeable and Shao Hu is strong and warlike. Even though my countrymen
call for me, I still cannot return."

"If Guan Zhong were able to exercise his knowledge in a country,"
said Bao Shu, / "could that country ever be[66] in disorder? Shao Hu may
be strong and warlike but how can he by himself plan against us?"

---

[62] A slightly different version of this story appears in the *Zuo zhuan*, Zhuang, 9 (Legge,
Ch'un Ts'eu, III, 9/6): "Bao Shu, leading an army, arrived [in Lu] and said, 'Zijiu [i.e.,
Gongzi Jiu] is a near relative of our prince. He requests that you execute him. Guan
[Zhong] and Shao [Hu] are his enemies. He requests that they be delivered to him so he may
satisfy [his desire for revenge].' [Lu] then killed Zijiu at Shengdou 生竇 [north of present-
day Geze 菏澤 Xian, Shandong] and Shao Hu died with him. Guan Zhong asked to be
held as a prisoner. Bao Shu received him and removed [his bonds] when they reached
Tangfou 堂阜 [a town on the border between Qi and Lu situated about thirty *li* northwest
of present-day Mengyin 蒙陰 Xian, Shandong]." See also the *Shi ji*, 32/6a10–b6
(Chavannes, *Mémoires historiques*, IV, pp. 48–49).

[63] This is a common formula used in the *Zuo zhuan* for introducing the comments of the
historian. This particular comment does not appear in the present *Zuo zhuan*.

[64] *Huo yueh* 或曰; this comment must have been inserted by Liu Xiang or some other
early editor to indicate that the material that follows was of different origin than the
preceding.

[65] This portion of the text is clearly a fragment taken from the middle of what must have
been a longer work. Since we do not have the material that originally preceded this story of
the expulsion of Xiaobo, we cannot state for certain the exact meaning of the reference to
"the following year." However, according to the next sentence, it was in the third year
after Xiaobo had fled to Ju that Duke Xiang met his death. Since the duke was killed in 686
B.C., Xiaobo must have been forced to flee to Ju about 689.

[66] Reading 謂 as 為 [Guo Moruo].

86.13
6a

Xiaobo replied, "Well, even though [Guan Zhong] is not able / to exercise his knowledge, does it mean he does not have it? And even though Shao Hu has not been able to win over the masses, does it mean he does not have enough friends[67] to make plans against us?" /

86.14

"When a country is in disorder," said Bao Shu, "wise men are unable to manage its internal affairs, and friends are unable to unite themselves. Thus you can make [your own] plans for the country." /

87.1

Thereupon chariots were ordered harnessed and with Bao Shu driving and Xiaobo riding with him, they left Ju.

Xiaobo said, "Now those two men will follow the orders of their prince. I cannot attempt this." /

87.2

He was about to get down when Bao Shu stepped on his foot and said, "Now is the time to succeed in this affair. If we do not succeed, I will die

87.3

because of it and you, My Lord, can[68] still / escape."

87.4

And so as they approached the outskirts of the capital, Bao Shu ordered twenty chariots to go before and ten to remain in the rear. / Bao Shu then told Xiaobo, "Now since there is doubt about [the succession] in the country, those two or three gentlemen [guarding the suburbs] will not offer any resistance to me.[69] But in case we do not succeed, I will barricade the road [while you escape]." /

87.5
5b

Bao Shu then addressed [the troops]: "If we are successful, listen for my orders. If we are not successful, saving the Gongzi comes first; dying

87.6

comes second. / With the complement of five chariots, I will proceed down the road."

Bao Shu then drove on ahead. Subsequently he entered the capital and expelled Gongzi Jiu. [During the battle] Guan Zhong shot at

87.7

Xiaobo / and hit him on the belt buckle. But afterward with Gongzi Jiu and Shao Hu he fled to Lu, and Duke Huan ascended the throne. Lu then attacked Qi [in an attempt] to reinstate Gongzi Jiu, but they were unable to do so.

In the second year [684 B.C.][70] after Duke Huan ascended the

---

[67] Emending 及 to 友 [Song and Guo Moruo].

[68] The character 之 here appears corrupt; the Yin commentary, which paraphrases the text, writes 可得. Xu would thus emend 之 to 可.

[69] This sentence is not clear. The Yin commentary says that the two or three gentlemen referred to were followers of Xiaobo. In view of the general context of Bao Shu's speech, this does not seem right. Therefore I have adopted Guo Moruo's interpretation with respect to them. Guo, however, would also emend 國 to 或 and 忍 to 認, thus making the passage read: "Perhaps none of those two or three gentlemen [guarding the suburbs] will recognize me."

[70] 二年; "the second year" should probably read 一年 or 元年, "the first year," i.e., 685 B.C. This is substantiated by the fact that the passage (7a8; 88.1) below makes a further reference to "the second year." This would be unnecessary if the text had originally read "second year" here.

87.8 throne, / he summoned Guan Zhong. When Guan Zhong arrived, the duke asked, "Can the altars of Land and Grain be made secure?"

Guan Zhong replied, "If you become lord protector to the king, the altars will be secure. Otherwise, they will not."

87.9 The duke said, "I would not / dare attain to such greatness. Just secure the altars of Land and Grain and that is all."

Guan Zhong again made the request, but the duke[71] said, " I can't."

Guan Zhong then took leave of the duke, saying, "Your saving me from death was my good fortune, but it was because I wished to make 87.10 the altars of Land and Grain secure that I / did not die for Jiu. If the altars are not made secure, I would not dare receive a salary[72] in the government of Qi after not having died for Jiu." /

87.11 Then he walked away. As he reached the gate, the duke called him 7a back and Guan / Zhong returned.

The duke, perspiring [under the strain], said,[73] "Since there is no help for it, I will strive to become lord protector."

87.12 Guan Zhong bowed down / twice, knocking his head on the ground and arose saying, "Today you will become that lord. I am eager to receive your orders."

He crossed to stand in the spot reserved for the chief minister and then ordered the five official bureaus[74] to carry on their affairs.

87.13 On another day the duke informed / Guan Zhong, "While there is no fighting going on among the feudal lords, I wish to strengthen our armed forces within the country."[75]

"That won't do," replied Guan Zhong. "The hundred surnames are suffering. Your Grace should first share [your resources] with the hun- 87.14 dred surnames and put your arms in storage. / Expending your wealth on men is better than expending it on arms. Qi's altars of Land and Grain are not yet secure. If Your Grace begins with arms rather than with men, you will neither be on good terms with the feudal lords abroad 88.1 nor on good terms / with the people at home."

"I agree," responded the duke. "The government can't do it yet."

In the second year [684 B.C.], the country was [still] in great disorder,

---

[71] That is, Duke Huan. Ding cites the passage above and below where the word *gong* 公, "duke," is used to show that here and in the next sentence the text should probably read *gong* rather than *jun* 君, "prince."

[72] Yu Yue would read 祿 as 錄 and interpret the sentence as meaning: "I would not dare take charge of the government of Qi after not having died for Jiu."

[73] The Yang edition mistakenly omits 曰.

[74] 五官; traditionally the five official bureaus were: the offices of the ministers of education (*situ* 司徒), military affairs (*sima* 司馬), works (*sikong* 司空), civil offices (*sishi* 司士), and justice (*sikou* 司寇).

[75] Emending 小 to 内 in order to accord with a similar passage (7b3; 88.5) below [Xu].

yet Duke Huan again told Guan Zhong,[76] "I wish to rebuild our armed forces."

Guan Zhong / again replied, "That won't do."

Paying no heed, however, the duke went ahead with the production of arms.

Once Duke Huan was drinking in a boat[77] with a lady from Song.[78] The woman [playfully] rocked the boat and frightened the duke, who became angry and sent her away. Song received her and married her to the lord of Cai.[79] /

The next year [683? B.C.] in anger the duke told Guan Zhong, "I wish to attack Song."

Guan Zhong said, "That won't do. I have heard that if internally the government / has not been strengthened, ventures abroad will be unsuccessful."

[However], the duke, paying no heed, consequently attacked Song. The feudal lords then raised arms / to help Song and severely defeated the troops of Qi.[80]

The duke returned in a rage and told Guan Zhong, "I requested you to strengthen our armed forces,[81] / but our knights have not been trained and weapons have not materialized. The feudal lords have therefore dared to help my enemy. Now let us strengthen our armed forces within the country."

"That won't do," said Guan Zhong. "The country of Qi is in danger.

[76] The phrase 桓公彌亂 is obviously corrupt. I have followed Xu, who would emend it to accord with the passage below (7b10; 88.8). Thus the Chinese text would read: 二年國彌亂, 桓公又告管仲.

[77] The Yang edition for 船 writes 舡 throughout this passage. The meaning is the same.

[78] 宋; a relatively small state situated south of present-day Shangqiu 商邱 Xian in eastern Henan, south of the Yellow River. Its rulers were the descendants of the Shang kings and carried on the sacrifices of the Shang dynasty.

[79] 蔡; a small state situated southwest of Shangcai 上蔡 Xian in east-central Henan.

[80] This story appears as a corruption of a well-known series of events that took place in the twenty-ninth year of Duke Huan (657 B.C.). According to the *Zuo zhuan*, Xi, 3 (Legge, *Ch'un Ts'eu*, V, 3/7): "The Lord of Qi went for a boat ride in the park with [the lady] Ji 姬 of Cai. She rocked the duke, who became frightened, changed color, and ordered her to stop. But she refused to do so. The duke became angry and sent her back [to Cai] but without breaking off [his relationship with her] completely. The men of Cai, however, married her off [to someone else]." The following year (656 B.C.), the *Zuo zhuan*, Xi, 4 (Legge, V, 4/1), records: "The Lord of Qi, with troops of the various feudal lords, invaded Cai. [The people of] Cai dispersed and subsequently [Qi and its allies] attacked Chu."

This same version of these events and their consequences appears in the *Shi ji*, 32/7b10–8a1 (Chavannes, *Mémoires historiques*, IV, p. 52). In these accounts the events occur near the end of the duke's reign rather than at the beginning; the lady is from Cai instead of Song; and the various lords, instead of joining against Qi, actually helped to crush the offending country, Cai.

[81] The Yang edition mistakenly omits 兵 before 革.

To rob the people of the essentials [of life] and encourage knights to [reckless] bravery is the basis for disorder at home.[82] And if you interfere with / the feudal lords abroad, people will become very resentful and knights who practice righteousness will not come to Qi. How then can you avoid danger?"

Bao Shu said, "Your Grace must follow Yiwu's / advice."

But the duke, paying no heed, thereupon ordered the strengthening of his armed forces within the four boundaries and greatly intensified the exactions at the customs stations and markets. He subsequently used [this revenue] to give salaries to those who were [recklessly] brave.

Bao Shu said / to Guan Zhong, "The other day the duke promised you that he would become lord protector. But now the country is in complete confusion. What are you going to do about it?"

"Our prince is a little wild," Guan Zhong replied, "but when he realizes [his mistakes] he will become very repentant.[83] Meanwhile we must wait a little / for him to come to [his senses]."[84]

"By the time he comes to [his senses]," said Bao Shu, "won't the country be lost?"

"Not quite," replied Guan Zhong. / "I can still secretly carry on the government within the country, and even if there are disorders, / we can still wait a while. Since among the advisers of the feudal lords abroad there are none like the two of us, no one will dare encroach upon [our country]." /

The next year [682? B.C.] those who contended for salaries at court slashed each other to pieces; the breaking of necks and slitting of throats went on uninterrupted. Bao Shu said to Guan Zhong, "A great number of men have died in the country. Won't this be harmful?"

Guan Zhong / replied, "How can we stop it? These, however, are all greedy people. What worries me is that [within the states] of the feudal lords none of those who practice righteousness are willing to enter Qi, and in Qi itself none of those who practice / righteousness are willing to enter the government. This is what worries me. Why should I care about the dead?"

The duke / again strengthened his armed forces within the country.

In the third year [683 B.C.], when Duke Huan was about to attack Lu,

---

[82] Following Wang Niansun, who would delete 外 as an interpolation taken from the following sentence.

[83] Reading 智 as 知 and emending 誨 to 悔 [Sun Xingyan and Wang Yinzhi].

[84] Wang Yinzhi would emend 及 to 反, thus having the phrase read: "We must wait a little for him to reflect on this himself."

he said, "Lu is a neighbor of mine; for this reason they were quick to help Song. Now I will punish them." /

89.1 "That won't do," said Guan Zhong. I have heard it said that the altars of Land and Grain will be safe only if the prince who possesses the territory does not devote himself to arms, is not resentful of insults, and does not make excuses for his mistakes. Whereas, if he does these things, the altars of Land and Grain will be endangered." /

89.2
8b But the duke, paying no heed, raised troops to attack Lu. He advanced to Changshao,[85] but Duke Zhuang of Lu [also] raised troops to repel him and severely defeated him.[86]

Duke Huan said, 'We are still deficient in arms. If I had three times as many [troops] to surround him, how could he withstand me?" /

89.3 In the fourth year [682 B.C.] he strengthened his arms, assembling 100,000[87] armored troops and 5,000 chariots. He then said to Guan Zhong, "Our knights are finally well trained and we are finally well

89.4 equipped with arms. I / wish to subjugate Lu."

Guan Zhong, sighing deeply, said, "The country of Qi is in danger. You do not compete [against others] with moral force but with [force of] arms. There are a number of states in the realm that can support 100,000

9.5 armored troops. / If we were to send our small force to subjugate the mighty forces [of the combined feudal lords], we would lose the support of the masses within our country. When the feudal lords are prepared for

9.6 us and / our own people are deceitful toward us, how can we expect our state to escape danger?"

But the duke, paying no heed, went ahead and attacked Lu.[88]

Lu did not dare fight and set up a [new] boundary fifty *li* from its

9.7 capital. / Lu then proposed that it be treated as a *guannei* vassal[89]

[85] 長勺; a place in Lu situated in present-day Shandong. Its exact location is unknown.

[86] According to the *Zuo zhuan*, Zhuang, 10 (Legge, *Ch'un Ts'eu*, III, 10/1), this battle took place in 684 B.C. instead of 683.

[87] According to several passages appearing later in this chapter and elsewhere in the *Guanzi*, the usual ratio of armored (infantry) troops to chariots was ten to one. Therefore Wang Yinzhi believes that 十萬, "100,000," should be emended to read 五萬, "50,000."

[88] From the context it would appear that this attack took place in 682 B.C. According to the *Shi ji*, 32/7al (Chavannes, *Mémoires historiques*, IV, p. 49), it took place in 681. See n. 90 below. The *Zuo zhuan*, Zhuang, 13 (Legge, *Ch'un Ts'eu*, III, 13/14), also records the conference at Ge 柯, which followed under the year 681.

[89] Inserting the character *hou* 侯 following *guannei* 關內. The *LSCQ*, XIX, 7/15a4, which contains a version of this story similar to that of the *Guanzi*, writes *guanneihou*. The *Hanfeizi*, XIX, 50/11b3–4 (Liao, *Han Fei Tzu*, II, pp. 305–306), gives some indication of the status of the *guannei* vassal: "Even though they disapprove our doings, we can always make them bring birds to visit our court." (Birds were a customary present when a vassal visited his lord). It would seem the *guannei* vassal enjoyed a certain amount of autonomy in local affairs, but was completely under the control of the dominant state in international matters.

rendering service to Qi [with the understanding that] Qi was not to invade Lu again.[90]

89.8
9a

Duke Huan agreed. The men of Lu then proposed a convenant / saying, "Lu is a small country. We definitely are not carrying swords while at the moment you are. Lest the feudal lords should hear that this is an armed encounter, it would be better for you to desist. We propose that you get rid of your arms."

89.9

"Agreed," said Duke Huan, / and ordered his followers not to carry their weapons.

"This won't do," said Guan Zhong. "The feudal lords bear resent-

89.10

ment against you. You can still withdraw from this. / If Lu is weakened by you,[91] the feudal lords will say you are greedy, and in case of future incidents lesser countries will remain steadfast [against you] while the greater countries will make preparations [for war]. This is not to

89.11

Qi's / advantage."

But the duke paid no heed.

Guan Zhong again warned him, "If you positively will not leave Lu, why don't you take your weapons? Cao Gui[92] is a man who is strong-willed and full of hate. He cannot be bound by a treaty." /

89.12

But Duke Huan, paying no heed, went ahead and met with [Duke Zhuang of Lu].

Duke Zhuang himself carried [a couple of] swords concealed against his chest. Cao Gui did the same. When they ascended the altar,[93] Duke Zhuang drew forth his swords and said, "The frontier of Lu is [now

89.13

only] fifty *li* from the capital.[94] / [If this goes on] it can only end in death."

---

[90] According to the *Shi ji*, 32/7a1–3 (Chavannes, *Mémoires historiques*, IV, pp. 49–50): "In the fifth year [681 B.C., Duke Huan] attacked Lu. Lu's army was defeated. Duke Zhuang of Lu proposed that he cede the town of Sui 遂 [to Qi] in order to obtain peace. Duke Huan agreed and met with Lu at Ge 柯 [situated in present-day Donga 東阿 Xian in eastern Shandong] to make a covenant."

[91] Following the Ancient edition, which for 君果弱魯君 writes 若魯弱於君 [Guo Moruo].

[92] 曹劌; the adviser to the duke of Lu who was responsible for the defeat of Qi at Changshao the year before. See the *Zuo zhuan*, Zhuang, 10 (Legge, *Ch'un Ts'eu*, III, 10/1). The *Shi ji*, 32/7a4, 33/9b6 (Chavannes, *Mémoires historiques*, IV, pp. 49–50, 110), and 86/1a–b, for Gui writes Mo 沫. The *Zhanguo ce*, 31/5a11–12, does the same. The *LSCQ*, XIX, 7/15a7–b11, writes Hui 翙. The *Guo yu* does not contain this story, but mentions Cao in connection with the battle of Changshao. Here his name is written the same as in this chapter of the *Guanzi*.

[93] The altar 壇 was made of packed earth with steps leading up from the sides. It was used for sacrificial purposes as well as for the swearing of covenants.

[94] In the *LSCQ* version, XIX, 7/15a–b11 (Wilhelm, *Frühling und Herbst*, p. 340), Duke Zhuang adds that the frontier was formerly 100 *li* from the capital.

While threatening[95] Duke Huan with [the sword in his] left hand, he held [the one in his] right against himself and continued, "Since I must die anyway, I will kill myself in front of you." /

Guan Zhong ran to his prince, but Cao Gui, drawing his sword and planting himself between the two steps [of the altar] said, "The two princes are about to change what they had planned; no one may advance." /

Guan Zhong called out, "Give them the territory and take the Wen [River][96] as the frontier."

Duke Huan agreed and, with the Wen fixed as the frontier, returned home.[97]

Upon his return, Duke Huan / strengthened his government but not his armed forces. He protected his own borders, ruled his people, put an end[98] to excesses, and demobilized his troops.

In the fifth year [681], Song [was about to] attack Qii.[99] / Duke Huan said to Guan Zhong and Bao Shu, "Now I have always desired to attack Song were it not for what might result from the feudal lords. Now since [the lord of] Qii is a descendant of the illustrious kings [of Xia], and Song is at present attacking him, / I wish to help him. How about it?"

Guan Zhong replied, "It won't do. I have heard that when the government within the country has not been strengthened, the promotion of righteousness abroad will not be trusted. If you would promote righteousness abroad, you should first put it into practice [at home], / and then the feudal lords may be made to depend on you."

"But," said Duke Huan, "if we do not help [Qii] in this, afterward there will be no reason for attacking Song."

[95] The Yang edition for 揕 mistakenly writes 椹. The *LSCQ* version, XIX, 7/15a–b11, writes 搏, "to seize," and reads: "Both Duke Zhuang and Cao Hui concealed swords against their chests. On reaching the top of the altar, Duke Zhuang with his left hand seized Duke Huan and with his right drew his sword and held it against himself."

[96] 汶; flows through Taian 泰安 Xian in eastern Shandong. It would have formed the northeast boundary of Lu.

[97] The *Zuo zhuan* gives none of the details of this affair. The *Gongyang zhuan*, however, deals with it at some length but presents a different version from that contained in the *Guanzi* and *LSCQ*. According to the *Gongyang zhuan*, Zhuang, 13 (Legge, *The Ch'un Ts'ew*, III, 13/14), it was only Cao Gui who threatened Duke Huan as he mounted the altar and forced him to agree to establishing the Wen River as the boundary line between Lu and Qi. The *Shi ji* versions cited above in n. 92 agree with the *Gongyang zhuan*.

[98] Reading 以 as 已 = 止 [Zhang Peilun].

[99] 杞; properly romanized "Qi." The special romanization of "Qii" here is to help distinguish it from Duke Huan's state of Qi 齊. Qii was a small state created by King Wu 武 of the Zhou to carry on the sacrifices of the Xia dynasty. It was situated near Qi 杞 Xian in northeast Henan southeast of the modern city of Kaifeng 開封. This attack is not mentioned in the *Zuo zhuan* or *Shi ji*.

Guan Zhong replied, "A prince among the feudal lords should not be greedy for territory. If he is, / he will have to devote himself to the use of arms. If he devotes himself to the use of arms, he will certainly bring distress to the people. If the people are distressed, / there will be a great deal of deceitfulness. If deceitfulness becomes prevalent,[100] [the prince] will not be trusted by his people. Now if he is not trusted by his people, / disorders will arise. If he takes [hasty] action within the country, he will endanger himself. But if he [first] makes thorough estimates[101] and then acts, he will be successful. For this reason those ancients who paid heed to the way of the former kings did not compete against others with [force of] arms."

"Then what is to be done about it?" asked Duke Huan.

Guan Zhong replied, / "In my opinion, we should not [attack Song], but rather you should order one of our men to be sent with valuable presents. If sending them presents does no good, you should receive [the lord of Qii] and enfeoff him." /

Duke Huan then questioned Bao Shu, "What about it?"

Bao Shu replied, "Your Grace should carry out Yiwu's advice."

The duke then ordered Cao Sun Xiu[102] to be sent to Song, but Song, paying no heed, went ahead and attacked Qii. /

Duke Huan then constructed [fortifications around] Yuanling[103] in order to enfeoff [the ruler of Qü] there. He gave him a hundred chariots and a thousand armored troops.

The following year [680 B.C.], the Di people[104] attacked Xing[105] and

---

[100] This passage is obviously corrupt. I have followed the suggested emendation of Dai, who says that the sentence 夫詐密而後動者勝 is out of place and should be transferred back to its original position below 內動則危於身 (10a2; 90.7).

[101] See n. 100, above, concerning the relocation of this sentence from the line above (10a1; 90.6). 詐 has also been emended to 計 [Dai and Tao].

[102] 曹孫宿; the Ancient, Liu, and Zhu editions for Xiu write Shu 叔. The *Xiao kuang*, VIII, 20/13a3 (1:106.2), and 18a10 (1:110.11), writes Xiu. According to Guo Moruo, *Guanzi*, I, p. 287, Cao was the name of this man's state. Sun was his clan name 氏, Xiu his personal name 名, and Shu his adult name 字. This, however, is all very hypothetical.

[103] 緣陵: later known as Yingling 營陵, situated seventy *li* southeast of present-day Changle 昌樂 Xian in north-central Shandong. According to the *Chunqiu* and *Zuo zhuan*, Zhuang, 14 (Legge, *Ch'un Ts'eu*, III, 14/1), the fortification of Yuanling did not occur until 646 B.C. The *Zuo zhuan* merely states: "In the spring of the fourteenth year, the feudal lords walled Yuanling and moved [the capital of] Qii to it. Because of an omission on the part of the historiographers there is no record of the men involved." The reason for the move is not given by the *Chunqiu* and *Zuo zhuan*, but Du Yu 杜預 (222–284) in his commentary says that it was to avoid the Yi people of the Huai region 淮夷. The *Guanzi* is most probably incorrect in attributing the move to an attack from Song.

[104] 狄; one of the so-called barbarian peoples who were spread over much of north China but who were particularly concentrated in Shanxi.

[105] 邢; a small state situated near present-day Xingtai 邢臺 Xian in southwest Hebei.

the Prince of Xing fled to[106] Qi. Duke Huan then constructed [fortifi-
cations around] Yi-yi[107] / in order to enfeoff [the ruler of Xing]. He gave
him 100 chariots and 1,000 men.

The following year [679 B.C.], the Di people attacked Weii[108] and the
prince of Weii fled to Xu.[109] Duke Huan also / enfeoffed him.

Xi Peng and Bin Xuwu[110] warned him, "This won't do. Those three
countries were lost because they remained too small. / Now you seek[111]
to enfeoff these lost countries. But when our country's [territory] is
exhausted [by conferring such fiefs], what then?" /

Duke Huan questioned Guan Zhong, "What about it?"

Guan Zhong said, "Since you have become famous for this sort of
action, you should live up to it in practice.[112] You / should do it."

The duke further questioned Bao Shu. Bao Shu said, "You should
carry out Yiwu's advice."

Duke Huan constructed [fortifications around] Chuqiu[113] in order to

---

[106] Reading 致 as 至 [Yao]. According to the *Zuo zhuan*, Min, 2 (Legge, *Ch'un Ts'eu*,
IV, 1/2), this attack took place in 661 B.C. On the advice of Guan Zhong, Qi then sent
forces to aid Xing.

[107] 夷儀; situated to the west of present-day Xingtai 邢臺 Xian in southwest Hebei.
According to the *Zuo zhuan*, Min, 2 (Legge, *Ch'un Ts'eu*, IV, 2/8): "During the first year of
Duke Xi, [659 B.C.], Duke Huan of Qi moved [the capital of] Xing to Yiyi."

[108] 衛; properly romanized "Wei." The special romanization of "Weii" here is to
distinguish it from the larger state of Wei 魏, which becomes important later on. Weii was
a relatively small state situated near present-day Qi 淇 Xian, north of the Yellow River in
northeast Henan. According to the *Zuo zhuan*, Min, 2 (Legge, ibid., IV, 2/7), which
records this event in some detail, the Di overran Weii in the twelfth month of 660 B.C.

[109] 盧; a town situated southeast of present-day Yanjin 延津 Xian in northeast Henan.
The town of Xu is not mentioned by either the *Zuo zhuan* or *Shi ji* in their accounts of this
affair. According to the *Zuo zhuan*, Min, 2 (Legge, ibid., IV, 2/7), part of the Weii people
managed to flee across the Yellow River to the state of Song. Those who remained behind
sought refuge in the town of Cao 曹 (situated near present-day Hua 滑 Xian in northeast
Henan), where they installed Duke Dai 戴 to take the place of their former ruler, Duke Yi
懿, who had been killed.

[110] 隰朋 and 賓胥無; two great officers of Qi.

[111] Emending 靳 to 蘄 [Sun Xingyan].

[112] There is wide disagreement among the commentators on the meaning of this
passage: 君有行之名,安得有其實. I have read 安 as a copulative particle similar to 則
and attempted to interpret the text as is. Guo Moruo would follow the Ancient, Liu, and
Zhu editions and transpose the two characters 名 and 實. He would further read 安 as 爰.
Thus the sentence would read: "Since you have the reality of the action, you have achieved
fame for it." Zhang Wenhu believes that the phrase 安得無其實 should be written
安得無其所. Thus his interpretation would read: "Since you have become famous for
this sort of action, how can you fail to live up to it?" None of these interpretations,
including my own, is very satisfactory.

[113] 楚丘; the new capital of Weii, situated in present-day Hua 滑 Xian in northeast
Henan, some distance to the east of the former capital of Zhaoge 朝歌. According to the
Zuo zhuan, Min, 2 (Legge, *Ch'un Ts'eu*, IV, 2/8), and *Shi ji*, 32/7b8–10 (Chavannes,
Mémoires historiques, IV, p. 52), Duke Huan helped Weii erect this new capital in 658 B.C.

enfeoff [the ruler of Weii]. He gave him 300 chariots and 5,000 armored troops.[114]

91.1   A year following the enfeoffment of Weii [678? B.C.], / Duke Huan questioned Guan Zhong, "What should I do?"

Guan Zhong replied, "You should strengthen the government within the country and encourage the people so that you can gain the trust of the feudal lords."

91.2   The prince agreed and thereupon lightened the taxes, / relaxed the exactions at the customs stations and markets, and created regulations governing levies and salaries. When he had finished this, Guan Zhong made a further request: "You should inquire after the sick,[115] and I would like to reward rather than punish. [If we can do this for] five years, the feudal lords can be made to support us." /

91.3   "Agreed," said the duke.

When he had put this into practice, Guan Zhong made a further request: "In the rites [involved in our relationships] with the feudal lords, let Qi present leopard skins when sending out [emissaries] and let the

91.4 lesser lords [merely] present deer / skins in return. Let Qi present horses when sending out [emissaries] and let the lesser lords present dogs in return."

Duke Huan agreed and carried it out. /

11a   Guan Zhong made a further request that rewards be given to [men] within the state [of Qi] as well as to the feudal lords [abroad].

91.5   "Agreed," said the duke, and carried it out.

Guan Zhong then gave rewards to [men] within the state [of Qi], while the duke gave them to the feudal lords [abroad]. He used valuable presents to congratulate those princes among the feudal lords who

91.6 excelled in carrying out their affairs. / [Guan Zhong] used[116] [presents of] clothing to congratulate those men from ranked officials on down who excelled [in their duties]. He presented seals to all ministers of the feudal lords who excelled in warning their princes, in order to show trust in their advice. /

91.7   When the duke had done this, he once more asked Guan Zhong, "What should I do?"

---

[114] Since the commonly given ratio is ten armored troops to one chariot (see n. 87, above), there appears to be a discrepancy here, but we do not know whether the figure 300 should read 500 or the figure 5,000 should read 3,000.

[115] According to *Guanzi*, XVIII, 54, inquiring after the sick 問病 was one of the nine acts of kindness to be performed within the first forty days of entering a country; however this does not seem to fit the context here. Yu Yue would emend 問 to 國. Thus the sentence would read: "Since the country is distressed, I would like to reward rather than punish."

[116] Following Xu, who would insert 以 after 者 to make this passage balance with the preceding one.

Guan Zhong replied, "Xi Peng is wise and quick-witted in argument.
You can order him to manage [relations with] states to the east.[117] / Bin
Xuwu is strong and good. You can order[118] him to manage [relations
with] lands to the west. The teachings of Weii [stress] opportunism[119]
and profit seeking. Gongzi / Kaifang[120] is a man who is shrewd and glib
of tongue. He cannot persevere but takes pleasure in starting things.
You should [send him to] travel in Weii. / The teachings of Lu [stress]
appreciation of the arts[121] and compliance with the rites. Jiyou[122] is a
man who is respectful and pure in heart, well versed in / the rites,[123] and
has considerable [talent] in matters involving petty details.[124] You
should [send him to] travel / in Lu. The teachings of Chu[125] are artful
and profit seeking. They are no good at anything of major significance
but all right in matters involving petty detail.[126] Meng Sun[127] is well
versed in the various teachings and is articulate[128] and clever in his

[117] These "states to the east" probably refer to those small feudal principalities such as
Lai 萊, which were controlled by Qi. See VIII, 20/16a12–16b1 (1:109.1–2), and nn. 168
and 169.

[118] Emending 以 to 令 to accord with the above passage [Yasui, Ding, and Guo
Moruo].

[119] Reading 危 as 恑 [Ding and Xu].

[120] 開方; a royal son of the state of Weii who left his own country to take service in Qi.
On the death of Duke Huan's successor, Xiao 孝, in 633 B.C., Kaifang rebelled against the
legitimate heir and helped raise Xiao's younger brother to the throne as Duke Zhao 昭.

[121] In its original meaning of "near" the character 邇 is unintelligible. I have followed
Yu Xingwu and Xu, who cite several examples where it is read similar to 藝, "arts."

[122] 季友; a son of Duke Huan (722–694 B.C.) of Lu. However, there is no record of this
man ever serving Duke Huan of Qi, though he made several trips to that country during
the years 657–647. The Xiao kuang, VIII, 20/13a3 (1:106.2), and 18a8 (1:110.10), when
presenting a similar list of men who served Duke Huan, gives two other names for what
appears to be this same man. The first passage mentions a Jilao 季勞, while the second
mentions Gongzi Ju 舉. Xu believes that the text here should also read Jilao. He adds that
Ju was probably the man's personal name while Jilao was his adult name. In this case the
man mentioned here would be a different person from the Jiyou of Lu.

[123] Emending 糧 to 禮 to accord with the Xiao kuang passage, VIII, 20/18a8 (1:110.10)
[Liu Ji and Sun Xingyan].

[124] The meaning of 小信 here and in the passage 11b2–3 (91.11–12) below is not clear.
Unfortunately, the commentators have remained silent on the matter and my interpretation is somewhat doubtful.

[125] 楚; the major state of south-central China, covering a large area in the north across
southern Shaanxi and Henan into western Anhui and in the south across eastern Sichuan,
northern Hunan, and western Jiangxi.

[126] In describing the attributes of the other countries, only one sentence was used. Here
there are two. Since this destroys the balance of composition, Zhang Wenhu believes this
second sentence is an interpolation taken from the following passage and should be
deleted.

[127] 蒙孫; the Xiao kuang, VIII, 20/13a3 (1:106.2) and 18a10 (1:110.11), when listing
these men, writes Cao Sun Xiu 曹孫宿 for Meng Sun. Sun Xingyan, Wang Niansun,
Zhang Binglin, and Guo Moruo all say Meng is a mistake for Cao.

[128] The Ancient edition for 文 writes 又. Zhang Peilun believes that 文 is an interpolation taken from the previous phrase 巧文 and should be deleted.

91.12   speech. He is no good at / anything of major significance but is all right in tying together matters involving petty detail. You [should send him to] travel in Chu. When the lesser lords have rendered service to us and the greater ones have joined us, then for the first time you will be able to

91.13   spread / your political control among them."

"Agreed," said the duke. He then sent the Gongzi Kaifang to travel in Weii, Jiyou to Lu, and Meng Sun to Chu.

In the fifth year [681 B.C.],[129] the feudal lords joined [Qi]. When the Di people launched an attack, Duke Huan issued a proclamation to the

91.14   feudal lords: / "I request help [to repulse] this attack. If the lords agree, the greater ones [should send] 200 chariots and 2,000 troops, the lesser

92.1   ones [should send] 100 chariots / and 1,000 troops."

The feudal lords all agreed. Qi, with 1,000 chariots and [10,000][130] troops as the vanguard,[131] challenged [the enemy] at Yuanling,[132] while [the feudal lords][133] fought in support. Consequently they defeated the Di. The captured chariots, armor, and goods were then given to the

92.2   lesser lords. Those nearest to the Di of the greater lords / divided up [the enemy's] outlying districts[134] but did not suppress their states completely.

None of the lords of the northern regions[135] had come, so Duke

92.3   Huan / met the lords of the southern regions at Shaoling.[136]
12a

He said, "The Di are unprincipled and have violated the orders of the son of Heaven by attacking small countries. For the sake of the son of

92.4   Heaven and to show respect for the mandate of Heaven, I ordered / [the feudal lords] to help [repulse] the attack. But none of the lords of the northern regions came. Thus, they did not obey the orders of the son of Heaven above and were not polite to the feudal lords below. I request that we punish the lords of the northern regions."

---

[129] Here the chronology again appears confused. The events that follow probably took place in 663 or 662 B.C. See n. 141, below.

[130] This passage is obviously corrupt, since the number of Qi's troops is missing. I have followed Igai and Yu Yue, who would insert 萬人. This phrase would then end with the word "troops."

[131] The Yang edition for 先 mistakenly writes 可.

[132] See n. 103, above.

[133] Yu Yue believes these words 諸侯 have been deleted from the text.

[134] Xian 縣. The *xian* as an administrative unit seems to have originated in Qin in 688 and 687 B.C., when four of them were established out of newly conquered territories. It is doubtful that the term was used in the area of Qi, however, until much later. See Bodde, *China's First Unifier*, pp. 238 ff.

[135] *Zhou* 州. According to tradition, Yu 禹 had divided China into nine regions. "Northern" regions probably refer to non-Chinese lords and those outside the alliance.

[136] 召陵; situated thirty-five *li* east of present-day Yancheng 郾城 Xian in east-central Henan.

92.5　　The feudal lords agreed. / Duke Huan then attacked Lingzhi[137] in the north and conquered Mount Fu.[138] He decapitated [the lord of] Guzhu[139] and subjugated[140] the Mountain Rong.[141]

　　Turning to Guan Zhong he asked, "What should I do from now on?"

92.6　　Guan Zhong replied, "You / should teach the feudal lords to collect provisions for the people and help those among the feudal lords who do not have sufficient arms by sending them [troops]. In this way, you can begin to extend your political control over them."

92.7　　Duke Huan / then issued a proclamation to the feudal lords that they must have provisions sufficient for three years and then[142] use any surplus to strengthen their arms. If their arms were not sufficient to conduct a military operation, they should inform Qi and Qi would help them by sending [troops]. /

92.8　　When he had done this, the duke again asked Guan Zhong, "What should I do?"

　　"You should harmonize [relations between] princes and ministers, fathers and sons," Guan Zhong replied. / "Then you will be able to extend your political control over them."

92.9
92b

　　"What is the way to harmonize [relations between them]?" asked the duke.

　　"The feudal lords should not on their own authority set up their concubines as legal wives or kill their great ministers," came the answer.

2.10　　"They should not on their own authority grant salaries to those who have not labored for their country / or [permit] members of the gentry and commoners on their own authority to abandon their wives. They should not manipulate boundary embankments, hoard grain, or prohibit the gathering of natural resources. Only after this has

---

[137]令支: a small state belonging to the Mountain Rong 山戎, situated west of present-day Qianan 遷安 Xian in northeast Hebei.

[138]This Mount Fu 鳧之山 is difficult to identify. There is a Mount Fu 鳧山 situated fifty *li* southwest of Zou 鄒 Xian in southwest Shandong. This, however, is far from the area of operation in this particular campaign, which was centered in northeast Hebei.

[139]孤竹; a small state situated in the vicinity of present-day Lulong 盧龍 Xian in northeast Hebei.

[140]The Ancient edition for *yu* 遇 writes 過. I have followed Tao and Guo Moruo in emending *yu* to 過.

[141]山戎; one of the non-Sinified peoples who inhabited the northeastern part of China proper. This subjugation of the Mountain Rong probably refers to the expedition led by Duke Huan against them in 663 or 662 B.C. See the *Shi ji*, 32/7b2 (Chavannes, *Memoires historiques*, IV, p. 51).

[142]The Yin commentary would read 安 (here translated as "then") with the phrase above. Thus it would interpret the sentence: "Duke Huan then issued a proclamation to the feudal lords that they must have provisions sufficient for three years in order to be secure. They could [then] use any surplus to strengthen their arms."

been in effect for a full year should you punish [those who do not obey]." [143]

92.11

The duke then announced this to the feudal lords, and the lords agreed.

After [these instructions] had been received and in effect for a full year, the men of Wu[144] attacked Gu.[145] Even before Duke Huan's

92.12

proclamation / to the feudal lords had reached everyone, the troops of the lords all arrived to wait upon Duke Huan. Duke Huan, with 1,000 chariots, met the lords at the border, but before all the troops from the minor lords [in Qi] could arrive, the men of Wu fled, and the lords all desisted. /

92.13

When Duke Huan returned home, he asked Guan Zhong, "What should I do from now on?"

Guan Zhong answered, "[Now] you can extend your political control.

92.14

Let [the entire realm] know / that if in the next two years you do not hear of the royal heirs practicing filial piety, loving their younger brothers, or being respectful toward the venerable good men of their countries, they can be disciplined for their lack of any one of these three [virtues]. If during [the next] three years you do not hear about any good deeds

93.1

performed by ministers / who have participated in the affairs of state of

13a

their feudal lords, they can be punished. / If a great officer does not warn the prince of his mistakes or bring forward members of the gentry or

93.2

commoners who have performed good deeds, / he can be punished. If from civil functionaries you hear of [exceptional] worthiness, filialness, or respect for elders on the part of members of the gentry or commoners, [those practicing these virtues] should be rewarded."

---

[143] These injunctions are reminiscent of those imposed upon the feudal lords by Duke Huan in the covenant signed at Kuiqiu 葵丘 in 651 B.C. According to the *Mengzi*, VIB, 7/3, which preserves the most detailed summary of the covenant: "The first injunction stated, 'Kill the unfilial; do not alter the royal heir; do not make a concubine your legal wife.' The second stated, 'Honor the worthy and care for the talented in order to give distinction to the virtuous.' The third stated, 'Respect the aged; be kind to the young; do not be forgetful of guests and travelers.' The fourth stated, 'Do not make the official posts of members of the gentry hereditary; do not let official business be concentrated in the hands of one person; when selecting members of the aristocracy [for office] be certain to obtain [the right man]; do not kill a great official on your own authority.' The fifth stated, 'Do not manipulate boundary embankments; do not prevent the sale of grain; do not enfeoff anyone without reporting it [to the Zhou king]."

[144] 吳; a large state covering most of present-day Anhui and Jiangsu provinces.

[145] 穀; a town in Qi that Duke Huan had walled as a fief for Guan Zhong in 662 B.C. Zang Lihe's *Zhongguo gujin diming dazidian* locates it near present-day Donga 東阿 Xian in west-central Shandong. This would place Gu deep inside Qi and a considerable distance from the borders of Wu. The *Zuo zhuan* contains no reference to the attack.

Duke Huan accepted [this advice] and carried it out. None of the lords who were near [Qi] failed to make requests [for help] / in their affairs. [Duke Huan] convened six military and three civil conferences[146] and reigned for forty-two years.

When Duke Huan / had been on the throne for nineteen years [667 B.C.], he relaxed the exactions at the customs stations and markets to one part in fifty. Salaries were paid in grain, and taxes were collected according to the land cultivated. He collected the taxes once in every two years. / For good years [the rate was] three parts in ten, for ordinary years, two parts in ten, and for bad years, one part in ten.[147] During those years in which there was famine he did not tax at all, but [waited] until the famine abated and then levied taxes. /

Duke Huan commissioned Bao Shu to make a record of those among the various[148] ministers who had performed good deeds, Yanzi[149] to

[146] The *Shi ji*, 32/9a11–12, says "three military and six civil conferences." The *Guo yu*, 6/10a4, and *Xiao kuang*, VIII, 20/14b3–4 (1.107.6–7), agree with the figures given here. According to Wei Zhao 韋昭 in his commentary to the *Guo yu*, 6/10a5–6, the six military conferences included Beiheng 北杏 in 681 B.C., Zhuan 鄄 in 680, Zhuan again in 679, Cheng 檉 in 651 (should read 659), Xian 鹹 in 647, and Huai 淮 in 644. The civil conferences included Yanggu 陽穀 in 657, Shouzhi 首止 in 655, and Kuiqiu in 651. However, Li Dongfang in his *Chunqiu Zhanguo*, pp. 16–20, lists some twenty-four conferences and twenty-eight examples of military activity in which Qi participated under Duke Huan, as recorded in the *Zuo zhuan*. The question then arises as to the origin of the figures six and three. The *Shi ji*, *Guo yu*, and *Xiao kuang* passages cited above all add the line 九合諸侯; 一匡天下, "Nine times he assembled the feudal lords, thereby bringing unity and order to the entire realm." These two phrases are also found in the *Lun yu*. The latter is contained in XIV, 18/2, the former in XIV, 17/2. Both Legge (*Confucian Analects*, p. 282) and Waley (*The Analects of Confucius*, p. 185) in their translations follow Zhu Xi 朱熹 (1130–1200), who interprets *jiu he* 九合 as a compound meaning "to assemble" (九 = 鳩 = 聚). Thus they interpret the *Lun yu* passage to read: "It was due to Guan Zhong that Duke Huan was able to assemble the feudal lords without resort to the use of his war chariots." In my opinion, *jiu he* should not be treated as a compound. As used by Confucius here, *jiu* is probably a symbolic number, simply indicating that there were a number of such assemblies. When the author of the *Guo yu*, however, compiled his text on the basis of the two *Lun yu* passages, XIV, 17, and XIV, 18, he took the meaning of *jiu* literally as "nine," and amplified it with the statement about the six military and three civil conferences. The *Xiao kuang*, *Da kuang*, and *Shi ji* then followed the *Guo yu*.

[147] The exact meaning of this passage in the text is not clear. I have interpreted it to mean that Duke Huan collected the taxes once every two years on the basis of the yield during that period. Yu Yue would interpret the passage to read: "He fixed the tax once every two years. For the first two-year period [the rate was] three parts in ten; for the second two-year period, it was two parts in ten; and for the third two-year period, it was one part in ten." Thus Yu believes the tax rate was calculated on a sliding scale extending over a six-year cycle.

[148] Emending 君 to 羣 [Wang Yinzhi and Xu].

[149] 晏子; The *Xiao kuang* chapter VIII, 20/13a4 (1:106.2), mentions a Yan Shang 匽尚.

make one of [gentlemen] not employed in office and persons engaged in agriculture who had performed good deeds, and Gaozi[150] / to make one of those among the artisans and merchants who had performed good deeds. Guozi[151] became chief justice.[152] Xi Peng managed [relations with] states to the east. / Bin Xuwu managed [relations with] lands to the west. Fu Zheng[153] became minister of housing.[154] All those who held office lived near the palace.[155] / Those not employed in office but engaged in agriculture lived near the [outer] gates [of the capital]. Artisans and traders lived near the market.

Every thirty *li* he set up a post house with supplies [for travelers] and placed an officer in charge of it. / Whenever a feudal lord wished [to send an emissary] to communicate [with Qi], a civil functionary would accompany the traveler [on his way] and order one man to haul [the traveler's baggage] in a cart. / If they stopped overnight, he would have men take care of the horses and feed [the traveler]with[156] the supplies [of the post house. In making up the bill] the guest and the officer [in charge of the post house] would divide a tally, [each taking half]. Upon arrival in the capital, each would submit[157] [his half of] the tally. / If [the officer] had been improper in expending [more or less than] the amount prescribed by custom,[158] it was considered a crime.

Whenever a commoner wished to communicate [with the court], a district civil functionary[159] / could be imprisoned for withholding the

---

[150] 高子; also known as Gao Xi 高傒 or Gao Jingzhong 高敬仲, a member of one of the two families, Gao 高 and Guo 國, which hereditarily held the highest official positions in Qi. The heads of these two families were known as the two watchmen 二守 of the Zhou king and were supposed to make periodic visits to the Zhou court to receive his orders. See the *Zuo zhuan*, Xi, 12 (Legge, *Ch'un Ts'eu*, V, 12/3), and Thatcher, *Structural Comparison*, p. 148. Gaozi was one of the earliest supporters of Duke Huan. See n. 53, above.

[151] 國子; the head of the Guo family, which, along with the Gao family, hereditarily held the most important political positions in Qi. See n. 150, above.

[152] *Li* 李; this is a rather curious term. It appears several times in the *Guanzi* (see, for example, VI, 16/9b2 (1:77.11), and XIV, 41/10b7 (2:82.13), and in the *Shi ji*, 27/5a1 (Chavannes, *Mémoires historiques*, III, p. 345). The *Shuowen tongxun dingsheng* says that it is a phonetic borrowing of *li* 理, "to control" or "to manage," and is actually the same as *li* 吏, an administrative functionary. The above translation is in accordance with the Yin commentary.

[153] 弗鄭; this name is probably corrupt. It is not cited elsewhere, and Fu seldom appears as the initial character in a name except as a corruption of *bi* 費 or *bi* 濞.

[154] *Zhai* 宅; I have not been able to find a clear reference to this office elsewhere. It may have been concerned with levying the taxes on dwellings.

[155] The Yang edition for 宮 mistakenly writes 公.

[156] Following the Ancient, Zhu, and Liu editions, which write 以 for 其.

[157] Emending 八 to 入 [Ding, Tao, and Guo Moruo].

[158] Emending 義 to 儀 [Ding and Guo Moruo].

[159] *Xiang li* 鄉吏.

communication for seven days. If a member of the gentry[160] wished to communicate [with the court], a civil functionary could be imprisoned for withholding the communication for five days. If the son of a nobleman wished to communicate [with the court], / a civil functionary could be imprisoned for withholding the communication for two days. The civil functionaries of the outer districts[161] always brought forward those among the feudal lords and members of the gentry who had performed good deeds. The extent of their ability was observed / and they were rewarded accordingly. If the reward was excessive, it was still not a crime.

[Duke Huan] ordered Bao / Shu to bring forth the great officers who had, in exhorting the country, achieved success[162] without [causing] later regrets. These were placed first. Those who had a well-ordered administration,[163] / who made fields out of wastelands and further had few[164] uprisings and were not arrogant in handling complaints, were placed next. / Those who, in exhorting the country, had achieved success but caused later regrets, who had a well-ordered administration yet were not able to make fields out of waste lands, and further had numerous uprisings and were arrogant in handling complaints, were placed last.[165] /

He ordered Yanzi to bring forth the sons of noblemen. Those who had demonstrated three[166] of the following—away from home were not profligate,[167] within the home were not extravagant, and with respect to friends maintained [differing forms of behavior] toward juniors and seniors—were placed first. / Those who had demonstrated two of these were placed next, and those who had demonstrated only one were placed last.

Among members of the gentry, those who had demonstrated three of the following—within the home were content, [outside the home] were respectful toward the aged and the honored, and did not neglect propriety in relations with others—were placed first. / Those who had

---

[160] The character 出 is clearly a corruption of 士 [Liu Ji and Wang Yinzhi].

[161] *Xian li* 縣吏.

[162] The meaning of 之 here is similar to 其 [Guo Moruo].

[163] Deleting 爲次 as an interpolation from the following passage [Wang Yinzhi].

[164] Inverting the characters 多不 [Liu Shipei].

[165] This entire passage is extremely corrupt. The four characters 行此三者 are obviously out of place here. I have followed Sun Shucheng and Xu, who would place them before the three characters 爲上舉 in the following passage, 14a9 (94.4).

[166] See n. 165, above.

[167] 仕, "to be employed in office," does not fit the context of this passage. I have followed Guo Moruo in emending it to 狂.

309

demonstrated two of these were placed next. Those who had demonstrated only one were placed last.

Among persons engaged in agriculture, those who had demonstrated three of the following—exerted themselves in their farming, fulfilled their obligations toward their fathers and elder brothers, and were extremely industrious in performing their duties—/ were placed first. Those who had demonstrated two of these were placed next. Those who had demonstrated only one were placed last.

He ordered Gaozi to bring forth the artisans and traders. Those who had demonstrated three of the following—fulfilled their obligations toward their fathers and elder brothers, served their elders and supported the aged, and respectfully carried out [their duties toward the ruler]—were placed first. / Those who had demonstrated two of these were placed next. Those who had demonstrated only one were placed last.

He ordered Guozi to decide criminal cases according to the actual circumstances. After the three great officers [Bao Shu, Yanzi, and Gaozi] had made their selections, [Duke Huan] had the outer districts send [the selectees to the capital]. Guan / Zhong brought them forward and recorded their comments. Then he presented them to the duke. At the end of the year, the duke elevated them. /

Guan Zhong told Bao Shu, "Those who have been guilty of the following three—in exhorting the country have not achieved success but caused later regrets, have not had a well-ordered administration and were unable to make fields out of wastelands, and furthermore had many uprisings and were arrogant in handling complaints—have committed / a crime and should not be pardoned."

He told Yanzi, "Among the sons of noblemen, those who have been guilty of the following three—have been extravagant at home, have fraternized with their inferiors, and have been gluttonous in their drinking and eating—have committed a crime and should not be pardoned. Among members of the gentry, / those who have been guilty of the following three—have been irregular in their comings and goings, have not respected the aged, but have concentrated instead on enriching [themselves]—have committed a crime and should not be pardoned. Among persons engaged in agriculture, those who have been guilty of the following three—in their comings and goings have not fulfilled their obligations toward their fathers and elder brothers, have exerted themselves in [pursuits] other than farming, and have not been industrious in performing their duties—have / committed a crime and should not be pardoned."

310

He told Gaozi,[168] "Among the artisans and traders, those who have been guilty of the following three—in their comings and goings have not fulfilled their obligations toward their fathers and elder brothers, have not respectfully carried out [their duties toward their ruler], and have abandoned the aged and endangered good order—have committed a crime and should not be pardoned."

Whenever there was someone / who was without fault toward his father and elder brothers and was praised in his subdistrict (*zhou* 州) or village (*li* 里), the civil functionaries were to bring him forward so the duke could employ him. Whenever there was someone who did well but had not been rewarded or who had faults but had not been punished, the civil functionaries [who were responsible] were not to be promoted but dismissed.[169] / Whenever there was someone who was without faults toward his father and elder brothers and yet had received no praise in his subdistrict or village, the civil functionaries were to bring him forward so that the ruler could employ him. If he did well, [the civil functionaries who brought him forward] were to be rewarded by their superiors; if he did not, these functionaries were to be punished. /

The duke stated to Guozi, "In all cases involving principles of righteousness between the honored and the lowly, inside [the family] the father is given complete [respect], outside [the family] the teacher is given complete [respect], / on high the prince is given complete [respect]. Whenever [any one of] these three is confronted by a rebel, he who will not die [for them] or who fails to recognize the rebel should not be pardoned. / When deciding criminal cases, the circumstances should be balanced against principles of righteousness, and principles of righteousness should be balanced against the salary status [of the person involved]. The status[170] / may be such that [the person involved] need not be held under restraint.[171] But if a [serious] crime,[172] / is involved, there can be no pardon."

[168] Emending Guozi to Gaozi to accord with the corresponding passage above [He Ruzhang and Tao].

[169] The two characters *lian yi* 廉意 are obviously corrupt. The sense of the passage demands some words implying punishment. I have followed Guo Moruo, who suggests that *lian yi* is a mistake for 廢棄.

[170] This final passage is extremely corrupt and ends very abruptly, indicating that the text is incomplete. The original ending was probably lost through mutilation or decay of the end of the bundle of slips or scroll. In order to derive any sense out of the passage at all, I have generally followed the interpretation of Guo Moruo, here deleting 易 above 祿 as an interpolation from the line above.

[171] Reading 斂 as 檢 [Guo Moruo].

[172] Emending 可 to 罪 as an interpolation taken from the above phrase [Wang Niansun].

311

Zhong Kuang
中匡

Introductory Comments

For the meaning of the title, *Zhong kuang*, see the discussion in the Introductory Comments to chapter VII, 18. This short chapter consists of three anecdotes concerning the relationship between Duke Huan and Guan Zhong, designed to convey the writer's Confucian political philosophy through imagined conversations between the two men. There are several other chapters in the *Guanzi* very similar to this in form, style, and content, but this one stands out from the others in that for some reason it was placed between the *Da kuang* and *Xiao kuang*, the major chapters in the *Guanzi* dealing with the exploits of Guan Zhong and Duke Huan.

Luo Genze (*Guanzi*, p. 63) says that it was probably written during the Warring States Period; I suspect it is quite late, perhaps even early Han. One passage, 2a1–3 (96.4–5), appears to reflect a statement in the *Hanfeizi*, XVII, 44/10a6–6, that the ancient sage rulers, including Shun 舜 and Yu 禹, had all risen to power by killing their former lords. Such a statement stands in sharp contrast to the generally accepted Confucian idealization of these men and would seem to be of late Legalist origin, Hanfeizi himself having died in 233 B.C. Furthermore, the chapter's general style and use of language support a late dating, as does its anecdotal form, which is very similar to that employed in such Han texts as the *Xin shu* of Jia Yi 賈誼 and *Shuo yuan* of Liu Xiang 劉向.

Translation

1:95.9
1a7

Guan Zhong took account of the national expenditures [and found] that two-thirds of them went for guests while only one-third went to the state. Becoming concerned, he reported the matter, but the duke said,

95.10

"My dear friend, how can you [talk] like this?/If guests from our neighboring states on entering [the country] are pleased and full of praise when they leave, we will have a glorious reputation throughout the entire realm. But if they are not pleased on entering/and do not

95.11

praise us when leaving, we will have a bad reputation throughout the entire realm. Land can be made to produce grain, trees can be made to produce goods. When the grain has been consumed, more can be grown. When goods have been dispersed, more can be gathered. For the prince, / it is his good name that counts. What does it matter about the money?"

"This is really brilliant of you," said Guan Zhong.

The duke asked, "Now that the people are prepared for military affairs, is it all right [to punish those large states that do not adhere to the proper way]?" [1]

"That won't do," was the reply. "Our arms / are not yet sufficient. I request that you lighten punishments in order to increase our [supply of] arms."

Thereafter, those whose crimes deserved the death penalty were not killed and those whose crimes deserved corporal penalties were not punished. They were made to redeem themselves by [supplying] arms instead. [2] Those whose crimes deserved the death penalty used rhinoceros-hide armor / and one halberd. Those whose crimes [3] deserved corporal penalties used a shield and one halberd. Those whose mistakes deserved punishments used one *jun* [4] of metal. Those who brought cases to court without due consideration used a bundle of arrows as a guarantee. [5] /

The duke said, "Now that our arms are sufficient, I desire to punish those large countries that do not adhere to the proper way. Will that be all right?"

The reply was, "Only after demonstrating your love for people within

[1] As both Zhang Peilun and Tao have pointed out there is something missing from the line 民辦軍事矣, 則可乎 since it does not fit the context of what follows. I have followed Tao by inserting the words 吾欲誅大國之不道者 before 則可乎, in accordance with the following passage 1b7–8 (96.1). The story that begins here seems to have been taken from the *Guo yu*, 6,/8a12 ff. See also the *Xiao kuang* chapter, VIII, 20/12b3 ff. (1 : 105.10 ff).

[2] According to the *Huainanzi*, 13/18b1–3 (Morgan, *Tao, the Great Luminant*, p. 172): "Duke Huan of Qi wished to launch a military expedition, but was short of arms. [Therefore] he ordered those with serious crimes to produce rhinoceros-hide armor and one halberd. Those with lighter crimes redeemed them with metal, according to the gravity of the offense. Those who entered into litigations but were not successful produced a bundle of arrows."

[3] Emending 罰 to 罪 [Wang Yinzhi].

[4] Emending 軍 to 鈞 [Wang Yinzhi]. The *Xiao kuang* chapter, VIII, 20/12b6 (1 : 105.11), states: 小罪人以金鈞, "Those with minor crimes should turn in one *jun* of metal." According to Swann (*Food and Money*, p. 364) a Han *jun* equaled 30 catties or 16 pounds, 2.2 ounces avoir.

[5] According to the *Zhou li*, 34/9b7 (Biot, *Tcheou-li*, II, pp. 310–311): "[The *da sikou* 大司寇], on the arrival of the two litigants in a civil case, prohibits discussion of the case until they have [each] turned in a bundle of arrows to the court. Then he will hear it."

96.2 your four borders [who do good] should / you express your hatred toward those without who do evil. Only after making the homes of your chief ministers and great officials safe, should you threaten enemy[6]

96.3 states. / Only after granting territory to smaller states, should you punish large states that do not adhere to the proper way. Only after elevating those who are worthy and of good character should you get rid of people who are dilatory in obeying the law and are of low character. It

96.4 was for this reason / that the former kings were certain to establish [a reputation for doing good] before[7] getting rid of [what they considered

2a bad]. / They were certain to provide people with benefits before doing any harm."

Duke Huan said, "The three kings of ancient times killed their own lords.[8] Now, however, when speaking about benevolence and

96.5 righteousness / we take them as models.[9] I do not understand the reason for this."

"In ancient times," came the reply, "Yu brought peace and good government to the entire realm, but when it came down to Jie, he threw it into disorder. Tang drove out Jie in order to secure the achievements of

96.6 Yu. Tang / brought peace and good government to the entire realm, but when it came down to Zhou, he threw it into disorder. King Wu attacked Zhou in order to secure the achievements of Tang. Moreover, from ancient times right down to the present, there has been no change in the good attacking evil.[10] Why should you have any doubts about it?" /

96.7 The duke again asked, "When states were lost in ancient times, how had [their rulers] failed?"

"They counted on gaining territory and precious things without considering how they might lose [the support of] the feudal lords. They counted on gaining wealth and stores of grain without considering how they might lose [the support of] the hundred surnames. They counted on

96.8 having the allegiance [of the people] / without considering how they

---

[6] Reading 救 as 仇 [Wang Yinzhi]. The *Xiao wen* chapter, XVI, 51/11b4 (2:109.2), in a similar passage writes: 可以危鄰之敵國, "Can you threaten neighboring countries."

[7] Deleting 必 after 後 both here and in the following sentence [Wang Yinzhi]. The similar passage in the *Xiao wen* chapter, XVI, 51/11b6–8 (2:109.2–3), lacks this 必.

[8] The three kings of ancient times referred to here are the founders of the Xia, Shang, and Zhou dynasties: Yu 禹, Tang 湯, and Wu 武.

[9] According to the *Hanfeizi*, XVII, 44/10a6–7 (Liao, *Han Fei Tzu*, II, p. 224): "Shun 舜 menaced Yao 堯, Yu menaced Shun, Tang banished Jie 桀, King Wu 武士 attacked Zhou 紂. These four kings were ministers who killed their own lords, yet the world has praised them."

[10] Xu would emend 伐 to 代, "replacing."

might be abandoned by them. Of these three things, one is sufficient to cause [one's territory] to be stripped away. Having all three leads to ruin. Those who in ancient times brought about the destruction of their states and the collapse of their altars of Land and Grain did not do it on purpose. It must have been that because of their little pleasures / they failed to realize they were falling upon evil ways."

Duke Huan said to Guan Zhong, "I wish to present a feast in your honor,[11] Zhongfu."[12] The duke prepared a guest house[13] for Zhongfu in order to offer him wine / and dug a new well, covering it over with sticks [to keep it clean].[14] After fasting for ten days, / he summoned Guan Zhong. When Guan Zhong arrived, the duke himself held up a *jue* 爵 goblet while his wife held a *zun* 尊 wine jar. / When they had finished drinking three rounds, Guan Zhong ran out [of the room].[15]

The duke angrily exclaimed, "I have fasted for ten days so that I might offer wine to Zhongfu. I feel I have done everything I could, but he left without even telling me. What is the meaning of this?" /

Bao Shu and Xi Peng[16] ran out and caught up with Guan Zhong on the road, saying, "The duke is angry."

Guan Zhong returned and, entering the hall, stood with his back to the door screen, but the duke refused to speak to him. Entering a little further, he stood in the center of the court, / but still the duke refused to speak. He then entered a little further and approached the hall. The duke said, "I fasted for ten days that I might offer you wine, Zhongfu, and consider myself free of any offense. But you left without telling me. I still do not understand / the meaning of this."

"I have heard," was the reply, "that those who immerse themselves in pleasure will bathe in sorrow. Those who are gluttonous in taste will be stingy in their conduct. Those who are dilatory in court will be lax in their government. Those who harm the state / will endanger the altars of Land and Grain. Hence I dared leave."

The duke at once descended from the hall saying, "It is not that I dare

---

[11] Following the Ancient, Liu, and Zhu editions, which have 其桓 after 仲父 [Guo Moruo].

[12] 仲父; one of Guan Zhong's several appellations. See VII, 18, n. 22.

[13] Deleting 與, in accordance with the Ancient and Zhu editions, and emending 管 to 官 = 館 [Guo Moruo].

[14] The well served to preserve the food and wine by keeping it cool and protecting it from flies.

[15] According to the *Zuo zhuan*, Xuan, 3 (Legge, *Ch'un Ts'eu*, VII, 2/4): "It is contrary to the rules of propriety for a minister, when waiting on his prince at a feast, to go beyond three goblets (*jue* 爵)."

[16] 鮑叔 and 隰朋; for these two men see VII, 18, and VIII, 20, passim.

presume I did all that I should. But, Zhongfu, you are getting old, and
97.2   even I am growing weak with age. It is only that I wished / to make you
feel at ease for a while."

"I have heard," came the reply, "that those who are strong should not
3a   be given to idleness, and those who are old / should not neglect their
duties. If you adhere to the way of Heaven, you are certain to be one who
97.3   will come to a good end. When the three kings failed / in this, it was not a
sudden thing of one day.[17] Why then should you neglect your duties?"

Guan Zhong walked away and the prince, in accordance with the
proper ceremony for a guest, bowed twice when seeing him off.

97.4   When Guan / Zhong came to court on the following day, the duke
said, "I wish to hear how the prince of a state establishes his credibility."

The reply was, "If his people love him and his neighboring countries
are on good terms with him, the world will trust him. This is what is
meant by the ruler of a country having credibility." /

97.5   "Good!" said the duke. "May I ask how I should begin so I may be
trusted?"

"The first stage lies in managing the self, the next in managing the
state, and the final one in managing the realm."

"May I ask about managing the self?"

"Guide your physical nature in order to extend[18] your years, your
97.6   mind, and your virtue. / Such is managing the self."

The duke said, "May I ask about managing the state?"

"Internally[19] elevate worthy individuals," came the reply, "and show
compassionate love for the hundred surnames. Externally restore those
countries that have been lost and provide successors for those families
that have been cut off without posterity. Raise up all the orphans of
97.7   [those officials who died for you]. / Lessen taxes and lighten punishments. Such is managing the state."[20]

["May[21] I ask about managing the realm?" said the duke.

The reply was], "Laws should be executed without cruelty.
Punishments should be scrupulously correct with no pardons. Officers

---

[17] The reference here is probably to Shun, Jie, and Zhou. See n. 9, above.

[18] Reading 長 as 長養 [Yu Xingwu and Guo Moruo].

[19] The character 遠, "in distant places," does not fit the context here. I have followed
Igai and Guo Songdao, who argue that the logical word here would be 内 in contrast to the
外, "externally," of the following sentence. Zhang Peilun would emend it to 選 to make
the sentence read: "Select and elevate worthy individuals . . ."

[20] Deleting 之大禮, since the presence of this phrase violates the pattern set by the
context above and below [Zhang Peilun]. The original rendering would have read: "Such
are the great principles of conduct for managing the state."

[21] The characters, 公曰請問爲天下, 對曰, have clearly been omitted here [Zhang
Peilun].

should be liberal and not harsh. Laws and procedures should not ignore[22] those[23] who are friendless and childless,[24] troubled and depressed. / Those who wish to leave [the country] or travel around should not be held back,[25] so that the people may travel freely.[26] / Such is managing the realm."

97.8

97.9
3b

[22] Reading 亡 as 忘 [Xu].
[23] Emending 皆 to 者 [Guo Moruo].
[24] Emending 苑濁 to 鰥獨 [Zhang Peilun and Guo Moruo].
[25] Reading 來 as 勑 [Yu Xingwu].
[26] Reading 世 as 泄 [Yu Yue and Guo Moruo].

Xiao Kuang

小匡

Introductory Comments

The meaning of the title, *Xiao kuang*, has been discussed in the Introductory Comments to the *Da kuang* (VII, 18). These two chapters, which constitute the longest and most detailed accounts of the political careers of Guan Zhong and Duke Huan, are similar in that both chapters relate the same basic story and are written in the form of a historical romance designed to propagandize the importance of rulers listening to their ministers. However, there are some major differences that indicate the two works are of different origins. As indicated in the Introductory Comments to VII, 18, the first part of the *Da kuang* (2b3–4a2; 83.13–85.3) is clearly based on the *Zuo zhuan*, and the material covered in it is not included in the *Xiao kuang*. The second part, while much closer to the *Xiao kuang* in terms of general coverage, also differs too much in detail to have been based on a common textual source. The *Xiao kuang* also goes into much more detail concerning the internal administration of Qi and Duke Huan's relations with the feudal lords.

The *Xiao kuang* is closely connected with the *Qi yu* 齊語 [Discourses of Qi], chapter 6 of the *Guo yu*. The two works parallel each other in presenting the same basic story, often in identically the same language, and are generally consistent in their use of particles, with one major exception that was pointed out to me in a letter from a young Canadian scholar, Gary Arbuckle. The *Qi yu* consistently uses the expression *ruo he* 若何, "what about it," where the *Xiao kuang* uses *nai he* 奈何. However, there are even more obvious differences. The *Xiao kuang* elaborates on numerous points covered only in a rather terse way by the *Qi yu* and has added to the text paralleling the *Qi yu* a brief coda (17a12–19a1; 110.14–111.5), which may or may not have been part of the original text. The phrasing frequently differs, and there are many discrepancies in the use of individual characters. Since these differences are too numerous to be dealt with except in a separate study, I have only mentioned them in the notes when they are pertinent to understanding the *Xiao kuang*.

The overall differences are so great that in spite of the obvious connection between the two texts, there can be no question about their coming from different authors. The only question is which came first. It is tempting to believe that the *Qi yu* deserves this honor since it is more sparse in composition than the *Xiao kuang* and is a better-known text. Most of the commentators assume this to be the case, and, in general, I would agree. This would place the composition of the *Xiao kuang* sometime between about 300 B.C., the generally accepted date for the *Guo yu*, and the first century B.C. However, it is possible that both date from about the same period (roughly 300 B.C.) and were based on a common source, rather than the *Xiao kuang* being taken directly from the *Qi yu*. This would account for some of their discrepancies in names and other details.

The policies of Guan Zhong and Duke Huan as described in the *Xiao kuang* and *Qi yu* have not been without some modern significance. Several years ago I received a letter from a Mr. Eugene W. Levich, who was then engaged in research on the 1930s Guangxi Clique of Bai Chongxi 白崇禧 and Li Zongren 李宗仁. In the letter Mr. Levich documents Bai's fascination with Guan Zhong's reforms and the organizational structure of Qi as described in this chapter and in the *Qi yu*. He went on to outline the politico-military policies and militia that were developed in Guangxi along these lines and states in part:

> Beginning in 1931, the Kwangsi Clique carried out what I believe were unique changes at that time in the structure and practice of local government. According to Pai Ch'ung-hsi, these changes were based upon the civil and military organization of the state of Ch'i during the Ch'un Ch'iu period . . . .
>
> By the start of the anti-Japanese War in 1937, Kwangsi had about a million trained militiamen . . . . The Fifth Route Army (organized from the Kwangsi militia) gave a good account of itself in the early stages of the war, particularly at Shanghai, and at Li Tsung-jen's startling victory at Taierhchuang.

Translation

When Duke Huan [685–643 B.C.] returned to Qi from Ju,[1] he ordered Bao Shuya[2] to become prime minister, but Bao Shu excused himself saying, "I would merely be an ordinary minister for you. Your kindness to me and your not letting me freeze or starve—all this / you have done for me. However, if you were to insist that I govern the state, I couldn't

[1] 莒: see VII, 18, n. 47.
[2] 鮑叔牙 or Bao Shu 鮑叔: oldest and closest associate of Guan Zhong 管仲 (Guan Yiwu 管夷吾). See VII, 18, n. 15.

do it. That is only for Guan Yiwu. There are five ways in which I am not as good as Guan Yiwu: in being compassionate and loving the people, / in governing the state and not losing control, in being loyal and trustworthy so bonds may be formed with the feudal lords,[3] in regulating propriety and righteous conduct to serve as a model / for the four corners [of the realm], and in standing before the headquarters wearing full armor and beating the drum[4] in order to enhance the bravery of all the hundred surnames. Now Guan Zhong is the father and mother of the people, and if one wishes / to keep children in order one cannot get rid of their parents."

The duke said, "Guan Yiwu himself shot at me, hitting my belt buckle. I nearly died from it. Now how can I employ him after that?"

"He was prompted to do this for his prince," said Bao Shu. / "If you were lenient and brought him back, he would also do the same for you."

"Then what should I do about it?"

"You should send someone to request him from Lu," Bao Shu replied.

"Now Shi Bo,"[5] said the duke, "is the minister with the brains behind Lu. / He will know that I intend to use [Guan Zhong] and certainly will not let me have him."

Bao Shu replied, "You should instruct our emissary to say, 'Our prince has a disobedient minister who is in your country. He wants him from you in order to execute him / before[6] the assembled ministers.' The duke of Lu will certainly agree. However, since Shi Bo knows Yiwu's ability, he will certainly offer him the government of Lu. Should Yiwu accept, then Lu will be able / to weaken Qi. Should he refuse, [Shi Bo] will realize he will return to Qi and will certainly kill him."

"But," asked the duke, "won't Yiwu accept?"

"He won't accept," Bao Shu replied. "Yiwu is single-minded in serving his prince." /

"Will he still be like this toward me?" asked the duke.

"It is not for you," came the reply, "but for our late prince and the altars of Land and Grain. If you wish to make the ancestral temples secure, then be quick about requesting him. Otherwise, / it will be too late."

The duke then sent Bao Shu to make peace between the two countries,

---

[3] The *Guo yu*, 6/1a11, for 諸侯, "feudal lords," writes 百姓, "hundred surnames."

[4] 執枹; lit., "holding the drumstick."

[5] 施伯; a great officer of Lu 魯. See VII, 18/7a6ff. (1:85.5ff.).

[6] Inserting 於 before 羣臣, in accordance with the Ancient and Zhu editions [Wang Niansun].

saying, "Gongzi Jiu[7] is a relative. We request that / you put him to death." The people of Lu therefore killed him. Again he said, "Guan Zhong is our enemy. We request that you let us have him to satisfy our desire [for revenge]."

The duke of Lu promised, but Shi Bo said to him, "Do not give him up! They will not kill him, they will use him in their government. Guan Zhong is one of the most worthy men in the world / and possesses great talent. If he were in Chu, Chu would obtain its goal in the world. If he were in Jin, Jin would obtain its goal in the world. If he were with the Di, the Di would obtain their goal in the world.[8] Now Qi seeks him, and if they get him, / he will certainly be a worry to Lu for a long time to come. Why don't you kill him and give them his corpse?"

"I agree," said the duke of Lu, and was about to kill Guan Zhong when Bao Shu advanced saying, "If we kill him in Qi, this is executing him for [crimes committed against] Qi, but if you kill him in Lu / this is executing him for [crimes committed against] Lu. The prince of our unworthy country wishes to obtain him alive to execute him for [crimes committed against] his country as a warning to the assembled ministers. If we do not obtain him alive, you will be collaborating with a rebel against our prince. / It will not be in accord with what the prince of our unworthy country has requested,[9] and I will not have been able to carry out my orders."

Thereupon the duke of Lu did not kill Guan Zhong, but subsequently trussed him up alive and put him in a cage to give to Qi. Bao Shu, receiving him, cried out three times. / Shi Bo, following, laughed at him and said to a great officer, "Guan Zhong certainly will not die. Now Bao Shu's goodness[10] will not permit him to kill a worthy man. / He is wise enough to know[11] how to elevate such a person in order to serve his own purposes. Bao Shu, advising Gongzi Xiaobo,[12] first entered and took control of Qi. Guan Zhong and Shao Hu,[13] serving Gongzi Jiu, entered later, / and were joined by Lu in attacking them. But [Bao Shu] was able to bring about Lu's defeat. This accomplishment depended

---

[7] 公子糾; the older brother of Duke Huan of Qi, who lost out in the struggle for the throne in spite of support from Lu and Guan Zhong.

[8] Chu 楚 was the major state in south-central China; Jin 晉 was a large state north of the Yellow River in the area of modern Shanxi and southern Hebei; the Di 狄 were a non-Sinified people spread over much of northern China with major concentrations in Shanxi.

[9] Emending 謂 to 請 [Wang Niansun].

[10] Emending 忍 to 志 = 任 [Zhang Wenhu and Guo Moruo].

[11] Inserting 知 after 智 [Hong and Xu].

[12] 公子小白; i.e., Duke Huan of Qi.

[13] 召忽; along with Bao Shu, Guan Zhong's chief associate in their attempt to settle the situation in Qi after the death of Duke Xi 僖 in 698 B.C. See VII, 18.

on[14] gaining or losing [the support of] Heaven, for in the affairs of
men we are equal. / Now Lu, in fear, has killed Gongzi Jiu and
Shao Hu, and imprisoned Guan Zhong, in order to give him to Qi.
Bao Shu knows there will be no evil consequences. / He will certainly
urge Guan Zhong to work for his prince desiring thereby to glorify his
[prince's] achievements [in stabilizing Qi] so the masses will be certain
to give him [their support]. / [Bao Shu's] success[15] in bringing about
[Jiu's] death is to be admired, but greater by far will be that displayed
in keeping [Guan Zhong] alive. / Bao Shu's wisdom will not let him
miss the opportunity to assist his prince through such a demonstration
of virtue." /

When they arrived at Tangfou,[16] Bao Shu purged Guan Zhong of evil
spirits by bathing him three times, and Duke Huan himself met him in
the suburbs. Guan Zhong, tucking up the chin straps of his cap and
scooping up[17] the skirt of his robe,[18] ordered a man / holding an axe to
stand behind him. The duke, after declining the axe three times, sent the
man away and said, "Let down your chin straps[19] and drop your robe. I
will see you."

Guan Zhong twice made obeisance, knocking his head on the ground
and said, / "I have received your favor. Should you kill me and confine
me to the Yellow Springs,[20] even in death I shall always be thankful."

The duke subsequently returned with him and treated him with
ceremony in the court. He toasted him three times and asked him about
carrying on the government, saying:[21]

In the past / our former prince, Duke Xiang,
Made lofty his pavilions and broad his ponds.
Wallowing in pleasure and drinking wine,
He hunted with net, and stringed arrow

---

[14] Emending 足 to 定 [Yu Yue].

[15] Deleting the character 力 following 得 [Zhang Peilun].

[16] 堂阜; see VII, 18, n. 62.

[17] The Yang edition for 搢 writes 捷. The meaning here is the same [Wang Niansun and Sun Xingyan].

[18] The Yin commentary explains that these actions indicate he was about to be executed. According to the *Zuo zhuan*, Ai, 15 (Legge, *Ch'un Ts'eu*, VII, 15/7): "A man of quality does not let his cap fall on the ground when he dies." Thus Guan Zhong was prepared to die as a common criminal.

[19] The Yang edition for 纓 writes 褸.

[20] That is, the netherworld.

[21] Again I wish to express my appreciation to Mr. Gary Arbuckle for pointing out that the following complaint against Duke Xiang 襄 (697–686 B.C.) is in the form of a chant. As he also noted, a similar statement in part appears in the *Zhuangzi*, VIII, 25/19a8–9 (Watson, *Chuang Tzu*, p. 289) concerning Duke Ling 靈 of Weii 衛 (534–493 B.C.).

322

Paying no attention to ruling the state.
He despised the gentry and ridiculed the sages,
Only women were honored.
Nine wives, [each] with six ladies-in-waiting, /
Ranked concubines by the thousands,
To be fed with millet and meat,
To be clothed in ornate embroidery,
While martial knights endured cold and hunger.
War horses had to wait for worn-out pleasure carriages,
Martial knights the left-overs of the ranked concubines. /
Actors, singing girls, and dwarf jesters occupied the fore,
While worthy gentlemen[22] and great officers remained behind.
Thus our country did not daily prosper / and monthly grow.
I fear the ancestral temples have not been swept, /
Nor the altars of Land and Grain provided with blood sacrifices.
Dare I ask, what is to be done?

Guanzi replied, "In ancient times our former kings, Zhao[23] and Mu[24] of Zhou, throughout their lives modeled themselves on the past accomplishments of Wen and Wu[25] and thereby achieved fame. / They united the various states and, having examined those among their people adhering to the moral way, set them up as examples to bring about the regulation of the people. They set standards for goodness so people could respond to them. They compared [wood blocks and bamboo slips], stringing them together to make books so that things could be traced back to the beginning and followed through to the end. / They encouraged the people with rewards, corrected them with punishments, and ranked[26] them according to [the color of] the hair on their heads.[27] / They bestowed favors in order to keep them content, and considered every aspect of their lives from beginning to end."

"How should I go about this?" asked the duke.

Guanzi replied, "In ancient times when the sage kings / governed their people, they divided the country proper (guo 國) into three parts and the outer territories (bi 鄙) into five parts. They fixed the dwelling places of the people and arranged their work in order to bring about their proper

---

[22] Inserting 士 after 賢, in accordance with the Ancient, Liu, and Zhu editions [Xu].
[23] 昭王; reigned 1052–1002 B.C.
[24] 穆王; reigned 1001–947 B.C.
[25] 文 and 武; the founders of the Zhou dynasty.
[26] Emending 冀 to 班 and 除 to 敘 = 序, in accordance with the Guo yu, 6/2b6 [Yu Yue and Song].
[27] That is, according to age.

regulation. They were careful in using the six handles [of power].[28] In such a way the nature of the people could be manipulated and the hundred surnames controlled." /

100.4

Duke Huan said, "What are the six handles?"

"To kill, to nurture, to honor, to degrade, to impoverish, to enrich—these are the six handles," replied Guanzi.

"What about dividing the country proper into three parts?" asked Duke Huan.

100.5
6b

Guanzi replied, "Organize the country proper / into twenty-one districts (*xiang* 鄉): six districts for merchants and artisans and fifteen for the gentry and peasants. Of these districts, you should command eleven,[29] Gaozi[30] five, and Guozi[31] five. Since [the operation of] the

100.6

country proper is divided into three parts, they should form / the three armies. Appoint ministers in charge of the three bureaus [administering the fifteen districts for the gentry and peasants under the command of yourself, Gaozi, and Guozi], three district supervisors (*xiang* 鄉) in charge of the markets, three clan elders (*zu* 族) in charge of the artisans, three wardens (*yu* 虞) in charge of the marshes, and three foresters (*heng* 衡) in charge of the mountains.

"Organize [the country proper] so five households will constitute a

100.7

neighborhood (*gui* 軌), / with each neighborhood having a leader (*zhang* 長); ten neighborhoods will constitute a village (*li* 里), with each village having an officer (*si* 司); four villages will constitute a community (*lian* 連), with each community having a chief (*zhang* 長); ten communities will constitute a district, with each district having a governor (*liang ren* 良人).[32] For every five districts[33] there will be a commanding general (*shuai* 帥)."

"What about dividing the outer territories into five parts?" asked Duke Huan.

---

[28] The *Guo yu*, 6/2b11, for *liu bing* 六秉 writes 六柄. According to the *Jing fa* (1.6.52): 執六枋(柄)以令天下, "Wield the six handles [of power] to command the realm." The Qin legal document unearthed at Shuihudi 睡虎地 in Hubei, *Wei li zhi dao* 爲吏之道 [How to be an Official] (p. 291), refers to "the handles of state [power]" 邦柄.

[29] For 十一, "eleven," the *Guo yu*, 6/4a13, writes 五, "five." Sun Shucheng believes this passage should accord with the *Guo yu* because the following passage, 6b6 (100.7), states: 五(三)鄉一帥, "For each five (originally 'three') districts there should be a commander." See n. 33, below.

[30] 高子; the head of one of the two noble families that hereditarily held the highest official positions in Qi. See VII, 18, n. 150.

[31] 國子; the head of the other family mentioned in n. 30 above.

[32] For a somewhat similar organizational structure, see I, 4/14a4–6 (1 : 13.6–7).

[33] Emending 三 to 五, in accordance with the Ancient, Liu, and Zhu editions and the *Guo yu*, 6/5a12 [Yasui, Dai, and Ding]. Accordingly, the commanders would be Duke Huan, Gaozi, and Guozi.

100.8 Guanzi / replied, "Organize [the outer territories] so five households will constitute a neighborhood with each neighborhood having a leader; six neighborhoods will constitute a camp (*yi* 邑) with each camp having an officer in charge; ten camps will constitute a military colony (*shuai* 率) with each colony having a commandant (*zhang* 長); ten military colonies will constitute a district with each district having a governor (*liang ren* 良人); three districts will constitute a dependency (*shu* 屬)

100.9 with each dependency / having a commanding general. For each five dependencies there will be a great officer. A military government will administer the dependencies, a civil government the districts. Each will maintain its separate administration and so there will be no confusion or laxity."

Duke Huan said, "What should I do about fixing the dwelling places
100.10 of the people / and arranging their work?"

Guanzi replied, "The gentry, peasants, artisans, and merchants, these four types of people, are the bedrock of the state. They should not be
100.11 allowed to dwell together in confusion. / If they do so, their speech will
a become distorted and their work disorganized. For this reason the sage kings, in situating the gentry, were certain to send them to places of leisure. In situating the farmers they were certain to send them to the fields. In situating the artisans they were certain to send them to the
00.12 bureaus responsible for them. / In situating the merchants they were certain to send them to the marketplaces.

00.13 "Since the gentry were made to[34] assemble and dwell together[35] in leisure, father with father spoke of righteousness / and son with son spoke of filial piety. Those who served the ruler spoke of respectfulness. The adults spoke of compassion and the young spoke of respect for elders. From dawn until late at night [adults] did this, thereby teaching their sons and younger brothers. From childhood, [the young] become
00.14 accustomed to it / and their hearts were at peace. They did not see something new and turn to it. For this reason fathers and elder brothers in teaching were effective without being severe, while sons and younger
1.1 brothers were able to learn without overexerting themselves. / Thus it was that the sons of the gentry always became gentlemen.

"Since farmers were made to assemble and dwell together, they came to pay careful attention to the four seasons, assess their needs,[36] provide

---

[34] Emending 今 to 令 here and below, in accordance with the Ancient, Liu, and Zhu editions as well as the *Guo yu*, 6/3a3 [Ding and Guo Moruo].

[35] Reading 州 as 周 here and below [Xu].

[36] The phrase 權節具備 is clearly corrupt. I have followed Liu Ji and Xu in emending it to: 權節其用.

101.2 tools,[37] and / compare[38] plows and plowshares, flails and scythes.[39] With the arrival of cold weather, they knocked down the old grain stalks and cleared the fields while awaiting the proper season. With the arrival

101.3
7b
of the time[40] for plowing, / they plowed deeply, planted evenly, and quickly covered over the new seeds. Before the rains they weeded and hoed, awaiting the seasonal rains. When the seasonal rains arrived, they

101.4 took their sickles and hoes under their arms to / work from dawn until dusk in the fields. They shed their jackets and commenced their labor. They separated the sprouts from the weeds and evened out the places

101.5 where the shoots were too thin or too thick. / On their heads they wore straw rain hats and on their bodies they wore clothes of coarse cloth. Their bodies became soaked and their feet muddy. Their hair and skin

101.6 were sunburned, and they exhausted the strength of their four limbs / in energetically working in the fields. From childhood they became accustomed to it, and their hearts were at peace. They did not see something new and turn to it. For this reason fathers and elder brothers in

101.7 their teaching / were effective without being severe, while sons and younger brothers were able to learn without overexerting themselves. Thus it was that the sons of farmers always became farmers.

"They remained simple and acquired no bad habits. When there were those among them who through their great talent were able to become

101.8 scholars, they could be relied upon. / Therefore, if they were used in agriculture, there was much grain. If they were used in office, there was much worthiness. For this reason the sage kings respected and were on good terms with farmers.[41] /

101.9
8a
"Since artisans were made to assemble and dwell together, / they came to examine their best materials and pay careful attention to the four seasons. They differentiated between the well and poorly made,

101.10 assessed their needs, discussed / and compared their estimates and procedures, and prized cutting instruments that were well made and sharp. They talked with each other about their business and showed each other

---

[37] This phrase 其械器用 is also corrupt, and again I have followed Liu Ji and Xu, emending the phrase to: 備其械器.

[38] The *SBBY* Zhao edition mistakenly writes 此 for 北.

[39] Emending 榖茇 to 枷茇 in accordance with the *Guo yu*, 6/3b9 [Sun Xingyan and Wang Shaolan].

[40] Emending 乃 to 及 [Yu Yue].

[41] There follow two sentences from the *Guo yu*, 6/4a7–8, which appear in the Yang but not in the Zhao edition and are clearly out of place here: 有司見之而不以告其罪五, 有司已於事而竣, "Those officers who observe [such talent] but do not report it commit a crime subject to the five [punishments]. The officers completed this business and then withdrew." Statements similar in content, but slightly different in wording, also appear later in this chapter, 10a4–11 (103.13–104.3).

326

their achievements. They displayed their skills to each other and esteemed each other's knowledge.[42] From dawn till late at night / they
worked at this, thereby teaching their sons and younger brothers. From
childhood they became accustomed to this and their hearts were at
peace. They did not see something new and turn to it. For this reason
fathers and elder brothers in their teaching / were effective without being
severe, while sons and younger brothers were able to learn without
overexerting themselves. Thus it was that the sons of artisans always
became artisans.

"Since merchants were made to assemble and dwell together, they
came to watch out for times of poor harvest and famine and paid careful
attention to the changes within the country. They took note of the four
seasons and examined the products of their districts / in order to know
their market value. They assumed burdens and bore responsibilities.
They yoked oxen and harnessed horses in order to encompass the four
quarters [of the realm]. They calculated the supply and then estimated
prices in order to exchange that which they had for that which they had
not. They bought / cheaply and sold dearly. For this reason, though
feathered banners were not sought after, they still arrived, and there was
a surplus of bamboo arrows within the country. Rarities frequently
arrived and precious things were easily[43] gathered. From dawn till late
at night they worked at this, thereby teaching their sons and younger
brothers. They talked to them / about profit, showed them the proper
seasons, and displayed [their goods] to them to let them know their
value. From childhood they became accustomed to this / and their
hearts were at peace. They did not see something new and turn to it. For
this reason fathers and elder brothers in teaching / were effective without
being severe, while sons and younger brothers were able to learn without
overexerting themselves. Thus it was that the sons of the merchants
always became merchants.

"If the land," [Guanzi continued], "is appraised and taxes are assessed [accordingly],[44] the people will not move away.[45] / If the government does not[46] treat old retainers as temporary guests, the people will
not be given to indolence. If proper times are set for entering mountains

---

[42] Deleting 事 [Ding, Tao, and Yao].

[43] Emending 物 to 易 [Yu Xingwu].

[44] Reading 政 as 征 [Liu Ji, Liu Shipei, and Xu). A similar passage appears in the *Xunzi*,
V, 9/6a2 (Dubs, *Hsüntze*, p. 132).

[45] Deleting the final particle 矣, in accordance with the *Guo yu*, 6/6b13–7a1 [Dai and
Xu].

[46] Emending 正旅舊 to 政不旅舊, in accordance with the *Guo yu*, 6/7a2 [Liu Ji and
Yao].

102.4 and marshes, the people will not enter them illegally. / If mountainous, hilly,[47] and level fields are equalized [for tax purposes], the people will not be resentful.[48] If you do not take the people from their seasonal work, the hundred surnames will be prosperous. If sacrificial animals are not seized[49] [from the people], cattle and horses will be raised."

102.5 Duke Huan asked another question. / "I wish to build up the government in order to seek an opportunity for [controlling] the realm. Can this be done?"

Guanzi replied, "It can."

"How should I begin?" asked the duke.

102.6 Guanzi replied, / "Begin with demonstrating your love for the people."

"How do I go about demonstrating love for the people?" said the duke.

"Set the ducal clan in order and let each family set its own clan in order," replied Guanzi. "If you unite them together in activities and have them share in the same prosperity, the people will be on good terms

102.7 with each other. / If you pardon old crimes and revive the old clans by establishing descendants for those who have none, the population will

102.8 increase. / If you decrease punishments and lighten levies and exactions,
9a the people will prosper. If in the districts you set up worthy scholars and have them teach the country, the people will have propriety. If you issue orders and do not change them, the people will be correct. This is the way to demonstrate your love for the people." /

102.9 "Once the people have been enriched and we are on good terms, can I employ them?" asked the duke.

Guanzi replied, "Develop resources and honor the artisans so there

102.10 will be enough[50] to meet the needs of the people. / Encourage industry and esteem worthiness in order to stimulate cooperation[51] among the people. Apply punishments without cruelty in order to relieve the hundred surnames. If you have no self-interest when executing them, the

102.11 masses will be satisfied. If your statements are sure to be reliable, / your orders will not be in vain. This is the way to employ the people."

Duke Huan said, "Once the dwelling places of the people have been fixed and their affairs have been arranged, I wish to direct my attention toward the feudal nobles of the world. Can this be done?" /

---

[47] Emending 井 to 阜 [Ding].
[48] Emending 慈 to 憾, in accordance with the *Guo yu*, 6/7a5 [Yasui].
[49] Reading 勞 as 撈 [Wang Niansun, Yasui, and Guo Moruo].
[50] Emending 止 to 足 [Wang Niansu and Guo Moruo].
[51] Emending 知 to 和 [Zhang Peilun].

"Not yet," replied Guanzi. "The hearts of the people are not at ease with us."

"How do we set them at ease?" asked the duke.

Guanzi replied, "Put the old laws in order. Select those that are good and use them in a conscientious manner. Be merciful to the people and give to those without resources. / Liberalize your government conscription and respect the hundred surnames. Then the country will be enriched and the people will be at ease."

The duke said, "Once the people are at ease, can it be done?"

"Not yet," replied Guanzi. / "Supposing you were to organize your troops and build up your arms, then the other great countries will also organize their troops / and build up their arms. If you were to launch an attack, the ministers of the feudal lords of the small countries would make preparations for defending their borders. / Thus it will be difficult for you to attain quickly your goals in the realm. If you wish to attain quickly your goals among the feudal lords of the realm, then [preparations] for war must be carried on in secret and a home base must be provided for administering [the army]." /

"What do we do about this?" asked the duke.

Guanzi replied, "Let your internal government serve as a home for the military command structure. Set up villages for Gaozi, Guozi, and yourself, thus dividing the country of Qi / into three parts in order to make three armies. Select worthy people to be village commandants.[52] Let the districts [organize] columns and squads[53] with company commanders (*zu zhang* 卒長) to direct their execution of orders. Furthermore, if hunting is used as a basis for rewards and punishments, / the hundred surnames will come to understand military affairs."

"Good!" said Duke Huan.

[52] The term *li jun* 里君, which I have translated as "village commandant," presents a problem. *Li jun* may indicate a special official at the top level of each of the three divisions who was placed in charge of organizing and coordinating military units at the village level. The use of *jun* here is suspect in itself, since in texts of this period it is usually reserved for the ruler or as an honorific appellation, but not as part of an ordinary administrative title. Zhang Peilun would therefore emend *li jun* to *li yin* 里尹, *yin* being a term frequently used for high-level officials. Both Yu Xingwu and Xu argue that *li jun* refers to a high level official citing the term *bai xing li ju* 百姓里居 (both would emend *ju* to *jun*) in the *Shang shu*, V, 10/10, which Legge translates as "men of honored name living in retirement," and Yu and Xu take as an official in charge of the offices. However, Yao believes *li jun* is the same as *li si* 里司, the officer in charge of the village referred to above, 6b5 (100.7). The *Yi Zhou shu*, VI, 16/28a3, also mentions a *li jun*, apparently meaning a village head.

[53] Traditionally a column 行 consisted of twenty-five men. A squad 伍 consisted of five men, one from each of the five households that made up the basic organizational unit in a village.

329

103.5

103.6
10a

103.7

103.8

103.9

103.10

103.11

Thereupon Guanzi organized five families to constitute a neighbor-hood (*gui* 軌) with a leader (*zhang* 長) in charge; ten neighborhoods to constitute a village (*li* 里) with an officer (*si* 司) in charge; / four villages to constitute a community (*lian* 連) with a chief in charge; ten com-munities to constitute a district (*xiang* 鄉) with each district having a governor (*liang ren* 良人) in charge of military orders. Since five families constituted a neighborhood, five men made up a squad (*wu* 伍) with the neighborhood leader to command it. Since ten neighborhoods constituted / a village, fifty men made up a platoon (*xiao rong* 小戎) with a village officer to command it. Since four villages constituted a community, two hundred men made up a company (*zu* 卒) with a community chief to command it. Since ten communities constituted a district, 2,000 men made up a regiment (*lü* 旅) / with the district gover-nor to command it. For every five districts there was a commanding general (*shuai* 帥).[54] Therefore 10,000 men made up an army with a commanding general of five districts to lead it. Thus there was the drum of the central army, the drum of Gaozi, / and the drum of Guozi.

Taking to the field in the spring was called the spring hunt (*sou* 蒐) and was where the regiments were formed. Taking to the fields in the autumn was called the autumn hunt (*xian* 獮) and was where the troops were trained. Accordingly, the administration of companies and squads was determined at the village level, while that of armies and regiments / was determined in the field.

When these instructions concerning internal administration had been completely carried out, people were ordered not to move around. Therefore men of the companies and squads became responsible for each other, and the families assisted[55] one another. When young, [troops] dwelled together. When they became adults, they traveled around together. At the sacrifices, they provided each other with sacrifi-cial meat. / In mourning for death, they condoled each other. Faced with calamity,[56] they grieved for each other and in dwelling together, they made each other happy. They worked together in harmony and cried together in sorrow. For this reason, in night fighting the sound of their voices was enough to prevent confusion. In day fighting the sight / of each other was enough for mutual recognition. Their happi-ness was enough to make them willing to die for each other. For this reason, in defense they were firm; in attack they were victorious.

Duke Huan had 30,000 of these trained soldiers to send abroad in the

[54] Emending 師 to 帥 both here and in the sentence below [Sun Xingyan, Wang Niansun, and Wang Shaolan].
[55] Emending 愛 to 受 [Ding and Xu].
[56] Emending 福 to 災, in accordance with the *Guo yu*, 6/5a5 [Yasui and Xu].

103.12
10b

realm / to[57] punish those [lords] who lacked the proper way and to make the house of Zhou secure. / None of the princes of the large states of the realm were able to stand against him.

103.13

At court during the first month the chiefs of the districts reported on affairs.[58] The duke personally questioned them, saying, "Is there anyone having residence in your / districts who is known in his district and village for practicing righteousness, for being good in his studies, for being intelligent and of good character, for being compassionate and filial toward his parents, and for providing leadership for the young? If there is, hereby report it. If there is and you do not report it, it is called

03.14

concealing / worthiness, and this crime is subject to the five [punishments]." The officers completed this business and then withdrew.

04.1

The duke again questioned them, saying, "Is there anyone in your districts who is energetic, courageous, and strong of limb, / and whose muscles and bones make him stand out in a crowd? If there is, hereby report it. If there is and you do not report it, it is called concealing talent, and this crime is subject to the five [punishments]." The officers completed this business and then withdrew.

04.2

The duke again questioned them, saying, "Is there anyone in your districts / who is not compassionate and filial toward his parents and does not provide leadership for the young in the districts and villages, but is arrogant and quick-tempered, licentious and cruel, and does not carry out the orders of his superiors? If there is, hereby report it. If there

4.3

is and you do not report it, it is called conniving with inferiors, / and this crime is subject to the five [punishments]." The officers completed this business and then withdrew.

4.4

Thereupon the district chiefs withdrew to cultivate virtue and advance the worthy. Duke Huan personally received them and subsequently employed them in offices. / He ordered the heads of offices to

a

provide periodic written reports on their achievements. / He further ordered them to pick out worthy individuals from their office and recommend them, stating, "Here is a man in our office who possesses

4.5

merit, is frugal / and virtuous, steadfast and obedient, upright and sincere in awaiting his opportunity to serve you. When employing the people, he is respectful in order to encourage them to state their criticisms,[59] thus enabling us to make up for defects in our administration." /

[57] Inserting 以 before 誅, in accordance with the grammatical pattern of the rest of the sentence [Xu].

[58] This sentence begins a new section, which is clearly indicated in the *Guo yu*, 6/5b11, by the beginning of a new paragraph.

[59] Emending 秉 to 謗, in accordance with the *Guo yu*, 6/6a11 [Wang Shaolan and Guo Moruo].

104.6   The duke had inquiries made throughout the districts and villages to
check on [those who had been recommended]. He then summoned and
104.7   sat with them, observing their character in order / to assess their achievements. If the facts indicated they could be appointed, he spent time with
them, asking hypothetical questions concerning the troubles facing the
104.8   country and how to avoid poverty.[60] / After they had withdrawn, he
conducted an investigation of their districts and villages in order to find
out about their abilities and [make sure] they had committed no major
mistakes. He then elevated them to become assistants to high-level
104.9   ministers. / This was called the threefold selection process.

Gaozi and Guozi withdrew to improve [the administration of] their
districts, whose officials withdrew to improve [the administration of]
104.10   their communities. Community officials / withdrew to improve [the administration of] their villages. Village officials withdrew to improve [the
administration of] their neighborhoods, whose officials then withdrew
and improved [the administration of] the households. For this reason
ordinary men who were good could be found and elevated, and those
104.11   who were not good could be found and punished. / Since the adminis-
11b   tration was completely organized, the district officials did not overstep
their chiefs and the court officials did not overstep their ranks. Men who
were morally weak were not included in the military ranks and women
104.12   who were morally weak were not married. Men / who divorced three
wives were expelled beyond the borders, and women who married three
104.13   times were made to pound grain. For this reason / the people were all
encouraged to do good. It was better for a man to do good in his village
104.14   than in his district and better to do good at home than in the village. / So
it was that no man dared speak of what was convenient for himself even
for a single morning. Since everyone's [achievements] were calculated at
the end of the year, no one dared quibble about them, and everyone was
successful throughout their entire lives.

105.1   At court during the first month / the great officers from the five
dependencies (*shu*) reported to the duke about their activities. He picked
out those with few accomplishments and reprimanded them, saying,
"Since your share of territory and allotment of people is the same as
those of others, why do you alone have so little accomplishment? Why
105.2   don't you come up to the others? Since your instruction / has been
poor, your administrative affairs are bound to lack order. I will be lenient the first and second time, but the third time there will be no
pardon."

---

[60] Emending 肉 to 疚 = 交 [Wang Niansun and Guo Moruo].

The duke questioned them again, "Is there anyone having residence in your dependencies / who is known in his district and village for practicing righteousness, for being good in his studies, for being intelligent and of good character, for being compassionate and filial / toward his parents, and for providing leadership for the young? If there is, hereby report it. If there is and you do not report it, it is called concealing worthiness and this crime is subject to the five [punishments]." The officers completed this business and then withdrew.

The duke again questioned them, saying, / "Is there anyone in your dependencies who is energetic, courageous, and strong of limb, and whose muscles and bones[61] make him stand out in a crowd? If there is, hereby report it. If there is and you do not report it, it is called concealing talent and is a crime subject to the five [punishments]." The officers completed this business / and then withdrew.

The duke again questioned them, saying, "Is there anyone in your dependencies who is not compassionate and filial toward his parents and does not provide leadership for the young in the districts and villages, but is arrogant and quick-tempered, licentious and cruel, and does not carry out the orders of his superiors? / If there is, hereby report it. If there is and you do not report it, it is called conniving with inferiors, and this crime is subject to the five [punishments]." The officers completed this business and then withdrew.

Thereupon the great officers of the five dependencies withdrew to improve [the administration of] their dependencies, whose officers withdrew to improve [the administration of] communities (*lian*).[62] Community officials withdrew / to improve [the administration of] their districts (*xiang*), whose officials then withdrew to improve [the administration of] their garrison areas (*zu* 卒).[63] Garrison area officials then withdrew to improve [the administration of] their camps, whose officers then withdrew to improve [the administration of] the households. For this reason ordinary people who were good could be found and elevated, and those who were not good could be found and punished. The

---

[61] Inserting 筋骨, in accordance with the duplicate passage 10b6 (104.1).

[62] The mention of communities (*lian* 連) here would seem to be a mistake since the community is only listed under the country proper in the previous description of state organization, 6b4–9 (100.6–9). *Lian* may be a mistake fo *xian* 縣, an outer district or region. The parallel passage in the *Guo yu*, 6/7b12, writes *xian*. According to the *Guo yu*, 6/7a9–10: "Three districts (*xiang* 鄉) constituted a region (*xian*) having a commanding general (*shuai* 帥). Ten regions constituted a dependency (*shu*) having a great official (*dafu* 大夫)."

[63] here again the text is not consistent with the organization of the dependency presented above, 6b4–9 (100.6–9). Instead, it follows the *Guo yu*, 6/7b12, writing of *zu* 卒 for *shuai* 率, "military colony."

105.8 administration was completely organized / and the country at peace. In defense the people were firm, in attack they were powerful. Since within the borders all was in good order, and the hundred surnames were on good terms [with the government], it was possible [for Duke Huan] to send forth expeditions to the four quarters of the realm and establish himself[64] as lord protector to the king.

105.9
12b
Duke Huan said, "Companies and squads / have been organized and matters completely arranged. I wish to direct my attention toward the feudal lords. Can this be done?"

"Not yet," replied Guanzi. "I have finished incorporating our military command structure within the internal administration, but our
105.10 state of Qi still has few / arms.[65] I wish to lighten[66] punishments[67] and replace them with [fines assessed in terms of] arms."

"How?" asked the duke.

Guanzi replied, "Issue regulations that those with serious crimes should turn in rhinoceros-hide armor and two halberds as the [required]
105.11 arms. Those with lighter crimes should turn in / a weapons rack, shield, and two heavy halberds. Those with minor crimes should turn in one *jun* (thirty catties) of metal. Accomplices whose crimes are light enough to
105.12 be pardoned should turn in half a *jun.* / When a person cannot be dissuaded from bringing a civil or criminal case to court, the judge should prohibit any action for three days,[68] and if the charges then prove to be unfounded, order [the complainant] to turn in a bundle of
105.13 arrows as punishment. / The good metal should be used to make lances, swords, spears, and halberds, and should all be tested on dogs and horses. The poorer metal should be made into axes and hatchets, hoes and scythes, saws and adzes, and should all be tested on wood and earth."

105.14 Duke / Huan said, "Our arms are now more than sufficient. I wish to direct my attention toward the feudal lords. Can it be done?"

"Not yet," replied Guan Zhong. "Since our internal administration is

---

[64] Emending 一 to 而 [Guo Moruo].

[65] The following story also appears in the previous chapter, VIII, 19/1b2–6 (1:95.13–14).

[66] Deleting 重 after 輕 [Ding].

[67] Emending 罪 to 爵 [Guo Moruo].

[68] The meaning of the phrase 正三禁之 is not all clear. Zhang Peilun would delete 正 as a corrupt repetition of the following character 三. I have read it as "judge," and generally followed Xu in basing my translation on a passage in the *Zhou li*, 34/9b7–10 (Biot, *Tcheou-li*, II, pp. 310–311): "[The *da sikou* 大司寇], on the arrival of the two litigants in a civil case, prohibits discussion of the case until they have [each] turned in a bundle of arrows to the court. Thereafter he hears the case. On presentation of both sets of charges in a criminal case, he prohibits imprisonment until [each] side has turned in a *jun* of metal. Three days later he convenes court and thereafter hears the case."

not yet complete, we are not prepared to take action abroad. Therefore, make Bao Shuya[69] / chief censor (*da jian* 大諫), Wangzi Chengfu[70] supreme commander (*jiang* 將), Xian Ziqi[71] chief justice (*li* 理), Ning Qi[72] minister of agriculture (*tian* 田), and Xi Peng[73] foreign minister (*xing,* 行). Have / Cao Sun Xiu[74] reside in Chu, Shang Rong 商容 in Song 宋, Jilao[75] in Lu, Xu Kaifeng[76] in Weii,[77] Yan Shang[78] in Yan,[79] and Shen You 審友 in Jin." /

[Guan Zhong] further sent eighty[80] gentlemen to travel abroad, providing them with chariots, horses, clothing, fur garments, an abundance of provisions, and plenty of money to travel around everywhere to the four corners [of the realm] in order to summon and recruit / its worthy gentlemen. They traveled to the four corners [of the realm], displaying items for amusement for sale to feudal lords in order to observe what these sovereigns and their subordinate officials valued and liked, and to determine those who were licentious[81] and disorderly so that they could be attacked[82] first. /

---

[69] Wang Niansun would emend Bao Shuya 鮑叔牙 to Dong Guoya 東郭牙, in accordance with other versions of the story found in the *Hanfeizi*, XII, 33/8b3–4 (Liao, *Han Fei Tzu*, II, p. 79), *LCSQ*, XVII, 4/9b13 (Wilhelm, *Frühling und Herbst*, p. 275), *Yanzi chunqiu*, 3/3b3, and *Xin xu*, 4/1a7. Zhang Peilun believes they may have been the same person.

[70] The *Zuo zhuan*, Wen, 11 (Legge, *Ch'un Ts'eu*, VI, 11/6), mentions a Wangzi (literally son of a king) Chengfu 王子成父 as serving Qi in 649 B.C. The *Yanzi chunqiu*, 3/3b2, and *Xin xu*, 4/1a10, for 成父 write 成甫.

[71] For Xian Ziqi 弦子旗 the *Hanfeizi*, XII, 33/8a12 (Liao, *Han Fei Tzu*, II, p. 78), writes Xian Shang 弦尚. The *LSCQ*, XVII, 4/10a5 (Wilhelm, *Frühling und Herbst*, p. 275), and the *Yanzi chunqiu*, 3/3b1, both write Xian Zhang 弦章.

[72] For Ning Qi 甯戚, the *Hanfeizi*, XII, 33/8b1 (Liao, *Han Fei Tzu*, II, p. 78), writes Ning Wu 甯武. The *LSCQ*, XVII, 4/9b9 (Wilhelm, *Frühling und Herbst*, p. 274), writes Ning Su 甯遬.

[73] 隰朋; see VII, 18/11a6 (1:91.7).

[74] For Cao Sun Xiu 曹孫宿, the Yang edition writes Cao Xiu Sun 曹宿孫. See also VII, 18, nn. 102 and 127.

[75] For Jilao 季勞 VII, 18/11a12 (1:91.10), writes Jiyou 季友. See also VII, 18, n. 122. As Song Xiangfeng and Guo Moruo point out, the characters *lao* and *you* were easily mistaken for each other in early script.

[76] Xu Kaifeng 徐開封 (the Yang edition writes Xu Xianfeng 徐閑封) should be written Weii Kaifang 衛開方 [Wang Niansun, Sun Xingyan, and Song]. See VII, 18/11a9 (1:91.9), and n. 120.

[77] 衛; properly romanized as Wei, but given this special spelling here in order to distinguish it from Wei 魏. Weii was a small state situated in northeast Henan. See VII, 18, n. 108.

[78] Yan Shang 匽尚 is probably the Yanzi 晏子 mentioned in VII, 18/13a11 (1:93.6), and n. 149.

[79] 燕: an important state located in northern Hebei, with its capital near the present site of Beijing.

[80] Emending 千 to 十, in accordance with the *Guo yu*, 6/8a7 [Wang Yinzhi].

[81] Reading 沈 as 淫, in accordance with the *Guo yu*, 6/9a11 [Liu Ji and Yasui].

[82] Reading 正 as 征, in accordance with the *Guo yu*, 6/9a11 [Liu Ji and Yasui].

106.5   "The external and internal situations have been settled," said the duke. "What about it?"

Guanzi replied, "Not yet. The neighboring countries are still not on friendly terms with us."

"What is to be done about that?" said the duke.

106.6   "Let us examine our borders,"[83] replied Guanzi, "return / seized territory, and rectify the boundaries. Let us not accept the goods of the feudal lords, but rather[84] give them presents of furs and silks[85] along with frequent[86] invitations to visit our court. By pacifying our neighbors in this way, they will feel friendly toward us."

106.7   Duke Huan said, "Our arms are more than sufficient, / and I wish to
13b   conduct an expedition to the south. Who should lead it?"[87]

"Make it [the lord of] Lu," replied Guanzi. "Return his seized territory of Chang[88] and Qian,[89] and it will cause [him to serve you like] a
106.8   breakwater against the sea, / a levy[90] against a rushing torrent,[91] or a redoubt in the midst of surrounding mountains."[92]

106.9   Duke Huan said, "I wish / to conduct an expedition to the west. Who should lead it?"

"Make it [the lord of Weii]," Guanzi replied. "Return his seized territories of Tai,[93] Yuan,[94] Gu, and Qili,[95] and it will cause [him to serve you like] a breakwater against the sea, a levy against a rushing torrent, or a redoubt in the midst of surrounding mountains."[96] /

[83] Following the yang edition, which for 場 writes 場.

[84] Emending 美 to 更 [Xu].

[85] Following the yang edition, which for 弊 writes 幣.

[86] Reading 極 as 亟 = 數 [Tao].

[87] The meaning of 主 is not clear. I have followed the interpretation of Yin Tongyang.

[88] 常; located southeast of modern Teng 滕 Xian in south-central Shandong. The *Guo yu*, 6/8b12, for Chang writes Tang 堂 or 棠, depending on the edition.

[89] 潜; I have been unable to locate this place, but it was probably in the same region as Chang.

[90] Emending 弊 to 蔽, in accordance with the *Guo yu*, 6/9a3 [Yasui, Zhang Peilun, and Xu]. This passage 使海 ... 有牢 is not clear. The commentators are of little help, and my translation is dubious.

[91] Reading 彌 as 瀰 [Yasui]. Guo Moruo and some of the other commentators would treat *jumi* 渠瀰 (the *Guo yu*, 6/9a5, for *mi* writes 弭), "rushing torrents" as the name of a lake or river.

[92] Emending 綱 to 緩 = 環 [Wang Niansun]. The *Guo yu*, 6/9a6, for 綱山 writes *huan shan* 環, which Guo Moruo and others would read as the name of a mountain in Qi.

[93] Deleting 吉, in accordance with the *Guo yu*, 6/9a2 [Wang Niansun]. The *Zhongguo gujin diming dacidian* of Zang Lihe locates Tai 臺 northeast of modern Licheng 歷城 Xian, near Jinan 濟南 in west-central Shandong. However, this seems too far east to have been part of Weii, which was located near modern Qi 淇 Xian in northeast Henan.

[94] 原; situated in modern Jiyuan 濟源 Xian in north-central Henan Province.

[95] I have not been able to locate either Gu 姑 or Qili 杀里. The *Guo yu*, 6/9a3, for Qili writes 漆里.

[96] For notes concerning the latter part of this sentence, see nn. 90 to 92, above.

336

06.10   "I wish to conduct an expedition to the north," said Duke Huan. "Who should lead it?"

    Guanzi replied, "Make it [the lord of] Yan. Return his seized territories of Chaifu and Feigou[97] and it will cause [him to serve you like] a 06.11 breakwater against the sea, a levy against a rushing torrent, / or a redoubt in the midst of surrounding mountains."[98]

    When the seized territories were returned and the boundaries rectified, the neighboring countries became very friendly. [The duke's] territory on the south extended to the north of Mount Dai,[99] on the west to 06.12 the Ji River,[100] on the north to the sea and on the east / to Jisui,[101] and covered an area of 360 *li* square. In the third year good order was established. By the fourth year his instructions had been carried out completely. In the fifth year the soldiers sent forth included thirty 06.13 thousand trained men and eight hundred[102] / war chariots.

    There were a number of feudal lords who were licentious[103] and *7a* disorderly and did not serve the son of Heaven. Thus / Duke Huan in the east went to the aid of Xuzhou[104] and divided the territory of Wu in half. He preserved Lu and invaded Cai,[105] cut up the territory of 6.14 Yue,[106] and in the south occupied / Song and Zheng[107] in order to attack Chu.[108] Crossing the Ru River,[109] he went beyond

---

[97] 柴夫 and 吠狗; I have not been able to locate either of these places.

[98] See nn. 90 to 92, above.

[99] 岱陰: probably the same as Mount Tai 泰山, one of the five sacred mountains. It is located south of Jinan 濟南 in west-central Shandong Province. The *Guo yu*, 6/9a7, writes Mount Tao 鮈山, but I have not been able to locate it.

[100] 濟; arises in Henan and flows into the Yellow River in Shandong. It formed part of the traditional boundary between the states of Qi and Lu.

[101] 紀隨; formerly part of the small state of Ji 紀, whose capital was located near present-day Shouguang 壽光 Xian in north-central Shandong. The *Guo yu*, 6/9a8, writes Jixi 紀鄙, a town formerly part of the state of Ji, located east of Linyi 臨淄 Xian in south-central Shandong. Xu believes the characters *sui* 隨 and *xi* 鄙 were interchangeable in early script.

[102] Wang Yinzhi would emend 八百, "800," to 六百, "600," in accordance with the previous statement (10a1; 103.6): 五十人為小戎, "50 men made up a platoon."

[103] Reading 沈 as 淫.

[104] 徐州: an area in northwest Jiangsu Province, which at this time was claimed by the state of Song. However, the much larger state of Wu 吳, occupying most of Jiangsu and Anhui, was the dominant power in the area.

[105] Emending 蔡陵 to 陵蔡 [Zhang Peilun]. For the state of Cai 蔡, see VII, 18, n. 79.

[106] 越; a large state occupying most of present-day Zhejiang, Jiangxi, and Fujian provinces.

[107] 鄭; a relatively small but important state situated in central Henan, south of the Yellow River.

[108] This attack probably took place in 656 B.C. and is the same as that mentioned in the *Zuo zhuan*, Xi, 4 (Legge, *Ch'un Ts'eu*, V, 4/1–5).

[109] 汝水; rises in central Henan and flows south into the Huai 淮 River.

Fangcheng[110] and sighted the Wen Mountains.[111] He forced [Chu] to
send tribute silk to the house of Zhou[112]/and after returning to
Chengzhou[113] sent sacrificial meat back to Longyue.[114] None of the
feudal lords of Jingzhou[115] failed to come to render service.

In the center [Duke Huan] helped the duke of Jin. He captured the
king of the Di people,/defeated the Humo,[116] smashed the Chuhe,[117]
and the mounted nomad bandits were subjugated for the first time. In
the north he attacked the Mountain Rong, brought Lingzhi[118] under
control, decapitated [the lord of] Guzhu,[119] and the nine Yi tribes[120]
for the first time became obedient. None of the lords of the sea
coast/failed to come to render service.

In the west he conquered and annexed the territory of the White
Di,[121] and subsequently reached the West River,[122] where he lashed

107.1

107.2

107.3

---

[110] Emending 方地 to 方城, in accordance with the *Guo yu*, 6/9a13 [Liu Ji and Wang
Niansun]. Fangcheng 方城 refers to a walled mountain pass northeast of the city of
Nanyang 南陽 in south-central Henan. See the *Zuo zhuan*, Xi, 4 (Legge, *Ch'un Ts'eu*, V,
4/3).

[111] 文山 (the *Guo yu*, 6/9b1, writes Min 汶山); the Wen Mountains are usually equated
with the Min (岷 or 汶) Mountains in northwest Sichuan, but again this appears
questionable because of the distance involved.

[112] Inserting 而反 after 周室, in accordance with the *Guo yu*, 6/9b2.

[113] 成州; the Zhou capital situated northwest of present-day Luoyang 洛陽 in Henan
Province.

[114] 隆嶽; that is, Mount Heng 衡山, a sacred mountain situated in the east-central
portion of Hunan Province. Yasui says that Chu was originally responsible for performing
sacrifices to this mountain on behalf of the Zhou, but stopped doing so as Zhou power
declined. The restitution of this sacrifice was a symbol of Chu's submission.

[115] 荊州 was one of the original nine divisions of China encompassing the modern
provinces of Hubei, Hunan, southeastern Sichuan, northeastern Guizhou, northeastern
Guangxi, and northern Guangdong.

[116] 胡貉; a branch of the Di people living in northeastern Shansi and west-central
Hebei.

[117] 屠何; also read "Tuhe," a non-Sinified tribe said to have been based in southwestern
Liaoning Province.

[118] 泠支; VII, 18/12a5 (1:92.5), for 泠 writes 令. A small state belonging to the
Mountain Rong 山戎. See VII, 18, nn. 137 and 141. According to the *Zhou li*, 33/6a1–3
(Biot, *Tcheou-li*, II, pp. 263–264), there are five major groups of Rong people.

[119] 孤竹; see VII, 18, n. 139.

[120] 九夷 here is a general term referring to all the non-Sinified people of northeastern
China.

[121] The White Di 白狄 who inhabited west-central Shanxi are distinguished from the
Red Di 赤狄 who lived in the southeastern part of the province.

[122] 西河; the term was used to refer to that part of the Yellow River which flows north
to south and forms the traditional boundaries between Shaanxi and Shanxi provinces.
However, this reading presents a problem, since both the Taihang and Bier Mountains,
mentioned in the following sentence, are east of the Yellow River. Therefore, it would
seem that if this account is to make sense, the White Di must have been holding territory
east of the Taihang Mountains, and the West River must refer to one of several large
streams flowing along the edge of the mountains and then off across the North China
Plain.

together boats [to transport the heavy chariots] and constructed rafts. Riding a raft, he crossed the river and reached Shichen,[123] where he hitched up the chariots and harnessed / the horses, passed through the valleys[124] of the Taihang[125] and Bier,[126] and took captive [the chief of] the Greater[127] Xia. Further to the west, he subjugated the Western Yu[128] of Liusha,[129] and for the first time the Rong people of Qin[130] were obedient. Therefore, even though the soldiers went forth only once, / their great accomplishments numbered twelve,[131] and as a consequence none of the eastern Yi, western Rong, southern Man,[132] northern Di, or / the feudal lords of the central states[133] failed to submit.

[Duke Huan] spread out a sacrificial feast for the feudal lords and drew up a covenant sealed with an oath[134] to the multitudinous[135] spirits above and below. / Thereafter he led the entire realm to make the House of Zhou secure and to convene a great court for the feudal lords at Yanggu.[136] He convened six military / and three civil conferences; nine times he assembled the feudal lords, thereby bringing unity and order to the entire realm.[137] Armor did not leave its wrappings,[138] and the arms did not leave their cases.[139] There were no bows in the bow cases / nor arrows in the quivers. [The feudal lords] desisted from military undertakings and carried on their affairs in a civilized way in paying court to the son of Heaven.

[123] For Shichen 石沈, the *Guo yu*, 6/9b8, writes 石枕. The Wei Zhao 韋昭 commentary simply states that Shichen was a place in Jin.

[124] Emending 貉 to 貉, in accordance with the *Guo yu*, 6/9b9 [Wang Niansun and Xu].

[125] The Taihang 大 (the *Guo yu*, 6/9b9, writes 太) 行 Mountains are a major range running in a northeasterly direction from northern Henan along the Shanxi-Hebei border into northern Hebei.

[126] 阜 (the *Guo yu*, 6/9b9, writes 辟) 耳; the name of a mountain chain in northwest Shanxi.

[127] Emending 秦 to 泰 = 大 [Liu Ji, Ding, Xu, and Ren Linbu]. The Great Xia 泰夏 are identified as the northwestern Rong 戎.

[128] The Western Yu 西虞 dwelled in northwest Shanxi.

[129] 流沙; lit., "flowing sands," i.e., the great Alashan and Gobi deserts of the Ningxia-Hui Autonomous Region and western Inner Mongolia.

[130] The state of Qin 秦 occupied the southern portion of Shaanxi and Gansu provinces.

[131] That is, their victories beginning with Xuzhou.

[132] 蠻; the collective name for the largest group of non-Sinified people living in the central Yangtze River valley and south-central China.

[133] Following the Yang edition, which for 中諸侯國 writes 中國諸侯.

[134] Inverting 誓要 to read 要誓 [Wang Niansun and Yasui].

[135] Emending 薦 to 庶, in accordance with the *Guo yu*, 6/9b5 [Wang Niansun and Yasui].

[136] 陽穀; situated southwest of Liaocheng 聊城 Xian in western Shandong Province. This is listed as one of the civil conferences and was held in 657 B.C. See VII, 18, n. 146.

[137] For a discussion of these conferences, see VII, 18, n. 146.

[138] Emending 壘 to 橐, in accordance with the *Guo yu*, 6/10a7 [Wang Niansun and Xu].

[139] Reading 胥 as 医 [Dai and Xu].

At the conference of Kuiqiu,[140] the son of Heaven sent the great officer Zai Kong 宰孔 to present sacrificial meat to Duke Huan, / saying, "I myself[141] have been sacrificing to Wen and Wu and now I am sending Zai Kong to present some of this sacrificial meat to you." There followed a second order: "Because of your humbleness and industry / I would like to see that you, my uncle, do not get down and perform obeisance."

Duke Huan summoned Guan Zhong and conferred with him about it. Guan Zhong replied, "If a prince fails to act as a prince or a minister as a minister, / it provides a basis for disorder."

Duke Huan said, "I have convened three civil and six military conferences; nine times I have assembled the feudal lords, thereby bringing unity and order to the entire realm. / In the north I reached Guzhu, the Mountain Rong, and Huimo,[142] and took captive [the chief of] the Greater[143] Xia. / In the west I reached Liusha and the Western Yu. In the south I reached Wu, Yue, Ba,[144] Zangke,[145] the Changbuyu,[146] Diaoti,[147] and Heichi.[148] None of the states belonging to the Yi people or the Jingzhou lords opposes my orders, but the central / states look down on me. How do I differ from those who in the three periods of ancient times received the mandate [of Heaven]?"

Guanzi replied, "The phoenix and *luan* bird have not appeared, while / hawks and owls abound, and the multitudinous spirits have not come forth. Divining by tortoise [shell] has failed to produce a prophecy, while fortunetellers[149] who cast lots with straws frequently hit the

---

[140] 葵丘; this incident is recorded in some detail in the *Zuo zhuan*, Xi (Legge, *Ch'un Ts'eu*, V, 9/1–2). For a discussion of the conference itself, see VII, 18, n. 143.

[141] Deleting the two characters 之命 [Ding and Xu].

[142] 穢 (the Yang edition writes 獩) 貉; a branch of the Mo people, who lived along the Korean border in Manchuria.

[143] Emending 秦 to 泰 [Li]. The directions given for some of the names listed in this and the following sentences do not accord with the above account.

[144] 巴; the area around Chongqing 重慶 in southeastern Sichuan Province.

[145] 牂(牂)牱(柯); situated near modern Dejiang 德江 Xian in northeastern Guizhou Province.

[146] 棖不庾; unidentified, but Zhang Peilun says the two characters 棖不 are a corruption of *mao* 髳 = 氊 and 庾 is a corruption of *yung* 庸. The Mao were one of the Qiang 羌 tribes that inhabited the Sichuan-Hubei region. Yong was the name of a small state near Zhushan 竹山 Xian in northwestern Hubei. It was later destroyed by Chu. Thus Changbuyu would be read, "the Mao of Yong."

[147] 雕題; a primitive tribe belonging to the Man people of south-central China. From the name it would appear they tattooed their foreheads.

[148] 黑齒; a primitive tribe of southern China said to have blackened their teeth with a plant, probably beetle nut.

[149] The Yang edition for 筮 mistakenly writes 筳.

mark.[150] / The seasonal rains and sweet dew have not fallen, but violent winds and cruel rains have been abundant. The five grains have not flourished, and the six domestic animals have failed to reproduce, while weeds and hellebore[151] have both been thriving. /

"Now, the phoenix is described as having foreparts that consist of virtue and righteousness while its hindparts [reflect] the brilliance[152] [of Heaven and Earth]. / When the ancients received the mandate [of Heaven], the dragon and tortoise appeared and the Yellow River gave forth its Chart; the Luo River produced its Writing and Earth produced its [fabulous] yellow horse.[153] Now, since these three prophecies of good fortune have not appeared, even though you may say you have received the mandate, isn't there something wrong here?" /

Duke Huan became afraid and went out to see the guests, saying, "The awesomeness of Heaven is never out of my thoughts, not even eight inches or a foot. Should I follow this order of the son of Heaven and not get down[154] / and make obeisance, I fear that I would be subverting [royal prerogatives], thereby bringing shame to the son of Heaven." Subsequently he got down and made obeisance. Rising, he received the awarded clothing, the great chariot, the dragon flag with its nine pennants and the red banners for his headquarters. When the son of Heaven presented sacrificial meat to Duke Huan and he got down to receive it, the feudal lords of the realm said that he was obedient.

Duke Huan was concerned about / the feudal lords of the realm. In Lu there was the rebellion of the wife of [Duke Zhuang] and Qingfu, leading to the murder of two princes, so the country was left without an heir to the throne.[155] When Duke Huan heard about it, he sent Gaozi to

[150] That is, the official diviners who read the cracks in tortoise shells after applying heat did not dare reveal their findings, while popular fortunetellers who practiced the lower form of divination of casting straws did not hesitate to produce their ominous forecasts.
[151] Emending 蘮 to 藟 [Yu Yue and Xu].
[152] Emending 日 to 明 [Ding].
[153] For the River Chart 河圖 and Luo Writing 雒(洛)書, see the Introductory Comments to chapter III, 8. According to the *Mozi*, V, 19/9a11 (Mei, *Motse*, p. 113), when the Shang dynasty fell to Wen and Wu of the Zhou, "The Yellow River produced its green chart 綠圖 and Earth its yellow horse 乘黃." This fabulous horse is described in later texts as having one horn on its head and two on its back.
[154] The Yang edition mistakenly writes 不 for 下.
[155] The bloody story of Qingfu 慶父 is presented in some detail in the *Zuo zhuan*, Zhuang, 32, and Min, 1–2 (Legge, *Ch'un Ts'eu*, III, 32/3–6, and IV, 1/2 and 2/3–5). After the death of Duke Zhuang 莊 in the autumn of 662 B.C., Qingfu, who was having illicit relations with the duke's wife Ai Jiang 哀姜 (a woman from the same Qi family as Wen Jiang 文姜, the wife of Duke Huan 桓 of Lu), plotted with her to seize the throne and murdered the legitimate heir, Ziban 子般, before he could be officially installed as duke of Lu. Fearing trouble, Qingfu fled, but later in 660 B.C. he arranged for the murder of Duke

108.7   preserve [the country].[156] / Men and women refrained from promiscuity and [the herds of] horses and cattle were kept intact. [People of Lu], bearing jade gifts, presented themselves, requesting that [Lu] be made a *guannei* vassal[157] [of Qi], but Duke Huan would not allow it. /

108.8   When the Di people attacked Xing,[158] Duke Huan constructed [fortifications around] Yiyi[159] in order to enfeoff [the ruler of Xing]. Men and women refrained from promiscuity and [the herds of] horses and cattle were kept intact. [People of Xing], bearing jade gifts, presented themselves, requesting that [Xing] be made a *guannei* vassal [of Qi], but Duke Huan would not allow it. /

108.9   When the Di people attacked Weii and its people fled, stopping temporarily at Cao,[160] Duke Huan built a wall around Chuqiu[161] in order to enfeoff [the ruler of Weii]. Since his animals were scattered and 108.10 lost, Duke Huan gave him three hundred head of good horses. / The
16a feudal lords of the realm said this was an act of benevolence.

    Thereupon the feudal lords of the realm knew that Duke Huan was not[162] working for himself alone, and for this reason they rallied to him 108.11 like people rushing to market. / Duke Huan, knowing that the feudal lords were rallying to him, consequently had them minimize presents to him, but was lavish in his ceremonies [welcoming them]. Therefore[163] the feudal lords of the realm used worn-out horses and old sheep as 108.12 presents, but Qi / used good horses in return. The feudal lords used plain silk[164] and four deer skins as presents, but Qi used ornate brocade and tiger and leopard skins in return. The emissaries of the feudal lords 108.13 entered with drooping bags, / but returned loaded down with bundles.

    Therefore he enticed[165] them with love and held them with benefits. He bound them by trustworthiness and demonstrated to them his

---

Min 閔, who had succeeded Zhuang to the throne of Lu. Ai Jiang fled to Chu, but was killed on orders from Qi. Qingfu, faced with execution, hanged himself.

[156] Both Zhang Peilun and Guo Moruo believe that the remainder of this paragraph, 男女…不使也, is an interpolation taken from the following paragraph and should be deleted. The comparable passage in the *Guo yu*, 6/10b8–10, lacks it.

[157] 關內之侯; for a discussion of this term, see VII, 18, n. 89.

[158] 邢; a small state situated west of present-day Xingtai 邢臺 Xian in southwestern Hebei Province.

[159] 夷儀; for a discussion of these events, see VII, 18, n. 107.

[160] 曹; a town situated in present-day Hua 滑 Xian in northeast Henan. See VII, 18, n. 109, for details of this incident.

[161] 楚丘; situated in present-day Hua Xian. See VII, 18, n. 113.

[162] Inserting 非 before 為, in accordance with the *Guo yu*, 6/11a5 [Xu].

[163] Deleting 使 following 故, in accordance with the *Guo yu*, 6/11a7 [Ding and Tao].

[164] Emending 縷 to 緩 and deleting 布, in accordance with chapter IX, 22/3a7 (2:2.3) [Liu Ji, Wang Niansun, and Xu].

[165] Emending 釣 to 鉤, in accordance with the Ancient and Zhu editions [Yasui and Guo Moruo].

military prowess. Consequently the lesser feudal lords of the realm served Duke Huan / and none dared turn against him. They rallied around him, reveled in his love, and yearned for his benefits. They trusted in his benevolence and feared his military prowess.

Duke Huan knew that most of the lesser feudal lords of the realm were allied with himself, so he / further extended his kindness.[166] Where grief was appropriate, he grieved for them. Where planning was appropriate, he planned for them. Where action was appropriate, he acted for them. He attacked Tan[167] and Lai[168] but did not annex them. The feudal lords said this / was an act of benevolence.

He imported Qi's fish and salt from / Eastern Lai,[169] and had [traders] inspected at the custom stations and markets, but did not charge them duties. He charged them ground rent[170] [in the markets], but did not tax [their goods] in order to bring profit to the feudal lords. / The feudal lords said this was an act of generosity.

He constructed [fortifications around] Cai, Yanling,[171] Peixia,[172] and Lingfuqiu[173] to garrison the territory of the Rong and Di in order to restrain their violence against the feudal lords. He constructed [fortifications around] Wulu,[174] Zhongmou,[175] Ye,[176] / Gaiyu,[177] and Mouqiu[178] to garrison Chinese territory in order to encourage[179] the central states.

His teachings were a great success, and for this reason the entire realm flocked to Duke Huan. The people of distant countries looked upon him

[166] Emending 忠 to 惠, in accordance with the Zhu edition [Guo Moruo].

[167] 譚; a small state situated in present-day Licheng Xian near the city of Jinan 濟南 in western Shandong.

[168] 萊; a small state belonging to the Yi people, situated in present-day Huang 黃 Xian, southwest of the city of Penglai 蓬萊 on the northeastern tip of the Shandong Peninsula.

[169] 東萊: the area around the city of Penglai.

[170] The Yang edition for 壏 writes 壚. The meaning is the same.

[171] 鄢陵; the *Guo yu*, 6/11b5, writes Ziyan 兹晏. Neither has been identified.

[172] 培夏; the *Guo yu*, 6/11b5, writes Fuxia 負夏, a territory said to belong to the eastern Yi. Neither has been identified.

[173] 靈父丘; the *Guo yu*, 6/11b5, writes 領釜丘. Neither has been identified.

[174] 五鹿; not identified.

[175] 中牟; situated in present-day Tangyin 湯陰 Xian, south of the city of Anyang 安陽 in northeast Henan.

[176] 鄴 situated in present-day Linzhang 臨漳 Xian, southeast of the city of Handan 韓鄲 in southern Hebei.

[177] 蓋與; I have been unable to identify a Gaiyu. Yu 與 may merely be a copula, though this would violate the usual structural pattern. Gai itself was a town in present-day Yishui 沂水 Xian in south-central Shandong.

[178] Emending 社丘 to 牡丘, in accordance with the *Guo yu*, 6/11b7 [Wang Yinzhi, Yasui, and Dai]. Mouqiu was situated in present-day Chiping 茌平 Xian in west-central Shandong province.

[179] For 勸, "encourage," the *Guo yu*, 6/11b, writes 權, "demonstrate his political power to."

109.5 as a father and mother / while those of nearby countries followed him like a flowing stream. Therefore the more[180] he extended the territory under his administration, the more he won the hearts of the multitude. Why was this? They cherished his civil administration and feared his military prowess because by having killed those who had failed to adhere to the proper way, making the house of Zhou secure, and having

109.6 no one in the entire realm / able to stand against him, he established himself in military affairs. By leaving in place the three forms of armament,[181] storing away the five types of weapons,[182] and crossing the Yellow River in ceremonial court attire without fear, he gained victory in civil affairs. /

109.7 For these reasons the princes of large states were humbled, while the lords of small states attached themselves to him; the princes of large states served him as though they were ministers and servants, while the lords of small states were content as though he were their father and

109.8 mother. Now, since / the princes of large states were not especially

17a honored and the lords of small / states were not despised, the former

109.9 were not arrogant and the latter were not afraid. To this end / he carved up large territories to benefit those whose territory was small. He took from those who had wealth and gave to those who lacked it. He looked after men of quality so they would not fail to achieve success and lesser

109.10 men so they would not fail in carrying out his orders. / Now such being the case, at home, they were obedient; when going out, they were successful. He did not take up arms, thereby following in the footsteps of Wen and Wu in the realm. /

109.11 Duke Huan was able to rely on the plans of his assembled ministers to enhance his wisdom. His chief minister (*xiang* 相) was Yiwu. His great

109.12 officers were Ning Qi, Xi / Peng, Bin Xuwu[183] and Bao Shuya. Using these five men, how could he fail! As a legacy to posterity and offering to the spirits of his ancestors, he set standards for righteousness, glorified virtue, perpetuated [clan] law, and provided [new lines of] succession [for families] which had been cut off without heirs. That he became lord

109.13 protector to the realm and / achieved a fame which was far-reaching and never to be obscured was only because there was an enlightened prince on high and a discerning minister below. /

109.14 When Duke Huan first met Guanzi in the suburbs and questioned

---

[180] The Yang edition for 滋 writes 兹. The meaning is the same.

[181] 三革; that is, men, horses, and chariots.

[182] 五兵; this term appears frequently in early texts, but the explanations provided by commentators vary. Usually their lists include five of the following: bows 弓, arrows 矢, spears 殳, lances 矛 or 戈, swords 刀 or 劍, halberds 鏚, battle-axes 釜, or shields 楯.

[183] 賓胥無; according to line 18b8 (111.2), Bin Xuwu became chief justice. In chapter VII, 18/13b1 (1:93.7), it says he managed relations with the lands to the west.

him, Guan Zhong declined appointment to office, but later he responded by dividing / the country proper into three parts and the outer territories into five.[184] He set up [the system of] five districts to promote education[185] and built up the five dependencies in order to sharpen [Qi's] military capability. He housed the military within / the political administration and utilized fines to procure weapons. In order to serve the House of Zhou, he applied military force against those lords who failed to adhere to the proper way.

Duke Huan was greatly pleased and thereupon fasted for ten days. He was about to make Guan Zhong chief minister, but Guan Zhong said, "I am a man [who should have been killed] by battle-axes and halberds, / but I have been lucky enough to hold on to my life and keep my body and neck together. This is my reward. I am not up to administering the government of the country."

"If you accept the government," said the duke, "I will be able to succeed. / If you do not, I fear I will fail completely." Guan Zhong agreed and, twice making obeisance, accepted the post of chief minister.

On the third day thereafter the duke said, "I have three great vices; in spite of these, / can I still run the country?"

"I have not yet heard about them," was the reply.

"Unfortunately," said the duke, "I like to hunt. When it is still dark I arrive at the bird site and only after the sun has set[186] and one can no longer see the birds do I return home. / Thus the emissaries of the feudal lords have no place[187] to reach me, and officials in charge of the various offices have no place to report."

"That's bad, / all right, but it is not vital," was the reply.

The duke said, "Unfortunately, I like wine and keep at it day and night. The emissaries of the feudal lords have no place to reach me, and officials in charge of the various offices have no place to report."

"That's bad, / all right, but it is not vital," was the reply.

"I have a serious vice," said the duke. "Unfortunately, I like women, and have not married off my aunts and sisters."[188]

"That's bad, all right, but it is not / vital," was the reply.

---

[184] Here begins a new section, not included in the *Guo yu*, which recapitulates the first part of the chapter and adds some additional anecdotes.

[185] That is, the groups of five districts for gentry and peasants that were assigned to Duke Huan, Gaozi, and Guozi. See 6b1 (100.5).

[186] Emending 田 to 日 [Yu Yue and Xu].

[187] The Yang edition mistakenly omits 所.

[188] Inserting 妹 following 姊 (姉) [Sun Xingyan, Yin Tongyang, and Xu]. According to the *Xunzi*, III, 7/13b5 (Dubs, *Hsüntze*, pp. 81–82): "Huan of Qi was the greatest of the five lord protectors, yet in his early days he killed his older brother and wrested the state from him. In internal affairs, he did not marry off seven aunts and sisters, and within the inner apartments there was dissipation and extravagance."

The duke, flushing in anger, said, "If these three things are all right, then what isn't all right?"

110.9   "Only if the ruler is too indecisive and slow to act / is it not all right," came the reply. "If he is too indecisive, he will lose the masses. If he is too slow to act, he will never be in time with his undertakings."

The duke said, "Good. Suppose you go to your lodging and on some other day I would like to talk things over with you."

110.10   "Right now is fine with me," was the reply. / "Why wait for another day?"

The duke said, "What is to be done?"

[Guan Zhong] replied, "Gongzi Ju[189] is a man who is of wide learning and understands the rites. He is studious and humble. I request that you
110.11   send him to live / in Lu to establish relations. Gonzi Kaifang is a man who is clever and sharp. I request you send him to live in Weii to establish relations. Cao Sun Xiu is a man of little integrity and finicky[190]
110.12   habits, but he is sufficiently respectful and glib of tongue,[191] / thus
18b   according with the manners of Jing.[192] I request that you send him to
110.13   live there in order to establish relations." / Subsequently he sent out the three emissaries and then withdrew.

When he had been chief minister for three months, [Guan Zhong] requested that they discuss the various offices, and the duke said, "I agree."

Guan Zhong said, "In terms of ascending and descending [ceremonial stairs], bowing and giving way to others, demeanor when advancing or
110.14   retreating, / and firmness or gentleness in argument, I am not equal to Xi Peng. I request that you make him grand foreign minister (*da xing* 大行). In terms of opening up grasslands and establishing[193] towns, cultivating the land and collecting grain, increasing the population, and
111.1   taking full advantage of the benefits of Earth, I am not equal to / Ning Qi. I request that you make him grand minister of agriculture (*da sitian* 大司田). In terms of preventing chariots from becoming stuck in their tracks or the troops from having to retrace their footsteps on the level plains and vast pasture lands, and beating the drum so the three armies
111.2   look on death as returning home, I am not equal to / Wangzi Chengfu. I request that you make him grand war minister (*da sima* 大司馬). In

---

[189] 公子舉; line 13a3 (106.2) above for the emissary to Lu writes Jilao 季勞 (see n. 75); VII, 18/11a12 (1:91.10), writes Jiyou 季友 (see VII, 18, n. 122).

[190] The Yang edition for 苟 writes 荷. The meaning remains the same [Dai].

[191] Emending 結 to 給 [Liu Ji and Xu].

[192] 荆; that is, the state of Chu.

[193] Emending 入 to 立 [Guo Moruo].

terms of judging fairly when trying cases and not killing those who are innocent nor making false accusations against those who are not guilty, I am not equal to Bin Xuwu. I request that you make him grand chief justice (*da sili* 大司理). In terms of not being afraid to incur the prince's anger, / of advancing criticism with certain loyalty and not avoiding death nor bowing before wealth and rank, I am not equal to Dong Guoya.[194] I request that you establish an office of grand censor (*da jian* 大諫) for him. I am not as good as any of these five men, / but I wouldn't want to change places with them. For if you wish to rule the country well and strengthen your arms, then these five men will do.[195] But if you wish / to become lord protector to the king, only I am equal to this."

"Good!" said Duke Huan.

[194] 東郭牙 12b12–13a1 (105.1) writes Bao Shuya instead of Dong Guoya. See n. 69, above.

[195] Emending 存 to 足, in accordance with a similar passage in the *LSCQ*, XVII, 4/10a8 [Yu Yue].

Ba Xing
霸形

Conditions Distinguishing A Lord Protector

Introductory Comments

It has been suggested by Zhang Peilun that the titles of this and the following chapter, IX, 23, have somehow been interchanged. Chapter IX, 23, opens with the sentence: 霸王之形, "There are [certain] conditions that distinguish a lord protector or king," using the same terminology as the above title. at the same time, the present title of IX, 23, *Ba yan* 霸言, "Conversations of the Lord Protector," fits the content here very well.

This chapter represents one of the better organized morality pieces in the *Guanzi*, presenting three new anecdotes about Duke Huan and Guan Zhong and a brief recapitulation of their military conquests as described in the *Xiao kuang*, VIII, 20, and chapter 6 of the *Guo yu*. The language and style is much better developed than that of either of those two works or the *Da kuang* or *Zhong kuang* and is reminiscent of the anecdotal literature of the Han. I suspect it is an early Han piece supplementing the tradition presented in the *Guo yu*. The connection would seem to be more likely with the *Guo yu* than the *Xiao kuang* chapter of the *Guanzi* because instead of *Xiao kuang*'s writing of Wen Shan 文山 (Wen Mountains), it accords with the *Guo yu* in writing Min Shan 汶山 (Min Mountains). It also uses the rather unusual expression *ruo he* 若何 ("What about it?") found in the *Guo yu* instead of the *nai he* 奈何 of the *Xiao kuang*.

Translation

2:1.7 *1a7* Duke Huan was sitting on the throne when Guan Zhong and Xi Peng[1] presented themselves. While they were standing at their leisure, two wild

[1] 隰朋: one of Duke Huan's most trusted ministers in charge of foreign affairs. See VII, 18/13a12 (1:93.7), and VIII, 20/13a2 (1:106.1) and 18b3–4 (110.14).

swans flew by.[2] Duke Huan sighed, saying, "Zhongfu,[3] now those wild swans fly south or north / according to the season, and, according to the season, come and go. In any direction, regardless of distance, they arrive anywhere they wish. Is it not just because they have wings that they are able to go where they please in the world?"

When Guan Zhong / and Xi Peng did not reply, Duke Huan asked, "Why don't you two answer?"

Guanzi replied, "You have a mind to become lord protector to the king, but I am not a minister to one. For this reason I dare not reply." /

"Zhongfu, how can this be?" said Duke Huan. / Why don't you speak out? Isn't there some direction for me to take? My having you, Zhongfu, is like those flying swans having wings. / It is like having a boat and oars when crossing a large river. If you, Zhongfu, will not say a single word to instruct me, even though I have ears, from whom shall I hear about the proper way so that I may take appropriate steps?" /

Guanzi replied, "If you, My Lord, wish to become lord protector to the king and undertake great affairs, you must attend to matters that are basic."

Duke Huan shifted his weight, adjusted the mat, and, folding his hands, inquired, "Dare I ask what is meant by / 'basic'?"

"The hundred surnames of Qi 齊 are your base," Guanzi replied, "but now they are extremely worried about starving, yet your taxes and exactions are heavy. They are terrified of death, yet your administration of punishments threatens them. They are grievously overworked, yet you initiate undertakings / in an untimely manner. If you were to lighten taxes and exactions, they would not be so worried about starvation. If you were to relax your administration of punishments, they would not be so terrified of death. If you were to initiate undertakings in a timely manner, they would not be so grievously overworked."

Duke Huan said, "I have listened to your words, Zhongfu, / and in regard to these three things, I shall obey orders. [However], since I do not dare act on my own authority, I will present [these recommendations] to [the spirits of] our former princes."

Thereupon he ordered the various officials / and officers in charge [of various bureaus] to scrape their tablets clean and ink their brushes. / The next day he held court for everyone before the gate[4] to the ancestral temple. He issued specific orders causing the grain tax to be one *zhong*

---

[2] A slightly different version of the following story occurs in chapter X, 26/3a ff. (2 : 16.14ff.).

[3] 仲父; that is, Guan Zhong.

[4] Reading 門朝 as 門廷 [Ding and Xu].

2.3 per hundred.[5] / The orphaned and young were not to be punished. Marshes and weirs were to be opened in season. [Traders] were to be inspected at the customs posts, but not charged a fee. [Merchants] were to be charged a ground rent[6] in the market place, but not taxed. Those

2.4 near at hand were to be treated with loyalty and trustworthiness / and those from afar with propriety and righteousness. When he had carried out these [policies] for several years, people came to him in a flowing stream.

Later on, Song 宋 attacked Qii 杞, and the Di 狄 attacked Xing 邢 and Weii 衛 but Duke Huan would not go to their rescue. He stripped

2.5 his body naked and bound up his chest claiming he was / ill. Summoning Guan Zhong, he said, "I have food for a thousand years, but I won't live to be a hundred. Now I am ill. Will you indulge me my pleasure?"

"I agree," Guanzi replied.

2.6 Thereupon / [Duke Huan] ordered him to hang up the rings for suspending[7] bells and musical stones and arranged [performances of] singing and dancing as well as the music of the reed organ (*yu* 竽) and the lute (*se* 瑟). Everyday for several weeks he killed tens of oxen [for feasts]. The assembled ministers approached him and issued a warning,

2.7 saying, "Song has attacked Qii and the Di / have attacked Xing and Weii. You have no choice but to rescue them."

Duke Huan replied, "I have food for a thousand years, but will not live to be a hundred. Now in addition I am ill. Will you indulge me my

2.8 pleasure? Besides, it isn't that they are attacking my / country, they are attacking my neighbors. It is none of your affair."

2b Song had already seized Qii, / and the Di had uprooted Xing and Weii when [one day] Duke Huan rose and walked among the frames [for suspending the bells and musical stones], with Guanzi following after.

2.9 On reaching a point west of the large bell, / Duke Huan faced south and stood still while Guan Zhong faced him to the north. When the great bell rang, Duke Huan looked at Guan Zhong[8] and exclaimed, "Pleasing, isn't it, Zhongfu?"

Guanzi responded, saying, "This is what your minister would call sad

2.10 rather than pleasing. / I have heard it said that when the ancients spoke

---

[5] A Han dynasty *zhong* 鍾 equaled about 3.6 U.S. bushels. The Yin commentary would read this passage to mean one *zhong* per hundred *shi* 石. A Han *shi* equaled about 18.1 U.S. dry quarts.

[6] Emending 書 to 廛(鄽, 壥), in accordance with a similar passage in the III, 10/19a11–12 (1:46.3): 關幾而不征, 市廛而不税. Similar passages also appear in the *Li ji*, IV, 5/10a3–4 (Legge, *Li Ki*, XXVII, p. 227), and the *Guanzi*, VIII, 20/16b1 (1:109.2).

[7] Reading 橫 as 環 [Guo Moruo].

[8] The Yang edition for 視管仲 writes 親管仲, "drew near to Guanzi...."

about pleasure among the bells and musical stones, it was not like this. Were a [single] word to drop from their mouths, orders were executed throughout the realm. When they amused themselves among the bells and musical stones, nowhere / were there worries about [enemy] arms. Now, in your affairs, when words drop from your mouth, orders cannot be executed throughout the realm. You stand among the bells and musical stones, but on all sides there are worries about [enemy] arms. This is what I / call sadness rather than pleasure."

"Good!" said Duke Huan. He thereupon cut down the hangings for the bells and musical stones, relinquished[9] the pleasure of singing and dancing, and emptied the palace of people. Duke Huan / [then] said, "I have already[10] cut down the hangings for the bells and musical stones and relinquished the pleasure of singing and dancing. May I ask what I should do first in order to run the country?"

Guanzi replied, "I beg to congratulate you on not having gone to the rescue when Song attacked Qii and the Di attacked Xing and Weii. / I have heard that when the feudal lords fight over territory, one should not take part in it. Now, why not arrange a place for those three princes to live?" /

Thereupon Duke Huan said, "I agree," and accordingly ordered that Qii be enfeoffed at Yuanling[11] with a hundred chariots and a thousand troops. Xing was enfeoffed at Yiyi[12] / with the same number of chariots and troops, while Weii was enfeoffed at Chuqiu[13] with five hundred chariots and five thousand troops.

Duke Huan said, "I have already arranged a place for the three princes to live. What more should I do now?" /

"I have heard," Guanzi replied, "that when the feudal lords are greedy for profit, one should not take part in it. Now, why not issue tiger and leopard skins and ornate brocades when sending envoys to the feudal lords, but order them to use plain silk and deer skins in return?"[14] /

"Agreed," said Duke Huan, and thereupon used tiger and leopard skins and ornate brocades when sending emissaries to the feudal lords.

---

[9] Reading 併 as 屏 [Yasui, Tao, and Yin Tongyang].

[10] Reading 以 as 已 [Xu].

[11] 緣陵; situated seventy *li* southeast of present-day Changluo 昌樂 Xian in north-central Shandong. See VII, 18, n. 103.

[12] 夷儀; situated to the west of present-day Xingtai 行臺 Xian in southwest Hebei. See VII, 18, n. 107.

[13] 楚丘; situated in present-day Hua 滑 Xian in northeast Henan. See VII, 18, n. 113.

[14] For other versions of this story, see VII, 18/10b11–12 (1:91.4), and VIII, 20/16a4–7 (1:108.11–13).

The feudal lords used plain silk and deer skins in return. Then for the first time [the duke's] orders were executed throughout the realm.

3.5 Following this, the men of Chu 楚 / assaulted Song and Zheng 鄭. They destroyed by fire the territory of Zheng and forbade damaged walls to be rebuilt or burned houses to be repaired, causing people to mourn
3.6 for their mates / and live like birds and rats in caves. They plundered the fields of Song and channeled together two rivers, damming them up so
3.7 the water could not flow to the east. / West of the Eastern Mountains,[15]
3b the water became so deep it covered the ruined walls and [one had to travel] four hundred *li* before finding a cultivable field.

[The king of] Chu wished to swallow up Song and Zheng, but was afraid, thinking,[16] "Qi's populace is so large and its arms so strong, it
3.8 certainly can do us harm." Thereupon / the king of Chu issued an order throughout the country saying, "Of those whom I consider brilliant[17] among the princes, none is the equal of Duke Huan. Of those whom I consider worthy among ministers, none is the equal of Guan Zhong.
3.9 Since I consider this prince brilliant / and his minister worthy, I wish to serve them. I will not be sparing in making an enfeoffed prince[18] of whoever is able to establish relations with Qi for me." Thereupon all the
3.10 worthy gentlemen of Chu / bundled up their most precious objects and silk in order to serve Qi, and there were none of Duke Huan's assistants on the left and right who did not receive [gifts of] precious objects and silk.

Thereupon Duke Huan summoned Guan Zhong saying, "I have
3.11 heard that when one is good to others, / they will be good to him. Now the king of Chu has been exceptionally good to me. If I am not good to him, I will violate the moral way. Zhongfu, how can I fail to go along and not establish relations with Chu?" /
3.12 "It won't do," Guanzi replied. "The men of Chu assaulted Song and Zheng. They destroyed by fire the territory of Zheng and forbade damaged walls to be rebuilt or burned houses to be repaired, causing
3.13 people / to mourn their mates and live like birds and rats in caves. They
4a plundered the fields of Song and channeled together two rivers, damming them up so the water could not flow to the east. West of the Eastern Mountains, the water has become so deep it covers the ruined walls and
3.14 [one has to travel] four hundred *li* / before finding a cultivable field. [The

[15] Dongshan 東山. Situated in northwestern Anhui.
[16] Deleting 曰 [Igai, Tao, and Li Zheming].
[17] Xu would read 明 as 尊, "Of those whom I esteem among princes...."
[18] Igai, Dai, and Guo Moruo would emend 君 to 賞, "I will not be sparing in granting an award of enfeoffment to...."

king of] Chu wishes to swallow Song and Zheng, but thinks your populace is so large and your arms so strong that Qi can certainly do him harm. This is an attempt to subdue Qi with political means while using military means to seize Song and Zheng. If we are not wise[19] enough to stop Chu from seizing / Song and Zheng, we will have neglected them. If we do stop Chu, then on the other hand, this will mean breaking faith with its [king]. When wisdom fails within and there are military complications without, / it is not a good situation."

"Good!" said Duke Huan. "But what should we do?"

Guanzi replied, "I beg you to raise troops to occupy Song and Zheng to the south, but issue orders to them, saying, 'Do not attack Chu. I[20] am going to meet with its [king].' / When you arrive at the meeting, you will make a request about the city walls of Zheng and the water in Song. If Chu agrees, we will have succeeded through political means. If Chu does not agree, we will then use military means."

Duke Huan said, "Good!" /

Subsequently he raised troops and occupied Song and Zheng to the south. He met with the king of Chu at Shaoling[21] and issued orders saying, "Do not hoard grain. Do not manipulate boundary embankments. Do not dispose of an heir-apparent on your own authority. Do not / set up a concubine as a legal wife."[22]

Availing himself [of this opportunity], he made his request to Chu concerning the city walls of Zheng and the water in Song. The men of Chu would not agree. Subsequently, [Duke Huan] withdrew seventy *li*, set up camp, and dispatched military personnel to erect walls in the area south of Zheng. He erected permanent[23] / walls [with an inscription] stating, "From here north to the Yellow River, Zheng may freely build walls." Consequently, Chu did not dare destroy them. To the east, he opened up the two rivers that had been channeled together through Song's fields so the water / would again flow eastward. Consequently, Chu did not dare obstruct them.

Subsequently, to the south, he attacked Chu[24] and passed through

---

[19] The Yang edition for 知 mistakenly writes 止.

[20] Reading 言 as 吾 [Guo Moruo].

[21] 召陵; situated thirty-five *li* east of present-day Yancheng 郾城 Xian in east-central Henan.

[22] These four prohibitions are included in a list that appears in chapter VII, 18/2b1–3 (1 : 92.10–11). A longer list appears in the *Mengzi*, VIB, 7/3, which attributes them to the Covenant at Kuiqiu 葵丘 proclaimed by Duke Huan in 651 B.C. See VII, 18, n. 143.

[23] The phrase 百代城 is very doubtful. Guo Moruo would emend 百 to 石 and 代 to 付 = 坿, "He erected stones to increase the height of the walls...."

[24] Emending 及 to 楚 [Guo Moruo].

Fangcheng,[25] crossed the Ru River,[26] and caught sight of the Min Mountains.[27] In the south he extended [his authority] to the princes of Wu[28] and Yue 越 and in the west attacked / Qin 秦. To the north, he attacked the Di, and turning to the east he restored the [territory of] the duke of Jin 晉 in the south.[29] Turning [again] to the north, he attacked Guzhu 孤竹 and on his way back he restored the [territory of] the duke of Yan 燕. He convened six military and three civil conferences, nine times / assembling the feudal lords.[30]

He resumed his position on the throne, and having already become lord protector, he repaired the bells and musical stones and again sought enjoyment. Guanzi said, "This is what I call [real] pleasure."

[25] 方成; an important fortified mountain pass leading into Chu, situated to the northeast of the city of Nanyang 南陽 in south-central Henan.

[26] 汝水; rises in central Henan and flows southeast into the Huai 淮. This crossing of the Ru should have occurred before passing through Fangcheng. See VIII, 20/14a2–3 (1:106.14), and the *Guo yu*, 6/9a13.

[27] 汶山; the identity of these mountains is not clear. The Yin commentary says they are the same as the Min 岷 Mountains in north-central Sichuan, but the great distance makes this seem unlikely. See VIII, 20/14a3 (1:106.14), and n. 111.

[28] Emending 楚 to 吳 [Zhang Peilun and Xu].

[29] According to VIII, 20/14a5 (1:107.1): "In the center [Duke Huan] helped the Duke of Jin."

[30] For further discussion of these meetings, see VII, 18, n. 146.

Ba Yan

霸言

CONVERSATIONS OF THE LORD PROTECTOR

Introductory Comments

As mentioned in the Introductory Comments to chapter IX, 22, the title of the present chapter should probably be *Ba xing* 霸形, "Conditions Distinguishing a Lord Protector," the present title of IX, 22, or *Ba wang xing* 霸王形, "Conditions Distinguishing a Lord Protector or King," which is more in line with the chapter's content. The text here begins with the sentence: 霸王之形 "There are [certain] conditions that distinguish a lord protector or king."

This is a rather difficult chapter. The style is frequently muddy and is distinguished by an excessive use of the character *fu* 夫 as an initial particle of accentuation, which I have usually translated as "now," "indeed," or "however," and sometimes, to avoid repetition, simply omitted.

The content is primarily Legalist with Daoist overtones, declaring (10b6; 9.13) in a very un-Confucian manner: "Now, control of a state does not lie [merely] in paying respect to tradition." It tends to stress political methods (*shu* 術) and military strategy rather than law, and in this sense it appears to be more in the tradition of Shen Buhai 申不害 (d. 337 B.C.) than Shang Yang 商鞅 (fl. 359–338 B.C.). I suspect this chapter represents an early political text of the Huang-Lao tradition, which developed during the third century B.C. as an amalgam of Legalist and Daoist ideas. Long Hui, in his article on the origins of the Mawangdui *Laozi* "B" silk manuscript (p. 26), expresses the belief that at least parts of the *Guanzi* are of Chu 楚 origin and connected with the Huang-Lao tradition. He points out the importance of timeliness in Huang-Lao thought and cites a passage (7a2–4; 6.10) from this chapter: "The sage is able to take advantage of the times, but is never able to go against them. Knowledge is good for formulating stratagems, but it is not as good as being timely," as an example of the Huang-Lao approach.

Of particular interest is that lines 10a3–7 (9.5–7) bear a stong resemblance to a statement attributed to Chao Cuo 晁錯 that appears in his biography in the *Qian Han shu*, 49/8a13–8b3.[1] Chao, who died in 154 B.C., was a native of Yingchuan 穎川, near the modern city of Kaifeng in northeast Henan. According to his biography, he studied the works of Shen Buhai and Shang Yang and was especially interested in methods of warfare (*bing fa* 兵法).[2] It is possible that this chapter may actually have been written by Chao, since its contents fit what we know of his ideological orientation. However, Chao's statement opens with the phrase 臣又問, "I have further heard." Therefore it is more likely that Chao was familiar with at least some portions of the present *Guanzi*, as was Jia Yi 賈誼, who died about fifteen years earlier, and in his statement is merely paraphrasing the *Guanzi*. This would then place the composition of this chapter sometime between the beginning of the third and the middle of the second centuries B.C.

Translation

2:4.12
4b12

5a

4.13

4.14

There are [certain] conditions that distinguish a lord protector or king. They model themselves on Heaven and follow the pattern of Earth. They transform men and change dynasties, / establish regulations for the realm, and rank the feudal lords. They treat everyone within the four seas as guest retainers and dependents, and, / at the proper moment, they set the entire realm in order. They reduce the size of large states and set to right those that behave in an unprincipled manner. They weaken those states that are strong and reduce the stature of those that are considered important. They bring unity to states wracked by rebellion and destroy / kings who indulge in violence. They execute criminals, demote those holding rank, and bind together their people. Thereafter they [are able to] rule them.

5.1

5.2

Now, [the ruler who] enriches[3] his own state is [merely] called a lord protector; / one who unifies and sets to right other[4] countries is called a king. Now, a [true] king is uniquely clearsighted. He does not seize control of states that share the same virtues nor establish his rule over those that are alike in adhering to the Way. / However, among those who struggle for [control of] the realm, it is the constant practice of violent kings to use their awesome power to overthrow and endanger others. /

---

[1] See n. 36, below.

[2] See Creel, *Shen Pu-hai*, pp. 258–263.

[3] Yu Xingwu would emend 豐 to 豊 = 體. Thus, "[The ruler] of states that keep their separate identity...."

[4] Emending 之 to 亡 [Yu Yue].

356

5.3   All princes [must] adhere to the Way, but lord protectors and kings [must also] have a sense of timeliness. To have one's own state in perfect order while those of one's neighbors fail to adhere to the Way is a major asset for becoming a lord protector or king. /

5.4
5b   Now, the survival of a state is affected by its neighbors. / Their military ventures determine their success or demise. When the entire realm is involved in such ventures, it is to the advantage of the sage
5.6   king. / Should his own state be in danger, he will know it [because of his clearsightedness].[5] The former kings became kings by taking advantage
5.7   of the injudicious actions of neighboring states. / Such actions [also] pleased the enemies of these neighbors.

Those who wish to utilize the political power of the realm must first
5.8   demonstrate their virtue to the feudal lords. / For this reason the former kings had that which they took, that which they gave, that in which they were yielding, and that in which they were uncompromising. Thereafter they were able to utilize the political power of the realm. /

5.9   Arms flourish on the basis of political power, and political power flourishes on the basis of territory. Therefore, when the feudal lords obtain the advantages of territory, political power follows. When they lose these advantages, their political power disappears. /

5.10   Those who would struggle for [control of] the realm must first struggle for men. Those who understand the great scheme of things will obtain them while those who concentrate on petty calculations will fail. Those who succeed in winning the masses of the realm become kings; those who win only half of them become [mere] lord protectors. /

5.11
5a   For this reason the sage kings were humble in performing the rites in order to bring the worthies of the realm under their sway and employ[6] them. They set equitable standards [for land taxes] in order to attract the
5.12   masses of the realm and make them their subjects. / That they were honored as sons of Heaven and their wealth encompassed the entire realm, yet later generations[7] never spoke of them as being greedy, was because their grand design prevailed. They used the resources of the
5.13   realm to benefit / its people and used the frightening force of their clear sight and majesty to pull together the political power of the realm. By
5.14   following the path of virtue, they secured / the allegiance of the feudal

---

[5] This paragraph is not clear and is the subject of some debate among the commentators. They all agree it basically means that it is to the advantage of a lord protector or king to have their neighbors fighting among themselves. I have generally followed Yasui's interpretation.

[6] Emending 王 to 壬 = 任 [Xu].

[7] Emending 伐 to 代 = 世 [Yasui, Yu Yue, Zhang Peilun, and Xu].

lords. By treating as evil the crime of sycophancy, they molded[8] the minds of the realm. They relied on the majesty of the realm to broaden the punitive force of a clearsighted king. / They attacked rebellious and disorderly states, rewarded meritorious effort, honored the virtue of worthies and sages, and made clear the conduct of the ruler himself to reassure the hundred surnames. /

When the former kings seized control of the realm, they [had mastered] political methods. Of such great virtue were these political methods that all things were said to have benefited from them. /

Now, those who make sure that their states never suffer calamities and accrue both fame and benefits are divine sages. Those whose states are faced with danger and destruction yet are able to persevere are / sages with clear sight. For this reason, the former kings emulated the divine sages and appreciated those with clear sight. / Indeed, when one word can cause a state to live forever, or, when unheeded, cause it to be lost, such is the word of a great sage.

Now, the clearsighted king attaches little importance to horses and jade. It is his government and army that are considered important. The incompetent ruler is not like this. He attaches little importance to giving people / a government, but considers it important to give them horses. He attaches little importance to giving them an army but considers it important to give them jade. He attaches importance to the guardhouses of his palace gates but little importance to the defense of his four borders. It is for this reason that [his territory] is pared away.

Political power is a major asset for being a divine sage. / Being uniquely clearsighted is the sharpest weapon in the realm. Making decisions on one's own is to have secret defenses. These three the sage takes as models. The sage / fears what is obscure; the stupid person fears what is clearly evident. The sage hates what is kept inside; the stupid person hates what is expressed in the open. / Before the sage will move, he must know [the situation]; the stupid person on encountering danger wavers and gives way. / The sage is able to take advantage of the times, but is never able to go against them. Knowledge is good for formulating stratagems, but it is not as good as being timely. / For those who are skilled in being timely, their days may be few but their achievements will be great.

Now, if stratagems are developed without someone in charge, there will be trouble. If undertakings lack full preparation, they will be a waste of time. For this reason the sage king pays heed to making his prepa-

---

[8] Reading 刑 as 型 [Guo Moruo].

rations complete and takes care to insure their timeliness. His undertakings prosper because he is prepared to await the proper time. / When the proper time arrives, he launches his armed forces, cutting through resistance to attack those who refuse to yield.[9] He destroys large states and carves up their territory. He treats the large as the root [problem] but the small as mere branches.[10] He assembles[11] the near to attack the far / and uses the large to drag along the small, the strong to coerce the weak, the many to bring along the few. His virtue benefits the hundred surnames; his majesty shakes the entire realm. His orders are carried out among the feudal lords with no opposition. / Of those near at hand, no one fails to submit; of those far removed, no one fails to obey.

Now, the clearsighted king in ruling the realm takes proper balance as his guiding principle. He represses the strong and assists the weak, restrains the violent and stops the corrupt, revives / states that have perished and stabilizes those that are endangered, and restores lines of succession where they have been broken. This is what the entire realm supports,[12] / what turns the feudal lords into allies, and what benefits the hundred surnames. It is for this reason that the realm / makes him its king.

Knowledge that covers the entire realm, order[13] that remains supreme throughout an entire age, talent capable of moving everything within the four seas—such are his aids to being a king. Since states possessing a thousand chariots obtain[14] his protection, the feudal lords can be made to serve / him as his subjects and the entire realm can be made his. When a state of ten thousand chariots loses his protection, it ceases to be one of his states.

When the entire realm is under his control, any state that acts on its own and is rebellious ceases to be one of his states. When the feudal lords all / accept his orders,[15] any state that acts on its own and stands apart ceases to be one of his states. When neighboring states all face danger, any state that acts on its own and wavers [in its allegiance] ceases to be one of his states. These three are the signs of a state that will perish. /

Now, if a state is large but its government is unimpressive, it will become like its government. If a state is small but its government is

[9] Emending 國 to 固 [Xu].
[10] The Yang edition for 摽 mistakenly writes 標.
[11] Emending 崟 to 榮 = 秦 = 湊 [Guo Moruo].
[12] Emending 載 to 戴 [Igai and Dai].
[13] Emending 繼 to 斷 [Igai, Zhang Peilun, and Liu Shipei].
[14] The Yang edition mistakenly inserts 可 before 得 [Dai].
[15] Igai and Wang Niansun would emend 令 to 合, "are united." This reading fits the context better.

impressive, it will grow larger. If it has become large but is not well managed, it will again / become small. If it has become strong but is not well ordered, it will again become weak. If it has developed a large population but it is not well ordered, its population will again become small. If it becomes honored but does not behave ceremoniously, it will again be slighted. / If it has become important, but abuses the regulations, it will again be treated lightly. / If it has become rich but is arrogant and dissolute, it will again become poor.

Therefore, when observing a state, [the clearsighted king] observes / its prince. When observing an army, he observes its generals. When observing its state of preparedness, he observes its fields. If its prince appears clearsighted, but is not; if its generals appear worthy, but are not; / if its people appear to be farming, but are not—if these three [essentials] for preserving [a state] are missing, such a state ceases to be one of his states.

If [a state's] territory is extensive but not well managed, / it is called being satisfied with [mere] land. If its population is large but not well ordered, it is called being satisfied with [merely] having people. If its armed forces are awesome but are not kept in check, it is called being satisfied with [mere] military prowess. If these three / satisfactions are not curbed, the state ceases to be one of his states.

If the territory is extensive but remains uncultivated, it is not his territory. If senior ministers (*qing* 卿) are honored but not submissive, they are not his senior ministers. / If the population is large but does not rally around him, they are not his people.

Now, to lack land yet desire to be rich will bring grief. To lack virtue yet desire to be king will bring danger. / To give little yet seek much will bring isolation. Indeed, if the throne is penurious[16] but subordinate officials profligate,[17] the state small but its capital large,[18] / there will be assassinations. To have the ruler revered and ministers humble, the throne majestic and subordinate officials respectful, orders carried out and people submissive—such is the goal of good order.

Should the realm have two sons of Heaven, a single state / two princes, or a single family two fathers, control would be impossible. Indeed if orders do not come from on high, they will not be carried out. If they do not emanate from a single source,[19] they will not be

---

[16] Emending 夾 to 狹 [Wang Niansun].

[17] Emending 亘 to 筧 = 寬 [Song and Zhang Peilun].

[18] The meaning here is somewhat ambiguous. Perhaps here 國, "state," should be read as "capital," and 都, "capital," as "regional cities."

[19] The Yang edition mistakenly writes 搏 for 搏 = 專 [Igai and Xu].

8.2   obeyed. / The people of Yao and Shun[20] were born to good order; those of Jie and Zhou[21] were born to disorder. Therefore [the responsibility for] order or disorder rests with the sovereign.

8.3   Now, a lord protector or king / begins by taking people as basic. If its base is in good order, the state will be secure; if it is in disorder, the state will be endangered. Therefore, if the sovereign is clearsighted, subordinate officials will be respectful. If the government is evenhanded, people will be at ease.[22] If the instruction of the knights is appropriate, the armed forces will vanquish the enemy. If these things can be

8.4   effected, / all undertakings will be well ordered. If the sovereign takes as his close associates those who are humane, he will never be endangered. If he employs the worthy, the feudal lords will be submissive.

  There are [certain] conditions that distinguish a lord protector or king. They are superior in terms of virtue and righteousness, wisdom and stratagems, armed forces and the conduct of warfare, [knowledge

8.5   of] the terrain and / maneuverability. Therefore they [are able] to rule [the realm].

8.6   Now, he who is skilled in manipulating states relies on the prominent
9a   position of large[23] states to reduce their influence, / on the power of strong states to weaken their influence, and on the characteristics of important states to lighten their influence. When strong[24] states are

8.7   numerous, he unites / with the strong to attack the weak in planning to become a lord protector. When strong states are few, he unites with the

8.8   small to attack the large in planning to become king. / When strong states are numerous, it is the wisdom of fools to talk about the influence of a king. When strong states are few, it is a defeatist strategy to proclaim the way of a lord protector.

.9   Now, the divine sage looks / at the condition of the realm and knows whether it is a time to be active or quiescent. He looks at the consequences of events and knows whether they represent the door to disaster or prosperity. If strong states are numerous, whoever takes the initiative will be in danger, while those who lag behind will reap the

.10   benefits. / When strong states are few, whoever takes the initiative will become king, while those who lag behind will be lost. When warring

[20] 堯 and 舜; ancient legendary rulers.
[21] 桀 and 紂; the last emperors of the Xia and Shang.
[22] Dai and Guo Moruo would emend *shi* 士, "knights," to *tu* 土, "land." Otherwise, the two sentences are out of balance. their revision would make the two sentences read, "If the government is evenhanded, people will be at ease on the land. If the instructions are appropriate, the armed forces will vanquish the enemy."
[23] Deleting 其, in accordance with the Ancient, Liu, and Zhu editions.
[24] The Yang edition mistakenly writes 弱 for 彊 [Zhang Peilun and Xu].

states are numerous, whoever lags behind may become lord protector. When warring states are few, whoever takes the initiative may become king.

The mind of the incompetent ruler[25] is undisciplined[26] so he does not assemble[27] / heroic[28] [knights], give way to the worthy,[29] or on the basis of age select [people from among] the masses. This is because of his greed for big things. / Thus a condition that distinguishes a king is magnanimity.

Now, the former kings, when struggling for [control of] the realm, relied on uprightness.[30] When establishing [their rule], they relied on having everything in its proper order. / When instituting good order, they relied on peaceful change. When setting up their government and issuing orders, they used the way of man. When awarding ranks and salaries, they used the way of Earth. / When initiating major undertakings, they used the way of Heaven.

For this reason, when the former kings launched punitive attacks, they attacked [only] those who opposed them and not those who were obedient, [only] those who posed a threat and not those who were compliant, [only] those who went to excess and not those who [merely] failed[31] to come up to standard. / Within the four boundaries, they were evenhanded in their employment of people. Feudal lords were brought together by using political power to summon them. For those who were near at hand but refused to submit, [the former kings] relied on [seizure of] their territory to make them suffer. / For those who were far removed and disobedient, they relied on punishments to threaten them. When [the feudal lords] were two-faced,[32] [the former kings] responded in a military way by attacking them. When [the feudal lords] were submissive, [the former kings] responded in a civil way by leaving them alone. / Both their military and civil responses were completely virtuous.

Now, there are [certain] conditions that produce importance or unimportance, strength or weakness. When the feudal lords are united, they

---

[25] The text of this passage is obviously corrupt, but none of the commentators provides a fully satisfactory revision. here I followed Guo Moruo in emending 夫王 to 失主.

[26] Reading 方 as 放 [Guo Moruo].

[27] Reading 弄 as 會 [Chen].

[28] Reading 列 as 烈 [Guo Moruo].

[29] Deleting the second 賢 as a reduplicated character [Chen and Guo Moruo].

[30] Emending 方心 to 方正 [Wang Niansun and Xu].

[31] Inserting 不 before 及 in accordance with the Ancient, Liu, and Zhu editions [Yasui, Dai, and Ding].

[32] Emending 一 to 二 = 貳 [Wang Niansun]. This passage is similar to the *Zuo zhuan*, Xi, 15 (Legge, *Ch'un Ts'eu*, V, 15/13): 貳而執之, 服而舍之. 德莫厚焉? "If he is two-faced, seize him; if he submits, let him go. What virtue could be greater than this?"

are strong; when they are isolated, they are weak. With all its capability, even a thoroughbred is bound to be exhausted when [challenged] by a hundred ordinary horses in succession.[33] / The most powerful state of its time[34] is bound to be weakened when attacked[35] by the entire realm.

A strong state achieves success by bringing together those that are small, but fails if it comes to depend on them. A small state achieves success by conserving its resources, / but fails if it breaks with its strong [neighbors]. Now, the large and small have their [separate] stratagems, and the strong and weak have their [different] conditions. To subjugate the near and use force against the far / is a condition distinguishing a state belonging to a king. To unite with the small to attack the large is a condition distinguishing rival states. To use the states bordering the four seas to attack other states bordering the four seas is a condition distinguishing the central states. To conserve its resources and serve / the strong so as to avoid offending them is a condition distinguishing small states.[36] From ancient times to the present, there has never been [a state] that was able to establish merit and fame[37] after having encountered [internal] difficulties, gone against the times and [attempted to] alter its condition. There has [also] never been [a state] / that did not suffer defeat after having encountered [internal] difficulties, gone against the times, and [attempted to] alter its condition.

Now, whoever wishes to become one of those who is able to attack princes by using their own subjects and establish order within the four seas cannot rely on the use of armed force alone to seize control. / Being certain to settle first on a plan, select advantageous terrain, take advantage of the balance [of power], develop close relations with allied states, and watch for the right moment to move—such are the political methods of a king.

Now, when the former kings engaged in punitive expeditions, their launching [of the attack] was certain to be just, and their use [of troops]

---

[33] Emending 伐 to 代 [Igai and Wang Niansun].

[34] Ibid.

[35] Emending 共 to 攻 [Ding].

[36] This passage is very similar to a statement of Chao Cuo 晁錯 (d. 154 b.c.), which appears in his biography in the *Qian Han shu*, 49, 8a13–8b3: "I have further heard that large and small states have different conditions, the strong and the weak have different ways of coping, and there are different forms of preparation depending on whether one is threatened or at ease. Now, to humble oneself to serve the strong is a condition distinguishing a small state. To unite the small to attack the large is a condition distinguishing rival states. To use the Man and the Yi to attack the Man and Yi is a condition distinguishing the central states." The Man 蠻 were a non-Sinified people living in the south of China. The Yi 夷 were a similar people inhabiting China's northeast.

[37] The Zhao edition mistakenly writes 先能 for 能先.

9.10
10b

was certain to be swift and violent. / They examined conditions to know what was possible, measured their strength to know when to attack, and considered[38] what was to be gained to know the proper time. For this reason, when the former kings engaged in punitive expeditions, they first

9.11

engaged [the enemy] in skirmishes / before a full-scale attack. They first launched full-scale attacks before seizing territory.

Therefore, those who are skilled in conducting attacks calculate numbers [of troops needed] to match the troops [of the enemy], food [needed] to match their food, and equipment [needed] to match their equipment. When matching numbers, if [the advantage in]

9.12

numbers / lies [with the enemy], they do not attack. When matching food, if [the advantage in] food lies [with the enemy], they do not attack. When matching equipment, if [the advantage in] equipment lies [with the enemy] they do not attack. They avoid [the enemy's] real strengths to

9.13

attack his deficiencies, strong points to attack / soft spots, and difficult targets to attack the easy.

Now, control[39] of a state does not lie [merely] in paying respect to tradition. Bringing order to a generation does not lie [merely] in being skilled in attack. Becoming a lord protector or king does not lie [merely]

9.14

in perfecting regulations.[40] Indeed, should their ventures / fail, their states will be endangered. If their punishments are excessive,[41] their political power will be toppled. If their stratagems are carelessly contrived, disasters will result. However, if their calculations are accurate, their strength will be reliable. If their achievements are real, fame will

10.1

follow. If their political power is taken seriously, / their orders will be carried out. Such is the [grand] scheme for ensuring security.

Now, states that struggle to be stronger than others must first struggle in terms of stratagems, conditions,[42] and political power. Stratagems are what cause a ruler to be liked one moment and hated another.

10.2
11a

Conditions / are what cause him to be taken lightly one moment and seriously another. Political power is what causes his armed forces to advance one moment and retreat another. Therefore, if he pays full

10.3

attention to stratagems, his desires / may be realized and his orders carried out. If he pays full attention to conditions, the territory of large countries may be seized and the armed forces of strong states contained.

---

[38] Reading 攻 as 玫 [Yasui].

[39] Both the Yang edition and the Ming print of the Zhao edition mistakenly write 搏 for 摶.

[40] Emending 曲 to 典 [Yu Yue, Wang Niansun, and Guo Moruo].

[41] Ding would emend 刑 to 形. Thus the phrase would read: "If they exceed their roles...."

[42] Emending 刑 to 形 here and below [Wang Niansun and Yasui].

10.4 If he pays full attention to political power, the armed forces of the realm may be reduced[43] and the feudal / princes brought to court.

Now, the divine sages looked at the condition [of various states] in the realm to know what stratagems to adopt for their generations, what their armed forces should attack, what territory should be returned, and what orders should be added.

10.5 Now, if armed forces are used to attack / those whom [a ruler] hates in order to benefit himself, neighboring countries will not rally around him. If his political power is applied against those whom [everyone] abhors and little profit accrues to him, he will become strong. /

0.6 Those who on their own destroy [an enemy] state and pass their strength on to later generations become kings. Those who on their own 0.7 destroy [an enemy] state but their strength / accrues to their neighbors will perish.

[43] Reading 齊 as 翦 [Guo Moruo].

Wen

問

QUERIES

Introductory Comments

Three separate fragments have been combined by an editor, probably Liu Xiang 劉向, to make up the *Wen*.[1] The first fragment (11b1–15a2; 10.10–13.12) consists of a rhymed prologue followed by a series of queries the ruler should present to his ministers when holding court. The effect of these queries following one upon another is to give this part of the chapter a unique form remarkably reminiscent of the *Tianwen* 天問 [Heavenly Questions] chapter of the *Chu ci*.[2]

There are, however, several notable differences between this *Guanzi* fragment and the *Tianwen*. The *Tianwen*, which Hawkes (*Ch'u Tz'u*, pp. 45–46) believes was originally written around the fifth century B.C. as a series of riddles, is an imaginative, literary work dealing primarily with natural phenomena and legendary history. The *Wen*, on the other hand, is a straightforward, practical work dealing with concrete political matters. The *Tianwen* is written in a rather archaic poetic style that combines four four-word phrases in a single, rhyming couplet.[3] In this first fragment, the *Wen* makes use of rhyme only in the prologue, is composed of sentences of varying length, some of them quite long and complicated in structure, and, for the most part, is written in a rather prosaic style. The individual queries in this chapter are roughly grouped according to related subject matter, with the first of a group usually introduced by the character *wen* 問, "inquire about." This device is not used by the author of the *Tianwen*. It seems to me that the author of

---

[1] For a special study of this portion of the chapter, see Utsunomiya Kiyoyoshi's article, *Kanshi Monben shiron*.

[2] This point may be clearly demonstrated by quoting a few lines from David Hawkes' translation (*Ch'u Tz'u*, p. 46): "Who was there to pass down the story of the beginning of things in the remote past? What means are there to examine what it was like before heaven above and earth below had taken shape? How is it possible to probe into that age when the light and darkness were still undivided? And how do we know of the chaos of insubstantial form?"

[3] The four-word phrase form is also used in the *Shi jing*.

the *Wen* may possibly have borrowed from the general literary form of the *Tianwen*, but did not copy it completely because he may have found that the rigid prosody of that work ill-fitted his subject matter.

The prologue serves as a sort of philosophical introduction to the queries representing a mixture of Confucian and Legalist ideas. The ruler is advised to promote Confucian-sounding "righteousness" and "virtue" and never abandon old retainers or kinsmen. At the same time, he is to establish Legalistic "constant standards" (*chang jing* 常經) and "political methods (*shu* 術) of the lord protector to the king," so that "the people will know where to stop and start."

The value of this fragment lies in its information on some of the social and political problems facing a ruler in pre-Han times. The first concern found in the questions deals with the orphans and widows of those who died in war. Apparently they were entitled either to grants of land or grain subsidies from the state. Concern is also expressed over delays in the law courts, debts accrued through loans, officials who, instead of performing their duties themselves, have left them to their servants, and the general moral standards of the population. A number of questions are posed regarding military affairs, the supply of draft animals, the manufacture and testing of weapons, and the fact that excess troops may be allowed to congregate in the hands of local officials or feudal landholders.

This portion of the text is very difficult to date, but the fact that it reflects both Legalist and Confucian ideas would seem to place it within the development of authoritarian Confucianism in the latter half of the third century B.C. It also seems likely that the author may have come from the state of Chu 楚. This is indicated somewhat by its similarity in form to the *Tianwen*, which is generally believed to be a product of that area. Even more indicative of Chu origin is the use of the term *gongyin* 工尹 (14a5–6; 13.1) for minister of works. *Yin* was the title given to chief ministers in the state of Chu. However, these points cannot be taken as conclusive.

The remainder of the chapter consists of two very short fragments that may or may not have been part of the same original work. The first (15a3–7; 13.13–14.1) appears to be part of a lost book or essay, *Zhi di jun* 制地君 [The Prince Who Rules in Accordance with Earth]. The text is very corrupt, and many of the emendations I have been forced to accept in order to make it readable at all can be considered no more than guesses. It is a curious piece in that its discussion of the Power of Earth (*di de* 地德) seems to reflect some offshoot of Five Phases thinking, with the term *di* incorporating some of the qualities of the earth phase (*tu* 土). The passage is really too short, however, to make possible any real attempt at analysis.

The remaining fragment (15a4–16a4; 14.1–14.11), which may have been added to that above because it too mentions Earth, is essentially a plea for free trade and, as such, is Confucian in outlook. The *Mengzi*, IB, 5/3, states that during the reign of King Wen 文 of the Zhou dynasty, "at the customs stations and markets, [strangers] were inspected but not [forced to] pay duties." Xunzi was also an advocate of free trade. According to V, 9/5b13 (Dubs, *Hsüntze*, p. 132): "At the customs stations and markets, [the king] inspects [strangers] but does not levy duties." Then he goes on to list the rich treasures—fine feathers, ivory, rhinoceros hides, copper, cinnabar, etc.—to be obtained from the four corners of the realm if this policy is carried out. The views expressed in this chapter of the *Guanzi* differ from those of Mencius and Xunzi only in that the author would merely limit the tax to one payment, so that those who had paid duties at the customs stations would not have to pay an additional tax in the marketplace.

The extreme brevity of these two fragments makes it difficult to say anything definite about their dating, except that in terms of ideological content, they would appear to be products of the late Warring States Period.

Translation

2:10.10
11b1 Whenever [the ruler] holds court, his queries should be concerned with basic principles. The great ministers will promote righteousness if ranks are bestowed on those who are virtuous. The knights will not fear death if salaries are given to those who are meritorious. If the sovereign 10.11 leads his knights with [the virtues] people / respect, harmony[4] will reign above and below. If he assigns tasks according to ability, people will esteem achievement. if he is judicious in making the punishment fit the crime, people will not be cynical about seeking justice through the 10.12 courts. / If he does not bring disorder to the altars of Land and Grain and the ancestral temples, people will have something to venerate. If he does not abandon his old [retainers] or forget his kinsmen, his great

---

[4] Zhang Peilun and Xu would insert 同 (*dewng*) after 和 in order to complete the rhyme with the final characters in the following sentences, 功 (*kweng*), 訟 (*grjewng*), and 宗 (*tsêwng*). The meaning would remain the same.

ministers will not become resentful.[5] / When initiating [military] ventures, if he understands the difficulties people [will encounter], the masses will not become rebellious. When this way [of government] is carried out, the state will have constant standards and men will know where to stop and start. / These are the political methods of the lord protector to the king.

After [mastering these], inquire about matters [of state]. Matters involving great merit should be put first. When dealing with the administration, begin with matters of detail. /

Inquire about the orphans of those who died in war. Are there any who do not yet have fields and houses? Inquire how many of the young and able-bodied[6] have not yet borne arms. / Inquire about the widows of those who died in war. What is the condition of their grain allowance?

Inquire about those who have achieved great merit on behalf of the country. In what official bureaus are they employed? / Inquire about the great officers of the subdistricts (*zhou* 州). Of what villages (*li* 里) are they members of the gentry? How can we learn about [the ability of] our present civil functionaries? Inquire why cases drag on for so long and if the decisions about punishments are consistent / and unalterable in their execution. Inquire why the present delay in affairs is so protracted, whether the five official bureaus[7] have regulations covering procedure, / and whether the heads[8] of these bureaus make consistent decisions.

Inquire how many persons are unmarried, widowed, destitute,[9] / and sick. Inquire about the exiles of the country. To what clans do the young people belong? Inquire about the honorable families[10] of the districts (*xiang* 鄉). / How many men are supported by them?

Inquire about the poor people of the towns (*yi* 邑). How many families have gone into debt in order to feed themselves? / Inquire how many families tend gardens in order to feed themselves. How many have

[5] This is reminiscent of the *Lun yu*, XVIII, 10, which says: "A virtuous prince never discards his kinsmen. Neither does he cause his great ministers to become resentful over not being used, or dismiss those who have been long in service (故舊) without grave cause."

[6] The Yang edition for 壯 mistakenly writes 仕.

[7] For these five official bureaus, see VII, 18, n. 74.

[8] Following Guo Moruo, who says that *du* 都 here means the head of a bureau or department. He cites the use of the term in XVIII, 57/7a7 (3:17.13), and XXIII, 78, 5b6–7 (3:87.7–8), as proof. This is an infrequent reading of the character, but it seems to fit the context of the sentence here.

[9] Emending 寡 to 窮 [Zhang Peilun and Xu].

[10] 良家, lit., "good families," i.e., well-to-do families who derived their incomes from land rather than trade or some less socially accepted source.

cleared land for cultivation, and how many families of the gentry cultivate [land] themselves? / Inquire about the poor people of the districts. What are their clan distinctions?

Inquire in how many families the chief heir takes care of[11] his brothers and poor cousins. / How many younger sons who served in office and possessed fields and estates [of their own] have now had them confiscated?[12]

How many young people in the districts and villages are noted for their filial piety? / How many younger sons whose parents are living do not take care of them but leave to marry [into other families]?[13]

How many of the members of the gentry[14] possessing fields are not employed [in office]? What[15] do the ones do who are civil functionaries? / How many of them possess fields but do not cultivate them? What do they do in their personal capacity? How many of the various[16] ministers have positions but do not yet have fields? / How many families of foreigners have come to serve us[17] but do not yet have fields and houses? How many of our country's young people have gone abroad?

How many impoverished members of the gentry are in debt[18] to great officers? / How many officials disparage performing clerical tasks and services[19] of a personal nature, and so use their private servants to substitute for them [at work]? / How many assistant[20] functionaries in the official bureaus have neither fields nor grain allowances and yet carry on managerial duties for nothing? How many of the various ministers have assumed[21] the duties of the great officers in charge of the bureaus?[22] / How many foreigners have come to visit in the houses of the great officers?

[11] Following the Yang edition, which writes 牧 for 收.

[12] Following the interpretation of Tao, who says the land had been confiscated (*ru* 入) after the younger sons had been demoted for committing crimes in office.

[13] Following Yu Yue's interpretation and reading 離 as 儷. The normal pattern in Chinese society was for the son to bring his wife home to become a member of his family. However, a son of a poor family or one not in line for an inheritance who had been able to marry a girl from a prosperous family might leave his own home to live in his wife's and then become an adopted member of her family.

[14] The *SBBY* reprint of the Zhao edition mistakenly prints 上 for 士.

[15] Deleting 惡 [Ding].

[16] Emending 君 to 羣 [Igai].

[17] Wang Yinzhi and Yasui would emend 從 to 徙, thus making the sentence read: "How many families of foreigners who have moved here do not yet have fields and houses?"

[18] Emending 責 to 債 [Zhu Changchun, Chen, and Tao].

[19] Emending 士 to 事 [Xu].

[20] Emending 承 to 丞 [Zhang Peilun].

[21] Reading 位 as 涖 [Wu Rulun and Jiang Han].

[22] 官大夫 was the name of a special rank in the state of Qin 秦. See the *LSCQ*, XXIV, 4/6b9. However, it is doubtful that the same meaning applies here.

370

12.3 How many young people in the districts lead others in working in the fields? / How many young people of the country do not serve their superiors, are extravagant in their clothing and food, and lead [other] young people away from tilling the fields to hunt with bow and arrow? Are there any men or women who are disorderly[23] and corrupt the young people of the districts? /

12.4 Inquire how many families have people who lend out grain and hold contracts in the form of tallies. Inquire about the country's latent re-

12.5 sources. In what ways can they meet the urgent [needs] of people? / What harm do people do in the districts and villages?

Inquire about members of the gentry who possess fields and houses.

2.6 How many are personally serving in the [armed] ranks? / How many younger sons bear arms and have formed columns (*hang* 行) and squads (*wu* 伍)?

Inquire about men and women who possess skills. How many are able

2.7 [to produce] / good equipment? How many women who have remained

3b [unmarried] at home occupy themselves with / [women's] work? Inquire[24] how many men in the country merely open their mouths to be fed. Inquire how many years' food there is for the entire population.[25] /

2.8 Inquire about the total number of war chariots. How many teams are there of privately owned draft horses yoked to privately owned vehicles?

How many of the gentry who have remained at home [rather than take up public office] have cultivated their conduct sufficiently to teach

2.9 others / and can be employed to lead the masses and oversee the hundred surnames? How many knights can be employed in time of emergency? How many artisans are there whose skill is sufficient for them to be of

2.10 advantage to the army away from home / or who, while remaining at home, can build walls and repair defense works? How many years will

2.11 grain for cities and military provisions last? / How many civil functionaries can be employed in times of emergency?

Have the great officers list the weapons. How many war chariots are there to go with the armored troops and how many chariots are used by the commanders to carry banners and flags, drums and cymbals, canopies and tents? /

.12 Have them list the implements for storing [weapons]. How is the

---

[23] The Yin commentary explains that this means they have improper relations with one another.

[24] Emending 冗 (Yang edition writes 宂) to 閒 [Ding and Yu Yue].

[25] 一民; the meaning of this term is not clear. Professor Qian Zhongshu suggested reading it as "average person."

workmanship[26] on the cases[27] for the bows and crossbows, sheaths for the double-edged swords[28] and spears, containers for thumb rings and bow strings, / and receptacles[29] for the lances and halberds? Why[30] have those [implements] not been made that should have been made? Examine the official bureaus where they[31] are made. / Concerning the completion of implements to be sent abroad or used at home, why is there delay in starting those that should have been started? What is the state of completion of the chariots and baggage wagons that are being built for the district commanders?[32] /

During the three seasons [of spring, summer, and autumn] the minister of works[33] should not cut timber for use. Since the various types of timber are then in the process of growth, the making of weapons should be limited to the winter time. Equipment of excellent quality[34] will then certainly be sufficient. /

Demand[35] that those persons who have surplus soldiers place them in the [regular] ranks in order to safeguard the constant standards of the state. / At the proper time, examine the physical condition of the horses and oxen of the commanders. Make a record of those that have become old or died. / How many of them go to the mountain grasslands and woodland marshes to eat grass? What was the total number that were sent out [to pasture], brought into [the stables], died, and were born?

Now, with regard to the width of city and suburban walls, / the depth of ditches and moats, and the height of outer and inner gates, if what should have been done was not done, the sovereign should inquire into it. The troops who guard the equipment [should see to it] that none of the

---

[26] This entire passage, 疏藏器 ··· 其厲何若, is extremely corrupt. Moreover, not only do the commentators show wide disagreement in their interpretation of individual characters, but on several problem points they make no comment at all. Assuming that the subject under discussion throughout the passage concerns implements for storing weapons (藏器), I have taken this as my point of departure when choosing among the various emendations and interpretations suggested by the commentators. Thus, for 厲, which has as its primary meaning "whetstone" and usually refers to grinding or sharpening, I have followed Zhang Binglin's interpretation of "good workmanship."

[27] Emending 張 to 帳 [Zhang Peilun and Guo Moruo].

[28] Emending the phrase 衣夾鋏 to read 夾鋏之衣 [Zhang Peilun and Guo Moruo]. 夾 is read as 鋏.

[29] Emending 緊 to 㮡 [Yao and Guo Moruo].

[30] Inverting the two characters 故向 [Ding and Xu].

[31] Reading 而 as 其 [Xu].

[32] Emending 師 to 帥 in order to accord with the passages above and below (13b11; 12.11 and 14a9; 13.3). The Guangxu 光緒 (1879) cutting of the Yang edition writes 帥.

[33] *Gongyin* 工尹; the chief ministers in Chu were called *yin*.

[34] The Yang edition for 完 mistakenly writes 兒.

[35] Following Zhang Binglin, who says 詭 means 責, "to demand." Guo Moruo agrees, but he would interpret 兵 to mean "arms." Thus he would read the sentence: "Demand that those men who have surplus arms distribute them among the [regular] ranks."

weapons are missing. When there is excessive rain, / each should have its storage place.

Inquire about the officers and civil functionaries in the armed forces[36] and eminent persons and gentlemen of the country. How many could be [depended upon] from first to last[37] in times of emergency? /

Now, military ventures are dangerous things. Being untimely in one's victories or unrighteous in one's acquisitions will not lead to good fortune. Defeats incurred through the neglect of [proper] stratagems / will endanger the country. [Therefore], pay careful attention to strategy in order to provide for the country's protection.[38]

Inquire what matters should be used [as a basis] for teaching and selecting men. Inquire how many years the administrative bureau heads / have directed[39] affairs. How many have increased their private estates by clearing the grasslands? What things should be especially noted in order to increase the benefits to human livelihood? / In what places should city and suburban walls be constructed, lesser walls[40] built, through roads obstructed, gates[41] blocked, and embankments and ditches deepened / in order to enhance people's defense of their locality? How many places have arrested robbers and rid themselves of those who do harm?[42] /

"The Prince Who Rules in Accordance with Earth"[43] says; "The

[36] Emending 兵官之吏 to read 兵之官吏, in accordance with the structure of the following phrase 國之豪士 [Xu].

[37] Yasui would interpret the two characters 先後 to mean "assist." Thus the sentence would read: "How many will be of assistance in time of emergency?"

[38] This short paragraph does not seem to fit the context here. Zhang Peilun suggests that it is a misplaced fragment from the lost chapter IX, 25, *Mo shi* 謀失 [On Stratagems against Defeat]. Guo Moruo agrees that it is a misplaced fragment, but says it probably belongs after the phrase 大度書曰, VI, 17/11a7 (1 : 79.6).

[39] Emending 位 to 涖.

[40] Emending 閘 to 闬 [Guo Moruo].

[41] Since this sentence is made up of a series of three character phrases, it is apparent that a character must be missing from the phrase 院闕. I have followed Chen and Guo Moruo in inserting 門 before 闕.

[42] The abruptness with which this portion of the text ends indicates without doubt that it is not complete.

[43] Here appears a definite break in the Chinese text, and in the Ancient edition the chapter ends at this point. *Zhi di jun* 制地君 may be the title of an ancient book or essay of which all trace is now lost except for this fragment. Other such titles appear in the *Guanzi*. For example, VI, 17/11a7 (1 : 79.6), cites a *Da du zhi shu* 大度之書, which may be rendered as the "Book of Important Procedures." XXIII, 80/13a11 (3 : 94.10), also cites a *Dao ruo mi* 道若秘 [The Way as the Mystery]. Guo Moruo believes that the fragment that follows here was inserted into the text by mistake. He suggests that the phrase should stop with *Zhi di* and that this was originally the name of a separate chapter of the *Guanzi*. When the greater portion of it was later lost, this remaining fragment was inserted here by mistake. Yasui would insert the character 子 after *jun*. Thus, if we combine these two suggestions, the text would read: "'On Ruling in Accordance with Earth.' A man of quality has said...."

correct way for managing a country takes the Power of Earth as its
guiding principle. The rules of propriety for the prince and minister and
the close relationship between father and son are all taken from the
[example of] Earth.[44] / It shelters and nourishes all men. The storehouses of the official depositories, which give strength to the army and
defend the country, [are all made of earth, as are] the ramparts of the city
and suburban walls that face outward toward the four extremities." /

Now,[45] the market is [the place] where the wealth of Heaven and
Earth is collected and where all men assemble to make profits. / When
the government[46] is [based on] this correct way, the people[47] will be
without anxieties;[48] men will fulfill their responsibilites toward Earth
and unite together / to defend their country. let each person hold his
position in accordance with his special ability. Do not employ slanderers, establish good order everywhere,[49] and let moral force create
close ties among the nine regions [of the empire].[50] /

The customs stations are [situated on] byways remote from [the
capitals of] the feudal lords, but they are gateways for [the entry of]
foreign wealth. Tens of thousands of people go through them. / Make
clear [the rules of] the road by repeatedly proclaiming them. Those who
have paid duties at the customs stations should not be taxed in the
marketplaces, and those who have been taxed in the marketplaces
should not pay duties at the customs stations. / Do not charge fees on
empty carts. Do not make those who are transporting their burden on
foot pay duties. [Do all this] in order that men will come from afar. Make
the same pronouncements[51] for all sixteen[52] highways. /

When foreign emissaries[53] are interviewed,[54] listen to their names,

13.14

14.1
14.2

14.3

14.4
15b

14.5

14.6

14.7

---

[44] Following He Ruzhang, who believes the phrase 其取之地, which appears three
lines below (15a7; 14.1), originally followed 父子之親 (15a4; 13.13) and was later
transferred to its present position by mistake.

[45] Emending 而 to 夫 [Zhang Peilun]. For the phrase 其取之地, see n. 44 above.

[46] Reading 正 as 政 [Guo Moruo].

[47] The character 荒 is unintelligible here. I have followed Yin Tongyang, Xu, and Guo
Moruo in emending it to 氓.

[48] Emending 苛 to 巫 [Guo Moruo].

[49] Reading 普 as 編 [Ding and Guo Moruo].

[50] Following Ding and Guo Moruo, who say that 九軍, lit., "nine armies," refers to the
九國 or 九州, "nine regions," into which the sage emperor Yu divided the empire.
However, the phrases in this sentence do not balance, and it is still probable that it suffers
from textual corruption.

[51] Emending 身 to 伸 or 申 [Yu Xingwu].

[52] Zhang Peilun would read "sixteen" as "eighteen," in accordance with the passage in
the *Zhou li*, 41/14b5 (Biot, *Tcheou-li*, II, p. 556): "Within the capital there are nine direct
avenues [running east and west]."

[53] Emending 事 to 使 [Guo Moruo].

[54] Emending 謹 to 覿 [Ding and Guo Moruo].

examine [the writing of] their names, their faces, and[55] the [nature of]
their business, / judge their virtue, and observe their pattern of conduct,[56] so that no one will be taken in by opportunists who [speciously]
give a sincere[57] appearance of virtue. / It is the duty, then, of those who
conduct this [examination] to see that the country is not misled.

Inform[58] the civil functionaries at the border: "Petty profit is harmful
to harmoniousness.[59] / Petty anger is harmful to righteousness.
Partial[60] trustworthiness is harmful to virtue. / Unite in harmony with
the states on our four borders in order to follow perfect[61] virtue, and
richly entertain[62] [the rulers of those states] from the four extremities." /

Order the officials [charged with] maintaining the law:[63] "In carrying
out the procedures, be certain to be clear. Do not[64] neglect the constant
standards."

[55] Emending 是 to 視 [Yu Yue].

[56] Following Guo Moruo, who would delete 外 as an interpolation growing out of a
mistaken reading of the word 則 as "then," instead of "pattern." His conclusion is
supported by the need for 則 (*tsek*) to end the above passage in order to complete the
rhyme with 德 (*tek*) in line 15b10 (14.8), below.

[57] Reading 困 as 悃 [Guo Moruo].

[58] 問 here is equivalent to 告 [Guo Moruo].

[59] Emending 信 to 和 [Kuo]. 和 (*gwa*) completes the rhyme with 義 (*ngia*) in the same
line below.

[60] Reading 邊 as 偏 [Yasui and Zhang Wenhu].

[61] The character *mao* 貌 is unintelligible here. It is probably a phonetic borrowing for
mao 兒, which in turn is a corruption of 完. See n. 34, above.

[62] Reading 鄉 as 饗 [Guo Moruo].

[63] Following the Zhu edition, which for *ri* 日 writes *yue* 曰 [Wang Niansun and Xu].

[64] The Yang edition mistakenly omits the character 無.

Jie

戒

ADMONITIONS

Introductory Comments

This chapter presents a series of stories concerning Duke Huan and Guan Zhong, including the well-known account of their deaths and the chaos that followed. All praise the standard Confucian virtues and belong to that tradition of propaganda literature aimed at convincing rulers to listen to the advice of good ministers. However, the first story is of particular interest because it is strongly Daoist in tone, stressing such concepts as the Way (*dao* 道) and the Power (*de* 德) as well as the ruler who rules through adhering to the natural order of things. A. C. Graham would link it to a more specific tradition, believing it is a surviving document of the school of Gaozi 告子, who seems to have been a contemporary of Mencius (371–279 B.C.) and is mentioned several times in the *Mengzi*.[1] As Graham points out (p. 228), the *Mengzi* provides us with three basic facts about Gaozi's thought: (1) He attained an "unmoved mind" 不動心 before Mencius himself. (2) He held that there is neither good nor bad in our natures. (3) He held that "benevolence" (*ren* 仁) is internal, not external; duty (righteousness; *yi* 義) is external, not internal.[2] Since all three of these ideas are either explicitly or implicitly expressed in this chapter, Graham's point appears well taken.

Graham also argues (p. 228) that this text comes from the same intellectual climate as the *Mengzi*. To support this argument, he cites the opening dialogue between Guan Zhong and Duke Huan regarding the duke's proposed tour of inspection as a variation of a similar story in the *Mengzi*, IB, 4/5–6, involving Duke Jing 景 and Yanzi 晏子. He states that the economic measures proposed by Guan Zhong (4a2–5; 17.11–12) are similar to those proposed by Mencius to King Xuan 宣 (*Mengzi*, IB, 5/3 and IA, 3/3–5), and that Guan Zhong's deathbed advice concerning his successor contains a statement (5a9; 18.13) similar to one attributed to Mencius (*Mengzi*, IVB, 16). With these arguments, Graham (p. 267) concludes that the chapter comes from

---

[1] See Graham, "On the Background of the Mencian Theory of Human Nature," p. 227.
[2] *Mengzi*, IIA, 2/2; VIA, 6/1; and VIA, 4/1.

some circle in Qi in the fourth or third century B.C. that shared the doctrines of Gaozi.

I would agree with Professor Graham in the sense that this text in general reflects the thinking of the idealistic wing of Confucianism, which was strongly represented in Qi during the early third century B.C. However, it should be pointed out that any direct connection between this text in its present form and the *Mengzi* is very tenuous. The *Guanzi* statement dealing with economics presents some of the same general ideas, but the treatment is very different. The same holds true for the deathbed statement.

I suspect that this chapter is made up of four separate stories composed of bits and pieces of a well-known tradition sometime after the death of Mencius in the late Warring States Period. Except for that unique section, which seems to represent the thought of Gaozi (1b4–3a2; 15.9–16.13), the remainder of the chapter fits much more closely the anecdotal literature of the end of the Warring States Period and the early Han than it does the *Mengzi* and the other more philosophical works of the late fourth and early third centuries B.C. The two stories, one beginning with Duke Huan's proposed tour and the Gaozi material and the other beginning with Duke Huan's shooting arrows, though very different in content, contain enough common phraseology to have been written by the same author, but there is no clear indication one way or the other about the remaining two.

Translation

When Duke Huan was about to make a tour of the east, he asked Guan Zhong about it, stating, "I [simply] wish[3] to travel to the east by way of[4] Zhuanfu[5] and south to Langye,[6] but the minister of military

---

[3] Reading 猶 as 欲 [Wang Yinzhi].

[4] The character 軸 is unintelligible here. I have followed Guo Moruo, who says it is a corruption of the two characters 東由. This section to 1b2 (15.8) appears to be a corrupted version of a story that appears in the *Yanzi chunqiu*, 4/1a3–12, and the *Mengzi*, IB, 4/5–6, where the two characters involved are Duke Jing 景公 (547–490 B.C.) of Qi and Yanzi 晏子 instead of Duke Huan and Guan Zhong. According to the *Mengzi*: "Formerly Duke Jing of Qi asked Yanzi, 'I wish to make an inspection tour to Zhuanfu 轉附 and Chaowu 朝儛 and then swing southward along the coast to Langye 琅邪. What shall I do to make my tour comparable to those of our former kings?' "

[5] The text reads Zhuanhu 轉斛. I have followed Wang Yinzhi and Guo Moruo in emending 斛 to 斛 = 附. Zhuanfu seems to have been a hill but its location is in doubt. Some commentators would place it in present-day Penglai 蓬莱, on the northern coast of the Shandong Peninsula, while others would place it in modern Zhucheng 諸城 Xian near Langyeh on the southern coast. See n. 6, below.

[6] 琅邪; the name of an area and a peak in Zhucheng 諸城 Xian on the southern coast of the Shandong Peninsula.

15.6   affairs[7] says [my trip] should be like the tours of the former kings. / What does this mean?"

Guan Zhong replied, "When the former kings made their tours, going out in the spring to check on nonessential activity[8] in agriculture was

15.7   called a spring tour.[9] / Going out in the fall to provide aid wherever people were short of provisions was called an end-of-the-year

1b   excursion.[10] / Now, when the army marches [along with the ruler], taking grain and provisions from the people, it is called being

15.8   destructive. / When [the ruler] follows his pleasure and does not repent, it is called being reckless. The former kings engaged in the business of spring tours and end-of-the-year excursions on behalf of others. They did not engage in destructive or reckless practices for their personal [pleasure]."

15.9   Duke Huan, leaving [his mat], bowed twice and / proclaimed, "This is a model to treasure!"

Guan Zhong resumed speaking to Duke Huan, "What has no wings yet flies is reputation. What has no roots yet remains firm is the true

15.10   self. / What lacks direction yet possesses a wealth of resources is life.[11] Your Grace should be firm in regard to your true self and cautious in

15.11   respect to your reputation / and strict [in respect to your habits][12] in order to show respect for life. This is called a flourishing of the Way."

Duke Huan, leaving [his mat], bowed twice and requested that [Guan

15.12   Zhong] continue. Guan Zhong resumed speaking to / Duke Huan: "No responsibility is heavier than that of the self, nothing is more dangerous to the road ahead than the mouth,[13] and no appointment lies beyond

---

[7]司馬; this probably refers to Wangzi Chengfu 王子成父, who is mentioned in both VII, 18, and VIII, 20, as being responsible for military affairs.

[8]不本 should probably be written 無本. Thus the sentence would read: "... when they went out in the spring to check if anything basic was lacking for agriculture...." The term appears elsewhere, XXIII, 78/9a10 (3:90.13), and XXIV, 83/10b12 (3:110.3), in a similar context.

[9] *You* 游; this term, in addition to its normal meaning "to travel," also had the specific meaning of a royal tour conducted during the spring of the year.

[10] According to the *Yanzi chunqiu*, 4/1a6–7: "Therefore when [the former kings] in the spring inspected the plowing and provided aid for those who were short [of seeds], they called it a spring tour (*you* 游). When in the fall they inspected the harvest and helped those who lacked provisions, they called it an autumn excursion (*yu* 豫)." The *Yanzi chunqiu*, 4/1a8, goes on to say that having one spring tour and one autumn excursion was the system followed by the feudal lords. A shorter version of this statement is to be found in the *Mengzi*, IB, 4/5.

[11] Graham ("Background of Mencian Theory," p. 229) would follow Guo Moruo in reading 生 as 性, "nature," i.e., "the qualities a thing has to start with." (Graham, p. 215).

[12] Inverting the two characters 以嚴 [Ding].

[13] Graham ("Background of Mencian Theory," p. 229) would emend 口 to 命 and translates the sentence as: "No road is as perilous as the life decreed for you."

15.13   [the end of] one's years.[14] / Only the virtuous prince is able to assume such a weighty responsibility in travelling the dangerous road to his ultimate appointment." /

2a   Duke Huan, leaving [his mat], bowed twice and said, "Will the master teach me what he meant by these words?" /

15.14   "Satisfaction of tastes, movement, and repose," replied Guan Zhong, "are the nourishment of life. Liking and disliking, pleasure and anger, sadness and joy are fluctuations in life. Sharpness of hearing, clarity of sight, and appropriate response to events are the capacities[15] of

6.1   life. / For this reason the sages were temperate in satisfying their tastes and timely in their movement and repose. They controlled fluctuations in the six moods,[16] and prohibited debauchery in music and sexual

6.2   pleasure. / To have depraved conduct banished from one's body, harsh words absent from one's mouth, and one's life quietly determined— such is the sage. Benevolence comes from within. Righteousness is

6.3   expressed without. / He is benevolent and therefore does not use the realm for his own profit. He is righteous and therefore does not use the realm to gain fame. He is benevolent and therefore does not attempt to

5.4   replace the king. / He is righteous and therefore turns over the government at age seventy.

"For this reason, the sage esteems the Power and plays down achievement, honors the Way and disdains the material world. Since the Way and the Power occupy his person, he is not misled by the material

.5   world. / For this reason, were his body to lie among the grass and weeds, he would have no feeling of concern. Were he to face south and sit in judgment on the entire realm, he would evince no sign of arrogance. /

.6   This being so, he can later serve as king of the realm. The reason it is called the Power is that he is quick without moving, knows without

.7   being told, is successful without doing anything, / and [people] arrive without being summoned. Such is the Power.

"Thus Heaven does not move, yet the four seasons revolve below, and

8   all things are transformed. / The prince does not move, yet his government and orders function below, and all things[17] are complete. The [sage's] mind does not move, yet it commands his four limbs,[18] ears and

9   eyes, and / in all things he adheres to his true self.[19] Few are his close

---

[14] Emending 而 to 之, in accordance with the syntax of the previous phrases and the text in the *Qunshu zhiyao* [Igai, Wang Niansun, and Sun Xingyan].

[15] Reading 德 as 得 [Yasui].

[16] That is, liking and disliking, pleasure and anger, sadness and joy.

[17] Emending 功 to 物 [Ding and Xu].

[18] The Yang edition for 肢 writes 枝. The meaning here is the same.

[19] The syntax of this sentence is out of balance with the two preceding it and is clearly corrupt. The translation is therefore doubtful.

associates, but many rally around him. This is called knowing people. Few are his undertakings, but his accomplishments are complete. This is called knowing how to employ [people]. / He need hear only a single word to relate all things together. This is called knowing the Way. Many words missing the point are not as good as his few. / Wide learning without self-reflection is certain to produce depravity. Filial piety and respect for elders are the progenitors of goodness. Loyalty and trustworthiness / are the basis[20] for communication. Those who internally fail to examine their filial piety and respect for elders are not strictly loyal and trustworthy in their external [relations], and abandon[21] these four constant [virtues] for the [mere] chanting of book learning will destroy themselves." /

On the following day Duke Huan was at the granary[22] shooting arrows when Guan Zhong / and Xi Peng[23] came to court. The duke, on seeing the two men, unstrung his bow, removed his arm guard, and greeted them, saying, "Now, the wild swans fly north in the spring and south in the fall, never missing a season.[24] Is it not just because they have wings / that they are able to go where they please in this world? But alas, the fact that I cannot do as I please in this world does not [seem to] worry you two."

Duke Huan then repeated what he had said, and when the two men failed / to reply, he said, "Since I have spoken, why don't you answer me?"

Guan Zhong replied, "Nowadays people suffer from overwork, yet their ruler employs them in an untimely fashion. People suffer from starvation, yet he demands heavy exactions from them. They suffer / from being killed, yet he intensifies his punishment of them. Such is the case, yet he further gathers around him those who are [merely] good-looking and keeps at a distance men of virtue. Swans may have wings and there may be boats and oars for crossing large rivers, but what does this have to do with you?" /

Duke Huan drew back, frowning, but Guan Zhong continued, "In the past when the former kings managed people, if people / were over-

---

[20] Emending 慶 to 度 = 託 [Igai and Guo Moruo].

[21] Reading 澤 as 舍 [Wang Niansun].

[22] The meaning of 廈 is not clear. I have retained its usual meaning following the explanation of the Yin commentary, which says that the duke was shooting there because birds would flock to the granary to eat the grain. However, Yasui explains it as a shooting screen, and Zhang Peilun says it is a borrowed character for 林, "forest," and was probably part of a place name.

[23] 隰朋; according to VII, 18, and VIII, 20, Xi Peng was an advisor of Duke Huan in charge of foreign affairs.

[24] For another version of this story, see IX, 22/1a (2:1.7).

worked, their sovereigns would employ them in a timely fashion so they would no longer suffer.[25] If people were starving, their sovereigns lightened their exactions so they would no longer suffer. If people were being killed, their sovereigns liberalized their punishments / so they would no longer suffer. Such being the case, they gathered around them men of virtue and kept at a distance those who were [merely] good-looking. Then everyone within the four boundaries looked upon their princes as being like parents, and from the four directions gravitated toward them like a flowing stream." /

The duke abandoned his shooting and, taking hold of the reins, mounted his chariot. He himself drove while Guan Zhong stood on his left and Xi Peng rode with them in the chariot.

On the third day of the tenth lunar month,[26] [Duke Huan] presented the two men to the ancestral temple[27] / and twice paying his respects by bowing his head said, "Since I have heard the words of these two gentlemen, my ears have become more sharp and my sight more clear. Since I dare not accept their advice on my own, I am presenting them to you, my ancestors." /

Guan Zhong and Xi Peng twice paid their respects by bowing their heads and said, "It is as if you were king. These are not the words of your ministers, but your own teachings." / Thereupon Guan Zhong and Duke Huan swore an oath of allegiance and issued an order saying, "Let the old and the weak suffer no punishment, but be forgiven three times and then judged. / Let [traders] be inspected at customs posts, but not charged duties.[28] Let [merchants] be charged a fee in the marketplace but not taxed.[29] Let the mountains and forests, marshes and weirs be opened and closed according to the season, but have no fees. / Let those who make bundles of grass and take salt from the marshes be treated the same as merchants when they transport these things to and fro."[30] /

---

[25] Emending 也 to 矣 to fit the pattern of the following sentences [Li].

[26] The phrase 朔月三日 does not make much sense. The *Shuo yuan*, 1/8a13, when relating the story, writes 正月之朝: "At the court of the first month...."

[27] The term 理官 also does not make much sense here. Igai, He Ruzhang, Zhang Peilun, and Xu would all emend 官, "office," to 宮, "palace" or "temple." Igai would emend 理 (*li*) to 釐 (*li*), the name of Duke Huan's father. Zhang and Xu would emend *li* to 祖, "ancestor." Chapter IX, 22/2a1 (2:2.2), in a different version of the story, writes 太廟, "ancestral temple." The *LSCQ*, XXIV, 2/3b4 (Wilhelm, *Frühling und Herbst*, p. 421), in another slightly different version simply writes 廟, "temple."

[28] Reading 正 as 征 both here and below, in accordance with similar statements: III, 10/19a11–12 (1:46.2–3), VIII, 20/16b1 (1:109.2), and IX, 22/2a3 (2:2.3).

[29] Following Guo Moruo, who says that 布 (*bu*) is a phonetic borrowing for 賦 (*fu*), which usually refers to taxes levied for military purposes.

[30] The text for this sentence appears to be corrupt and the translation is somewhat forced.

17.13   For three years Duke Huan instructed his people, and in the fourth year selected the worthy to become leaders. In the fifth year he began raising an army[31] and arranged his chariots in battle order. Subsequently, to the south he attacked Chu 楚, reaching[32] Shicheng.[33] To the north he attacked the Mountain Rong

17.14   山戎,/ taking away winter onions[34] and soybeans[35] to distribute to the realm. Finally, he three times assisted[36] the son of Heaven and nine times assembled the feudal lords. /

18.1   Duke Huan was about to leave home, but had not filled *ding* 鼎 vessels with food for presents. The Zhongfu Zhuzi[37] said to the palace women, "Why don't we follow him. Our prince is about to go on an expedition." /

18.2   The palace women all followed him, but the duke became angry, saying, "Who said I was going on an expedition?" /

4b   "We heard it from the Zhongfu Zhuzi," replied the palace women.

18.3   The duke summoned the Zhongfu Zhuzi and said, / "How did you hear I was going on an expedition?"

"I heard that when you are planning to leave but have not filled *ding* vessels with food for presents, it is because there are either internal problems or trouble abroad.[38] Now you, My Lord, are leaving home,

18.4   but have not filled *ding* vessels with food for presents. / Since you have no internal problems, I knew you were about to go on an expedition."

The duke said, "Good! This is not something I would have discussed

18.5   with you, but your words are to the point. / Therefore I will tell you

---

[31] Emending 車 to 軍 [Yasui].

[32] Deleting 門 [Ding and Yao].

[33] 施城 is identified by the Yin commentary as a city in Chu, but there seems to be no collaboration for this statement, Hong and Yao would emend 施 to 方 (*fang*). Fangcheng was a famous fortified pass belonging to Chu, located northeast of the present-day city of Nanyang 南陽 in south-central Henan. See VIII, 20, n. 110, and IX, 22/4b5 (2 : 4.7).

[34] The Yang edition for 蒠 writes a variant form of the character, 苍.

[35] *Rongshu* 戎叔(叔 = 菽); these events are mentioned in the *Zuo zhuan*, Zhuang, 31 (Legge, *Ch'un Ts'eu*, III, 31/4). See also the *Guliang zhuan* for more details.

[36] The phrase 三匡天子 is unusual. I have followed Guo Moruo, who would read 匡 as 轉 in reference to the three civil conferences listed in VII, 18, n. 146. Yasui, in accordance with the *Lun yu*, XIV, 18/2, and the *Guanzi*, VIII, 20/14b4 (1 : 107.6–7), would emend the passage to read 一匡天下. Thus, "Finally, he brought unity and order to the entire realm and nine times assembled the feudal lords."

[37] 中婦諸子; a slightly different version of this story is contained in XII, 35/11b5ff. (2 : 54.2ff.), where the character 婦 is written *qin* 寢. Yasui explains the Zhongfu Zhuzi as the female officer in charge of the women's quarters. Zhang Wenhu believes it refers to one of the duke's female relatives living in the palace.

[38] That is, since he had not packed food for presents, she knew that he was not paying a ceremonial visit to either one of the other lords or the Zhou king.

382

about it. I wish to have the feudal lords visit me, but they have not come. What should I do about it?" /

18.6 "Judging from my own case," said the Zhongfu Zhuzi, "if I had not properly served guests when receiving them, I would never have obtained [gifts] of cloth from people. Perhaps the reason [for the lords not visiting you] to an even greater extent lies in your not paying attention to them." [39] /

18.7
18.8 The next day when Guan Zhong appeared in court, the duke told him about what had happened, and Guan Zhong said, / "This is the advice of a sage. You must follow it."

18.9
5a Guan Zhong was sick in bed and when Duke Huan went to visit him the duke asked, "You have become very ill, Zhongfu. Should you fail to recover, and it is our misfortune that you do not arise from this illness, to whom should I transfer the government?" [40]

18.10 Guan / Zhong had not yet replied when Duke Huan continued, "What about Bao Shu?" [41]

"Bao Shu is a man of quality," replied Guan Zhong, "but if he were to attempt to apply his way of doing things to a state of a thousand
18.11 chariots, people would not accept it. / Even though he cannot take over the government, as a person he is extremely strong in liking what is good and hating what is evil. If he were to see a single evil deed, he would not forget it to the end of his life." /

18.12 "Then who can do it?" said Duke Huan.

"Xi Peng can," replied Guan Zhong. "Peng is a person who is good at adhering to the goals[42] of his ruler while seeking information from subordinate officials. I have heard that those who bestow virtue on
18.13 others are called / benevolent (ren 仁), while those who bestow wealth on others are called good (liang 良). Those who use their skills to vanquish others are never able to make people submit, while those who use their skills to nourish people never have people who do not submit.
18.14 There / are things he does not know about the government of the state and the affairs of the royal house, but definitely Peng is the one.

[39] The meaning of this sentence in the text is not clear. None of the commentators provides a satisfactory explanation, and my translation is dubious.

[40] Different versions of this well-known story about the deaths of Guan Zhong and Duke Huan appear in several other texts, including the *Guanzi*, XI, 32/11a6–12b6 (2:40.6–41.11); the *LSCQ*, I, 4/9a7–10a9 (Wilhelm, *Frühling und Herbst*, pp. 9–11), and XVI, 3/6b1–7b10 (Wilhelm, pp. 240–244); and the *Hanfeizi*, II, 7b6–8a3 (Liao, *Han Fei Tzu*, I, p. 50), and III, 10/7b12–8b13 (Liao, I, pp. 89–92).

[41] 鮑叔; Guan Zhong's closest associate and an early supporter of Duke Huan. See the beginning of VII, 18, and VIII, 20.

[42] Reading 識 as 志 [Xu]. The *LSCQ*, I, 4/9b5, for 識 writes 志.

19.1
5b

Moreover, Peng is a person / who does not forget his duke's household when at home, nor his own family while residing in the household of the duke. In serving you he will not be of two minds, but will also not forget his own person. He presented the gifts that he received from the state of Qi to relieve[43] fifty destitute[44] households / without anyone knowing it. Such is his great benevolence! That's Peng!" /

19.2

19.3

The duke again asked, "If by misfortune I lose you, Zhongfu, will those few great officers still be able to ensure the country's peace?"

19.4

Guan Zhong replied, / "My Lord, I beg you to make your own[45] evaluation.[46] Bao Shuya[47] is a person who admires straightforwardness, Bin Xuwu[48] admires skill, Ning Qi[49] / is able in affairs, and Sun Zai[50] is glib of tongue. The capabilities[51] of these four gentlemen are superior to those of all[52] other men."

19.5

"If I bring them together," said the duke, "and make them my ministers, how can they fail to ensure the country's peace?" /

19.6

19.7

6a

19.8

"Bao Shu is a person who admires straightforwardness, but he is not capable of being flexible for the sake of the country. Bin / Xuwu is a person who admires skill, but he too is not capable of being flexible for the sake of the country. / Ning Qi is a person who is able in affairs, but he is not capable of [knowing when] to stop. Sun Zai / is a person who is glib of tongue, but he is not capable of being trusted with secrets. I have heard that only if one is flexible and keeps good faith with the hundred surnames in the ebb and flow of fortune[53] / can the state be ensured of peace. Do not hesitate. Peng can do it. Peng is a person who is certain to measure both his strength before moving and ability before acting."

19.9

As he finished speaking, he heaved a deep sigh and continued,

---

[43] Emending 握 to 振 [Wang Yinzhi].

[44] Reading 路 as 露 [Wang Yinzhi].

[45] The Zhao edition mistakenly writes 巳 for 己.

[46] Reading 覺 as 舊 [Zhang Peilun and Guo Moruo].

[47] 鮑叔牙; that is, Bao Shu. See n. 41, above.

[48] 賓胥無; according to VIII, 20/18b7–8 (1:111.2), Bin Xuwu served as chief justice.

[49] 寗戚; according to VIII, 20/18b4–5 (1:110.14–111.1), Ning Qi served as minister of agriculture.

[50] 孫在; Liu Shipei would emend Sun Zai to Sun Xu 孫宿 to correspond with the name of one of the men listed in VIII, 20/18a10 (1:110.11), Cao Sun Xu 曹孫宿, who served as emissary to the state of Chu.

[51] This sentence is unintelligible as it stands. I have followed Guo Moruo in emending 孰 to 執.

[52] Reading 一 as 皆 [Wang Yinzhi].

[53] According to the Yi jing, III, 23/3b2 (Wilhelm, I ching, II, p. 141): 尹子尚消息盈虛天行也. "The man of quality respects the ebb and flow of fortune (lit., increase and decrease, fullness and emptiness) for they are the course of Heaven."

19.10 "Heaven / produced Peng to be a tongue for me. The body may die, but the tongue will live on in him."

[After pausing for a bit], Guan Zhong spoke, "Now, the states of

19.11 Jiang and Huang[54] / are close to Chu. If I should die, you must return

19.12 them to Chu as a matter of trust. Should you fail to return them, / Chu will certainly take them for its own. Should this happen, you would have to come to their rescue, for if you were to prove unable to save them, this would be the beginning of disorder." /

19.13 "I promise," said Duke Huan.

Guan Zhong then spoke again. "In the eastern suburb a dog is

6b snarling.[55] / Morning and evening it wishes to bite me, but it is fettered,[56] and I won't allow it. Now, Yi Ya[57] is one who is incapable

19.14 of / loving his son. How will he be able to love you? You must get rid of him."

"I promise," said the duke. /

20.1 Guanzi spoke again. "In the northern suburbs a dog is snarling. Morning and evening it wishes to bite me, but it is fettered, and I won't allow it. Now, Shu Diao[58] is one who does not even love his own body.

20.2 How will he be able to love you? You must get rid of / him."

"I promise," said the duke.

Guanzi spoke again, "In the western suburbs a dog is snarling. Morning and evening it wishes to bite me, but it is fettered, and I won't allow it. Now, the Gongzi Kaifang of Weii[59] left his position as heir

[54] Jiang 江 and Huang 黄 were two small states situated in southwestern Henan Province. According the the *Guliang zhuan*, Xi, 12 (Legge, *Ch'un Ts'eu*, V, 12/2): "At a conference at Guan 貫 [held in 658], Guan Zhong told Duke Huan, 'Jiang and Huang are far from Qi but near Chu. Chu considers them within its sphere of interest. Should Chu attack them, but we prove unable to come to their rescue, you will cease to be honored by the feudal lords.' When Guan Zhong died, Chu attacked Jiang and wiped out Huang, but Duke Huan was unable to save them." The *Chunqiu*, Xi, 12 (Legge, *Ch'un Ts'eu*, V, p. 12), gives 648 B.C. as the date for the attack on Huang, but Guan Zhong is not supposed to have died until 645.

[55] Reading 嘽嘽 as 唯唯 here and below [Wang Niansun].

[56] Reading 猳 as 枂 here and below [Xu].

[57] According to the *Guanzi*, XI, 32, and *Hanfeizi*, II, 7, and III, 10, versions of this story, Yi Ya 易牙 was in charge of the duke's kitchen. When he learned that the duke had never tasted human flesh, he killed his own son and presented the steamed head to the duke.

[58] According to the *Guanzi*, XI, 32, and *Hanfeizi*, II, 7, and III, 10, versions of the story, Shu Diao 豎刁 had castrated himself so he could serve in the women's quarters of the duke's palace.

[59] Gongzi Kaifang of Weii 衛公子開方 was heir apparent to the small state of Weii 衛 situated in northeastern Henan Province. He left his own state to serve Duke Huan, but on the death of Duke Huan's successor, Duke Xiao 孝 in 633 B.C. raised a rebellion against the legitimate heir and helped raise Xiao's younger brother to the throne as Duke Zhao 昭. See VII, 18, n. 120.

20.3 apparent to a thousand chariots / to serve you. What he wants[60] from you[61] is to gain more than a thousand chariots. You must get rid of him." /

20.4 "I promise," said the duke.

Guanzi subsequently died, and ten months after his death, Xi Peng also died. Duke Huan had gotten rid of Yi Ya, Shu Diao, and Gongzi

20.5 Kaifang of Weii. However, since his five tastes were not satisfied, / he restored Yi Ya. Since the inner palace had fallen into disorder, he restored Shu Diao. Since beguiling words and humble phrases were absent from his side, he restored Gongzi Kaifang of Weii.

Since Duke Huan did not measure his strength within nor weigh his

20.6 relations abroad, / he used his energy to attack his neighbors on all four
7a sides. When the duke died, his six sons vied to be placed on the throne. Yi Ya allied with Gongzi [Kaifang] of Weii externally[62] and Shu Diao internally. Consequently, they together killed the various functionaries [supporting the legitimate heir] and placed Gongzi Wukui[63] on the throne.

20.7 Therefore, seven days after the duke died, / he had not yet been placed in a coffin.[64] After nine months, he had not yet been buried. Duke Xiao fled to Song and Duke Xiang of Song led the feudal lords to attack Qi. They fought a battle at Yan[65] and inflicted a severe defeat on the troops of Qi. They killed Gongzi Wukui and, having placed Duke Xiao on the

20.8 throne, returned home. / Duke Xiang ruled for twenty-three years and Duke Huan for forty-two.

[60] Deleting 也 after 願 [Hong].

[61] Deleting 是 after 與 [Wang Niansun].

[62] Inserting 外 before 與 [Ding and Tao].

[63] 無虧; one of Duke Huan's six sons by different wives. He was killed shortly after this attempt to seize the throne. The legitimate heir who had fled to the state of Song 宋 was then returned with the help of duke Xiang 襄 (650–637) B.C. of Song to assume the throne as Duke Xiao 孝 (642–633). For a description of these events, which took place in 643–642, see the *Zuo zhuan*, Xi, 27–28 (Legge, *Ch'un Tz'eu*, V, 17/5 and 18/2, 3, and 5).

[64] According to the *Zuo zhuan*, Xi, 17 (Legge, *Ch'un Ts'eu*, 5, 17/5), it was sixty-seven days before Duke Huan was placed in his coffin.

[65] 甗; situated near the present-day city of Jinan 濟南 in west-central Shandong Province.

Di Tu

地圖

ON MAPS

Introductory Comments

Di tu is the first chapter of the *Duan yu* 短語 [Short Discourses] section and one of the shortest in the *Guanzi*. Consisting of two short fragments from some unknown military text, it is of interest primarily because the first of the fragments represents one of the earliest and most detailed discussions of terrain maps in China.

The oldest surviving Chinese maps were discovered during the 1973–74 excavations of the Mawangdui tomb no. III located near Changsha in Hunan Povince. The tomb, which belonged to a man who died in 168 B.C., contained a fabulous store of artifacts and documents written on silk and bamboo, including three maps painted on silk. These maps have been discussed in considerable detail in *Wen wu* during 1975 and 1976[1] and in articles by A. Gutkind Bulling and Cao Wanru.[2] The first of them is chiefly topographical, covering the Changsha marquisate, which included the southern part of modern Hunan and adjoining areas of Guangdong and Guangxi. The second is a military map showing where troops had been stationed throughout the marquisate. The third is a political map, locating the marquisate's cities and towns. These three maps indicate that advanced skill in cartography already existed in China by the middle of the second century B.C.

The development of Chinese cartography seems to have begun about the sixth century B.C. or perhaps slightly before, since our earliest reference to what is probably a map or chart is contained in a chapter of the *Shang shu* known as the *Luo gao* 洛告 [The Announcement Concerning Luo], V, 13/3, a text generally believed to predate Confucius.[3] According to the *Luo gao*, the duke of Zhou went out to find a suitable location for a capital. On reaching the city of Luo he

---

[1] These discussions appearing in *Wen wu*, 1975, nos. 2 and 6, and 1976, no. 1, have been summarized by Jeffery K. Riegel in *Early China*, 2 (1976): 69–72.

[2] A. Gutkind Bulling, "Ancient Chinese Maps," pp. 16–25, and Cao Wanru, "Maps 2,000 Years Ago," pp. 251–255.

[3] See Creel, *Confucius*, p. 295.

found that divination indicated it to be the best site, and sent back a messenger to the king with a map (*tu* 圖) and record of the divinations. It is impossible to tell the nature of this map, though it may have resembled the charts of the later geomancers.[4] In any case, it must have presented some visual description of the actual terrain.

By the fourth and third centuries B.C., maps seem to have become quite common. The *Zhanguo ce*, 19/2b, in its account of the state of Zhao 趙 during the late fourth century, mentions a map (*di tu* 地圖) that outlined the territory of the various states of the empire. The first clearly datable reference to a map (*di tu*) involves an incident that took place in 227 B.C. when a certain Jing Ke 荊 軻 presented a map to the king of Qin 秦 during an attempt to assassinate him.[5]

None of these references, however, tells us very much about the content of maps in pre-Han times. For this we must turn to the *Zhou li*.[6] Selected references to different types of maps mentioned in that work are as follows:

1. A possible population map is referred to in 10/1a8–9 (Biot, *Tcheou-li*, I, p. 192): "The director general of the masses (*da situ* 大司徒) presides over the preparation of maps (*tu*) relating to the territory of [feudal] states and [the registration of] the number of their people."

2. Area and resource maps are referred to in 33/6a1–3 (Biot, II, pp. 263–264): "The deputy in charge of the regions (*zhifang shi* 職方氏) presides over the maps (*tu*) of the empire [assisting the king] in keeping control of his territory. He distinguishes [the area of] the country's [feudal] states, cities, and outlying districts, and those of the people of the Four Yi 夷, Eight Man 蠻, Seven Min 閩, Nine Mo 貉, Five Rong 戎, and Six Di 狄, as well as the quantity and importance of materials of value, nine grains, and six domestic animals."

3. Area maps are further mentioned in 15/7b10 (Biot, I, 336–337): "The grand officer in charge of the outlying areas (*suiren* 遂人) presides over the wastelands of the state. Using a map (*tu*) of the territory, he outlines the fields and wastelands."

4. The existence of special resource maps is indicated in 16/8a5–7 (Biot, I, p. 377): "The officer in charge of minerals (*gongren* 卝人) presides over areas [containing] metals, jade, tin, and [valuable] stones and issues strict prohibitions in order that they may be preserved. If there is any occasion to exploit them he makes a map (*di tu*) of the

---

[4] See Needham, *Science and Civilisation*, II, pp. 359–363.

[5] This story is recounted in detail in the *Shi ji*, 86/13a–b (translated by Bodde, *Statesman, Patriot, and General*, pp. 33–34).

[6] Unfortunately this text is difficult to date. It may go back to the fourth century B.C., but is more likely a product of the third or even early second century B.C.

area containing these things in order to present it [to the workers]."

5. A type of terrain map is described in 30/8a1–2 (Biot, II, pp. 198–199): "The officer in charge of obstacles (*sixian* 司 險) presides over maps (*tu*) of the nine regions [of the empire] in order that [the king] can be completely informed about obstructions presented by its mountains, forests, rivers, and marshes, so that roads may be cut through them." It is this latter type of terrain map designed for military purposes that is described in the first section of *Guanzi*, X, 27.

With the beginning of the second paragraph there is a sharp shift in subject matter to a discussion of the various responsibilities attached to those connected with military affairs, thereby seeming to indicate that what follows is probably a separate fragment. However, as described in the Introductory Comments to chapter II, 6, both fragments have close counterparts in the last two paragraphs of the *Wang bing* 王兵 text unearthed at Yinqueshan 銀雀山, Linyi 臨邑 Xian, Shandong in 1972. Paragraph 7 of the *Wang bing* reconstruction, which was published in the 1976, no. 12, issue of *Wen wu* (pp. 40–41), is similar in its general content to the first paragraph of this chapter without, however, specifically mentioning the term for maps. Instead it merely speaks of *di xing* 地形, "terrain." Paragraph 8 is closer in content and terminology to the passage 7b6–8a2 (20.2–6) of the second part of this chapter, but again it is abbreviated in form and there is considerable difference in individual characters.

The brevity of this chapter makes it difficult to say anything about its date of composition. It seems clear that it must predate 134 B.C., the date of the Yinqueshan tomb from which the *Wang bing* text was recovered. Furthermore, as pointed out previously, the later part of the Warring States Period through the early Han was the time when works on military theory and strategy enjoyed their highest popularity. Luo Genze (*Guanzi*, p. 77) states it could not date before the middle of the Warring States Period because it uses the term *xiang shi* 相室 to refer to the premier, or chief minister of state.[7]

Translation

·20.11
·9   All military commanders must first examine and come to know maps.[8] They must know thoroughly the location of winding, gatelike

---

[7] See Luo Genze's comments on use of the word *hsiang* in his *Guanzi tanyuan*, pp. 26–29.

[8] Cf. *Guanzi*, II, 6/6b2–4 (1:27.3–4): "Therefore, in military affairs it is the duty of military commanders to examine maps, consult with the court astronomer, estimate accumulated stores, organize the brave knights, acquire a broad knowledge of the realm, and determine strategy."

defiles,[9] streams that may inundate their chariots, famous mountains,[10]
passable valleys, arterial / rivers, highlands, and hills. They must also
know where grasses, trees, and rushes grow, the distances of roads, the
size of city and suburban walls, famous and deserted towns, / and barren
and fertile land. They should thoroughly store up [in their minds] the
location of ways in and out of the terrain. / Then afterward they can
march their armies and raid towns. In the disposition [of troops] they
will know what lies ahead and behind, and will not lose the advantages
of the terrain. This is the constant [value] of maps.

They must know thoroughly the number of men, the bearing of their
knights, and the quality of their weapons. / This then is to know the
outward condition [of the troops]. To know their outward condition is
not as good as knowing their ability, and knowing their ability is not as
good as knowing their thoughts.

Therefore three factors are necessary to command troops, namely,
the intelligence of the ruler,[11] the knowledge of his chief ministers, and
the capacity of his generals. / [Therefore, when orders are about to be
issued to send out the knights, the time will be calculated to the day.][12]

It is the responsibility of the ruler of men initially to make certain
which country may be attacked, to see to it that the various ministers,
great functionaries, fathers and elder brothers, / attendants, and advisers
are prevented from discussing the success or failure [of a mission].

It is the responsibility of the chief minister of state (*xiang shi* 相室) to
make sure that no one dares conceal worthiness or indulge in favoritism
when judging merit or applying rewards and punishments, / to expend

---

[9] *Huan yuan zhi xian* 轘轅之險. *Huan* is read as *huan* 環. *Yuan* originally meant the
thills or shafts of a chariot. When the chariot was unhitched, it was allowed to roll
backward with the rear end touching the ground and the thills pointing skyward. Two of
these placed opposite each other were used to form a gate before the king's tent while he
was on a military expedition. Thus the term *yuan* later came to be applied to the gates
outside an office or headquarters. The reference here is to a narrow, steepsided, and
winding pass. Huanyuan is also the name of a mountain situated southeast of Yanshi
偃師 Xian in northern Henan Province. It is famous for a particularly dangerous pass,
from which it derived its name. The road through the pass is described as having twelve
switchback turns.

[10] *Ming shan* 名山. This term usually refers to the five sacred mountains: Tai 泰 Shan in
Shandong, Heng 衡 Shan in Hunan, Hua 華 Shan in Shaanxi, Heng 恆 Shan in Hebei, and
Song 嵩 Shan in Henan; and the five guardian peaks: Guiji 會稽 Shan in Zhejiang, Yi 沂
Shan in Shandong, Yiwulü 醫無閭 Shan in Liaoning, and Huo 霍 Shan in Shanxi.

[11] *Zhu* 主. I have interpreted *chu* here to refer to the "ruler of men" (*ren zhu* 人主) of line
7b9 (21.1) below. This would be the king and would be distinct from the "military
commander" (*bing zhu* 兵主), i.e., "general" of lines 7a9 (20.11) and 8a2 (21.5).

[12] This sentence appears to be out of context. Perhaps it represents a misplaced slip that
was inserted here because it contained the character 將 (here an adverbial particle), which
also appears in the preceding line with the meaning of "general."

390

goods and wealth in order to supply the demands of the army, and to see to it that the various functionaries are respectful and dare not be remiss or act in a depraved manner when waiting upon the orders of the prince. /

It is the duty of the military commander to repair the weapons, select trained knights, prepare instructions to be carried out, organize troops in their units of five and ten,[13] be broadly informed about [the state of] the realm, and examine and take charge of strategy.

[13] Groups of five (*wu* 伍) and ten (*shi* 什) served as the basic units of conscription for labor or military purposes. Since conscription was supposed to be based on one man per household, units of five and ten households also served as basic administrative units.

Can Huan

IN CONSIDERATION OF EVIL CONSEQUENCES

Introductory Comments

The first two paragraphs (8a5–13; 21.9–13) of this short chapter concerning rulers who are either violent and reckless or irresolute and weak seem to have little connection with the rest of the essay, which deals with military affairs. Therefore Igai, Zhang Peilun, and Guo Moruo believe it is probably a misplaced portion of the *Fa fa*, VI, 16. The content of lines 10a10–10b6 (1:78.7–11) of that chapter largely parallels these two paragraphs and much of the wording is identical. I suspect that this material represents a duplicate slip or part of a lost explanation that was attached to this chapter because the passage immediately preceding this material in IV, 16, refers to evil consequences (*huan* 患), as does the title here.

The section dealing with military affairs is of special interest because of its close association with two other documents. As mentioned in the Introductory Comments to chapter II, 6, over half (8a12–9a5; 21.13–22.8) of this section is covered by the reconstructed *Wang bing* 王兵 text found in a Han dynasty tomb dating from about 134 B.C. and unearthed at Yinqueshan 銀雀山, Linyi 臨邑 Xian, Shandong. The *Wang bing* counterpart to this text differs in that it is more abbreviated in content and frequently uses different characters, but the closeness of the two texts is readily apparent. Part of this same section covered by the *Wang bing* material (9a2–5; 22.5–7) also appears in II, 6/5b9–6a1 (1:26.8–10).

Another passage (9a8–9b3; 22.8–12) is duplicated with some minor variations in an address to the emperor by Chao Cuo 鼂錯 (d. 154 B.C.), which is contained in his biography in the *Qian Han shu*, 49/8a7–13. According to Chao, the passage in question is a quotation taken from a work entitled *Bing fa* 兵法 [Methods of Warfare]. Luo Genze (*Guanzi* p. 77) concludes therefore that this chapter was taken from a work on military affairs written by Chao. I would doubt this very much since this quotation immediately precedes another passage that duplicates a part of *Guanzi*, IX, 23, and is introduced by the phrase "I have further heard," 臣又問. As discussed in the Introductory Comments to IX, 23, it appears more likely that Chao, who was known for his interests in Legalist and military writings, was familiar with at least some of the chapters that later came to make up our present *Guanzi*. It is also very possible that this chapter at one time was also known by the very common title, *Bing fa*, or that both the author of this chapter and Chao Cuo took their material from a common source. Again, this chapter is very difficult to date, but it is probable that both sections date from the late Warring States Period.

Translation

2:21.9
8a5

The violent and reckless among rulers of men are always subject to attack; the irresolute and weak are always killed. What is being violent and reckless? It is called being violent and reckless when [the ruler] is irresponsible in applying punishments and killing others. What is being irresolute and weak? It is called being irresolute and weak when [the ruler] finds it difficult to apply punishments and kill others. / Both of these fail in one respect or the other.

21.10

Those who are irresponsible in applying punishments always kill the innocent while those who find difficulty in applying punishments are remiss in dealing with the guilty. Now, when the throne kills the innocent, those whose way of conduct is correct are no longer safe. When it is remiss in dealing with the guilty, those whose way of conduct is wicked / will not reform. If those whose way of conduct is correct are no longer safe, men of talent and ability will flee. If those whose behavior is wicked do not reform, the various ministers will form factions. When men of talent and ability flee, it sets the stage for external / difficulty. When the various ministers form factions, it sets the stage for internal disorder. Therefore it is said: "Those who are violent and reckless are subject to attack while those who are irresolute and weak are killed." /

21.11

21.12

21.13
b

Nothing is more important than the armed forces in determining whether a prince is despised or respected or whether his country is safe or endangered. The reason for this is that when punishing an aggressor state, it is necessary to use armed forces. When restraining perverse people, it is necessary to apply punishments. Thus the armed forces are used externally to / punish aggression and internally to restrain wickedness. Therefore armed forces are the primary factor in ensuring respect for the ruler and the safety of the state. They are indispensable.

21.14

The rulers of our time are not like this. Externally they do not [know how to] use armed forces, so if they wish to punish aggression / their

22.1

territory is certain to be lost. Internally they do not [know how to] use punishments, so if they wish to restrain wickedness, their states are certain to be thrown into disorder.

Now, whenever calculating [expense incurred by] the use of armed forces, three [mobilizations] to warn [the enemy] equal / one expedition. Three expeditions equal one stationing of troops abroad. Three stationings of troops abroad equal one war. Therefore, while the troops needed for one incident / may consume ten years of accumulated stores, the expense of one war may exhaust the achievements of several generations.

Now, if swords are crossed and armed forces engaged so that afterward one must continue to provide for them, / this is to vanquish oneself.[1] If one attacks a city or lays siege to a town so its occupants [are forced to] exchange their sons for food and crack their bones for cooking, such an attack / is merely to uproot oneself.

For this reason the sage conducts few punitive expeditions yet effects a great ordering [of the realm]. He does not neglect the seasons of Heaven or ignore / the benefits of Earth. Even though[2] his expenses are heavy, the amount is certain[3] to have been derived from detailed planning. Therefore detailed plans must be settled before / armed forces are dispatched beyond the borders. If this has not been the case, battles will be self-defeating and attacks self-destructive.

If one gains [control over] the masses but does not win their hearts, it is the same as if one were acting alone. / If the weapons are not well-made and sharp, it is the same as being empty-handed.[4] If shields are not strong and tightly woven, it is the same as being without armor.[5] If crossbows cannot shoot a long distance, / it is the same as [merely] having a dagger. If the archers are not able to hit the target, it is the same as being without arrows.[6] If they hit the mark but cannot pierce it, it is the same as having arrows without heads. To command untrained men is the same as being without armor. / To oppose long-distance arrows with [mere] daggers is the same as sitting and waiting for death.

22.2
22.3
22.4
22.5
9a
22.6
22.7
22.8
22.9
22.10

---

[1] Ding and Xu would emend 自勝 to 自敗, "to defeat oneself." The meaning is essentially the same.

[2] This passage 不失天時...自毀者也, which for the most part parallels II, 6/5b9–6a1 (1:26.8–10), is clearly corrupt here. I have largely followed Igai and Guo Moruo in emending 用日維夢 to 用費雖多.

[3] Emending 不 to 必 [Ding].

[4] The biography of Chao Cuo 晁錯 in the *Qian Han shu*, 49/8a7–13, appears to cite an abbreviated version of this passage, which Chao attributes to a work entitled *Bing fa* [Methods of Warfare]. The *Qian Han shu*, 49/8a7, for 無操 writes 空手. The meaning is the same.

[5] The *Qian Han shu*, 49/8a8, for 儀 writes 祖裼, "having the arms exposed."

[6] The *Qian Han shu*, 49/8a9, for 無矢 writes 亡矢, "losing one's arrows."

Therefore, whenever there is a major inspection of the armed forces, it is first / necessary to inspect their weapons, and then inspect the troops, their generals, and their ruler. Therefore it is said, "Having weapons that are of very poor quality / and not sharp is to give one's troops to others.[7] Having troops that are useless is to give one's generals to the enemy. Having generals / who do not understand arms is to give the ruler to the enemy. Failing to stockpile and pay attention to arms[8] is to give the state to others."

However, if the weapons for one [army][9] are complete, a punitive expedition[10] will be all that is needed for the realm to have no heart for war. / If weapons for two [armies] are complete, a warning[11] is all that will be necessary to keep the realm from defending its cities. / If the weapons for three [armies] are complete, a royal tour of inspection[12] is all that will be necessary to keep the realm from assembling its [armed] masses.

Having no heart for war means that [the realm] knows that war will / not lead to victory.[13] Therefore [the text] says that [the realm] will have no heart for war. Being kept from defending their cities means that the realm knows that its cities will be uprooted. Therefore the text says that [the realm] will be kept from defending its cities. To be kept from assembling its [armed] masses means that [the realm] knows that its masses will be scattered. Therefore [the text] says that [the realm] will be kept from assembling its [armed] masses.

---

[7] *Qian Han shu*, 49/8a10, writes 故兵法曰器械不利以其卒予敵也, "Therefore the *Bing fa* says, 'Having weapons that are not sharp is to give the troops to the enemy.'"

[8] The *Qian Han shu*, 49/8a12, writes 君不擇將, "Failure of the prince to select [good] generals...."

[9] The meaning of 一器, 二器, and 三器 in this and the following sentence is not clear.

[10] Emending 往 to 征 [Zhang Peilun].

[11] Reading 驚 as 警.

[12] Yasui would interpret 游 to read "roving emissaries."

[13] This final paragraph is probably part of an old commentary incorporated into the text by mistake.

Zhi Fen
制分

ON RULING AND THE ASSIGNMENT OF
RESPONSIBILITIES

Introductory Comments

The title of this chapter is the same as that of the *Hanfeizi*, XX, 55, which W. K. Liao (*Han Fei Tzu*, II, p. 330) translates as "Regulations and Distinctions." However, in this chapter, *zhi* involves the entire question of rule; *fen* means the assignment of responsibilities and / or allotments. The text falls into the category of *bing fa* 兵法 and is another of the military works appearing in this section of the *Guanzi*. Its use of both Daoist and Legalist terminology would also seem to indicate that its author belonged to the Huang-Lao tradition.

On the basis of its general literary style, I suspect the chapter is rather late, possibly as early as the middle of the third century B.C., but more likely early Han. The text also contains a brief reference to an ox butcher named Tan 坦, who, with his ability to carve up nine oxen in a single morning, is reminiscent of Cook Ding 庖丁 in chapter II, 3, of the *Zhuangzi*. A slightly different version of the *Guanzi* story appears in the biography of Jia Yi 賈誼 (201–169 B.C.) in the *Qian Han shu*, 48/8b11–9a1, where the ox butcher is called Tu 吐 instead of Tan. Jia Yi was very familiar with at least portions of the present *Guanzi*, and cites it by name on occasion, but whether or not he based his story on this particular chapter is impossible to tell. A version similar to that of the *Guanzi* is to be found in the *Huainanzi*, 11/b7–8. Since the *Huainanzi* was produced before 122 B.C., it would seem fairly certain that this chapter dates before then, and may have been a product of the Huang-Lao writers from the old Chu area.

Translation

2:23.4
9b12
23.5

Whenever armed forces prevail in battle it is because [the prince], having sages and worthy knights, does not / begrudge them honors and ranks; having those who are steeped in the Way and political methods

10a and possess knowledge and ability, he does / not begrudge them offices and ranks; having those who are [skilled in the arts of war] and possess great strength, he does not begrudge them large salaries; having those with sharp ears and clear sight, he does not begrudge them money and wealth.

Now, it was only after the day of their deaths that Boyi and Shuqi[1]
3.6 became famous, / but their previous conduct had already been extremely virtuous. It was only after the morning of *jiazi*[2] that King Wu was victorious, but his previous government had already been very skillfully managed. /

3.7 If[3] a wall were built surrounding an area even ten feet square or ten people had gathered together, [the prince who is skilled in the use of his armed forces] would have learned about it within five days. Therefore, if even a small punitive operation were to take place within a thousand
.8 *li*, / he would know all about it. If it were a large operation, he would
.9 know about it anywhere in the entire realm. / He [would be able to] learn about these things within five[4] days because he would disburse money and wealth to employ those with sharp ears and clear sight.
.10 Therefore, / those who are skilled in the use of their armed forces do not [need] to penetrate the ramparts [of their enemies] to have eyes and ears.

Their troops are not aroused [with loud calls], carelessly assembled, recklessly moved about, or advanced without regard to the opposition. If they are aroused [with loud calls], the enemy will be forewarned. If
11 they are carelessly assembled, / their mass [strength] will be useless. If they are recklessly moved about, the troops will be exhausted. If they are advanced without regard for the opposition, valiant knights will be crushed.

Now, those who use their armed forces to attack a strong point will
12 always encounter stiff opposition.[5] / If they take advantage of weak

[1] Boyi 伯夷 and Shuqi 叔齊 were brothers whose father was the king of Guzhu 孤竹, a small state northwest of Hebei. When the father appointed the younger brother, Shuqi, his heir, Shuqi refused to accept the throne out of respect for his elder brother. Boyi, however, also refused to accept the throne because it would have violated the wishes of his father. Both men, in order to avoid assuming the throne, fled to Zhou; but on learning that Zhou had rebelled against the Shang, they refused to remain there, preferring instead to starve to death in the mountains.

[2] 甲子; the cyclical characters for the date on which King 武 Wu of the Zhou overthrew the Shang Dynasty.

[3] The passage 故小征. . . 日五間之 is clearly corrupt. I have followed Igai in rearranging it to read: 築堵之牆, 十人之聚, 日五間之. 故小征千理徧知之. Also, reading 間 as 俔 [Yasui].

[4] Emending 一 to 五 [Guo].

[5] The Zhao edition writes *ren* 韌. The Yang edition writes *ren* 軔. Both characters describe a strong obstacle.

points,[6] they will move like the spirits. If they attack strong points, then even the weak will become strong, but if they take advantage of weak points, then even the strong will become weak. / Therefore treat [the enemy's] strength as strength and their weakness as weakness. When ox butcher Tan 屠牛坦 in one morning carved up nine oxen but his knife could still engrave iron,[7] / it was because it traveled between the joints. Therefore, if the way of Heaven is not followed, mere subjugation will not suffice to make [the enemy] subservient.

If human activities are in a state of wild disorder, ten [men] may destroy a hundred. / If the preparation of weapons is not [properly] carried out, half [the usual number] can rout [an enemy] twice its size. Therefore those who would compete with military force do not march against well-constructed walls and moats.[8] / Those who possess the Way do not march against [states] that have lost their prince.[9]

Now, since no one knows when he will arrive, / there is no way to defend against[10] him. Since no one knows when he will leave, there is no way to prevent it. Even though the enemy may mass [their forces], they will be unable to stop or control him.

Maintaining order / is the way to prosperity, but it does not necessarily mean prosperity [in itself].[11] It is necessary to understand the activities that create prosperity before being able to be prosperous. Prosperity is the way to strength, / but it does not necessarily mean strength. It is necessary to understand the stratagems involved in acquiring strength before being able to be strong. Strength is the way to victory, but it does not necessarily mean victory. It is necessary to understand the principles of victory before being able to be victorious. / Victory is the way to rule, but victory does not necessarily mean rule. It

23.13
23.14

24.1

24.2

24.3
11a

24.4

24.5

24.6

---

[6] The Yang edition mistakenly writes 瑕 for 瑕 [Dai and Xu].

[7] Reading 莫 as 篡 [Yasui]. This story is reminiscent of that in the *Zhuangzi*, II, 3/1b2–2b11 (Watson, *Chuang Tzu* pp. 50–51), about Cook Ding 庖丁, who used his knife for nineteen years without it ever becoming dull. The *Yinyi* 音義 commentary of Lu Deming 陸德明 (A.D. 556–627) cites this passage from the *Guanzi*, writing 弟毛, "shave hairs," for 莫鐵. The *Huainanzi*, 11/10b7–8, also cites this story, but for 屠牛坦 writes 屠牛吐, "ox butcher Tu," and also writes 弟毛 for 莫鐵. The biography of Jia Yi in the *Qian Han shu*, 48/8b11–9a1, states that ox butcher Tan carved up twelve oxen in a morning instead of the nine given here.

[8] Ding would delete 池, "moats," following 城 as an interpolation, maintaining that its presence destroys the rhyme pattern of 城 (*djieng*), "walls," and 君 (*kjwen*), "prince." The additional character also destroys the balance with the sentence that follows.

[9] Such action, being in violation of the rites, would offend the other feudal lords. Furthermore, it being a time of crisis, the enemy might be prepared for an invasion.

[10] The Yang edition mistakenly writes 圖 for 圍 [Xu].

[11] Inverting the two characters 治而, in accordance with the Ancient and Zhu editions and the pattern of the sentences that follow [Igai and Wang Niansun].

is necessary to understand the assignment of responsibilities involved in ruling before being able to rule.

For this reason there are weapons for maintaining order within the state, activities for making a state prosperous, stratagems for making a state strong, principles for making a state victorious, / and the assignment of responsibilities for ruling the realm.

Jun Chen, Shang

君臣上

THE PRINCE AND HIS MINISTERS, PART I

Introductory Comments

This essay is the first of two chapters bearing the title *Jun chen* and dealing with the relationship between the prince and his ministers. *Jun chen* is also the title of chapter V, 23, of the *Shangjun shu*. However, even though the general subject is the same, these two *Guanzi* chapters differ greatly in tone from that of the *Shangjun shu*. The difference is made particularly evident by this chapter's stress on temperance in the application of laws and punishments.

The general style of this chapter tends to be somewhat verbose and pedantic, and the sentence patterns are often long and complicated. Guo Moruo believes it to be a work of the Qin or Han because of the reference (15b9; 28.9) to the five censors (*heng* 橫), which he equates with two Qin institutions: the *yushi dafu* 御史大夫, a censorate connected with the central government, and the *jian yushi* 監御史, an office responsible for overseeing the work of officials at the regional level. The Han continued this system of censors when it took over the governmental structure of the Qin. Luo Genze attributes the work to the late Warring States Period because it uses *zhu* 主 to mean ruler and *xiang* 相 for the chief minister, and because it implies much more mass involvement in government than possible in the earlier period.

Perhaps the most interesting aspect of this chapter is the degree of responsibility the author would assign to officials, leaving the ruler with only the function of overall command. This would seem to reflect the growing complexity of government and particularly the influence of Legalism characteristic of the late Warring States Period. Therefore, even though this chapter is clearly a work with Confucian orientation, it comes from a period when Legalist ideas of administrative structure were beginning to take hold. I would generally date the work about the middle of the third century B.C.

Translation

:24.10
1a12

The [true] prince cultivates a way of remaining above the [various] offices and not discussing their internal affairs. [True] ministers coordinate the internal affairs / of the [various] offices but do not discuss matters lying outside them.

4.11
1b

If the way of the prince is not clear, those who receive his orders will be in doubt. If political power and procedure are not unified, those who practice[1] righteousness will be led astray. When people have doubts and are led astray, their minds are in a quandary. / Moreover, if the sovereign is unable to establish order, a gulf will be created between himself and the hundred surnames. It will be as if a notice had been posted [instructing them to do something] and then [suddenly] they were ordered to stop. /

4.12

Thus the enlightened prince is one who is able to make this way [of governance] serve as the pattern for the state and applies it to the hundred surnames so as to instruct[2] his officials and transform those below. / The loyal minister is one who, on high, is able to give honest advice, and below, directs his efforts toward the people so they will practice righteousness and follow orders. When the sovereign acts in accord with this way while his subjects earnestly pursue their occupations, / and both the sovereign and his subjects harbor mutual aspirations, it is like being able to sight along three markers[3] [to determine] who is deviant in his behavior.

4.13

4.14

1

The *sefu*[4] in charge of civil functionaries is responsible for official matters. / The *sefu* in charge of people is responsible for education. He conducts education among the hundred surnames, judges the recalcitrant, and issues rewards to the trustworthy and sincere. / Since being made to feel as one with the prince and his ministers is the cause of their sincerity, they can[5] be used in both defensive and offensive warfare.

2

3

[1] Emending 修 to 循 here and in line 11b8 (24.14), below [Wang Niansun].

[2] Reading 飾 as 飭 [Yasui and Xu].

[3] According to He Ruzhang, Zhu Kezhen, and Guo Moruo, the three markers (*san biao* 参表) possibly refer to a three-point system of fixing the four directions, using the rising and setting sun as reference points. First, a pole is planted in the earth and a second is planted ten paces from the first in line with the rising sun. At sunset, a third pole is planted ten paces from the first in line with the setting sun. A fourth pole is then planted halfway between the second and third poles. A line between the second and third poles establishes an east-west axis, and that between the first and fourth establishes one running north and south. For a slightly garbled description of this system, see the *Huainanzi*, 3/18a11ff.

[4] The *sefu* 嗇夫 was a type of official mentioned in the *Zhou li* who has varying responsibilities. This sentence, 吏嗇夫任事, is clearly out of place here and belongs at the beginning of the next paragraph (12a3; 25.3).

[5] Inserting 可 before 以 [Xu].

When such is the case, the work of the *sefu* in charge of people is complete.

[The *sefu* in charge of civil functionaries is responsible for official matters.]⁶ He adheres completely to the prescribed / rules and conducts his affairs in accordance with the statutes. When judging cases involving laws and punishments or weights and measures, he states the charges in writing and avoids self-interest when rendering judgment, relying on the facts as proof. / When such is the case, the work of the *sefu* in charge of civil functionaries is complete.

After the *sefu* in charge of people has been successful in educating [the hundred surnames] and the *sefu* in charge of civil functionaries has been successful in making them adhere to the statutes, even persons who are sincere, upright, loyal, and trustworthy / will not be considered especially good, and even persons who are pleasure-seeking, self-indulgent, lazy, and arrogant will be unable to cause failure.⁷ When such / is the case, the work of the prince is complete.

Therefore the prince relies on the activities [of the *sefu*] and takes advantage of their work to examine [his officials] in accordance with proper procedures. / Those who do well, he rewards with the honors of ranks and titles. However, if the fields are rich but the people are disaffected, he punishes those who have gone to excess with the shame of dismissal / or death so his people will not be oppressed. Whether he kills them or lets them live, [the prince] does not violate [proper procedures] so no one among the people abandons his allegiance to him. / This is precisely because the sovereign has clear laws and his subjects have their constant work. /

Heaven has its constant representations,⁸ Earth has its constant form, and man has constant rules of propriety, which, once established, never change. These are called the three constants. Uniting them together into one / is the way of the prince. Maintaining distinctions and performing his tasks is the duty of the minister. If the prince neglects his way, it will be impossible for him to possess his state. If the minister neglects his duty, / it will be impossible for him to maintain his position.

Thus the sovereign should never be reckless in caring for his subjects, and they should never be remiss in serving the sovereign. Never reckless in caring for his subjects, the sovereign makes himself clear when proclaiming laws and instituting procedures.⁹ / Never remiss in serving

---

⁶ See n. 4, above.

⁷ The meaning of the text here is not entirely clear. I have generally followed the interpretation of Liu Ji.

⁸ *Xiang* 象; i.e., the sun, moon, and stars.

⁹ Deleting 所 as a corrupted reduplication of the preceding 則 [Guo Moruo].

25.4
25.5
25.6
25.7
25.8
25.9
12b
25.10
25.11
25.12
25.13
25.14

the sovereign, his subjects are conscientious in cultivating righteousness and following orders.

If the sovereign makes himself clear, and his subjects are conscientious, sovereign and subject will be united in their virtue and accentuate their respective positions. If the prince does not lack prestige and his subjects / do not neglect production, no one will claim to be the more virtuous. Thus the sovereign pays heed to virtue while his subjects preserve moderation. If propriety and righteousness are perfectly manifested on high / so goodness extends downward to the people, the hundred surnames will extend their allegiance upward to the ruler and expend their full energies on agriculture below.

Therefore it is said: "When the brilliance of the prince is fully trusted, the five officers[10] are stern, the gentry above corruption, the peasants simple, and the merchants and artisans honest, / the sovereign and his subjects will be as one,[11] and the sexes will be kept separate. The people will have a basis for their existence, and the three generations[12] will all observe the regulations."

Now, / the prince should cherish virtue in others while the minister looks to the sovereign for his life. The sovereign should measure achievement and provide sufficient emoluments / while the minister accepts employment and occupies [his position] in order to instruct [others].

If the governmental policies proclaimed are equitable, and the people obtain enough from their production [to meet their needs], the state will flourish. If salaries are bestowed[13] / on the basis of hard work, the people will not trust to luck for their livelihood. If the punishments are equitable, there will be no resentments below. If terminology is precise and distinctions are clear, the people will have no doubts about the way [of proper governance]. / This way [of governance] is the means by which the sovereign leads his people.

Thus, both the way [of proper governance] and virtue emanate from the prince. Regulations and orders are circulated[14] by the chief minister (*xiang* 相). The various activities are arranged by officials. / The efforts

---

[10] *Wu guan* 五官; the officers of the five traditional bureaus or departments of government. Their titles changed with the dynasties, but according to the *Zhou li*, they were: (1) the minister of education 地官司徒; (2) the minister of rites 春官宗伯; (3) the minister of war 夏官司馬; (4) the minister of justice 秋官司寇; and (5) the minister of works 司空 or 考工記.

[11] Yu Xingwu would read 體 as 分; thus, "will maintain their distinctions."

[12] That is, the father, grandfather, and grandson [Yasui and Zhang Peilun].

[13] The Zhao edition mistakenly writes 受 for 授 [Yasui].

[14] The Zhao edition mistakenly writes 傳 for 傅 = 敷 [Yu Xingwu].

of the hundred surnames are devoted to awaiting orders and then acting [on them]. /

26.9   Therefore nothing is more precious to a prince than his word, nothing more cherished on the part of a minister than his effort. When
26.10   words / move downward, and effort moves upward, the way of the ruler and minister is complete.

Thus, when the ruler defines [the tasks of government], the chief
26.11   minister attends to them. When the chief minister defines them, / officials attend to them. When the officials define them, the people render their service.

Furthermore, in order to determine [the true from the false], there are tallies[15] and tokens,[16] personal and public seals,[17] statutes and laws,
26.12   and plans and records. / These make clear the way of public good so as to eliminate wicked and false schemes.

Assessing talent, measuring ability, considering virtue, and promot-
26.13   ing those [with these attributes] is the way of the sovereign. / Focusing his thoughts, being of one mind [with the prince], attending to his tasks,
14a   and never considering himself overworked is the duty of the subject. / If the prince meddles in the affairs of the offices below, the responsible
26.14   officials will shirk their duties. / If ministers work together to dominate what lies beyond their offices[18] on high, the ruler will lose prestige.

27.1   For this reason, the prince who possesses the [proper] way / rectifies his virtue in order to manage his people and does not speak about his own wisdom and ability or sharpness of hearing and keenness of sight. It is the task of the subject to provide wisdom and ability, sharpness of hearing, and keenness of sight. It is by means of the way of the sovereign that wisdom and ability, sharpness of hearing, and keenness of sight are
27.2   employed. / The person on high clarifies this way, while those below attend to their tasks. Sovereign and subject are divided in their differing responsibilities, but come together again to form a unity.

27.3   Thus, the person who recognizes skill in others is the prince; / those

---

[15] Tallies (*fu* 符) were made of various materials, including metal and bamboo. Usually the whole tally was inscribed with characters, then broken in two, with one piece being given to a prospective correspondent. When that person wished to send a message, he would send along his half of the tally to prove the message was authentic.

[16] Tokens (*jie* 節) included insignia of rank, flags, staffs, or other symbols of authority issued by the ruler to authenticate a special mission.

[17] *Yin xi* 印璽; from the Qin on, *xi* was used to designate an imperial seal, but according to the Wei Zhao 韋昭 (204–273) commentary to the the *Guo yu*, 5/4b2, it was used in pre-Qin times to indicate the seal of a great officer. Yin simply means a mark and refers to seals in general. I believe that here *xi* probably refers to the seal of an office, while *yin* refers to one belonging to an individual.

[18] Inserting 官 after 於 [Guo Moruo].

404

who are skilled themselves serve others. If the prince [exercises] his own
skills, he will lack good judgment. / If he lacks good judgment, he will
constantly be [overly] generous with rewards and incapable of inflicting
punishment. Such is a state with no law. Its people will form factions,
and below, vie with one another in showing off / their cleverness in order
to fulfill their personal ambitions. When laws and regulations have a
constant standard, the people do not split up [into factions], but unite
with their sovereign and exert themselves fully in giving him their
loyalty.

Thus, it is not the discussion of wisdom and ability but the administration of court[19] affairs and the solution of national problems / that are
the responsibility of great ministers. They do not discuss sharpness of
hearing or keenness of sight, but in the promotion of skilled persons,
the punishment of wickedness and falsehood, and seeing and hearing
[everything], [their duties] are manifold.

This is why the [true] prince sits at the source of the myriad of things
and is the one who assigns tasks for all living beings. / He selects the
worthy, assesses the talented, and treats them according to the law.
Having elevated and obtained [the service of] these men, he sits back
and watches[20] over [his people], and his wealth is more than can be
absorbed. /

If his officials do not fulfill their responsibilities, they may run back
and forth receiving [his orders] but their failures will remain beyond
repair. However, a state is never lacking in gentlemen able to assume
responsibilities. It is only that the intelligence of the sovereign / is not
sufficient to realize this. Thus, the enlightened prince is careful to know
which of his ministers is capable of fulfilling his responsibilities.

Therefore it is said: / "The ruler himself is the basis for rectifying
virtue; officials[21] are the means [for providing him] with ears and eyes."
When [the ruler] has established his own [virtue], the people will be
transformed. When his virtue has been rectified, the officials / will be well
regulated. In regulating officials and transforming the people, the most
important factor is the sovereign. Therefore, the virtuous prince does
not seek [regulation and transformation] to come from the people, [but
rather from himself].

Thus, if the sovereign meddles in the affairs of his subjects, he is said to

---

[19] Emending 順 to 朝. The use of 順 destroys the syntactical balance of the sentence
[Guo Moruo].

[20] Emending 收 to 牧 [Guo Moruo].

[21] Deleting 治 as an interpolation taken from the following passage [Wang Yinzhi and
Guo Moruo].

405

27.12
15a
be domineering. / If his subjects meddle in the affairs of their sovereign, they are said to be presumptuous. When a sovereign is domineering, he is disruptive; when subjects are presumptuous, they are seditious. If a state [is beset by] conduct that is disruptive and seditious, perverse and

27.13
recalcitrant, / there will be a failure of discipline in the gentry's control over the people.

27.14
Thus, / to differentiate relationships and correctly maintain social distinctions is called establishing order. To accord with order and not neglect it is called having the proper way. When the proper way and virtue are fixed, the people will have rules. The prince who possesses the

28.1
proper way is one who is skilled in / establishing clear laws and does not violate them for reasons of self-interest, while the prince who lacks the proper way is one who, having already established laws, abandons them to pursue his self-interest.

If the sovereign relaxes the laws to pursue his self-interest, his

28.2
ministers / will put forth self-interest as being synonymous with public good, [maintaining that] to avoid violating the way of public good one

28.3
must not violate the way of self-interest / and that self-interest is inherent in carrying out the way of public good. If this goes on for a long time without [the ruler] realizing [what is happening], is it conceivable that wicked hearts will not accumulate? If wicked hearts accumulate, at the

28.4
worst there will be the disasters of usurpation / and murder of the sovereign; at the very least, there will [still] be the chaos of partisanship and civil war.

15b
This is so because the virtue of the ruler has not been established / and the state lacks constant laws. If the virtue of the ruler has not been

28.5
established, his women / will be able to corrupt his thinking. If the state lacks constant laws, great ministers will dare to usurp his authority and

28.6
will avail themselves of the ability of females to spy upon[22] / his true state of affairs. The women, enjoying his favor, will avail themselves of

28.7
the knowledge of males to bring in outside forces. Thereupon, / they will cast out the consort and endanger the heir apparent. The armed forces will create disturbances within the palace in order to summon insurgents from abroad. This is the ultimate proof that the prince is in danger. /

28.8
For this reason, the prince who possesses the proper way has the five officers at the top to shepherd his people so that the masses will not dare transgress the rules in their conduct. Below, he has the five censors[23] to

[22] Reading 規 as 窺 [Ding and Yasui].
[23] Guo Moruo equates these censors 橫 (or 衡) with the central government's *yushi dafu* 御史大夫 and its regional *jian yushi* 監御史, both of which were responsible for overseeing the work of other officials during the Qin period.

406

28.9   oversee his officials so that those in charge will not dare part from / the law when serving him. The court has fixed measures and proper rules of decorum to uphold the honor of the ruler's position. His clothing,

28.10   including mourning caps, are completely covered by regulation, / so that the prince will be established as the embodiment of law. The prince, taking firm grasp of the law, issues his orders. Responsible officials

16a   receive his commands and carry them out, / while the hundred surnames follow their sovereign, fully adhering to established customs. Once this

28.11   has been in practice for some time, it becomes the norm. / Those who violate established custom or part from accepted teaching are considered as malefactors by the masses, so the sovereign may rest at ease.

     When the son of Heaven issues orders to the realm, and the feudal

8.12   lords receive them from him; / when great ministers accept orders from their princes, and sons accept them from their parents; when inferiors obey their superiors, and younger brothers obey their elder brothers— the ultimate in obedience will prevail.

     When there are standard beam and weight for weighing, standard *dou* and *hu*[24] for measuring, standard *zhang* and *chi*[25] for bolts of

8.13   cloth,[26] / standard lengths for spears and other weapons,[27] and when writing uses common characters,[28] and vehicles have the same axle width—the ultimate in having standards will prevail.

     Those who are obedient will expose[29] those who are recalcitrant, and those who adhere to the standards will expose those who are perverse.

.14   This is like / having a lighted torch when searching for something at night. People who are wicked and false will have no place to hide. This is the way in which the former kings unified the hearts of their people. /

---

[24] A Han *dou* 斗 equaled 1.81 U.S. dry quarts. A *hu* 斛, consisting of ten *dou*, equaled 18.1 U.S. dry quarts or .565 U.S. bushels (Swann, *Food and Money*, p. 364).

[25] A Han *zhang* 丈, consisting of ten *chi* 尺, equaled 7 feet, 6.94 inches (ibid., p. 362).

[26] Reading 緯 as 淳 [Igai, Wang Niansun, and Hong]. The term appears in *Zhou li*, 7/7a2 (Biot, *Tcheou-li*, I, p. 146), where it says that the administrator of the interior (*neicai* 内宰) assists the empress in establishing a market in the capital and 出其度量淳制. The Zheng Xuan 鄭玄 commentary explains this passage as meaning: "He issues [standards] for linear and capacity measurement and for the width and length of bolts of cloth."

[27] The *Zhou li*, 39–40 (Biot, ibid. II, pp. 456–514), discusses the standard measurements for various weapons.

[28] Reading 名 as 文. The *Zhong yong*, 28/3, says: "Now, throughout the empire, vehicles have the same axle width, writing uses the same characters, and conduct has the same rules." Here 文 is written instead of 名. Jiang Han and Xu cite a passage in the *Zhou li*, 37/10b5 (Biot, ibid., II, p. 407), which states that in the ninth year, the grand officer in charge of travel (*da xingren* 大行人) 諭書名, 聽聲音: "compares the characters (名) used in writing and determines their pronunciation." The Zheng Xuan commentary says that 名 means 文.

[29] Emending 獨 to 燭 here and in the following phrase [Zhang Peilun].

29.1   Thus, whatever his goodness, the son of Heaven concedes his virtue to Heaven. Whatever their goodness, the feudal lords offer[30] it to the son of Heaven. Whatever their goodness, the great ministers present it
29.2   to their princes. Whatever their goodness, the people / consider it to have come from their fathers and offer it to their elders. This is the source of both the proper way and the law, and is the basis of good order.

Thus, the one who makes a single inquiry[31] covering the entire year is
29.3   the prince, / the one who conducts seasonal investigations is the chief
16b   minister, the one who conducts monthly examinations is the official, and the one who pays heed to the strength of his four limbs, practices the business of agriculture, and thereby awaits orders is the common man.

29.4   Thus, the gentry measure out [the fruits of] their efforts among their fathers and elder brothers, / and make their speech adhere to the ideas of the prince and his ministers so that officials, in judging their virtue and ability, will treat them generously. Great officers check on affairs in the various offices but do not discuss external matters, while the chief
29.5   minister / makes constant preparations for them.

The chief minister manages important affairs, while the various[32] officials handle ordinary matters.[33] They measure accomplishments, discuss[34] their good points, and submit requests for corrective action where they have doubts. /

29.6   Subsequently, the prince brings forth the laws and jade tallies from
29.7   the illustrious archives to verify [the activities of his officials].[35] / He stands on the third step [leading into the audience hall] and, facing

---

[30] Emending 慶 to 薦 here and below, in accordance with a similar passage in the *Li ji*, XIV, 24/17a5–7 (Legge, *Li Ki*; XXVIII, p. 233) [Wang Niansun].

[31] Reading 言 as 問 [Yu Yue]. Chen Huan would emend 一言 to 省, in accordance with a similar passage in the *Shang shu*, V, 4/35, 王省惟歲, 卿士惟月, 師尹惟日: "The king scrutinized the year, high ministers the months, and lower officials the days. According to the *Shangjun shu*, V, 24/11a2–5 (Duyvendak, *Lord Shang*, p. 320); "... officials exert sole authority and take decisions a thousand *li* away [from the ruler]. In the twelfth month, to confirm it, they make a report in which the affairs of the whole year have separate entries, but as the ruler gives but one hearing, although he sees doubtful cases, he cannot determine whether an official is capable or not."

[32] Reading 者 as 諸 [Yin Tongyang and Yu Xingwu].

[33] Reading 士 as 事 [Yin Zhizhang and He Ruzhang].

[34] Emending 義 to 議 [Igai, Ding, and Guo].

[35] This sentence is not clear, and it appears likely that something has been omitted before the 而, which begins it. The illustrious archives (*mingfu* 明府) probably represent the same institution as the *taifu* 太府 mentioned in chapter I, 4/15a1–3 (1 : 14.3): "On the day of the great court, the governors of the five districts and the great officers of the five dependencies all acquaint themselves with the laws before the prince. The grand scribe 太史 then proclaims the laws and deposits a record of them in the grand archives (*taifu*)."

408

south, receives important documents. Thereby, the sovereign has his
29.8 leisure, and the officials fulfill / their responsibilities. The seasonal orders
are not excessive, and the gentry is respectful in supplying [the prince
with his due]. This is only because [36] the sovereign has his laws and
regulations, while his subjects have their separate tasks. /

29.9 The way [of good government] produces[37] sincere men, but it is not
17a inherent in them. However, the sage king and enlightened prince understand this well and thus lead [others]. Thus, there is the constant way for
29.10 administering / the people, and there are constant methods for producing wealth. The way [of good government] is the most important of all
things. If the prince grasps its importance and behaves accordingly,
29.11 even though among his subjects there may be wicked / and false hearts,
no one will dare kill him.[38]

Now, the way [of good government] is intangible. When men [who
possess it] exist, it becomes pervasive. However, when men [who possess it]
29.12 are gone, it is stifled. If it is not present,[39] there is no way / to bring order
to the people or produce wealth. When people are well administered and
wealth is cultivated, prosperity accrues to the sovereign. This being the
case, we understand that the enlightened prince is one who emphasizes
the way [of administering the people] and the methods [for producing
29.13 wealth] while deemphasizing [the power of] the state.[40] / Therefore,
whether one is prince of a single state or king of the realm, it is the way
[of good government] that makes him [truly] so.

29.14 Whether they be great kings / of the realm or petty princes of a single
state, the way [of good government] brings them together. This being the
30.1 case, they are able to obtain / from the people what they desire and
7b eliminate what they hate. Since they are able to obtain what they desire
from the people, the worthy and talented adhere to them. Since they are
able to eliminate what they hate from the people, wickedness and
30.2 falsehood are reduced. It is as though they were casting / [their people] in
metal or molding them in clay. Their control depends on putting forth
effort. /

30.3 For this reason, if [the sovereign] seeks to provide for [his people],

---

[36] Transposing 唯此 to read 此唯 [Ding].

[37] Emending 姓 to 性 = 生 [Yasui, Dai, and Tao].

[38] Wang Niansun and Xu would emend 殺 to 試, in accordance with a similar passage
in chapter XI, 31/3b6–7 (2:33.10). Thus, "No one would dare attempt [evil deeds]."

[39] Reading 是 as 則 [Wang Yinzhi].

[40] The position of 知, "understand," in this sentence makes it difficult to interpret. Tao
would write: 是以明君知之，重道法而輕其國也："This being the case, the
enlightened prince understands. He emphasizes the way [of administering the people] and
the methods [for producing wealth] and deemphasizes [the power of] the state."

kindness and generosity [alone] are incapable of fulfilling their needs. If he seeks to subjugate them, severity and awesome power / are incapable of terrifying them. If severity and awesome power are not capable of terrifying them, and kindness and generosity are not capable of fulfilling their needs, there will be a gulf between [the ruler's] words and reality.

If he is not reluctant to reward those who are good, the people will not seek profit on their own. / If he is not hesitant to punish those who make mistakes, people will not resent his awesome power. If he does not go to excess in inflicting his awesome power and punishment on the people, / people will give their allegiance to their sovereign. It is just as when Heaven sends down the right amount of rain, the marsh is lowered by one foot and growing things rise one foot. / In this way [the sovereign] controls the people by not controlling them; he serves the people by not serving them. Aloof and unhindered, such is the position of the ruler. /

When the former kings inhabited the world, the people compared them to a divine power because they derived[41] their goodness from the people. Now, when the people are listened to individually, they are stupid. / However, when they are listened to collectively, they are sagelike.[42] Even though [a ruler] may have the virtue of a Tang 湯 or Wu 武, he will still be in agreement with what people in the marketplace say. /

Hence, the enlightened prince accords with the hearts of the people, is at ease with their natures, and proceeds from a consensus of the masses. Hence, his orders are put forth with no resistance while punishments are established but not applied. / The former kings were skilled at being as one with the people. Since they were as one with their people, they relied on their state to preserve their state and their people to preserve their people. This being so, the people / would not easily commit wrongs.

Even though one is an enlightened prince, beyond a hundred paces [his voice] cannot be heard. Situated behind walls, he cannot be seen. / Consequently, when [a ruler] has the reputation of being an enlightened prince, it is because he is skilled in utilizing his ministers, and his ministers are skilled in rendering loyalty to him. Their trust perpetuates / trust. Their skill transmits skill. Hence, within the four seas, whatever they possess is well administered.

Thus, when the enlightened prince promotes his subjects, he fully understands their weaknesses / and strengths. Knowing their limits, he

---

[41] Emending 牧 to 收 [Tao].
[42] According to the *Shang shu*, II, 3/7: 天聰明自我民聰明, "Heaven hears and sees as my people hear and see."

then[43] employs them according to the task. When a worthy person serves his ruler, he must fully understand his own weaknesses and strengths. Knowing what his strength cannot accomplish, / he then measures his ability when accepting office. The sovereign uses this to nurture his subjects; subjects use this to serve their sovereign. / When superior and inferior communicate their expectations of what is correct, men and women of the hundred surnames share in maintaining good order.

---

[43] Reading 若 as 乃 here and below [Yu Yue].

Jun Chen Xia
君臣下

THE PRINCE AND HIS MINISTERS, PART II

Introductory Comments

This is the second of the two chapters entitled *Jun chen*. *Jun chen* is also the title of chapter V, 23, of the *Shangjun shu* (Duyvendak, *Lord Shang*, p. 314), and the opening sentence of this and the *Shangjun shu* chapter even begin in much the same way: "In ancient times before there were princes and ministers, superiors and inferiors. . . ." However, as in the case of *Jun chen shang*, this chapter is much more Confucian in its content than the *Shang jun shu*. It is best known for the opening statement that describes how primitive society came to develop governmental structures and standards of behavior. Although these two *Jun chen* chapters are similar in their general point of view, they differ in specific content and in style, with this chapter appearing to be more tightly structured than *Jun chen shang*. For this reason, and despite their common ideological base, I tend to believe that they are the products of different authors. They were probably produced during the middle of the third century B.C. by writers belonging to that later authoritarian wing of Confucianism represented by Xunzi.

Translation

2:31.8
1a7

In ancient times there were no distinctions between prince and minister or superior and inferior, nor did there exist the union of husband and wife or man and mate. People lived like beasts and dwelt together in herds, using their strength to attack one another. Consequently, the

31.9

clever / cheated the stupid, and the strong maltreated the weak. The old and young, orphaned and alone were thus unable to obtain the means to subsist. Therefore the wise took advantage of the strength of the masses to restrain the cruelty of the strong, and violence against people was brought to an end. On behalf of the people, they promoted [policies]

31.10

that were beneficial and eliminated / those that were harmful. They established correct standards of virtue for the people so the people took them as their teachers. It was because of this that political methods of the

Way and virtuous conduct emanated from worthies, and, as adherence to righteousness and proper order took shape in the minds of the people, / they turned to the moral way.

As contradictions arose between what people said and what they did and distinctions emerged between right and wrong,[1] rewards and punishments were implemented, / superior and inferior status was instituted, the people came to constitute a political entity, and a national capital was established. / Therefore, what makes a state a state is the fact that the people have come to form a political entity. What makes a prince a prince is the fact that he issues rewards and punishments.

Excessive rewards / result in shortages; excessive punishments result in cruelty. Shortages of resources and cruelty in the issuance of orders are causes for losing the [support of] the people. For this reason the enlightened prince takes care to see that the people are taught to remain in their places so they may be well governed at home, / victorious in battle, and firm in defense.

Now, if rewards become too costly, the sovereign cannot afford them. If punishments become too cruel, his subjects will not trust him. / For this reason the enlightened prince is one who sets forth rules of propriety for feasts and funerals, ranking them in different categories. He disciplines [his subjects] in accordance with the eight concerns of government,[2] uses clothing to indicate [their ranks], / enriches them with salaries,[3] and honors them in accordance with royal regulations. Thus the people give their allegiance to the prince and he is able to employ them. /

When the people are employed, [control of] the realm is attainable. If the realm adheres to the moral way, it will achieve [its goals]; otherwise, it will not, Now, water rushes upward forming waves, but when it reaches the peak of its crest, / it dies down again. The authority of [the prince] is definitely like this. Therefore, if [the prince] comforts [his people] with benevolence and makes them fearful [of punishment] through his awesomeness, / the entire realm will be his.

When a state that adheres to the moral way issues instructions and orders, men and women will give their complete allegiance to their sovereign. When it proclaims laws and issues statutes, worthy gentlemen

---

[1] Emending 違 to 諉 = 是 and deleting 是 as a reduplication [Xu and Guo Moruo]. Also deleting 之 [Zhang Peilun and Guo Moruo].

[2] According to the *Hong fan* 洪範 chapter of the *Shang shu*, V, 4/7, the eight concerns of government 八政 consisted of: (1) food 食, (2) commodities 貨, (3) sacrifices 祀, (4) public works 司空, (5) education 司徒, (6) justice 司寇, (7) guests 賓, and the military 師.

[3] Emending 裏 to 稟 [Wang Yinzhi].

and heroic knights will devote all their efforts and abilities to their

sovereign. / Within a thousand *li*, [even] minor fines involving silk cloth or money[4] or the tax on a single *mou* of land can be made known to everyone. Those who wield the battle-axe and halberd will not dare refuse to implement punishment; those who are charged with [the

bestowing of] carriages and caps will not dare / decline to make awards. Obedient,[5] they are like the children of a single father or the members of a single household, because their duties and the rules of propriety are clear.

Now, if inferiors / do not support their superiors and ministers do not support the prince, worthy men will not come [to court]. / If worthy men do not come, the hundred surnames will not be employed. If the hundred surnames are not employed, [control of] the realm will not be attained. Therefore it is said: "If there is interference with [the prince's]

beneficence, the prince will be in danger. / If there is interference with his discussion of matters, persons of merit will be in danger. If there is interference with his orders, officials will be in danger. If there is interference with his punishments, the hundred surnames will be in

danger." / Thus the enlightened prince is one who takes care to prohibit malicious interference. If on high there are no arguments supporting malicious interference, there will be no thought of risking[6] it below.

It is called misrule whenever a person who functions as a prince turns

his back on the moral way and ignores the law, while enjoying the pursuit of his selfish interests. / It is called usurpation of higher authority[7] whenever a person who functions as a minister changes established practices and deviates from the constant standards, while engaging in clever rhetoric[8] in order to curry favor with his sovereign.

When misrule becomes extreme, it leads to cruelty; when the usurpation of higher authority becomes extreme, it leads to treason.[9] / When these

---

[4] The phrase 束布 is not clear. I have followed the Yin commentary. However, Liu Ji and Yasui would interpret it to mean a bundle of cloth. Xu would emend 布 to 矢, "arrows," in accordance with the *Xiao kuang*, chapter VII, 20/12b8 (1:105.12): "When a person cannot be dissuaded from bringing a civil or criminal case to court, the judge should prohibit any action for three days, and if the charges then prove to be unfounded, order [the complainant] to turn in a bundle of arrows as punishment. Thus the passage here would read:..., [even] minor fines involving a bundle of arrows...."

[5] Emending 墳 to 壙(隤) [Chen, Ding, Yasui, and Zhang Peilun].

[6] Reading 異 as 翼, in accordance with the Yang, Ancient, Liu, and Zhu editions.

[7] Yu Xingwu would read 騰 as 匿, "concealing evil."

[8] Emending 官 to 言 [Wang Yinzhi and Yu Xingwu].

[9] Reading 北 as 背 [Wang Niansun, Igai, and Sun Xingyan].

two[10] occur at the same time,[11] enemies will hatch their plots against [the prince].

If[12] he is charitable and generous[13] in order to provide relief [in times of] disorder, the hundred surnames will be happy. / If he selects those who are worthy and advances those with talent so there is propriety, filial piety, and respect for elders, then wickedness and falseness will be prevented. If he restrains licentiousness and sloth and keeps men and women separate, improper relations and disorderly conduct / will be prevented. If righteous conduct is practiced by both the honored and the lowly and no one oversteps the bounds of proper relationships and ranks, those having merit will be encouraged. If the state has constant forms, and traditional laws are not relegated to obscurity, those below will not possess resentful hearts. These five are the way to make virtue flourish, correct mistakes, preserve / the state, and settle the people.

Now, a prince may make serious mistakes; a minister may commit major crimes. The state is what [the prince] possesses; the people are what he rules. If [the prince] who possesses a state and rules his people / tries to administer them through those they hate, he will be committing his first mistake. The people have their three duties.[14] If [the prince] does not keep his people informed of them, they will not be his people. / If the people are not his people, they can be used neither in defense nor attack. This is his second mistake.

Now, a minister receives a high rank and large salary from the prince and supervises important offices. If he turns his back on these offices, / neglects his duties, suits his actions to the prince's expression, compliers with the prince's [personal] desires, and caters to him in order to gain influence over him, he will be committing a major crime. /

When a prince makes major mistakes and does not reform, it is called perversity. When a minister commits crimes and is not punished, it is called fomenting disorder. If the prince is perverse / and the minister foments disorder, it is only a matter of sitting and waiting for the state to collapse. /

For this reason, the prince who adheres to the moral way holds fast to what is fundamental, his chief minister (*xiang* 相) holds fast to what is important, and his great officers (*dafu* 大夫) hold fast to the law.

[10] Emending 四, "four," to 兩 [Zhang Peilun and Guo Moruo].

[11] Emending 敗 to 則 [Wang Niansun and Xu].

[12] Deleting 則 as an interpolation from the preceding passage [Yasui and Xu].

[13] Reading 猶 as 游 [Wang Niansun].

[14] *San wu* 三務; according to the Yin commentary, these refer to the seasonal tasks associated with spring, summer, and fall.

Thereby they shepherd the multitude of ministers. His ministers expend their wisdom and exhaust their strength in serving their sovereign. When these four / responsibilities are met there is good government. If they are altered, there is anarchy. Therefore it is absolutely necessary that they be clearly established and strictly observed.[15]

In ancient times, the sage kings treated the livelihood of the people as fundamental and carefully studied the causes of disaster and prosperity. / For this reason, they treated minor details with care and distinguished right[16] from wrong in order to get to the root of matters. Hence people prone to reckless, evil, and deceitful behavior dared not attempt it. / This is the way to institute[17] propriety and rectify the people.

In ancient times there were two expressions: "The walls have ears" and "Unseen bandits are at your side." The walls have ears" means that secret plans have leaked out. / "Unseen bandits are at your side" is to say that concealed usurpers[18] are winning over the hearts of your people. When secret plans have leaked out, it is because designing women have ferreted out the true state of the ruler's affairs[19] to assist roving conspirators.[20] / When concealed usurpers win over the hearts of the people,[21] it is because those who were formerly honored but later reduced in rank chase about in their service. /

When an enlightened prince is on high, specious attendants cannot corrupt his thinking because punishments are applied to [even] those closest to him. Great ministers are unable to encroach upon / his authority because it is clear that those who form cliques and factions will be executed. He who acts as the prince of men is able to keep his distance from slander and cajolery, eliminate factions, and see to it that those licentious and perverse drifters who wander around in search of salaries, are not given ranks or positions / at court. Such is the way to prevent deceit, restrain evil, enrich the state, and preserve one's life.

He who acts as the sovereign controls his various ministers and the hundred surnames and establishes harmony [among them] through men attached to him at the center. / Thus men attached to the center serve as

---

[15] Reversing the order of the two characters 守固 [Ding and Yasui].

[16] Emending 違 to 韙 = 是 [Ding and Guo Moruo].

[17] Inserting 制 before 禮, in accordance with the Yin commentary [Ding and Xu].

[18] The meaning of 疑 is not clear. I have generally followed Guo Moruo, who says it means 僭擬.

[19] Reading 請 as 情 [Fang, Ding, Tao, and Yao].

[20] For a similar statement in the preceding chapter, see X, 30, 15b1–7 (2:28.4–7).

[21] The Yang edition mistakenly writes 者 for 之.

intermediaries between ordinary ministers and the ruler. The dissemination of regulations and orders among the people must be carried out by men attached to the center. If those attached to the center / are quick to implement [regulations and orders that the sovereign wants] implemented slowly, they could be usurping his majestic power. If they are slow to implement [regulations and orders that the sovereign wants] implemented immediately, they could be seeking to show kindness to the people. When majestic power and [the power] to show kindness to the people are transferred to / his subordinates, the sovereign will be in danger.

Knowledge about those who are worthy or unworthy must be conveyed to the sovereign by men associated with him at the center. Contributions of wealth and labor to the sovereign must be made through men associated with him at the center. If they are able to substitute those who are unworthy for those who are worthy, / they will be able to create[22] factions below. Furthermore,[23] if they are able to offer up the wealth and labor of the people to entice[24] the ruler, they will be able to appear as hardworking to their superior.[25] / They will have [gained the support of] both their superior and their subordinates in order to promote their self-interest on all sides. When [the sovereign's system of] ranks and regulations cannot be implemented, the sovereign will be in danger. /

Those who are ahead of their prince in extending favors encroach upon [his authority to] bestow rewards and preempt [his right to] show kindness.[26] Those who are ahead of their prince in the application of what [people] hate, encroach upon /[his authority to] punish and preempt his majestic power. Those who circulate false rumors outside the court threaten their prince, and those who obstruct orders so they are not issued isolate him. / If one of these [evils] is committed and the sovereign[27] does not know of it, then it is only a matter of sitting and waiting for the state to be endangered.

It is in the way of Heaven and nature of man that the divine and sagely become kings, the benevolent and wise become princes, and the warlike and brave / become [military] leaders (*zhang* 長). It is in the grand

[22] Emending 威 to 成 [Wang Niansun].
[23] Reading 有 as 又 [Liu Ji, Zhao, Tao, and Xu].
[24] The Yang edition mistakenly writes 陷 for 啗 [Wang Yinzhi].
[25] Emending 下 to 上 [Tao].
[26] Emending 實 to 惠 [Ding and Xu].
[27] Deleting 下 in accordance with the Ancient, Liu, and Zhu editions [Yasui and Wang Niansun].

scheme of things that those who comprehend the way of Heaven and the nature of man become men of substance, while those lacking[28] [in such comprehension] become followers. /

Accordingly, those who lead the way in using their minds do not participate in ordinary affairs of state. Those who are personally involved in such affairs do not determine the way [in which the state is to be governed]. / For this reason, he who serves as the sovereign belabors his mind but not his physical strength. The hundred surnames belabor their physical strength but not their minds.[29]

When the distinctions between prince and minister, superior and inferior are fixed, rules of propriety and sumptuary regulations are established. Accordingly, it is in the nature of things for ordinary men / to serve the sovereign, for physical strength to serve intelligence, and for the body[30] to serve the mind. It is the way of the mind to [consider matters] back and forth, / but the way of the body to rush about [doing things]. Those who [consider matters] back and forth devote themselves to management. Those who rush about devote themselves to labor. Those who devote themselves / to labor are represented by squareness; those who devote themselves to management are represented by roundness.[31] What is round revolves. What revolves is comprehensive. When there is comprehensiveness, there is harmony. What is square / is steadfast. What is steadfast is stable. When there is stability there is credibility. When the prince maintains harmony by extending benefits [to the people][32] and ministers maintain credibility by practicing restraint, there will be no profligacy on the part of either the sovereign or his subordinates. / Therefore it is said: "Those who act as a prince of men manage a benevolent [government]; those who serve as a minister among men safeguard their credibility." This / refers to the proper conduct of the sovereign and his subordinates.

The prince, in occupying the capital of his state, is like the mind in the body. When moral conduct (*dao de* 道德) is certain on / high, the hundred surnames will be transformed below. When a sincere[33] mind

---

[28] Emending 寵 to 窮 [Ding].

[29] This passage is very reminiscent of the famous statement in the *Mengzi*, IIIA, 4/6: 古曰，或勞心，或勞力，勞心者治人，勞力者治於人，"Hence there is a saying, 'Some labor with their minds and some with their strength. Those who labor with their minds rule others; those who labor with their strength are ruled by others.'"

[30] Reading 刑 as 形 [Liu Ji, Hong, and Wang Niansun].

[31] This statement accords with the concept of Heaven being round and Earth being square.

[32] Guo Moruo would emend 利, "benefits," to 制. Thus, "When the prince maintains harmony through [good] management."

[33] Emending 戒 to 成 = 誠 [Wang Niansun].

takes shape within, it will be manifested without. Rectification [of his own conduct] is the means by which [the prince] makes his virtue clear. It is because he follows this principle that [the prince] knows what is 35.6 suitable / for himself and what is suitable for the people. When he realizes that something is not suitable for the people and withdraws to correct himself, it is because he has returned to this basic 35.7 [principle]. / Since he demands much of himself, his virtuous conduct is [fully] established. Since he demands little of others, the people freely give to him. /

35.8 Therefore he who acts as a prince of men should concentrate on what lies above. He who serves as a minister among men should concentrate on what lies below. He who concentrates on what lies above should take note of the seasons of Heaven and devote his attention to the labor of the people. He who concentrates on what lies below should develop the 35.9 fruits of Earth and see that there is sufficient / to meet material needs. Therefore the way of the enlightened prince lies in being able to set forth major duties, pay attention to the seasons, accord proper ceremony toward the gods above and be righteous in his conduct toward those 5.10 who serve him below. / The conduct[34] of a loyal minister lies in being able to hold to the law and never curry favor [from those in high station]. Above, they rectify the mistakes of the ruler; below, they relieve the misery of the people. /

a If an enlightened prince is on high and he is served by loyal ministers, 5.11 they will keep the people in line / through [proper] administration and punishments and lead them along with the benefits of clothing and food. Therefore, since [the people] are sincere, they are easy to manage; since they are simple-minded, they are easy to keep in check. /

5.12 The man of quality (*junzi* 君子) is paid according to his adherence to the moral way, the ordinary person according to his strength. Such is the distinction between them.[35] When [the former] lacks real authority, there is no way for him to establish his own majestic power. When [the latter] is unable to act [on his own], there is no way for him to initiate his 5.13 own affairs. / Under such circumstances, the state will be at peace and depravity will decline.

When the man of quality is paid according to his adherence to the moral way, righteous conduct is subjected to careful scrutiny and 5.14 propriety is clearly observed. / When righteous conduct is subjected to careful scrutiny and propriety is clearly observed, no one oversteps the proper relationship and rank [appropriate to him]. Even though there

[34] Deleting 所 [Ding and Xu].
[35] Emending 民 to 也 [Igai, Wu Zhizhong, Li Zheming, and Xu].

are great officers [commanding] squadrons of chariots (*pian* 偏)[36] and companies of troops (*zu* 卒),[37] if they dare not harbor opportunistic thoughts, the sovereign will not be in danger. / If the common people are paid according to their strength,[38] they will be engaged in essential production. When those engaged in essential production constitute the bulk of the population, it will be diligent in obeying orders. In such a way the enlightened prince establishes his affairs,[39] and the sovereign's control of the people is like the seasons' control of the grasses and trees. /

If the people are impeded [in their work], he opens the way for them; if they move ahead too quickly, he slows[40] them down. / When he clears the way for them, they move; when he restrains them, they stop. Only[41] / the enlightened prince is capable of both clearing the way and restraining them. When he clears the way for them, men of quality act in accordance with the rules of propriety. When he restrains them, ordinary men devote themselves to agriculture. When men of quality act in accordance with the rules of propriety, the sovereign is revered and the people are submissive. / When ordinary people devote themselves to agriculture, there will be an abundance of wealth and sufficient supplies. When the sovereign is revered and the people are submissive, wealth is abundant and supplies are sufficient. Being complete in these four, [a prince] will have no difficulty in becoming a king within a short period of time.

The four limbs / and the six passages (*liu dao*)[42] are the basic components of the self. The four principals (*si zheng*)[43] and the five official bureaus (*wu guan*)[44] are the basic components of the state. If the four limbs do not function properly or the six passages / are not clear, it is called having a deficiency. If the four principals are not correct in their behavior and the five official bureaus do not carry out their administrative functions, it is called anarchy. For this reason, the prince selects his wife from another clan. He establishes [the categories of] "wife's retinue," [45] "concubine," and "palace woman," and for all of them has laws and regulations / in order to control his inner apartments. He

36.1

36.2
6b

36.3

36.4

36.5

36.6

36.7

---

[36] A *pian* is described as being a unit of twenty-five chariots [Igai and Yu Yue].

[37] A *zu* is described as being a unit of one hundred troops [Igai and Yu Yue].

[38] The Yang edition mistakenly omits the character 則 after 力 [Xu and Guo Moruo].

[39] Reading 世 as 事 [Guo Moruo].

[40] Deleting 通 following 流 as an interpolation from the Yin commentary [Igai, Wang Yinzhi, and Guo Moruo].

[41] Emending 雖 to 唯 [Igai and Dai].

[42] 六道; that is, the eyes, ears, nose, and mouth.

[43] 四正; that is, the prince and minister, father and son.

[44] 五官; see VII, 18, n. 74, and X, 30, n. 10.

[45] 姪娣; that is, the ladies-in-waiting and younger sisters of the wife who accompany her to her new home.

makes it clear that the sexes are to be kept separate and jealousy is to be restrained so there will be no wickedness on their part. Under these circumstances, there is no communication between those residing within the palace and those residing without, slander and intrigue do not arise, the words of a wife have no effect on official / matters, and the various ministers and their sons and younger brothers have no relations with those within the palace. This is the way in which the former kings made virtue clear and contained wickedness, made the public good understood, and eliminated[46] selfish behavior.

When establishing[47] positions for your most respected and favorite [sons], do not, accordingly, depose your legitimate heir / or violate the standards of righteous behavior. Adhere to the rules of propriety in dealing with [children] for whom you feel personal affection and never allow the authority [of these children] to match [that of the heir apparent]. Even though the ranks and positions [of these children] are to be honored, at no time should they fail / to carry out the rules of propriety. The heir apparent[48] should be the most handsomely appointed of all. Enhance his prestige by adorning him with [special] clothing, and distinguish [his position] by means of ornate banners. / Thus no gulf will be created between the older and younger brothers, and slanderers will not dare open their mouths.

Now, in appointing a chief minister, apply standards of virtue when considering his accomplishments. Clarify the extent of his adherence to the law when examining his meritorious service. When he has been evaluated and found fitting,[49] promote him everywhere. Show your respect for his authority and make clear your trust in him. / In this way, the people under him will have no apprehension about being killed if they were to admonish him, and those in humble positions[50] / will have no anxious or resentful hearts. Such being the case, the country will be at peace, and there will be no intrigue among the people.

In selecting the worthy and pursuing the talented, promote to [high]

---

[46] Emending 咸 to 箴 [Ding, Yu Yue, Xu, and Guo Moruo].

[47] The Yang edition mistakenly writes 妾 for 立 [Liu Ji, Zhang Peilun, Liu Shipei, Zhang Binlin, and Xu].

[48] Emending 選 to 適 [Guo Moruo].

[49] This passage *can wu xiang de* 參伍相德 is not entirely clear. I have generally followed Yasui, Yu Xingwu (Jilin Institute), and Zhao Shouzheng in reading *can wu* (lit., "three-five") as "to measure" or "judge." *De* 德 is read as *de* 得 [Li Zheming and Xu]. Roger Ames, in his *The Art of Rulership*, p. 78 and n. 41, points out that the term appears in the *Huainanzi* (20/4b10ff), with *can* referring to the family, nation, and officialdom, and *wu* referring to the five relationships: ruler and minister, father and child, husband and wife, senior and junior, and friends. Thus, he translates the sentence, "Where they measure up to the *ts'an* (*can*) *wu*, promote them everywhere."

[50] Reading 聚 as 鯫 or 緅 and 立 as 位 [Guo Moruo].

37.1
7b

rank those possessing virtue, / but not those who lack it. Promote to office those possessing ability, but not those who lack it. Put virtue ahead of meritorious service. Do not let seniority become a

37.2

hindrance.[51] / Such being the case, the sovereign will encounter no difficulties and the people will not trust to luck in providing for their livelihood.

37.3

There are four reasons for a state / to fall into anarchy. There are two reasons for it to perish. The palace will be in disorder if within the inner apartments there are concubines who presume[52] to be the wife. The [royal] family will be in disorder if there are ordinary sons who presume to be the heir apparent. The court will be in disorder if there are ordinary

37.4

ministers who presume to be the chief minister. / There will be disorder among the masses if those who become officials lack ability.[53] If no distinctions are made in the case of these four, the ruler will lose his identity. If the various ministers form factions in order to espouse their

37.5

selfish interests, he will lose [the support of] the noble clans. / If ministers charged with state secrets make secret agreements and hatch plots behind closed doors in order to deal with him, he will lose the help [of

37.6

those outside the court]. / Loss of clan [support] within and help from without are [two reasons for a state] to perish.

Therefore, [the position of] the wife must be secure, sons must be correct, the chief minister must be straightforward, firm, and obedient, officials must be loyal,[54] trustworthy, and respectful. Therefore it is

37.7

said: / "He who acts as the sovereign will be in danger if one of the following occurs—there is disorder in the palace, there is disorder among brothers, / there is disorder among great ministers, there is dis-

37.8
8a

order among the middle-level people,[55] or there is disorder among the little people. / Disorder in the palace arises[56] from jealous squabbling. Disorder among brothers arises from their factional partisan-

---

[51] Inverting the two characters 傷年 in accordance with the interpretation of the Yin commentary.

[52] Reading 疑 as 擬 here and below [Igai, Song Xiangfeng, and Zhang Peilun].

[53] The preceding passage is very reminiscent of the *Hanfeizi*, XVII, 44/11b5–8 (Liao, *Han Fei Tzu*, II, p. 228): "To have sons of concubines who presume to be the heir apparent, to have concubines among one's consorts who presume to be the wife, to have ordinary ministers within the court who presume to be the chief minister, and to have favorites among one's ministers who presume to be a ruler—these four constitute dangers to the state. Having favorites in the inner apartments who rival the queen, having favorites without who divide the government, having younger sons who compete with the heir apparent, and having great ministers who presume to be the ruler—such is the way to anarchy."

[54] Emending 中 to 忠, in accordance with the *Qunshu zhiyao*.

[55] Middle-level people 中民 were probably low-level officials and public functionaries.

[56] Reading 曰 as 于 = 由于 here and below [Guo Moruo].

422

ship. Disorder among great ministers arises from their political manipulations.[57] / Disorder among middle-level people arises from fear and suspicion.[58] Disorder among little people arises from a shortage of material resources. A shortage of material resources produces meanness. Fear and suspicion produce insolence. / Political manipulation, factional partisanship, and jealous squabbling produce rebellion.

Therefore, rectify titles, investigate suspicions, and punish or execute even those who are closest to you. Then the inner apartments will be stabilized. / Make your great ministers obedient by [stressing] achievement. Make your middle-level people obedient by [stressing virtuous] behavior. Make the little people obedient by [stressing their agricultural] duties. Then the state will prosper. /

Examine the seasons of Heaven and search out the nature of Earth in order to make full use of the strength of the people. Restrict the production of luxuries and encourage work in agriculture in order to give employment to those with nothing to do. / Then the little people will be well governed. On high, keep account of them in order to set figures [for taxation]. / Below, place them in units of five and ten households (*shi wu* 十伍) in order to tax them. When the time[59] [for paying taxes] arrives, employ criminal sanctions to strengthen their / desire [to comply].

In the districts (*xiang* 鄉), establish teachers (*shi* 師) [for members of the gentry] so they may complete their studies. Give them official positions in accordance with their ability and promote them on reaching the required years of service. Then the local gentry / will restore [virtuous] conduct. Having weighed their virtue, measured their achievements, and observed[60] that of which they are capable, investigate the opinions[61] of the masses about them and employ them to carry out the responsibilities connected with the altars of Land / and Grain. If this is done, the local gentry will then revert to their proper nature.

[57] Reading 述 as 術 [Yu Xingwu].
[58] Emending 諄 to 誖 [Zhang Wenhu].
[59] Emending 其 to 期 [Zhang Wenhu].
[60] Reading 勸 as 觀 [Yu Xingwu].
[61] Reading 風 as 諷 [Ding and Xu].

Xiao Cheng
小稱

Minor Appraisals

Introductory Comments

Although this is a relatively short chapter, it contains a number of textual problems as well as problems of interpretation. Even the meaning of the title is not clear. The term *cheng* appears in line 9b12 (39.5) where it clearly means "to judge" or "to appraise" one's mistakes. However, it is not at all clear why the contents of this chapter should be referred to as *xiao*, "minor," "small," or "petty." It is possible that *xiao cheng* here refers to the appraisal or critique of individual character, the general subject of the chapter, as opposed to appraisals involving major political questions or the grand scheme of things.

The chapter is divided into two distinct parts, the first, 8b/11 (38.6)–11a6 (40.6), which contains three short sections presenting Guanzi's advice on the need for self-criticism and cultivation of individual character; and the second, 11a6 (40.6) to the end, which presents two anecdotes concerning Guan Zhong and Duke Huan, including the well-known story of Guan Zhong's death and Duke Huan's tragic end. The two parts are very different in style and content, the first part written in a relatively terse essay style, while the second adheres to the more loosely written anecdotal style common to the end of the Warring States Period and the early Han.

The three sections of the first part are quite consistent in language, style, and content and are probably the work of a single author writing in the early part of the third century B.C. Shi Yishen believes that this first part probably belonged originally to the lost chapter, XIX, 61, *Xiu shen* 修身 [On Cultivating the Self].

There are numerous pre-Han versions of the story of Guan Zhong's death and the disasters that subsequently befell Duke Huan and the state of Qi, beginning with the *Zuo zhuan*, Xi, 17 (Legge, *Ch'un Ts'eu*, V, 17/5), and including the *Hanfeizi*, II, 7/78b–8a (Liao, *Han Fei Tzu*, I, p. 50), and III, 10/7b–8b (Liao, I, pp. 89–92), and the *Lüshi chunqiu*, I, 4/9a–10a (Wilhelm, *Frühling and Herbst*, pp. 9–11) and XVI, 3/6b–7b (Wilhelm, pp. 240–244). The story also appears in the *Guanzi*, X, 26.

424

However, the version that appears here, as well as the second little anecdote that ends the chapter, are both connected with the *Lüshi chunqiu*. The latter, with minor variations in wording, forms part of a longer discussion of Guan Zhong and Duke Huan in XXIII, 2/3b (Wilhelm, p. 406). The former (XVI, 3/6b–7b) is a more involved version of what appears here. I suspect that the two *Guanzi* versions are earlier and formed the basis for those in the *Lüshi chunqiu*, which was put together about 240 B.C., but I doubt that they could be much earlier than the beginning of the third century B.C.

Translation

Guanzi said, "Worry about not doing what is right.[1] Don't worry that others will not know about you. When cinnabar and malachite exist in the mountains, people come to know about it and extract them. When beautiful pearls lie in the depths, people come to know about it / and gather them. For this reason, I may make mistakes, but the people do not make mistakes in their criticism. / Since people have a very clear perception of things, there is no escape.[2] Therefore, when I do well, they praise me; when I make mistakes, they blame me. / When faced with the people's praise or blame, there is no point in seeking further opinion from the members of one's family. / Therefore the former kings stood in awe of the people.

"When establishing their reputations, those who listened to others always became strong; those who rejected them always became weak. Even though / one might be a son of Heaven or feudal lord, if he has gained a [bad] reputation among all the people and they have rejected him, he will lose his land and [be forced to] flee. Therefore the former kings stood in awe of the people. /

"What are the sharpest [organs] of the body? The ears[3] and eyes are the sharpest. The sages relied on this sharpness. Therefore they treated the people with great respect, / and their own reputations flourished. I also rely on [this sharpness]. The sages relied on it [to do] good. If I were to rely on it [to do] evil, how could I expect to acquire[4] a good

[1] Reading 之 as 是 [Xu].
[2] The following four characters 以爲不善 are troublesome. I have followed the *Qunshu zhiyao* in deleting them. Guo Moruo believes they were originally part of the Yin Commentary. Most commentators, including Liu Ji, Zhao Yongxian, Yasui, Zhang Wenhu, and Wu Rulun, believe they should be read in conjunction with the preceding phrase 豈可遁逃. Thus the sentence would read: "Since people have a very clear perception of things, there is no way to avoid their recognizing what is bad."
[3] Emending 氣 to 耳 [Guo Moruo].
[4] Emending 來 to 求 [Wang Niansun and Igai].

425

38.14   reputation? / If I were to rely on it to do evil, even those who love me would be unable to make it possible for me [to acquire a good reputation].[5]

39.1   "Mao / Qiang and Xi Shi[6] were the most beautiful women in the world. But had their faces been filled with hatred, they could not have been considered attractive. On the other hand, since my face is [already]

39.2   quite ugly, were / I filled with hatred so it appeared on my face and ugly words issued from my mouth, how could I divest myself of the reality of

39.9   evil and thereby seek a good reputation? / [Therefore[7] the enlightened
10a8   kings were careful that their ears should be sensitive to sounds and their

39.10   eyes should be sensitive to [people's] dispositions. / Since their possession of the realm depended on these two, how could they fail to be

39.3   concerned about them?][8] / In such a way, [the former kings were able to]
9b9   shorten what was too long, lengthen what was too short, drain[9] what was too full, and fill what was too empty." /

39.4   Guanzi said: "The best thing is to criticize oneself. Then the people will not have to criticize. The people will criticize those who are

39.5   unable / to criticize themselves. Therefore, being able to judge one's own mistakes represents strength. Cultivating one's moral integrity rep-

39.6   resents wisdom.[10] / Not blaming evil on others represents goodness.
10a   Therefore, when the enlightened kings made mistakes, they took the blame themselves. When they did well, they gave credit to the people.

39.7   When there are mistakes and one takes the blame oneself, / one becomes cautious. When things are done well and credit is given to the people, they are happy. Making the people happy and being cautious themselves—these are the means by which the enlightened kings /

39.8   governed the people.

"Now Jie and Zhou[11] were not like this. When things were done well, they took credit for it themselves. When there were mistakes, they

[5] Here I have followed the Zhao edition's rendering of this passage. The Yang edition mistakenly writes 我託可惡, 我託可惡以來 (求) 美名又可得乎, 愛且不能爲我能也

[6] According to tradition 毛嬙 and 西施 lived in the state of Yue during the 5th century B.C.

[7] Following Igai and Guo Moruo who believe the line (10a8–11; 39.9) 故明王懼聲以感耳, 懼氣以感目. 以此二者有天下矣, 可毋慎乎 represents a misplaced passage, which should be inserted here.

[8] The following sentence in the text 甚矣, 百姓之惡人之有餘忌, does not seem to fit the context here. I have followed Igai, who believes it constitutes a misplaced passage that should follow the phrase (10a8; 39.9) 此其所以失身也: "These are the ways in which they brought about their own demise."

[9] Emending 洫 to 泄 [Dai and Zhang Peilun].

[10] Reading 惠 as 慧 [Ding].

[11] 桀 and 紂 were the last kings of the Xia and Shang whose evil deeds were supposed to have brought about the fall of these dynasties.

blamed them on the people. Since they blamed them on the people, the people became angry. Since they took the credit [when things were done well], / they became arrogant. Making the people angry and becoming arrogant themselves—these were the ways in which they / brought about their own demise.[12] [Intense[13] is the hatred of the hundred surnames for people who indulge in excessive malice.] /

"The craftsman[14] had an intuitive grasp of how to use his axe and adze. Therefore he could cut along the marking line.[15] Yi[16] had an intuitive grasp of how to use / his bow and arrow. Therefore, when shooting, he could hit the mark. Zaofu[17] had an intuitive grasp of how to use reins and whip. Therefore he could catch swift beasts and reach distant roads. / The realm never remains in a perpetual state of anarchy or good order. When there are evil persons, there is anarchy; when there are good people, there is order. When goodness pervades [the whole society],[18] it is because [good people] have exercised their influence on it." /

Guanzi said: "One will never lose [the support] of others if one cultivates [the virtues of] reverence and humility, respect and love, and is politely yielding, devoid of resentment, and uncontentious when meeting them. / However,[19] if one is filled with resentment, ready to fight for any advantage, and lacking in humility, it will be difficult to protect[20] oneself. Great indeed is the way of reverence and humility, respect and love! When blessed with good fortune, [these virtues] may be expressed in / the sacrifices [to one's ancestors].[21] When faced with hard times, they may be expressed in the practice of mourning. In a grand way, they may be used without amplification to govern the entire realm. In a lesser way, they may be used without moderation to regulate a single individual. /

"Whether applied to the capital, the various Chinese states, the states

[12] See n. 7 for deleted passage.

[13] See n. 8 for insert.

[14] The craftsman probably refers to Xi Zhong 奚仲, who was famous for his skill in constructing chariots. See XX, 64/6a3 (3:33.5).

[15] Following the Zhao (*SBBY*) edition, which accords with the *Taiping yulan*, 823/9b2 [Wang Niansun]. Zhang Peilun and Xu would follow the Yang edition, which for 斷 writes 料: "Therefore the marking line could fulfill its role as a measure."

[16] 羿; China's most famous archer of antiquity. See XX, 64/5b4 (3:32.13).

[17] 造夫; the legendary charioteer of the Zhou King Mu 穆 (trad. 1001–945 B.C.). See XX, 64/5b10 (3:33.20).

[18] Reading 旣 as 盡.

[19] Deleting 嘗試 as an interpolation taken from the following passage, 10b9 (39.2) [Ding, Zhang Wenhu, and Guo Moruo].

[20] Emending 得 to 保 [Guo Moruo].

[21] The Yang edition mistakenly writes 察 for 祭 [Wang Niansun and Yasui].

of the Man and Yi,[22] or even beasts and insects, everything depends on [these virtues] for the existence of order or disorder. The person who is enriched by them is honorable; / the one who rejects them is shameful. A person who is conscientious and never remiss in carrying them out may even transform the Yi or Mo[23] people and make them love him. / One who deliberately rejects them may even transform brothers or parents and cause them to hate him. Therefore[24] the self causes one to be loved / or hated and one's reputation [in respect to these virtues] is what brings one honor or shame. Their effect on reputations and affairs is like that of Heaven and Earth. / Therefore the former kings spoke of [this phenomenon as] 'the Way.' "

When Guan Zhong fell ill, Duke Huan went to visit him saying, "Zhongfu, your illness has become very serious. Should / you fail to recover from this illness, what instructions will you have for me?"

"Had there been no such order from you," replied Guan Zhong, "I definitely[25] would have brought the matter up myself. / It is only that you will probably not be able to do [what I say]."

"If you, Zhongfu, were to order me to go to the east," said the duke, "I would go east. If you commanded me to go to the west, I would go west. Were you to give me orders, / would I dare not follow them?"

Guan Zhong, adjusting his clothing and cap, arose and replied, "I want you to send Yi Ya, Shu Diao, Tang Wu, and Gongzi Kaifang far away.[26] / Now, Yi Ya harmonizes tastes[27] to serve Your Grace, and when you said that the only thing you had never tasted was steamed child, he thereupon cooked up his son's head[28] and presented it to you. It is human nature to love one's children. If he does not love his son, how can he have any love for / you?

40.3
40.4
11a
40.5
40.6
40.7
40.8
40.9
40.10
11b
40.11

---

[22] 蠻夷; that is, states belonging to the non-Sinified people of southern and north-eastern China.

[23] 貉; that is, a non-Sinified people of the north noted for their ferocity.

[24] Deleting 之 [Yu Yue].

[25] Inverting the two characters 故臣, and reading 故 as 固 [Wang Yinzhi].

[26] Yi Ya 易牙, Shu Diao 豎刀, and Gongzi Kaifang 公子開方 are dealt with at length in *Guanzi*, X, 26/6b–7a (2:19.13–20.6), and other pre-Han versions of this story concerning the deaths of Guan Zhong and Duke Huan mentioned in the Introductory Comments. Tang Wu 堂巫 appears only in the *LSCQ*, XIV, 3/6b–7b (Wilhelm, *Frühling und Herbst*, pp. 242–244), version of the story, where his name is given as Chang Zhi Wu 常之巫, lit., the Sorcerer of Chang. Since the characters *chang* 常 and *tang* 堂 are similar in form, this difference is undoubtedly due to a scribal error, and both texts are referring to the same person. The *Zuo zhuan*, Xi, 17 (Legge, *Ch'un Ts'eu* V, 17/5), in recounting the death of Duke Huan mentions a Yung Wu 雍巫, whom Xu believes to be the same as Tang Wu. Most commentators, however, believe Yung Wu was another name for Yi Ya.

[27] Emending 和 to 味, in accordance with the *Qunshu zhiyao* [Sun Xingyan and Xu].

[28] Following the *Qunshu zhiyao* and the *Hanfeizi*, II, 7/7b8, and III, 10/8a13, versions of this story, which for 其首子, "his eldest son," write 其子首.

"Your Grace takes pleasure in his harem[29] and thus is very jealous [concerning his women]. Shu Diao castrated himself so he could serve you by managing the harem. It is human nature to love one's body. If he does not love his body, how can be love you? Gongzi Kaifang / has served Your Grace for fifteen years without returning to see his family even though the distance between Qi 齊 and Weii 衛 does not exceed a few days of travel. [If[30] he does not love his parents, how can there by any love for you?] I have heard that those who perform their duties under false pretenses[31] will not last for long, and those who attempt to conceal their lack of an honorable purpose / will not long endure. Those who do not lead good lives, in death will certainly come to no good end." /

"Good," said the duke.

After Guan Zhong died and was buried, the duke summoned[32] the four and eliminated their positions. However, after dismissing Tang Wu, [the duke] suffered a nervous breakdown,[33] / and after dismissing Yi Ya, he had no taste for food. After dismissing Shu Diao, there was confusion in the palace, and after dismissing Gongzi Kaifang, the court became unmanageable.

"Alas!" said Duke Huan, "even the Sage / could be wrong!"

He then restored the four men, but a year after their return to court, the four launched a coup. They confined the duke to a single room and refused to let him leave. / One of his wives subsequently managed to enter the room through a small hole. "I am famished," he moaned, "and wish to eat; I am thirsty and wish to drink, but they won't let me have anything. What could be the reason for this?"

The woman replied, "Those four men—Yi Ya, Shu / Diao, Tang Wu, and Gongzi Kaifang—have divided the state of Qi. The roads have already been blocked for ten days, and Gongzi Kaifang has already signed an agreement giving seven hundred *she*[34] / to Weii. Food will be unobtainable."

"Alas!" the duke sighed, "that it should come to this! The words of the Sage were so wise! / If, on dying, I had not known any better, it would

[29] Emending 宮 to 內, in accordance with the Zhu edition [Wang Yinzhi].

[30] Inserting 於親之不愛焉能有於公, in accordance with the *Qunshu zhiyao* [Wang Niansun].

[31] Reading 爲 as 偽 [Wang Yinzhi and Yu Xingwu].

[32] Emending 憎, "hated," to 召, in accordance with the *Qunshu zhiyao* [Sun Xingyan and Wang Niansun].

[33] Deleting 兵 following 起, in accordance with the *Qunshu zhiyao* and *LSCQ*, XVI, 3/7a6 [Igai and Wang Niansun].

[34] 社; this probably refers to a rural area possessing a small altar to Land. According to the *Shuowen jienzi*, it contained twenty-five households. See *Guanzi*, I, 5/20b3 (1:19.11).

be all right, but having known, how will I be able to face Zhongfu in the netherworld?"

41.7 He then took up a plain white head scarf and, wrapping it around his head, died. / It was only after he had been dead for eleven days and worms began crawling out from around his door, that people knew Duke Huan was dead. They covered[35] him over with a leaf from the south[36] gate. It was because he did not employ worthy people toward the end of his life that Duke Huan could be dead for eleven days and
41.8 worms crawl out from around his door before / anyone claimed [his
12b body].

The four men, Duke Huan, Guan Zhong, Bao Shuya,[37] and Ning Qi[38] were drinking [wine]. When they were quite drunk, Duke Huan
41.9 said to Bao Shuya, "Why[39] don't you rise and / drink to my long life?"

Bao Shuya lifted his cup and rose, saying, "May Your Grace never forget being exiled in Ju.[40] May Guanzi never forget being bound in
41.10 Lu.[41] May / Ning Qi never forget feeding the oxen from under your chariot."[42]

Duke Huan then left his mat and, bowing twice, said, "If these two great officers and I never forget your words, our country's altars of Land and Grain will certainly never be endangered."

---

[35] Emending 葬 to 蓋, in accordance with the *LSCQ*, XVI, 3/7b6, which goes on to say that the duke was not buried for three months.

[36] Reading 楊 as 陽 [Yin Tongyang].

[37] 鮑叔牙 or Bao Shu 鮑叔 was Guan Zhong's closest associate and early supporter. See the beginning of chapters VII, 18, and VIII, 20.

[38] 甯戚; according to VIII, 20/18b4–5 (1 : 110.14–111.1), Ning Qi served Duke Huan as minister of agriculture.

[39] Emending 闔 to 盍, in accordance with the *Qunshu zhiyao* [Sun Xingyan and Liu Shipei]. In the *LSCQ* version of this story, XXIII, 2/3b7, 盍 is written 何. The translation would remain the same.

[40] Emending 出如莒時 to 出而在於莒, in accordance with the *Qunshu zhiyao* [Wang Niansun and Xu]. Ju 莒 was a small principality located in present-day south-central Shandong where Duke Huan sought refuge during the struggle for succession before he gained the throne. See chapters VII, 18, and VIII, 20, for details.

[41] This refers to the fact that after his failure to place Duke Huan's rival, Gongzi Jiu 公子糾, on the throne, Guan Zhong was detained by his former ally, the Duke of Lu 魯, and threatened with death. Again see chapters VII, 18, and VIII, 20.

[42] According to Gao You's 高誘 commentary to the *LSCQ* version of this story, XXIII, 2/3b11, when Duke Huan once went out into the suburbs to meet some guests at night, Ning Qi crawled under his chariot to feed the oxen. The duke, realizing he was a worthy person, then promoted him.

Si Cheng
四稱

FOUR APPRAISALS

Introductory Comments

This relatively short chapter attempts to enumerate the good and bad characteristics of princes and ministers of the past through a dialogue between Duke Huan and Guanzi. It is a well-integrated essay, written in a rather terse style with extensive use of rhyme. Traditionally feudalistic in content, it stresses standard Confucian virtues for both the prince and the minister. It is difficult to make any statement about its date of composition, but its general content and style lead me to believe it is probably a work of the pre-Han period, perhaps middle of the third century B.C. It is interesting that this chapter should have the unusual distinction of being quoted in its entirety in the *Cefu yuangui* (242/2a8–4b2), a Song dynasty encyclopedia on government compiled between the years 1005 and 1013.

Translation

Duke Huan questioned Guanzi, "I am young, weak, and very confused and do not understand the rationale for [coping with] the feudal lords on our four borders. Shouldn't you tell me in detail about princes of old who have mastered the way [of good government] so I[1] / may gain a lesson from their example?"

Guanzi replied, "You have a complete grasp of my abilities. Why do you demean yourself with such an order?" /

Duke Huan again stated the question, "Zhongfu, I am young, weak, and very confused and do not understand the rationale for [coping with] the feudal lords on our four borders. Shouldn't you inform me in detail about princes of old who have mastered the way [of good government] so I may / gain a lesson from their example?"

"I have heard Xu Bo[2] say," Guanzi replied, "that the princes of old who mastered the way [of good government] paid respect to [the god of]

---

[1] Emending 亦 to 以 both here and in the repeat of the question below [Zhang Wenhu and Tao].

[2] 徐伯; this person is unidentified.

their mountains and rivers, revered their ancestral temples and altars of Land and Grain, and, remaining loyal to their great ministers of the past, / provided them with rich [sacrifices].[3] They affirmed [the positions of] their ministers involved in military affairs and made wide use of their abilities. They engaged in discussions with sages at the fore and upright and honest men on both sides. / Above and below, order was maintained[4] everywhere, punishments and administrative matters[5] were thoroughly investigated, and there were no mistakes in the conduct of activities related to the four seasons. The people too were without cares. The five grains flourished, harmony reigned both at home and abroad, the feudal lords were submissive, the country was at peace, and there was no need / for the armed forces. [Princes who had mastered the way of good government] gave[6] presents of silk [to the feudal lords] in appreciation of their virtuous conduct and explained to them their orders in order to establish norms of behavior. These can indeed / be said to have been princes of old who mastered the way [of good government]."

"Very good!" said Duke Huan.

"Zhongfu, since you have told me about the princes of old who mastered the way [of good government]," said Duke Huan, "shouldn't you tell me in detail about the princes of old who lacked / the way [of good government] so I may gain a lesson from their example?"

"Now," Guanzi replied, "given your goodness and broad understanding, and the fact that you already clearly[7] understand[8] the way to do what is good, what reason is there for you to further inquire about what is bad?" /

"How can you say that?" said Duke Huan. "How would I know the beauty of hemming black[9] [clothing] with black or the advantages of

---

[3] There appears to be a problem with the final part of this sentence: 至乃... 富之. Guo Moruo points out that the series of rhymes beginning with 稷 and continuing through 之 to 式 (13a9; 42.6) is broken here. I have attempted to follow the original wording. According to I, 1/1b5–8 (1 : 1.12–13): "If the spirits are not honored, crude common folk will take no notice of them. If the mountain and river gods are not respected, orders intended to inspire awe will go unheeded. If the ancestral temples are not revered, the people will emulate the sovereign [in their lack of respect]. If ancestors and great men of the past are not venerated, filial piety and respect for elders will be lacking."

[4] Reading 飾 as 飭 [Yasui].

[5] Reading 正 as 政. The Ancient, Liu, and Zhu editions all write 政.

[6] Reading 受 as 授 here and below.

[7] Reading 官 as 宣 = 明 [Xu].

[8] Reading 職 as 識 [Xu].

[9] Emending 繻 to 緇 both here and below [Wang Niansun]. Zhang Peilun would emend 繻 to 繢, in accordance with the *Cefu yuangui*, 242/2b9. Thus the sentence would read: "How would I know the beauty of hemming embroidered clothing with embroidered material or the advantages of hemming plain [clothing] with plain material?" The character 素 can mean either white or plain, i.e., undyed.

2.10 hemming white [clothing] with white? / Zhongfu, you have already told me about the good but not the bad. How can I know the good points of what is good?"

2.11 "I have heard Xu Bo say," replied Guanzi, / "that the princes of old who lacked the way [of good government] constructed enormous palaces and high pavilions, but they refused to employ good ministers, and their companions[10] consisted of slanderers and thieves. Unable to

2.12 manage even their own household, they relied / on others to scheme for them. Since their administrative orders were deplorable, [the situation] was as black as night. Like wild animals, [their people] had no place to

2.13 go.[11] / They ignored[12] the way of Heaven and failed to learn from the example of [other rulers] surrounding them on all four sides. Not even able to manage themselves,[13] it was as if they were crazy. Curses expressed the resentment of the masses, few of whom avoided total destruction.

.14 "Bringing forward their court jesters[14] and [sounding] a profusion of / bells and drums, [these profligate princes] gave themselves over to gambling and amusing themselves with musicians while they slaugh-

7 tered their good / ministers. They dallied with their women, hunted animals, netted and shot birds, and treated their senior relatives with

1 extreme violence. They galloped / their horses without restraint, joking and laughing. Since their administration was already perverse beyond repair, their application of punishments and fines was extremely cruel. They considered the reduction of the number of people within their

2 countries as a matter of considerable achievement. Like / a leaking cauldron, how could [their countries] fail to become empty? These can indeed be said to be princes of old who lacked the way [of good government]."

"Very good!" said Duke Huan.

3 "Zhongfu, since you have already / told me about princes of old who mastered the way [of good government] as well as those who lacked it," said Duke Huan, "shouldn't you tell in detail about ministers of old who mastered the way so I may gain a lesson from their example?"

4 "I have heard Xu Bo say," replied Guanzi, / "that ministers of old

---

[10] Emending 舍 to 予 = 與 [Sun Yirang].

[11] Emending 朝 to 就, in accordance with the *Cefu Yuangui*, 242/3a4 [Dai and Guo Moruo]. The subject of this sentence is not clear. I have interpreted it as being the people, but it could be the princes who lacked the way. Thus the sentence would read: "Like wild animals, there was no place for them to go."

[12] Emending 脩 to 循 [Wang Niansun].

[13] Emending 家 to 身 [Yasui].

[14] Emending 諛 to 俳, in accordance with the Ancient, Liu, and Zhu editions and the *Cefu yuangui*, 242/3a6 [Yasui and Dai].

433

who mastered the way [of good government], after being inducted as ministers, attached no value to serving those to the right or left [of their princes]. Their princes, knowing this, appointed them to office. Otherwise, they let them be. If there were matters to be attended to, they were certain / to put all their efforts into planning for [the good of] the state. They adhered to ancestral virtues and drew clear distinctions between what conformed or was contrary to them. They recommended men of worth and refused to engage in slander or intrigue. They were righteous in serving their prince, / causing those below to exercise propriety. They were friendly toward the honored and lowly alike as though they were older or younger brothers. Their loyalty to the state caused both those above and below to gain positions [for which they were suited]. /

"When at home, they were thoughtful.[15] When they spoke, it was to devise a plan. When they moved, it was to serve [their princes]. When they resided in a state, / it became rich. When they held a position in an army, it was victorious. When meeting with difficulties, they took charge. Even though they might die, they had no regrets. Near to their prince, they acted as a support. Far from him, they acted as a prop. Their [words] were righteous when communicating with allies, and their [actions] were humble when living among them. When assuming office, they took charge. When drinking and feasting, they were easy-going,[16] / but refrained from criticizing their princes or detracting from[17] their statements. When their princes committed mistakes, they presented their warnings with no hesitation. When their princes were beset by worries, these ministers assumed their burdens. These can indeed be said to have been ministers of old who had mastered the way [of good government]." /

"Very good!" said Duke Huan.

"Zhongfu, since you have told me about the ministers of old who mastered the way [of good government]," said Duke Huan, "shouldn't you tell me in detail about the ministers of old who lacked the way [of good government] so I may gain a lesson from their example?" /

"I have heard Xu Bo say," replied Guanzi, "that ministers of old who lacked the way [of good government], after being inducted as ministers, attached great value to serving those to the right and left [of their

---

[15] Deleting 義 following 思 and 謨 following 謀 in the next phrase. The series here is made up of six four-character phrases. Since these two characters destroy the balance, they would appear to be later interpolations [Zhang Wenhu and Xu].

[16] Xu would read 慈 as 省: "They engaged in the proper pursuit of information."

[17] Following the Zhao edition, which writes 毀. The Yang edition and *Cefu yuangui*, 242/3b9, write 諱, "obscuring."

princes]. They were ingratiating in their speech in order to obtain
11   advancement and strove never to neglect[18] their own interest. / They
knew how to advance but not retreat and capitalized on the kindness [of
their princes] to promote their own importance. They honored goods
12   and bribes and looked down on ranks and position. / On advancing they
would say they could help; on retreating they would say nothing could
be done. When they brought failure upon their princes, they all would
say, 'It's not my fault.' /

13   "They would flock together with other disreputable persons to attack
those who were worthy. When they met someone of high station,[19] [they
chased after him] as if he were some valuable goods. When they met
someone of low station, [they would treat him] as a passing
14   stranger. / Greedy for goods and bribes, contentious when drinking and
feasting, they did not associate with good people but only with those
who could be of service to them. Rude and arrogant, they had no respect
for others. Instead of maintaining friendly relations with good men, they
1   fraternized[20] with slanderers and thieves. / Instead of resolving disputes,
they encouraged men to engage in litigation.[21]

"Steeped in wine, they were in constant violation of the rules of
2   etiquette.[22] / They refused to follow[23] ancient traditions, altered the
constant standards of the state, acted on their own authority to create
false[24] orders, confused[25] their princes, and seized political power from
them in order to protect those whom they honored and grant favors to
3   those whom they esteemed. They removed good men from office[26] / and
rendered assistance[27] to unscrupulous merchants. On entering the
court, they exceeded their status and on leaving it, formed
4   factions. / The flow of goods and bribes into the court, and intimacy
while drinking and feasting, all served to confuse their princes.
[Moreover], if their princes met with misfortune,[28] each [of these minis-
ters] would serve himself alone. These can indeed be said to be ministers
of old who lacked the way [of good government]." /

"Very good!" said Duke Huan.

[18] Reading 亡 as 忘 [Yu Xingwu and Xu].
[19] Emending 賢 to 貴 [Ding and Yu Yue].
[20] Emending 鬫 to 通 [Ding, Yu Yue, and Xu]. The *Cefu yuangui*, 242/4a8, writes 通.
[21] Emending 通 to 詔 [Wang Niansun, Liu Shipei, and Xu]. The *Cefu yuangui*, 242/4a8,
also writes 訟.
[22] Reading 義 as 儀 [Yu Xingwu].
[23] Emending 修 to 循 [Wang Niansun and Xu].
[24] Reading 為 as 偽 [Xu].
[25] Reading 或 as 惑 [Yasui, Dai, and Xu].
[26] Emending 損 to 捐 [Yasui, Yu Yue, and Dai].
[27] Emending 捕 to 輔 [Guo Moruo].
[28] Emending 過 to 禍 [Guo Moruo].

BIBLIOGRAPHY

ABBREVIATIONS

Abbreviations have been used for the following collections and individual Chinese works:

CQZZ, Chunqiu Zuo zhuan 春秋左傳.

CSJC, Congshu jicheng 叢書集成 [Complete Collection of Collected Works]. Shanghai: Commercial Press, 1935–1937.

GXJBCS, Guoxue jiben congshu 國學基本叢書 [Collection of Basic Works in Chinese Studies]. Shanghai: Commercial Press, 1933, 1936.

LSCQ, Lüshi chunqiu 呂氏春秋.

SBBY, Sibu beiyao 四部備要 [Collection of Important Works in Four Categories]. Shanghai: Zhonghua Shuju 中華書局, 1927–1935.

SBCK, Sibu congkan 四部叢刊 [Collected Reprints of Works in Four Categories]. 3 ser. Shanghai: Commercial Press, 1920–1936.

SKQSZM, Siku quanshu zongmu 四庫全書總目 [Complete Catalogue of All Books in the Four Libraries]. Compiled by Ji Yun 紀昀 and others, 1782. Shanghai: Datong Shuju 大東書局, 1930.

WYWK, Wanyou wenku 萬有文庫 [Universal Treasury of Literature]. 2 ser. Shanghai: Commercial Press, 1929–1935.

COMMENTATORS

Chen Huan 陳奐 (1786–1863). Notes contained in Dai Wang, *Guanzi jiaozheng*.

Dai Wang 戴望 (1837–1873). *Guanzi jiaozheng* 管子校正 [The *Guanzi*, Collated and Corrected]. Pub. in 1873.

Ding Shihan 丁士涵 (19th century). Notes contained in Dai Wang, *Guanzi jiaozheng*. Guo Moruo (*Guanzi jijiao*, I, 19) believes Ding's work was never published.

Fang Bao 方苞 (1668–1749). *Shanding Guanzi* 刪定管子 [The *Guanzi* Reedited]. Contained in *Kangxitang shiliu zhong* 抗希堂十六種, 1746.

Gu Guangqi 顧廣圻 (1776–1835). Notes contained in Dai Wang's *Guanzi jiaozheng*, Wu Rulun's *Diankan Guanzi duben*, and Guo Moruo's *Guanzi jijiao*.

Guo Moruo 郭沫若 (1892–1978), Wen Yiduo 聞一多 (1899–1945), and Xu Weiyu 許維遹 (d. 1951). *Guanzi jijiao* 管子集校 [Collected Collations of the *Guanzi*]. Beijing: Koxue Chubanshe 科學出版社, 1956.

Guo Songdao 郭嵩燾 (1818–1891). *Du Guan zhaji* 讀管札記 [Notes on Reading the *Guanzi*]. These notes were appended to the manuscript of Yan Changyao 顏昌嶢 (1870–c. 1940) *Guanzi jiaoshi* 管子校釋 [Collations and Explanations of the *Guanzi*] by Guo Songdao's son, Guo Dachi 郭大痴. Yan's manuscript was later damaged but Guo's notes were largely preserved

436

and have been incorporated into the *Guanzi jijiao*.

He Ruzhang 何如璋 (fl. 1886). *Guanzi xiyi* 管子析疑 [Resolution of Doubtful Passages in the *Guanzi*]. Manuscript in Shanghaishi Lishi Wenxian Tushuguan 上海市歷史文獻圖書館, dated 1886. Notes contained in Guo Moruo, *Guanzi jijiao*.

Hong Yixuan 洪頤烜 (1761–1837). *Guanzi yizheng* 管子義證 [Evidence for Meanings in the *Guanzi*]. *Jixuezhai congshu* 積學齋叢書 ed. of 1812.

Huang Zhen 黃震 (fl. 1270). *Huangshi richao* 黃氏日鈔 [Daily Notes of Mr. Huang]. Reprint of 1767.

Hui Dong 惠棟 (1697–1758). Notes contained in Guo Moruo, *Guanzi jijiao*.

Igai Hikohiro 猪飼彦博 (1761–1845). *Kanshi hosei* 管子補正 [Supplementary Corrections to the *Guanzi*]. First pub. 1798. Tokyo reprint of 1911.

Jiang Han 江瀚 (1853–1931). *Guanzi shixiao* 管子識小 [Distinction of Details in the *Guanzi*]. Pub. at end of Guangxu period (1875–1907). Contained in *Shiwengshanfang zhaji* 石翁山房札記.

Jilin Sheng Zhexue Shehuikexue Yanjiusuo 吉林省哲學社會科學研究所 [Jilin Provincial Institute for Philosophy and Social Science]. *Guanzi xuanzhu* 管子選注 [*Guanzi*, Selections with Commentary]. Jilin: Renmin Chubanshe 吉林人民出版社, 1975. Work assisted by Yu Xingwu 于省吾.

Jin Tinggui 金廷桂 (20th century). *Guanzi canjie* 管子參解 [*Guanzi*, Collated and Explained]. Pub. 1922.

Li Zheming 李哲明 (1857–?). *Guanzi jiaoyi* 管子校義 [Collated Meanings of the *Guanzi*]. Beiping, 1931.

Liu Ji 劉績 (fl. 1012?). *Guanzi buzhu* 管子補注 [Supplementary Commentary to the *Guanzi*]. *Zhongdu sizi* 中都四子 ed. of 1579.

Liu Shipei 劉師培 (1884–1919). *Guanzi jiaobu* 管子斠補 [Emendations of the *Guanzi*]. Contained in *Liu Shenshu yishu* 劉申叔遺書, 1912.

Ma Feibai 馬非百 [Yuancai 元材] (1896–). *Guanzi Qingzhong pien xinquan* 管子輕重篇新詮 [New Explanation of the *Qingzhong* Chapters of the *Guanzi*]. Beijing; Zhonghua Shuju 中華書局, 1979.

———. "*Guanzi Nei ye* pien jizhu" 管子內業篇集註 [Collected Annotations of the *Nei ye* chapter of the *Guanzi*]. Unpublished manuscript.

Mei Shixiang 梅士享 (17th century). *Quanxu Guanzi chengshu* 詮叙管子成書 [Complete Text of the *Guanzi*, Annotated and Rearranged]. Pub. in 1625.

Ren Linbu 任林圃 (20th century). Notes contained in Guo Moruo, *Guanzi jijiao*.

Shi Yishen 石一參 (20th century) *Guanzi jinquan* 管子今詮 [Modern Commentary on the *Guanzi*]. Changsha: Commercial Press, 1938.

Song Xiangfeng 宋翔鳳 (1766–1860). *Guanzi shiwu* 管子識誤 [A Record of Mistakes in the *Guanzi*]. Postscript dated 1879. Contained in *Chou Qin zhuzi jiaozhu shizhong* 周秦諸子校注十種, 1912.

Sun Shucheng 孫蜀丞 (20th century). Former professor, Furen University, Beijing. Notes contained in Guo Moruo, *Guanzi jijiao*.

Sun Xingyan 孫星衍 (1753–1818). Notes contained in Hong Yixuan, *Guanzi yizheng*.

Sun Yirang 孫詒讓 (1848–1908). *Zhayi* 札迻 [Study Notes]. Pub. 1894.

Sun Yutang 孫毓棠 (20th century). Former professor Qinghua University. Notes contained in Guo Moruo *Guanzi jijiao*.

Tan Jiefu 譚戒甫 (1888–?). Professor, Wuhan University. Notes contained in Guo Moruo, *Guanzi jijiao*.

Tang Jinggao 唐敬杲 (20th century). *Guanzi* 管子. Taipei: Commercial Press, 1957. Twenty chapters with notes.

Tang Lan 唐蘭 (1900–). Former acting president, Beijing University. Notes contained in Guo Moruo, *Guanzi jijiao*.

Tao Hongqing 陶鴻慶 (1895–?). *Du Guanzi zhaji* 讀管子札記 [Notes on Reading the *Guanzi*]. Posthumously published notes contained in *Du zhuzi zhashe* (probably should be *zhaji*) 讀諸子札社(札記). Wenzi Tongmengshe 文子同盟社, n.d.

Wang Niansun 王念孫 (1744–1832). *Guanzi zazhi* 管子雜誌 [Miscellaneous Notes on the *Guanzi*]. Contained in his *Dushu zazhi* 讀書雜誌. First pub. 1812–1832. *GXJBCS* reprint of 1933.

Wang Shaolan 王紹蘭 (1760–1835). *Guanzi Di yuan pien zhu* 管子地員篇注 [Commentary on the *Di yuan* chapter of the *Guanzi*]. Completed in 1834; originally pub. in 1891. Beiping: Laixunge Shudian 來薰閣書店 ed. Other notes cited in Dai Wang, *Guanzi jiaozheng*.

Wang Yinzhi 王引之 (1766–1834). Notes contained in Wang Niansun, *Guanzi zazhi*.

Wen Yiduo 聞一多 (1899–1945). See Guo Moruo, *Guanzi jijiao*.

Wu Rulun 吳汝綸 (1840–1903). *Diankan Guanzi duben* 點勘管子讀本 [A Verified Guanzi Reader]. Contained in his *Tongcheng Wu Xianzheng diankan qunshu* 桐城吳先生點勘羣書, n.d.

Wu Zhizhong 吳志忠 (Qing). Notes contained in Dai Wang, *Guanzi jiaozheng*.

Xu Weiyu 許維遹 (d. 1951). See Guo Moruo, *Guanzi jijiao*.

Yan Changyao 顏昌嶢 (1870–c. 1940). See Guo Songdao.

Yang Shuda 楊樹達 (1885–?). Notes contained in Guo Moruo, *Guanzi jijiao*.

Yao Yonggai 姚永概 (1866–1923). *Shenyixuan biji* 慎宜軒筆記 [Notes of Yao Yonggai]. Pub. 1926.

Yasui Kō 安井衡 [Sokken 息軒] (1799–1876). *Kanshi sanko* 管子纂詁 [The *Guanzi*, Edited and Annotated]. Pub. 1864.

Yin Tongyang 尹桐陽 (20th century. *Guanzi xinshi* 管子新釋 [New Explanation of the *Guanzi*]. Pub. 1928.

Yin Zhizhang 尹知章 (d. A.D. 718). Commentary contained in most modern editions under the name of Fang Xuanling 房玄齡 (578–648).

Yu Xingwu 于省吾 (1896–). *Guanzi xinzheng* 管子新證 [New Evidence Concerning the *Guanzi*]. Contained in *Shuangjianyi zhuzi xinzcheng* 雙劍誃諸子新證. Beijing, 1940. See also *Jilin Sheng Zhexue Shehuikexue Yanjiusuo*.

Yu Yue 俞越 (1821–1906). *Guanzi pingyi* 管子平議 [Running Commentary on the *Guanzi*]. Contained in *Zhuzi pingyi* 諸子平議. Pub. 1870.

Zang Yong 臧庸 (1767–1811). Notes contained in Dai Wang, *Guanzi jiaozheng*.

Zhang Bang 張榜 [Binwang 賓王] (late Ming). *Guanzi zuan* 管子纂 [*Guanzi* Reedited]. Contained in his *Sizi zuan* 四子纂. Pub. 1611.

Zhang Binglin 章炳麟 (1868–1936). *Guanzi yuyi* 管子餘義 [Further Meanings in the *Guanzi*]. Shiwenshe 石文社, 1919.

Zhang Dejun 張德鈞 (20th century). Notes contained in Guo Moruo, *Guanzi jijiao*.

Zhang Peilun 張佩綸 (1848–1903). *Guanzi xue* 管子學 [Studies on the *Guanzi*]. Privately pub. 1928 (?).

Zhang Wenhu 張文虎 (1808–1885). *Shuyishi suibi* 舒藝室隨筆 [Running Notes from the Shuyi Study]. Contained in *Fupouji* 覆瓿集, 1860.

Zhao Shouzheng 趙守正. *Guanzi zhuyi* 管子注譯 [*Guanzi* with Notes and Translation into Modern Chinese]. Vol. I. Nanning, Guangxi: Guangxi Renmin Chubanshe 廣西人民出版社, 1982.

Zhao Yongxian 趙用賢 (1535–1596). *Guan Han heko* 管韓合刻 [Combined Printing of the *Guanzi* and *Hanfeizi*]. Pub. 1582. See *SBBY* ed. of *Guanzi*.

Zhi Weicheng 支偉成 (20th century). *Guanzi tongshi* 管子通釋 [Comprehensive Explanation of the *Guanzi*]. Shanghai: Taitong Tushuju, 泰東圖書局, 1924.

Zhongguo Renmin Daxue, Beijing Jingji Xueyuan, *Guanzi* Sixiang Yenjiuzu 中國人民大學, 北京經濟學院, 管子思想研究組 [Chinese Peoples' University, Beijing Economics Institute, *Guanzi* Economic Thought Study Group]. *Guanzi jingji pianwen zhuyi* 管子經濟篇文注譯 [Economic Sections of the *Guanzi* with Notes and Translation into Modern Chinese]. Nanchang: Jiangxi Renmin Chubanshe 江西人民出版社, 1980.

Zhu Changchun 朱長春 (16th century). *Guanzi jue* 管子權 [Bridge to the *Guanzi*]. Notes cited by Zhao Yongxian in *Guan Han heko*.

Zhu Kezhen 竺可楨 (1890–?). Cited by Guo Moruo, *Guanzi jijiao*.

Zhu Yanghe 朱養和 (fl. early 17th century). *Guanzi pingzhu* 管子評註 [Running Commentary on Guanzi]. Huazhai 花齋 ed. of *Guanzi*, first pub. 1625. Contained in *Shizi quanshu* 十子全書 reprint of 1804.

OLDER WORKS IN CHINESE AND JAPANESE

Beitang shuchao 北堂書鈔 [Abstracts from Books in the Northern Hall]. Encyclopedia comp. by Yu Shinan 虞世南 (558–638). Nanhai Kongshi Sanshisanwan Juan Tang 南海孔氏三十三萬卷堂 ed. of 1888.

Bie lu 別錄 [Separate Lists]. Comp. by Liu Xiang 劉向 (77–6 B.C.) and Liu Xin 劉歆 (d. A.D. 23). Descriptive lists of books prepared while cataloguing the Han imperial library. Now lost.

Bi Song lou cangshu zhi 百宋樓藏書志 [Treatise on Books Stored in the Two Hundred Song Editions Tower]. Comp. by Lu Xinyuan 陸心源 (1834–1894). Shiwan Juan Lou 十萬卷樓 ed. of 1882.

Bohu tong 白虎通 [The Comprehensive Discussions in the White Tiger Hall]. Comp. by Ban Gu 班固 (A.D. 32–92) in about 80 A.D. Lu Wenchao 盧文弨 ed. of 1784. *CSJC*. Trans. by Tjan, *Po Hu T'ung*.

439

Bohu tong de lun 白虎通德論 [The Comprehensive Discussions of Virtue in the White Tiger Hall]. Comp. by Ban Gu 班固 (A.D. 32–92). Yuan dynasty ed. *SBCK.*

Bo Kong liu tie 白孔六帖 [Kong's Supplement to Bo Juyi's 白居易 Encyclopedia on Notes to the Classics]. Comp. by Kong Chuan 孔傳 (12th century). Taipei: Xinxing Shuju 新興書局, 1969 reprint.

Cefu yuangui 册府元龜 [Models from the Storehouse of Literature]. Comp. by Wang Qinruo 王欽若, Yang Yi 楊億, and others between 1005 and 1013. Beijing: Zhonghua Shuju 中華書局, 1960.

Cheng 稱 [Balancing]. Text prefixed to the *Laozi* "B" silk manuscript discovered at Mawangdui. See Tang Lan, *Mawangdui chutu Laozi Yi ben juanqian guyi shu de yanjiu.*

Chijing zhai shumu 持靜齋書目 [Catalogue of Chijing's Study]. Comp. by Ding Richang 丁日昌 (1823–1882), whose sobriquet was Chijing. Beiping: Laixun Ge Shudian 來薰閣書店 ed., 1934.

Chongwen zongmu 崇文總目 [Complete Catalogue of Honored Writings]. Comp. by Wang Yaochen 王堯臣 and others between 1034 and 1038. Now lost.

Chongwen zongmu fubuyi 崇文總目附補遺 [Complete Catalogue of Honored Writings, Reconstructed]. Reconstruction of the above by Qian Dongyuan 錢東垣 and others, c. 1799. *CSJC* ed.

Chu ci 楚辭 [Songs of Chu]. Attributed to Qu Yuan 屈原 (4th century B.C.). *SBBY* (*Chuci buzhu* 楚辭補注) ed. Trans. by D. Hawkes, *Ch'u Tz'u, The Songs of the South.*

Chunqiu 春秋 [Spring and Autumn Annals]. Traditionally ed. by Confucius (551–479 B.C.). James Legge, *Ch'un Ts'eu with Tso Chuen, The Chinese Classics*, vol. V, pts. 1–2, contains text and trans.

Chunqiu fanlu 春秋繁露 [Luxuriant Dew of the Spring and Autumn Annals]. By Dong Zhongshu 董仲舒 (179?–104? B.C.). *SBBY* ed.

Chunqiu Zuo zhuan leijie 春秋左傳類解 [Classified Explanations of the *Chunqiu and Zuo zhuan*]. Liu Ji 劉績 of Jiangxia 江夏, Hupei. Pub. during Ming, Jiajing period (1522–1566).

Chuxue ji 初學記 [Records for Beginning Students]. Encyclopedia comp. by Xu Jian 徐堅 (659–729) and others. Guxiang Ge 古香閣 (Xiuzhen 袖珍) ed., n.d.

Da Dai li ji 大戴禮記 [Record of Rites of the Elder Tai]. Compilation attributed to Dai De 戴德 (A.D. 1st century). *CSJC* ed. Trans. by Richard Wilhelm, *Li Gi.*

Dao yuan 道原 [Dao, the Origin]. Prefixed to the *Laozi* "B" silk manuscript discovered at Mawangdui. See Tang Lan, *Mawangdui chutu Laozi Yi ben juanqian guyi shu de yanjiu.*

Da xue 大學 [Great Learning]. James Legge, *The Great Learning, The Chinese Classics*, vol. I, contains text and translation.

Dengxizi 登析子 [Book of the Master Deng Xi]. Attributed to a 6th century B.C. official in Zheng. Probably Han. *SBBY* ed.

Erya 爾雅 [Literary Expositor]. Zhou word list stabilized during Qin and Han. Compiler unknown. *SBBY* ed.

Fengsu tongyi 風俗通義 [Popular Traditions and Customs]. By Ying Shao 應劭 (fl. 178–196). Beijing: Centre franco-chinois d'études sinologiques ed., 1943.

Gongyang zhuan 公羊傳 [Gongyang Commentary to the Chunqiu]. Attributed to Gongyang Gao 公羊高 (5th century B.C.), probably composed during 3rd and 2nd centuries B.C. *Songben Chunqiu Gongyang zhuan zhusu fu jiaokan ji* 宋本春秋公羊傳注疏附校勘記 ed. of 1887. Partially trans. by James Legge, *Ch'un Ts'eu Tso Chuen, The Chinese Classics*, vol. V, pts. 1–2.

Guang yun 廣韻 (Expanded Rhyme Dictionary]. Revised and enlarged version of other rhymed dictionaries. Comp. by Chen Pengnian 陳彭年 and others in 1011. *SBBY* ed.

Guangshi zhilüe 管氏指略 [Summary of the Main Points of Mr. Guan]. By Du You 杜佑 (735–812). Now lost.

Guanzi 管子 [The Book of Master Guan]. Ed. by Liu Xiang 劉向 c. 26 B.C. See editions listed below.

Guanzi. Ancient (*guben* 古本) ed. See Introduction, p. 35, for ancient, ten-line edition of Liu Ji's *Guanzi buzhu*.

Guanzi. Cai Quiandao 蔡潛道 (Mobao Tang 墨寶堂) ed. See Introduction, p. 34.

Guanzi. Hua Zhai 花齋 [Flowery Studio] ed. See Zhu Yanghe.

Guanzi. Ling Ruxiang 凌如享 ed. of 1620. Photographic reprint by Song Zheyuan 宋哲元, 1937.

Guanzi. Liu 劉 ed. See Liu Ji and Introduction, pp. 35–39, for Yellow Paper of Liu Ji, *Guanzi buzhu*.

Guanzi. Yang Chen 楊忱 ed. See Introduction, pp. 33–34.

Guanzi. Zhao 趙 ed. See Zhao Yongxian and Introduction, p. 35.

Guanzi. Zhu 朱 ed. See Introduction, p. 36, for Zhu Dongguang, 朱東光 *Zhongdu sizi* 中都四子 ed. (pub. 1579) of Liu Ji, *Guanzi buzhu*.

Guanzi buzhu 管子補注 [Supplementary Commentary to the *Guanzi* by Liu Ji 劉績 (fl. 1012?). Zhu Dongguang, 朱東光 *Zhongdu sizi* 中都四子 ed. of 1579.

Guanzi yaolüe 管子要略 [Summary of the *Guanzi*]. By Ding Du 丁度 (990–1053). Now lost.

Guiguzi 鬼谷子 [The Book of the Master of Devil Valley]. Anon. Partly 4th or 3d century B.C., partly Han and later. *SBBY* ed.

Gujin shulu 古今書錄 [List of Ancient and Modern Books]. By Wu Qiung 毋煚 (8th century A.D.). Pub. soon after 721. Now lost.

Guliang zhuan 穀梁傳 [Guliang Commentary to the *Chunqiu*]. Attributed to Guliang Chi 穀梁志 (5th century B.C.), probably composed during the 3d or 2d century B.C. *Song ben Chunqiu Kuliang zhuan zhusu fu jiaokanji* 宋本春秋穀梁傳注疏附校勘記 ed. of 1887.

Guo yu 國語 [Discourses of the States]. Anon. compilation of the 4th or early 3d century B.C. *SBBY* ed.

Hanfeizi 韓非子 [The Book of Master Fei from the State of Han]. Comp. by the followers of Hanfeizi (d. 233 B.C.). *SBBY* ed. Trans. by W. K. Liao, *The Complete Works of Han Fei Tzu.*

Han ji 漢紀 [Records of the Han]. By Xun Yue 荀悦 (148–209). *SBCK* ed. Partial trans. by Ch'i-yün Ch'en, *Hsün Yüeh.*

Han Shi waizhuan 韓詩外傳 [Han's *Shi jing* Anecdotes]. By Han Ying 韓嬰 (fl. 157 B.C.). *CSJC* ed. Trans. by Robert James R. Hightower, *Han shih wai chuan.*

Han shu buzhu 漢書補註 [Supplementary Commentary to the *Han shu*]. By Wang Xianqian 王先謙 (1842–1917). Originally pub. in Changsha in 1900. *GXJBCS* ed.

Heguanzi 鶡冠子 [Book of Master Heguan]. Attributed to a Daoist from the state of Chu who lived during Zhou times. Probably composed during the Han with later additions. *SBBY* ed.

Huainan honglie jijie 淮南鴻烈集解 [Collected Explanations on the Illustrious Teachings of Huainan]. By Liu Wendian 劉文典 (1893–?). Shanghai: Commercial Press, 1921.

Huainanzi 淮南子 [Book of the King of Huainan]. Comp. by scholars at the court of Liu An 劉安 (d. 122 B.C.). *SBBY* ed. Partial trans. by E. Morgan, *Tao, the Great Luminant*; Benjamin E. Wallacker, *The Huai-nan-tzu, Book Eleven*; and Charles Le Blanc, "The Idea of Resonance (*Kan-ying*) in the *Huai-nan-tzu*."

Huang Di si jing 黃帝四經 [Four Canons of the Yellow Emperor]. Lost text, which Tang Lan in his *Mawangdui chutu Laozi Yi ben juanqian guyi shu de yanjiu* identifies as composed of the four texts prefixed to the *Laozi* "B" silk manuscript discovered at Mawangdui.

Hubei tongzhi 湖北通志 [Hubei Provincial Gazetteer]. Comp. by Zhang Zhongshi 張仲炘 and Yang Chengxi 楊承禧. Taipei: Huawen Shuju 華文書局 ed. of 1967.

Jijie. See Shi ji jijie.

Jing fa 經法 [The Scriptures and Law]. Prefixed to the *Laozi* "B" silk manuscript discovered at Mawangdui. See Tang Lan, *Mawangdui chutu Laozi Yi ben juanqian guyi shu de yanjiu.*

Jiu Tang shu 舊唐書 [Old History of the Tang Dynasty]. Comp. by Liu Xu 劉昫 (887–946) and others. Completed in 945. *SBBY* ed.

Junzhai dushu zhi. See Zhaode xiansheng junzhai dushu zhi.

Laozi 老子 or *Dao de jing* 道德經 [The Book of the Old Master or Canon of the Way and the Power]. By anon. Daoist writer of 4th or 3d century B.C. *SBBY* ed. Trans. by A. Waley, *They Way and Its Power.*

Laozi "A" 老子甲本. Silk manuscript discovered at Mawangdui. See *Wenwu* 文物 (1974), no. 11, pp. 8–14, for modern transcription.

Laozi "B" 老子乙本, silk manuscript discovered at Mawangdui. See *Wenwu* 文物 (1974), no. 11, pp. 15–20, for a modern transcription. See also Robert G. Henricks, "Examining the Ma-wang-tui silk texts of the *Lao-tzu*," for a translation and study.

442

Liao shi 遼史 [History of the Liao Dynasty]. Traditionally ascribed to Tuotuo 托托 (1313–1355). *SBBY* ed.

Liezi 列子 [The Book of Master Lie]. Anon. Daoist fragments from 4th and 3d centuries B.C., put together with new material in 4th century A.D. Compiler unknown. *SBBY* ed. Trans. by A. C. Graham, *The Book of Lieh-tzu*. See also Anton Forke, *Yang Chu's Garden of Pleasure*.

Li ji 禮記 [Record of Rites]. Compilation attributed to Dai Sheng 戴聖 (1st century A.D.). *SBBY* (*Li ji Zheng zhu* 禮記鄭注) ed. Trans. by James Legge, *The Li Ki*.

Li ji zhusu 禮記注疏 [Commentaries on the *Li ji*]. By Kong Yingda 孔穎達 (574–684). Maiwangxian Guan 脈望仙館 ed. of 1887.

Liu tao 六韜（弢）[Six Bow Cases]. Attributed to Lü Wang 呂望 of the Zhou ·dynasty. Present text probably for the most part a post-Han forgery. *SBCK* ed. Remnants found in Linyi Xian tomb. See *Wenwu* 文物 (1974), no. 2, pp. 15–35.

Longkan shoujian 龍龕手鑑 [Hand Mirror of Dragon Coffins]. By Xingjun 行均. Pub. in 997. *SBCK* ed., ser. 2.

Lun yu 論語 [The Analects of Confucius]. Comp. by followers of Confucius (551–479 B.C.) during 5th century B.C. James Legge, *Confucian Analects*, *The Chinese Classics*, vol. I, contains text and trans. See also A. Waley, *The Analects of Confucius*. See also *Lun yu Heshi deng jijie* 論語何氏等集解. *SBBY* ed.

Lüshi chunqiu (*LSCQ*) 呂氏春秋 [The Spring and Autumn Annals of Mr. Lü]. Comp. under Lü Buwei 呂不韋 (d. 235 B.C.) about 240 B.C. *SBBY* ed. Trans. by R. Wilhelm, *Frühling und Herbst des Lü Bu We*.

Mengzi 孟子 [The Book of Mencius]. Comp. by followers of Mencius (371–289 B.C.). James Legge, *The Works of Meneius*, *The Chinese Classics*, vol. II, contains text and trans.

Mozi 墨子 [The Book of Master Mo]. Comp. by followers of Mo Di 墨翟 (c. 479 – c. 381 B.C.). *SBBY* ed. Partial trans. by Y. P. Mei, *The Ethical and Political Works of Motse*.

Nan Qi shu 南齊書 [History of the Southern Qi Dynasty]. Comp. by Xiao Zixian 蕭子顯 (489–537). *SBBY* ed.

Nihonkoku genzaisho mokuroku 日本國現在書目錄 [Catalogue of Present Books in Japan]. Comp. by Fujiwara no Sukeyo 藤原佐世 (d. 898). See Onagaya Keikichi, *Nihonkoku genzaisho mokuroku kaisetsukō*.

Qian Han shu 前漢書 [History of the Former Han Dynasty]. Comp. by Ban Gu 班固 (A.D. 32–92). *SBBY* ed. Trans. by H. Dubs, *The History of the Former Han Dynasty*.

Qi lu 七錄 [Seven Lists]. Comp. by Ruan Xiaoxu 阮孝緒 (479–536). Descriptive catalogue in 12 *juan*. Now lost.

Qi lüe 七略 [Seven Summaries]. Comp. by Liu Xin 劉歆 (d. A.D. 23). Catalogue based on *Bie lu*, prepared by Liu Xiang and Liu Xin while engaged in cataloguing the imperial library. Now lost.

Qin legal documents from Yunmeng Xian, Hubei. See *Shuihudi Qin mu zhujian*.

Qinding gujin tushu jicheng 欽定古今圖書集成 [Complete Collection of Ancient and Modern Illustrations and Books Made on Imperial Order]. Shanghai: Zhonghua Shuju 中華書局 ed., 1934.

Quan shanggu Sandai Qin Han Sanguo Liuchao wen 全上古三代 秦漢三國六朝文 [Complete Collection of Prose from the Three Periods of Remote Antiquity and the Periods of the Qin, Han, Three Kingdoms, and Six Dynasties]. Comp. by Yan Kejun 嚴可均 (1762–1843). Shanghai: Yixue Shuju 醫學書局 ed., 1930.

Qunshu huiji 羣書會記 [Collected Records of Assembled Books]. Comp. by Zheng Qiao 鄭樵 (1104–1162). Presented in 1149. Lost.

Qunshu zhiyao 羣書治要 [Important Passages from Assembled Books]. Comp. by Wei Zheng 魏徵 (580–643) in 631. *SBCK* ed.

Sanshi shi 三十時 [The Thirty Periods]. Unpub. text recovered from a Han tomb at Yinxueshan in Linyi Xian, Shandong.

Shanben shushi cangshu zhi 善本書室藏書志 [Treatise on Books Stored in the Rare Book Room]. Comp. By Ding Bing 丁丙 (1832–1899). *Qiantang Dingshi* 錢塘丁氏 ed. of 1901.

Shangjun shu 商君書 [Book of Lord Shang]. Comp. by followers of Shang Yang 商鞅 (fl. 359–338 B.C.). *SBBY* ed. Trans. by J. J. L. Duyvendak, *The Book of Lord Shang*.

Shang shu 尚書 (*Shu jing* 書經) [Book of History]. Collection of documents, some of which may go back to 10th century B.C.; others are 4th century A.D. forgeries. James Legge, *The Shoo King or The Book of Historical Documents, The Chinese Classics*, vol. III, contains text and trans.

Shenzi 申子 [Book of Master Shen]. Comp. by the followers of Shen Buhai 申不害 (d. 337 B.C.). Now lost. Recollected and trans. by H. G. Creel, *Shen Pu-hai*.

Shi da jing 十大經 [Ten Great Scriptures]. Prefixed to the *Laozi* "B" silk manuscript discovered at Mawangdui. See Tang Lan, *Mawangdui chutu Laozi yiben juanqian guyi shu de yanjiu*.

Shi ji 史記 [Records of the Historian]. Comp. by Sima Qian 司馬遷 (145–86? B.C.) and his father, Sima Tan 司馬談 (180?–110 B.C.). *SBBY* ed. Partial trans. by Ed. Chavannes, *Les mémoires historiques de Se-ma Ts'ien*; Burton Watson, *Records of the Grand Historian of China*; and Yang Hsien and Gladys Yang, *Records of the Historian*.

Shi ji jijie 史記集解 [Collected Explanations to the *Shi ji*], by Pei Yin 斐駰 (5th century A.D.). A commentary pub. c. A.D. 440. Incorporated in *SBBY* ed. of *Shi ji*.

Shi jing 詩經 [The Bookes of Odes]. Anon. collection of 11th to 7th centuries B.C. Bernhard Karlgren, *The Book of Odes*, contains text and trans. See also Arthur Waley, *The Book of Songs*.

Shi ji zhengyi 史記正義 [Rectification of Meanings in the *Shi ji*]. By Zhang Shoujie 張守節 (8th century A.D.). A commentary pub. A.D. 737. Incorporated in *SBBY* ed. of *Shi ji*.

Shiwen. See *Zhou li shiwen*.

Shuihudi Qin mu zhujian 睡虎地秦墓竹簡 [Bamboo Documents from the Shuihudi Qin Dynasty Tomb]. Beijing: Wenwu Chubanshe 文物出版社, 1978.

Shui jing zhu 水經注 [Commentary on the Canon of Rivers and Streams]. By Li Daoyuan 酈道元 (d. A.D. 527). Wang Xianqian 王先謙 (1842–1918) ed. *SBBY*.

Shuowen jiezi 説文解字 [Analytical Dictionary of Characters]. By Xu Shen 許慎 (d. A.D. 120?). *SBBY* ed.

Shuowen tongxun dingsheng 説文通訓定聲 [Definitions and Pronunciations of the *Shuowen*]. By Zhu Junsheng 朱駿聲 (1788–1858). Shanghai: Shijie Shuju 世界書局 ed. of 1936.

Shuo yuan 説苑 [Garden of Discourses]. By Liu Xiang 劉向 (77–6 B.C.) *SBBY* ed.

Sima fa 司馬法 [Methods of the Minister of War]. Attributed to Rang Ju 穰苴 of the 6th century B.C. Present text probably Han or post-Han forgery. *SBBY* ed.

Song shi 宋史 [History of the Song Dynasty]. Traditionally edited by Toto 托托 (1313–1355), actually by Ouyang Xuan 歐陽玄 (1274/5-1358). Pub. in 1354. *SBBY* ed.

Song Yuan jiuben shu jingyan lu 宋元舊本書經眼錄 [Record of Personally Examined Old Editions from the Song and Yuan]. By Mo Youzhi 莫友芝 (1811–1871). Pub. in 1873. Cited in Guo Moruo, *Guanzi jijiao*.

Sui shu 隋書 [History of the Sui Dynasty]. Comp. by Wei Zheng 魏徵 (580–643) and others. Completed in 636. *SBBY* ed.

Sun Bin bingfa 孫臏兵法 [Sun Bin's Methods of Warfare]. Attributed to Sun Bin (fl. 357–320 B.C.). A lost text, whose remnants were recovered from a Han tomb in Linyi Xian, Shandong, and pub. by the Wenwu Chubanshe 文物出版社 of Beijing in 1975.

Sunzi 孫子 [The Book of Master Sun]. Also known as *Bing fa* [The Art of War]. Comp. by followers of Sun Wu 孫吳 (d. 496 B.C.?). *SBBY* ed. Trans. by L. Giles, *Sun Tzu on the Art of War*. See also Samuel B. Griffith, *Sun Tsu: The Art of War*.

Taiping yulan 太平御覽 [Imperial Survey of the Taiping Period]. Comp. by Li Fang 李昉 and others in 983. *GXJBSC* ed.

Tai xuan 太玄 [The Great Mystery]. By Yang Xiung 揚雄 (53 B.C.–A.D. 18). *SBCK* ed.

Tang yun 唐韻 [Rhyme Dictionary of the Tang Dynasty]. Originally comp. by Lu Fayan 陸法言 in 601. Pub. in 751 as *Tang yun*. Revised and enlarged as *Guang yun* in 1011.

Tong dian 通典 [Comprehensive Collection of Documents]. By Du You 杜佑 (735–812). *WYWK* ed., ser. 2.

Tongjian waiji 通鑑外紀 [Unofficial Records of the Universal Mirror of History]. By Liu Shu 劉恕 (1032–1078). Cited by *SKQSZM*, 101/1a.

Tong zhi 通志 [Comprehensive Collection of Treatises]. by Zheng Qiao 鄭樵 (1104–1162). Completed c. 1161. *WYWK* ed., ser. 2.

Wang bing 王兵 [Armed Forces of the King]. Text discovered at Linyi Xian. Reconstruction published in *Wenwu* 文物 (1976), no. 12, pp. 36–43.

Wei li zhi dao 爲吏之道 [How to be an Official]. See *Shuihudi Qin mu zhujian.*

Wen shi 文釋 [Literary Comments]. By Jiang Suizhi 江邃之 (fl. A.D. 420). Now lost.

Wenxian tongkao 文獻通考 [Comprehensive Examination of Writings]. By Ma Duanlin 馬端臨 (fl. 1254–1322). *WYWK* ed., ser. 2.

Wen xin diao long 文心雕龍 [The Literary Mind and the Carving of Dragons]. By Liu Xie 劉勰 (c. 465–522). *SBBY* ed. Trans. by Vicent Shih, *The Literary Mind and the Carving of Dragons.*

Wen xuan 文選 [Anthology: Poetry and Prose Written 246 B.C.–A.D. 502]. Comp. by Xiao Tong 蕭統 (501–531). *SBBY* (Hu 胡) ed.

Wenzi 文子 [Book of Master Wen]. Attributed to a Xin Jin 辛鈃 of the Zhou dynasty; probably post-Han. *SBBY* ed.

Wushi xizhai shumu 吳氏西齋書目 [Catalogue of Mr. Wu's Western Studio]. Comp. by Wu Jing 吳競 (d. 749). Now lost.

Wu Yue chunqiu 吳越春秋 [Spring and Autumn Annals of Wu and Yue]. Comp. from earlier sources by Zhao Ye 趙曄 (fl. A.D. 40). *SBCK* ed.

Wuzi 吳子 [The Book of Master Wu]. Attributed to Wu Qi 吳起 (d. 381 B.C.). *SBBY* ed. Trans. by Samuel B. Griffith, *Sun Tzu: The Art of War.*

Xin shu 新書 [New History]. By Jia Yi 賈誼 (201–169 B.C.). *SBBY* ed.

Xin Tang shu 新唐書 [New History of the Tang Dynasty]. Comp. by Ouyang Xiu 歐陽修 (1007–1072) and Song Qi 宋祁 (998–1061) during 1045–1060. *SBBY* ed.

Xian Qin yun du 先秦韻讀 [A Study of Pre-Qin Rhymes]. By Jiang Yougao 江有誥 (d. 1851). Contained in his *Jiangshi yinxue shi shu* 江氏音學十書 [Ten Works on Phonology by Mr. Jiang]. Chengdu: Sichuan Renmin Chubanshe 四川人民出版社 ed. of 1957.

Xin xu 新序 [New Preface]. By Liu Xiang 劉向 (77–6 B.C.). Beiping: Centre franco-chinois d'études sinologiques, 1946.

Xunzi 荀子 [Book of Master Xun]. Comp. by followers of Xun Qing 荀卿 (c. 298–238 B.C.). *SBBY* ed. Partial trans. by H. Dubs, *The Works of Hsüntze.*

Yan tie lun 鹽鐵論 [Discourses on Salt and Iron]. By Huan Kuan 恒寬 (fl. 81–73 B.C.). *SBBY* ed. Partial trans. by Esson M. Gale, *Discourses on Salt and Iron.* See also Gale, Boodberg, and Lin for additional chapters in *Journal of the North China Branch of the Royal Asiatic Society*, 65 (1934): 73–110.

Yanzi chunqiu 晏子春秋 [Spring and Autumn Annals of Master Yan]. Anon. compilation of 4th or 3rd century B.C.(?). Ed. by Liu Xiang 劉向, c. 26 B.C. *SBBY* ed.

Yi jing 易經 [Book of Changes]. Zhou dynasty divination text supplemented during the Han. *SBBY* (*Zhou yi Wang Han zhu* 周易王韓注) ed. Trans. by R. Wilhelm, *The I Ching, or Book of Changes.*

Yi jing (benyi) 易經（本義） [(Original Meaning of) the Book of Changes]. Ed. by Zhu Xi 朱熹 (1130–1200). *Jieziyuan chongding jianben wujing* 芥子園 重訂監本五經 ed., n.d.

Yi lin zhu 意林注 [Commentary to the Forest of Ideas]. By Zhou Guangye 周廣業 (1730–1798). *Juxue xuan congshu* 聚學軒叢書 ed. of 1903.

Yi long tu 易龍圖 [Dragon Chart of the Book of Changes]. By Chen Tuan 陳摶 (c. 906–989). Now lost.

Yingshu yulu 楹書隅錄 [Initial Catalogue of the Yang Library]. Comp. by Yang Shaohe 楊紹和 (1831–1876). Prefaces dated 1869 and 1871.

Yiwen leizhu 藝文類聚 [Literature, Classified]. Encyclopedia comp. by Ouyang Xun 歐陽詢 (557–641) and others. Huayang Hongda Tang 華陽宏達堂 ed. of 1879.

Yi xue qimeng 易學啓蒙 [Application of the Book of Changes for Beginners]. By Zhu Xi 朱熹 (1120–1200). Hu Fangping 胡方平 (13th century), *Yi xue qimeng tongshi* 易學啓蒙通釋 [Comprehensive Explanation of the Application of the Book of Changes for Beginners] ed. Contained in the *Tongzhi tang jingjie* 通志堂經解.

Yi Zhou shu 逸周書 [Lost Books of the Zhou]. Collection of supposedly early documents recovered from a tomb about A.D. 281; appears to contain some genuine Zhou material as well as later forgeries. *SBBY* ed.

Yi zhuan 易傳 [Commentary on the Book of Changes]. By Guan Lang 關朗 (fl. 477–500). Now lost.

Yu hai 玉海 [Ocean of Jade]. Encyclopedia comp. by Wang Yinglin 王應麟 (1223–1296). Zhejiang Shuju 浙江書局 ed. of 1883.

Zhanguo ce 戰國策 [Intrigues of the Warring States]. Anon. collection of 3d century B.C. *SBBY* ed. Trans. by J. I. Crump, Jr., *Chan-Kuo Ts'e*.

Zhaode xiansheng junzhai dushu zhi 昭德先生郡齋讀書志 [Treatise by Mr. Zhaode on Books Read in the Prefectural Studio]. Comp. by Chao Gongwu 晁公武 (d. 1175), whose sobriquet was Zhaode. *SBCK* ed., ser. 3.

Zhengyi. See *Shi ji zhengyi*.

Zhizhai shulu jieti 直齋書錄解題 [Zhizhai's Descriptive Catalogue]. Comp. by Chen Zhensun 陳振孫 (fl. 1234), whose sobriquet was Zhizhai. *GXJBCS* ed.

Zhongxing guange shumu 中興館閣書目 [Catalogue of Official Libraries during the Southern Song Restoration]. Comp. in 1178. Now lost.

Zhong yong 中庸 [Doctrine of the Mean]. Attributed to Zisi 子思, the grandson of Confucius, 5th century B.C. James Legge, *The Doctrine of the Mean*, *The Chinese Classics*, vol. I, contains text and trnaslation.

Zhou li 周禮 [Rites of Zhou]. Anon. Work probably comp. during 3d or 2d century B.C.; also known as *Zhou guan* 周官 [Office of the Zhou]. *SBBY* (*Chou li Zheng zhu* 鄭注) ed. Trans. by E. Biot, *Le Tcheou-li ou Rites des Tcheou*.

Zhou li shiwen 周禮釋文 [Explanations on the *Zhou li* Text]. By Lu Deming 陸德明 (early 7th century). Contained in *Zhou li zhusu*.

Zhou li zhusu 周禮注疏 [Commentaries on the *Zhou li*]. By Jia Gongyan 賈公彥 (fl. 650–655). Maiwangxian Guan 脈望仙館 ed. of 1887.

Zhuangzi 莊子 [Book of Master Zhuang]. Comp. by the followers of Zhuang Zhou 莊周 (c. 369 – c. 286 B.C.). *SBBY* ed. Trans. by Burton Watson, *The Complete Works of Chuang Tzu*.

Zi chao 子鈔 [Extracts from the Philosophers]. By Yu Zhongrong 庾仲容

(476–549). Now lost.

Zi lüe 子略 [Summary of the Philosophers]. By Gao Sisun 高似孫 (fl. 1184). *SBBY* ed.

Ziwei ji 紫微集 [Collected Works of Zang Nie]. By Zhang Nie (1096–1148). Contained in *Hubei xianzheng yishu* 胡北先生遺書. Mianyang 沔陽, Hubei, 1932.

Zuo zhuan 左傳 [Mr. Zuo's Commentary to the *Chunqiu*]. Comp. 4th century B.C. James Legge, *The Chinese Classics*, vol. V, pts. 1–2, contains text and trans.

RECENT WORKS IN CHINESE AND JAPANESE

Aihara Shunji 相原俊二. *Kanshi sho to gogyō setsu* 管子書と五行説 [The Book of *Guanzi* and the Doctrine of Five Phases]. *Tōyōgakuhō* 東洋學報, 5 (1978): 59–91.

Chen Mengjia 陳夢家. *Wuxing zhi qiyuan* 五行之起源 [On the Origin of the Five Elements]. *Yanjing xuebao* 燕京學報, 24 (1938): 35ff.

Chou Fa-kao (Zhou Fagao) 周法高. *Hanzi gujin yinhui* 漢字古今音彙 [A Pronouncing Dictionary of Chinese Characters in Archaic and Ancient Chinese, Mandarin and Cantonese]. Hong Kong: Chinese University Press, 1979.

Gu Jiegang 顧頡剛 and Yang Xiangkui 楊向奎. *San huang kao* 三皇考 [On the Three Sovereigns], *Gu shi bien* 古史辨, 7B. Shanghai: Kaiming Shudian 開明書店, 1941.

Guo Moruo 郭沫若. *Chimi pien de yanjiu* 侈靡篇研究 [A Study of the *Chimi* Chapter, *Guanzi*, XII, 35]. *Lishi yanjiu* 歷史研究, 3 (1954): 27–62.

———. *Song Xing Yin Wen yizhu kao* 宋鈃尹文遺著考 [On Remnants of the Writings of Song Xing and Yin Wen]. Contained in *Qingtong shidai* 青銅時代. Chongqing: Wenzhi Chubanshe 文治出版社, 1945.

Huang Han 黃漢. *Guanzi jingji sixiang* 管子經濟思想 [Economic Thought in the *Guanzi*]. Shanghai: Commercial Press, 1936. Trans. contained in Maverick, *Economic Dialogues*, pp. 213–403.

Jiang Liangfu 姜亮夫. *Lidai mingren nian li bei zhuan zongbiao* 歷代名人年里碑傳總表 [Complete Table of the Year, Native Village, Stone Tablets, and Biographies of Famous Men of History]. Shanghai: Commercial Press, 1937.

Jin Shoushen 金受申. *Jixiapai zhi yanjiu* 稷下派之研究 [A Study of the Jixia School]. Shanghai: Commercial Press, 1930.

Johnson, Wallace (Zhuang Weisun 莊爲斯). *Guanzi yinde* 管子引得 [A Concordance to the *Kuan-tzu*]. Taipei: Chinese Materials and Research Aids Service Center, 1970.

Kimita Rentarō 公田連太郎. *Kanshi* 管子 [*Guanzi*]. Japanese translation with original Chinese text. Contained in *Kokuyaku kambun taisei, kei shi shi bu* 國譯漢文大成, 經子史部, 19. Tokyo: Kokumin Bunko Kankōkai 國民文庫刊行會, 1924.

448

Koyanagi Shigeta 小柳司氣太. *Kanshi* 管子 [*Guanzi*]. Japanese translation with notes; original Chinese text on top margin of each page. Contained in *Kambun sōsho* 漢文叢書, 6. Tokyo: Miura Osamu 三浦理, 1922.

———. *Kanshi no honbun hihyō* 管子の本文批評 [Textual Criticism of the *Guanzi*]. Contained in *Zoku tōyō shisō no kenkyū* 續東洋思想の研究, pp. 1–18. Tokyo: Morikita Shoten 森北書店, 1943.

———. *Kanshi to shurei* 管子と周禮 [The *Guanzi* and the *Zhou li*]. Contained in *Tōyō shisō no kenkyū* 東洋思想の研究, pp. 215–226. Tokyo: Morikita Shoten 森北書店, 1942.

Li Dongfang 黎東方. *Chunqiu Zhanguo pien* 春秋戰國篇 [On the Spring and Autumn and Warring States Periods]. Chongqing: Commercial Press, 1944.

Li Yumin 李裕民. *Mawangdui Hanmu boshu chaoxie niandai kao* 馬王堆漢墓帛書抄寫年代考 [Examination of the Copy Date for the Silk Manuscripts from the Han Tombs of at Mawangdui]. *Kaogu yu wenwu* 考古與文物 (1981), no. 4, pp. 99–101.

Ling Xiang 凌襄. *Shilun Mawangdui Hanmu boshu Yi Yin jiuzhu* 試論馬王堆漢墓帛書伊尹九主 [An Exploratory Discussion of the Mawangdui Han Tomb Silk Manuscript, Yi Yin on the Nine Types of Rulers Section]. *Wenwu* 文物 (1974), no. 11, pp. 21–27.

Long Hui 龍晦. *Mawangdui chutu Laozi Yi ben juanqian guyi shu tanyuan* 馬王堆出土老子乙本前古佚書探原 ["A Philological Study of the Lost Ancient Treatise Found at the Head of the Manuscript of the *Lao Tzu* (Text B) Unearthed at Ma-Wang-Tui"]. *Kaogu xuebao* 考古學報 (1975), no. 2, pp. 23–32.

Lou Liangle 婁良樂. *Guanzi pingyi* 管子評議 [Critique of the *Guanzi*]. Privately published in Taiwan about 1977.

Luo Genze 羅根澤. *Guanzi tanyuan* 管子探原 [On the Origin of the *Guanzi*]. Shanghai: Zhonghua Shuju 中華書局, 1931.

Luo Jizu 羅繼祖. *Guanzi buzhu zuozhe Liu Ji de shidai wenti* 管子補注作者劉績的時代問題 [The Problem of the Date for Liu Ji, the Author of the *Guanzi buzhu*]. *Shixue jikan* 史學集刊, 2 (1956): 31–33.

Machida Saburō 町田三郎. *Kanshi no shisō (Gaigen rui o chūshin ni shite)* 管子之思想 (外言類を中心にくて) [The Thought of the *Guanzi* (Taking the *Wai yen* Section as the Core)]. *Shūkan tōyogaku* 週刊東洋學, 7 (1962): 45–57.

———. *Kanshi Yōkan ko* 管子幼官考 [An Examination of the *You guan* Chapter of the *Guanzi*]. *Tōyō gaku* 東洋學, 1 (1959): 13–24.

———. *Kanshi yompen ni tsuite* 管子四篇について [Concerning Four Chapters of the *Guanzi* (36–38 and 49)]. *Bunka* 文化, 25 (1961): 75–102.

Matsumoto Kazuo 松田一男. *Kanshi* 管子 [*Guanzi*]. Japanese translation. Tokyo: Tokuma Shoten 德間書店, 1973.

Onagaya Keikichi 小長谷惠吉. *Nihonkoku genzaisho mokuroku kaisetsukō* 日本國現在書目錄解説稿 [Draft Explanation of Catalogue of Present Books in Japan]. Tokyo: Kunitachi Hon no Kai くにたち本の會, 1936.

Qian Mu 錢穆. *Xian-Qin zhuzi xinian* 先秦諸子繫年 [Chronological Studies of

Pre-Qin Philosophers]. 2 vols. Hong Kong: Hong Kong University Press, 1956.

Qindu Xianyang gucheng yizhi de diaocha he shijue 秦都咸陽故城遺址的調查和試掘 [Investigation and Trial Excavations of the Remains of the Ancient Capital of the Qin Dynasty, Xianyang]. *Kaogu* 考古, 6 (1962): 281–289.

Qiu Xigui 裘錫圭. *Mawangdui Laozi Jia Yi pen juanqianhou yishu yu Daofajia* 馬王堆老子甲乙本卷前後逸書與道法家 [The Lost Texts Attached to the Front and Back of the *Laozi* "A" and "B" Texts from Mawangdui and the Daoist-Legalist School]. *Zhongguo zhexue* 中國哲學. Second collection, pp. 68–84. Beijing: Sanlian Shudian 三聯書店, 1980.

Shigezawa Toshirō 重澤俊郎. *Kanshi kyūhai shikai* 管子九敗私解 ["On the *Guanzi's* Animadversion on *Jiu bai*"]. Kyōtō Daigaku *Bungakubu, Gojūshunen kinen ronshū* 京都大學文學部五十週年紀念論集 (1956), pp. 43–54.

Sun Shande 孫善德. *Shandong Haiyang chutu yipi Qi daohua* 山東海陽出土一批齊刀化 [A Group of Knife Money Remains Unearthed in Haiyang Xian, Shandong]. *Wenwu* 文物 (1980), no. 2, pp. 69–72.

Takeuchi Yoshio 武内義雄. *Shina shisō shi* 支那思想史 [A History of Chinese Thought]. Tokyo: Iwanami Shoten 岩波書店, 1936.

Tang Lan 唐蘭. *Mawangdui chutu Laozi Yi ben juanqian guyi shu de yanjiu* 馬王堆出土老子乙本卷前古佚書的研究 ["A Study of the Lost Ancient Book Found at the head of the *Lao Tzu* (Text B) Unearthed at Mawangtui and Its Relation to the Struggle between the Confucians and Legalists in Early Han]. *Kaogu Xuebao* 考古學報 (1975), no. 1, pp. 7–38.

Toda Toyosaburō 戶田豊三郎. *Gogyō setsu seiritsu no ichikōsatsu* 五行説成の一考察 [A Study of the Formation of the Five Phases Theory]. *Shinagaku kenkyū* 支那學研究, 12 (March 1955): 38–45.

Utsunomiya Kiyoyoshi 宇都宮清吉. *Kanshi Monben shiron* 管子問篇試論 [Discussion of the *Wen* Chapter of the *Guanzi*]. *Tōyōshi kenkyū* 東洋史研究, 22 (1964), no. 4, pp. 475–487.

Xiao Gongquan 蕭公權. *Zhongguo zhengzhi sixiang shi* 中國政治思想史 [History of Chinese Political Thought]. 2 vols. Chongqing: Commercial Press, 1945–1946. See Hsiao Kung-chuan for translation of vol. 1.

Xu Qingyu 徐慶譽, *Guanzi zhengzhi sixiang de tantao* 管子政治思想的探討 [An Examination of the Political Thought of the *Guanzi*]. *Journal of Oriental Studies*, 2 (January 1955): 72–88.

Yu Dunkang 余敦康. *Lun Guan Zhong xuepai* 論管仲學派 [On the School of Guan Zhong]. *Zhongguo zhexue* 中國哲學. Second collection, pp. 39–67. Beijing: Sanlian Shudian 三聯書店, 1980. Trans. by Ai Ping in *Studies in Chinese Philosophy* (Winter 1982–1983), pp. 3–60.

Zang Lihe 臧勵龢. *Zhongguo gujin diming dazidian* 中國古今地名大辭典 [Comprehensive Dictionary of Ancient and Modern Chinese Place Names]. Shanghai: Commercial Press, 1930.

Zhang Xincheng 張心澂. *Weishu tongkao* 偽書通考 [Comprehensive

Examination of Forged Books]. 2 vols. Changsha: Commercial Press, 1939.

Zhou Fagao 周法高. See Chou Fa-kao.

Zhu Huo 朱活. *Tan Shandong Haiyang chutu de Qiguo daohua* 談山東 海陽出土的齊國刀化 [On the Remnants of Qi Knife Money Unearthed in Haiyang Xian, Shandong]. *Wenwu* 文物 (1980), no. 2, pp. 63–68.

WORKS IN OTHER LANGUAGES

Ames, Roger T. *The Art of Rulership: A Study in Ancient Chinese Political Thought.* Honolulu: University of Hawaii Press, 1983.

Barnard, Noel. "A Preliminary Study of the Ch'u Silk Manuscript." *Monumenta Serica*, 17 (1958), no. 1, pp. 1–11.

Biot, Edouard. *Le Tcheou-li ou Rites des Tcheou.* 2 vols. plus index. Paris: L'Imprimerie Nationale, 1851.

Bodde, Derk. *China's First Unifier: A Study of the Ch'in Dynasty as Seen in the Life of Li Ssu (280?–208 B.C.).* Leiden: E. J. Brill, 1938.

———. *Essays on Chinese Civilization.* Princeton: Princeton University Press, 1981.

———. *Statesman, Patriot, and General in Ancient China.* New Haven: American Oriental Society, 1940.

Bulling, A. Gutkind. "Ancient Chinese Maps, Two Maps Discovered in a Han Dynasty Tomb from the Second Century B.C." *Expedition*, Museum of the University of Pennsylvania, vol. 20, no. 2 (Winter 1978): 16–25.

Cammann, Schuyler. "The Magic Square of Three in Old Chinese Philosophy and Religion." *History of Religions*, I, 1 (June 1961): 37–80.

Cāṇakya (Kautilya). *Cāṇakya-nīti-śāstra* [Cāṇakya's Science of Political Conduct]. See Kressler, *Stimmen indischer Lebensklugheit.*

Cao Wanru. "Maps 2,000 Years Ago and Ancient Cartographical Rules." *Ancient China's Technology and Science*, comp. by the Institute of the History of Natural Sciences, Chinese Academy of Sciences. Beijing: Foreign Languages Press, 1983.

Chartley, Herbert. "The Date of the Hsia Calendar Hsia Hsiao Cheng." *The Journal of the Royal Asiatic Society of Great Britain and Ireland* (October 1938), pp. 523–533.

Chavannes, Edouard. *Les mémoires historiques de Se-ma Ts'ien.* 5 vols. Paris: Ernest Leroux, 1895–1905.

Ch'en, Ch'i-yün. *Hsün Yüeh (A.D. 148–209): The Life and Reflections of an Early Medieval Confucian.* Cambridge: Cambridge University Press, 1975.

———. *Hsün Yüeh and the Mind of Late Han China: A Translation of the Shen-chien, with Introduction and Annotations.* Princeton: Princeton University Press, 1980.

Creel, Herrlee Glessner. *Confucius, The Man and the Myth.* New York: John Day Co., 1949.

———. *Shen Pu-hai, A Chinese Political Philosopher of the Fourth Century B.C.* Chicago: University of Chicago Press, 1974.

———. *What Is Taoism? and Other Studies in Chinese Cultural History.* Chicago: University of Chicago Press, 1970.

Crump, J. I., Jr. *Chan-Kuo Ts'e.* Oxford: Clarendon Press, 1970.

———. *Intrigues: Studies of the Chan-kuo Ts'e.* Ann Arbor: The University of Michigan Press, 1964.

De Francis, John, and Sun, E-Tu Zen. *Chinese Social History: Translations of Selected Studies.* Washington, D.C.: American Council of learned Societies, 1956.

Dubs, Homer H. *The History of the Former Han Dynasty.* 3 vols. Baltimore: Waverly Press, 1938, 1944, 1955.

———. *The Works of Hsüntze.* London: Arthur Probsthain, 1928.

Duyvendak, J. J. L. *The Book of Lord Shang.* London: Arthur Probsthain, 1928.

Egan, Ronald C. "Narratives in *Tso chuan.*" *Harvard Journal of Asiatic Studies,* 37 (1977), no. 2, pp. 323–352.

Forke, Anton. *Yang Chu's Garden of Pleasure.* London: John Murray, 1912.

Fung Yu-lan. *A History of Chinese Philosophy.* Trans. by Derk Bodde. 2 vols. Princeton: Princeton University Press, 1953.

Gale, Esson M. *Discourses on Salt and Iron.* Leyden: E. J. Brill, 1931.

Gale, Esson M.; Boodberg, P. A.; and Lin, T. C. "Discourses on Salt and Iron" (chapters in addition to above). *Journal of the North China Branch of the Royal Asiatic Society,* 65 (1934): 73–110.

Gardner, Charles Sidney. *Chinese Traditional Historiography.* Cambridge: Harvard University Press, 1938.

Giles, Lionel. *Sun Tzu on the Art of War.* London: Luzac & Co., 1910.

Graham, A. C. "The Background of the Mencian Theory of Human Nature." *The Tsing Hua Journal of Chinese Studies* 清華學報, n.s., VI, 1–2 (December 1967): 214–271.

———. *The Book of Lieh-tzu.* London: John Murray, 1960.

Granet, Marcel. *Danses et légendes de la Chine ancienne.* 2 vols. Paris: Librairie Felix Alcan, 1926.

———. *Festivals and Songs of Ancient China.* Trans. from the French by E. D. Edwards. London: George Routledge & Sons, Ltd., 1932.

Griffith, Samuel B. *Sun Tzu: The Art of War.* New York: Oxford University Press, 1963.

Haloun, Gustav. "Legalist Fragments: Part I; *Kuan-tsï* 55 and Related Texts." *Asia Major,* n.s. 2, pt. 1 (April 1951): 85–120.

———. "Das Ti-tsï-tsï, Frühkonfuzianische Fragmente II." *Asia Major,* 9 (1933): 467–502.

Hawkes, David. *Ch'u Tz'u: The Songs of the South.* Oxford: Clarendon Press, 1959.

Henricks, Robert G. "Examining the Ma-wang-tui Silk Texts of the *Lao-tzu* with Special Note of Their Differences from the Wang Pi Text." *T'oung Pao,* 65 (1979): 166–169.

Hightower, James Robert. *Han shih wai chuan: Han Ying's Illustrations of the Didactic Application of the Classic of Songs.* Cambridge: Harvard University Press, 1952.

452

Ho, Ting Guang. "Kwantze, Seventh Century B.C.: A Study of His Economic Ideas, with Reference to Recent Economic Thought." Ph.D. dissertation, American University, Washington, D.C., 1935.

Hsiao, Kung-chuan. *A History of Chinese Political Thought.* Vol. I, *From the Beginnings to the Sixth Century A.D.* Trans. by F. W. Mote. Princeton: Princeton University Press, 1979.

Hulsewé, A. F. P. "The Ch'in Documents Discovered in Hupei in 1975." *T'oung Pao,* 64 (1978): 175–217.

———. *Remnants of Han Law.* Vol. I. Leiden: E. J. Brill, 1955.

Jan Yün-hua. "The Silk Manuscripts of Taoism." *T'oung Pao,* 63 (1977): 65–84.

Karlgren, Bernhard. "The Authenticity of Ancient Chinese Texts." *Bulletin of the Museum of Far Eastern Antiquities,* 1 (1929): 165–183.

———. *The Book of Odes.* Stockholm: Museum of Far Eastern Antiquities, 1950.

———. *Grammata Serica Recensa.* Stockholm: Museum of Far Eastern Antiquities, 1950.

———. "Legends and Cults in Ancient China." *Bulletin of the Museum of Far Eastern Antiquities,* 18 (1946): 199–365.

———. *On the Authenticity and Nature of the Tso Chuan.* Göteborg: Elanders Boktryckeri Aktiebolag, 1926.

Kautilya. See Cāṇakya.

Keith, A. Berriedale. *A History of Sanskrit Literature.* Oxford: Clarendon Press, 1928.

Kracke, Edward A., Jr. *Civil Service in Early Sung China, 960–1067.* Cambridge: Harvard University Press, 1953.

Kressler, Oskar. *Stimmen indischer Lebensklugheit.* Trans. of *Vṛddha-Cāṇakya* version of *Cāṇakya-nīti-śāstra.* Frankfurt a.M.: Druckerei August Osterrieth, 1904.

Le Blanc, Charles Y. "The Idea of Resonance (*Kan-ying*) in the *Huan-nan Tzu:* With a Translation and Analysis of Huai-nan Tzu Chapter Six." Ph.D. dissertation, University of Pennsylvania, 1978.

Legge, James. *The Chinese Classics.* 8 vols., with Chinese text and translation. Oxford: Clarendon Press, 1893–1895. Reissued in 5 vol. by the Hong Kong University Press, 1961, with a biographical note of James Legge by L. T. Ride, notes on *Mencius* by Arthur Waley, and *Concordance Tables.* Vol. I contains: *Confucian Analect (Lun yu), The Great learning (Da xue),* and *The Doctrine of the Mean (Zhong young).* Vol. II contains *The Works of Mencius (Mengzi).* Vol. III, pts. 1 and 2, contains *The Shoo King or The Book of Historical Documents (Shang shu).* Vol. IV, pts. 1 and 2, contains *The She King or The Book of Poetry (Shi jing).* Vol. V, pts. 1 and 2, contains *The Ch'un Ts'eu, with Tso Chuen (Chunqiu Zuo zhuan).*

———. *The Li Ki, The Sacred books of the East.* Vols. XXVII and XXVIII. London: Oxford University Press, 1885.

Liao, W. K. *The Complete Works of Han Fei Tzu: A Classic of Chinese Legalism.* 2 vols. London: Arthur Probsthain, 1939, 1959.

Lin, Paul J. *A Translation of Lao Tzu's Tao Te Ching and Wang Pi's*

Commentary. Michigan Papers in Chinese Studies, 30. Ann Arbor: Center for Chinese Studies, University of Michigan, 1977.

van der Loon, Piet. "On the Transmission of the *Kuan-tzu.*" *T'oung Pao*, II, 41 (1952): 357–393.

Margoulies, Georges. *Le kou-wen chinois*. Paris: Paul Geuthner, 1925.

Maspero, Henri. *China in Antiquity*. Trans. from the French by Frank A. Kierman, Jr. Amherst: University of Massachusetts Press, 1978.

———. "La chronologie des rois de Ts'i au IVe siècle avant notre ère." *T'oung Pao*, II, 25 (1927): 367–386.

———. "Le Ming-T'ang et la crise religieuse chinoise avant les Han." *Mélanges Chinois et Bouddhiques*, 9 (1948–1951): 1–71.

———. Review of Gustav Haloun, *Seit wann kannten die Chinese die Tocharer oder Indogermanen überhaupt?* (part 1, Leipzig: Verlag der *Asia Major*, 1926.) *Journal Asiatique*, 210 (1927): 144–152.

Maverick, Lewis; T'an Po-fu; and Wen Kung-wen. *Economic Dialogues in Ancient China: Selections from the Kuan-tzu*. Carbondale, Ill.: Lewis A. Maverick, 1954.

Mei, Yi-pao. *The Ethical and Political Works of Motse*. London: Arthur Probsthain, 1929.

Morgan, Evan. *A Guide to Wenli Styles and Chinese Ideals*. Shanghai: Probsthain & Co., 1912.

———. *Tao, the Great Luminant*. Shanghai: Kelly & Walsh, 1933.

Needham, Joseph. *Science and Civilisation in China*. 9 vols. Cambridge: Cambridge University Press, 1954– .

Rickett, W. Allyn. "An Early Chinese Calendar Chart: *Kuan-tzu*, III, 8 (*Yu Kuan* 幼官)." *T'oung Pao*, 48 (1960): 195–251.

———. *Kuan-tzu, a Repository of Early Chinese Thought*. Hong Kong: Hong Kong University Press, 1965.

Riegel, Jeffry K. "Mawangdui Tomb Three: Documents." *Early China*, 2 (Fall 1976): 68–72.

———. "A Summary of Some Recent *Wenwu* and *Kaogu* Articles on Mawangdui Tombs Two and Three." *Early China*, 1 (Fall 1975): 10–15.

Rosen, Sydney. "Changing Conceptions of Hegemon in Pre-Ch'in China." *Ancient China: Studies in Early Civilization*, ed. by Roy and Tsien. Hong Kong, 1978.

———. "In Search of the Historical Kuan Chung." *Journal of Asian Studies*, XXXV, 3 (May 1976): 431–440.

Roth, Harold David. "The Textual History of the *Huainan Tzu*." Ph.D. dissertation, University of Toronto, 1981.

Shafer, Robert. "Linguistics in History." *Journal of the American Oriental Society*, 67 (1947): 296–305.

Shih, Vincent Yu-cheng. *The Literary Mind and the Carving of Dragons*. New York: Columbia University Press, 1959.

Shteyn (Stein), Viktor M. *Guan-tze: Issledovanie i perevod* [*Guanzi*: A Study and Translation]. Moscow: Izdatelstvo Vostochnoi Literaturi, 1959.

Soothill, William Edward. *The Hall of Light: A Study of Early Kingship*. London: Lutterworth Press, 1951.

Swann, Nancy Lee. *Food and Money in Ancient China*. Princeton: Princeton University Press, 1950.

Tchang, Matthias. *Synchronismes chinois*. Shanghai: Imprimerie de la Mission Catholique, 1905.

Thatcher, Melvin P. "A Structural Comparison of the Central Governments of Ch'u, Ch'i and Chin." *Monumenta Serica*, 33 (1977–1978): 140–161.

Tjan Tjoe Som (Tseng Chu-sen). *Po Hu T'ung, The comprehensive Discussions in the White Tiger Hall*. 2 vols. Leiden: E. J. Brill, 1949, 1952.

Tu Wei-ming. "The 'Thought of Huang-Lao': A Reflection on the Lao Tzu and Huang Ti Texts in the Silk Manuscripts of Ma-wang-tui." *Journal of Asian Studies*, 39, no. 1 (November 1979): 95–110.

Waley, Arthur. *The Analects of Confucius*. London: George Allen & Unwin Ltd., 1956.

———. *The Book of Songs*. London: George Allen & Unwin Ltd., 1954.

———. *The Way and Its Power*. London: George Allen & Unwin Ltd., 1934.

Walker, Richard Louis. *The Multi-State System of Ancient China*. Hamden, Conn.: The Shoe String Press, 1953.

Wallacker, Benjamin E. *the Huai-nan-tzu, Book Eleven: Behavior, Culture, and the Cosmos*. New Haven: American Oriental Society, 1962.

Wang Yü-ch'üan. *Early Chinese Coinage*. New York: The American Numismatic Society, 1951.

Watson, Burton. *The Complete Works of Chuang Tzu*. New York: Columbia University Press, 1968.

———. *Early Chinese Literature*. New York: Columbia University Press, 1962.

———. *Records of the Grand Historian of China*. 2 vols. New York: Columbia University Press, 1961.

Wilhelm, Richard. *Frühling und Herbst des Lü Bu We*. Jena: Eugen Diederichs, 1928.

———. *The I Ching or Book of Changes*. Trans. from the German by Cary F. Baynes. 2 vols. New York: Pantheon Books, 1950.

———. *Li Gi, Das Buch der Sitte des älteren und jüngeren Dai*. Jena: Eugen Diederichs, 1930.

Yang, Hsien-yi, and Yang, Gladys. *Records of the Historian*. Hong Kong: Commercial Press, 1974.

INDEX

He tu 河圖 (River Chart), 154–156, 155n, 158, 169, 341, 341n

heads. See *zhang*

heads of household. See *zhang jia*

headquarters unit. See *zhang*

hearing, 186, 206, 211, 349, 379, 404–405. *See also* ears

heart. See *xin*

Heaven (*tian* 天), 52, 56, 56n, 62–64, 64n, 69, 74–75, 77, 77n, 81, 81n, 82–85, 89, 113, 116–117, 128, 133, 137–138, 144, 147, 150, 155, 158, 158n, 166, 166n, 176, 183, 192, 199, 203–204, 206, 210, 212–214, 212n, 216, 285, 316, 322, 340–341, 356, 362, 374, 379, 385, 394, 398, 402, 408, 410, 417, 419, 423, 428

Heguanzi (*see* Bib., Older), 113n

Hei Di 黑帝 (Black Emperor), 167n, 182n. *See also* Hei Hou

Hei Hou 黑后 (Black Ruler), 161, 182. *See also* Hei Di, Xieguang Ji

Heichi 黑齒 (people), 340

heirs, 184, 184n, 222, 286, 306, 306n, 341, 344, 353, 370, 385–386, 406, 421–422

Helü 闔閭 (king of Wu; 514–496 B.C.), 83n, 168n

hemp, 55, 103, 108, 121, 227, 243

heng 橫 (censor), 400, 406. See also *jian* and *jian yushi*

heng 衡 (forester), 324

Heng Shan 恆山 (Mount Heng, sacred mountain in Hebei), 390n

Heng Shan 衡山 (Mount Heng, sacred mountain in Hunan), 338n, 390n

Henricks, Robert G., 20n

heterodoxy, 236, 253–254, 407

historical romance, 10, 282–283, 318

Ho, Ting Guang (*see* Bib., Western), 15n

Hong fan 洪範 (chapter of *Shang shu*), 150n, 158n, 413n

Hong Yixuan (*see* Bib., Com.), 41

honor, 78. See also *rong*, ranks and honors

horses, 70, 76, 77n, 114, 118, 120, 211–212, 228, 254, 302, 308, 323, 327–328, 334–335, 339, 342, 358, 363, 371–372, 433

horticulture, 103, 195, 231

Houji 后稷 (minister of agriculture under Shun), 264–265n

households. See *jia*

Houtu 后土 (Master of Earth), 148n

Hsiao Kung-chuan (*see* Bib., Western), 3n, 16–17. *See also* Xiao Gongquan

Hsü Chung-shu (*see* Bib., Recent, de Francis and Sun, *Chinese Social History*),

162n

Hua Shan 華山 (Mount Hua), 390n

Huai 淮 (place), 307n

Huainan 淮南 (Han feudal state), 23

Huainan honglie jijie (*see* Bib., Older), 270n

Huainanzi (*see* Bib., Older), 23, 65n, 68n, 71nn, 72n, 73n, 75nn, 87n, 110n, 150, 159, 159n, 160, 162–163, 166, 168, 175n, 179n, 184n, 189n, 190n, 202n, 206n, 212n, 214n, 269–270, 276n, 313n, 396, 398n, 401n

Huan 桓 (duke of Lu; 711–694 B.C.), 287, 287nn, 288

Huan 桓 (duke of Qi; 685–643 B.C.), 4, 5–6, 9–12, 13, 13n, 77n, 83n, 137, 147, 168n, 172n, 182n, 258n, 279–354 *passim*, 376–386 *passim*, 424–435 *passim*; death of, 386, 386n, 424–425, 429–430

Huan Yuan 環淵 (Jixia Academy philosopher), 19

huang 皇 (sovereign), 165, 171, 268, 270

Huang 黃 (state), 385

Huang Di 黃帝 (Yellow Emperor), 20, 167nn, 168n, 170n, 220n, 265. *See also* Huang Hou

Huang Di si jing (*see* Bib., Older), 21

Huang Han (*see* Bib., Recent), 15n

Huang Hou 黃后 (Yellow Ruler), 161, 166, 170. *See also* Earth Star, Hanshu Niu, Huang Di

Huang Lao 黃老 (school of thought), 3, 19–21, 20n, 165, 190n, 216, 241, 268, 355, 396.

Huang Zhen (*see* Bib., Com.), 8, 41

Huanyuan 轘轅 (pass and mountain), 390n

Hui Shi 惠施 (4th cent. B.C. philosopher), 72n

Huimo 穢貉 (people), 340

Hulsewé, A.F.P., 20n, 105n, 114n, 120n

human goodness. See *ren*

human nature, 66, 84, 95, 124, 324, 410, 418, 428

Humo 胡貉 (people), 338

hundred surnames. See *bai xing*

hunger, 81, 196, 199, 200, 227, 229–230, 243, 257, 319, 323, 349, 380, 429

hunting, 212, 222, 322, 330, 345, 371, 380, 433

Huo Shan 霍山 (sacred mountain in Shanxi), 390n

husband, 88, 145, 197, 204, 233n, 412

Igai Hikohiro (*see* Bib., Com.), 42

illness, 196, 284, 302, 350, 369, 383, 428–429

illustrious archives. See *ming fu*

impartiality, 56, 56n, 65, 74, 75, 84, 138, 144–145, 145n, 147, 197. *See also* self-interest

individual tract. See *fu*

indolence, 62, 66, 78, 82, 212, 222, 315–316, 350, 402, 415

inspections or inquiries, 95, 108, 129–130, 132, 139, 178, 185, 187, 192, 227–229, 234, 260, 323, 331–333, 364, 368–374, 395, 407–408, 423

instruction, 62, 66, 96–97, 113, 130, 132, 140, 182, 188, 194, 197, 205, 226, 258, 273, 277, 325–328, 332, 377, 349, 361, 371, 373, 379, 381, 401, 403, 412–413, 431–435 *passim*. See also *wu jiao*

integrity. See *lian*

interstate relations, 69, 88, 109–110, 133, 145, 219, 233, 245–246, 358–359, 266, 287–306, 306n, 307–308, 312–315, 320–322, 335–344, 346, 350–354, 356–365, 382–383, 386, 393–395, 432. *See also* feudal lords

jade, 62, 69n, 111–112, 211 217, 228, 230, 232, 342, 358

jails, 194–195

Jan Yün-hua (*see* Bib., Western), 20n, 21n

jesters, 433

ji 紀 (discipline, rules, and regulations), 137, 139, 323–324, 406

Ji 姬 (lady of Cai), 295n

Ji 濟 (river), 337

jia 家 (household), 56, 92–93, 95, 103–104n, 119–120, 228, 229, 237, 324–325, 332–333, 414, 433

Jia Gongyan (*see* Bib., Older, *Zhou li zhusu*), 149

Jia Yi (*see* Bib., Older, *Xin shu*), 5, 14, 16, 60, 76n, 312, 359, 396

jian 諫 (censor), 335, 347

jian ai 兼愛 (universal love), 110, 110n, 136, 140

Jian yuan si 諫怨思 (Admonishment Against Resentful Thoughts), 78n. See *also* Dongfang Suo

jian yushi 監御史 (Qin regional censor), 400, 406n

jiang 將 (general or supreme commander), 109–110, 109n, 134, 189, 218, 245, 335, 360, 390–391, 395

Jiang 江 (state), 385, 385n

Jiang Liangfu (*see* Bib., Recent), 15n, 33n

Jiang Suizhi (*see* Bib., Older, *Wen shi*), 28n

Jiang Yougao (*see* Bib., Older, *Xian Qin

yun du), 46

jiao 角 (musical note), 176

jie 解 (explanatory chapters), 4, 58, 60–61, 99, 136–137

jie 節 (tokens indicating rank), 404

Jie 桀. *See* Jie Gui

Jie Gui 桀癸 (last king of the Xia; trad. 1818–1766 B.C.), 83, 83n, 85, 205, 205n, 219, 314, 361, 426

Jie Yu 接輿 (Jixia Academy scholar), 19

Jilao 季勞 (emissary to Lu; *see also* Jiyou), 303n, 335, 346n

Jilin Sheng Zhexue Shehuikexue Yanjiusuo (*see* Bib., Com.), 42, 115

Jin 晉 (state), 16, 322, 225, 338, 339n, 354, 534n

Jin Shoushen (*see* Bib., Recent), 19n

jing 經 (standards, precepts, or guides to action), 55, 100, 122, 131, 137–139, 195, 197, 236, 244, 253, 256–257, 264, 367, 369, 375, 393. See also *chang* and *si jing*

jing 靜 (quiescence, tranquillity, or repose), 165, 170, 176, 178, 180–182, 192, 195, 202, 207–208, 339, 339, 393, 361, 379

Jing 景 (duke of Qi, 547–490 B.C.), 79n, 291n 377n

Jing 景 (Han emperor; 156–141 B.C.), 225, 376

Jing 荆 (state of Chu), 246. *See also* Chu

Jing fa (*see* Bib., Older), 21, 126n, 216, 241, 246n

Jing Ke 荆軻 (would-be assassin of Qin king), 388

Jing yan 經言 (Canonical Statements; section of the *Guanzi*), 4, 5n, 6n, 14n, 193

jingtian 井田 (well field), 114, 120n, 122n

Jingzhou 荆州 (division of ancient China), 338, 340

jishu 計數 (mensuration), 128–130

Jisui 紀隨 (place), 337

Jiu 糾 or 紏 (elder brother of Duke Huan of Qi), 8, 285–286, 289–290, 292n, 293–294, 321–322, 430n

jiu 九 (nine), 179, 280

Jiu bai 九敗 (Nine Ways to Failure, section of chapter I, 4), 99–100, 109–113, 174n

jiu ben 九本 (nine bases of government), 172–173

Jiu fu 九府 (Nine Treasuries), 6, 6n

jiu gu 九穀 (nine grains), 388

jiu guo 九國 (nine regions), 374n. See also *jiu zhou*

jiu qi 九器 (nine weapons), 187

jiu shu 九數 (nine propositions), 174

Jiu Tang shu (*see* Bib., Older), 27, 29n

punishments, 51, 53–56, 64–66, 66n, 69,
78, 84, 91–93, 95–96, 98, 100–102,
104–107, 109, 113, 127, 133–134, 139,
142–144, 171, 181, 188, 188n, 189, 189n,
190, 190n, 191, 191n, 196, 199–200, 207,
222–223, 226, 231, 233, 235, 242,
245–247, 250, 252–253, 256, 266,
272–273, 288, 302, 306, 308, 310–311,
313, 316, 321, 323, 328, 332–334, 345,
347, 349, 356, 362, 364, 368–369,
380–381, 390, 393–394, 397, 400,
402–403, 405, 410, 413–415, 417, 419,
423, 432. *See also* law

qi 畿 (royal domain), 114
qi 七 (seven), 178
qi 氣 (vital force or spirit), 64, 128, 139, 170,
170n, 175–178, 180, 182, 192, 216
Qi 齊 (state), 3, 5–6, 9, 9n, 12, 15n, 16, 18,
18n 19–20, 279–311 *passim*, 318–354
passim, 376–386 *passim*, 424–430 *passim*
Qi 杞 (state). *See* Qii
Qi fa 七法: Seven Standards (chapter II, 6),
24, 125–126, 128n, 128–130; seven standards, 174n, 267n
Qi guan 七觀 (Seven Points to Observe;
section of chapter I, 4), 113
qi ji 七機 (Seven Crucial Concerns), 174,
174nn
Qi lu (*see* Bib., Older), 26–27, 26n, 27n
Qi lüe (*see* Bib., Older), 7n, 24n, 25–26,
26n, 270
qi sheng 七勝 (seven victories), 173, 173n,
222
qi shu 七數 (seven calculations), 276, 276n
qi ti 七體 (seven forms of righteous conduct), 193, 195–196
Qi yu 齊語 (chapter 6 of the *Guo yu*),
318–319. See also *Guo yu*
Qian 潛 (territory), 336
Qian Dongyuan (*see* Bib., Older, *Chongwen zongmu fubuyi*), 28n
Qian Han shu (*see* Bib., Older), 3n, 7, 23,
24n, 25, 37, 120n, 153n, 225, 267n, 270,
271n, 356, 363n, 394nn, 395nn, 396, 398n
Qian Mu (*see* Bib., Recent), 15n
Qian Zhongshu 錢鍾書, 371n
Qiang 羌 (people), 340n
qie 篋 (box-shaped measure), 121
Qii 杞 (state), 299–300, 299n, 350–351
Qili 杞里 (territory), 336
qilin 麒麟 (mystical animal), 170n
Qin 秦 (state), 3, 12, 75n, 339, 354, 388
qin bing 寢兵 (disarmament), 109, 109n
Qin Shi Huangdi 秦始皇帝 (First Em-

peror of the Qin), 3, 154
Qinding gujin tushu jicheng (*see* Bib.,
Older), 155n
qing 卿 (minister of state, chief or senior
minister), 184, 314, 332, 360
Qing Di 青帝 (Green Emperor), 167nn,
176n. *See also* Qing Hou
Qing Feng 慶封 (Qi official), 291n
Qing Hou 青后 (Green Ruler), 161,
166–167n, 176. *See also* Ling Weiyang,
Qing Di, Wood Star
qing xiang 卿相 (prime minister), 102, 168,
173
Qing zhong 輕重 (Light and Heavy), 3, 5, 6,
6n
Qinghua (Tsinghua) University 清華大學,
42
qiu 丘 (section consisting of four colonies
邑), 114, 115n
Qiu Xigui (*see* Bib., Recent), 21n, 22, 22n
Qu yan 區言 (Minor Statements; section of
the *Guanzi*), 5
quan 權 (political power), 45, 193, 195,
198–199, 232, 237, 243, 260, 357–358,
362, 364–365, 401
*Quan shanggu Sandai Qin Han Sanguo
Liuchao wen* (*see* Bib., Older), 78n
quan sheng 全生 (living to the full), 110,
110n
quiescence. See *jing*
Qunshu huiji (*see* Bib., Older), 33n
Qunshu zhiyao (*see* Bib., Older), 28, 28n,
80n, 90n, 96n, 143nn, 194nn, 379nn,
422nn, 425n, 428nn, 429nn, 430nn
Ququi 渠丘 (man of Qi), 289n

rain, 65, 133, 135, 138, 177, 187, 277, 326,
341, 410.
ranks and honors, 54, 65, 74, 79, 81–82,
83n, 85, 98, 101–102, 105, 108, 110–112,
116–117, 131, 140, 145, 147, 171, 177,
197–198, 208, 209, 217, 220, 223,
232–233, 235, 238–239, 243–245, 247,
254–256, 258, 261, 264–265, 275n, 286,
309, 311, 323, 332, 346–347, 356, 360,
362, 368, 386, 402, 413, 415–417, 419,
421, 434–435; selling of, 225, 232
reality. See *shi*
rebellion, 139, 146, 188, 195, 226, 235, 243,
246, 256, 286, 288–289, 291, 309, 311,
321, 341, 356, 358–359, 369, 406, 414,
416, 429–430
reciprocity. See *shu*
records, 131, 207, 209, 280, 323, 404
red, 178, 189

Way. See *Dao*

wealth, 52, 54, 57, 66, 68–69, 74, 81–82, 85, 93, 95, 108, 111, 135, 140, 144, 174, 195, 204, 207–208, 217, 223, 227, 230–232, 237–239, 242, 244, 246, 255, 263, 294, 314, 344, 347, 374, 378, 391, 297, 405, 409, 417, 420. *See also* prosperity

weapons, 95, 108–109, 109n, 115, 127–128, 132–134, 143, 171, 180, 182, 186–192, 191n, 247–248, 258, 261, 172–278 *passim*, 294, 297–298, 300–302, 313, 322, 334, 339, 407, 414

weaving, 76, 183

wei 威: majestic or awesome power or authority, 55, 65, 80, 88, 96, 101–102, 130–131, 135, 142, 172–175, 185, 190, 194–195, 196, 209, 222, 226, 236, 242, 245, 247, 272, 341, 356–358, 359, 360, 410, 413, 417, 419; prestige, 142, 191, 252, 260, 266, 278, 404, 421

wei 尉 (village commandant), 103–105, 231n

Wei 威 (king of Qi; 357–320 B.C.), 125, 267

Wei 魏 (state), 335n

Wei 衛 (state). *See* Weii

Wei bing zhi shu 爲兵之數 (Art of Conducting Warfare; section of chapter II, 6), 132–133

Wei li zhi dao 爲吏之道 (Qin document from Shuihudi), 324n

Wei Mou 魏牟 (Warring States hedonist philosopher), 174n

Wei Zhao 韋昭 (*Guo yu* commentator; 204–273), 307n, 339n, 404n

Wei Zheng (*see* Bib., Older, *Qunshu zhiyao*), 28, 37

weights (*cheng* 稱), 213, 402. *See also* measurements

Weii (Wei) 衛 (state), 76n, 301, 301n, 303–304, 335–336, 342, 346, 350–351, 429

Weii Kaifang 衛開方. *See* Kaifang

Weizi 微子 (minister to Zhou, last Shang king), 207, 207n

wells, 122, 170, 176, 178, 180, 182, 231, 315

well-field. See *jingtian*

Wen 文 (Han emperor; 179–157 B.C.), 225. *See also* Liu Heng

Wen 文 (Zhou king; trad. d. 1135 B.C.), 67, 67n, 68n, 83n, 168n, 220, 220n, 323, 323n, 340, 344, 368

Wen Jiang 文姜 (wife of Duke Huan of Lu), 287, 341n

Wen Mountains 文山, 338. *See also* Min Mountains

Wen River 汶水, 299

Wen shi (*see* Bib., Older) 28n

Wen xin diao long (*see* Bib., Older), 26

Wen xuan (*see* Bib., Older), 28n, 78n

Wen Yiduo (*see* Bib., Com.), 42

Wenwu 文物 (journal), 387, 387n, 389

Wenxian tongkao (*see* Bib., Older), 29n, 33n, 40n

Wenzi (*see* Bib., Older), 51, 71n, 72n

West River. *See* Xi He

Western Yu. *See* Xi Yu

white, 179, 180n, 189

White Emperor. *See* Bai Di

White Ruler. *See* Bai Hou

wickedness, 82, 89, 96–97, 112, 130–131, 143, 147, 194, 195, 199–200, 225–226, 228, 238–239, 244, 261, 266, 383, 393–394, 404, 506, 407, 409, 415, 421

widows, 101, 103, 196, 367, 369

wife, 61–64, 72, 145, 194, 204, 223, 258, 287, 305, 306n, 315, 323, 332, 353, 370n, 406, 412, 420–422, 429

Wilhelm, Richard, 158n

wind, 65, 133, 135, 138, 140, 187, 274, 277, 341

wine, 315, 322, 345, 430, 435

winter. *See* seasons

wisdom, 20, 88, 88n, 93, 111, 133, 202, 207–209, 211, 218, 220–223, 239, 262, 287, 290, 293, 321–322, 353, 361, 390, 404–405, 412, 416–417, 426

wisdom literature, 58

witch doctors, 96

women, 88, 95, 103–104, 110, 135, 143, 145, 176, 180, 191, 200, 211–212, 226, 231, 242, 247, 272, 284, 295, 287, 315, 323, 332, 342, 345, 353, 369, 371, 382, 403, 406, 411–413, 415–416, 420, 422–423, 426, 429, 433

wood, 334; (phase) 157, 157n, 176

Wood star (Jupiter), 176n. *See also* Ling Weiyang

words, 57, 71, 75, 90, 172, 206, 213, 349, 351, 379, 404, 358, 426. *See also* speech

worthy. See *xian*

writing, 209, 214, 224, 349, 375, 402, 407–409. *See also* bamboo slips and silk scrolls

wu 五: five, 156, 156n, 157, 157n, 169; five punishments, 331, 334

wu 伍: group of five, 103, 119, 171, 180, 391n; squad, 329–330, 333, 371, 422

Wu 武 (Zhou king; trad. 1134–1116 B.C.), 67n, 81n, 84–85, 147, 205, 205n, 207n, 220, 220n, 236, 236n, 299n, 314, 314n,

LIBRARY OF CONGRESS CATALOGING IN PUBLICATION DATA

Kuan, Chung, d. 645 B.C.
  Guanzi: political, economic, and philosophical essays from early China.

  (Princeton library of Asian translations)
  Translation of: Kuan-tzu/Kuan Chung.
  Parallel title in Chinese characters.
  "In 1955, I revised part of my translation of the Guanzi's surviving seventy-six
chapters and submitted eight of them as a Ph.D. dissertation to the University of
Pennsylvania ... In 1965 the University of Hong Kong Press published my Kuan-tzu:
A repository of early Chinese thought, which contained twelve chapters, including the
original eight of my dissertation"—Pref.
  Bibliography: p.
  Includes index.
  1. Philosophy, Chinese. I. Rickett, W. Allyn, 1921—   . II. Title.
III. Title: Kuan-tzu. IV. Series.

B128.K832E57 1985   181'.11   84-15094
ISBN 0-691-06605-1 (v. 1: alk. paper)